# Advanced Techniques in the Analysis and Prediction of Students' Behaviour in Technology-Enhanced Learning Contexts

# Advanced Techniques in the Analysis and Prediction of Students' Behaviour in Technology-Enhanced Learning Contexts

Editors

**Juan A. Gómez-Pulido**
**Young Park**
**Ricardo Soto**

MDPI • Basel • Beijing • Wuhan • Barcelona • Belgrade • Manchester • Tokyo • Cluj • Tianjin

*Editors*
Juan A. Gómez-Pulido
Universidad de Extremadura
Spain

Young Park
Bradley University
USA

Ricardo Soto
Pontificia Universidad Católica de Valparaíso
Chile

*Editorial Office*
MDPI
St. Alban-Anlage 66
4052 Basel, Switzerland

This is a reprint of articles from the Special Issue published online in the open access journal *Applied Sciences* (ISSN 2076-3417) (available at: https://www.mdpi.com/journal/applsci/special_issues/Techniques_Analysis_Prediction).

For citation purposes, cite each article independently as indicated on the article page online and as indicated below:

LastName, A.A.; LastName, B.B.; LastName, C.C. Article Title. *Journal Name* **Year**, *Volume Number*, Page Range.

ISBN 978-3-0365-2115-2 (Hbk)
ISBN 978-3-0365-2116-9 (PDF)

© 2021 by the authors. Articles in this book are Open Access and distributed under the Creative Commons Attribution (CC BY) license, which allows users to download, copy and build upon published articles, as long as the author and publisher are properly credited, which ensures maximum dissemination and a wider impact of our publications.

The book as a whole is distributed by MDPI under the terms and conditions of the Creative Commons license CC BY-NC-ND.

# Contents

About the Editors . . . . . . . . . . . . . . . . . . . . . . . . . . . . . . . . . . . . . . . . . . . . . . . . . . . . . . . . . . . vii

**Juan A. Gómez-Pulido, Young Park and Ricardo Soto**
Advanced Techniques in the Analysis and Prediction of Students' Behaviour in Technology-Enhanced Learning Contexts
Reprinted from: *Appl. Sci.* **2020**, *10*, 6178, doi:10.3390/app10186178 . . . . . . . . . . . . . . . . . . 1

**Maria Tsiakmaki, Georgios Kostopoulos, Sotiris Kotsiantis and Omiros Ragos**
Implementing AutoML in Educational Data Mining for Prediction Tasks
Reprinted from: *Appl. Sci.* **2020**, *10*, 90, doi:10.3390/app10010090 . . . . . . . . . . . . . . . . . . . 7

**Raza Hasan, Sellappan Palaniappan, Salman Mahmood, Ali Abbas, Kamal Uddin Sarker and Mian Usman Sattar**
Predicting Student Performance in Higher Educational Institutions Using Video Learning Analytics and Data Mining Techniques
Reprinted from: *Appl. Sci.* **2020**, *10*, 3894, doi:10.3390/app10113894 . . . . . . . . . . . . . . . . . . 35

**Javier López-Zambrano, Juan A. Lara and Cristóbal Romero**
Towards Portability of Models for Predicting Students' Final Performance in University Courses Starting from Moodle Logs
Reprinted from: *Appl. Sci.* **2020**, *10*, 354, doi:10.3390/app10010354 . . . . . . . . . . . . . . . . . . . 55

**Yenny Villuendas-Rey, Carmen F. Rey-Benguría, Oscar Camacho-Nieto and Cornelio Yáñez-Márquez**
Prediction of High Capabilities in the Development of Kindergarten Children
Reprinted from: *Appl. Sci.* **2020**, *10*, 2710, doi:10.3390/app10082710 . . . . . . . . . . . . . . . . . . 79

**Luiz Antonio Buschetto Macarini, Cristian Cechinel, Matheus Francisco Batista Machado, Vinicius Faria Culmant Ramos, Roberto Munoz**
Predicting Students Success in Blended Learning—Evaluating Different Interactions Inside Learning Management Systems
Reprinted from: *Appl. Sci.* **2019**, *9*, 5523, doi:10.3390/app9245523 . . . . . . . . . . . . . . . . . . . 99

**Sunbok Lee and Jae Young Chung**
The Machine Learning-Based Dropout Early Warning System for Improving the Performance of Dropout Prediction
Reprinted from: *Appl. Sci.* **2019**, *9*, 3093, doi:10.3390/app9153093 . . . . . . . . . . . . . . . . . . . 123

**Emanuel Queiroga, João Ladislau Lopes, Kristofer Kappel, Marilton Aguiar, Ricardo Matsumura Araújo, Roberto Munoz, Rodolfo Villarroel, Cristian Cechinel**
A Learning Analytics Approach to Identify Students at Risk of Dropout: A Case Study with a Technical Distance Education Course
Reprinted from: *Appl. Sci.* **2020**, *10*, 3998, doi:10.3390/app10113998 . . . . . . . . . . . . . . . . . . 137

**David Bañeres, M. Elena Rodríguez, Ana Elena Guerrero-Roldán and Abdulkadir Karadeniz**
An Early Warning System to Detect At-Risk Students in Online Higher Education
Reprinted from: *Appl. Sci.* **2020**, *10*, 4427, doi:10.3390/app10134427 . . . . . . . . . . . . . . . . . . 157

**Jan Skalka and Martin Drlik**
Automated Assessment and Microlearning Units as Predictors of At-Risk Students and Students' Outcomes in the Introductory Programming Courses
Reprinted from: *Appl. Sci.* **2020**, *10*, 4566, doi:10.3390/app10134566 . . . . . . . . . . . . . . . . . . 185

**F. José Racero, Salvador Bueno and M. Dolores Gallego**
Predicting Students' Behavioral Intention to Use Open Source Software: A Combined View of the Technology Acceptance Model and Self-Determination Theory
Reprinted from: *Appl. Sci.* **2020**, *10*, 2711, doi:10.3390/app10082711 . . . . . . . . . . . . . . . . . **209**

**Yousef A. M. Qasem, Shahla Asadi, Rusli Abdullah, Yusmadi Yah, Rodziah Atan, Mohammed A. Al-Sharafi and Amr Abdullatif Yassin**
A Multi-Analytical Approach to Predict the Determinants of Cloud Computing Adoption in Higher Education Institutions
Reprinted from: *Appl. Sci.* **2020**, *10*, 4905, doi:10.3390/app10144905 . . . . . . . . . . . . . . . . . **225**

**Zoltán Balogh and Michal Kuchárik**
Predicting Student Grades Based on Their Usage of LMS Moodle Using Petri Nets
Reprinted from: *Appl. Sci.* **2019**, *9*, 4211, doi:10.3390/app9204211 . . . . . . . . . . . . . . . . . . . **259**

**Hongxu Wei, Richard J. Hauer and Xuquan Zhai**
The Relationship between the Facial Expression of People in University Campus and Host-City Variables
Reprinted from: *Appl. Sci.* **2020**, *10*, 1474, doi:10.3390/app10041474 . . . . . . . . . . . . . . . . . **275**

**Jose Ramon Saura, Ana Reyes-Menendez and Dag R. Bennett**
How to Extract Meaningful Insights from UGC: A Knowledge-Based Method Applied to Education
Reprinted from: *Appl. Sci.* **2019**, *9*, 4603, doi:10.3390/app9214603 . . . . . . . . . . . . . . . . . . . **293**

**Manuel Rodríguez-Martín, Pablo Rodríguez-Gonzálvez, Alberto Sánchez-Patrocinio and Javier Ramón Sánchez**
Short CFD Simulation Activities in the Context of Fluid-Mechanical Learning in a Multidisciplinary Student Body
Reprinted from: *Appl. Sci.* **2019**, *9*, 4809, doi:10.3390/app9224809 . . . . . . . . . . . . . . . . . . . **309**

**Shan-Hui Chao, Jinzhang Jiang, Chia-Hsuan Hsu, Yi-Te Chiang, Eric Ng and Wei-Ta Fang**
Technology-Enhanced Learning for Graduate Students: Exploring the Correlation of Media Richness and Creativity of Computer-Mediated Communication and Face-to-Face Communication
Reprinted from: *Appl. Sci.* **2020**, *10*, 1602, doi:10.3390/app10051602 . . . . . . . . . . . . . . . . . **327**

**Juan L. Rastrollo-Guerrero, Juan A. Gómez-Pulido, and Arturo Durán-Domínguez**
Analyzing and Predicting Students' Performance by Means of Machine Learning: A Review
Reprinted from: *Appl. Sci.* **2020**, *10*, 1042, doi:10.3390/app10031042 . . . . . . . . . . . . . . . . . **345**

# About the Editors

**Juan A. Gómez-Pulido** received a PhD degree from the Complutense University, Madrid, Spain, in 1993. He is currently a full professor in the Department of Technologies of Computers and Communications, University of Extremadura, Spain. He has authored or co-authored 70 ISI journals, almost 100 book chapters, and 300 peer-reviewed conference proceedings. He has participated in 19 funded research projects, leading some of them. His current main research efforts revolve around predicting students' performance, although he also works on hot topics about machine learning, bioinformatics, and reconfigurable and embedded computing based on FPGA devices, optimization, and evolutionary computing.

**Young Park** (PhD) is currently a professor and a graduate advisor in the Department of Computer Science and Information Systems, Bradley University, USA. He also worked at the University of Windsor in Canada, New York University, and Soonchunhyang University in South Korea. His teaching is geared toward students' personalized learning. His main research areas include recommender systems, Web search, data mining, and software engineering. He has conducted research on topics such as personalized recommender systems and prediction systems in the education sector, among others. Specifically, he is working to develop software that predicts personalized grades and areas of improvement.

**Ricardo Soto** received a PhD degree in computer science from the University of Nantes, France, in 2009. He is currently a Full Professor and the Head of the Computer Science Department, Pontical Catholic University of Valparaíso, Chile. His main areas of research interest include metaheuristics, global optimization, and autonomous search. In this context, he has published more than 200 scientific papers in different international conferences and journals, some of them top-ranked in computer science, operational research, and artificial intelligence. Most of these papers are based on the resolution of real-world and academic optimization problems, some of them related to learning processes.

*Editorial*

# Advanced Techniques in the Analysis and Prediction of Students' Behaviour in Technology-Enhanced Learning Contexts

**Juan A. Gómez-Pulido [1,*], Young Park [2] and Ricardo Soto [3]**

[1] Department of Technologies of Computers and Communications, University of Extremadura, 10003 Cáceres, Spain
[2] Department of Computer Science and Information Systems, Bradley University, Peoria, IL 61625, USA; young@fsmail.bradley.edu
[3] School of Computer Engineering, Pontificia Universidad Católica de Valparaíso, 4059 Valparaiso, Chile; ricardo.soto@pucv.cl
* Correspondence: jangomez@unex.es

Received: 16 August 2020; Accepted: 2 September 2020; Published: 5 September 2020

**Abstract:** The development and promotion of teaching-enhanced learning tools in the academic field is leading to the collection of a large amount of data generated from the usual activity of students and teachers. The analysis of these data is an opportunity to improve many aspects of the learning process: recommendations of activities, dropout prediction, performance and knowledge analysis, resources optimization, etc. However, these improvements would not be possible without the application of computer science techniques that have demonstrated a high effectiveness for this purpose: data mining, big data, machine learning, deep learning, collaborative filtering, and recommender systems, among other fields related to intelligent systems. This Special Issue provides 17 papers that show advances in the analysis, prediction, and recommendation of applications propelled by artificial intelligence, big data, and machine learning in the teaching-enhanced learning context.

**Keywords:** teaching-enhanced learning and teaching; personalized learning; intelligent tutoring systems; data mining and big data analysis; intelligent systems; machine and deep learning; recommender systems; software tools; performance prediction; knowledge analysis

## 1. Introduction

Analysing and predicting individuals' behaviour are important topics in academic environments, especially after the increasing development and deployment of software tools for supporting learning stages. The automation of many processes involved in the usual students' activity allows for processing massive volumes of data collected from teaching-enhanced learning (TEL) platforms, leading to useful applications for academic personnel. In this way, monitoring and analysing students' behaviour are key activities required for the improvement of students' learning.

Recommendations of activities, dropout prediction, performance and knowledge analysis, and resources optimization, among other students-centred interests, are complex tasks that involve many elements that need to be considered. Therefore, it becomes necessary that these efforts search for support from other fields in the computational science that have demonstrated a high effectiveness when handling data and processes that are strongly interconnected. Data mining, big data, machine learning (ML), deep learning, collaborative filtering, and recommender systems, among other fields related to intelligent systems, allow for the development of advanced techniques that provide a significant potential for the above purposes, leading to new applications and more effective approaches in the analysis and prediction of the students' behaviour in academic contexts.

This Special Issue provides a collection of papers of original advances in the analysis, prediction, and recommendation of applications propelled by artificial intelligence, big data, and machine learning, especially in the TEL context.

## 2. Summary of the Contributions in This Special Issue

Although each paper published in this Special Issue covers different topics, we can identify three groups where the papers can be classified according to their main focus: performance and behaviour prediction, dropout and risk prediction, and intelligent analysis of different learning aspects. However, some of these papers could be classified into more than one of these groups. Finally, a review article is also provided to get a wide perspective of this field.

With regard to performance and behaviour prediction, we find four contributions.

The first article in this group is entitled "Implementing AutoML in Educational Data Mining for Prediction Tasks" [1], by Maria Tsiakmaki, Georgios Kostopoulos, Sotiris Kotsiantis and Omiros Ragos. This research focuses on examining the potential use of advanced ML strategies on educational settings from the perspective of hyperparameter optimization, because of the complexity of ML when it is applied for a given problem formulation and it must be optimally configured. To this end, the authors analyze the effectiveness of automated ML (autoML) for the task of predicting students' learning outcomes based on their participation in online learning platforms, limiting the search space to tree-based and rule-based models. After carrying out many experiments, the performance of AutoML is verified. This proposal allows educators and instructors in educational data mining (EDM) to perform experiments with good parameter configurations, thus achieving highly accurate results.

The second article in this group is entitled "Predicting Student Performance in Higher Educational Institutions Using Video Learning Analytics and Data Mining Techniques" [2], by Raza Hasan, Sellappan Palaniappan, Salman Mahmood, Ali Abbas, Kamal Uddin Sarker, and Mian Usman Sattar. The authors have developed a system for predicting student's overall performance at the end of the semester using video learning analytics and data mining techniques. They consider video-based learning with flipped teaching to improve student's academic performance. Particularly, the authors applied eight classification algorithms (where random forest obtained the best results) to data collected from the student information system, learning management system and mobile applications. Additionally, they used genetic search, principle component analysis, rule inducer and multivariate projection to improve different aspects of the study.

The third article in this group is entitled "Towards Portability of Models for Predicting Students' Final Performance in University Courses Starting from Moodle Logs" [3], by Javier López-Zambrano, Juan A. Lara, and Cristóbal Romero. This work focuses on the data sources rather than the prediction techniques. Particularly, the work studies the portability of prediction models obtained directly from Moodle logs, according to grouping similar courses by degree or level of usage of activities or using numerical or categorical attributes. To this end, the authors apply a classification algorithm to the datasets in order to obtain decision tree models and test their portability to other courses by comparing the obtained accuracies. The authors conclude that the prediction models can be transferred to different courses under some circumstances.

The fourth article in this group is entitled "Prediction of High Capabilities in the Development of Kindergarten Children" [4], by Yenny Villuendas-Rey, Carmen F. Rey-Benguría, Oscar Camacho-Nieto, and Cornelio Yáñez-Márquez. This paper focuses on a type of the student's behaviour: the early detection of high capabilities, particularly at kindergartens, when the students are children. The prediction of such students is difficult, due to its low number and the focus of the teachers in the learning process. The authors propose a prediction algorithm based on Nearest Neighbor able to tackle this problem with satisfactory results.

With regard to dropout and risk prediction prediction, we find five contributions.

The first article in this group is entitled "Predicting Students Success in Blended Learning-Evaluating Different Interactions Inside Learning Management Systems" [5], by Luiz Antonio

Buschetto Macarini, Cristian Cechinel, Matheus Francisco Batista Machado, Vinicius Faria Culmant Ramos, and Roberto Munoz. The authors apply ML techniques for detecting at-risk students earlier in courses involving algorithms and programming topics in undergraduate programs, where dropout and failure rates are usually high. This research finds the best combination of datasets collected from Moodle (considering cognitive, social and teaching presence) and classification algorithms. The best ML model was able to detect students at-risk in the first week of the course.

The second article in this group is entitled "The Machine Learning-Based Dropout Early Warning System for Improving the Performance of Dropout Prediction" [6], by Sunbok Lee and Jae Young Chung. This researc tries to identify students who are at risk of dropping out of school. To this end, the authors developed a dropout early warning system characterized by two features. On the one hand, the system addresses the class imbalance issue using the synthetic minority oversampling techniques (SMOTE) and the ensemble methods in ML. On the other hand, the system evaluates the trained classifiers with both receiver operating characteristic (ROC) and precision–recall (PR) curves. The authors trained random forest, boosted decision tree, random forest with SMOTE, and boosted decision tree with SMOTE by using large datasets. Among these ML techniques, boosted decision tree obtained the best results.

The third article in this group is entitled "A Learning Analytics Approach to Identify Students at Risk of Dropout: A Case Study with a Technical Distance Education Course" [7], by Emanuel Marques Queiroga, João Ladislau Lopes, Kristofer Kappel, Marilton Aguiar, Ricardo Matsumura Araújo, Roberto Munoz, Rodolfo Villarroel, and Cristian Cechinel. This article continues in the line of the early prediction of at-risk students. Here, the authors consider students' interactions with the virtual learning environment as data source. With the goal of maximizing the prediction results, the authors apply an elitist genetic algorithm for tuning the hyperparameters of some classifiers: classic decision tree (DT), random forest (RF), multilayer perceptron (MLP), logistic regression (LG), and the meta-algorithm AdaBoost (ADA).

The fourth article in this group is entitled "An Early Warning System to Detect At-Risk Students in Online Higher Education" [8], by David Bañeres, M. Elena Rodríguez, Ana Elena Guerrero-Roldán, and Abdulkadir Karadeniz. The authors centered the research effort on finding accurate predictive models to identify at-risk students. The authors considered several classifiers, whose prediction quality was evaluated by a proposed method. Furthermore, they developed an early warning system tested in a real educational setting, which demonstrated accuracy and usefulness for detecting at-risk students in online higher education. This system shows different dashboards where students and teachers can analyze the information and perform some interventions to reduce at-risk situations.

The fifth article in this group is entitled "Automated Assessment and Microlearning Units as Predictors of At-Risk Students and Students' Outcomes in the Introductory Programming Courses" [9], by Jan Skalka and Martin Drlik. This work predicts at-risk students particularly in the context of introductory programming courses, where some students with limited programming skills can be discouraged by key aspects as the ability to think abstractly, solve problems, and design solutions. This work analyzed the automated source code assessment of assignments and the implementation of a set of microlearning units as predictors of at-risk students and students' outcomes. The authors found a significant contribution of automated code assessment in students' learning outcomes and proved a certain dependence between the students' activity and achievement in the activities and final students' outcomes.

With regard to intelligent analysis of different learning aspects, we find seven contributions.

The first article in this group is entitled "Predicting Students' Behavioral Intention to Use Open Source Software: A Combined View of the Technology Acceptance Model and Self-Determination Theory" [10], by F. José Racero, Salvador Bueno and M. Dolores Gallego. This work focuses on students' behavioral intention to continue using open source software (OSS) after be trained in it. This intention is predicted by applying Self-Determination Theory and the technological acceptance model (TAM). The dataset was built collecting data from a survey. The results obtained by the model confirmed the influence of the intrinsic motivations, autonomy and relatedness, to improve perceptions with regard to the usefulness of OSS and, therefore, on the intention to continue considering OSS.

The second article in this group is entitled "A Multi-Analytical Approach to Predict the Determinants of Cloud Computing Adoption in Higher Education Institutions" [11], by Yousef A. M. Qasem, Shahla Asadi, Rusli Abdullah, Yusmadi Yah, Rodziah Atan, Mohammed A. Al-Sharafi, and Amr Abdullatif Yassin. This work predicts the key aspects that influence on the managers of higher education institutions for adopting cloud computing as services provider. To this end, a variance-based structural equation modeling (PLS-SEM) and an artificial neural network (ANN) were applied to data collected from 134 managers involved in the decision making of the institutions. The PLS-SEM approch was used for extracting the significant relationships among the identified factors, whereas ANN ranked the normalized importance among those factors. It is interesting to know that technology readiness is the most important predictor for cloud computing adoption, followed by security and competitive pressure. Furthermore, the authors present an innovative approach useful for decision-makers to develop stategies for adopting cloud computing services.

The third article in this group is entitled "Predicting Student Grades Based on Their Usage of LMS Moodle Using Petri Nets" [12], by Zoltán Balogh and Michal Kuchárik. In this paper, the data source is the popular learning management system (LMS) Moodle. This platform provides the information needed for analyzing the correlations between access to materials and the final grade in order to predict student's grades. According to the highest correlation, a model with Petri nets predicts what grade the student would get based on their usage of Moodle.

The fourth article in this group is entitled "The Relationship between the Facial Expression of People in University Campus and Host-City Variables" [13], by Hongxu Wei, Richard J. Hauer and Xuquan Zhai. The authors evaluate the public attitude towards university campuses and detect the relationship with host-city variables by using data about facial expression scores on social networks. It is interesting to know this attitude since it matters for the resource investment to sustainable science and technology. To this end, ML techniques area applied on datasets composed of 4327 selfies collected from social networks. The photos provide scores of happy and sad facial expressions and a positive response index was calculated. After analyzing some interesting results, the main conclusion is that people tend to show positive expression at campuses in cities with more education infrastructures but fewer residences and internet users.

The fifth article in this group is entitled "How to Extract Meaningful Insights from UGC: A Knowledge-Based Method Applied to Education" [14], by Jose Ramon Saura, Ana Reyes-Menendez, and Dag R. Benn. Students and teachers are a rich source of user generated content (UGC) on social networks and digital platforms. The vast amount of this type of data can supply useful knowledge by extracting and visualizing samples of readily available content, particularly the tweets published in Twitter. The authors apply latent dirichlet allocation (LDA) to identify topics, which are then subjected to sentiment analysis by using ML and a data visualization algorithm for complex networks. This research allows practitioners to improve short-term education strategies and interventions.

The sixth article in this group is entitled "Short CFD Simulation Activities in the Context of Fluid-Mechanical Learning in a Multidisciplinary Student Body" [15], by Manuel Rodríguez-Martín, Pablo Rodríguez-Gonzálvez, Alberto Sánchez-Patrocinio, and Javier Ramón Sánchez. The learning goal in this research was the instruction of students in fluid simulation tools in industrial engineering bachelors. These tools usually require long training times. Therefore, the authors propose a methodology based on short lessons, whose statistical results show a good acceptance in many terms. Furthermore, a ML technique was applied to find group peculiarities and differences among them in order to identify the need for further personalization of the learning activity.

The seventh article in this group is entitled "Technology-Enhanced Learning for Graduate Students: Exploring the Correlation of Media Richness and Creativity of Computer-Mediated Communication and Face-to-Face Communication" [16], by Shan-Hui Chao, Jinzhang Jiang, Chia-Hsuan Hsu, Yi-Te Chiang, Eric Ng, and Wei-Ta Fang. This article explores and compares the differences in potential creative thinking that media richness had on learners in creativity training by considering computer-mediated communication and face-to-face communication. The authors found that the computer-mediated communication format shows better fluency, flexibility, and originality dimensions of creative thinking than the face-to-face format. Moreover, the computer-mediated format provides a greater level of media richness perception.

Finally, this special issue includes the review article entitled "Analyzing and Predicting Students' Performance by Means of Machine Learning: A Review" [17], by Juan L. Rastrollo-Guerrero, Juan A. Gómez-Pulido, and Arturo Durán-Domínguez. This article provides a wide perspective in the field of predicting students' performance. Many promising algorithms and methods focused on predicting students' performance have been investigated, hence the need to provide a detailed review. In this article, almost 70 papers were analyzed to show different techniques and objectives, mainly in the context of the artificial intelligence (AI).

**Author Contributions:** The authors have contributed equally to the conceptualization, writing, supervision and editing of this manuscript. All authors have read and agreed to the published version of the manuscript.

**Funding:** This research received no external funding.

**Acknowledgments:** We would like to acknowledge all of the authors and peer reviewers for their contributions to this Special Issue. We would also like to thank the editorial board of Applied Sciences for trusting our proposal of Special Issue and the editorial team at MDPI for the help in handling the editorial process.

**Conflicts of Interest:** The authors declare no conflict of interest.

## References

1. Tsiakmaki, M.; Kostopoulos, G.; Kotsiantis, S.; Ragos, O. Implementing AutoML in Educational Data Mining for Prediction Tasks. *Appl. Sci.* **2020**, *10*, 90. [CrossRef]
2. Hasan, R.; Palaniappan, S.; Mahmood, S.; Abbas, A.; Sarker, K.U.; Sattar, M.U. Predicting Student Performance in Higher Educational Institutions Using Video Learning Analytics and Data Mining Techniques. *Appl. Sci.* **2020**, *10*, 3894. [CrossRef]
3. López-Zambrano, J.; Lara, J.A.; Romero, C. Towards Portability of Models for Predicting Students' Final Performance in University Courses Starting from Moodle Logs. *Appl. Sci.* **2020**, *10*, 354. [CrossRef]
4. Villuendas-Rey, Y.; Rey-Benguría, C.F.; Camacho-Nieto, O.; Yáñez-Márquez, C. Prediction of High Capabilities in the Development of Kindergarten Children. *Appl. Sci.* **2020**, *10*, 2710. [CrossRef]
5. Buschetto Macarini, L.A.; Cechinel, C.; Batista Machado, M.F.; Faria Culmant Ramos, V.; Munoz, R. Predicting Students Success in Blended Learning—Evaluating Different Interactions Inside Learning Management Systems. *Appl. Sci.* **2019**, *9*, 5523. [CrossRef]
6. Lee, S.; Chung, J.Y. The Machine Learning-Based Dropout Early Warning System for Improving the Performance of Dropout Prediction. *Appl. Sci.* **2019**, *9*, 93. [CrossRef]
7. Queiroga, E.M.; Lopes, J.L.; Kappel, K.; Aguiar, M.; Araújo, R.M.; Munoz, R.; Villarroel, R.; Cechinel, C. A Learning Analytics Approach to Identify Students at Risk of Dropout: A Case Study with a Technical Distance Education Course. *Appl. Sci.* **2020**, *10*, 3998. [CrossRef]
8. Bañeres, D.; Rodríguez, M.E.; Guerrero-Roldán, A.E.; Karadeniz, A. An Early Warning System to Detect At-Risk Students in Online Higher Education. *Appl. Sci.* **2020**, *10*, 4427. [CrossRef]
9. Skalka, J.; Drlik, M. Automated Assessment and Microlearning Units as Predictors of At-Risk Students and Students' Outcomes in the Introductory Programming Courses. *Appl. Sci.* **2020**, *10*, 4566. [CrossRef]
10. Racero, F.J.; Bueno, S.; Gallego, M.D. Predicting Students' Behavioral Intention to Use Open Source Software: A Combined View of the Technology Acceptance Model and Self-Determination Theory. *Appl. Sci.* **2020**, *10*, 2711. [CrossRef]
11. Qasem, Y.A.M.; Asadi, S.; Abdullah, R.; Yah, Y.; Atan, R.; Al-Sharafi, M.A.; Yassin, A.A. A Multi-Analytical Approach to Predict the Determinants of Cloud Computing Adoption in Higher Education Institutions. *Appl. Sci.* **2020**, *10*, 4905. [CrossRef]
12. Balogh, Z.; Kuchárik, M. Predicting Student Grades Based on Their Usage of LMS Moodle Using Petri Nets. *Appl. Sci.* **2019**, *9*, 4211. [CrossRef]

13. Wei, H.; Hauer, R.J.; Zhai, X. The Relationship between the Facial Expression of People in University Campus and Host-City Variables. *Appl. Sci.* **2020**, *10*, 1474. [CrossRef]
14. Saura, J.R.; Reyes-Menendez, A.; Bennett, D.R. How to Extract Meaningful Insights from UGC: A Knowledge-Based Method Applied to Education. *Appl. Sci.* **2019**, *9*, 4603. [CrossRef]
15. Rodríguez-Martín, M.; Rodríguez-Gonzálvez, P.; Sánchez-Patrocinio, A.; Sánchez, J.R. Short CFD Simulation Activities in the Context of Fluid-Mechanical Learning in a Multidisciplinary Student Body. *Appl. Sci.* **2019**, *9*, 4809. [CrossRef]
16. Chao, S.H.; Jiang, J.; Hsu, C.H.; Chiang, Y.T.; Ng, E.; Fang, W.T. Technology-Enhanced Learning for Graduate Students: Exploring the Correlation of Media Richness and Creativity of Computer-Mediated Communication and Face-to-Face Communication. *Appl. Sci.* **2020**, *10*, 1602. [CrossRef]
17. Rastrollo-Guerrero, J.L.; Gómez-Pulido, J.A.; Durán-Domínguez, A. Analyzing and Predicting Students' Performance by Means of Machine Learning: A Review. *Appl. Sci.* **2020**, *10*, 42. [CrossRef]

© 2020 by the authors. Licensee MDPI, Basel, Switzerland. This article is an open access article distributed under the terms and conditions of the Creative Commons Attribution (CC BY) license (http://creativecommons.org/licenses/by/4.0/).

Article

# Implementing AutoML in Educational Data Mining for Prediction Tasks

**Maria Tsiakmaki, Georgios Kostopoulos, Sotiris Kotsiantis * and Omiros Ragos**

Department of Mathematics, University of Patras, 26504 Rio Patras, Greece; m.tsiakmaki@gmail.com (M.T.); kostg@sch.gr (G.K.); ragos@math.upatras.gr (O.R.)
* Correspondence: sotos@math.upatras.gr

Received: 29 November 2019; Accepted: 17 December 2019; Published: 20 December 2019

**Abstract:** Educational Data Mining (EDM) has emerged over the last two decades, concerning with the development and implementation of data mining methods in order to facilitate the analysis of vast amounts of data originating from a wide variety of educational contexts. Predicting students' progression and learning outcomes, such as dropout, performance and course grades, is regarded among the most important tasks of the EDM field. Therefore, applying appropriate machine learning algorithms for building accurate predictive models is of outmost importance for both educators and data scientists. Considering the high-dimensional input space and the complexity of machine learning algorithms, the process of building accurate and robust learning models requires advanced data science skills, while is time-consuming and error-prone in most cases. In addition, choosing the proper method for a given problem formulation and configuring the optimal parameters' values for a specific model is a demanding task, whilst it is often very difficult to understand and explain the produced results. In this context, the main purpose of the present study is to examine the potential use of advanced machine learning strategies on educational settings from the perspective of hyperparameter optimization. More specifically, we investigate the effectiveness of automated Machine Learning (autoML) for the task of predicting students' learning outcomes based on their participation in online learning platforms. At the same time, we limit the search space to tree-based and rule-based models in order to achieving transparent and interpretable results. To this end, a plethora of experiments were carried out, revealing that autoML tools achieve consistently superior results. Hopefully our work will help nonexpert users (e.g., educators and instructors) in the field of EDM to conduct experiments with appropriate automated parameter configurations, thus achieving highly accurate and comprehensible results.

**Keywords:** automatic machine learning; educational data mining; Bayesian optimization; early performance prediction

## 1. Introduction

Educational Data Mining (EDM) is the research field of using data mining methods and tools in educational settings [1,2]. Its main objective is to analyze these environments in order to find appropriate solutions to educational research issues [3], all of which are directed to improve teaching and learning [4]. Their results help students improve their learning performance, provide personalized recommendations, enhance the teaching performance, evaluate learning effectiveness, organize institutional resources and educational offer and many more [1,5].

Three common concerns that employ EDM techniques are the detection of whether a student is going to pass or fail a certain course, the prediction of students' final marks and the identification of students that are likely to drop out. The ability to predict students' performance and their underlying learning difficulties is a significant task and leads to benefits for both students and educational institutions [6]. With a view to encouraging those students, remedial actions could be organized, such as early alerts and advising interventions [7]. In addition, the critical analysis of the reasons for failure and dropouts assist educators to improve their pedagogical basis and teaching approach [8]. Moreover, when used effectively, they can help institutions enhance learning experiences, develop appropriate strategies and ultimately, reduce dropout rates [9]. As such, we consider that effective tools for predicting student failures can be beneficial, especially at an early stage.

Related studies encompass a large collection of data mining tasks for studying different aspects of these problems. They include algorithms for attribute selection, association rule learning, classification and regression. Most of these methods depend on a wide range of hyperparameter choices with varying degrees of complexity and dimensions, which make them difficult for non-machine-learning experts to apply and even more to reason about. Meanwhile, the rapid development and the wide distribution of machine learning applications also point out the necessity of advanced data science skills in the relevant fields. Therefore, the need for machine learning methods that automate several of these design choices has been identified. The research area that promises to reduce the human input and effort on these processes is called automated Machine Learning or autoML. In experiments with several datasets, results from sophisticated automated optimization approaches compared favorably with results published from human experts inputs and the state of the art [10–13]. AutoML allows non-experts, such as educators and instructors, to conduct experiments and produce complex and effective learning models that ultimately support educational institutions.

At the same time, the need to provide transparent and explainable ML systems is also a factor to consider [14]. Such an effort aims to help scientists and nonexperts to understand and analyze ML models, their operational mechanism and the choices made towards their decision-making processes. Generally, it can be argued that methods that provide more linguistic models, such as rule and tree-based classifiers, are considered to be more comprehensible [15]. On the other hand, methods that are easy to understand and interpret tend to have lower predictive accuracy [16]. However, practical experience has demonstrated that, for some cases, the explainability feature is more important than the predictive accuracy [14,15]. AutoML could tackle the performance-transparency trade-off, providing tuned hyperparameters that improve the overall performance of the selected methods.

In the above context, our present work investigates the use of autoML in order to automate any part of the process of building machine learning models for the above mentioned three tasks: predict students who are prone to pass of fail, student's final grade and students at risk of dropout. We present a comparative study on classic educational data mining techniques and autoML. To equally highlight the importance of producing interpretable and explainable machine learning models [14,16], we restrict the configuration space by allowing only tree-based and rule-based classifiers (the choice of the classifier itself is considered as a hyperparameter). We prove that in most cases, the application of autoML on educational data improves model performance over traditional approaches. To the best of our knowledge, there is no research that demonstrates the use of advanced machine learning strategies to educational settings.

This paper is organized as follows. Section 2 is devoted to related work. We present a collection of studies that investigate the student's performance employing data mining techniques. Section 3 briefly introduces the Bayesian optimization search strategy that allows the efficient hyperparameter configuration. Section 4 describes our proposed approach. Section 5 illustrates our results. In Section 6 we discuss our findings, while Section 7 concludes our research considering some thoughts for future work.

## 2. Related Work

Predicting students' learning behavior and outcomes is regarded among the most important tasks of the EDM field. The main interest is mainly focused on three forms of predictive problems [17]. Predicting student performance (i.e., whether a student will pass or fail a course) covers a very wide area of research in the EDM field [18]. In addition, a plethora of studies has been published with the aim of predicting students who are prone to drop out from a course, a very important problem, which principally concerns distance learning [19]. Finally, another common problem on prediction is estimating students' grades in a specific test, an exam or a course [20].

## 2.1. Related Work on Predicting Student Academic Performance

Mueen et al. (2016) employed Naïve Bayes (NB), Neural Networks (NNs), and Decision Trees (DTS) classification algorithms to predict the performance of undergraduate students [21]. The dataset was collected from two courses, both supported by a Learning Management System (LMS). The information retrieved included the access to teaching material, the performance on course assignments and the participation in discussion fora. The experimental results revealed that NB classifier outperformed the other two methods.

Student performance prediction models were also constructed and compared in a similar study [22]. Demographic features, academic background and behavioral metrics for student and parent participation in the learning process were exploited for this purpose. Apart from Artificial Neural Network (ANN), NB and DTS algorithms, the authors also compared several ensemble methods such as Bagging, Boosting and Random Forest (RF). The ANN model outperformed the other data mining techniques, while Boosting was the best ensemble method.

The prediction of whether a student should be considered as qualified or not was the research objective of Kaur et al. (2015) [23]. The authors experimented with four attribute evaluation methods and five classification algorithms, using a sample dataset of 152 regular high school students. The Multilayer Perceptron (MLP) was the best performing classifier among all other methods.

Guo et al. (2015) developed a prewarning system for students at risk of failing on the basis of a deep learning multiclass classification model [24]. The deep neural system developed in this work was a six-layer, fully connected feed-forward neural network with Rectified Linear Units (ReLU). The output layer was composed of five neurons with Softmax as a classifier. Each node on the output layer represented the students' final score {O, A, B, C, D}. The results showed that the proposed architecture acquired the highest accuracy values compared to three familiar classification algorithms: NB, MLP and Support Vector Machine (SVM).

The objective of Saa's study (2016) was to discover relations between students' personal and social factors, as well as their educational performance using data mining tasks [25]. The authors collected 270 records through online questionnaires and tested four classification algorithms, while the values of the class attribute were: excellent, very good, good, and pass. The best performing method was the Classification and Regression Tree (CART) classifier, scoring an accuracy measure of 40%.

In another comparative study regarding the effectiveness of EDM techniques [26], the authors compared four methods to predict students that are likely to fail in introductory programming courses at early stages. In addition, they demonstrated the importance of data preprocessing and algorithms fine-tuning tasks in the effectiveness of these techniques. Finally, the fine-tuned SVM was the best performer.

Predicting students' graduation performance at the end of a degree program was one of the three research goals examined by Asif et al. (2017) [27]. The data used comprised students' marks for all the courses in the four years of the program and variables related to students' pre-admission marks. The graduation mark (the class attribute) was divided into five possible values: A, B, C, D, E. The authors used several classification algorithms (DTS, k-Nearest Neighbor (kNN), NB, NNs and RF), while the maximum accuracy score (83.65%) was obtained by NB.

Finally, a recent study indicated the effectiveness of semisupervised learning (SSL) methods in students' performance prediction [28]. The authors evaluated the performance of SSL algorithms, namely Self-Training, Democratic, De-Tri-Training, Tri-Training, Co-Training, RAndom Subspace CO-training (RASCO) and Rel-RASCO. The best overall averaged accuracy score was obtained by Tri-Training algorithm with a C4.5 Decision Tree as the base classifier. Moreover, the Tri-Training algorithm performed better than the C4.5 Decision Tree supervised algorithm trained on the full dataset.

## 2.2. Related Work on Predicting Student Grade

Personalized multiple regression-based methods and matrix factorization approaches based on recommender systems were used by Elbadrawy et al. (2016) to forecast students' grades in future courses and in-class assessments [29]. Briefly, the first method was the course-specific regression, which predicted the grade that a student will achieve in a specific course as a sparse linear combination of the grades that the student obtained in past courses. The second method was the personalized linear multiregression, which employed a linear combination of k regression models, weighted on a per-student basis. The third method was a standard matrix factorization approach that approximated the observed entries of the student–course grade matrix. The fourth method was matrix factorization based on factorization machines. The evaluations showed that the factorization machines produced lower error rates for the next-term grade prediction.

Predicting student performance was also the main focus of the study conducted by Xu et al. (2017) [30]. Their goal was to predict the final cumulative Grade Point Average (GPA) of a student, given his/her background and performance states of the known grades and the predictions for the courses that have not been taken. For enabling such progressive predictions, the authors proposed a two-layer architecture. The first layer implements the base predictors for each course, given the performance state of graduate students on courses relevant to the targeted course. For discovering the relevant courses, a course clustering method was developed. In the second layer, ensemble-based predictors were developed, able to keep improving themselves by accumulating new student data over time. The authors' architecture was compared with four classic machine learning algorithms, named Linear Regression (LR), Logistic Regression (LogR), RF and kNN. The proposed method yielded the best prediction performance.

Predicting students' final grade was one of the two research goals also by Strecht et al. (2015) [31]. The authors evaluated various popular regression algorithms, i.e., Ordinary Least Squares, SVM, CART, kNN, RF and AdaBoost R2. The experiments were carried out using administrate data from the university's Student Information System (SIS) of Porto, concerning approximately 700 courses. The algorithms with best results overall were SVM, RF and AdaBoost R2.

The proposed method by Meier et al. (2015) made personalized and timely predictions of the grade of each student in a class [32]. Using data obtained from a pilot course, the authors' methodology suggested that it was effective to perform early in-class assessments such as quizzes, which result in timely performance prediction for each student. The study compared their proposed algorithm against four different prediction methods: two simple benchmarks; Single performance assessment and past assessments and weights and two well-known data mining algorithms; Linear Regression (LR) employing the Ordinary Least Squares (OLS) method and kNN algorithm (k = 7). The error of the proposed method decreased approximately linearly as more homework and in-class exam results were added to the model.

Sweeney et al. (2016) also presented the problem of student performance prediction as a regression task [33]. They explored three classes of methods for predicting the next-term grade of students. These were (1) simple baselines, (2) Matrix Factorization (MF)-based methods, and (3) common regression models. For the third category of methods, four different regression models were tested: RF, Stochastic Gradient Descent (SGD), kNN and personalized LR. The obtained results revealed that a hybrid of the RF model and the MF-based Factorization Machine (FM) was the best performer.

The first study that applied Semi-Supervised Regression (SSR) methods for regression tasks in educational settings was carried out by Kostopoulos et al. (2019) [34]. In order to predict final grades in a distance learning course, the authors proposed a Multi-Scheme Semi-Supervised Regression Approach (MSSRA) employing RF and a set of three k-NN algorithms as the base regressors. A plethora of features related to students' characteristics, academic performance and interactions within the learning platform throughout the academic year formed the training set. The results indicated that the proposed algorithm outperformed typical classical regression methods.

Finally, a recent study utilized eight familiar supervised learning algorithms – LR, Random Forests (RF), Sequential Minimal Optimization algorithm for regression problems (SMOreg), 5-NN, M5 Rules, M5, Gaussian processes (GP), Bagging – for predicting students' marks [35]. The training data contained selected demographic variables, students' first semester grades along with the number of examination attempts per course. The reported results seem rather satisfactory, ranging from 1.217 to 1.943. It was observed that RF, Bagging and SMOreg took precedence over the other methods.

### 2.3. Related Work on Predicting Student Dropout

One interested study used data gathered from 419 high schools students in Mexico [36]. The authors carried out experiments to predict dropout at different steps of the course, to select the best indicators of dropout. Results showed that their classifier (named ICRM2) could predict student dropout within the first 4–6 weeks of the course.

Student retention and the identification of potential problems as early as possible was the main aim of Zhang et al. (2010) [37]. The authors used data from the Thames Valley University systems that were related to the background and the academic activities of the students. Three algorithms, namely NB, SVM and DTS, were chosen and different configurations for each algorithm were tested in order to find the optimum result. Finally, NB was reported to have achieved the highest prediction accuracy.

Moreover, Delen (2010) used five years of institutional data along with several popular data mining techniques (four individual and three ensemble techniques), in order to build models to predict and explain the reasons behind students dropping out [38]. The data contained variables related to students' academic, financial, and demographic characteristics. The SVM produced the best results when compared to ANN, DTS and LogR. The information fusion-type ensemble model produced the best results when compared with the Bagging and Boosting ensembles.

Lykourentzou et al. (2009) presented a dropout prediction method for e-learning courses, based on three machine learning techniques: NNs, SVM and the probabilistic ensemble simplified fuzzy ARTMAP [39]. The results of these techniques were combined using three decision schemes. The dataset consisted of demographic attributes, prior academic performances, time-varying characteristics depicting the students' progress during the courses, as well as their level of engagement with the e-learning procedure. The decision scheme where a student was considered to be a dropout if at least one technique has classified this student as such, was reported to be the most appropriate solution for achieving and maintaining high accuracy, sensitivity and precision results in predicting at-risk students.

Superby et al. (2006) applied NNs, discriminant analysis, DTS and RF on survey data from three universities, to classify new students in low-risk, medium-risk, and high-risk categories [40]. The authors found that the scholastic history and socio-family background were the most significant predictors of students at risk. The least bad result of the four methods was reported by the NNs method, reaching the total rate of correctly classified students up to 57.35%.

Herzog's study (2006) examined the predictive accuracy of the DTS and NNs over the problem of predicting college freshmen retention [41]. The author used three sources to produce the data set: the institutional student information system for student demographic; the American College Test (ACT)'s Student Profile Section for parent income data; and the National Student Clearinghouse for identifying transfer-out students. Overall prediction results showed that the DTS and NNS performed substantially better to the LR baseline. Also, the different results from the three NNs variations confirmed the importance of exploring available setup options.

Finally, a recent study explored the usage of semi-supervised techniques for the task of drop out prediction [42]. The dataset consisted of 2 classes of 344 instances characterized by 12 attributes. The authors compared familiar SSL techniques, Self-Training, Co-Training, Democratic Co-Training, Tri-Training, RASCO and Rel-RASCO. In their two separate experiments, C4.5 and NB were the base classifiers, while C4.5 was the dominant supervised algorithm. The results revealed that Tri-Training (C4.5) algorithm outperformed the rest SSL algorithms as well as the supervised C4.5 Decision Tree.

To sum up, various researchers have investigated the problem of student's performance prediction employing a plethora of data mining techniques. The results reveal that there is a strong relationship between students' logged activities in LMSs and their academic achievements. Most of the proposed prediction models achieved notable results (accuracy is more than 80%). However, a variation in the outperformers is observed; i.e., there is no method that can be thought of or shown to be better than others for educational settings (Table 1). Even more, to the best of our knowledge, there is no research that demonstrates the use of advanced machine learning strategies to these settings, such as the autoML.

**Table 1.** Data mining algorithms as applied in educational settings.

| Paper | Prediction Task | Metrics | Methods Compared | Outperformers |
|---|---|---|---|---|
| *Related work on predicting student academic performance* | | | | |
| [21] | Binary Classification | Accuracy, Precision, Recall, Specificity | NB, NNs, DTs | NB |
| [22] | Binary Classification | Accuracy, Precision, Recall, F-measure | ANN, NB, DTs, RF, Bagging, Boosting | ANN and Boosting |
| [23] | Binary Classification | Accuracy, Precision, Recall, F-measure, ROC Area | NB, MLPs, SMO, J48, REPTree | MLP |
| [24] | Multiclass Classification | Accuracy | NB, MLPs, SVM | Deep Neural Network |
| [25] | Multiclass Classification | Accuracy, Precision, Recall | C4.5, NB, ID3, CART, CHAID | CART |
| [26] | Binary Classification | F-measure | NNs, J48, SVM, NB | SVM fine-tuned |
| [27] | Multiclass Classification | Accuracy, Kappa | DTs, NB, NNs, Rule Induction, 1-NN, RF | NB |
| [28] | Binary Classification | Accuracy, Specificity | De-Tri-Training, Self-Training, Democratic, Tri-Training, Co-Training, RASCO, Rel-RASCO, C4.5 | Tri-Training (C4.5 as base learner) |
| *Related work on predicting student grade* | | | | |
| [29] | Regression course grades | RMSE, MAE | Regression-based methods, Matrix factorization–based methods | Factorization machine |
| | Assessments Grades | | | Depending on the records |
| [30] | Regression GPA | MAE | LR, LogR, RF, kNN | Proposed architecture |
| [31] | Regression course grades | RMSE | SVM, RF, AB.R2, kNN, OLS, CART | SVM |
| [32] | Regression course grades | Average absolute prediction error | Single performance assessment proposed architecture and Past Assessments, Weights, LR, 7-NN | Proposed architecture |
| [33] | Regression course grades | RMSE, MAE | Simple baselines, MF-based methods, regression models {RF, SGD, kNN, personalized LR} | Authors' proposed hybrid model (FM-RF) |
| [34] | Regression course grades | MAE, RAE, RMSE, PCC | IBk, M5Rules, M5 Model Tree, LR, SMOreg, k-NN, RF, MSSRA | Proposed method (MSSRA) |
| [35] | Regression course grades | MAE | LR, RF, 5NN, M5 Rules, M5, SMOreg, GP, Bagging | RF, Bagging, SMOreg |
| *Related work on predicting student dropout* | | | | |
| [36] | Classification (dropout) | Accuracy, TP rate, TN rate, GM | NB, SMO, IBk, JRip, J48, ICRM2 | Proposed architecture (ICRM2) |
| [37] | Classification (dropout) | Accuracy | NB, SVM, DTs | NB |

Table 1. Cont.

| Paper | Prediction Task | Metrics | Methods Compared | Outperformers |
|---|---|---|---|---|
| | | *Related work on predicting student dropout* | | |
| [38] | Classification (dropout) | Accuracy | ANN, SVM DTs, LR, Information fusion, Bagging, Boosting | Information fusion |
| [39] | Classification (dropout) | Accuracy, Sensitivity, Precision | 3 decision schemes based on NN, SVM, and ARTMAP | Decision scheme 1 |
| [40] | Classification (dropout) | Accuracy | NNs, DTs, RF, Discriminant Analysis | NNs |
| [41] | Classification (dropout) | Accuracy | NNs, DTs, LR | DTs |
| [42] | Classification (dropout) | Accuracy, Sensitivity | Self-Training, Co-Training, Democratic Co-Training, Tri-Training, RASCO, Rel-RASCO, C4.5 | Tri-Training (C4.5) |

## 3. Introduction to Bayesian Optimization for Hyperparameter Optimization

For the prediction of students' academic performance, we explore the use of autoML to automatically find the optimal learning model without human intervention. The task of constructing a learning model usually includes supplementary processes; the attributes selection, learning algorithm selection, and their hyperparameter optimization. Therefore, to model the problem of automatically tuning the machine learning pipeline for obtaining the optimal performance result (i.e., the goal of autoML), the overall hyperparameter configuration space covers the choice between various preprocessing and machine learning algorithms along with their relevant hyperparameters.

This optimization problem is currently addressed by various techniques. During this section, we will briefly discuss algorithms that are part of a powerful and popular approach, referred to as "black-box optimization" techniques. More specifically, our focus will be the Bayesian optimization algorithm, as this is the method that we employ for our experiments. We will also refer to prominent autoML software packages and to the importance of autoML, especially for the non-ML-expert users. At first, we provide some definitions related to both optimization and hyperparameter optimization problem.

### 3.1. Definitions

In general, optimization refers to the process of finding the best result under specified circumstances [43]. More formally, it is the (automatic) process of finding the value or a set of values of a function (a real valued function called the objective function) that maximizes (or minimizes) its result. It is consistent with the principle of maximum expected utility or minimum expected loss (risk) [44]. It is well known that there is no single method that can solve every optimization problem efficiently. It can be challenging to choose the best method for a given problem formulation, usually complex and computationally expensive processes are required. However, optimization methods can obtain high quality results with reasonable efforts.

In machine learning systems, the targets of automation include mechanisms that optimize machine learning pipelines, such as the feature engineering, model selection, hyperparameter selection, etc. The problem of identifying values for the hyperparameters that optimize the system's performance is called the problem of hyperparameter optimization [45]. Hyperparameters are the parameters whose values are set before the beginning of the learning process, e.g., the number of neighbor's k in the nearest neighbor algorithm, or the depth of the tree in tree-structured algorithms. In contrast, model parameters are parameters that are learned during the training process, e.g., the weights of neurons in a neural network. The central focus of autoML is the hyperparameter optimization (HPO) of machine learning processes.

Formally, the general statement of the hyperparameter optimization problem is defined as [44]:

$$x^* = \operatorname*{argmin}_{x \in X} f(x) \tag{1}$$

where $f$ is the objective function, given a set of hyperparameters $x$ from a hyperparameters space X. We are interested in finding $x^*$ set that minimizes the expected loss (the value of $f(x)$). One important property of this function f is that its evaluation is expensive (costly) or even impossible to compute [46].

To make $f$ more clear, consider the context of machine learning applications, where, for example, the function $f$ can be a system that predicts student dropout rates (e.g., a set of preprocessing and classification algorithms) with adjustable parameters $x$ (e.g., the learning algorithm or the depth of the tree when tree structured algorithms are tested), and an observable metric $y = f(x)$, on data collected from learning systems (e.g., data from a learning management system).

As manual tuning is an error-prone process that also requires time and experts in the field [47], various automatic configuration methods have been proposed. A popular approach is to treat the problem as black-box optimization. Grid search has been the traditional and the most basic, yet extremely costly method. A fairly efficient alternative is random search [48]. Other families of methods that have been applied are gradient-based algorithms [49], racing algorithms, e.g., [50], evolutionary optimization algorithms [51], and population-based search, e.g., [52]. Next, we will try to focus on another strategy employed to obtain the optimal set of hyperparameters, that of Bayesian optimization. Our research also leverages the advances of this method.

### 3.2. Bayesian Optimization

Bayesian optimization is an effective strategy for minimizing (or maximizing) objective functions that are costly to evaluate. The main advantage of this method is that it uses previous results in order to pick the next point to try, while dealing with the dilemma of exploration and exploitation. As such, it reaches the optimal solution with less number of evaluations [44,53].

Bayesian optimization uses the famous Bayes theorem. The theorem states that the posterior probability of a model M given data D $P(M|D)$ is proportional to the likelihood of D given M $P(D|M)$ multiplied by the prior probability $P(M)$. As for the hyperparameter optimization problem, model M should not be mistaken with the output model of machine learning algorithms. On the contrary, M is actually a regression model that represents our assumptions about $f$ [54]:

$$P(f|D_{i:t}) \propto P(D_{i:t}|f)P(f) \tag{2}$$

where $D_{i:t} = \{x_{i:t}, f(x_{i:t})\}$ defines our accumulated observations of the objective function $f$ on sequences of data samples $x_{i:t}$ [44]. The prior prescribes our belief (what we think we know) over a space of objective functions. The likelihood captures how likely the data we observed are, given our belief about the prior. These two combined, give us the posterior, which represents our belief about the objective function $f$. Additionally, the posterior conceptualizes the *surrogate* function, the function used to estimate $f$.

As it is much easier to optimize the surrogate probability model than the objective function, the Bayesian optimization selects the next set of hyperparameters to evaluate based on its performance on the surrogate. During the execution, the accuracy of the surrogate model is increased by continually incorporating the evaluations on the objective function.

The Bayesian optimization is considered as a sequential design strategy (formally Sequential model-based optimization (SMBO)) [10,55]. At first, a surrogate probabilistic regression model of the objective function is built. Until a budget limit is being reached, new samples of hyperparameters are sequentially selected. These new samples are selected by optimizing an acquisition function S, which uses the surrogate model. Each suggested sample is applied on the true objective function and produce new evaluations. The new observations are used to update the surrogate model (Algorithm 1). There are several variants of the SMBO formalism, which are specified by the selection of the probabilistic model and the criteria (acquisition function) used to select the next hyperparameters.

In the model-based optimization literature, the most recognized choices for the surrogate model are the Gaussian Processes [56], Tree Parzen Estimators (TPE) [10,57], and Random Forests [58]. In this research, we selected Random Forests for our experiments. Some of the advantages of this method is that it can represent the uncertainty of a given prediction, and that it can handle categorical and conditional parameters [59]. Hutter et al. [54] suggested that tree-based models (i.e., TPE and Random Forests) work best for large configuration spaces and complicated optimization problems. The same conclusions are marked by the authors of [60]. They further notice that, in their experiment, Random Forests could obtain results of four more configurations at that same time budget compared to TPE and GP. The reason is their support on small number of folds at the cross- validation procedure. Random Forests are used by the Sequential Model-based Algorithm Configuration (SMAC) library (https://github.com/automl/SMAC3).

---

**Algorithm 1:** The sequential model-based optimization algorithm

---

Input: $f, M_0, T, S, H := \emptyset$
Output: $x^*$ from $H$ with minimal $c$

1:     Function SMBO
2:     for $t := 1$ to T do
3:         $x^* := argmin\ S(x, M_{t-1})$;
4:         c:= evaluateCost $(f(x^*))$;
5:         $H := H \cup \{(x^*, c)\}$;
6:         $M_t :=$ fitNewModel $(H)$;
7:     end for

---

The role of the acquisition function is to decide which point the surrogate model should evaluate next. It determines the utility of the candidate data points, trading off exploration and exploitation. Exploration favors new, uncertain areas in the objective space. Exploitation benefits areas that are already known to have advantageous results [11]. The Expected Improvement is considered to be among the typically used acquisition functions [61]. Other strategies have also been suggested, such as the upper confidence bound (UCB), the Probability of Improvement [62], and the more recent proposed Gaussian process upper confidence bounds (GP-UCB) [63].

Several open-source Bayesian optimization software packages exist for various stages of autoML. Some libraries that can be used to optimize hyperparameters are Spearmint (https://github.com/JasperSnoek/spearmint) [11], Metric Optimization Engine (MOE) [64], Hyperopt [13], Sequential Model-based Algorithm Configuration (SMAC) [59]. SMAC framework enabled the autoML frameworks: Auto-WEKA and Auto-sklearn.

### 3.3. Use Cases

In the context of machine learning, each time we try a different set of hyperparameters, we build a model using the training dataset and create the predictions based on the validation dataset and the evaluation metric. Considering the high dimensional search space and the complexity of models, such as deep neural networks or ensemble methods, the specific process is practically intractable to be done by hand, while in most cases it requires advanced data science skills. Therefore, autoML processes make machine learning more accessible, while reducing the human expertise that is required and, finally, improving the performance of the model [45]. Moreover, automatic tuning is reproducible and generally supports the fair comparison of the produced results [57], while in the case that the search space is limited by design to specific learning algorithms, the produced results can be more transparent and interpretable to the end users, as our study shows.

## 4. Method

*4.1. Research Goal*

The goal of this study is to examine the potential yield of advanced machine learning strategies to improve the prediction of student's performance based on their participation in online learning platforms. Specifically, we investigated the effectiveness of the Automated Machine Learning (autoML) in conjunction with educational data to early predict students' final performance. We experimented using autoML for the tasks of algorithm selection, hyperparameter tuning, feature selection and preprocessing. Furthermore, to achieve explainable machine learning decisions, we made available only tree and rule-based classifiers in the configuration space for the task of selecting a learning algorithm. We examined log data obtained from several blended courses that were using the Moodle platform. We studied whether, and to what extent, the use of the autoML could leverage the performance of the predictions and provide reasonable results rather early when compared with standard ML algorithms. Our work will hopefully help nonexpert users, such as teachers, to conduct experiments with the most appropriate settings and hence achieve improved results.

*4.2. Procedure*

The selected compulsory courses "Physical Chemistry I", "Physics III (Electricity—Magnetism)" and "Analytical Chemistry Laboratory" were held in the spring semester of 2017–2018 at the Aristotle University of Thessaloniki (Table 2). In total, 591 students attended the courses, 322 of which were male, and 269 females (mean = 295.5, standard deviation = 26.5). The total number of students of the first course was 282 (122 females and 160 male), in the second 180 (90 females and 90 male), and in the third 129 (57 females and 72 male). The final grade was based on weighted averages of grades that students received at the online assignments and the final examination. The students attended the courses between February 2018 and July 2018.

Table 2. Summary statistics for each course.

| Course | Female | Male | Total | Course Modules in Moodle |
|---|---|---|---|---|
| Physical Chemistry I | 122 | 160 | 282 | forum, resource, page, assign, folder |
| Physics III | 90 | 90 | 180 | forum, resource, page, assign |
| Analytical Chemistry Lab | 57 | 72 | 129 | forum, resource, page, assign, folder, URL |
| **Total** | **269** | **322** | **591** | |

For all courses, the face-to-face teaching was supported with online resources and activities over the Moodle learning platform. All of the material of the courses was added into sections as web pages, files or URLs. The materials were available to the students until the end of the semester. Most sections also contained learning activities that were evaluated for a grade. Each Moodle course preserved the default Announcements forum. Announcements were created by making posts in that forum. It should be noted that the courses were not directed or specially designed for the conduction of the experiments that are described in the research.

*4.3. Data Collection*

For the collection of the datasets, we developed a custom plugin for Moodle (Figure 1). The implemented extension computes an outline report of the course's activities. For each student, the outline calculates the number of views for each available module (e.g., activity, resource, folders, forum), the grades of each activity (e.g., assign, workshop, choice, quiz), the number of created posts (if any), aggregated event counters, and her/his final grade. By default, the report is computed from the course starting date to the current date, but results can also be filtered by a specified date. Data are exported in various formats and for regression and classification machine learning tasks. Most of the data are retrieved from the log's table in conjunction with aggregate functions.

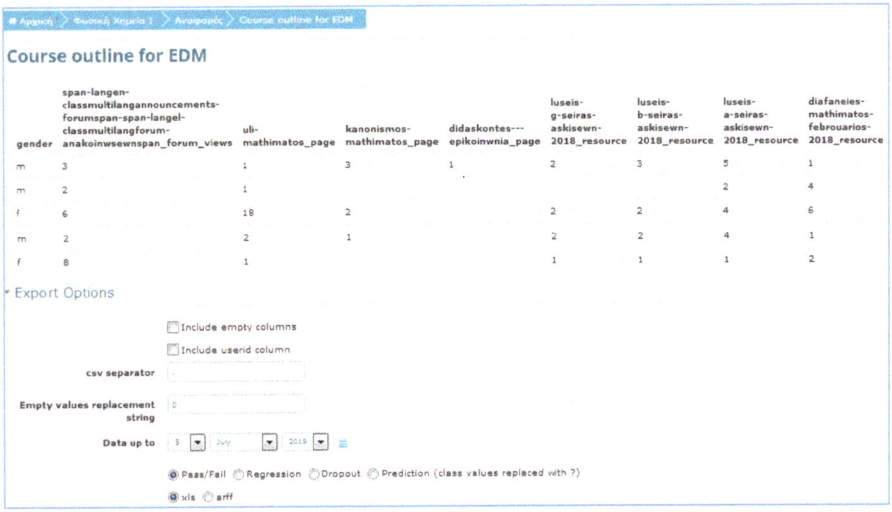

**Figure 1.** Screenshot of the custom report plugin on Moodle. The report outline lists all the available learning activities of the course (modules) along with a corresponding score for each participant (student). Scores are calculated according to the resource type (e.g., for the 'page' module we count the total number of student access). The report can be exported in two formats (arff, xls) and for various data mining tasks (classification, regression). Results can be calculated until a specified date.

For each machine learning experiment (dropout, pass/fail, regression) we collected six samples of the exported reports, one for each month of the semester. We aimed at experimenting in order to be aware of the precision of the results at the time and to predict failures as soon as possible during the semester. Table 3 lists the total number of logs that were available per course in the Moodle platform. In total, more than 130,000 log events were parsed. As it is expected, the number of events is increased during the semester (Figure 2). The students' interest in the course varies, depending on the course activities. In general, course registrations start in February, final examinations take place in June, and final grades are announced by professors in July. An exception is the "Physical Chemistry I" course, by which the logged interactions had not started until March. As such, we will not build models for the first period.

**Table 3.** Number of activity logs per month for each course (separate and aggregated). e.g., 7617 records were created for Physical Chemistry I in the logs table during the third month (April), and 9692 records were created until the end of the third month (i.e., 2075 + 7617).

|  | February 2018 | March 2018 | April 2018 | May 2018 | June 2018 | July 2018 |
|---|---|---|---|---|---|---|
| Physical Chemistry I | 0 | 2075 | 7617 | 13,175 | 9298 | 787 |
|  | 0 | 2075 | 9692 | 22,867 | 32,165 | 32,952 |
| Physics III | 1156 | 8007 | 7259 | 10,369 | 7760 | 617 |
|  | 1156 | 9163 | 16,422 | 26,791 | 34,551 | 35,168 |
| Analytical Chemistry Lab | 5800 | 28,564 | 8499 | 17,054 | 1623 | 416 |
|  | 5800 | 34,364 | 42,863 | 59,917 | 61,540 | 61,956 |

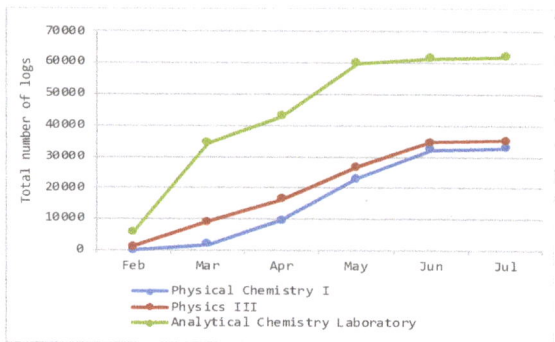

**Figure 2.** The total number of logs per month for each course. Logged activities are increased during the semester, as could be expected.

*4.4. Data Analysis*

Data related to 6 types of learning activities were collected and they are presented in Table 4. For each module, we calculated a numeric representation. Specifically, for the forum module, we counted the total number of times a student viewed the forum threads. Respectively, we counted the number of times a page, a resource, a folder, and a URL module had been accessed by each student. For the assign module, we counted the number of times a student accessed its description, and the grade that s/he took using the 0–10 scale. We also include a counter that aggregates the number of times a student viewed the course (course total views) and the total number of every kind of log written for a student for the specific course (course total activity). We were not able to examine additional demographic values apart from gender. The class attribute was the final grade that the student achieved, transformed to 0–10 scale, or nominal according to the supervised machine learning problem in question. Students that finally succeeded in a course are the ones that scored above or equal to 5. Dropout students were considered to be the ones whose final grade was an empty value. The dataset does not contain missing values. Students that did not access a learning activity score for 0. Learning resources that were not accessed by any student were not included in the experiments.

**Table 4.** Variables extracted from students' Moodle use for each course.

| Physical Chemistry I | Physics III | Analytical Chemistry Lab | Description | Possible Values |
|---|---|---|---|---|
| gender | gender | gender | Student's gender | {female, male} |
| 1 forum<br>7 pages<br>17 resources<br>2 folders<br>8 assign views | 1 forum<br>6 pages<br>15 resources<br>9 assign views | 1 forum<br>2 pages<br>4 resources<br>17 folders<br>1 URL<br>8 assign views | Total number of times a student accessed the resource | 0 or positive integer |
| 3 assigns | 9 assigns | 8 assigns | Student grade | [0,10] |
| course total views | course total views | course total views | The total number of course views for an individual student | 0 or positive integer |
| course total activity | course total activity | course total activity | The total number of every kind of log written for an individual student | 0 or positive integer |
| 42 attributes | 44 attributes | 45 attributes | | |

The descriptive statistics are represented in Table 5. The mean (average) and standard deviation of the final grades in "Physical Chemistry I" were, respectively, 3.98 and 2.92, in "Physics III" 3.62 and 3.17, while in "Analytical Chemistry Laboratory" 6.27 and 2.73. The 48% of students passed the first course, 41% the second and 81% the third course. Only the 28% of students dropped out of the first course, 24% dropped out of the second and 6% dropped out of the third. It is concluded that Physical Chemistry I and Physics III were more challenging courses, while the high grades on average in the laboratory of Analytical Chemistry affirm that this course was easier.

Table 5. Descriptive statistics for each course.

|  | Regression | | | | Classification | | Classification | |
| --- | --- | --- | --- | --- | --- | --- | --- | --- |
|  | Min | Max | Mean | Std | Pass | Fail | Dropout | No Dropout |
| Physical Chemistry I | 0 | 10 | 3.98 | 2.92 | 134 | 148 | 78 | 204 |
| Physics III | 0 | 10 | 3.62 | 3.17 | 74 | 106 | 44 | 136 |
| Analytical Chemistry Lab | 0 | 10 | 6.27 | 2.73 | 105 | 24 | 8 | 121 |

*4.5. Feature Importance*

During our research, additional procedures to understand more comprehensively the datasets were performed. More specifically, we used extremely randomized trees [65] to evaluate the importance of features on the classification and regression tasks (We used ExtraTreesClassifier and ExtraTreesRegressor ensemble methods from sklearn Python library, that return the feature importance (e.g., see https://scikit-learn.org/stable/modules/generated/sklearn.ensemble.ExtraTreesClassifier.html)). We therefore indicated the informative features for each course (Figure 3). Table 6 summarizes the results found by listing the module categories that were estimated above each average per course and per task.

Table 6. Features above the average importance per course and per task.

|  | Physical Chemistry I | Physics III | Analytical Chemistry Lab |
| --- | --- | --- | --- |
| Classification (Pass/Fail) | 14<br>total views, 3 assign views, total activity, 4 resources, 3 assigns, 1 folder, forums | 13<br>2 assign, 4 assign views, 4 resources, total views, total activity, gender | 10<br>8 assigns, 1 resources, 1 assign views |
| Regression | 9<br>total views, 2 assign views, total activity, 2 resources, 3 assigns | 14<br>3 assign, 5 assign views, 3 resource, total views, total activity, gender | 7<br>7 assigns |
| Classification (Dropout/No Dropout) | 17<br>total views, 3 assign views, total activity, 5 resources, 3 assigns, 1 folder, 1 forum, 2 pages | 10<br>1 assign, 5 assign views, 2 resources, total views, total activity | 15<br>7 assign, 5 folder, 3 assign views, total views |
| Common Important Features | 9<br>total views, total activity, 2 assign views, 2 resources, 2 assigns | 8<br>total views, total activity, 1 resource, 4 assign views, 1 assign | 6<br>6 assigns |

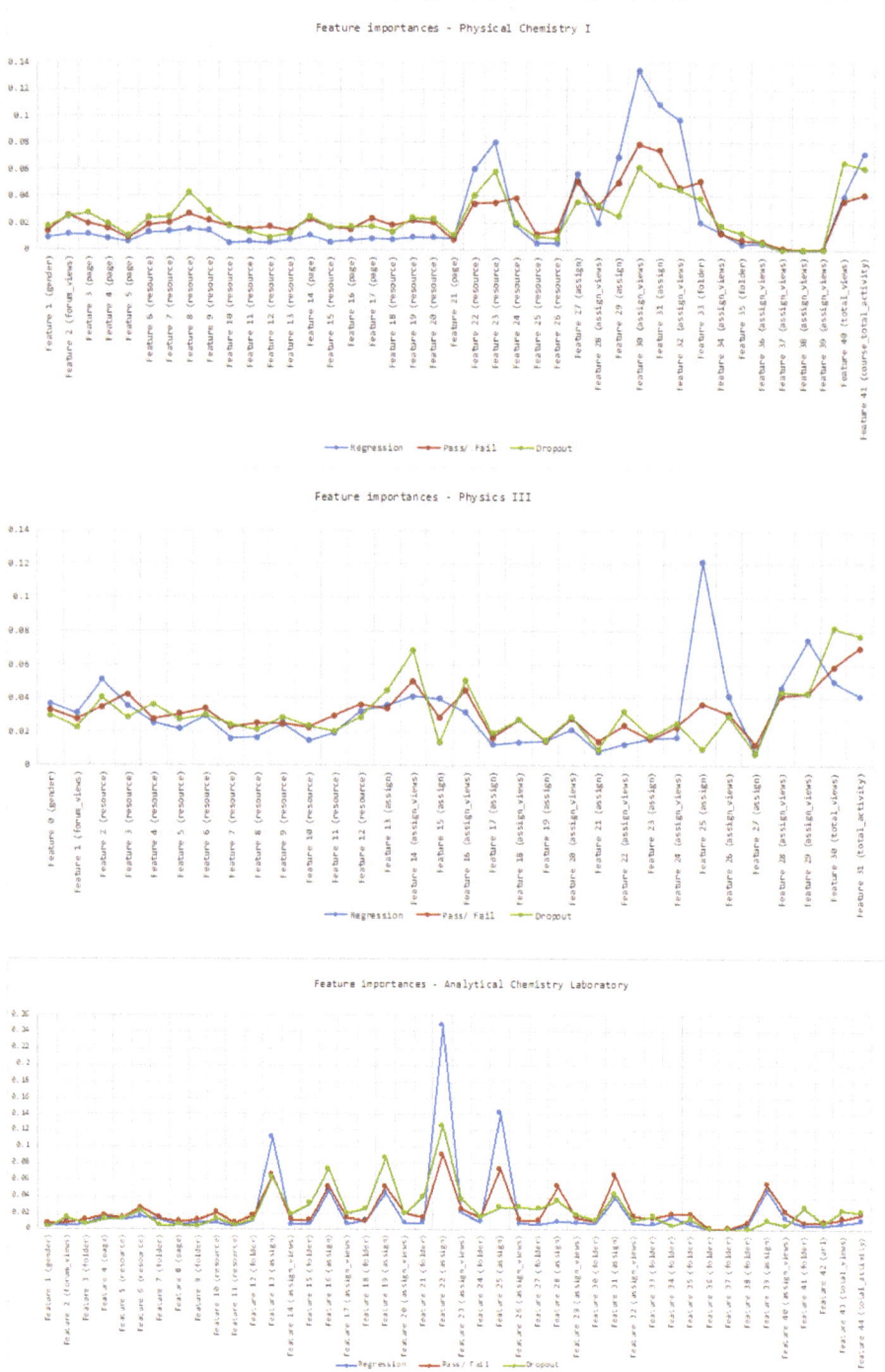

**Figure 3.** The plot suggests the features that are informative for each task.

However, such data approaches rarely can lead to conclusive results. As expected, features related to assignment grades were far more informative that views counters when considering regression tasks. A representative example is the laboratory course of Analytical Chemistry; as such type of courses concentrate on conducting assignments related to the theory of a related course. In-class exams were indicated as good predictors also by Meier et al. [32]. On the other hand, pass/fail classification tasks list among the effective and some features that are related to how many times a student accessed resources and pages. It is worth noting that among the high rated documents are the ones related to result announcements. Features 22 and 23 of the "Physical Chemistry I" course are related to resources were the results of the handwritten exams and the final grades were listed. Finally, dropout classification tasks list the widest variety of features among its important compared to the other tasks. Seventeen out of 42 features have estimated importance above the average of all the feature importance at the "Physical Chemistry I" course.

### 4.6. Evaluation Measures

For evaluating the performance of the classification models, we calculated the accuracy metric, which is defined in accordance to the confusion matrix (Table 7) as follows:

$$\text{Accuracy} = \frac{TP + TN}{TP + FP + FN + TN} \tag{3}$$

Table 7. Confusion matrix.

|  |  | Predicted Class | |
| --- | --- | --- | --- |
|  |  | Fail/Dropout | Pass/No Dropout |
| Actual class | Fail/Dropout | TP | FN |
|  | Pass/No Dropout | FP | TN |

In addition, in order to evaluate the regression models, we make use of the Mean Absolute Error (MAE) measure, which is defined as follows:

$$\text{MAE} = \frac{\sum_{t=1} |\hat{G}_{ij} - G_{ij}|}{N} \tag{4}$$

Finally, the dropout classification accuracy was measured with the Receiver Operating Characteristic (ROC), since it is appropriate for datasets with imbalanced class distributions [66,67]. The ROC Curve is a two-dimensional graph that illustrates the performance trade-off of a given classification model [68].

Given such experimental set-up, it is necessary to use a statistical test to verify whether the improvement is statistically significant or not. We apply the paired, one tailed $t$-test to compare the maximum accuracy (or minimum error) obtained by a set of classic machine learning algorithms using their default parameter values (marked with a star *), with the results when using autoML. All $t$-tests have been performed with a significance level of $\alpha = 0.05$. As such, if the $p$-value is inferior or equal to 0.05, we conclude that the difference is significant.

### 4.7. Environment

To apply the data mining techniques, we used the WEKA implementation [69] without customizing the default parameter values. In addition, we employed the Auto-WEKA [70], the autoML implementation for WEKA that uses SMAC to determine the classifier with the best performance.

During the experiments, the classic algorithms were executed using the 10-fold cross-validation method. Therefore, each dataset was divided into 10 equally sized subsets (folds). The method was repeated 10 times, and for each time 9 of the 10 subsets were used to form the training set, and the remaining 1 was used as the test/validation set.

*4.8. ML Algorithms*

For our study we used various classification and regression techniques for predicting the final student performance. We made sure to choose one representative example out of the six main categories of learners, i.e., Bayes classifiers, rule-based, tree-based, function-based, lazy and meta classifiers [71].

1. Bayes classifiers: Based on the Bayes theorem, the Bayes classifiers constitute a simple approach that often achieves impressive results. Naïve Bayes is a well-known probabilistic induction method [72].
2. Rule-based classifiers: In general, rule-based classifiers classify records by using a collection of "if … then … " rules. PART uses separate-and-conquer. In each iteration the algorithm builds a partial C4.5 decision tree and makes the "best" leaf into a rule [73]. M5Rules is a rule learning algorithm for regression problems. It builds a model tree using M5 and makes the "best" leaf into a rule [74].
3. Tree-based classifiers: Tree-based classifiers is another approach to the problem of learning. An example is Random Forest classifier that generates a large number of random trees (i.e., forest) and uses the majority voting to classify a new instance [75].
4. Function-cased classifiers: Function-based classifiers build a discriminant function that separates selected instances as widely as possible. SMO and SMOreg implement the support vector machine for classification [76–78] and regression [79,80] respectively.
5. Lazy classifiers: Lazy learners do not train a specific model. At the prediction time, they evaluate an unknown instance based on the most related instances stored as training data. IBk is the k-nearest neighbor's classifier that is able to analyze the closest k number of training instances (nearest neighbors) and returns the most common class or the mean of k nearest neighbors for the classification and regression task respectively [81].
6. Meta classifiers: Meta classifiers either enhance a single classifier or combine several classifiers. Bagging predictors is a method for generating multiple versions of a predictor and using them in order to get an aggregated predictor [82].

On the other hand, Auto-WEKA was restricted to use tree-based classifiers – Decision Stump, J48, Logistic model tree (LMT), REPTree, RT and M5P – and rule-based classifiers – JRip, One Rule (OneR), PART and M5Rules.

## 5. Results

In this section, we present the main results of our experiments that were outlined in Section 4. We will show that the application of autoML technique in educational datasets significantly improves the efficiency of classic machine learning algorithms.

*5.1. Predicting Pass/Fail Students*

At first, we conducted a series of experiments to identify the effectiveness of classic data mining algorithms to predict students that are likely to fail at early enough stages. We performed 6 classic machine-learning algorithms on the datasets of 3 courses, split into chronological sets (month A, month B, etc.). An exception is the "Physical Chemistry I" course, which did not have any logs on the first month, and as such, we did not conduct experiments during that period. Tables 8–10 present the effectiveness results, represented by the accuracy measure.

We observe that Bagging and the Random Forest ensemble algorithms outperform the others in most cases in the first course, Naïve Bayes, PART and IBk algorithms outperform the others in most cases in the second course, and SMO and Random Forest algorithms outperform the others in most cases in the third course. In total, SMO and Random Forest are noted to be among the best performers 9 times and Bagging 7 times. As such, we could not conclude one best performer for our given datasets.

Table 8. Overall accuracy results regarding the "Physical Chemistry I" course and Pass/Fail classification task.

|  | February 2018 | March 2018 | April 2018 | May 2018 | June 2018 | July 2018 |
|---|---|---|---|---|---|---|
| Naïve Bayes | - | 59.22 | 68.09 | 75.18 | 75.18 | 75.18 |
| Random Forest | - | 62.06 | 78.01 * | 82.62 * | 81.56 * | 81.56 * |
| Bagging | - | 62.4 | 74.47 | 81.21 | 81.21 | 81.20 |
| PART | - | 63.12 * | 73.76 | 72.70 | 75.89 | 74.11 |
| SMO | - | 58.16 | 74.82 | 79.43 | 80.85 | 80.14 |
| IBk-5NN | - | 59.93 | 70.92 | 78.01 | 79.43 | 79.08 |
| Auto-WEKA | - | 66.67<br>Random Tree | 81.20<br>LMT | 83.68<br>LMT | 82.27<br>REPTree | 81.56<br>PART |

$t$-test: $p$-value = 0.0365, a = 0.05.

Table 9. Overall accuracy results regarding the "Physics III" course and Pass/Fail classification task.

|  | February 2018 | March 2018 | April 2018 | May 2018 | June 2018 | July 2018 |
|---|---|---|---|---|---|---|
| Naïve Bayes | 53.33 | 61.67 | 61.67 | 63.33 | 67.78 * | 67.78 * |
| Random Forest | 52.78 | 54.44 | 60.56 | 60.00 | 61.67 | 60.56 |
| Bagging | 57.22 | 57.78 | 60.56 | 61.11 | 66.67 | 62.22 |
| PART | 62.22 * | 63.33 * | 58.89 | 62.22 | 55.00 | 52.22 |
| SMO | 56.11 | 61.67 | 64.44 * | 65.56 * | 64.44 | 63.89 |
| IBk-5NN | 56.67 | 58.89 | 60.56 | 60.56 | 60.56 | 60.00 |
| Auto-WEKA | 61.11<br>PART | 73.33<br>J48 | 66.67<br>OneR | 69.44<br>LMT | 71.11<br>J48 | 70.56<br>JRip |

$t$-test: $p$-value = 0.0317, a = 0.05.

Table 10. Overall accuracy results regarding the "Analytical Chemistry Laboratory" course and Pass/Fail classification task.

|  | February 2018 | March 2018 | April 2018 | May 2018 | June 2018 | July 2018 |
|---|---|---|---|---|---|---|
| Naïve Bayes | 61.24 | 63.57 | 66.67 | 83.72 | 84.50 | 84.50 |
| Random Forest | 78.29 | 85.27 * | 86.05 * | 90.70 * | 90.70 | 89.92 |
| Bagging | 79.84 | 85.27 * | 84.50 | 88.37 | 88.37 | 88.37 |
| PART | 72.09 | 76.74 | 75.97 | 86.04 | 86.82 | 86.82 |
| SMO | 81.40 | 86.05 | 86.05 * | 89.92 | 91.47 * | 90.70 * |
| IBk-5NN | 75.19 | 85.27 * | 84.50 | 89.92 | 89.92 | 89.92 |
| Auto-WEKA | 81.40<br>LMT | 86.82<br>JRip | 86.05<br>LMT | 93.02<br>LMT | 93.02<br>LMT | 93.02<br>LMT |

$t$-test: $p$-value = 0.0223, a = 0.05.

In addition, we used Auto WEKA to run automated machine learning experiments for the corresponding datasets. From the results, we identify that in most cases, the accuracy was significantly increased. Auto-WEKA was able to optimize the results up to 10% (Figure 4). The suggested classifiers and hyperparameters again vary across the datasets, including LMT, J48, PART, and JRip, to name a few. Overall, tree-based classifiers were suggested the most. More specifically, the LMT method was the outperformer 8 out of 17 times.

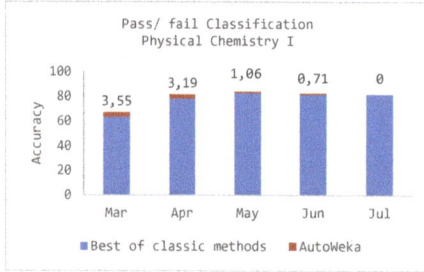
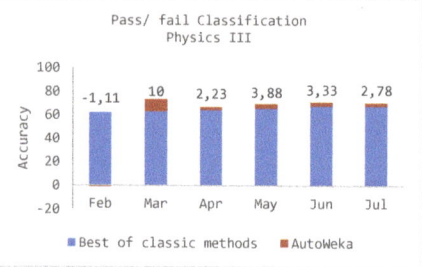
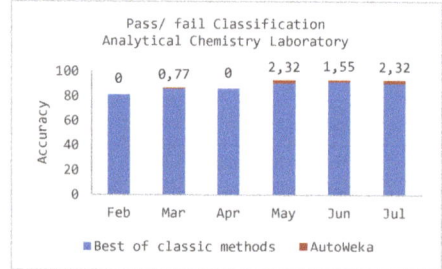

**Figure 4.** Comparative results of the effectiveness of autoML over classic EDM methods. The results indicate that in most cases, the effectiveness of the best classic classifier was improved when we applied autoML.

Finally, by applying the *t*-test on the results as shown in Tables 8–10, we obtained the following *p*-values: "Physical Chemistry I" *p*-value = 0.0365; "Physics III" *p*-value = 0.0317; Analytical Chemistry Laboratory *p*-value = 0.0223. Thus, we can conclude that the autoML presents a statistically significant increase when applied to specific educational datasets.

## 5.2. Predicting Students' Academic Performance

In addition, we conducted a series of experiments to identify the effectiveness of classic data mining algorithms to predict students' grades at early enough stages. Next, we compared the results with the predictions given by models created by applying the autoML. Similar to Section 5.1, the experiments comprise of six phases, one for each month of the semester. Tables 11–13 present the regression results, represented by the mean absolute error measure.

Depending on the dataset, we observe that Bagging and the Random Forest algorithms outperform the others in most cases in the first course, Bagging and SMOreg algorithms outperform the others in most cases in the second course, and Random Forest algorithm outperforms the others in most cases in the third course. In total, Bagging is noted to be among the best performers 10 times, Random Forest 9 times, and SMOreg 5 times. Overall, from the predictions generated we could not conclude one best performer for our given datasets.

In addition, we used Auto-WEKA to run the automated machine learning experiments for the corresponding datasets. From the results, we identify that in all cases, the mean absolute error was significantly decreased. Auto-WEKA was able to minimize the error from 0.0188 to 0.4055 (Figure 5). The suggested classifiers and hyperparameters again vary across the datasets, including M5P, Random Tree, REPTree and M5Rules. Overall, tree-based methods were primarily suggested. More specifically, the M5P and Random Tree were the outperformers 5 out of 17 times.

**Table 11.** Overall MAE results regarding the "Physical Chemistry I" course and regression task.

|               | February 2018 | March 2018 | April 2018 | May 2018 | June 2018 | July 2018 |
|---------------|---------------|------------|------------|----------|-----------|-----------|
| Random Forest | -             | 2.4264     | 1.9346     | 1.7334 * | 1.5784 *  | 1.5731 *  |
| M5Rules       | -             | 2.4504     | 2.0541     | 1.8244   | 1.8169    | 1.782     |
| Bagging       | -             | 2.3903 *   | 1.901 *    | 1.7495   | 1.6081    | 1.6136    |
| SMOreg        | -             | 2.4604     | 2.1352     | 1.9962   | 1.8998    | 1.9037    |
| IBk-5NN       | -             | 2.4433     | 2.1556     | 1.9011   | 1.7521    | 1.774     |
| Auto-WEKA     | -             | 1.9848 REPTree | 1.8822 Random Tree | 1.6715 M5P | 1.4017 Random Tree | 1.4255 Random Tree |

$t$-test: $p$-value = 0.0366, a = 0.05.

**Table 12.** Overall MAE results regarding the "Physics III" course and regression task.

|               | February 2018 | March 2018 | April 2018 | May 2018 | June 2018 | July 2018 |
|---------------|---------------|------------|------------|----------|-----------|-----------|
| Random Forest | 2.944         | 2.676      | 2.6011     | 2.507    | 2.4429    | 2.4946    |
| M5Rules       | 2.8632 *      | 2.6879     | 2.6901     | 2.5311   | 2.5291    | 2.5235    |
| Bagging       | 2.8638        | 2.6932     | 2.5707     | 2.5179   | 2.4094 *  | 2.3855 *  |
| SMOreg        | 3.1291        | 2.6246     | 2.5372 *   | 2.3305 * | 2.4123    | 2.4305    |
| IBk-5NN       | 2.8962        | 2.5815 *   | 2.5832     | 2.5777   | 2.5059    | 2.5448    |
| Auto-WEKA     | 2.8194 M5P    | 2.0091 M5Rules | 2.2386 Random Tree | 2.1743 REPTree | 2.2015 M5P | 2.1276 M5Rules |

$t$-test: $p$-value = 0.0021, a = 0.05.

**Table 13.** Overall MAE results regarding the "Analytical Chemistry Lab" course and regression task.

|               | February 2018 | March 2018 | April 2018 | May 2018 | June 2018 | July 2018 |
|---------------|---------------|------------|------------|----------|-----------|-----------|
| Random Forest | 2.1137        | 1.7123 *   | 1.62 *     | 1.381 *  | 1.3825 *  | 1.3864 *  |
| M5Rules       | 2.1347        | 1.9989     | 1.6982     | 1.4233   | 1.5202    | 1.5492    |
| Bagging       | 2.0715 *      | 1.795      | 1.7555     | 1.4894   | 1.4902    | 1.4864    |
| SMOreg        | 2.1972        | 1.9377     | 1.7385     | 1.5705   | 1.5401    | 1.5303    |
| IBk-5NN       | 2.3073        | 1.8891     | 1.7302     | 1.4574   | 1.4434    | 1.4426    |
| Auto-WEKA     | 1.7935 REPTree | 1.6067 REPTree | 1.4947 M5P | 1.2135 M5Rules | 1.0402 M5P | 1.2135 M5Rules |

$t$-test: $p$-value = 0.0016, a = 0.05.

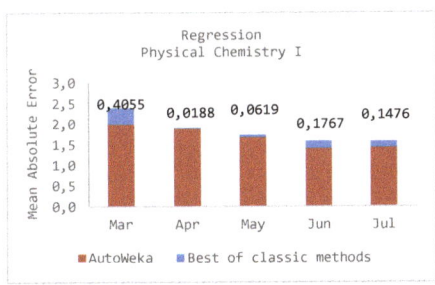

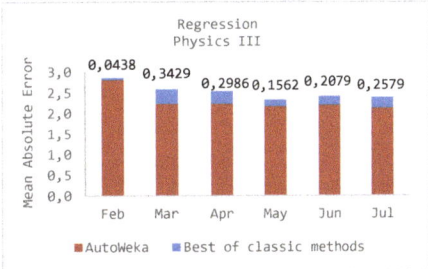

**Figure 5.** *Cont.*

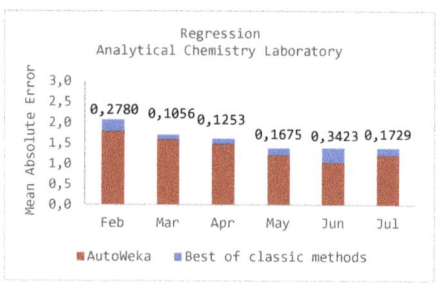

**Figure 5.** Comparative results of the effectiveness of autoML over classic ML methods. The results indicate that in all cases, the effectiveness of the best classic classifier was improved when we applied autoML.

Finally, by applying the *t*-test on the results as shown in Tables 11–13, we obtained the following *p*-values: "Physical Chemistry I" *p*-value = 0.0366; "Physics III" *p*-value = 0.0021; Analytical Chemistry Laboratory *p*-value = 0.0016. Similarly, a statistically significant decrease was observed in the overall measurements.

## 5.3. Predicting Dropout Students

Lastly, we conducted a series of experiments to identify the effectiveness of classic data mining algorithms to predict students that are likely to drop out at early enough stages. We compared the results with the predictions given by models created by applying the autoML. Similar to Sections 5.1 and 5.2, the experiments consist of six phases, one for each month of the semester. As the Analytical Chemistry Laboratory course displays a large level of class imbalance—the dropout class represents the 6% of the dataset—we did not include it in this category of experiments. Since it is easy to get high accuracy without actually making useful predictions in imbalanced datasets [66,83], for the drop out problem we used the ROC measure to compare the results of the classifiers. For the same reason, in Auto-WEKA we set the 'area above ROC' as the metric to optimize. Tables 14 and 15 present the drop results.

Depending on the dataset, we observe that SMO and Bagging algorithms outperform the others in most cases in the first course, and Bagging algorithm outperforms the others in most cases in the second course. In total, Bagging is noted to be among the best performers 7 times, and SMO 4 times. We could not result in one best performer.

**Table 14.** Overall ROC area results regarding the "Physical Chemistry I" course and dropout classification task.

|  | February 2018 | March 2018 | April 2018 | May 2018 | June 2018 | July 2018 |
|---|---|---|---|---|---|---|
| Naïve Bayes | - | 0.520 | 0.731 | 0.793 * | 0.817 | 0.817 |
| Random Forest | - | 0.569 | 0.763 | 0.777 | 0.871 * | 0.869 * |
| Bagging | - | 0.512 | 0.774 * | 0.791 | 0.860 | 0.854 |
| PART | - | 0.599 * | 0.710 | 0.740 | 0.796 | 0.787 |
| SMO | - | 0.500 | 0.500 | 0.688 | 0.820 | 0.818 |
| IBk-5NN | - | 0.594 | 0.700 | 0.758 | 0.804 | 0.811 |
| Auto-WEKA | - | 0.801 J48 | 0.863 LMT | 0.828 LMT | 0.928 LMT | 0.896 LMT |

*t*-test: *p*-value = 0.0308, a = 0.05.

**Table 15.** Overall ROC area results regarding the "Physics III" course and dropout classification task.

|  | February 2018 | March 2018 | April 2018 | May 2018 | June 2018 | July 2018 |
|---|---|---|---|---|---|---|
| Naïve Bayes | 0.463 | 0.680 | 0.710 * | 0.699 | 0.743 | 0.744 |
| Random Forest | 0.487 | 0.697 | 0.704 | 0.689 | 0.708 | 0.716 |
| Bagging | 0.495 | 0.723 * | 0.690 | 0.702 | 0.747 * | 0.760 * |
| PART | 0.477 | 0.590 | 0.660 | 0.722 * | 0.651 | 0.742 |
| SMO | 0.500 * | 0.500 | 0.500 | 0.500 | 0.496 | 0.496 |
| IBk-5NN | 0.486 | 0.649 | 0.632 | 0.655 | 0.740 | 0.737 |
| Auto-WEKA | 0.545 Decision Stump | 0.883 Random Tree | 0.778 Random Tree | 0.801 J48 | 0.842 LMT | 0.784 LMT |

*t*-test: *p*-value = 0.0039, a = 0.05.

Auto-WEKA experiments again proved to be more effective. From the results, we identify that in all cases, the ROCK curve measure was increased. Auto-WEKA was able to optimize the results from 0.018 to 0.202 (Figure 6). The suggested classifiers and hyperparameters again vary across the datasets, including LMT, Random Tree, and J48. Overall, only tree-based algorithms were suggested. More specifically, the LMT was the outperformer 6 out of 17 times.

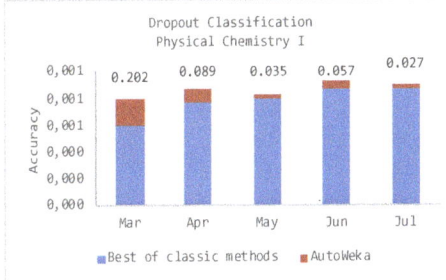
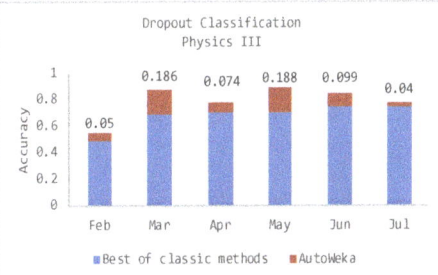

**Figure 6.** Comparative results of the effectiveness of autoML over classic ML methods. The results indicate that in all cases, the effectiveness of the best classic classifier was improved when we applied autoML.

Finally, by applying the *t*-test on the results as shown in Tables 14 and 15, we obtained the following *p*-values: "Physical Chemistry I" *p*-value = 0.0308; "Physics III" *p*-value = 0.0039. A statistically significant increase was observed in all courses.

## 6. Discussion

The results illustrated in previous sections unveil the effectiveness of the autoML methods in educational data mining processes. Without any human intervention, the suggested models report performance often much better of classic supervised learning techniques with default hyperparameters settings. Even from the early half of the semester, predictions have satisfactory values. The result models can help educators and instructors to identify weak students, improve retention and reduce academic failure rates. It can also lead to improved educational outcomes.

Finding appropriate models and hyperparameter configurations is one of the most difficult processes when building a machine learning solution and indeed, it is central to the pursuit of precision. The main advantage of autoML and tools like Auto-WEKA is that they provide an out-of-the-box mechanism to build reliable machine learning models without the need for advanced data science knowledge. People in IT, educational administration, teaching, research or learning support roles, who want to explore how their students perform, are not always experts in educational data mining. Therefore, despite having basic knowledge, novice ML users can converge easily to a suitable algorithm and its related hyperparameter settings and develop trusted machine learning models to support their educational institutions.

In our comparative study we focus on classification and regression using educational data. We evaluated widely known ML algorithms from 6 different categories versus 2 allowed categories in Auto-WEKA, on 51 datasets exported from 3 compulsory courses, using the Moodle LMS as a complement to face-to-face lectures. For each course, we collected 6 samples of data—one for each month of the semester—in order to predict students' final performance as soon as possible. The total number of students (591) who attended the courses produced more than 130,000 log events between February 2018 and July 2018. Logs were triggered by a variety of learning modules that structured the courses—fora, pages, resources, assignments, folders, and URLs. Assignment grades were scaled to a common metric. The final performance for each ML task—pass/fail, regression and dropout—was adjusted to represent the class attribute appropriately.

We further indicated the informative features for each course using the extremely randomized trees. We concluded that attributes related to assignment grades were more important than views counters when performing regression tasks. For pass/fail classification, apart from assignment grades, some features related to how many times a student accessed a resource or a page also had high importance scores. Lastly, dropout classification tasks yielded the widest variety of features among its important compared with the other tasks.

As previous studies have shown [17,84,85], there is no algorithm that is the best across all classification problems. A similar conclusion was reached by our experiments, as we could not result in one best performer in our educational data mining tasks illustrated in Section 5. We applied 6 well known supervised machine learning algorithms—Naïve Bayes, Random Forest, Bagging, PART/M5Rules, SMO/SMOreg and IBk—one representative of the six main learners' categories. Each time we compared the performance of the classic models with the calculated by Auto-WEKA model. Auto-WEKA was set to allow only ten tree or rule-based classifiers. The automated one was in most cases better. Significant differences calculated by $t$-test were marked. We did not conclude an overall winner classifier suggested by the Auto-WEKA tool either. However, when we grouped the proposed classifiers under the 6 learner's categories, it was clear that Auto-WEKA suggestions were mostly tree-based classifiers (Table 16).

**Table 16.** Classic outperformers and Auto-WEKA suggestions grouped under 6 learners' categories. Twelve out of 17 proposed Auto-WEKA classifiers (71%) were tree classifiers. Similarly, 14 out of 17 regressors (82%) and 11 out of 11 (100%) suggested dropout models also belong to the tree classifiers category.

|  | Pass/Fail | | Regression | | Dropout | |
|---|---|---|---|---|---|---|
|  | Best of Classic Methods | Auto-WEKA | Best of Classic Methods | Auto-WEKA | Best of Classic Methods | Auto-WEKA |
| bayes | 5% | - | Not applicable | Not applicable | 12% | - |
| functions | 27% | - | 19% | - | 4% | - |
| lazy | 9% | - | 7% | - | 8% | - |
| meta | 21% | - | 37% | - | 32% | - |
| rules | 9% | 29% | 4% | 18% | 12% | 0% |
| tree | 27% | 71% | 33% | 82% | 32% | 100% |
|  | functions/trees | trees | meta | trees | meta/trees | trees |

There are several advantages to using decision trees in classification and prediction applications. Decision trees models are easy to interpret and explain [14]. Compared to other algorithms, they require less effort for data preparation during pre-processing. A decision tree does not require normalization of data nor scaling of data.

Finally, automated hyperparameter optimization familiarized us with a wide range of models and configurations that were practically applied to our settings [10]. It allowed us to test models with many variables that would be complicated to be tuned by hand.

However, some limitations should also be noted. First, it was not clear what was the appropriate time limit that imposed on our (relatively small) datasets. We marked differences between the suggested models for the same datasets when Auto-WEKA was executed e.g., for 5 min and when it was executed for 1 or 2 h. In limited cases, as the time limit increased, the performance was not necessarily better. This behavior is probably due to the fact that the parameter space is too large to explore, and different randomizations (e.g., during the train/test splitting, or in the underline SMAC optimizer that is used) allow to explore a smaller or a larger part of it. Another possible explanation is the fact that datasets of such size are prone to overfitting and underfitting. In any case, the suggested model was generally beneficial over using default values. Secondly, autoML methods, by definition, take much longer to train. Such an effect could be afforded due to the reliability of the results.

## 7. Conclusions and Future Research Directions

This study has investigated the effectiveness of autoML techniques for the early identification of students' performance in three compulsory courses supported by the Moodle e-learning platform. In our experimental evaluation, we focused on classification and regression. We further limited the configuration space of autoML methods to allow only tree and rule-based classifiers, in order to enhance the interpretability and explainability of the resulting models. Our results provide evidence that tools optimizing hyperparameters rather than choosing default values achieve state-of-the-art performance in educational settings as well. The comparison we made reveals that in the majority of cases, hyperparameter optimization results in better performances than default values for a set of classic learning models. We also noted that in most cases, the proposed configuration included tree-based classifiers. On this basis, we believe that autoML procedures and tools like Auto-WEKA can help people in education—both experts and novices in the field of data science.

Moreover, the proposed method may serve as a significant aid in the early estimation students' performance, and thus enabling timely support and effective intervention strategies. Appropriate software extensions within learning management systems could be built, to enable non-expert users benefit from autoML. Meanwhile, such tools should not lack transparency. It is essential to incorporate features that enable the interpretability and explainability of the produced results to a certain extent. Understanding why a student is prone to fail can help to better align the learning activities and support with the students' needs. This assumption could be addressed in future studies. Overall, the potential use of automatic machine learning methods in the educational field opens up new horizons for educators so as to enhance their use of data coming from educational settings, and ultimately improve academic results.

**Author Contributions:** S.K. and O.R. conceived and designed the experiments; M.T. performed the experiments; M.T. and G.K. analyzed the data; S.K. contributed analysis tools; M.T. wrote the paper. All authors have read and agreed to the published version of the manuscript.

**Funding:** This research received no external funding.

**Conflicts of Interest:** The authors declare no conflict of interest.

## References

1. Romero, C.; Ventura, S. Data mining in education. *Wiley Interdiscip. Rev. Data Min. Knowl. Discov.* **2013**, *3*, 12–27. [CrossRef]
2. Bakhshinategh, B.; Zaiane, O.R.; ElAtia, S.; Ipperciel, D. Educational data mining applications and tasks: A survey of the last 10 years. *Educ. Inf. Technol.* **2018**, *23*, 537–553. [CrossRef]

3. Romero, C.; Ventura, S. Educational data mining: A review of the state of the art. *IEEE Trans. Syst. Man Cybern. Part C Appl. Rev.* **2010**, *40*, 601–618. [CrossRef]
4. Bousbia, N.; Belamri, I. Which Contribution Does EDM Provide to Computer-Based Learning Environments? In *Educational Data Mining*; Springer: Basel, Switzerland, 2014; pp. 3–28.
5. Romero, C.; Ventura, S. Educational data science in massive open online courses. *Wiley Interdiscip. Rev. Data Min. Knowl. Discov.* **2017**, *7*, e1187. [CrossRef]
6. Wolff, A.; Zdrahal, Z.; Herrmannova, D.; Knoth, P. Predicting student performance from combined data sources. In *Educational Data Mining*; Springer: Basel, Switzerland, 2014; pp. 175–202.
7. Campbell, J.P.; DeBlois, P.B.; Oblinger, D.G. Academic analytics: A new tool for a new era. *Educ. Rev.* **2007**, *42*, 40–57.
8. Romero, C.; Ventura, S. Educational data mining: A survey from 1995 to 2005. *Expert Syst. Appl.* **2007**, *33*, 135–146. [CrossRef]
9. Daniel, B. Big Data and analytics in higher education: Opportunities and challenges. *Br. J. Educ. Technol.* **2015**, *46*, 904–920. [CrossRef]
10. Bergstra, J.S.; Bardenet, R.; Bengio, Y.; Kégl, B. Algorithms for hyper-parameter optimization. In *Advances in Neural Information Processing Systems*; Curran Associates Inc.: New York, NY, USA, 2011.
11. Snoek, J.; Larochelle, H.; Adams, R.P. Practical bayesian optimization of machine learning algorithms. In *NIPS'12 Proceedings of the 25th International Conference on Neural Information Processing Systems*; Curran Associates Inc.: New York, NY, USA, 2012.
12. Thornton, C.; Hutter, F.; Hoos, H.H.; Leyton-Brown, K. Auto-WEKA: Combined selection and hyperparameter optimization of classification algorithms. In Proceedings of the 19th ACM SIGKDD International Conference on Knowledge Discovery and Data Mining, Chicago, IL, USA, 11–14 August 2013.
13. Bergstra, J.; Yamins, D.; Cox, D.D. Hyperopt: A python library for optimizing the hyperparameters of machine learning algorithms. In Proceedings of the 12th Python in Science Conference, Brussels, Belgium, 21–25 August 2013.
14. Galitsky, B. Customers' Retention Requires an Explainability Feature in Machine Learning Systems They Use. In Proceedings of the 2018 AAAI Spring Symposium Series, Palo Alto, CA, USA, 26–28 March 2018.
15. Martens, D.; Vanthienen, J.; Verbeke, W.; Baesens, B. Performance of classification models from a user perspective. *Decis. Support Syst.* **2011**, *51*, 782–793. [CrossRef]
16. Došilović, F.K.; Brčić, M.; Hlupić, N. Explainable artificial intelligence: A survey. In *2018 41st International Convention on Information and Communication Technology, Electronics and Microelectronics (MIPRO)*; IEEE: Opatija, Croatia, 2018.
17. Hämäläinen, W.; Vinni, M. Classifiers for educational data mining. In *Handbook of Educational Data Mining*; CRC Press: Boca Raton, FL, USA, 2010; pp. 57–74.
18. Conijn, R.; Snijders, C.; Kleingeld, A.; Matzat, U. Predicting student performance from LMS data: A comparison of 17 blended courses using Moodle LMS. *IEEE Trans. Learn. Technol.* **2016**, *10*, 17–29. [CrossRef]
19. Márquez-Vera, C.; Cano, A.; Romero, C.; Ventura, S. Predicting student failure at school using genetic programming and different data mining approaches with high dimensional and imbalanced data. *Appl. Intell.* **2013**, *38*, 315–330. [CrossRef]
20. Moreno-Marcos, P.M.; Alario-Hoyos, C.; Muñoz-Merino, P.J.; Kloos, C.D. Prediction in MOOCs: A review and future research directions. *IEEE Trans. Learn. Technol.* **2018**, *12*. [CrossRef]
21. Mueen, A.; Zafar, B.; Manzoor, U. Modeling and predicting students' academic performance using data mining techniques. *Int. J. Mod. Educ. Comput. Sci.* **2016**, *8*, 36–42. [CrossRef]
22. Amrieh, E.A.; Hamtini, T.; Aljarah, I. Mining educational data to predict student's academic performance using ensemble methods. *Int. J. Database Theory Appl.* **2016**, *9*, 119–136. [CrossRef]
23. Kaur, P.; Singh, M.; Josan, G.S. Classification and prediction based data mining algorithms to predict slow learners in education sector. *Procedia Comput. Sci.* **2015**, *57*, 500–508. [CrossRef]
24. Guo, B.; Zhang, R.; Xu, G.; Shi, C.; Yang, L. Predicting students performance in educational data mining. In Proceedings of the 2015 International Symposium on Educational Technology (ISET), Wuhan, China, 27–29 July 2015.
25. Saa, A.A. Educational data mining & students' performance prediction. *Int. J. Adv. Comput. Sci. Appl.* **2016**, *7*, 212–220.

26. Costa, E.B.; Fonseca, B.; Santana, M.A.; de Araújo, F.F.; Rego, J. Evaluating the effectiveness of educational data mining techniques for early prediction of students' academic failure in introductory programming courses. *Comput. Hum. Behav.* **2017**, *73*, 247–256. [CrossRef]
27. Asif, R.; Merceron, A.; Ali, S.A.; Haider, N.G. Analyzing undergraduate students' performance using educational data mining. *Comput. Educ.* **2017**, *113*, 177–194. [CrossRef]
28. Kostopoulos, G.; Kotsiantis, S.; Pintelas, P. Predicting student performance in distance higher education using semi-supervised techniques. In *Model and Data Engineering*; Springer: New York, NY, USA, 2015; pp. 259–270.
29. Elbadrawy, A.; Polyzou, A.; Ren, Z.; Sweeney, M.; Karypis, G.; Rangwala, H. Predicting student performance using personalized analytics. *Computer* **2016**, *49*, 61–69. [CrossRef]
30. Xu, J.; Moon, K.H.; van der Schaar, M. A machine learning approach for tracking and predicting student performance in degree programs. *IEEE J. Sel. Top. Signal Process.* **2017**, *11*, 742–753. [CrossRef]
31. Strecht, P.; Cruz, L.; Soares, C.; Mendes-Moreira, J.; Abreu, R. A Comparative Study of Classification and Regression Algorithms for Modelling Students' Academic Performance. In Proceedings of the 8th International Conference on Educational Data Mining, Madrid, Spain, 26–29 June 2015.
32. Meier, Y.; Xu, J.; Atan, O.; van der Schaar, M. Personalized grade prediction: A data mining approach. In Proceedings of the 2015 IEEE International Conference on Data Mining, Atlantic City, NJ, USA, 14–17 November 2015.
33. Sweeney, M.; Rangwala, H.; Lester, J.; Johri, A. Next-term student performance prediction: A recommender systems approach. *arXiv* **2016**, arXiv:1604.01840.
34. Kostopoulos, G.; Kotsiantis, S.; Fazakis, N.; Koutsonikos, G.; Pierrakeas, C. A Semi-Supervised Regression Algorithm for Grade Prediction of Students in Distance Learning Courses. *Int. J. Artif. Intell. Tools* **2019**, *28*, 1940001. [CrossRef]
35. Tsiakmaki, M.; Kostopoulos, G.; Koutsonikos, G.; Pierrakeas, C.; Kotsiantis, S.; Ragos, O. Predicting University Students' Grades Based on Previous Academic Achievements. In Proceedings of the 2018 9th International Conference on Information, Intelligence, Systems and Applications (IISA), Zakynthos, Greece, 23–25 July 2018.
36. Márquez-Vera, C.; Cano, A.; Romero, C.; Noaman, A.Y.M.; Fardoun, H.M.; Ventura, S. Early dropout prediction using data mining: A case study with high school students. *Expert Syst.* **2016**, *33*, 107–124. [CrossRef]
37. Zhang, Y.; Oussena, S.; Clark, T.; Kim, H. Use Data Mining to Improve Student Retention in Higher Education-A Case Study. In Proceedings of the 12th International Conference on Enterprise Information Systems, Volume 1, DISI, Funchal, Madeira, Portugal, 8–12 June 2010.
38. Delen, D. A comparative analysis of machine learning techniques for student retention management. *Decis. Support Syst.* **2010**, *49*, 498–506. [CrossRef]
39. Lykourentzou, I.; Giannoukos, I.; Nikolopoulos, V.; Mpardis, G.; Loumos, V. Dropout prediction in e-learning courses through the combination of machine learning techniques. *Comput. Educ.* **2009**, *53*, 950–965. [CrossRef]
40. Superby, J.-F.; Vandamme, J.P.; Meskens, N. Determination of factors influencing the achievement of the first-year university students using data mining methods. In Proceedings of the Workshop on Educational Data Mining, Jhongli, Taiwan, 26–30 June 2006.
41. Herzog, S. Estimating student retention and degree-completion time: Decision trees and neural networks vis-à-vis regression. *New Dir. Inst. Res.* **2006**, *2006*, 17–33. [CrossRef]
42. Kostopoulos, G.; Kotsiantis, S.; Pintelas, P. Estimating student dropout in distance higher education using semi-supervised techniques. In Proceedings of the 19th Panhellenic Conference on Informatics, Athens, Greece, 1–3 October 2015.
43. Rao, S.S. *Engineering Optimization: Theory and Practice*; John Wiley & Sons: Toronto, ON, Canada, 2009.
44. Brochu, E. *Interactive Bayesian Optimization: Learning User Preferences for Graphics and Animation*; University of British Columbia: Vancouver, BC, Canada, 2010.
45. Feurer, M.; Hutter, F. Hyperparameter Optimization. In *Automated Machine Learning: Methods, Systems, Challenges*; Springer: New York, NY, USA, 2019; pp. 3–33.
46. Brochu, E.; Cora, V.M.; de Freitas, N. A tutorial on Bayesian optimization of expensive cost functions, with application to active user modeling and hierarchical reinforcement learning. *arXiv* **2010**, arXiv:1012.2599.

47. Hutter, F.; Kotthoff, L.; Vanschoren, J. *Automated Machine Learning-Methods, Systems, Challenges*; Springer: New York, NY, USA, 2019.
48. Bergstra, J.; Bengio, Y. Random search for hyper-parameter optimization. *J. Mach. Learn. Res.* **2012**, *13*, 281–305.
49. Bengio, Y. Gradient-based optimization of hyperparameters. *Neural Comput.* **2000**, *12*, 1889–1900. [CrossRef]
50. Maron, O.; Moore, A.W. The racing algorithm: Model selection for lazy learners. *Artif. Intell. Rev.* **1997**, *11*, 193–225. [CrossRef]
51. Simon, D. *Evolutionary Optimization Algorithms*; Wiley: Hoboken, NJ, USA, 2013.
52. Guo, X.C.; Yang, J.H.; Wu, C.G.; Wang, C.Y.; Liang, Y.C. A novel LS-SVMs hyper-parameter selection based on particle swarm optimization. *Neurocomputing* **2008**, *71*, 3211–3215. [CrossRef]
53. Dewancker, I.; McCourt, M.; Clark, S. Bayesian Optimization Primer; SigOpt. 2015. Available online: https://app.sigopt.com/static/pdf/SigOpt_Bayesian_Optimization_Primer.pdf (accessed on 12 June 2019).
54. Hutter, F.; Lücke, J.; Schmidt-Thieme, L. Beyond manual tuning of hyperparameters. *Künstliche Intell.* **2015**, *29*, 329–337. [CrossRef]
55. Shahriari, B.; Swersky, K.; Wang, Z.; Adams, R.P.; de Freitas, N. Taking the human out of the loop: A review of bayesian optimization. *Proc. IEEE* **2016**, *104*, 148–175. [CrossRef]
56. Williams, C.K.I.; Rasmussen, C.E. *Gaussian Processes for Machine Learning*; MIT Press: Cambridge, MA, USA, 2006; Volume 2.
57. Bergstra, J.; Yamins, D.; Cox, D.D. Making a Science of Model Search: Hyperparameter Optimization in Hundreds of Dimensions for Vision Architectures. In Proceedings of the 30th International Conference on International Conference on Machine Learning, Atlanta, GA, USA, 16–21 June 2013.
58. Breiman, L.; Friedman, J.; Olshen, R.; Stone, C. *Classification and Regression Trees*; Wadsworth Int. Group: Belmont, CA, USA, 1984; Volume 37, pp. 237–251.
59. Hutter, F.; Hoos, H.H.; Leyton-Brown, K. Sequential model-based optimization for general algorithm configuration. In Proceedings of the International Conference on Learning and Intelligent Optimization, Rome, Italy, 17–21 January 2011.
60. Eggensperger, K.; Feurer, M.; Hutter, F.; Bergstra, J.; Snoek, J.; Hoos, H.; Leyton-Brown, K. Towards an empirical foundation for assessing bayesian optimization of hyperparameters. In Proceedings of the NIPS Workshop on Bayesian Optimization in Theory and Practice, Lake Tahoe, NV, USA, 10 December 2013.
61. Jones, D.R.; Schonlau, M.; Welch, W.J. Efficient global optimization of expensive black-box functions. *J. Glob. Optim.* **1998**, *13*, 455–492. [CrossRef]
62. Kushner, H.J. A new method of locating the maximum point of an arbitrary multipeak curve in the presence of noise. *J. Basic Eng.* **1964**, *86*, 97–106. [CrossRef]
63. Srinivas, N.; Krause, A.; Kakade, S.M.; Seeger, M. Gaussian process optimization in the bandit setting: No regret and experimental design. *arXiv* **2009**, arXiv:0912.3995.
64. Clark, S.; Liu, E.; Frazier, P.; Wang, J.; Oktay, D.; Vesdapunt, N. MOE: A Global, Black Box Optimization Engine for Real World Metric Optimization. 2014. Available online: https://github.com/Yelp/MOE (accessed on 12 June 2019).
65. Geurts, P.; Ernst, D.; Wehenkel, L. Extremely randomized trees. *Mach. Learn.* **2006**, *63*, 3–42. [CrossRef]
66. Jeni, L.A.; Cohn, J.F.; de la Torre, F. Facing imbalanced data–recommendations for the use of performance metrics. In Proceedings of the 2013 Humaine Association Conference on Affective Computing and Intelligent Interaction, Geneva, Switzerland, 2–5 September 2013.
67. Ling, C.X.; Huang, J.; Zhang, H. AUC: A better measure than accuracy in comparing learning algorithms. In Proceedings of the Conference of the Canadian Society for Computational Studies of Intelligence, Halifax, NS, Canada, 11–13 June 2003.
68. Provost, F.; Fawcett, T. Analysis and Visualization of Classifier Performance: Comparison under Imprecise Class and Cost Distributions. In Proceedings of the Third International Conference on Knowledge Discovery and Data Mining, Newport Beach, CA, USA, 14–17 August 1997.
69. Frank, E.; Hall, M.A.; Witten, I.H. *The WEKA Workbench. Online Appendix for Data Mining: Practical Machine Learning Tools and Techniques*, 4th ed.; Morgan Kaufmann: Massachusetts, MA, USA, 2016.
70. Kotthoff, L.; Thornton, C.; Hoos, H.H.; Hutter, F.; Leyton-Brown, K. Auto-WEKA 2.0: Automatic model selection and hyperparameter optimization in WEKA. *J. Mach. Learn. Res.* **2017**, *18*, 826–830.

71. Witten, I.H.; Frank, E.; Hall, M.A.; Pal, C.J. *Data Mining: Practical machine learning tools and techniques*; Morgan Kaufmann: Massachusetts, MA, USA, 2016.
72. John, G.H.; Langley, P. Estimating continuous distributions in Bayesian classifiers. In Proceedings of the Eleventh Conference on Uncertainty in Artificial Intelligence, Montreal, QC, Canada, 18–20 August 1995.
73. Eibe, F.; Witten, I.H. *Generating Accurate Rule Sets without Global Optimization*; University of Waikato, Department of Computer Science: Hamilton, New Zealand, 1998.
74. Holmes, G.; Hall, M.; Prank, E. Generating rule sets from model trees. In Proceedings of the Australasian Joint Conference on Artificial Intelligence, Sydney, Australia, 6–10 December 1999.
75. Breiman, L. Random forests. *Mach. Learn.* **2001**, *45*, 5–32. [CrossRef]
76. Platt, J. Fast Training of Support Vector Machines using Sequential Minimal Optimization. In *Advances in Kernel Methods—Support Vector Learning*; Schoelkopf, B., Burges, C., Smola, A., Eds.; MIT Press: Massachusetts, MA, USA, 1998.
77. Keerthi, S.S.; Shevade, S.K.; Bhattacharyya, C.; Murthy, K.R.K. Improvements to Platt's SMO Algorithm for SVM Classifier Design. *Neural Comput.* **2001**, *13*, 637–649. [CrossRef]
78. Hastie, T.; Tibshirani, R. Classification by Pairwise Coupling. In *Advances in Neural Information Processing Systems*; MIT Press: Massachusetts, MA, USA, 1998.
79. Shevade, S.K.; Keerthi, S.S.; Bhattacharyya, C.; Murthy, K.R.K. Improvements to the SMO Algorithm for SVM Regression. *IEEE Transactions on Neural Netw.* **2000**, *11*. [CrossRef]
80. Smola, A.J.; Schoelkopf, B. *A Tutorial on Support Vector Regression*; Kluwer Academic Publishers: Dordrecht, The Netherlands, 1998.
81. Aha, D.; Kibler, D. Instance-based learning algorithms. *Mach. Learn.* **1991**, *6*, 37–66. [CrossRef]
82. Breiman, L. Bagging predictors. *Mach. Learn.* **1996**, *24*, 123–140. [CrossRef]
83. Kim, B.-H.; Vizitei, E.; Ganapathi, V. GritNet: Student performance prediction with deep learning. *arXiv* **2018**, arXiv:1804.07405.
84. Caruana, R.; Niculescu-Mizil, A. An empirical comparison of supervised learning algorithms. In Proceedings of the 23rd International Conference on Machine Learning, Pittsburgh, PA, USA, 25–29 June 2006.
85. Wolpert, D.H.; Macready, W.G. No free lunch theorems for optimization. *IEEE Trans. Evol. Comput.* **1997**, *1*, 67–82. [CrossRef]

© 2019 by the authors. Licensee MDPI, Basel, Switzerland. This article is an open access article distributed under the terms and conditions of the Creative Commons Attribution (CC BY) license (http://creativecommons.org/licenses/by/4.0/).

*Article*

# Predicting Student Performance in Higher Educational Institutions Using Video Learning Analytics and Data Mining Techniques

**Raza Hasan [1,2,*], Sellappan Palaniappan [1], Salman Mahmood [1], Ali Abbas [2], Kamal Uddin Sarker [3] and Mian Usman Sattar [1]**

1. Department of Information Technology, School of Science and Engineering, Malaysia University of Science and Technology, Petaling Jaya 47810, Selangor, Malaysia; sell@must.edu.my (S.P.); salman.mahmood@pg.must.edu.my (S.M.); mian.usman@phd.must.edu.my (M.U.S.)
2. Department of Computing, Middle East College, Knowledge Oasis Muscat, P.B. No. 79, Al Rusayl 124, Oman; aabbas@mec.edu.om
3. Faculty of Ocean Engineering Technology and Informatics (FTKKI), University Malaysia Terengganu, Kuala Terengganu 21030, Terengganu, Malaysia; ku_sarker@yahoo.com
* Correspondence: raza.hasan@pg.must.edu.my; Tel.: +968-98199513

Received: 4 May 2020; Accepted: 3 June 2020; Published: 4 June 2020

**Abstract:** Technology and innovation empower higher educational institutions (HEI) to use different types of learning systems—video learning is one such system. Analyzing the footprints left behind from these online interactions is useful for understanding the effectiveness of this kind of learning. Video-based learning with flipped teaching can help improve student's academic performance. This study was carried out with 772 examples of students registered in e-commerce and e-commerce technologies modules at an HEI. The study aimed to predict student's overall performance at the end of the semester using video learning analytics and data mining techniques. Data from the student information system, learning management system and mobile applications were analyzed using eight different classification algorithms. Furthermore, data transformation and preprocessing techniques were carried out to reduce the features. Moreover, genetic search and principle component analysis were carried out to further reduce the features. Additionally, the CN2 Rule Inducer and multivariate projection can be used to assist faculty in interpreting the rules to gain insights into student interactions. The results showed that Random Forest accurately predicted successful students at the end of the class with an accuracy of 88.3% with an equal width and information gain ratio.

**Keywords:** classification algorithms; data preprocessing; data mining; data transformation; student academic performance; video learning analytics

## 1. Introduction

Digitalization has infiltrated into every aspect of life. Emerging new technologies have an impact on our lives and change the way we do our daily work, raising our performance to a new height. The technology used in education has allowed educators to implement new theories to enhance the teaching and learning process. This shift from "traditional learning" has led to a model in which learning can take place outside the classroom, facilitating different learner attributes such as visual, verbal, aural and solitary learning within the "blended learning" approach [1]. Educators use innovative technologies to cater to different learners with blended learning, and learners can use these technologies to improve their cognitive abilities to excel in the courses being taught [2]. Educators use virtual classrooms, webinars, links, simulations or any other online mechanism to deliver the information [3].

In blended learning environments (BLE), the approach to education is a flipped classroom, where content is provided through the Internet in advance before the commencement of the class [4]. The flipped classroom enables students to come to the class prepared, and the educator uses activities in the class that can clear the doubts of the students, as well as helping them in their assessments and the concepts learned from the content provided to them in the form of discussions or activities. The content that is usually provided by the educator for the flipped classroom includes reading along with questions and answers, created video lectures, demonstration videos, an online class discussion room, lecture slides, tutorials and reading from textbooks or reference books [5].

The adoption of flipped classrooms by higher education institutions (HEI) has rapidly increased in recent years [6]. The crucial factor in flipped classrooms is the electronic support that the HEI uses to disseminate knowledge among the learners. Encouraging learners to learn at their own pace, including through video lectures, frees up classroom time for more applied learning or active learning. Educators take support from various educational technologies to replicate the virtual classroom.

At Middle East College (MEC), different systems are in place to store student information. The student information system (SIS) stores the related academic data; the learning management system (LMS)—i.e., Moodle—is used as an e-learning tool to disseminate knowledge at the same time as online behavior is stored in the logs for each student; and the video streaming server (VSS) is used alongside Moodle to share video lectures to the students [7]. As mobile culture is on the rise, an in-house built mobile application—eDify—has been developed to share video lectures to students since spring 2019, enhancing the teaching and learning process. With the use of eDify, the collection of students' video interactions was made easy, providing valuable information about the learners. The data which these systems hold about the learners can be useful for enhancing the teaching and learning process. Learning analytics (LA) help HEIs to gain useful insights about their learners interacting with the system [8–11]. When videos are used to provide useful information about the learners, it is called video learning analytics (VLA) [10,12–14].

The study aimed to use systems such as SIS, LMS and eDify to explore students' overall performance at the end of the semester. Education data mining is used to elucidate this issue as this uses predictive analysis on the data [8,15,16]. The majority of the research suggests that the classification model can be used to predict success in HEIs using data related to student profiles and data logs from Moodle [17–19]. Similarly, research has been carried out to predict student performance using videos, but little work has been done on using both systems to predict the students' academic performance. The study attempts to predict student performance in HEIs using video learning analytics and data mining techniques to help faculty, learners and the management to make better decisions.

The contribution of this paper is threefold: (1) when the classification model is formed using interaction data from different systems used in the learning setting, we determine which algorithm and preprocessing techniques are best for predicting successful students; (2) we determine the impacts that feature selection techniques have on classification performance; and (3) we determine which features have greater importance in the prediction of student performance.

This paper is organized as follows: Section 2 presents a literature review and an overview of related works in this field. Section 3 presents the methodology used in the study. Section 4 presents the results. Section 5 presents the discussion on the study. Finally, Section 6 draws a conclusion and proposes future research.

## 2. Literature Review and Related Works

*2.1. Learning Analytics*

LA is defined as the usage of data, statistical analysis, and explanatory and predictive models to gain insight and act on complex issues. LA involves the data analysis of the learners and their activities to enhance the student learning experience [20]. Implementing LA allows higher education institutions to understand their learners and the barriers to their learning, thus ensuring institutional success and retaining a larger and more diverse student population, which is important for operational facilities, fundraising and admissions. Student success is a key factor in improving academic institutions' resource management.

LA is the measurement, collection, analysis and reporting of data about learners. Understanding context is important for the purposes of optimization and learning and for the environments in which learning occurs [21], as shown in Figure 1.

**Figure 1.** Learning analytics cycle.

Several studies have been conducted on LA to understand the students' learning behaviors and to optimize the learning process. Thus, HEIs will able to identify the learners' behavior and patterns to detect low achievers or students who are at-risk. Early warning systems are investigated in order to achieve these objectives. Predictive modelling is usually used to predict the learners' end-of-term academic performance, with the data from different online learning systems being evaluated [22]. Purdue university uses course signals which allow faculty to provide real-time feedback to the students. Grades, demographic data, learning management system (LMS) interaction data, grade history and students' effort are measured with the help of LA. A personalized email is used to communicate with students about their current status with the help of traffic lights. The system helps to retain information, and performance outcomes are thus evaluated [23]. Predictive analysis using PredictED emails students about their behavior to predict their end-of-semester grades with the help of LMS access logs [24]. An LA study showed that students' online activities correlate with their performance in the course, and a prediction can be made regarding the possible outcome of their performance at the end of the course [25]. The study suggests that LA plays a vital role in affecting students' perspectives and the way they learn in the different online settings [26]. LA not only provides the educator with insights on the outcomes of the course, but also provides an opportunity for self-evaluation for the students [9,27].

*2.2. Video Learning Analytics*

VLA enables us to understand and improve the effectiveness of video-based learning (VBL) as a tool and its related practices [28]. Flipped teaching is an important component of VBL, where an educator uploads a video lecture. The evaluation of this type of education can be enhanced through LA and can predict the students' overall performance in the course. With the rapidly changing environments in teaching and learning, different technologies in VLA can help stakeholders, educators and learners to understand the data generated by these videos. Different research has been carried out to understand this relationship. Regarding the use of YouTube to upload lectures, quantitative data were analyzed by using the trends of the video interactions [13]. The researcher used student interactions in the analyzed video to understand the students' behavior and tried to predict the outcomes of their final scores with the help of machine learning. These interactions within the video are called the "Clickstream" [28,29]. Researchers use different data mining algorithms to predict student performance or for grade prediction [12].

*2.3. Educational Data Mining*

Data mining (DM) refers to the discovery of associable patterns from large datasets. It is a powerful tool in artificial intelligence (AI) and facilitates the categorization of data into different dimensions, identifying relationships and categorizing the information. This allows stakeholders to use the information extracted from DM and can help improve decision-making. Educational data mining (EDM) is a growing discipline which is used to discover meaningful and useful knowledge from data extracted from educational settings. Applying DM techniques, EDM provides researchers with a better understanding of student behavior and the settings in which learning happens, as shown in Figure 2 [18,30].

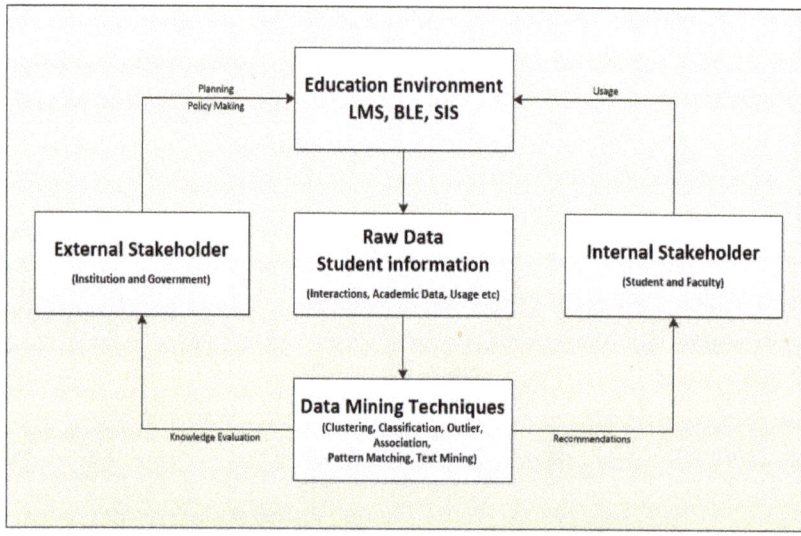

**Figure 2.** The cycle of applying data mining in education [31].

The EDM process converts raw data from different systems used in HEIs into useful information that has a potential impact on educational practice and research [32]. It is also referred to as Knowledge Discovery in Databases (KDD) due to the hierarchical nature of the data used [18,30]. The methods used for KDD or EDM are as follows.

2.3.1. Prediction

This is a widely used technique in EDM. Here, historical data are used in terms of student grades, demographic data, etc., to predict the future outcomes of the students' results. Many studies have been carried out in which classification is most the commonly used method to make predictions. In order to achieve their research targets, researchers have used the Decision Tree, Random Forest, Naïve Bayes, Support Vector Machines, Linear Regression or Logistic Regression models, and K means approaches [33–38]. The studies mainly suggest the prediction of students' academic performance either before the classes, at the middle of the session or at the end of the term.

2.3.2. Clustering

This is a process of finding and grouping a set of objects, called a cluster, in the same group based on similar traits. This technique is used in EDM, where student participation in online forums, discussion groups or chats is studied. Studies show that classification should be used after clustering. Researchers have used similar algorithms as those for prediction to determine students' academic success [39–42].

2.3.3. Relationship

This method is used to look for similar patterns from multiple tables as compared to other methods. The methods commonly used to investigate relationships are association, correlation, and sequential patterns. The study suggests that, in EDM, an association rule should be used to predict students' end-of-semester exam results and performance using heuristic algorithms [43,44].

2.3.4. Distillation

This recognizes and classifies features of the data, depicted in the form of a visualization for human inference [18,36,45].

*2.4. State-Of-The-Art*

EDM aims to predict student performance either using demographic data or socio-economic data or online activity on the learning management system at different educational levels. A problem arises when the data are imbalanced or where researchers have used other techniques alongside a simple classification method such as data balancing, cost-sensitive learning and genetic programing [8,46]. Early dropout studies have been conducted by researchers to determine the factors that can influence student retention. Here, classical classification methods were also used to predict early dropout. Feature selection plays a vital role in the accuracy of the classification algorithms. The genetic algorithm was used and obtained 10 attributes out of 27, and the efficiency was improved [47,48]. For our study into handling imbalanced data, we use the K-fold cross-validation technique; to reduce features, we use ranking and scoring, the genetic search algorithm, principle component analysis and the multiview learning approach using multivariate projection along with the CN2 Rule induction for easier interpretation, as the multiview learning approach uses sparse data where a high percentage of the variable's cells do not contain actual data.

HEIs use different learning systems and the amount of data accumulated from these systems is enormous. The LA provides the analysis of data from these systems and finds meaningful patterns which can be helpful for educators and learners. From the literature review and related works, it is evident that, when analyzing student academic performance prediction, LA is a widely used method in EDM. The classification technique is also used to classify the parameters used for the prediction and success of the model. Due to innovative teaching and learning pedagogies and the implementation of flipped classrooms, the use of VBL is on the increase, where students can study prior to the class at their own leisure and come prepared to the class. Little research has been carried out on VLA and on determining students' attitude and behavior towards VBL. Educators apply different settings within or outside the classroom to create an effective learning experience for learners. For effective knowledge transfer, an educator needs a predictive model to understand the future outcomes for each student. This will help the educator to identify the methods which should be applied, to identify poorly performing students and provide better support to the students to obtain good grades at an early stage.

## 3. Methodology

The study is exploratory in nature. The quantitative prediction method is used for the study.

*3.1. Educational Datamining Model*

According to the literature review in the previous section, some of the important activities are recognized in educational datamining, as shown in Figure 3. The classification method is used to predict student academic performance as a widely used method in prediction, as shown in the literature review. For this study, we also use the classification method, and the data are gathered from multiple systems which are already running in the HEI: student academic information is gathered from the student information system (SIS), student online activity from LMS Moodle and student video interactions data from eDify (mobile application). The algorithms used for this study are based on the frequently used algorithms form the existing literature: Classification Tree, Random Forest, k-Nearest Neighbors (kNN), Support Vector Machine (SVM), Logistic Regression, Naïve Bayes, Neural Network and CN2 Rule Induction.

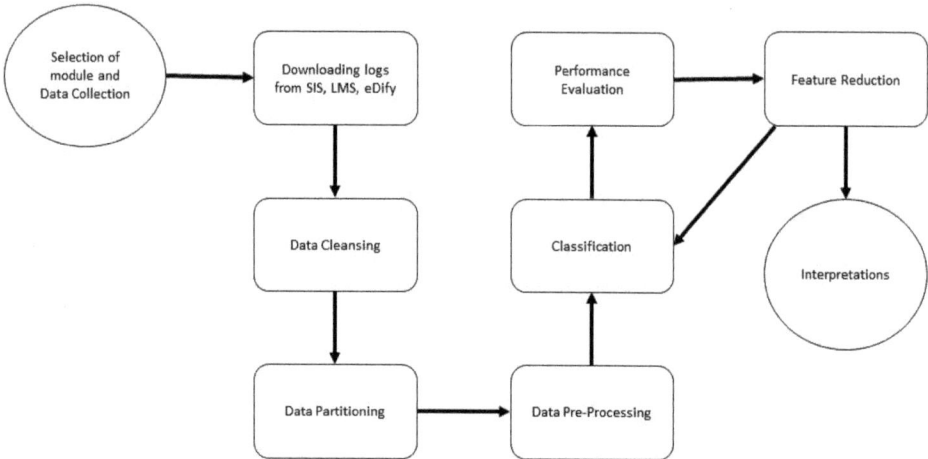

**Figure 3.** The cycle of applying educational data mining in research.

*3.2. Module Selection*

The study was conducted at a private HEI in Oman with a dataset consisting of 772 instances of students registered in the sixth semester. The modules chosen were e-commerce (COMP 1008) and e-commerce technologies (COMP 0382). The reason for choosing these modules was that the modules are offered in different specializations, sharing the same course content and yielding the maximum number of students necessary for making the dataset.

*3.3. Data Collection*

Before starting data collection for any research, ethical approval is necessary. For this study, informed consent was obtained from the applicants, explaining the purpose of study and the description. There were "no potential risks" or discomfort while using eDify, but if the applicant, for any reason, felt discomfort or risk, they were able to withdraw from the study at any time. To ensure confidentiality and privacy, all the information from the study was coded to protect applicant names. No names or other identifying information were used when discussing or reporting data. Once the data was fully analyzed, it was destroyed. This research was voluntary and the applicant retained the right to withdraw from participation at any time; this was also communicated to the students when the semester started.

The data were collected from the Spring 2019 and Fall 2019 semesters after the implementation of eDify (mobile application) supporting VBL and by capturing students' video interactions. Eight lecture videos were used in the module, but for study purposes, the data from all lecture videos were used.

*3.4. Data Cleansing*

In this activity, unnecessary data were cleansed and data were separated from information which was not relevant for the analysis. Historical data for each student registered in the two modules were considered for the study. In total, 19 features were selected for study, from which 12 features and one meta attribute was used from SIS; Moodle yielded two features related to the online activity within and outside the campus; and four features were selected from eDify.

*3.5. Data Partionioning*

After the data cleansing activity, data partitioning was performed. Relevant data were extracted and combined for further analysis, as shown in Table 1.

**Table 1.** List of extracted features and description. GPA: grade point average.

| No | Category | Feature | Values | Description |
|---|---|---|---|---|
| 1 | | Applicant | Text + Numeric | Student ID for identification and mapping |
| 2 | | Cumulative Grade Point Average (CGPA) | * 0.00–4.00 | Student overall GPA |
| 3 | | Attempt Count | Low (1), Medium (2) and High (>2) | Status of the student attempts in the module |
| 4 | Student Academic Information | High Risk | Yes/No | A student having a high failure rate in the same module |
| 5 | | Term Exceed at Risk | Yes/No | Shows the students' progression in the degree plan |
| 6 | | At Risk | Yes/No | A student failed two or more modules previously |
| 7 | | Student Success Centre (SSC) | Yes/No | Student referred to SSC for any assistance |
| 8 | | Other Modules | Low (1), Medium (2) and High (>2) | Student register for other modules |
| 9 | | Plagiarism Count | * Numeric Value | Students have been accused of any plagiarism |
| 10 | | Coursework 1 (CW1) | * 1–100 | Marks obtained in CW1 |
| 11 | | Coursework 2 (CW2) | * 1–100 | Marks obtained in CW2 |
| 12 | | End Semester Examination (ESE) | * 1–100 | Marks obtained in ESE |
| 13 | Students Activity | Activity on Campus | * Time spent in minutes | Student Moodle activity on campus |
| 14 | | Activity Off Campus | * Time spent in minutes | Student Moodle activity off campus |
| 15 | | Played | * No. of times video played | eDify access and played video |
| 16 | Student Video Interactions | Paused | * No. of times video paused | eDify access and paused the video |
| 17 | | Likes/Dislikes | Yes/No | eDify access and either liked or disliked video |
| 18 | | Segment | * No. of segments rewind | eDify access and most-watched segment mapped with ESE |
| 19 | Result (Target Variable) | | * Numeric value | Overall marks obtained in the module |

## 3.6. Data Pre-Processing

The main reason for testing several algorithms on the dataset was that their performance varies for the selected features. The study suggested that algorithms behave differently; depending on the dataset, the efficiency and performance may also vary. With this approach, it is easier to identify any one algorithm which suits the dataset with better accuracy and performance. For this purpose, a similar approach was used for this study. For the study, the Orange data mining tool was used in accordance with the process shown in Figure 4 [49].

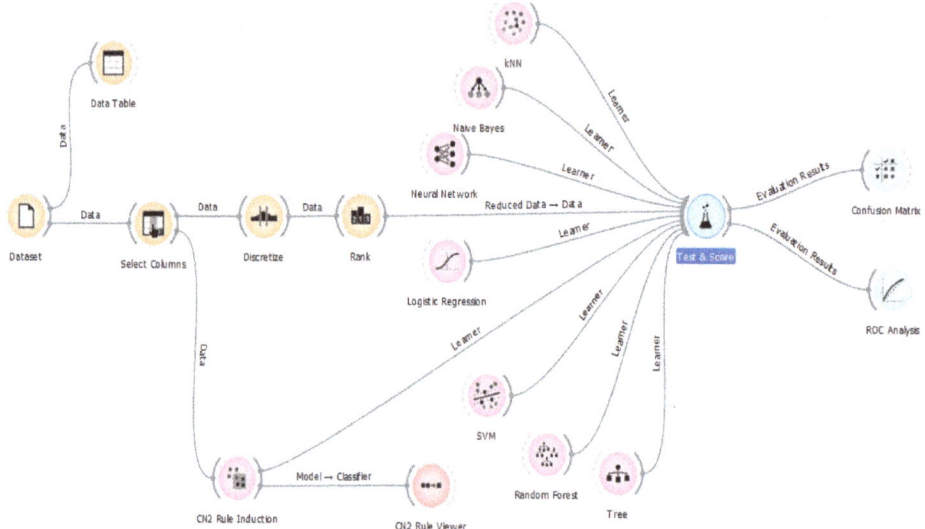

**Figure 4.** Data mining process.

Pre-processing methods were used to transform raw data collected from these systems into an understandable form. Table 1 shows the features selected from SIS, where CGPA is converted into nominal order as excellent, very good, good, fair, adequate, or poor/fail; plagiarism count into low, medium, or high; coursework (CW)1 into pass or fail; CW2 into pass or fail; and end-of-semester evaluation (ESE) into pass or fail. Online activity was captured from Moodle in terms of minutes and is converted into nominal order as follows: activity on campus—low, medium, or high; and activity off campus—low, medium, or high. From eDify, four features—played, paused, likes/dislikes and segment—were selected, and discretization was applied on the continuous data to transform them into categorical data.

The dataset was fed into the analyzer, and the select column widget was used to select the features from the available variables. Student ID is the meta attribute, and the result was selected as the target variable. The discretize widget was used to transform the variable into categorical data in order to be used in the study. The rank widget scoring technique was used for feature selection, which could be used further for prediction. Information gain, gain ratio, and the Gini decrease weight were compared for the performance of the prediction model. Furthermore, the investigation of the feature selection proceeded using the genetic algorithm, and principle component analysis (PCA) was used to further reduce the features. Multivariate projection was used as an optimization method that finds a linear projection and associated scatterplot that best separates instances of separate classes, uncovering feature interactions and providing information about intra-class similarities.

## 3.7. Performance Evaluation

The performance of the classification algorithms was determined in the study; performance was based on the four standard evaluation metrics for accuracy, sensitivity, specificity and f-measure. A 10-fold cross-validation for comparison with the baseline method was used, splitting the data into 10 folds and using nine folds for training and one fold for testing. Confusion metrics were used for the analysis of supervised learning, where each column of the matrix represents the instances in a predicted class, while each row represents the instances in an actual class to avoid mislabeling as shown in Table 2.

Table 2. Sample confusion matrix.

|        |        | Predictions |        |
|--------|--------|-------------|--------|
|        |        | Failed      | Passed |
| Actual | Failed | a           | b      |
|        | Passed | c           | d      |

The entries in the confusion matrix have the following meaning in the context of a data mining problem: a is the correct negative prediction, also called true negative (TN), classified as failed by the model; b is the incorrect positive prediction, also called false positive (FP), classified as passed by the model; c is the incorrect negative prediction, also called false negative (FN), classified as failed by the model; and d is the correct positive prediction, also called true positive (TP), classified as passed by the model.

The performance metrics according to this confusion matrix are calculated as follows.

### 3.7.1. Accuracy

The accuracy (AC) is the proportion of the total number of predictions that were correct. It is determined using the following equation:

$$AC = (d + a)/(d + a + b + c), \quad (1)$$

### 3.7.2. Sensitivity

The recall or TP rate is the proportion of positive cases that were correctly identified, as calculated using the following equation:

$$\text{Sensitivity} = d/(d + c), \quad (2)$$

### 3.7.3. Specificity

The TN rate is the proportion of negatives cases that were correctly classified as negative, as calculated using the following equation:

$$\text{Specificity} = a/(a + b), \quad (3)$$

### 3.7.4. F-Measure

The confusion matrix belongs to a binary classification, returning a value of either "passed" or "failed". The sensitivity and specificity measures may lead to biased comments in the evaluation of the model, as calculated using the following equation:

$$\text{F-measure} = 2d/(2d + 2b + c), \quad (4)$$

## 4. Results

A supervised data classification technique was used to determine the best prediction model that fit the requirements for giving an optimal result. For analysis, the same set of classification algorithms, performance metrics and the 10-fold cross-validation method were used.

*4.1. No Feature Selection and Transformation*

The CN2 Rule Inducer and Random Forest algorithm exhibited a performance rate of 85.1%, as shown in Table 3. Further investigating the performance metrics of the CN2 Rule Inducer showed good sensitivity, levelling-out the lower specificity and giving a good F-measure score. When no data transformation and no feature selection were undertaken, the CN2 rule inducer showed the highest classification accuracy.

**Table 3.** Data transformation (none), feature selection (none).

| Algorithm | Accuracy | Sensitivity | Specificity | F-Measure |
|---|---|---|---|---|
| CN2 Rule Inducer | 0.851 | 0.960 | 0.870 | 0.913 |
| Random Forest | 0.851 | 0.952 | 0.875 | 0.912 |
| Log. Reg. | 0.847 | 0.992 | 0.846 | 0.913 |
| Tree | 0.843 | 0.939 | 0.876 | 0.907 |
| kNN | 0.841 | 0.939 | 0.874 | 0.905 |
| Naïve Bayes | 0.821 | 0.957 | 0.844 | 0.897 |
| Neural Network | 0.811 | 1.00 | 0.811 | 0.896 |
| SVM | 0.785 | 0.927 | 0.829 | 0.875 |

*4.2. No Feature Selection and Equal Frequency Transformation*

When data transformation was applied with equal frequency, the Random Forest algorithm predicted with an accuracy of 85%, as shown in Table 4. The predicted scores were similar to the previous results when no data transformation and no feature selection were applied, as shown in Table 3.

**Table 4.** Data transformation (equal frequency), feature selection (none).

| Algorithm | Accuracy | Sensitivity | Specificity | F-Measure |
|---|---|---|---|---|
| Random Forest | 0.850 | 0.911 | 0.873 | 0.911 |
| Log. Reg. | 0.846 | 0.992 | 0.845 | 0.913 |
| kNN | 0.837 | 0.939 | 0.870 | 0.903 |
| Tree | 0.837 | 0.936 | 0.872 | 0.903 |
| CN2 Rule Inducer | 0.837 | 0.938 | 0.871 | 0.903 |
| SVM | 0.820 | 0.960 | 0.841 | 0.896 |
| Neural Network | 0.811 | 1.00 | 0.811 | 0.896 |
| Naïve Bayes | 0.804 | 0.931 | 0.844 | 0.885 |

*4.3. No Feature Selection and Equal Width Transformation*

When data transformation was applied with equal width, the Random Forest predicted with an accuracy of 85.5%, as shown in Table 5. From the analysis, it was found that the equal width data transformation technique can be further investigated with feature selection, as the result showed slight improvements.

**Table 5.** Data transformation (equal width), feature selection (none).

| Algorithm | Accuracy | Sensitivity | Specificity | F-Measure |
|---|---|---|---|---|
| Random Forest | 0.855 | 0.973 | 0.865 | 0.916 |
| Log. Reg. | 0.846 | 0.990 | 0.846 | 0.912 |
| kNN | 0.842 | 0.971 | 0.854 | 0.909 |
| Tree | 0.842 | 0.955 | 0.864 | 0.907 |
| CN2 Rule Inducer | 0.842 | 0.957 | 0.863 | 0.908 |
| SVM | 0.820 | 0.958 | 0.842 | 0.896 |
| Naïve Bayes | 0.811 | 0.935 | 0.848 | 0.889 |
| Neural Network | 0.811 | 1.00 | 0.811 | 0.896 |

*4.4. Information Gain Feature Selection and Equal Width Transformation*

The tree-based algorithm showed improvements in accuracy when a data transformation of equal width was applied with the ranking technique, utilizing the scoring methods provided by the Orange data mining tool. The accuracy of Random Forest increased from 85.5% to 87.6%, the CN2 Rule Inducer increased from 85.1% to 87.3%, and Classification Tree increased from 84.3% to 87.2% when the information gain feature was selected. The nine selected features were found in all the three scoring methods—CW1, ESE, CW2, likes, paused, played, segment, Moodle on campus and Moodle off campus. SVM performed worse compared to others, but the accuracy of SVM was slightly improved from 82% to 82.5%, as shown in Table 6.

**Table 6.** Data transformation (equal width), feature selection (information gain).

| Algorithm | Accuracy | Sensitivity | Specificity | F-Measure |
|---|---|---|---|---|
| Random Forest | 0.876 | 0.981 | 0.883 | 0.930 |
| CN2 Rule Inducer | 0.873 | 0.978 | 0.883 | 0.928 |
| Tree | 0.872 | 0.978 | 0.881 | 0.927 |
| Log. Reg. | 0.870 | 0.992 | 0.871 | 0.928 |
| kNN | 0.864 | 0.961 | 0.886 | 0.922 |
| Naïve Bayes | 0.835 | 0.935 | 0.876 | 0.905 |
| Neural Network | 0.835 | 1.00 | 0.835 | 0.910 |
| SVM | 0.825 | 0.949 | 0.857 | 0.901 |

*4.5. Information Gain Ratio Feature Selection and Equal Width Transformation*

Random Forest's accuracy was improved by 0.7% with better sensitivity and F-measure when the equal width data transformation technique and information gain ratio technique were applied. The CN2 Rule Inducer improved by 0.1% with less sensitivity and better specificity. Interestingly, Classification Tree, Logistic Regression, Naïve Bayes, Neural Network and SVM showed no sign of improvement and remained unchanged. kNN's performance was decreased by 3% from the previous example, as shown in Table 7.

**Table 7.** Data transformation (equal width), feature selection (information gain ratio).

| Algorithm | Accuracy | Sensitivity | Specificity | F-Measure |
|---|---|---|---|---|
| Random Forest | 0.883 | 0.975 | 0.895 | 0.933 |
| CN2 Rule Inducer | 0.874 | 0.964 | 0.894 | 0.928 |
| Tree | 0.872 | 0.978 | 0.881 | 0.927 |
| Log. Reg. | 0.870 | 0.992 | 0.871 | 0.928 |
| Naïve Bayes | 0.835 | 0.935 | 0.876 | 0.905 |
| Neural Network | 0.835 | 1.00 | 0.835 | 0.910 |
| kNN | 0.834 | 0.922 | 0.884 | 0.903 |
| SVM | 0.825 | 0.949 | 0.857 | 0.901 |

## 4.6. Gini Decrease Feature Selection and Equal Width Transformation

Data transformation with equal width and the feature selection of Gini decrease reduced the overall accuracy of all the selected algorithms in the study, except the Neural Network, as shown in Table 8. Although kNN performed well compared to the other classification algorithms, its accuracy was less than the information gain, as shown in Table 6. Thus, the Gini decrease method was omitted as the accuracy was not enhanced, as shown in Table 8.

**Table 8.** Data transformation (equal width), feature selection (Gini decrease).

| Algorithm | Accuracy | Sensitivity | Specificity | F-Measure |
|---|---|---|---|---|
| kNN | 0.838 | 0.989 | 0.844 | 0.911 |
| Neural Network | 0.835 | 1.00 | 0.835 | 0.910 |
| Log. Reg. | 0.832 | 0.995 | 0.835 | 0.908 |
| Tree | 0.829 | 0.980 | 0.842 | 0.905 |
| CN2 Rule Inducer | 0.829 | 0.980 | 0.842 | 0.905 |
| Random Forest | 0.828 | 0.980 | 0.840 | 0.905 |
| Naïve Bayes | 0.807 | 0.941 | 0.845 | 0.891 |
| SVM | 0.773 | 0.913 | 0.832 | 0.871 |

## 4.7. Feature Selection Using Genetic Algorithm and Classification

Due to the limitation of the Orange tool to run the genetic algorithm for feature selection, Weka (Waikato Environment for Knowledge Analysis) was used on the same dataset for feature selection using genetic search. Before applying classification algorithms in Orange, relevant features were selected by using feature selection method. Feature selection was performed by using the genetic algorithm, and applicant, at-risk, CW1, CW2, ESE and played were selected. Tree predicted with an accuracy of 87.4%, as shown in Table 9. Feature selection using the genetic search reduced the features to six as compared to the information gain ratio feature selection technique and equal width transformation, but the accuracy was not improved, as shown in Table 7.

**Table 9.** Feature selection using genetic algorithm and classification.

| Algorithm | Accuracy | Sensitivity | Specificity | F-Measure |
|---|---|---|---|---|
| Tree | 0.874 | 0.997 | 0.748 | 0.93 |
| Log. Reg. | 0.871 | 0.992 | 0.74 | 0.928 |
| kNN | 0.867 | 0.983 | 0.717 | 0.926 |
| SVM | 0.867 | 0.989 | 0.748 | 0.926 |
| Naïve Bayes | 0.847 | 0.952 | 0.685 | 0.912 |
| Random Forest | 0.835 | 1 | 1 | 0.91 |
| CN2 Rule Inducer | 0.834 | 0.922 | 0.884 | 0.903 |
| Neural Network | 0.828 | 0.98 | 0.84 | 0.905 |

## 4.8. Principal Component Analysis

A principle component analysis (PCA) was undertaken to reduce the number of variables from 19 to eight components with a variance of 95.6%, as shown in Figure 5. Table 10 shows the PCA component variances.

PC1 shows that a video being played and paused and the segment correspond to the behavior of a video being watched. PC2 shows that a video being played and the segment correspond to the behavior of a video being watched and rewound. PC3 shows that CGPA indicates high academic achievers. PC4 shows that at risk, ESE and likes correspond to the behavior of a student being at risk; those who scored fewer marks in the ESE will like video content. PC5 shows that plagiarized, likes and Moodle activity outside campus correspond to the behavior of a student who is weak in academic writing but likes the video and watches the video outside the campus. PC6 shows that attempt count, at risk, plagiarized, CW1, CW2 and Moodle activity in campus correspond to the behavior of a weak student that spends time on Moodle inside the campus to get better grades in the ESE. PC7 shows that not at risk, plagiarized, CW1, ESE and Moodle activity outside the campus correspond to the behavior of weak students who spend time on Moodle activities outside the campus. PC8 shows that not at risk, plagiarized, CW1, CW2, likes, Moodle activity inside the campus, and less Moodle activity outside the campus correspond to the behavior of weak students, with the attributes in common that they spend time on Moodle both inside and outside the campus.

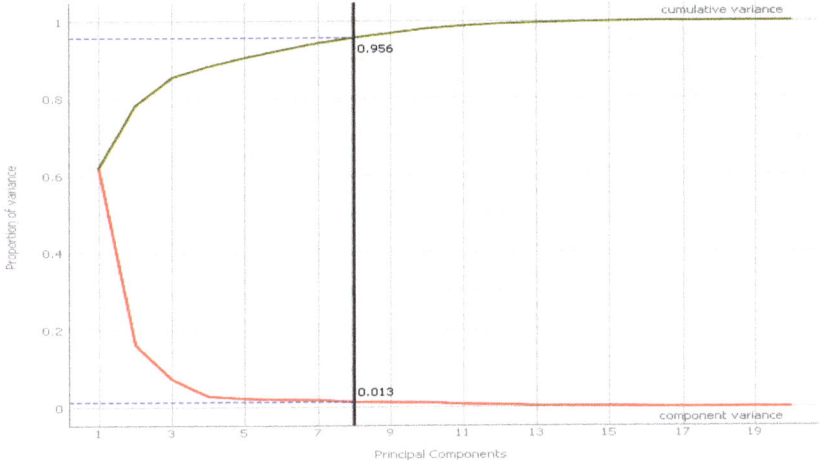

**Figure 5.** Principal component analysis (PCA) selection.

Table 10. PCA variances.

| Component | PC1 | PC2 | PC3 | PC4 | PC5 | PC6 | PC7 | PC8 |
|---|---|---|---|---|---|---|---|---|
| CGPA | 0.013 | −0.003 | **0.998** | −0.028 | 0.011 | 0.017 | −0.024 | −0.014 |
| Attempt Count | 0.002 | −0.004 | 0.007 | 0.031 | 0.005 | **0.145** | 0.067 | −0.082 |
| High Risk = 1 | −0.007 | 0.005 | −0.014 | −0.117 | 0.017 | −0.151 | 0.025 | 0.044 |
| High Risk = 2 | 0.007 | −0.005 | 0.014 | 0.117 | −0.017 | 0.151 | −0.025 | −0.044 |
| Term Exceeded = 1 | −0.006 | −0.002 | −0.015 | −0.005 | 0.005 | −0.012 | −0.019 | 0.050 |
| Term Exceeded = 2 | 0.006 | 0.002 | 0.015 | 0.005 | −0.005 | 0.012 | 0.019 | −0.050 |
| At Risk = 1 | −0.020 | 0.010 | 0.016 | −0.204 | 0.057 | −0.534 | **0.154** | **0.261** |
| At Risk = 2 | 0.020 | −0.010 | −0.016 | 0.204 | −0.057 | 0.534 | −0.154 | −0.261 |
| At Risk SSC = 1 | 0.000 | 0.004 | 0.004 | −0.027 | −0.003 | −0.049 | 0.016 | 0.002 |
| At Risk SSC = 2 | 0.000 | −0.004 | −0.004 | 0.027 | 0.003 | 0.049 | −0.016 | −0.002 |
| Other Module Count | −0.008 | 0.013 | −0.011 | 0.075 | 0.071 | −0.284 | −0.265 | 0.043 |
| Plagiarism | 0.016 | −0.005 | 0.003 | 0.027 | **0.242** | **0.287** | **0.172** | **0.346** |
| CW1 = 1 | −0.011 | −0.005 | −0.012 | −0.065 | 0.038 | −0.132 | −0.113 | −0.446 |
| CW1 = 2 | 0.011 | 0.005 | 0.012 | 0.065 | −0.038 | **0.132** | **0.113** | **0.446** |
| CW2 = 1 | −0.004 | −0.003 | −0.007 | −0.084 | 0.066 | −0.109 | −0.075 | −0.311 |
| CW2 = 2 | 0.004 | 0.003 | 0.007 | 0.084 | −0.066 | **0.109** | 0.075 | **0.311** |
| ESE = 1 | −0.004 | 0.059 | −0.025 | −0.638 | −0.002 | **0.232** | −0.130 | 0.052 |
| ESE = 2 | 0.004 | −0.059 | 0.025 | **0.638** | 0.002 | −0.232 | **0.130** | −0.052 |
| Played | **0.398** | **0.582** | −0.002 | 0.039 | −0.022 | −0.020 | 0.006 | −0.010 |
| Paused | **0.825** | −0.560 | −0.014 | −0.060 | 0.001 | −0.024 | −0.012 | 0.002 |
| Likes | 0.008 | 0.013 | −0.012 | **0.134** | **0.522** | −0.019 | −0.748 | **0.235** |
| Segment | **0.398** | **0.582** | −0.002 | 0.039 | −0.022 | −0.020 | 0.006 | −0.010 |
| Moodle Online In campus = 1 | −0.009 | 0.008 | 0.011 | −0.094 | 0.012 | −0.104 | −0.047 | −0.130 |
| Moodle Online In campus = 2 | 0.009 | −0.008 | −0.011 | 0.094 | −0.012 | **0.104** | 0.047 | **0.130** |
| Moodle Outside campus = 1 | −0.012 | −0.017 | 0.004 | 0.033 | −0.568 | −0.046 | −0.325 | **0.144** |
| Moodle Outside campus = 2 | 0.012 | 0.017 | −0.004 | −0.033 | **0.568** | 0.046 | **0.325** | −0.144 |

## 4.9. Multivariate Projection

Multivariate visualization is one of the tools used in datamining and provides the starting point in an explorative study. With an increasing number of features, it requires some automatic means of finding good projections that would optimize criteria of quality and expose any inherit structure in the data. FreeViz is used for multivariate projection, which optimizes the linear projection and displays the projected data in a scatterplot. The target projection is found through a gradient optimization approach [50]. Figure 6 depicts the multivariant projection on the dataset; based on the target variable, the projection is made, and two clusters are easily visible. First, the cluster "pass" identified students that passed the module, with relationships in CW1, CW2, ESE, played, paused, likes, segment and Moodle activity either on campus or outside, all of which play a significant role in their overall pass performance; the second cluster, "fail", identified students that failed the module, with relationships in at risk, SSC, high risk, term exceed, at risk, attempt count, CGPA and Moodle activity within the campus.

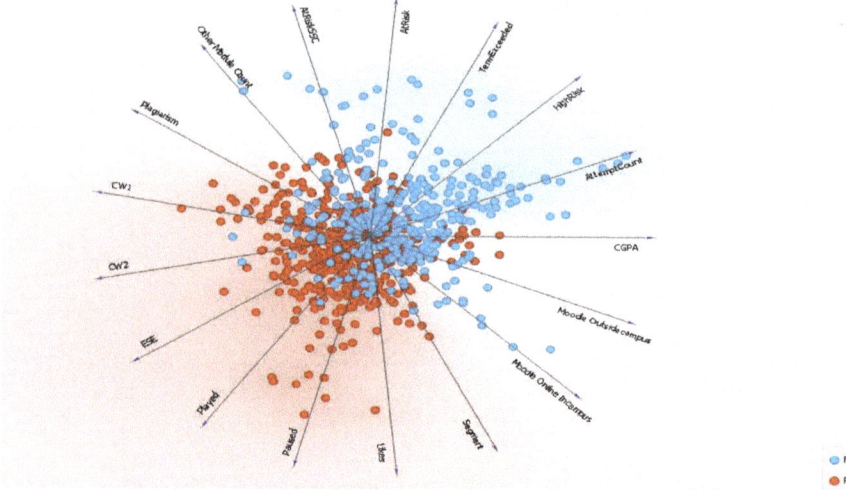

**Figure 6.** Multivariate projection.

## 4.10. CN2 Rule Viewer

CN2 Rule Inducer has a closer accuracy to Random Forest; Table 11 depicts the rules set by CN2 Rule Inducer. Out of 45 rules, only 23 rules were selected based on either Moodle activity or video interactions or both. The reason for selecting CN2 Rule Inducer was because it is easier to interpret for non-expert users of data mining. For this case, it would be easier for a faculty member to determine the probabilities of student interactions within the learning setting systems. The interpretation of the rules set by CN2 Rule inducer is that there is a high probability—92%—that a student will pass the module if the student is available on Moodle when active on campus and he/she played the video at least three times or more. A student is likely to pass the module with a probability of 75% if there is Moodle activity in and outside the campus. A student has a high chance of passing the end-of-semester examination if they engaged in the activities outside the campus on Moodle, played the video more than once and paused the video at least three times or more, with a probability of 94%. A student spending time on Moodle activities on campus has a fair chance of passing the module, with a probability of 83%. The student is likely to pass the module if they use Moodle outside the campus and like a video which they paused either twice or more. A video being paused more than or equal to 10 times and accessing Moodle outside the campus indicates a probability of 67% that the student will not be successful at the end semester examination. A student playing a video equal to or more than five times and exhibiting activity Moodle outside the campus has a probability of 90% of passing the module. If the student pauses a video more than or equal to four times and has low Moodle activity, they are likely to pass the module with a probability of 83%. If a student likes the video content equal to or more than twice with little Moodle activity outside the campus, they have a chance of 88% of passing the module. A student has a probability of 87% of passing the module if the student has Moodle activity outside the campus and played the video at least twice. Students' CW1 marks are important, as if the student failed the CW1 and played the video equal to or less than twice along with rewinding to capture the concepts, they have a chance of 75% of passing the module. A student playing the video content many times, such as more than or equal to five times, and pausing the video many times has a 91% chance of passing the module. A student who engages in rewinding and listening to the content many times has high chances, at 93%, of passing the module. For video content, a student who pauses the videos many times and moves slowly to gather the concepts has an 80% probability of passing the module, but if the frequency is more than or equal to 13 times, the student has an 83% chance of failing the end-of-semester examination. If a student failed in CW1 and exhibits low activity on Moodle on campus, there are high chances of failure in the module, at 90%. If a student plays the video content at least twice, with a low activity on Moodle outside the campus, and pauses the video much more than seven times, they have high chances of passing the module, at 90%. If a student passed in CW1, plays the video at least twice, exhibits a high activity on Moodle outside campus and likes the video more than once, they have high chances of passing the module at 80%. If a student pauses the video less than four times, exhibits a high activity on Moodle outside campus and plays the video more than twice, they have high chances of passing the module, at 90%. Playing video content more than or equal to five times gives a high probability of 83% that the student will fail in the module. Similarly, if the video is paused more than or equal to seven times, the probability goes to 62%. Playing a video up to four times results in a probability of 71% of a student passing the module. It is evident from the analysis and visualization projection (Figure 5) that videos being played, paused, segments and likes along with either in-campus or off-campus use can enhance learning as compared to the normal setting in which this opportunity was not available.

Table 11. Rules set by CN2.

| No. | IF Conditions | THEN Class | Probability |
| --- | --- | --- | --- |
| 1 | ESE≠Fail AND Activity on campus=LOW AND Played≥3 | Result = Passed | 92% |
| 2 | ESE≠Fail AND Activity on campus=LOW AND Activity out campus=LOW | Result = Passed | 75% |
| 3 | ESE≠Fail AND Activity out campus=LOW AND Paused≥3 AND Played≤2 | Result = Passed | 94% |
| 4 | ESE≠Fail AND Activity on campus=LOW | Result = Passed | 83% |
| 5 | ESE≠Fail AND Activity out campus=LOW AND Likes≥1 AND Paused≥2 | Result = Passed | 94% |
| 6 | ESE≠Fail AND Activity out campus=LOW AND Paused≥10 | Result = Failed | 67% |
| 7 | ESE≠Fail AND Played≥5 AND Activity out campus=LOW | Result = Passed | 90% |
| 8 | ESE≠Fail AND Activity out campus=LOW AND Paused≥4 | Result = Passed | 83% |
| 9 | ESE≠Fail AND Activity out campus=LOW AND Likes≥2 | Result = Passed | 88% |
| 10 | ESE≠Fail AND Activity out campus=LOW AND Played≥2 | Result = Passed | 87% |
| 11 | ESE≠Fail AND Played≤2 AND CW1≠Fail AND Segment≥1 | Result = Passed | 75% |
| 12 | ESE≠Fail AND Played≥5 AND Paused≤7 | Result = Passed | 91% |
| 13 | ESE≠Fail AND CW1=Fail AND Segment≥2 | Result = Passed | 83% |
| 14 | ESE≠Fail AND Paused≥10 | Result = Passed | 80% |
| 15 | Paused≥13 | Result = Failed | 83% |
| 16 | CW1 = Fail AND Activity on campus≠LOW | Result = Failed | 90% |
| 17 | Played≤2 AND Activity out campus≠LOW AND Paused≥7 | Result = Passed | 90% |
| 18 | Played≤2 AND CW1≠Fail AND Activity out campus≠LOW AND Paused≥6 | Result = Failed | 83% |
| 19 | CW1≠Fail AND Played≤2 AND Activity out campus≠LOW AND Likes≥1 | Result = Passed | 80% |
| 20 | Paused≤4 AND Activity out campus≠LOW AND Played≥2 | Result = Passed | 90% |
| 21 | Played≥5 | Result = Failed | 83% |
| 22 | Played≥3 | Result = Passed | 71% |
| 23 | Paused≥7 | Result = Failed | 62% |

## 5. Discussion

The study was conducted to create a model that can predict students' end-of-semester academic performance in the modules e-commerce (COMP 1008) and e-commerce technologies (COMP 0382). End-of-semester results from these two modules were taken into consideration as the performance indicators and were considered as target features. The data of students from these modules was collected using three different systems such as SIS (student academics), LMS (online activities) and eDify (video interactions). Firstly, the performance of the most widely used classification algorithms was compared using the complete dataset. Secondly, data transformation and feature selection techniques were applied to the dataset to determine the impact on the performance on the classification algorithms. Lastly, we reduced the features and determined the appropriate features that can be used in order to predict the students' end-of-semester performance. Four performance metrics—accuracy, sensitivity, specificity and F-Measure—were evaluated in order to compare the performance of the classification models.

The effect of data transformation on classification performance was tested by converting the features into a categorical form using the techniques of equal width and equal frequency. Results indicated that models with categorical data performed better than those with continuous data. Observation showed that equal width data transformation performance results were better compared with equal frequency data transformation.

The impact of feature election on classification performance was tested. For this purpose, a ranking and scoring technique was used with three feature selection methods: information gain, information gain ratio and Gini decrease. Nine features were determined from ranking and scoring techniques—CW1, ESE, CW2, likes, paused, played, segment, Moodle on campus and Moodle off campus—and were tested regarding the performance of the classification models.

Moreover, feature selection using the genetic algorithm was used to further reduce the features. The features were reduced from nine to six: applicant, at risk, CW1, CW2, ESE and played. Here, a meta attribute was selected and the Moodle activity feature was not selected. The performance of the classification model accuracy was less than the data transformation method and the information gain ratio selection technique. Then, a PCA analysis was performed to reduce the features with a variance of 95.6%; PCA derived eight component solutions. The feature selection method enables the prediction model to be interpreted more easily. However, PCA resulted in one fewer component, and it is difficult to interpret for a normal faculty member from a different specialization field.

Furthermore, multivariate projection using a gradient optimization approach and CN2 Rule viewer was used to interpret the relationship within the dataset and the features. Relationship, features that were extracted with help of data transformation method and information gain ratio selection technique showed a resemblance which enhances the understanding for the novice users..

From the results of this study, we can conclude that Random Forest provides a high classification accuracy rate in conditions where equal width data transformation method and information gain ratio selection techniques were used (Table 7). The Random Forest outperformed the other selected algorithms in predicting successful students. The confusion matrix for 10-fold cross-validation derived via Random Forest is provided in Table 12. The classification model correctly predicted 629 students out of 645 students, with an accuracy of 88.3%.

Table 12. Sample confusion matrix.

| | | Predictions | | |
| --- | --- | --- | --- | --- |
| | | Failed | Passed | Σ |
| Actual | Failed | 53 | 74 | 127 |
| | Passed | 16 | 629 | 645 |
| | Σ | 69 | 703 | 772 |

## 6. Conclusions and Future Works

In this study, a supervised data classification model is proposed with the aim of predicting student academic performance at the end of the semester. Two modules were selected for the study based on the similarity of the course content. The dataset consisted of student academic data gathered from SIS (student academics) and performance in the modules using two different learning environments; i.e., Moodle (LMS) and eDify (mobile application). Activities performed by students in Moodle on campus and outside campus were used. Video interactions (clickstreams) of students in eDify were used for prediction. In total, 18 features and one meta attribute were used to form the dataset, 12 features were extracted from SIS, 2 from Moodle, four from eDify and one result was used as the target feature for prediction. The dataset consisted of 772 samples from one academic year. The complete dataset was tested with eight classification algorithms derived from the literature review and related works.

The Tree-based classification model—specifically, Random Forest—outperformed the other techniques with an accuracy of 88.3%. This accuracy was achieved using the equal width data transformation method and information gain ratio selection technique. To identify which features have greater importance in the prediction of student performance, features were reduced using the genetic algorithm and PCA. The result was inconclusive as the reduced features have low significance in predicting student performance. Multivariate analysis was conducted to inspect the correlations, and nine variables were selected using scoring and ranking techniques to successfully predict the students' academic performance. Thus, the results obtained with reduced features were better than those using all the features. The CN2 Rule Inducer algorithm was the second-best performing algorithm, showing 87.4% accuracy. The reason for using CN2 Rule Viewer is that it provides rules induction with probability, which is easier to interpret for non-expert users such as faculty who can therefore easily relate to the situation, as shown in Table 12.

For future work, a dashboard with data representations from these virtual learning environments would help in projecting the students' performance and interactions. Predicting the students' performance and outcomes on a weekly basis could help faculty to identify poor-performing students. This can act as an early alert system for faculty to intervene with any problems faced by the students within the module. Students could also self-assess their own performance within the module with the help of a dashboard.

**Author Contributions:** R.H. contributed to the investigation and project administration. S.P. contributed to the supervision- S.M. contributed to the visualization. M.U.S. contributed to the resources and writing—review and editing. A.A. and K.U.S. contributed to the collected data and conducted the pre-processing of the input data. All authors have read and agreed to the published version of the manuscript.

**Funding:** This research received no external funding.

**Acknowledgments:** The authors would like to thank Middle East College, Oman for the experimental data. The authors are thankful to the Head of Computing Department, Mounir Dhibi (MEC), for his support and encouragement to carry out this study.

**Conflicts of Interest:** The authors declare no conflict of interest.

## References

1. Castro, R. Blended learning in higher education: Trends and capabilities. *Educ. Inf. Technol.* **2019**, *24*, 2523–2546. [CrossRef]
2. Ali, M.F.; Joyes, G.; Ellison, L. Using blended learning to enhance students' cognitive presence. In Proceedings of the 2013 International Conference on Informatics and Creative Multimedia, ICICM 2013, Kuala Lumpur, 4–6 September 2013.
3. Cleveland-Innes, M.; Wilton, D. *Guide to Blended Learning*; Commonwealth of Learning: Burnbay, BC, Canada, 2018, ISBN 9781894975940.
4. Medina, L.C. Blended learning: Deficits and prospects in higher education. *Australas. J. Educ. Technol.* **2018**, *34*. [CrossRef]

5. Schmidt, S.M.P.; Ralph, D.L. The flipped classroom: A twist on teaching. *Contemp. Issues Educ. Res.* **2016**, *9*. [CrossRef]
6. Graham, C.R.; Woodfield, W.; Harrison, J.B. A framework for institutional adoption and implementation of blended learning in higher education. *Internet High. Educ.* **2013**, *18*, 4–14. [CrossRef]
7. Hasan, R.; Palaniappan, S.; Mahmood, S.; Shah, B.; Abbas, A.; Sarker, K.U. Enhancing the teaching and learning process using video streaming servers and forecasting techniques. *Sustainability* **2019**, *11*, 2049. [CrossRef]
8. Romero, C.; Ventura, S. Educational data mining and learning analytics: An updated survey. *Wiley Interdiscip. Rev. Data Min. Knowl. Discov.* **2020**, *10*, e1355. [CrossRef]
9. Naidu, V.R.; Singh, B.; Hasan, R.; Al Hadrami, G. Learning analytics for smart classrooms in higher education. *IJAEDU- Int. E-J. Adv. Educ.* **2017**, 440–446. [CrossRef]
10. Lester, J.; Klein, C.; Rangwala, H.; Johri, A. Learning analytics in higher education. *ASHE High. Educ. Rep.* **2017**, *43*, 9–135. [CrossRef]
11. Atif, A.; Richards, D.; Bilgin, A.; Marrone, M. Learning analytics in higher education: A summary of tools and approaches. In Proceedings of the 30th Annual conference on Australian Society for Computers in Learning in Tertiary Education, ASCILITE 2013, Sydney, Australia, 1–4 December 2013.
12. Yang, T.Y.; Brinton, C.G.; Joe-Wong, C.; Chiang, M. Behavior-based grade prediction for MOOCs via time series neural networks. *IEEE J. Sel. Top. Signal Process.* **2017**, *11*, 716–728. [CrossRef]
13. Lau, K.H.V.; Farooque, P.; Leydon, G.; Schwartz, M.L.; Sadler, R.M.; Moeller, J.J. Using learning analytics to evaluate a video-based lecture series. *Med. Teach.* **2018**, *40*, 91–98. [CrossRef]
14. Hasan, R.; Palaniappan, S.; Mahmood, S.; Naidu, V.R.; Agarwal, A.; Singh, B.; Sarker, K.U.; Abbas, A.; Sattar, M.U. A review: Emerging trends of big data in higher educational institutions. In *Micro-Electronics and Telecommunication Engineering*; Lecture Notes in Networks and Systems; Springer: Singapore, 2020; Volume 106, pp. 289–297. [CrossRef]
15. Chaudhury, P.; Tripaty, H.K. An empirical study on attribute selection of student performance prediction model. *Int. J. Learn. Technol.* **2017**, *12*, 241–252. [CrossRef]
16. Romero, C.; Ventura, S. Data mining in education. *Wiley Interdiscip. Rev. Data Min. Knowl. Discov.* **2013**, *3*, 12–27. [CrossRef]
17. Romero, C.; López, M.I.; Luna, J.M.; Ventura, S. Predicting students' final performance from participation in on-line discussion forums. *Comput. Educ.* **2013**, *68*, 458–472. [CrossRef]
18. Hasan, R.; Palaniappan, S.; Raziff, A.R.A.; Mahmood, S.; Sarker, K.U. Student academic performance prediction by using decision tree algorithm. In Proceedings of the 2018 4th International Conference on Computer and Information Sciences: Revolutionising Digital Landscape for Sustainable Smart Society, ICCOINS 2018—Proceedings, IEEE, Kuala Lumpur, Malaysia, 13–14 August 2018; pp. 1–5.
19. Shana, J.; Venkatachalam, T. Identifying key performance indicators and predicting the result from student data. *Int. J. Comput. Appl.* **2011**, *25*. [CrossRef]
20. Kash, B.R.P.; Thappa, D.M.H.; Kavitha, V. Big data in educational data mining and learning analytics. *Int. J. Innov. Res. Comput. Commun. Eng.* **2015**, *2*, 7515–7520. [CrossRef]
21. Siemens, G.; Gasevic, D. Guest editorial - learning and knowledge analytics. *Educ. Technol. Soc.* **2012**, *15*, 1–2.
22. Akçapınar, G.; Altun, A.; Aşkar, P. Using learning analytics to develop early-warning system for at-risk students. *Int. J. Educ. Technol. High. Educ.* **2019**, *16*, 1–20. [CrossRef]
23. Arnold, K.E.; Pistilli, M.D. Course signals at Purdue: Using learning analytics to increase student success. In Proceedings of the ACM International Conference Proceeding Series, Vancouver, BC, Canada, 29 April –2 May 012.
24. Corrigan, O.; Smeaton, A.F.; Glynn, M.; Smyth, S. Using educational analytics to improve test performance. In Proceedings of the Lecture Notes in Computer Science (Including Subseries Lecture Notes in Artificial Intelligence and Lecture Notes in Bioinformatics), Toledo, Spain, 15–18 September 2015.
25. Saqr, M.; Fors, U.; Tedre, M. How learning analytics can early predict under-achieving students in a blended medical education course. *Med. Teach.* **2017**, *15*, 1–11. [CrossRef]
26. Chatti, M.A.; Schroeder, U.; Jarke, M. LaaN: Convergence of knowledge management and technology-enhanced learning. *IEEE Trans. Learn. Technol.* **2012**, *5*, 177–189. [CrossRef]

27. Hadhrami, G.A. Al learning analytics dashboard to improve students' performance and success. *IOSR J. Res. Method Educ.* **2017**, *7*, 39–45. [CrossRef]
28. Giannakos, M.N.; Chorianopoulos, K.; Chrisochoides, N. Making sense of video analytics: Lessons learned from clickstream interactions, attitudes, and learning outcome in a video-assisted course. *Int. Rev. Res. Open Distance Learn.* **2015**, *16*. [CrossRef]
29. Hasnine, M.N.; Akcapinar, G.; Flanagan, B.; Majumdar, R.; Mouri, K.; Ogata, H. Towards final scores prediction over clickstream using machine learning methods. In Proceedings of the ICCE 2018—26th International Conference on Computers in Education, Workshop Proceedings, Manila, Philippines, 26–30 November 2018.
30. Hasan, R.; Palaniappan, S.; Mahmood, S.; Abbas, A.; Sarker, K.U. Modelling and predicting student's academic performance using classification data mining techniques. *Int. J. Bus. Inf. Syst.* **2020**, *1*, 1. [CrossRef]
31. Romero, C.; Ventura, S. Educational data mining: A survey from 1995 to 2005. *Expert Syst. Appl.* **2007**, *33*, 135–146. [CrossRef]
32. Romero, C.; Ventura, S.; De Bra, P. Knowledge discovery with genetic programming for providing feedback to courseware authors. *User Model. User-Adapt. Interact.* **2004**, *14*, 425–464. [CrossRef]
33. Yaacob, W.F.W.; Nasir, S.A.M.; Yaacob, W.F.W.; Sobri, N.M. Supervised data mining approach for predicting student performance. *Indones. J. Electr. Eng. Comput. Sci.* **2019**, *16*, 1584–1592. [CrossRef]
34. Shetty, I.D.; Shetty, D.; Roundhal, S. Student performance prediction. *Int. J. Comput. Appl. Technol. Res.* **2019**, *8*, 157–160. [CrossRef]
35. Abu Zohair, L.M. Prediction of Student's performance by modelling small dataset size. *Int. J. Educ. Technol. High. Educ.* **2019**, *16*. [CrossRef]
36. Daud, A.; Aljohani, N.R.; Abbasi, R.A.; Lytras, M.D.; Abbas, F.; Alowibdi, J.S. Predicting student performance using advanced learning analytics. In Proceedings of the 26th International Conference on World Wide Web Companion—WWW '17 Companion, Perth, Australia, 7 April 2017; ACM Press: New York, NY, USA, 2017; pp. 415–421.
37. Tomasevic, N.; Gvozdenovic, N.; Vranes, S. An overview and comparison of supervised data mining techniques for student exam performance prediction. *Comput. Educ.* **2020**, *143*, 103676. [CrossRef]
38. Saa, A.A.; Al-Emran, M.; Shaalan, K. Mining student information system records to predict students' academic performance. In *Advances in Intelligent Systems and Computing*; Springer: Berlin, Germany, 2020; pp. 229–239. ISBN 9783030141172.
39. López, M.I.; Luna, J.M.; Romero, C.; Ventura, S. Classification via clustering for predicting final marks based on student participation in forums. In Proceedings of the 5th International Conference on Educational Data Mining, EDM 2012, Chania, Greece, 19–21 June 2012.
40. Yassein, N.A.; M Helali, R.G.; Mohomad, S.B. Predicting student academic performance in KSA using data mining techniques. *J. Inf. Technol. Softw. Eng.* **2017**, *7*, 1–15. [CrossRef]
41. Govindasamy, K.; Velmurugan, T. Analysis of student academic performance using clustering techniques. *Int. J. Pure Appl. Math.* **2018**, *119*, 309–322.
42. Veeramuthu, P.; Periyasamy, R.; Sugasini, V.; Patti, P. Analysis of student result using clustering techniques. *Int. J. Comput. Sci. Inf. Technol.* **2014**, *5*, 5092–5094.
43. Saneifar, R.; Saniee Abadeh, M. Association Rule Discovery for Student Performance Prediction Using Metaheuristic Algorithms. *Comput. Sci. Inf. Technol. (CS & IT)* **2015**, *5*, 115–123.
44. Chandrakar, O.; Saini, J.R. Predicting examination results using association rule mining. *Int. J. Comput. Appl.* **2015**, *116*, 7–10. [CrossRef]
45. Ferguson, R.; Macfadyen, L.P.; Clow, D.; Tynan, B.; Alexander, S.; Dawson, S. Setting learning analytics in context: Overcoming the barriers to large-scale adoption. *J. Learn. Anal.* **2014**, *1*, 120–144. [CrossRef]
46. Márquez-Vera, C.; Cano, A.; Romero, C.; Ventura, S. Predicting student failure at school using genetic programming and different data mining approaches with high dimensional and imbalanced data. *Appl. Intell.* **2013**, *38*, 315–330. [CrossRef]
47. Márquez-Vera, C.; Cano, A.; Romero, C.; Noaman, A.Y.M.; Mousa Fardoun, H.; Ventura, S. Early dropout prediction using data mining: A case study with high school students. *Expert Syst.* **2016**, *33*, 107–124. [CrossRef]
48. Cano, A.; Leonard, J.D. Interpretable multiview early warning system adapted to underrepresented student populations. *IEEE Trans. Learn. Technol.* **2019**, *12*, 198–211. [CrossRef]

49. Demšar, J.; Curk, T.; Erjavec, A.; Gorup, Č.; Hočevar, T.; Milutinovič, M.; Možina, M.; Polajnar, M.; Toplak, M.; Starič, A.; et al. Orange: Data mining toolbox in python. *J. Mach. Learn. Res.* **2013**, *14*, 2349–2353.
50. Demšar, J.; Leban, G.; Zupan, B. FreeViz-An intelligent multivariate visualization approach to explorative analysis of biomedical data. *J. Biomed. Inform.* **2007**, *40*, 661–671. [CrossRef]

© 2020 by the authors. Licensee MDPI, Basel, Switzerland. This article is an open access article distributed under the terms and conditions of the Creative Commons Attribution (CC BY) license (http://creativecommons.org/licenses/by/4.0/).

*Article*

# Towards Portability of Models for Predicting Students' Final Performance in University Courses Starting from Moodle Logs

**Javier López-Zambrano [1,2], Juan A. Lara [3] and Cristóbal Romero [2,*]**

1. Escuela Superior Politécnica Agropecuaria de Manabí (ESPAM MFL), Faculty of Computing, SISCOM Group, 131205 Calceta, Ecuador; jlopez.ec@outlook.com or jlopez@espam.edu.ec
2. Department of Computer Science and Numerical Analysis, University of Córdoba (UCO), 14014 Córdoba, Andalucía, Spain
3. Department of Computer Science, Madrid Open University (UDIMA), 28400 Madrid, Spain; juanalfonso.lara@udima.es
* Correspondence: cromero@uco.es

Received: 27 November 2019; Accepted: 31 December 2019; Published: 3 January 2020

**Abstract:** Predicting students' academic performance is one of the older challenges faced by the educational scientific community. However, most of the research carried out in this area has focused on obtaining the best accuracy models for their specific single courses and only a few works have tried to discover under which circumstances a prediction model built on a source course can be used in other different but similar courses. Our motivation in this work is to study the portability of models obtained directly from Moodle logs of 24 university courses. The proposed method intends to check if grouping similar courses by the degree or the similar level of usage of activities provided by the Moodle logs, and if the use of numerical or categorical attributes affect in the portability of the prediction models. We have carried out two experiments by executing the well-known classification algorithm over all the datasets of the courses in order to obtain decision tree models and to test their portability to the other courses by comparing the obtained accuracy and loss of accuracy evaluation measures. The results obtained show that it is only feasible to directly transfer predictive models or apply them to different courses with an acceptable accuracy and without losing portability under some circumstances.

**Keywords:** Educational Data Mining; predicting student performance; student model portability

## 1. Introduction

The use of web-based education systems or e-learning systems has grown exponentially in the last years, spurred by the fact that neither students nor teachers are bound to any specific location and that this form of computer-based education is virtually independent of a specific hardware platform. Adopting these e-learning systems in higher educational institution can provide us with enormous quantities of data that describe the behavior of students. In particular, Learning Management Systems (LMSs) are becoming much more common in universities, community colleges, schools, and businesses, and are even used by individual instructors in order to add web technology to their courses and supplement traditional face-to-face courses. One of the most popular LMS is Moodle [1], a free and open-source learning management system that allows the creation of completely virtual courses (electronic learning, e-learning) or courses that are partially virtual (blended learning, b-learning). Moodle accumulate a vast amount of information, which is very valuable for analyzing students' behavior and could create a gold mine of educational data. Moodle keeps detailed logs of all events that students perform and keeps track of what materials students have accessed. However, due to the huge quantities of log data that Moodle can generate daily, it is very difficult to analyze them, thus, it is necessary to use Educational Data Mining (EDM) and Learning Analytics (LA) tools [2]. EDM and LA techniques discover useful, new, valid, and comprehensible knowledge from educational data in order to resolve educational problems [3]. There is a wide range of EDM/LA tasks or applications, but one of the oldest and most important ones is to predict student performance [4]. The objective of prediction is to estimate the unknown value of a variable that describes the student. In education the values normally predicted are performance, knowledge, score, or mark [5]. This value can be numerical/continuous value (regression task) or categorical/discrete value (classification task). In fact, nowadays, there is a great interest in analyzing and mining students' usage/interaction information gathered by Moodle for predicting students' final mark in blended learning [6,7]. Blended learning combines the e-learning and the classical face-to-face learning environments. It has been termed as blended learning, hybrid, or mixed learning [8]. Since either pure e-learning or traditional learning hold some weaknesses and strengths, it is better to mix the strengths of both learning environments into a new method of instruction delivery called blended learning.

Most of the research about predicting students' performance has focused on scenarios that assume that the training and test data are drawn from the same course [9]. As a matter of fact, the obtained/discovered models are mostly built on the samples that researchers have ready at hand, whether it is the current population of students at a university developing a model, the current user base of the adaptive learning system for which the model is being built, or just students who are relatively easy to survey or observe [10]. However, in real educational environments, we historical data are not always available from all the courses. Let us imagine, for example, the case of a new course that is taught for the first time in an institution. Here, we would not have data for training model for predicting student performance. Yet, it is fair that the tutors and students of this new subject have the chance to work with predictive models that notify them of possible unwanted at risk situations such as student drop out. Thus, model portability can be very useful to create and use transferable models of other similar course in which we have a prediction model.

The idea of Portability is that knowledge extracted from a specific environment can be applied directly to another different environment. Within the educational sphere, this idea has great applicability, as it permits to use a model discovered on a previous course (source) to an ongoing course (target) that does not have a model for any reason whatsoever, and to apply these models with certain guarantees to this new course [11]. Most of the previous works related with model portability use a Transfer Learning (TL) approach in which there is a tune-up process, usually based on deep learning approaches, so that the updated model is transferred from one course to another, as shown in [12,13]. Other different works use a Generalization approach that tries to discover one single general model that fit to all the exited courses [14,15]. This is the reason why, in this paper, we have used the term "portability" instead of the related terms "transferability" and "generalization", since we think that it better describes the direct application of a model obtained with one dataset to a different dataset. In this regard, the goal of this research is to study the portability of predictive models between courses taught via blended-learning (b-learning) in formal university education. These predictive models try to predict whether a student will succeed or not in a certain course (pass or fail) starting to the log data generated from the student interactions with Moodle LMS. Specifically, the problem we want to resolve is: if we have available data for different university courses, could we use or apply the performance prediction model obtained in one specific course in other different course (in which we do not have enough data or we do not have a prediction model) without losing much accuracy. However, due to that the number of courses in a University can be large, and thus, the number of combinations will be huge, and it seems logical to think that good model portability only occurs between similar courses. This is why, in this paper, we propose to group courses in two different ways; our main objective in this paper is to answer the following two research questions:

Can the models obtained in one (source) course be used in other different similar (target) courses of the same degree, while maintaining an acceptable predictive quality?

Can the models obtained in one (source) course be used in other different (target) courses that make a similar level of usage of Moodle activities/resources?

The rest of the document is arranged in the following order: Section 2 reviews the literature related to this research. Section 3 describes the data and experiments. The results are shown in Section 4. Section 5 discusses the results obtained. Finally, Section 6 presents the conclusions and suggests future lines of research.

## 2. Background

Within the EDM and LA scientific community, several works have been published that discuss the difficulty of achieving generalizable and portable models. In [14], the authors suggested that it is imperative for learning analytics research to account for the diverse ways technology is adopted and applied in a course-specific context. The differences in technology use, especially those related to whether and how learners use the learning management system, require consideration before the log-data can be merged to create a generalized model for predicting academic success. In [16], the authors stated that the portability of the prediction models across courses is low. In addition, they show that for the purpose of early intervention or when in-between assessment grades are taken into account, LMS data are of little (additional) value.

Nevertheless, Baker [10] considered that one of the challenges for the future of EDM is what he called the "Generalizability" problem or "The New York City and Marfa" problem. In his words, Learning Analytics models are mostly built on the samples that we have ready at hand, whether it is the current population of students at a university developing a model, the current user base of the adaptive learning system we are building the model for, or just students who are relatively easy to survey or observe. However, what happens when the population changes? He defined this problem in three steps: (1) Build an automated detector for a commonly-seen outcome or measure; (2) Collect a new population distinct from the original population; and (3) Demonstrate that the detector works for the new population with degradation of quality under 0.1 in terms of AUC ROC (Area Under the ROC -Receiver Operating Characteristic- Curve) and remaining better than chance (AUC ROC > 0.5).

In this regard, there are works that have demonstrated the possibility of replicating EDM models. In [17], they presented an open-source software toolkit, the MOOC (Massive Open Online Course) Replication Framework (MORF), and show that it is useful for replication of machine learned models in the domain of the learning sciences, in spite of experimental, methodological, and data barriers. This work demonstrates an approach to end-to-end machine learning replication, which is relevant to any domain with large, complex, or multi-format, privacy-protected data with a consistent schema.

What Baker [10] defined as "Generalizability" is, in reality, closely related to the concept of Transfer Learning (TL). Boyer and Veeramachaneni [11] defined TL as the attempt to transfer information (training data samples or models) from a previous course to establish a predictive model for an ongoing course. According to Hunt et al. [18], TL enables us to transfer the knowledge from a related (source) task that has already been learned, to a new (target) task. This idea breaks with the traditional view of attempting to learn a predictive model from the data from the on-going course itself, known as in-situ learning.

As listed in [11], there are various types of TL, among which are: (a) Naive Transfer Learning, when using samples from a previous course to help predict students' performance in a new course; (b) Inductive Transfer Learning, when certain class labels are available as attributes for the target course; and (c) Transductive Transfer Learning, where no labels are available for the target course data.

Transfer learning has been applied in the field of EDM and LA in different applications. In [18], they proposed an approach for predicting graduation rates in degree programs by leveraging data across multiple degree programs. There are also TL-based works for dropout prediction. In [12], they developed a framework to define classification problems across courses, provide proof that ensemble methods allow for the development of high-performing predictive models, and show that these techniques can be used across platforms, as well as across courses. Nevertheless, this study neither mentions each course topic nor does it analyze the transferability of the models. However, in [13] they proposed two alternative transfer methods based on representation learning with auto-encoders: a passive approach using transductive principal component analysis and an active approach that uses a correlation alignment loss term. With these methods, they investigate the transferability of dropout prediction across similar and dissimilar MOOCs and compare with known methods. Results show improved model transferability and suggest that the methods are capable of automatically learning a feature representation that expresses common predictive characteristics of MOOCs. A detailed description of the most relevant works in TL can be found in the survey presented in [9], and more recently, in the survey described in [19].

Domain Adaptation (DA) has gained ground in TL, being a particular case of TL that leverages labeled data in one or more related source domains, to learn a classifier for unseen or unlabeled data in a target domain [20]. In this regard, [21] propose an algorithm, called DiAd, which adapts a classifier trained on a course with labelled data by selectively choosing instances from a new course (with no label data) that are most dissimilar to the course with labelled data and on which the classifier is very confident of classification. A complete review of DA techniques can be found in [20] and [22].

Contextualizing our work in relation to the rest of the related research, we may affirm that our research is innovative and very interesting because it deals with one of the six challenges on EDM/LA community recently presented by Baker [10] named the "The New York City and Marfa Problem". Our work focuses on traditional university courses that use blended learning, while most of the previous works focus on MOOCs [11–13,21]. Although our research is very related to TL, as it fits the definitions of [11,18], it is not our goal to propose or study a specific tune-technique, similar to the latest research on DA [21], but only to study the direct portability of prediction models. To do so, we will follow the idea demonstrated in [13], but instead of carrying out tests with two subjects to prove the reliability of the method, our goal is to carry out a complete study with a greater number of courses in order to study the degree of model portability between subjects. Given that our study does not focus on any concrete technique, rather it studies the degree of portability of models; we use a direct transfer, also called Naive in [11]. This type of transfer has innumerable benefits such as simplicity and immediacy, which can aid other researchers in easily replicating our study with their own data. Additionally, studies such as [13] have demonstrated that this type of direct approach obtains better results than other approaches such as instance-based learning and even in-situ learning approaches. Taking all of this into account, and based on the extent of the authors' knowledge, this is the first study that measures the degree of model portability in blended learning university courses (not MOOCs), focusing on how portability of model is affected when using course of the same degrees and courses with similar level of usage of Moodle.

## 3. Materials and Methods

In this section, we describe the data used and the experiments we have conducted in order to answer the initial research questions.

*3.1. Data Description and Preprocessing*

We have downloaded the Moodle log files generated by 3235 students in 24 courses in different bachelor's degrees of University of Cordoba (UCO) in Spain as shown in Table 1. These courses can be from year 1 to year 4 of the bachelor's degree (most of them from year 1) and they have different numbers of students (#Stds in Table 1) ranging from 50 (minimum) to 302 (maximum). We have categorized each course depending on how many different Moodle's activities are used in each course, having three different usage levels (Low, Medium, and High), denoted LMS Level in Table 1, having found a medium level in most courses. We have defined three levels of usage according to the number of activities used in the course:

- Low level: The course only uses one type of activity or even none of them.
- Medium level: The course uses two different types of activities.

- High level: The course uses three or more different types of activities.

Table 1. Information about the courses.

| Course Name | Code | Degree | Year | #Stds | LMS Level |
|---|---|---|---|---|---|
| Introduction to programming | IP | Computer | 1 | 289 | High |
| Programming methodology | PM | Computer | 1 | 233 | High |
| Professional computer tools | PCT | Computer | 1 | 124 | Medium |
| DataBases | DB | Computer | 2 | 58 | Medium |
| Human Computer Interfaces | HCI | Computer | 2 | 260 | High |
| Information Systems | InS | Computer | 2 | 188 | Medium |
| Software Engineering | SE | Computer | 2 | 58 | Medium |
| Interactive Systems | IS | Computer | 3 | 84 | High |
| Requirement engineering | RE | Computer | 3 | 86 | Medium |
| Software Design and Construction | SDC | Computer | 3 | 50 | Medium |
| Primary Education in the School System | PESS | Education | 1 | 205 | Medium |
| Knowledge of the Social and Cultural Environment | KSCE | Education | 1 | 302 | Low |
| Primary Education Planning and Innovation | PEPI | Education | 2 | 117 | Medium |
| Psychoeducational Care for the Cultural Diversity of Early Childhood Education | PECE | Education | 4 | 55 | Medium |
| Hermeneutics of the Work of Art | HWA | Education | 4 | 83 | Low |
| Spanish Social and Cultural Media | SSCM | Education | 4 | 58 | Medium |
| Introduction to Psychology | IPs | Education | 4 | 91 | High |
| Introduction to Computer Science | ICS1 | Electrical Engineering | 1 | 100 | Low |
| Introduction to Computer Science | ICS2 | Electronic Engineering | 1 | 198 | High |
| Introduction to Computer Science | ICS3 | Civil Engineering | 1 | 85 | Low |
| Introduction to Computer Science | ICS4 | Mining Engineering | 1 | 77 | Low |
| Mathematics Analysis I | MA1 | Physics | 1 | 155 | Low |
| Mathematical Analysis II | MA2 | Physics | 1 | 160 | Low |
| Mathematical Methods | MM | Physics | 1 | 119 | Low |

Finally, it is important to notice that the class (final marks) of the students in these courses is not unbalanced, that is, there are not many differences between the number of students who pass the course and the number of students who fail the course. In addition, although all courses have a little imbalance (between 50%–70% for each class), this is not a problem for most machine learning algorithms since standard performance evaluation measures remain effective in those scenarios with such a little imbalance rate [23].

In order to preprocess the Moodle's log files and to add the course final marks, we have developed a specific Java GUI (Graphical User Interface) tool for preprocessing this type of files [24]. This is a visual and easy-to-use tool for preparing both the raw Excel students' data files directly downloaded from Moodle's courses interface and the Excel students mark files provided by instructors.

Firstly, it shows the content of the Excel files and allows selecting the specific columns where the required information is located: Name of the students, Date and Events (Moodle events) in the Log file and Name of student and Marks (final mark in the course that has a value between 0 and 10) in the Grades file. It joins the information about each student (events and mark) and it anonymizes the data by deleting the name of the students. Next, it allows the user to select what events (all of them or just a few) should be used as attributes in the final dataset. In our case, we have only selected 50 attributes (see Table 2) from all the events that appear in our logs files (we have removed all the instructor's and administrator's events). As can be seen from Table 2, we have considered attributes related to the interactions of students with assignments, choices, forums, pages, quizzes, wikis, and others.

Then, the specific starting and ending date of the course can be established in order to count only the number of events that occurred between these dates for each student. Next, it is possible to transform these values defined in a continuous domain/range into discrete or categorical values. This tool provides the option of performing a manual discretization (by specifying the cut points) as well as traditional techniques such as equal-width or equal-frequency. In our case, we are going to generate two different datasets for each course: one continuous dataset (with numerical values in all the attributes less the class attribute) and another discretized datasets (with categorical values in all the attributes). We have discretized all the Moodle's attributes using the equal-width method (it divides the data into $k$ intervals of equal size) with the two labels HIGH and LOW. Moreover, we have manually discretized the students' final grade attribute, that is, the class to predict in our classification problem, to two values or labels: FAIL (if the mark is lower than 5) and PASS (if the mark is greater or equal than 5). Finally, this tool allows us to generate a preprocessed data file in. ARFF (Attribute-Relation File Format) format for doing data mining. It is important to notice that all the data used has been treated according to academic ethics. In fact, firstly we requested the instructors of each course to download the log files of their courses from Moodle together with an excel file with the final marks of the students. Then, we signed a declaration for each course stating that we would use the data only for researching purposes and would anonymize them after integrating the students' events with their corresponding final marks as a previous step to the application of data mining algorithms.

Table 2. List of Moodle logs attributes/events used.

| Assignments | | Folders | | Quizzes | |
|---|---|---|---|---|---|
| 1. | assign submit | 17. | folder view | 34. | quiz attempt |
| 2. | assign submit for grading | 18. | folder view all | 35. | quiz close attempt |
| 3. | assign view | **Forums** | | 36. | quiz continue attempt |
| 4. | assign view all | | | 37. | quiz review |
| 5. | assignment upload | 19. | forum add discussion | 38. | quiz view |
| 6. | assignment view | 20. | forum add post | 39. | quiz view all |
| 7. | assignment view all | 21. | forum mark read | 40. | quiz view summary |
| **Choices** | | 22. | forum search | **Resources** | |
| | | 23. | forum subscribe | | |
| 8. | choice choose | 24. | forum subscribe all | 41. | resource view |
| 9. | choice choose again | 25. | forum unsubscribe | 42. | resource view all |
| 10. | choice report | 26. | forum view discussion | **Urls** | |
| 11. | choice view | 27. | forum view forum | | |
| 12. | choice view all | 28. | forum view forums | 43. | url view |
| **Courses** | | **Pages** | | 44. | url view all |
| | | | | **Wikis** | |
| 13. | course enroll | 29. | page view | | |
| 14. | course user report | 30. | page view all | 45. | wiki edit |
| 15. | course view | **Questionnaires** | | 46. | wiki info |
| 16. | course view section | | | 47. | wiki links |
| | | 31. | questionnaire submit | 48. | wiki update |
| | | 32. | questionnaire view | 49. | wiki view |
| | | 33. | questionnaire view all | 50. | wiki view all |

*3.2. Experimentation*

For each of the mentioned 24 UCO courses, we have considered two datasets: one of them in which we have used continuous values of attributes (called Numerical Dataset); and the other one in which we have used discretized values of those attributes (called Discretized Dataset). This means we had 48 datasets in total. In order to answer the two research questions described in the Introduction section, we conducted two types of experiments that we will describe in detail later (denoted "Experiment 1" and "Experiment 2") in which we categorize the courses into different groups. In those experiments, for each of the 48 datasets, we have measured the portability of each obtained model to the rest of the courses of the same group. We have used WEKA (Waikato Environment for Knowledge Analysis) [25] because it is a well-known open-source machine learning tool that provides a huge number of classification algorithms and evaluation measures. In fact, we have compared the portability of the models obtained by using the J48 classification algorithm, the AUC and the loss of AUC (difference in two AUC values) as evaluation performance measures. An explanation of the key points in which this choice is based can be found in the coming paragraphs.

We have used the well-known J48 classification algorithm, namely, the Weka version of the C4.5 algorithm [26]. J48 is a re-implementation in Java programming language of C4.5 release 8 (hence the name J48). We have selected this algorithm for two main reasons. The first one is that it is a popular white box classifier that provides a decision tree as model output. Decision trees are very interpretable or comprehensible models that explain the predictions in the form of IF-THEN rules in a decision tree [27] and it has been widely used in education for predicting student performance. The second one is that C4.5 became quite popular after ranking #1 in the Top 10 Algorithms in Data Mining pre-eminent paper published by Springer LNCS in 2008 [28].

We have used AUC and AUC loss as evaluation measures of the performance of the classifier because: (a) AUC is one of the evaluation measures most commonly used for assessing students' performance predictive models [29–31]; and, (b) AUC loss is also proposed by Baker in his Learning Analytics Prizes [10] as the evaluation measure for testing whether or not his transfer challenge has been solved. The Area Under the ROC Curve (AUC) is a universal statistical indicator for describing the accuracy of a model regarding predicting a phenomenon [32]. It has been widely used in education research for comparing classification algorithms and models [33,34] instead of other well-known evaluation measures such as Accuracy, F-measure, Sensitivity, Precision, etc. AUC can be defined as the probability that a classifier will rank a randomly chosen positive instance higher than a randomly chosen negative one (assuming 'positive' ranks higher than 'negative'). It is often used as a measure of the quality of the classification models. A random classifier has an area under the curve of 0.5, while AUC for a perfect classifier is equal to 1. In practice, most of the classification models have an AUC between 0.5 and 1. We have also calculated the AUC loss or difference between the two AUC values obtained when applying the model over the source dataset and when applying over the target dataset.

The general procedure of our experiments has been summarized in Figure 1, where we graphically show the main steps of the experiments by using a flow diagram.

An overall explanation of the main steps (see Figure 2) of our experiments is:

- Firstly, Moodle logs have to be pre-processed (step 1) in order to obtain numerical and discretized datasets according to the format expected in the data mining tool to be used, Weka.
- Then, for each course dataset (numerical and discretized), the algorithm J48 is run in order to obtain a general prediction model (step 2) to be used in portability experiments.
- Next, courses are grouped according to 2 different criteria to conduct two types of experiments (step 3); for the first experiment (named "Experiment 1"), related courses are grouped by the area of knowledge (attribute "Degree" in Table 1); for the second experiment ("Experiment 2"), groups of courses are built according to the Moodle usage ("Moodle Usage" in Table 1).
- In each experiment, each model is selected (step 4) and tested against the rest of the datasets of courses belonging to the same group (step 5), repeating this process for each course.
- Finally, AUC values are obtained and AUC loss values are calculated when using the model against the rest of the courses of the same group (step 6).

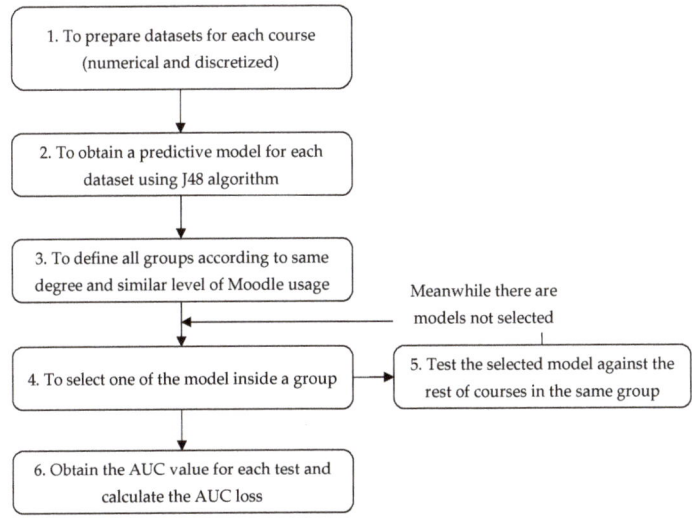

**Figure 1.** Experiments procedure steps.

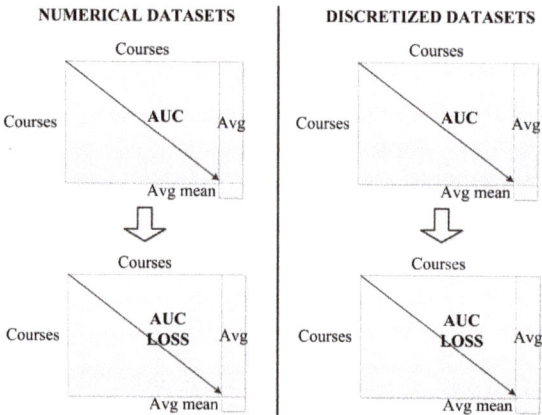

**Figure 2.** Visual description of the results in four tables.

In the next two subsections, we provide a more detailed explanation of how we have grouped similar courses in the two experiments.

3.2.1. Groups of Experiment 1

In this portability test, four groups of similar courses were used, according to the degree they belong to, as shown in Table 3. Our idea is that all courses of the same degree must be related and can be similar in the subjects.

**Table 3.** List of groups by degree.

| N. | Group | N. of Subjects |
|---|---|---|
| 1 | Computer | 10 |
| 2 | Education | 7 |
| 3 | Engineering | 4 |
| 4 | Physics | 3 |

It is noticeable in Table 3 that there are a higher number of courses in the Computer degree and in the Education degree, than in the Engineering and Physics degrees. In general, both Science and Humanities areas are considered in this study.

3.2.2. Groups of Experiment 2

In this portability experiment, three groups of similar courses were used, according to the respective Moodle usage level, as shown in Table 4. Moodle is an LMS that provides different types of activities (assignments, chat, choice, database, forum, glossary, lesson, quiz, survey, wiki, workshop, etc.). Our idea is that courses that use similar activities will have the same level of usage and these activities are related to the fact of passing or failing the course [2,6].

**Table 4.** List of groups by Moodle usage.

| N. | Group | Number of Subjects |
|---|---|---|
| 1 | High | 6 |
| 2 | Medium | 10 |
| 3 | Low | 8 |

It is important to notice that the most popular activities in our 24 courses are assignments, forums, and quizzes. Normally, low level courses only use one of these three kinds of activities, medium level courses use two of them, and high level courses use all three mentioned types of activities or even more.

## 4. Results

In this section we show the results obtained from the two sets of experiments carried out. We present the AUC and the loss of AUC in four different matrixes (two for numerical datasets and two for discretized datasets) for each group of similar courses (see Figure 2). In the upper part, we show two matrixes containing the AUC metric values that we have obtained when testing each course model (row) against the rest of the courses datasets (columns) using the numerical and the discretized datasets. The matrix main diagonal values correspond to the tests carried out for each course model against its own dataset, which means those AUC values (the highest ones) constitute the reference value (in green color) when compared with the rest of the courses. We have also calculated the average AUC values for each course (column denoted as "*avg*" in the tables) and the overall mean value for the group (cell denoted as "*avg mean*" in the tables). In the lower part, we show two matrixes showing the difference values between the highest AUC (row), which is considered to be the reference value, and the AUC values obtained when applying the corresponding model to each of the rest of the courses in the same group (column) using the numerical and the discretized datasets. Finally, our analysis focused on finding the best or highest AUC values and the best or lowest rates of AUC loss in each group of similar courses. Thus, we highlighted (in bold) the highest AUC values (without considering the reference value) and the lowest AUC loss values, which will represent the lowest portability loss, and thus the best results.

### 4.1. Experiment 1

In this experiment we assess the portability of prediction models between courses belonging to the same degree, having considered four different groups (Computer, Education, Engineering, and Physics). Firstly, we have obtained 24 prediction models (one for each course) and then we have tested them with the other courses' datasets of the same group, which in this case is a total of 174 numerical and 174 discretized datasets. Thus, we have carried out a total of 348 executions of J48 algorithm for obtaining each AUC value and then calculated the AUC loss versus the reference model.

For the Computer group, we can observe from Table 5 that the best AUC value (0.896) when transferring a prediction model to a different course corresponds to the PM (refer to Table 1 for course names abbreviations) course model when tested against the DB course numerical dataset. However, we can observe that the overall mean value for AUC measure with discretized datasets is 0.56, which means that the predictive ability of models when used in other subjects of this group is lightly above randomness. Something similar happens with numerical datasets, where the average value is 0.57. We can also observe that the lowest (best) AUC loss in discretized dataset is close to the perfect portability (0.006). This value is obtained when using the PM model against the RE subject. Overall, we can observe that AUC loss is better in the discretized dataset than in the numerical one (0.23 versus 0.33 in average). We can also highlight that the best average values in terms of portability loss are obtained for DB course in numerical dataset and PM course in discretized datasets (0.10 in both cases).

For the Education group, we can observe from Table 6 that the best AUC value (0.708) is obtained when using the prediction model of PESS course against the SSCM course discretized datasets. The overall average AUC for this group's discretized dataset (0.56) is very similar to that for the numerical datasets (0.57). In addition, we noticed that portability loss (AUC loss) is near-perfect (0.003) when testing the PEPI model against HWA course dataset in the discretized datasets. The overall average portability loss for discretized dataset experiments is 0.29, much better than the mean value obtained for numerical dataset experiments (0.39). We can also highlight that the best average values in terms of portability loss correspond to PEPI course (0.30 for numerical datasets and 0.11 for discretized datasets).

For the Engineering group, we can observe from Table 7 that the best AUC value (0.636) is obtained for ICS2 course prediction model when tested against ICS1 course discretized dataset. In this experiment, we can observe that the overall average value of AUC is again better in the numerical dataset (0.59) than in the discretized one (0.56), with both values staying above randomness. In addition, we can observe that the best portability loss value of 0.126 is obtained for ICS2 course model when tested against ICS1 course dataset in discretized datasets. Again, we obtain better results in the discretized than in the numerical dataset (0.24 versus 0.30) in terms of portability loss. We can also highlight that the best course average portability loss values are obtained for ICS3 in numerical dataset (0.20) and for ICS1 subject in discretized dataset (0.22).

Finally, for the Physics group, we can see in Table 8 that the highest AUC value (0.641) corresponds to the MM course prediction model when tested against the MA2 course numerical dataset. This value is very close to the overall mean value for the numerical dataset (0.68), which outperforms the overall AUC mean value for the discretized dataset (0.60). If we look at the portability loss values, we notice that the best (the lowest) AUC loss value of 0.009 is obtained when testing the MM course model against MA1 course discretized dataset. In this group, again, the global mean values are better for the discretized dataset than for the numerical one (0.09 versus 0.28), which means that the portability loss rate is particularly lower in this experiment in the discretized dataset compared to the numerical one. We can also highlight that the best course portability loss values are obtained for MM course model in both the numerical (0.21) and discretized (0.04) datasets.

*4.2. Experiment 2*

In this experiment we assess the portability of prediction models between courses with a similar level of usage of Moodle activities. In fact, we have considered three different groups (High, Medium, and Low). Firstly, we have obtained 24 prediction models (one for each course), and then, we tested them with other courses datasets of the same group, in this case a total of 204 numerical and 204 discretized datasets. Thus, we have carried out a total of 400 executions of J48 algorithm for obtaining each AUC value and then calculating the AUC loss versus the reference model.

For the high level group, as we can see from Table 9, the best value for AUC measure (0.656) is obtained when testing the IS course prediction model against the PM course discretized dataset. In this experiment (and equal than in the previous ones), the overall AUC means values are very similar for numerical (0.58) and discretized datasets (0.57). If we have a look at portability loss values, we can see that the best AUC loss value (0.061) is obtained when testing the ICS2 model against IS discretized dataset. In general, the average mean of AUC loss is better for the discretized datasets than for the numerical datasets (0.24 versus 0.37). Finally, we highlighted the average values of AUC loss for the ICS2 course, which are the lowest both in numerical datasets (0.25) and in discretized datasets (0.10).

For the medium level group, we can observe from Table 10 that the best AUC value of 0.792 corresponds to the prediction model of SDC course when tested against the discretized dataset of the SSCM course. The global average AUC value for this discretized category (0.53) is very similar to the global AUC value for numerical datasets (0.55). Regarding portability loss, we can see that the best value (0.009) belongs to DB prediction model when tested against PEPI discretized dataset. Moreover, again, the portability loss is better in the discretized datasets (0.25) than in the numerical datasets (0.38). Finally, we would also like to highlight the good average AUC loss results obtained by the InS course prediction model with the numerical datasets (0.12) and DB course prediction model in the discretized datasets (0.14).

Finally, for the low level group, we can see from Table 11 that the best AUC measure value (0.758) is obtained when testing the ICS3 prediction model against the HWA numerical dataset. The global average value for the numerical dataset (0.57) is a bit better than the obtained value by the discretized dataset (0.54). We can also notice that the best portability loss value is obtained when testing the MM model against HWA discretized dataset (0.028). The overall mean value for portability loss measure is also better for discretized than for numerical datasets (0.22 versus 0.34). Additionally, the best course prediction model on average values in terms of portability loss correspond to KSCE for numerical dataset (0.16) and MM for the discretized dataset (0.12).

Table 5. AUC Results and Loss in Portability in Computer degree group.

### AUC (Numerical Datasets)

| Course | HCI | IS | IP | PM | DB | SDC | PCT | RE | SE | InS | avg |
|---|---|---|---|---|---|---|---|---|---|---|---|
| HCI | 0.943 | 0.510 | 0.555 | 0.524 | 0.505 | 0.507 | 0.576 | 0.500 | 0.491 | 0.460 | 0.56 |
| IS | 0.522 | 0.966 | 0.526 | 0.522 | 0.521 | 0.604 | 0.483 | 0.691 | 0.491 | 0.482 | 0.58 |
| IP | 0.524 | 0.616 | 0.931 | 0.652 | 0.608 | 0.562 | 0.495 | 0.493 | 0.442 | 0.590 | 0.59 |
| PM | 0.514 | 0.500 | 0.687 | 0.915 | 0.896 | 0.550 | 0.554 | 0.518 | 0.530 | 0.544 | 0.62 |
| DB | 0.527 | 0.249 | 0.513 | 0.564 | 0.601 | 0.574 | 0.425 | 0.544 | 0.593 | 0.477 | 0.51 |
| SDC | 0.510 | 0.660 | 0.492 | 0.523 | 0.572 | 0.844 | 0.599 | 0.558 | 0.467 | 0.514 | 0.57 |
| PCT | 0.510 | 0.660 | 0.492 | 0.523 | 0.572 | 0.599 | 0.844 | 0.558 | 0.467 | 0.514 | 0.57 |
| RE | 0.490 | 0.563 | 0.491 | 0.521 | 0.515 | 0.525 | 0.561 | 0.992 | 0.491 | 0.551 | 0.57 |
| SE | 0.515 | 0.408 | 0.603 | 0.504 | 0.508 | 0.557 | 0.475 | 0.623 | 0.978 | 0.429 | 0.56 |
| InS | 0.479 | 0.481 | 0.533 | 0.551 | 0.544 | 0.572 | 0.501 | 0.610 | 0.525 | 0.673 | 0.55 |
| avg mean | | | | | | | | | | | 0.57 |

### AUC LOSS (Numerical Datasets)

| Course | HCI | IS | IP | PM | DB | SDC | PCT | RE | SE | InS | avg |
|---|---|---|---|---|---|---|---|---|---|---|---|
| HCI | - | 0.432 | 0.388 | 0.418 | 0.437 | 0.436 | 0.367 | 0.443 | 0.452 | 0.483 | 0.43 |
| IS | 0.444 | - | 0.440 | 0.444 | 0.445 | 0.363 | 0.483 | 0.276 | 0.475 | 0.484 | 0.43 |
| IP | 0.408 | 0.315 | - | 0.279 | 0.323 | 0.370 | 0.436 | 0.439 | 0.489 | 0.341 | 0.38 |
| PM | 0.401 | 0.415 | 0.228 | - | 0.019 | 0.365 | 0.361 | 0.397 | 0.385 | 0.370 | 0.33 |
| DB | 0.074 | 0.352 | 0.087 | 0.037 | - | 0.027 | 0.176 | 0.057 | 0.008 | 0.124 | 0.10 |
| SDC | 0.335 | 0.184 | 0.352 | 0.321 | 0.272 | - | 0.245 | 0.287 | 0.377 | 0.330 | 0.30 |
| PCT | 0.335 | 0.184 | 0.352 | 0.321 | 0.272 | 0.245 | - | 0.287 | 0.377 | 0.330 | 0.30 |
| RE | 0.501 | 0.429 | 0.501 | 0.470 | 0.476 | 0.467 | 0.431 | - | 0.501 | 0.441 | 0.47 |
| SE | 0.464 | 0.570 | 0.375 | 0.474 | 0.470 | 0.422 | 0.503 | 0.356 | - | 0.549 | 0.46 |
| InS | 0.193 | 0.192 | 0.140 | 0.122 | 0.128 | 0.101 | 0.172 | 0.063 | 0.148 | - | 0.14 |
| avg mean | | | | | | | | | | | 0.33 |

### AUC (Discretized Datasets)

| Course | HCI | IS | IP | PM | DB | SDC | PCT | RE | SE | InS | avg |
|---|---|---|---|---|---|---|---|---|---|---|---|
| HCI | 0.769 | 0.621 | 0.496 | 0.570 | 0.590 | 0.541 | 0.543 | 0.510 | 0.561 | 0.525 | 0.57 |
| IS | 0.557 | 0.854 | 0.643 | 0.551 | 0.513 | 0.573 | 0.545 | 0.534 | 0.460 | 0.687 | 0.59 |
| IP | 0.496 | 0.501 | 0.827 | 0.674 | 0.621 | 0.478 | 0.500 | 0.500 | 0.434 | 0.541 | 0.56 |
| PM | 0.550 | 0.622 | 0.598 | 0.715 | 0.646 | 0.682 | 0.562 | 0.710 | 0.542 | 0.597 | 0.62 |
| DB | 0.469 | 0.490 | 0.450 | 0.593 | 0.602 | 0.508 | 0.471 | 0.575 | 0.444 | 0.466 | 0.51 |
| SDC | 0.475 | 0.626 | 0.523 | 0.484 | 0.484 | 0.783 | 0.544 | 0.605 | 0.481 | 0.579 | 0.56 |
| PCT | 0.475 | 0.626 | 0.523 | 0.484 | 0.484 | 0.544 | 0.783 | 0.605 | 0.481 | 0.579 | 0.56 |
| RE | 0.499 | 0.549 | 0.444 | 0.516 | 0.547 | 0.620 | 0.514 | 0.845 | 0.582 | 0.508 | 0.56 |
| SE | 0.441 | 0.558 | 0.462 | 0.446 | 0.471 | 0.477 | 0.511 | 0.569 | 0.729 | 0.463 | 0.51 |
| InS | 0.492 | 0.634 | 0.546 | 0.606 | 0.570 | 0.578 | 0.533 | 0.565 | 0.510 | 0.792 | 0.58 |
| avg mean | | | | | | | | | | | 0.56 |

### AUC LOSS (Discretized Datasets)

| Course | HCI | IS | IP | PM | DB | SDC | PCT | RE | SE | InS | avg |
|---|---|---|---|---|---|---|---|---|---|---|---|
| HCI | - | 0.148 | 0.273 | 0.200 | 0.179 | 0.228 | 0.226 | 0.260 | 0.208 | 0.245 | 0.22 |
| IS | 0.297 | - | 0.211 | 0.303 | 0.341 | 0.281 | 0.309 | 0.321 | 0.394 | 0.167 | 0.29 |
| IP | 0.331 | 0.326 | - | 0.153 | 0.206 | 0.349 | 0.327 | 0.327 | 0.393 | 0.286 | 0.30 |
| PM | 0.165 | 0.094 | 0.118 | - | 0.069 | 0.034 | 0.153 | 0.006 | 0.173 | 0.119 | 0.10 |
| DB | 0.134 | 0.112 | 0.152 | 0.009 | - | 0.094 | 0.131 | 0.027 | 0.158 | 0.136 | 0.11 |
| SDC | 0.308 | 0.157 | 0.260 | 0.298 | 0.299 | - | 0.239 | 0.178 | 0.302 | 0.204 | 0.25 |
| PCT | 0.308 | 0.157 | 0.260 | 0.298 | 0.299 | 0.239 | - | 0.178 | 0.302 | 0.204 | 0.25 |
| RE | 0.346 | 0.296 | 0.400 | 0.329 | 0.297 | 0.225 | 0.331 | - | 0.263 | 0.337 | 0.31 |
| SE | 0.288 | 0.171 | 0.267 | 0.283 | 0.258 | 0.252 | 0.218 | 0.160 | - | 0.266 | 0.24 |
| InS | 0.300 | 0.158 | 0.246 | 0.186 | 0.222 | 0.215 | 0.259 | 0.227 | 0.282 | - | 0.23 |
| avg mean | | | | | | | | | | | 0.23 |

Table 6. AUC Results and Loss in Portability in Education degree group.

| | AUC (Numerical Datasets) | | | | | | | | AUC (Discretized Datasets) | | | | | | |
|---|---|---|---|---|---|---|---|---|---|---|---|---|---|---|---|
| Course | PESS | SSCM | PEPI | PECE | HWA | KSCE | IPs | avg | PESS | SSCM | PEPI | PECE | HWA | KSCE | IPs | avg |
| PESS | 0.938 | 0.554 | 0.553 | 0.548 | **0.667** | 0.558 | 0.535 | 0.62 | 0.805 | **0.708** | 0.526 | 0.331 | 0.500 | 0.525 | 0.611 | 0.57 |
| SSCM | 0.629 | 0.843 | 0.574 | 0.395 | 0.667 | 0.530 | 0.522 | 0.59 | 0.560 | 0.839 | 0.466 | 0.366 | 0.500 | 0.500 | 0.515 | 0.54 |
| PEPI | 0.490 | 0.587 | 0.839 | 0.562 | 0.556 | 0.499 | 0.552 | 0.58 | 0.483 | 0.572 | 0.670 | 0.568 | 0.667 | 0.460 | 0.597 | 0.57 |
| PECE | 0.447 | 0.265 | 0.463 | 0.972 | 0.333 | 0.467 | 0.541 | 0.50 | 0.308 | 0.342 | 0.515 | 0.749 | 0.500 | 0.500 | 0.465 | 0.48 |
| HWA | 0.493 | 0.533 | 0.441 | 0.574 | 1.000 | 0.543 | 0.534 | 0.59 | 0.549 | 0.569 | 0.549 | 0.488 | 0.778 | 0.532 | 0.515 | 0.57 |
| KSCE | 0.531 | 0.575 | 0.459 | 0.516 | 0.354 | 0.817 | 0.500 | 0.54 | 0.550 | 0.679 | 0.523 | 0.472 | 0.608 | 0.931 | 0.583 | 0.62 |
| IPs | 0.586 | 0.322 | 0.643 | 0.519 | 0.528 | 0.625 | 0.921 | 0.59 | 0.556 | 0.500 | 0.505 | 0.498 | 0.618 | 0.542 | 0.884 | 0.59 |
| | | | | | | | avg mean | 0.57 | | | | | | | avg mean | 0.56 |

| | AUC LOSS (Numerical Datasets) | | | | | | | | AUC LOSS (Discretized Datasets) | | | | | | |
|---|---|---|---|---|---|---|---|---|---|---|---|---|---|---|---|
| Course | PESS | SSCM | PEPI | PECE | HWA | KSCE | IPs | avg | PESS | SSCM | PEPI | PECE | HWA | KSCE | IPs | avg |
| PESS | - | 0.384 | 0.385 | 0.390 | 0.271 | 0.380 | 0.403 | 0.37 | - | 0.097 | 0.279 | 0.474 | 0.305 | 0.280 | 0.195 | 0.27 |
| SSCM | 0.214 | - | 0.269 | 0.448 | 0.176 | 0.313 | 0.321 | 0.29 | 0.279 | - | 0.373 | 0.473 | 0.339 | 0.339 | 0.324 | 0.35 |
| PEPI | 0.349 | 0.253 | - | 0.277 | 0.283 | 0.340 | 0.288 | **0.30** | 0.187 | 0.099 | - | 0.102 | 0.003 | 0.210 | 0.073 | **0.11** |
| PECE | 0.526 | 0.707 | 0.509 | - | 0.639 | 0.505 | 0.431 | 0.55 | 0.442 | 0.408 | 0.234 | - | 0.249 | 0.249 | 0.285 | 0.31 |
| HWA | 0.507 | 0.468 | 0.559 | 0.426 | - | 0.457 | 0.466 | 0.48 | 0.229 | 0.210 | 0.229 | 0.290 | - | 0.246 | 0.263 | 0.24 |
| KSCE | 0.286 | **0.243** | 0.358 | 0.301 | 0.463 | - | 0.317 | 0.33 | 0.381 | 0.253 | 0.408 | 0.459 | 0.323 | - | 0.348 | 0.36 |
| IPs | 0.336 | 0.600 | 0.278 | 0.402 | 0.393 | 0.296 | - | 0.38 | 0.329 | 0.385 | 0.379 | 0.386 | 0.266 | 0.342 | - | 0.35 |
| | | | | | | | avg mean | 0.39 | | | | | | | avg mean | 0.29 |

Table 7. AUC Results and Loss in Portability in Engineering degree group.

| | AUC (Numerical Datasets) | | | | | AUC (Discretized Datasets) | | | | |
|---|---|---|---|---|---|---|---|---|---|---|
| Course | ICS1 | ICS2 | ICS3 | ICS4 | avg | ICS1 | ICS2 | ICS3 | ICS4 | avg |
| ICS1 | 0.958 | 0.477 | 0.464 | 0.569 | 0.62 | 0.742 | 0.535 | 0.554 | 0.474 | 0.58 |
| ICS2 | **0.576** | 0.789 | 0.504 | 0.557 | 0.61 | **0.636** | 0.761 | 0.523 | 0.402 | 0.58 |
| ICS3 | 0.544 | 0.547 | 0.739 | 0.525 | 0.59 | 0.446 | 0.506 | 0.739 | 0.514 | 0.55 |
| ICS4 | 0.410 | 0.477 | 0.542 | 0.790 | 0.55 | 0.428 | 0.455 | 0.483 | 0.685 | 0.51 |
| | | | | avg mean | 0.59 | | | | avg mean | 0.56 |
| | AUC LOSS (Numerical Datasets) | | | | | AUC LOSS (Discretized Datasets) | | | | |
| Course | ICS1 | ICS2 | ICS3 | ICS4 | avg | ICS1 | ICS2 | ICS3 | ICS4 | avg |
| ICS1 | - | 0.480 | 0.494 | 0.389 | 0.45 | - | 0.206 | 0.187 | 0.268 | **0.22** |
| ICS2 | 0.213 | - | 0.285 | 0.231 | 0.24 | **0.126** | - | 0.238 | 0.359 | 0.24 |
| ICS3 | 0.195 | **0.192** | - | 0.214 | **0.20** | 0.293 | 0.233 | - | 0.225 | 0.25 |
| ICS4 | 0.380 | 0.314 | 0.248 | - | 0.31 | 0.257 | 0.230 | 0.202 | - | 0.23 |
| | | | | avg mean | 0.30 | | | | avg mean | 0.24 |

Table 8. AUC Results and Loss in Portability in Physics degree group.

| | AUC (Numerical Datasets) | | | | AUC (Discretized Datasets) | | | |
|---|---|---|---|---|---|---|---|---|
| Course | MM | MA1 | MA2 | avg | MM | MA1 | MA2 | avg |
| MM | 0.807 | 0.559 | **0.641** | 0.67 | 0.639 | **0.630** | 0.563 | 0.61 |
| MA1 | 0.542 | 0.880 | 0.591 | 0.67 | 0.578 | 0.697 | 0.603 | 0.63 |
| MA2 | 0.574 | 0.592 | 0.905 | 0.69 | 0.546 | 0.525 | 0.642 | 0.57 |
| | | | avg mean | 0.68 | | | avg mean | 0.60 |
| | AUC LOSS (Numerical Datasets) | | | | AUC LOSS (Discretized Datasets) | | | |
| Course | MM | MA1 | MA2 | avg | MM | MA1 | MA2 | avg |
| MM | - | 0.249 | 0.166 | **0.21** | - | **0.009** | 0.076 | **0.04** |
| MA1 | 0.337 | - | 0.288 | 0.31 | 0.119 | - | 0.094 | 0.11 |
| MA2 | 0.331 | 0.313 | - | 0.32 | 0.096 | 0.117 | - | 0.11 |
| | | | avg mean | 0.28 | | | avg mean | 0.09 |

Table 9. AUC Results and Loss in Portability in high level of usage of Moodle group.

| | AUC (Numerical Datasets) | | | | | | | AUC (Discretized Datasets) | | | | | |
|---|---|---|---|---|---|---|---|---|---|---|---|---|---|
| Course | HCI | IS | ICS2 | IP | PM | IPs | avg | HCI | IS | ICS2 | IP | PM | IPs | avg |
| HCI | 0.943 | 0.510 | 0.522 | 0.538 | 0.524 | 0.457 | 0.58 | 0.769 | 0.621 | 0.569 | 0.417 | 0.570 | 0.550 | 0.58 |
| IS | 0.485 | 0.927 | 0.494 | 0.470 | 0.606 | 0.520 | 0.58 | 0.479 | 0.816 | 0.577 | 0.555 | 0.656 | 0.596 | 0.61 |
| ICS2 | 0.514 | 0.590 | 0.783 | 0.500 | 0.569 | 0.513 | 0.58 | 0.503 | 0.558 | 0.619 | 0.485 | 0.516 | 0.552 | 0.54 |
| IP | 0.484 | 0.420 | 0.472 | 0.862 | 0.490 | 0.627 | 0.56 | 0.519 | 0.576 | 0.535 | 0.761 | 0.491 | 0.409 | 0.55 |
| PM | 0.514 | 0.489 | 0.530 | 0.618 | 0.899 | 0.610 | 0.61 | 0.574 | 0.488 | 0.522 | 0.592 | 0.793 | 0.480 | 0.57 |
| IPs | 0.516 | 0.529 | 0.514 | 0.427 | 0.597 | 0.921 | 0.58 | 0.507 | 0.638 | 0.485 | 0.514 | 0.460 | 0.884 | 0.58 |
| | avg mean | | | | | | 0.58 | avg mean | | | | | | 0.57 |
| | AUC LOSS (Numerical Datasets) | | | | | | | AUC LOSS (Discretized Datasets) | | | | | | |
| Course | HCI | IS | ICS2 | IP | PM | IPs | avg | HCI | IS | ICS2 | IP | PM | IPs | avg |
| HCI | - | 0.432 | 0.421 | 0.404 | 0.418 | 0.486 | 0.43 | - | 0.148 | 0.201 | 0.352 | 0.200 | 0.220 | 0.22 |
| IS | 0.442 | - | 0.433 | 0.457 | 0.321 | 0.407 | 0.41 | 0.337 | - | 0.238 | 0.260 | 0.160 | 0.219 | 0.24 |
| ICS2 | 0.270 | 0.193 | - | 0.283 | 0.215 | 0.271 | 0.25 | 0.116 | 0.061 | - | 0.134 | 0.103 | 0.067 | 0.10 |
| IP | 0.378 | 0.441 | 0.390 | - | 0.371 | 0.235 | 0.36 | 0.242 | 0.184 | 0.225 | - | 0.269 | 0.352 | 0.25 |
| PM | 0.385 | 0.410 | 0.369 | 0.281 | - | 0.290 | 0.35 | 0.219 | 0.305 | 0.271 | 0.200 | - | 0.313 | 0.26 |
| IPs | 0.405 | 0.392 | 0.407 | 0.495 | 0.324 | - | 0.40 | 0.377 | 0.246 | 0.400 | 0.370 | 0.424 | - | 0.36 |
| | avg mean | | | | | | 0.37 | avg mean | | | | | | 0.24 |

Table 10. AUC Results and Loss in Portability in medium level of usage of Moodle group.

### AUC (Numerical Datasets)

| Course | SSCM | DB | SDC | PCT | RE | SE | InS | PECE | PESS | PEPI | avg |
|---|---|---|---|---|---|---|---|---|---|---|---|
| SSCM | 0.839 | 0.521 | 0.549 | 0.464 | 0.500 | 0.489 | 0.546 | 0.366 | 0.560 | 0.466 | 0.53 |
| DB | 0.223 | 0.976 | 0.535 | 0.457 | 0.670 | 0.581 | 0.517 | 0.456 | 0.544 | 0.539 | 0.55 |
| SDC | 0.610 | 0.467 | 0.809 | 0.504 | 0.558 | 0.496 | 0.456 | 0.571 | 0.514 | 0.467 | 0.55 |
| PCT | 0.495 | 0.337 | 0.585 | 0.891 | 0.612 | 0.382 | 0.492 | 0.422 | 0.324 | 0.431 | 0.50 |
| RE | 0.456 | 0.329 | 0.553 | 0.579 | 0.956 | 0.473 | 0.577 | 0.465 | 0.607 | 0.487 | 0.55 |
| SE | 0.417 | 0.611 | 0.559 | 0.486 | 0.614 | 0.964 | 0.494 | 0.517 | 0.665 | 0.542 | 0.59 |
| InS | 0.605 | 0.671 | 0.583 | 0.486 | 0.610 | 0.533 | 0.704 | 0.564 | 0.684 | 0.494 | 0.59 |
| PECE | 0.265 | 0.520 | 0.371 | 0.505 | 0.281 | 0.471 | 0.548 | 0.972 | 0.447 | 0.463 | 0.48 |
| PESS | 0.554 | 0.471 | 0.547 | 0.509 | 0.579 | 0.579 | 0.582 | 0.548 | 0.938 | 0.553 | 0.59 |
| PEPI | 0.587 | 0.323 | 0.574 | 0.540 | 0.499 | 0.481 | 0.542 | 0.562 | 0.490 | 0.839 | 0.54 |
| avg mean | | | | | | | | | | | 0.55 |

### AUC LOSS (Numerical Datasets)

| Course | SSCM | DB | SDC | PCT | RE | SE | InS | PECE | PESS | PEPI | avg |
|---|---|---|---|---|---|---|---|---|---|---|---|
| SSCM | - | 0.318 | 0.290 | 0.375 | 0.339 | 0.350 | 0.293 | 0.473 | 0.279 | 0.373 | 0.34 |
| DB | 0.754 | - | 0.441 | 0.519 | 0.307 | 0.395 | 0.459 | 0.520 | 0.432 | 0.437 | 0.47 |
| SDC | 0.199 | 0.342 | - | 0.305 | 0.252 | 0.313 | 0.353 | 0.238 | 0.296 | 0.342 | 0.29 |
| PCT | 0.397 | 0.554 | 0.306 | - | 0.279 | 0.509 | 0.399 | 0.469 | 0.568 | 0.460 | 0.44 |
| RE | 0.500 | 0.627 | 0.403 | 0.377 | - | 0.483 | 0.379 | 0.491 | 0.350 | 0.469 | 0.45 |
| SE | 0.548 | 0.353 | 0.405 | 0.478 | 0.351 | - | 0.470 | 0.447 | 0.299 | 0.422 | 0.42 |
| InS | 0.100 | 0.033 | 0.121 | 0.218 | 0.094 | 0.171 | - | 0.140 | 0.021 | 0.210 | 0.12 |
| PECE | 0.707 | 0.452 | 0.602 | 0.467 | 0.691 | 0.501 | 0.424 | - | 0.526 | 0.509 | 0.54 |
| PESS | 0.384 | 0.467 | 0.391 | 0.429 | 0.359 | 0.359 | 0.356 | 0.390 | - | 0.385 | 0.39 |
| PEPI | 0.253 | 0.516 | 0.265 | 0.299 | 0.341 | 0.358 | 0.297 | 0.277 | 0.349 | - | 0.33 |
| avg mean | | | | | | | | | | | 0.38 |

### AUC (Discretized Datasets)

| Course | SSCM | DB | SDC | PCT | RE | SE | InS | PECE | PESS | PEPI | avg |
|---|---|---|---|---|---|---|---|---|---|---|---|
| SSCM | 0.843 | 0.492 | 0.698 | 0.514 | 0.635 | 0.513 | 0.583 | 0.395 | 0.629 | 0.574 | 0.59 |
| DB | 0.422 | 0.652 | 0.551 | 0.476 | 0.500 | 0.510 | 0.499 | 0.500 | 0.500 | 0.643 | 0.53 |
| SDC | 0.792 | 0.430 | 0.924 | 0.531 | 0.610 | 0.484 | 0.622 | 0.268 | 0.664 | 0.506 | 0.58 |
| PCT | 0.683 | 0.447 | 0.567 | 0.712 | 0.553 | 0.470 | 0.551 | 0.286 | 0.569 | 0.500 | 0.53 |
| RE | 0.491 | 0.529 | 0.614 | 0.508 | 0.756 | 0.545 | 0.569 | 0.521 | 0.597 | 0.542 | 0.57 |
| SE | 0.425 | 0.500 | 0.375 | 0.473 | 0.431 | 0.718 | 0.451 | 0.000 | 0.272 | 0.556 | 0.42 |
| InS | 0.512 | 0.429 | 0.625 | 0.528 | 0.454 | 0.500 | 0.761 | 0.610 | 0.432 | 0.502 | 0.54 |
| PECE | 0.342 | 0.553 | 0.550 | 0.468 | 0.559 | 0.530 | 0.463 | 0.749 | 0.308 | 0.515 | 0.50 |
| PESS | 0.708 | 0.461 | 0.618 | 0.519 | 0.518 | 0.465 | 0.606 | 0.331 | 0.805 | 0.526 | 0.56 |
| PEPI | 0.572 | 0.500 | 0.435 | 0.505 | 0.454 | 0.504 | 0.590 | 0.568 | 0.483 | 0.712 | 0.53 |
| avg mean | | | | | | | | | | | 0.53 |

### AUC LOSS (Discretized Datasets)

| Course | SSCM | DB | SDC | PCT | RE | SE | InS | PECE | PESS | PEPI | avg |
|---|---|---|---|---|---|---|---|---|---|---|---|
| SSCM | - | 0.351 | 0.145 | 0.329 | 0.208 | 0.330 | 0.260 | 0.448 | 0.214 | 0.269 | 0.28 |
| DB | 0.230 | - | 0.101 | 0.176 | 0.152 | 0.142 | 0.153 | 0.152 | 0.152 | 0.009 | 0.14 |
| SDC | 0.132 | 0.494 | - | 0.393 | 0.314 | 0.440 | 0.302 | 0.656 | 0.261 | 0.418 | 0.38 |
| PCT | 0.029 | 0.265 | 0.145 | - | 0.159 | 0.242 | 0.161 | 0.426 | 0.143 | 0.212 | 0.20 |
| RE | 0.265 | 0.227 | 0.142 | 0.248 | - | 0.211 | 0.187 | 0.235 | 0.160 | 0.214 | 0.21 |
| SE | 0.294 | 0.218 | 0.343 | 0.245 | 0.287 | - | 0.267 | 0.718 | 0.447 | 0.162 | 0.33 |
| InS | 0.249 | 0.332 | 0.136 | 0.233 | 0.307 | 0.261 | - | 0.151 | 0.330 | 0.259 | 0.25 |
| PECE | 0.408 | 0.196 | 0.200 | 0.281 | 0.191 | 0.219 | 0.286 | - | 0.442 | 0.234 | 0.27 |
| PESS | 0.097 | 0.344 | 0.187 | 0.286 | 0.287 | 0.340 | 0.199 | 0.474 | - | 0.279 | 0.28 |
| PEPI | 0.141 | 0.212 | 0.278 | 0.207 | 0.258 | 0.208 | 0.122 | 0.144 | 0.229 | - | 0.20 |
| avg mean | | | | | | | | | | | 0.25 |

Table 11. AUC Results and Loss in Portability in low level of usage of Moodle group.

| | AUC (Numerical Datasets) | | | | | | | | | AUC (Discretized Datasets) | | | | | | | |
|---|---|---|---|---|---|---|---|---|---|---|---|---|---|---|---|---|---|
| Course | ICS1 | MM | MA1 | MA2 | KSCE | HWA | ICS3 | ICS4 | avg | ICS1 | MM | MA1 | MA2 | KSCE | HWA | ICS3 | ICS4 | avg |
| ICS1 | 0.917 | 0.524 | 0.523 | 0.512 | 0.653 | 0.498 | 0.491 | 0.404 | 0.57 | 0.761 | 0.480 | 0.485 | 0.448 | 0.531 | 0.597 | 0.470 | 0.591 | 0.55 |
| MM | 0.501 | 0.807 | 0.559 | 0.683 | 0.347 | 0.475 | 0.519 | 0.461 | 0.54 | 0.639 | 0.688 | 0.630 | 0.530 | 0.559 | 0.660 | 0.538 | 0.444 | 0.59 |
| MA1 | 0.676 | 0.542 | 0.880 | 0.447 | 0.674 | 0.519 | 0.505 | 0.481 | 0.59 | 0.644 | 0.578 | 0.697 | 0.556 | 0.568 | 0.333 | 0.472 | 0.485 | 0.54 |
| MA2 | 0.519 | 0.607 | 0.574 | 0.905 | 0.486 | 0.496 | 0.521 | 0.489 | 0.57 | 0.457 | 0.526 | 0.532 | 0.642 | 0.484 | 0.451 | 0.518 | 0.519 | 0.52 |
| KSCE | 0.594 | 0.554 | 0.563 | 0.354 | 0.705 | 0.663 | 0.545 | 0.522 | 0.56 | 0.674 | 0.560 | 0.574 | 0.422 | 0.931 | 0.608 | 0.570 | 0.445 | 0.60 |
| HWA | 0.490 | 0.434 | 0.489 | 0.428 | 0.590 | 1.000 | 0.522 | 0.512 | 0.56 | 0.628 | 0.516 | 0.547 | 0.492 | 0.532 | 0.778 | 0.522 | 0.516 | 0.57 |
| ICS3 | 0.554 | 0.562 | 0.457 | 0.426 | 0.653 | 0.758 | 0.938 | 0.527 | 0.61 | 0.375 | 0.428 | 0.454 | 0.510 | 0.456 | 0.528 | 0.707 | 0.502 | 0.49 |
| ICS4 | 0.414 | 0.563 | 0.539 | 0.550 | 0.472 | 0.521 | 0.495 | 0.771 | 0.54 | 0.410 | 0.443 | 0.390 | 0.475 | 0.452 | 0.500 | 0.460 | 0.682 | 0.48 |
| avg mean | | | | | | | | | 0.57 | | | | | | | | | 0.54 |

| | AUC LOSS (Numerical Datasets) | | | | | | | | | AUC LOSS (Discretized Datasets) | | | | | | | |
|---|---|---|---|---|---|---|---|---|---|---|---|---|---|---|---|---|---|
| Course | ICS1 | MM | MA1 | MA2 | KSCE | HWA | ICS3 | ICS4 | avg | ICS1 | MM | MA1 | MA2 | KSCE | HWA | ICS3 | ICS4 | avg |
| ICS1 | - | 0.393 | 0.394 | 0.406 | 0.264 | 0.419 | 0.426 | 0.513 | 0.40 | - | 0.281 | 0.276 | 0.313 | 0.230 | 0.164 | 0.291 | 0.170 | 0.25 |
| MM | 0.307 | - | 0.249 | 0.125 | 0.460 | 0.332 | 0.288 | 0.347 | 0.30 | 0.048 | - | 0.057 | 0.158 | 0.129 | 0.028 | 0.150 | 0.244 | 0.12 |
| MA1 | 0.204 | 0.337 | - | 0.433 | 0.206 | 0.361 | 0.374 | 0.399 | 0.33 | 0.053 | 0.119 | - | 0.142 | 0.129 | 0.364 | 0.225 | 0.212 | 0.18 |
| MA2 | 0.386 | 0.298 | 0.331 | - | 0.419 | 0.409 | 0.384 | 0.416 | 0.38 | 0.185 | 0.116 | 0.110 | - | 0.158 | 0.191 | 0.124 | 0.123 | 0.14 |
| KSCE | 0.112 | 0.151 | 0.142 | 0.351 | - | 0.042 | 0.160 | 0.183 | 0.16 | 0.258 | 0.371 | 0.357 | 0.510 | - | 0.323 | 0.361 | 0.486 | 0.38 |
| HWA | 0.511 | 0.566 | 0.511 | 0.573 | 0.410 | - | 0.478 | 0.488 | 0.51 | 0.150 | 0.262 | 0.231 | 0.287 | 0.246 | - | 0.256 | 0.262 | 0.24 |
| ICS3 | 0.384 | 0.376 | 0.481 | 0.513 | 0.285 | 0.180 | - | 0.411 | 0.38 | 0.333 | 0.280 | 0.253 | 0.197 | 0.251 | 0.179 | - | 0.205 | 0.24 |
| ICS4 | 0.357 | 0.208 | 0.232 | 0.222 | 0.299 | 0.250 | 0.277 | - | 0.26 | 0.273 | 0.239 | 0.292 | 0.207 | 0.230 | 0.182 | 0.222 | - | 0.23 |
| avg mean | | | | | | | | | 0.34 | | | | | | | | | 0.22 |

## 5. Discussion

About the obtained accuracy of the student performance prediction models, as we can see in previous section tables for Experiments 1 and 2, it is noticeable that average AUC values are always a little better in the case of the numerical datasets than the discretized datasets. It is logical and expected that the models' predictive power is higher when we use numerical values. In Experiment 1, the average AUC highest values are obtained for the Physics group, having 0.68 for the numerical dataset and 0.60 for the discretized one. In Experiment 2 the highest values are found in the High group, obtaining values of 0.58 for the numerical dataset and 0.57 for the discretized dataset. Thus, in general the average AUC values are not high and only a little higher than a change (0.5). If we have a look at the maximum values for AUC, there is not a clear rule that we can obtain since we have found similar good values in both experiments: 0.89 in Computer group of experiment 1 with numerical datasets and 0.79 in medium level group of experiment 2 with discretized datasets. We can conclude that the accuracy of the prediction models when we transfer them to other different courses are not very high (but higher than a chance, AUC > 0.5), it is a little higher when using numerical values (but only slightly) and similar results are obtained in both experiments. We think that this can be in part due to the number of students vary a lot of from one course to another, ranging from 50 (minimum) to 302 (maximum) and the number of attributes vary from one dataset to another.

When assessing the models' portability, we have also used the AUC loss as an indicator of portability loss. According to Baker [10], prediction models are portable as long as their portability loss values stay around 0.1 (and AUC is kept above randomness). In general, in our two experiments, we have only obtained these good values in one group, namely, the Physics group with discrete datasets with 0.60 AUC average value and 0.09 AUC loss average. Thus, this group of courses fit the Baker's rule for model portability. However, if we look at specific cases, we also found that some specific models that applied to specific courses datasets obtain good results and fit the Baker's rule. For instance, in Experiment 1, the minimum values of portability loss was 0.008 for the numerical dataset (Computer group; DB transfer to SE) and 0.006 for discretized dataset (Computer group; PM transfer to RE). In Experiment 2, the minimum value of portability loss was 0.021 for numerical dataset (Medium group; InS transfer to PESS) and 0.009 for discretized dataset (Medium group; DB transfer to PEPI). These results indicate that some particular prediction models are applicable to some other different courses. However, we are more interested in finding if a model can be correctly transferred to all the rest of the courses in its group, and thus, we have a look at portability loss average values ("$avg$" loss column). In this regard, we have also found some good results, and the best four prediction models are described below. In Experiment 1, we have obtained good average results for the DB prediction model in the numerical dataset (average loss of 0.10) and the MM prediction model in the discretized dataset (0.04). Some similar results were obtained in Experiment 2 with InS prediction model in the numerical case (0.12) and ICS2 prediction model in the case of discretized dataset (0.10). It is important to highlight that those best four models not only present average portability loss values close to 0.10, but they all also keep average values of AUC above randomness. Thus, it indicates that those models are portables and they can be used to correctly predict in the rest of the courses in their group and we can conclude that they meet the conditions established in the portability challenge defined by Baker in The Baker Learning Analytics Prizes [10]. We also checked if these courses are very similar (number of students, number of types of activity, teachers in charge of the course, etc.), having only found some similarities in the group of Physics (which obtained the best average mean AUC Loss). In particular, we noticed that the instructors in charge of the three Mathematics courses in the Physics group were the same and they used the same methodology and evaluation approach in all their courses.

Next, we will show and comment those best four decision trees prediction models. The discovered knowledge from a decision tree can be extracted and presented in the form of classification IF-THEN rules. One rule is created for each path from the root to a leaf node. Each attribute-value pair along a given path forms a conjunction in the rule antecedent (IF part). The leaf node holds the class prediction, forming the rule consequent (THEN) part. In our case, we will show the J48 pruned tree that Weka provides when training a classification prediction model. We have added the word "**THEN**" to the output of Weka in order to make easier the reading of each rule.

*5.1. Best Models of Experiment 1*

In Figure 3 we can see the best decision tree for Computer group with numerical datasets that is the prediction model of DB course. It is a big tree (27 nodes in total) that consists of eight leaf nodes or rules for the *Pass* class and six rules for the *Fail* class. We can see that all the attributes or Moodle events counts are about assignment, choice, forum, page, and resource. In most of the branches that lead to *Pass* leaf nodes, we can see "greater than" conditions over attributes and "less or equal than" condition in the attributes of branches that lead to *Fail* classification. Thus, we can conclude that in this prediction model to have a minimum threshold number of events in these activities seem to be much related with students' success in the course.

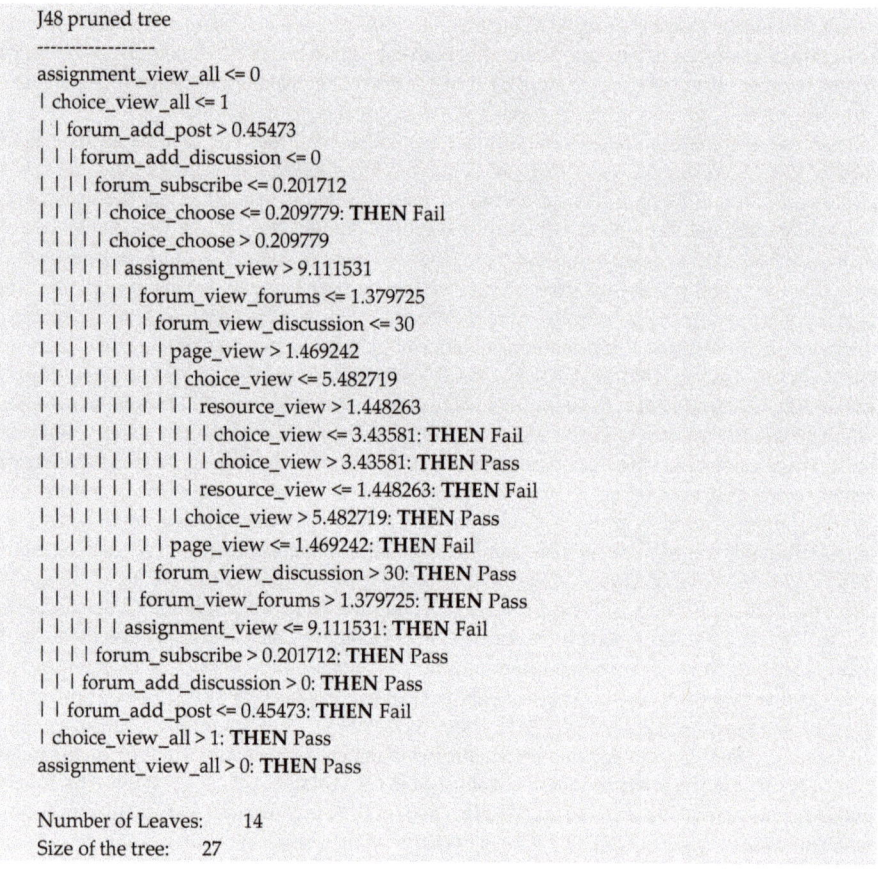

**Figure 3.** Best model of the Computer group with numerical dataset—Subject DB.

Figure 4 shows the best decision tree in the Physic group with discretized dataset, that is, the prediction model of the MM course. It is a small decision tree (11 nodes in total) with five leaf nodes labeled with the *Pass* value and only one leaf node with the label *Fail*. The attributes or events that appear in the tree are about page, resource, and forum. Thus, thanks to the little number or rules and the high comprehensibility of the two labels (HIGH and LOW) the tree is very interpretable and usable by an instructor. For example, if we analyze the branch leading to that *Fail* leaf node, we can see that students that showed a low number of events with pages, resources, and forums are quite likely to fail the course.

```
J48 pruned tree
------------------
page_view = Low
|  resource_view = Low
|  |  forum_view_forums = Low
|  |  |  resource_view_all = Low
|  |  |  |  resource_view = Low: THEN Fail
|  |  |  |  resource_view = High: THEN Pass
|  |  |  resource_view_all = High: THEN Pass
|  |  forum_view_forums = High: THEN Pass
|  resource_view = High: THEN Pass
page_view = High: THEN Pass

Number of Leaves:      6
Size of the tree:     11
```

**Figure 4.** Best Model of the Physics group with discretized dataset—Subject MM.

*5.2. Best Models of Experiment 2*

In Figure 5, we show the best decision tree in the medium level group with numerical datasets, that is, the prediction model of the Ins course. It is a medium size tree (15 nodes in total) that has three rules or leaf nodes for *Pass* class and five rules for *Fail*. The attributes or events that appear in this tree are about forum, page, and choice. Most of the branches that lead to *Pass* show that students must have a greater number of events in these attributes than a specific threshold. The rest of paths lead to students' fail.

```
J48 pruned tree
------------------
forum_view_forums <= 0.937213
|  page_view <= 1.866007: THEN Fail
|  page_view > 1.866007
|  |  choice_view_all <= 0.496039
|  |  |  forum_view_forum <= 4: THEN Fail
|  |  |  forum_view_forum > 4: THEN Pass
|  |  choice_view_all > 0.496039: THEN Pass
forum_view_forums > 0.937213
|  choice_view <= 2.576183: THEN Fail
|  choice_view > 2.576183
|  |  forum_add_discussion <= 0: THEN Fail
|  |  forum_add_discussion > 0
|  |  |  choice_view_all <= 0.496039: THEN Fail
|  |  |  choice_view_all > 0.496039: THEN Pass

Number of Leaves:      8
Size of the tree: 15
```

**Figure 5.** Best model of the Medium group with numerical dataset—Subject InS.

Figure 6 show the best decision tree obtained in the high level group with discretized dataset, which is the prediction model of ICS2 course. It is a small tree (only nine nodes in total) that has three leaf nodes or rules for predicting when the students *Pass* and two rules for *Fail*. In this model, the attributes or Moodle events that appear in the rules are about forum, resource, and choice activities. Again, most of the branches that lead to *Pass* show that student must have a greater number of events in these attributes than a specific threshold. The rest of paths lead to students' fail.

```
J48 pruned tree
------------------
forum_view_forum = Low
|  forum_view_discussion = Low
|  |  resource_view= Low: THEN Fail
|  |  resource_view= High: THEN Pass
|  forum_view_discussion = High: THEN Pass
forum_view_forum = High
|  choice_view = Low: THEN Fail
|  choice_view = High: THEN Pass

Number of Leaves:    5
Size of the tree:    9
```

**Figure 6.** Best Model of the High group with discretized dataset—Subject ICS2.

## 6. Conclusions and Future Research

This paper presents a detailed study about the portability of predictive models between universities courses. To our knowledge, this work is one of the first exhaustive studies about portability of performance prediction models with blended university courses, and thus, we hope that it can be of help to other researchers who are also interested in developing models for portability solutions in their educational institutions.

In order to answer to our two research questions, we have carried out two experiments executing the J48 classification algorithms over 24 courses in order to obtain the AUC and AUC loss of the models when applying to different courses of the same group by using numerical and discretized datasets. Starting of the results obtained in our experiments, the answers to our two research questions are:

a.  How feasible it is to directly apply predictive models between courses belonging to the same degree. By analyzing the results shown in Tables 5–8, we can see that the average AUC values are not very high (both in numerical and discretized datasets), but when we used discretized datasets, the obtained models are better in terms of AUC loss or portability loss, in spite of the fact that numerical datasets present the best AUC values, which is something that we expected in advance. In fact, portability loss values are inside the interval from 0.09 to 0.28 for the discretized datasets and we obtained good portability loss results in the Computer group and in the Physics group.

b.  How feasible it is to directly apply predictive models between courses that make a similar level of usage of Moodle. By analyzing the results shown in Tables 9–11, we can see that again, the best AUC values are obtained with the numerical datasets but they are not very high. However, the best lowest portability loss values are obtained with the discretized datasets in the range from 0.22 to 0.25. In this experiment, we did not find results as good as in the first one, but nevertheless, the results obtained are inside an acceptable range.

In conclusion, the results obtained in our experiments with our 24 university courses show that it is only feasible to directly transfer predictive models or apply them to different courses with an acceptable accuracy and without losing portability under some circumstances. In our case, only when we have used discretized datasets and the transfer is between courses of the same degree, although only in two specific degrees of the four degrees tested, the loss portability is feasible. Additionally, we have shown the four best prediction models obtained in each experiment (1 and 2) and type of dataset (numerical and discretized). We have obtained that the most important attributes or Moodle events that appear in the decision trees are about forums, assignments, choices, resource, and page. However, it is important to remark that prediction models when using discretized datasets not only provide the lowest AUC loss values, that is, the best portability, but they also provide smaller decision trees than numerical ones and they only use two comprehensible values (HIGH and LOW) in their attributes (instead of continues values with threshold) that make them much easier to interpret and transfer to other courses.

A limitation of this work is the fact that the best obtained models (decision trees) might not be directly actionable by the teachers of the other courses since those models may include activities or actions that their courses do not have. We have technically solved this problem by executing J48 as Wrapper classifier that addresses incompatible training and test data by building a mapping between the training data that a classifier has been built with and the incoming test instances' structure. Model attributes that are not found in the incoming instances receive missing values. We have to do it because there are some cases when the source course and the target course do not exactly use the same attributes (they do not have the same events in their logs). We also think that this issue can be one of the reasons why we have obtained low accuracy values when applying a model to other courses that use different activities.

Finally, this work is a first step in our research. The experimental results obtained show that new strategies must be explored in order to get more conclusive results. In the future, we want to carry out new experiments by using much more additional courses and other degrees in order to check how generalizable our results can be. We are also very interested in the next potential lines or future research lines:

- To use a low number of higher-level attributes proposed by pedagogues and instructors (such as ontology-based attributes) in order to analyze whether using only few high level semantic sets that remain same in all the course datasets has a positive influence on portability results.
- To use other factors (apart from the degree and the level of Moodle usage) that can be used to group different courses and analyze how portable the models are inside those groups, for example, the number of students, the number of assessment tasks, the methodology used by the instructor, etc. Furthermore, if we have a higher number of different courses, we can do groups inside groups, for example, for each degree, to group the course by the level of Moodle usage and the same used activities.

**Author Contributions:** Conceptualization, C.R., J.A.L., and J.L.-Z.; methodology, C.R. and J.A.L.; software, J.L.-Z.; validation, C.R., J.A.L. and J.L.-Z.; formal analysis, C.R.; investigation, J.L.-Z.; resources, C.R., and J.L.-Z.; data curation, J.L.-Z.; writing—original draft preparation, J.A.L. and J.L.-Z.; writing—review and editing, C.R., and J.A.L.; visualization, J.L.-Z.; supervision, C.R. and J.A.L.; project administration, C.R.; funding acquisition, C.R. All authors have read and agreed to the published version of the manuscript.

**Funding:** This research is supported by projects of the Spanish Ministry of Science and Technology TIN2017-83445-P.

**Conflicts of Interest:** The authors declare no conflict of interest.

## References

1. Dougiamas, M.; Taylor, P. Moodle: Using learning communities to create an open source course management system. In *EdMedia: World Conference on Educational Media and Technology*; The LearnTechLib: Waynesville, NC, USA, 2003; pp. 171–178.
2. Romero, C.; Ventura, S.; García, E. Data mining in course management systems: Moodle case study and tutorial. *Comput. Educ.* **2008**, *51*, 368–384. [CrossRef]
3. Romero, C.; Ventura, S. 2020. Educational Data mining and Learning Analytics: An updated survey. In *Wiley Interdisciplinary Reviews: Data Mining and Knowledge Discovery*; John Wiley and Sons: Hoboken, NJ, USA, 2011.

4. Romero, C.; Ventura, S. Data mining in education. *Wiley Interdiscip. Rev. Data Min. Knowl. Dis.* **2013**, *3*, 12–27. [CrossRef]
5. Romero, C.; Ventura, S. Educational data mining: A review of the state of the art. *IEEE Trans. Syst. Man Cybern. Part C (Appl. Rev.)* **2010**, *40*, 601–618. [CrossRef]
6. Romero, C.; Espejo, P.G.; Zafra, A.; Romero, J.R.; Ventura, S. Web usage mining for predicting final marks of students that use Moodle courses. *Comput. Appl. Eng. Educ.* **2013**, *21*, 135–146. [CrossRef]
7. Luna, J.M.; Castro, C.; Romero, C. MDM tool: A data mining framework integrated into Moodle. *Comput. Appl. Eng. Educ.* **2017**, *25*, 90–102. [CrossRef]
8. Tayebinik, M.; Puteh, M. Blended Learning or E-learning? *Int. Mag. Adv. Comput. Sci. Telecommun.* **2013**, *3*, 103–110.
9. Pan, S.J.; Yang, Q. A Survey on Transfer Learning. *IEEE Trans. Knowl. Data Eng.* **2010**, *22*, 1345–1359. [CrossRef]
10. Baker, R.S. Challenges for the Future of Educational Data Mining: The Baker Learning Analytics Prizes. *J. Educ. Data Min.* **2019**, *11*, 1–17.
11. Boyer, S.; Veeramachaneni, K. Transfer learning for predictive models in massive open online courses. In *Artificial Intelligence in Education. AIED 2015. Lecture Notes in Computer Science*; Conati, C., Heffernan, N., Mitrovic, A., Verdejo, M., Eds.; Springer: Cham, Switzerland, 2015; Volume 9112.
12. Boyer, S.; Veeramachaneni, K. Robust predictive models on MOOCs: Transferring knowledge across courses. In Proceedings of the 9th International Conference on Educational Data Mining, Raleigh, NC, USA, 29 June–2 July 2016; pp. 298–305.
13. Ding, M.; Wang, Y.; Hemberg, E.; O'Reilly, U.-M. Transfer learning using representation learning in massive open online courses. In Proceedings of the 9th International Conference on Learning Analytics & Knowledge (LAK19), Empe, AZ, USA, 4–8 March 2019; ACM: New York, NY, USA, 2019; pp. 145–154.
14. Gašević, D.; Dawson, S.; Rogers, T.; Gasevic, D. Learning Analytics should not promote one size fits all: The effects of instructional conditions in predicting academic success. *Int. High. Educ.* **2016**, *28*, 68–84. [CrossRef]
15. Kidzinsk, L.; Sharma, K.; Boroujeni, M.S.; Dillenbourg, P. On generalizability of MOOC models. In Proceedings of the 9th International Conference on Educational Data Mining (EDM), Raleigh, NC, USA, 29 June–2 July 2016; International Educational Data Mining Society: Buffalo, NY, USA, 2016.
16. Conijn, R.; Snijders, C.; Kleingeld, A.; Matzat, U. Predicting Student Performance from LMS Data: A Comparison of 17 Blended Courses Using Moodle LMS. *IEEE Trans. Learn. Technol.* **2017**, *10*, 10–29. [CrossRef]
17. Gardner, J.; Yang, Y.; Baker, R.S.; Brooks, C. Enabling end-to-end machine learning replicability: A case study in educational data mining. In Proceedings of the 1st Enabling Reproducibility in Machine Learning Workshop, Stockholmsmässan, Sweden, 25 June 2018.
18. Hunt, X.J.; Kabul, I.K.; Silva, J. Transfer learning for education data. In Proceedings of the ACM SIGKDD Conference, El Halifax, NS, Canada, 17 August 2017.
19. Weiss, K.; Khoshgoftaar, T.M.; Wang, D. A survey on transfer learning. *J. Big Data* **2016**, *3*, 9. [CrossRef]
20. Csurka, G.A. Comprehensive survey on domain adaptation for visual applications. A comprehensive survey on domain adaptation for visual applications. In *Domain Adaptation in Computer Vision Applications. Advances in Computer Vision and Pattern Recognition*; Csurka, G., Ed.; Springer: Cham, Switzerland, 2017.
21. Zeng, Z.; Chaturvedi, S.; Bhat, S.; Roth, D. DiAd: Domain adaptation for learning at scale. In Proceedings of the 9th International Conference on Learning Analytics & Knowledge (LAK19), Empe, AZ, USA, 4–8 March 2019; ACM: New York, NY, USA, 2019; pp. 185–194.
22. Sun, S.; Shi, H.; Wu, Y. A survey of multi-source domain adaptation. *Inform. Fusion* **2015**, *24*, 84–92. [CrossRef]
23. Japkowicz, N.; Stephen, S. The class imbalance problem: A systematic study. *Intell. Data Anal.* **2002**, *6*, 429–449. [CrossRef]
24. López-Zambrano, J.; Martinez, J.A.; Rojas, J.; Romero, C. A tool for preprocessing moodle data sets. In Proceedings of the 11th International Conference on Educational Data Mining, Buffalo, NY, USA, 15–18 July 2018; pp. 488–489.
25. Witten, I.H.; Frank, E.; Hall, M.A.; Pal, C.J. *Data Mining: Practical Machine Learning Tools and Techniques*; Morgan Kaufmann Publishers: San Francisco, CA, USA, 2016.
26. Quinlan, R. *C4.5: Programs for Machine Learning*; Morgan Kaufmann Publishers: San Mateo, CA, USA, 1993.

27. Hamoud, A.; Hashim, A.S.; Awadh, W.A. Predicting Student Performance in Higher Education Institutions Using Decision Tree Analysis. *Int. J. Interact. Multimed. Artif. Intell.* **2018**, *5*, 26–31. [CrossRef]
28. Wu, X.; Kumar, V.; Quinlan, J.R.; Ghosh, J.; Yang, Q.; Motoda, H.; McLachlan, G.J.; Ng, A.; Liu, B.; Philip, S.Y.; et al. Top 10 algorithms in data mining. *Knowl. Inform. Syst.* **2008**, *14*, 1–37. [CrossRef]
29. Thai-Nghe, N.; Busche, A.; Schmidt-Thieme, L. Improving academic performance prediction by dealing with class imbalance. In Proceedings of the 9th International Conference on Intelligent Systems Design and Applications, Pisa, Italy, 30 November–2 December 2009; pp. 878–883.
30. Käser, T.; Hallinen, N.R.; Schwartz, D.L. Modeling exploration strategies to predict student performance within a learning environment and beyond. In Proceedings of the 7th International Learning Analytics & Knowledge Conference, Vancouver, BC, Canada, 13–17 March 2017; pp. 31–40.
31. Santoso, L.W. The analysis of student performance using data mining. In *Advances in Computer Communication and Computational Sciences*; Springer: Berlin/Heidelberg, Germany, 2019; pp. 559–573.
32. Fawcett, T. An introduction to ROC analysis. *Pattern Recognit. Lett.* **2006**, *27*, 861–874. [CrossRef]
33. Gamulin, J.; Gamulin, O.; Kermek, D. Comparing classification models in the final exam performance prediction. In Proceedings of the 37th IEEE International Convention on Information and Communication Technology, Electronics and Microelectronics (MIPRO), Opatija, Croatia, 26–30 May 2014; pp. 663–668.
34. Whitehill, J.; Mohan, K.; Seaton, D.; Rosen, Y.; Tingley, D. MOOC Dropout Prediction: How to Measure Accuracy? In Proceedings of the Fourth Association for Computing Machinery on Learning @ Scale, Cambridge, MA, USA, 20–21 April 2017.

© 2020 by the authors. Licensee MDPI, Basel, Switzerland. This article is an open access article distributed under the terms and conditions of the Creative Commons Attribution (CC BY) license (http://creativecommons.org/licenses/by/4.0/).

Article

# Prediction of High Capabilities in the Development of Kindergarten Children

Yenny Villuendas-Rey [1], Carmen F. Rey-Benguría [2], Oscar Camacho-Nieto [1] and Cornelio Yáñez-Márquez [3,*]

[1] Centro de Innovación y Desarrollo Tecnológico en Cómputo, Instituto Politécnico Nacional, Ciudad de México 07700, Mexico; yenny.villuendas@gmail.com (Y.V.-R.); oscarc@cic.ipn.mx (O.C.-N.)
[2] Center for Pedagogical Studies and Department of Computer Sciences of the University of Ciego de Ávila, Ciego de Ávila 67100, Cuba; carmenrb2008@gmail.com
[3] Centro de Investigación en Computación, Instituto Politécnico Nacional, Ciudad de México 07700, Mexico
* Correspondence: coryanez@gmail.com; Tel.: +52-555-729-6000 (ext. 56505)

Received: 24 March 2020; Accepted: 2 April 2020; Published: 14 April 2020

**Abstract:** Analysis and prediction of children's behavior in kindergarten is a current need of the Cuban educational system. Despite such an early age, the kindergarten institutions are devoted to facilitate the integral children development. However, the early detection of high capabilities in a child is not always accomplished accurately; due to teachers being mostly focused on the performance of the children that are lagging behind to achieve their age range's stated goals. In addition, the amount of children with high capabilities is usually low, which makes the prediction an imbalanced data problem. Thus, such children tend to be misguided and overlaid, with a negative impact in their sociological development. The purpose of this research is to propose an efficient algorithm that enhances the prediction in the kindergarten children data. We obtain a useful set of instances and features, thus improving the Nearest Neighbor accuracy according to the Area under the Receiving Operating Characteristic curve measure. The obtained results are of great interest for Cuban educational system, regarding the rapidly and precise prediction of the presence or absence of high capabilities for integral personality development in kindergarten children.

**Keywords:** student performance; kindergarten children; nearest neighbor; imbalanced data

## 1. Introduction

The goal for children in the earliest stages of childhood in Cuba is to achieve the maximum possible integral development in each child. This goal imposes a challenge regarding the attention to the diverse kinds of children within the Cuban children's institutions belonging to the Ministry of Education. To this end there is a marked interest in detecting children that possess high development potential, since seldom do these children receive an education that is tailored to their potential.

Children with high development potential need specific learning strategies so that their development can be enhanced [1–3]. Cuban pedagogy wagers on teaching styles that respect individual differences and grant each child the ability to assimilate knowledge at his or her own pace, in a personalized way and according to each individual's needs. In this sense, several advances have been made in Cuba regarding attention to children with learning difficulties as well as those with special needs such as blind, deaf and motor-impaired children. However, attention to kindergarten children with high development potential has not received the same amount of attention, neither theoretical nor practical, in Cuba.

Among the causes of this phenomenon is the fact that high-capabilities children do not represent a threat for the performance scores of educational institutions. This results in teachers focusing on helping the children that are lagging behind to achieve their age range's stated goals; leaving high-capabilities children without specialized attention.

In addition, the theoretical foundation of high capabilities in the early stages of childhood has not been fully developed. Most research aimed at superior potential detection focuses on children over five years old [4,5], leaving a void in researching detection at an early age [6]. High capabilities can show up in fields so apart from each other, such as music and mathematics, which makes it a complex phenomenon that is hard to define and identify [7]. Even though psychological studies have been carried out to detect it, most of them involves the use of complex tests that need to be interpreted by highly-qualified personnel [6].

The absence of easily measurable indicators turns early detection of children with high capabilities into a nearly impossible task for the personnel in charge of preschool education in Cuba. This results in an affectation to the differentiated attention process that such children need, since their detection and further access to pedagogical attention is compromised. In several occasions, this lesser pedagogical stimulation results in the children not reaching their full intellectual potential and underachieving [2,8,9]. Additionally, the lack of differentiated attention results in a lessened social development in these children, who can end up isolated from their peers and therefore lacking the expected social skills for their age [10,11].

We want to emphasize that, in Cuba, that the strategies for the pedagogical management of children with high-potential exist, and are detailed in the methodological procedures of the education system. However, they are useless if the educational personnel in charge do not detect the children with high-potential, that is, if they do not detect the child, they do not apply what is established, and the development of the child is affected.

It is for these reasons that the Center for Pedagogical Studies of the University of Ciego de Ávila is undertaking field research aimed at improving pedagogical attention for high-potential children, which are classified as having special educational needs according to the Cuban educational system. This study aims to use easily measurable and understandable indicators along with advanced pattern recognition and data mining techniques as tools to determine the characteristics of gifted children. Thus, these children would be identified earlier and the design and application of pedagogical strategies tailored to them would become easier. In this way, the expectation is to achieve the best possible development for each child.

One of the requirements of computer-aided prediction in educational environments is the decision explanation capability of the used model. The Nearest Neighbor (NN) classifier [12] is one of the simplest yet accurate algorithms for non-parametric prediction, and its ability of returning the neighbors of an unclassified pattern makes it very suitable for soft sciences prediction problems. The NN classifier had been used previously to successfully solve educational problems in Cuba, such as family classification [13].

However, the NN classifier heavily depends on the dissimilarity function used. To detect children with high capabilities, the design of a specific dissimilarity function is needed, in order to successfully compare the children descriptions. To address this issue, the present paper includes the design of a specific dissimilarity function for the NN classifier in the detection of children with high capabilities for the integral personality development.

NN classifier is also sensitive to noisy features and mislabeled or outlier training instances, but these drawbacks may be overcome by the elimination of irrelevant features and instances. To preprocess the kindergarten children data, we propose a novel algorithm that selects both relevant features and instances. Our proposal integrates some elements of the Rough Set Theory [14] and a structuration strategy of logical-combinatorial pattern recognition [15].

## 2. Materials and Methods

### 2.1. The Kindergarten Children Data

The Cuban children of five years of age carried out their studies on the kindergarten facilities of the Cuban educational system. All of them are government facilities. The Cuban educational system is under two ministries: the Ministry of Education, and the Ministry of Superior Education. The last one is just for university and postgraduate education, while the former includes all other forms of education. The Ministry of Education includes special facilities for children with social and behavioral maladies (SBAM), as well as special facilities for children with disabilities (blind, deaf, motor problems, mental retardation, among others). Most of the educational population is under regular facilities, divided into four stages: nursery school (1–5 years old), elementary (6–11 years old), secondary (12–14 years old) and high school (15–17 years old, non-mandatory). Our research is focused on children of the preschool year, that is, children of five years old. Such children can be in classrooms at nursery school facilities or in classrooms at elementary school facilities. It is important to mention that the preschool year is the first mandatory school year in Cuba. Therefore, all children must be in the corresponding classroom.

The study of which features potentially intervene in the presence of high capabilities for development in children was the first step in this research. For this purpose, pedagogical and sociological research was taken into account [3–5,8,16], as well as the professional experience of teaching personnel at the preschool level. In addition, other situations that may influence detection such as environmental and socioeconomic factors were analyzed [2].

The process for data integration considered several sources of data: Data stored in school records (related to children performance and behavior), data collected from questionnaires and interviews to families (related to lifestyle, antecedents and others) and data stored in municipality records (related to environmental and socioeconomic factors). We want to emphasize that all such data were collected with the consent of the parents and the corresponding authorities. In addition, all surveys and questionnaires were carried out by qualified personnel, and all the instruments used had the corresponding validation. Figure 1 shows the data integration process.

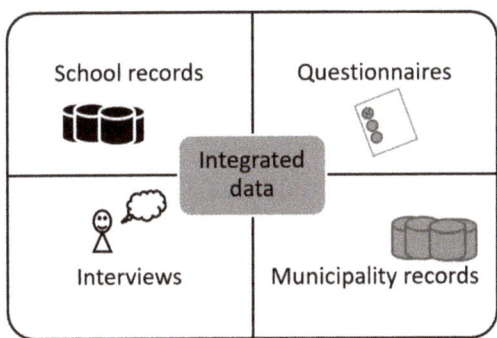

**Figure 1.** Data integration process.

The collected features are divided into five groups. The first one is related to the child and its antecedents. The features considered in this group were the child's age, its gender, whether its family supports its development (family), whether someone in the family has a history of high potential (antecedents), whether the child received schooling prior to entering preschool (prior education) and the performance of the teaching agent in charge of the child (performance).

The second group of features alludes to the attributes of the child's environment. These are the nutritional status of the child (nutrition), the hygiene level of the household (hygiene), the presence of healthy lifestyles at home (lifestyle), the structural conditions of the dwelling (dwelling) and the characteristics of the home's neighborhood (environment, considered as favorable, average or socially challenging).

The third attribute group evaluates the product of the child's activity within its educational institution. For this purpose, the situations considered were the quality of the child's schoolwork (quality), the quickness with which the child solved the required tasks (speed), the originality of the child's proposed solutions (originality) and the tendency to help other children with their tasks in addition to their own (help).

The fourth group of attributes focuses on characterizing the child's relationship with their educational environment. In this sense, the features analyzed are the level of interest and participation of the child in collective playtime (play), the child's tendency to interact with other children or to remain alone (relationships), whether the child prefers the company of an adult to that of other children (adult) and whether the child is active and energetic (activity).

The fifth feature group takes into account subjective aspects related to the perception that the child has of itself and of its environment. In this group are included: whether the child shows a heightened curiosity about its surroundings (curiosity), whether it shows a high level of interest in its environment (interest), whether the child becomes easily bored with simple tasks (boredom), whether the child feels superior to its peers (superiority) and its self-esteem level (self-esteem, measured as low or high). In all, 24 potential attributes were considered and are shown in Table 1.

**Table 1.** Description of the attributes used in the process of automatic detection of kindergarten children with high development capabilities.

| Group | No. | Name | Description |
|---|---|---|---|
| 1 | 1 | age | Age, in months, of the child (from 56 to 68 months) |
| | 2 | sex | Gender of the child (Male/Female) |
| | 3 | family | Whether the family encourages the child's development (Yes/No) |
| | 4 | antecedents | Whether there exists a history of high potential in the family (Yes/No) |
| | 5 | prior education | Did the child receive previous educational attention? (Yes/No) |
| | 6 | performance | Quality of the teacher's performance (Very good/Good/Average) |
| 2 | 7 | nutrition | The nutritional status of the child (Well nurtured/Poorly nurtured) |
| | 8 | environment | How is the environment, neighborhood or place where the child is growing up (Socially challenging/Average/ Favorable) |
| | 9 | house | Condition of the dwelling where the child lives (Good/Average/Bad) |
| | 10 | hygiene | Hygiene conditions of the dwelling (Good/Poor) |
| | 11 | lifestyle | Lifestyle of the family (Healthy/Unhealthy) |
| 3 | 12 | originality | Does the child like to be different or non-repetitive? (Yes/No) |
| | 13 | help | Does the child like to help other children with their tasks, in addition to its own? (Yes/No) |
| | 14 | quality | The quality of the child's schoolwork (Very good/Good/Average/Poor) |
| | 15 | speed | The speed with which the child works (Fast/Average/Slow) |
| 4 | 16 | activity | Is the child active and energetic? (Yes/No) |
| | 17 | relationships | Does the child enjoy the company of its peers or does it prefer to be alone? (Socializes well/Usually alone) |
| | 18 | adult | Whether the child prefers the company of an adult over being with other children (Yes/No) |
| | 19 | play | Interest and participation of the child in collective play (High/Low) |
| 5 | 20 | curiosity | Whether the child is curious and likes to learn new things (Yes/No) |
| | 21 | interest | Whether the child shows interest in its surroundings (Yes/No) |
| | 22 | boredom | Is the child easily bored when faced with easy tasks? (Yes/No) |
| | 23 | self-esteem | The degree of self-esteem that the child has (High/Low) |
| | 24 | superiority | Does the child feel superior to his peers? (Yes/No) |

Taking into account the attributes that are potentially influential in the characterization of high-capabilities Cuban preschool children, a data collection process was undertaken.

For this purpose, these features were evaluated in children from five preschool classrooms in the municipality of Ciego de Ávila, Cuba, in the school years 2014–2018. The teaching personnel was in charge of the description of its own students, except for attribute #6, performance, which was input by the administrative staff in charge of the teachers, according to the performance evaluation of each worker. In total, we obtained the description of 1032 children. Of them, 91 were marked as having high-potential, for an imbalance ratio of 11.34.

It is important to mention that during the data collection process, not every attribute was able to be obtained for every student; in the majority of cases, this was because the teacher was unable to find the right information or was unsure about its accuracy. This resulted in the presence of missing values in the description of the children.

## 2.2. Data Mining Algorithms

In order to perform automated detection of high-capabilities children, data mining and pattern recognition techniques were employed. It is known that not every pattern classifier is able to explain its inner workings [17]. It is for this reason that for this research it was decided to use a classifier (Nearest Neighbor, NN) [12] that is able to explain how it arrived at a determined prediction.

NN was proposed by Cover and Hart back in 1967. It stores a set of training instances, and when a new instance arrives, it computes its distance (or dissimilarity) with respect to every instance in the training set. Then, it classifies the novel instance with the class of its closest (nearest) instance.

In addition, the presence of missing values represents a challenge for most classification algorithms [18], which complicates their application to problems presenting this kind of data. Along with this, most classifiers assume the presence of either numerical or categorical attributes, and are not prepared to deal with mixed data. In the problem of detecting high-capabilities Cuban preschoolers we have 23 categorical features, one numerical feature (age) and several incomplete descriptions. This makes the application of some pattern classifiers difficult.

To apply the Nearest Neighbor classifier to the data we need to define, with the support of educational specialists, a dissimilarity function to compare children descriptions. The designed function is non-symmetric, given that the feature comparison criterion of feature "house" is non-symmetric. Having two children description $n_i$ and $n_j$ the dissimilarity function to compare them is given as:

$$d(n_i, n_j) = \sum_{k=1}^{l} d_k(n_i, n_j) \qquad (1)$$

where $l$ denotes the amount of features, and $d_k$ is the feature comparison criterion for the k-th feature.

For the numeric attribute "age", we used normalized difference as comparison criterion, as in Equation (2). $max_k$ and $min_k$ denote the maximum and minimum values of the k-th feature.

$$d_k(n_i, n_j) = \frac{|n_i[k] - n_j[k]|}{max_k - min_k} \qquad (2)$$

Additionally, we used classical comparison criteria, as in Equation (3) for the categorical features with two admissible values (features 2, 3, 4, 5, 7, 10–13 and 16–24). For the other features, we used the comparison criterion defined in the corresponding table.

$$d_k(n_i, n_j) = \begin{cases} 1 \text{ if } n_i[k] \neq n_j[k] \\ 0 \text{ if } n_i[k] = n_j[k] \end{cases} \qquad (3)$$

To handle missing values (denoted by "?"), we decided to set the dissimilarity value $d_k(n_i, n_j) = 0.5$ if $n_i[k] =? \lor n_j[k] = $ "?", as numeric and categorical comparison criteria are defined between the [0,1] interval. For the feature "speed", we use the feature values dissimilarity matrix showed in Table 2 as comparison criterion.

Table 2. Comparison criterion for feature "speed".

|         | Quick | Average | Slow |
|---------|-------|---------|------|
| Quick   | 0     | 0.5     | 1    |
| Average | 0.5   | 0       | 0.5  |
| Slow    | 1     | 0.5     | 0    |

In addition, features "quality", "performance", "environment" and "house" have comparison criteria showed in Tables 3–6, respectively.

Table 3. Comparison criterion for feature "work quality".

|           | Very Good | Good | Regular | Bad |
|-----------|-----------|------|---------|-----|
| Very Good | 0         | 0.1  | 0.4     | 1   |
| Good      | 0.1       | 0    | 0.2     | 0.7 |
| Regular   | 0.4       | 0.2  | 0       | 0.6 |
| Bad       | 1         | 0.7  | 0.6     | 0   |

Table 4. Comparison criterion for feature "teacher".

|           | Very Good | Good | Average |
|-----------|-----------|------|---------|
| Very Good | 0         | 0.4  | 1       |
| Good      | 0.4       | 0    | 0.4     |
| Average   | 1         | 0.6  | 0       |

The similarities among feature values for the attributes "environment" and "house" were determined according to the criteria of specialist of the Municipal Investment Unit of Dwelling (UMIV), in Ciego de Avila, Cuba.

Table 5. Comparison criterion for feature "environment".

|                      | Favorable | Average | Socially Challenging |
|----------------------|-----------|---------|----------------------|
| Favorable            | 0         | 0.5     | 1                    |
| Average              | 0.5       | 0       | 0.5                  |
| Socially challenging | 1         | 0.5     | 0                    |

Table 6. Comparison criterion for feature "house".

|         | Good | Average | Bad |
|---------|------|---------|-----|
| Good    | 0    | 0.7     | 1   |
| Average | 0.3  | 0       | 0.5 |
| Bad     | 1    | 0.6     | 0   |

As mentioned earlier, the Nearest Neighbor classifier is sensitive to noisy or mislabeled instances, as well as to irrelevant attributes. To overcome these drawbacks, we propose a novel algorithm for selecting both useful cases and features. The proposed algorithm is described in the next section.

## 3. Data Preprocessing

The proposed algorithm is based on Rough Set Theory (RST), and it is inspired in some elements of selecting pools of classifiers. The next section is devoted to the explanation of some basic RST concepts.

### 3.1. Fundamentals of Rough Set Theory

Pawlak introduced Rough Set Theory in 1982 [14] to deal with vague and imprecise information. Since then, it have been successfully applied to data preprocessing in both cases and attributes selection [19]. Let $A$ be a set of features and a non-empty set $U$ (universe) of instances described by the features in $A$; the pair $(U,A)$ is denoted as the information system. If every element of $U$ has also an additional decision feature $c$, then it is obtained a decision system, $DS(U, A \cup \{c\})$, where $c \notin A$ [14].

Classical (often called Pawlak's) RST considers that a feature $A_i \in A$ distinguishes an instance $x$ from another instance $y$, and it is denoted by $Distinguishes(A_i, x, y)$, if and only if all their feature vales are different; that is, $Distinguishes(A_i, x, y) \leftrightarrow x(i) \neq y(i), \forall A_i \in A$.

Every subset of features $B$ of $A$ has associated a binary inseparability relation $IND_B(U)$, which is formed by the set of pairs of instances indistinguishable by the relation; that is, the instances having the same feature values in the set of features B. Formally, $IND_B(U) = \{(x, y) \in U \times U : \sim Distinguishes(B_i, x, y), \forall B_i \in B\}$. An inseparability or indiscernibility relation defined by forming subsets of elements from U having the same feature values for a subset of features $B \subseteq A$, is an equivalence relation.

The indistinguishable instances form an equivalence class. The equivalence class of an instance $x$ with respect to the indiscernibility relation induced by the features in $B$, is denoted by $[x]_B$.

RST incorporates a very interesting concept, the reduct definition. A reduct is a set of features $B \subseteq A$ such that $IND_B(X) = IND_A(X)$; that is, both $B$ and $A$ generate the same partition of the universe $U$. In Pawlak's words "a reduct is the minimal set of attributes that enables the same classification of elements of the universe as the whole set of attributes. In other words, attributes that do not belong to a reduct are superfluous with regard to classification of elements of the universe" [14].

Following these considerations, the computation of the set of reducts in a dataset is a kind of feature selection (by deleting those features, which do not belong to the obtained reducts), and have been extensively used [20]. In this research, we include the computation of all reducts to perform feature selection the proposed algorithm.

RST also considers that every concept can be roughly approximated. Let it be a decision system $DS = (U, A \cup \{c\})$ and let it be the sets $B$ and $X$ such that $B \subseteq A$ and $X \subseteq U$. The concept $X$ can be roughly approximated using the information contained in $B$ by constructing the $B$-inferior (B-lower) and $B$-superior (B-upper) approximations, denoted by $INF_B(X)$ and $SUP_B(X)$, respectively; and defined as follows: $INF_B(X) = \{x \in U : [x]_B \subseteq X\}$ and $SUP_B(X) = \{x \in U : [x]_B \cap X \neq \emptyset\}$. The instances in $INF_B(X)$ are with certainty members of $X$ while the instances in $SUP_B(X)$ are possible members of $X$. The limit region for the concept $X$ is computed as $LIM_B(X) = SUP_B(X) - INF_B(X)$.

The information in the lower and upper approximations of a rough set have been used for the task of selecting relevant instances [21]. In this paper, we also used that information. However, we use Minimum Neighborhood Rough Sets (MNRS) [21] instead of Pawlak's.

*3.2. Proposed Preprocessing Technique*

The proposed algorithm consists of three phases. The first phase consists of the parallel selection of relevant features and relevant instances of the training set. Then, the second phase obtains a candidate training sets, composed by the selected features and instances. Finally, the candidate training sets are merged in the third phase of the algorithm. As the main highlights of the algorithm, we consider its ability to handle mixed and incomplete datasets, with class imbalance. The three phases of the proposed algorithm, named FIS-SM (Feature and Instance Selection, with Sigmoid Merging) are described in detail in the next subsections.

3.2.1. Parallel Computation of Relevant Features and Instances

The algorithm starts by executing two separated processes over the training set: selection of relevant feature sets, and selection of relevant instances (Figure 2). The selection of relevant feature sets consist on the computation of all reducts of the training sets, using the LEX algorithm [22].

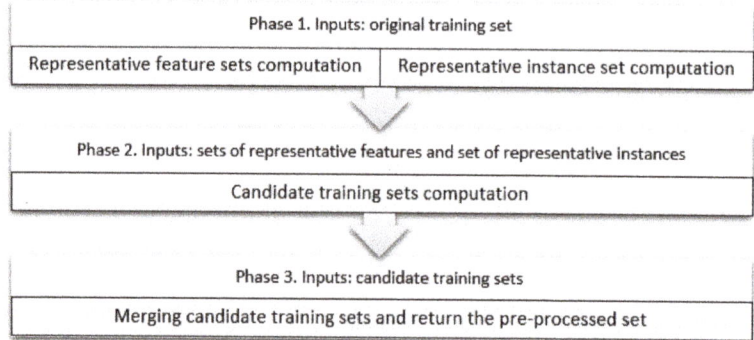

**Figure 2.** Schematic of the proposed algorithm.

On the other hand, to remove irrelevant instances, we decide to preserve decision boundaries, to keep as much as possible the minority class examples. We introduce a condensation algorithm, based on Minimum Neighborhood Rough Sets (MNRS) [21]. We selected MNRS due to its ability of handling missing and incomplete decision systems, and non-symmetric similarity functions. Those characteristics make MNRS very suitable to solving the preprocessing of the Cuban kindergarten data.

In a Minimum Neighborhood Rough Set, the positive and limit regions of the decision classes are computed according to the relations between instances in a Maximum Similarity Graph (MSG). A MSG is a directed graph such that each instance is connected with its most similar instance. Formally, two instances x and y belonging to the set X, for an arc in a MSG if and only if $sim(x.y) = max\{sim(x,z)\} \forall z \in X$ where $sim(,)$ is a similarity function. The connected components of such graphs are named compact sets. Let $\theta$ be the arcs in a MSG, the lower approximation of a decision class $Y_i$ with respect to the feature set $A$, is defined as:

$$INF_A(Y_i) = \{x \in Y_i : \forall (x,y) \in \theta, \ y \in Y_i\} \tag{4}$$

The limit region of a decision class $Y_i$ is is given by the following:

$$LIM_A(Y_i) = \{x \in Y_i : \exists (x,y) \in \theta, \ y \not\in Y_i\} \tag{5}$$

The algorithm proposed for selecting relevant instances consist on computing the limit region of each decision class, and using compact sets [15] to structure each class. Compact sets are the connected components of a Maximum Similarity Graph, and they have been used for instance selection, with very good results [23].

Let be U a universe of instances and a similarity function $sim(x,y)$ where $x, y \in U$. A subset $cs \neq \emptyset$ from U is a compact set if and only if:

(a) $\forall x_j \in U \left[ x_i \in cs \wedge \left( \begin{array}{c} \max_{\substack{x_k \in U \\ x_k \neq x_i}} \{sim(x_i, x_k)\} = sim(x_i, x_j) \\ \vee \max_{\substack{x_k \in U \\ x_k \neq x_i}} \{sim(x_k, x_i)\} = sim(x_j, x_i) \end{array} \right) \right] \Rightarrow x_j \in cs$

(b) $\forall x_i, x_j \in cs, \exists x_{i_1}, \cdots, x_{i_q} \in cs \left[ \begin{array}{c} x_i = x_{i_1} \wedge x_j = x_{i_q} \wedge \forall p \{1, \cdots, q-1\} \\ \left[ \begin{array}{c} \max_{\substack{x_k \in U \\ x_k \neq x_{i_p}}} \{sim(x_{i_p}, x_t)\} = sim(x_{i_p}, x_{i_{p+1}}) \\ \vee \max_{\substack{x_k \in U \\ x_k \neq x_{i_p}}} \{sim(x_{i_{p+1}}, x_t)\} = sim(x_{i_{p+1}}, x_{i_p}) \end{array} \right] \end{array} \right]$

(c) Every isolated instance is a degenerated compact set.

After computed the compact sets, for each of them the algorithm finds a representative prototype, which is added to the prototype set, along with the instances in the limit region. This guarantees the preservation of the decision boundaries, as well as the inner representation of the class structure. The representative prototypes are computed as the instances that maximize the average similarity with respect to all instances in the compact set.

The pseudo code of the main steps for the proposed instance selection algorithm is presented as follows in Algorithm 1.

**Algorithm 1.** Pseudocode of the proposed algorithm.

Algorithm to compute the representative instance set
Inputs: training set X
Output: representative set C
Steps:
1. $C = \emptyset$
2. For each decision class $Y_i$

   $C = C \cup LIM(Y_i)$ (as in Equation (5))
   Structure $Y_i$ in compact sets.
   For each compact set CS
   $C = C \cup r$ where $r = \underset{x \in CS}{\operatorname{argmax}} \left\{ \frac{\sum_{y \in CS} sim(x,y)}{|CS|} \right\}$

3. Return C

The obtained representative instance set along with the set of all reducts is given as inputs to the second phase of the proposed algorithms.

### 3.2.2. Computation of Candidate Training Sets

The second phase of the algorithm begins with the representation of the selected instances using only the features in the minimal reducts sets. That is, every minimal reduct will be used as the feature set to represent the selected instances (Figure 3) obtaining as many candidate training sets as minimal reducts computed.

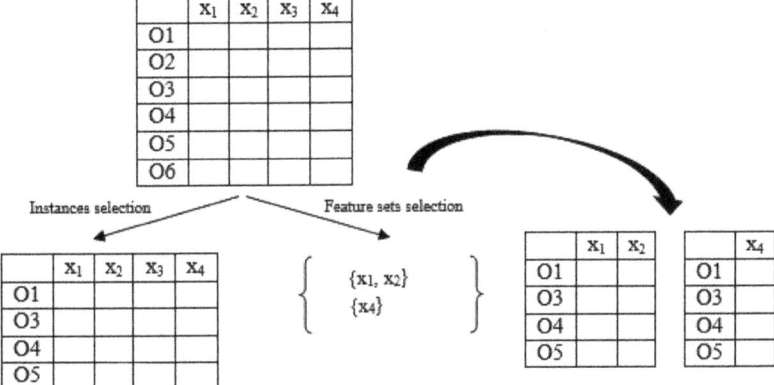

**Figure 3.** Representation of the selected instances according to the reducts in the feature sets.

Then, each candidate training set is postprocessed, by the application of the CSE algorithm [23] for further instance selection (Figure 4). Our proposal uses the CSE algorithm for additional instance selection because CSE is able to handle mixed and incomplete data descriptions, and preserves the inner structure of classes, due to it has the property of been subclass consistent [23].

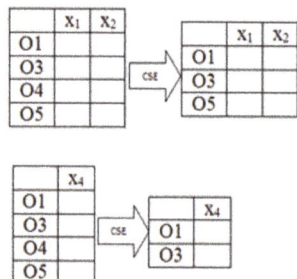

**Figure 4.** Additional instance selection in the candidate training sets.

### 3.2.3. Merging of Candidate Training Sets

Although the application of extra instance selection in the second phase of the algorithm may cause some information loss, the merging phase compensates it. When two candidate training sets are merged, the resulting set contains the instances and features of both parent sets (Figure 5).

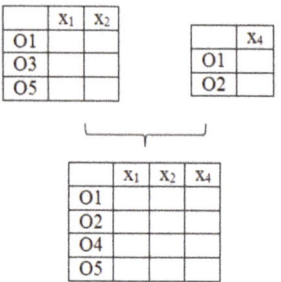

**Figure 5.** Merging of two candidate training sets.

We viewed the merging process of candidate training sets as an equivalent of the selection of classifiers to form a classifier ensemble. In classifier selection to form ensembles, there is a pool of candidate classifiers, and they must be combined to form an ensemble [24]. In the merging process, there is a pool of candidate training sets, and they must be merged to form the final training set (Figure 6).

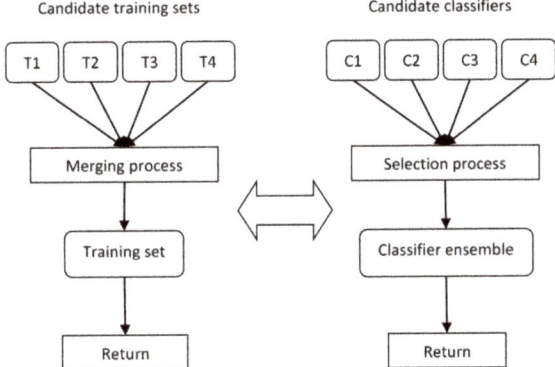

**Figure 6.** Resemblance between classifier ensemble selection (right) and candidate training set merging (left).

To carry out the merging phase, we introduced a novel procedure (Algorithm 2), inspired in the SA algorithm [25] to select a classifier ensemble form a pool of classifiers. SA uses classifier correlation and diversity to guide the selection.

---

**Algorithm 2.** Pseudocode of the proposed merging strategy.

---

Merging of candidate training sets
Inputs: $\Phi$: correlation measure, $T$: set of candidate training sets, $O$: original training set
Output: preprocessed training set *tbest*
Steps:

1. Consider $tbest \in T$ as the candidate training set with higher consistency factor (Equation (7)) and *best* as the associated consistency factor value.
2. *possible = true*
3. Select the candidate training set $t \in T$ less correlated with *tbest*, as $L = \mathrm{argmin}_{t \in T} \Phi(tbest, t)$
4. While $(best < \gamma(L \cup tbest))$ and (possible)

    $tbest = L \cup tbest$
    Select the most accurate candidate training set to merge with the current *tbest*,
    $S = \mathrm{argmax}_{t \in T} Sig(tbest \cup t)$, where $Sig(tbest \cup t) = \frac{1}{|O|} \sum_{o \in O} sigmoid(\rho)$.
    If $\gamma(tbest \cup S) > \gamma(tbest)$ then $tbest \leftarrow tbest \cup L$
    else *possible = false*

5. Return *tbest*

---

We considered the RST measure consistency factor [14] as a degree of performance of the candidate training sets. The consistency factor ($\gamma$) considers the amount of instances in the lower approximation of concepts, with respect to the total amount of instances. Thus, the graters $\gamma$, greater amount of instances certainly belong to their classes.

Let us considered a set of instances $X$ described by a set of features $A$, and a decision attribute $c$. The partition of the set $X$ according to the decision attribute form the set $Y = \{Y_1, \ldots, Y_k\}$. The lower approximation of the corresponding decision system $DS(X, A \cup c)$ is given by:

$$INF_A(Y) = \cup_{Y_i \in Y} INF_A(Y_i) \qquad (6)$$

Then, the consistency factor of the decision system is defined as:

$$\gamma(A, Y) = \frac{|INF_A(Y)|}{|X|} \qquad (7)$$

Taking into consideration the values of the consistency factor, we considered the candidate training set with higher $\gamma$ as the current best, *tbest*.

Then, the procedure selects the less correlated candidate training set, with respect to *tbest*. If the merging of both sets outperforms the $\gamma$ of *tbest*, *tbest* is replaced by the resultant training set, and an iterative process is carried out until no improvements are achieved. Otherwise, *tbest* is returned as the final preprocessed training set.

We used the sigmoid function as well as in [25] to potentiate the correct classification of as much instances as possible. For this task, we computed the Nearest Neighbor classification of the instances in the original (unprocessed) training set and we followed a procedure based on the sigmoid function. If both candidate training sets correctly classifies a case belonging to the original training set, then $\rho = 5$. On the contrary, if both of them give an incorrect classification, $\rho = -5$. Finally, if only one correctly classifies the case, $\rho = 0$.

We used the Q measure recommended in [26] as a training set correlation measure. The Q measure has as advantages that it is independent of the amount of sets to considered, and obtained a zero value for independent training sets. By considered the correlation of the candidate training sets, the proposed merging strategy avoided fusions with no direct impact on the classifier accuracy.

## 4. Results and Discussion

In this section, we investigated the performance of the proposed FIS-SM algorithm for data preprocessing. We carried out two different numerical experiments. The first addressed the suitability of FIS-SM in selecting relevant instances and feature to solve the classification of Cuban kindergarten children with high capabilities. The second experiment evaluates the performance of the proposal over international datasets.

### 4.1. Results for Educational Data

As we were dealing with an imbalanced dataset, with imbalance ratio IR = 8.1, we used as a classifier performance measure the Area under the ROC curve (AUC). AUC is a performance measure that takes into consideration the amount of correctly classified instances of positive and negative classes [27]. This characteristic makes AUC suitable for the evaluation of classifier performance in imbalanced datasets, due to its lack of bias in favor of the majority class.

The AUC is based on the computation of two measures: the True Positive Rate (recall or sensitivity) and the True Negative Rate (specificity).

Table 7. Confusion matrix for a two-class classification problem.

| Examples | Classified as | |
|---|---|---|
| | Positive | Negative |
| Positive | True positive (*tp*) | False negative (*fn*) |
| Negative | False positive (*fp*) | True negative (*tn*) |

Let us consider the confusion matrix of Table 7. The True Positive Rate (TPR) and True Negative Rate (TNR) are computed as follows:

$$TPR = \frac{tp}{tp + fn} \qquad (8)$$

$$TNR = \frac{tn}{tn + fp} \qquad (9)$$

Accordingly, the Area under the ROC curve for a discrete classifier is computed as:

$$AUC = \frac{TPR + TNR}{2} \tag{10}$$

In addition to classifier performance, we computed the instance reduction rate and feature reduction rate. As the Nearest Neighbor classifier stores the training set in memory, and also compares the new instances to be classified with the ones stored in the training set, both instance and feature reduction measures indicate the amount of computational cost saved with the preprocessing algorithm.

We compared FIS-SM with respect to previously reported algorithms. Several genetic based algorithms were selected [28], such as the Genetic Algorithm proposed by Ishibushi and Nakashima (IN-GA) [29], the Genetic Algorithm proposed by Kuncheva and Jain (KJ-GA) [30] and the Genetic Algorithm proponed by Ahn, Kim and Han (AKH-GA) [31]. The hybrid Evolutionary Instance Selection enhanced by Rough set based Feature Selection (EIS-RFS) algorithm [19] was also selected for comparison. In addition, the deterministic algorithm for instance and feature selection proposed by Villuendas-Rey et al., the Testors and Compact set based Combined Selection (TCCS) [32] were considered in the comparison.

We also computed the results of the NN classifier without any preprocessing (ONN). The parameters for the compared algorithms are shown in Table 8. We used the corresponding papers for such parameter configuration.

Table 8. Parameters used by algorithms under comparison.

| Algorithm | Parameters |
|---|---|
| AKH-GA | Iterations: 20<br>Population count: 200 individuals<br>Crossover probability: 0.7<br>Mutation probability: 0.1 per bit |
| EIS-RFS | MAX_EVALUATIONS: 10,000<br>Population count: 50<br>Crossover probability: 1.0<br>Mutation probability: 0.005 per bit<br>a: 0.5, b: 0.75<br>MaxGamma: 1.0<br>UpdateFS: 100 |
| IN-GA | Iterations: 500<br>Population count: 50 individuals<br>Crossover probability: 1.0<br>Mutation probability for features: 0.01 per bit<br>Mutation probability for instances: $p(1 \rightarrow 0) = 0.1$ and $p(0 \rightarrow 1) = 0.01$ |
| KJ-GA | Iterations: 100<br>Population count: 10 individuals<br>Crossover probability: 1.0<br>Mutation probability: 0.1 per bit |
| TCCS | No user-defined parameter |

In Table 9 we show the results of the compared algorithms over the kindergarten dataset. We highlight in bold the best results.

Table 9. Performance of the algorithms to predict high capabilities in kindergarten children.

| Algorithm | ONN | TCCS | EIS-RFS | AKH-GA | IN-GA | KJ-GA | FIS-SM |
|---|---|---|---|---|---|---|---|
| AUC | 0.94 | 0.94 | 0.93 | 0.87 | 0.64 | 0.76 | **0.95** |
| Instance Reduction | 0.00 | 0.70 | 0.44 | 0.45 | 0.21 | 0.68 | **0.93** |
| Feature Reduction | 0.00 | 0.52 | 0.00 | 0.71 | 0.52 | 0.43 | **0.73** |

The results show that the proposed FIS-SM increased the classifier performance according to the AUC measure, using fewer instances and features. FIS-SM obtained an AUC very close to the perfect classification, with less than 7% of instances and with almost 27% of features. Having a reduced set of instances and features decreased the computational cost of the Nearest Neighbor classifier, and reduced the execution time. Let $n$ be the number of instances and $m$ the number of features in the training set. The classification cost of NN classifier was bounded by $O(n \times m)$, due to each instance to be classified need to be compared using a similarity function with an average cost of $O(m)$, with respect to every instance in the training set. Considering the results of the proposed FIS-SM, the cost after preprocessing will be $O(0.93 \times n \times 0.73 \times m)$.

In addition, the FIS-SM algorithm outperformed all compared algorithms according to AUC, instance reduction and feature reduction. The above results show the high quality of the proposed algorithm, and its ability to obtain a useful set of both cases and features in mixed, incomplete and imbalanced scenarios.

Considering the experiments carried out, we selected as relevant the features that were included in at least one fold. Therefore, our research points out that features 4, 13, 18, 19, 20, 21, 22 and 24 (antecedents, help, adult, play, curiosity, interest, boredom and superiority) are relevant to determine if a child has or has not high-potential for development.

Having an accurate automatic classification of kindergarten children allows the educational personnel to improve the pedagogical attention for high-potential children. The automatic classification alerts the personnel of the presence of gifted children, and the design and application of pedagogical strategies tailored to them would become easier. In addition, we see that the number of high-potential children in a classroom is usually very low. In the data collected from 2014 to 2018, the classroom having the greater number of such children only have four of them. Therefore, guaranteeing an automatic classification with high AUC (as the 0.95 obtained by our proposal) is a significant result, and a major aid to educational personnel in charge of the children.

*4.2. Results for Repository Data*

In addition to the excellent results obtained over the Cuban kindergarten dataset, we also consider that it was necessary to test the performance of the proposed algorithm over well-known repository datasets. To accomplish this task, we selected eight datasets from the UCI Machine Learning repository [33]. Table 10 gives the description of them. The IR column represents the imbalance ratio of the dataset, computed as the ratio between the instances in the majority and minority classes.

Table 10. Description of repository databases.

| Datasets | Nominal Attributes | Numeric Attributes | Instances | Classes | Missing Values | Imbalance Ratio |
|---|---|---|---|---|---|---|
| breast-w | 0 | 9 | 699 | 2 | | 1.90 |
| credit-a | 9 | 6 | 690 | 2 | x | 1.25 |
| diabetes | 0 | 8 | 768 | 2 | | 1.87 |
| heart-c | 7 | 6 | 303 | 5 | x | 1.20 |
| hepatitis | 13 | 6 | 155 | 2 | x | 3.87 |
| labor | 6 | 8 | 57 | 2 | | 1.86 |
| wine | 0 | 13 | 178 | 3 | x | 1.47 |
| zoo | 16 | 1 | 101 | 7 | | 10.46 |

To consider the imbalanced class scenario, we included five datasets having $IR > 1.5$. We also considered among the selected datasets seven having mixed numerical and categorical features, and five incomplete datasets.

To apply the NN classifier over the repository data, we selected as the dissimilarity function the HEOM dissimilarity [34]. We used the five-fold cross validation procedure and averaged the results. We selected five-fold cross validation due to its suitability for handling the imbalanced nature of some of the datasets [35].

As in the previous experiment, we computed the instance reduction ratio and the feature reduction ratio for the Nearest Neighbor classifier. However, to compare the classifier performance we could not use the Area under the ROC curve measure.

As the AUC is only applicable for a two class problems and we were dealing with several multiclass imbalanced data problems, and it is well known that classifier accuracy is biased to favor the majority class, we considered the computation of the average accuracy by classes (Avg_Acc) as a classifier performance measure [36].

Let be $Y = \{Y_1, \cdots, Y_l\}$ the set of classes the averaged accuracy by classes is computed by:

$$Avg\_Acc = \frac{1}{|Y|} \sum_{Y_i \in Y} \frac{1}{|Y_i|} \sum_{x \in Y_i} well(x)$$
$$well(x) = \begin{cases} 1 & \text{if } x \text{ is correctly classified} \\ 0 & \text{otherwise} \end{cases} \quad (11)$$

We considered that the computation of the average accuracy by classes eliminates the bias of the traditional classifier accuracy and allows us to compare the classifier performance over multiclass imbalanced datasets. This computation is also provided in the summary results of the Explorer module of the Weka software [37].

Table 11 offers the Avg_Acc results of the Nearest Neighbor classifier without preprocessing (ONN), as well as the results of TCCS, EIS-RFS and the proposed FIS-SM. Best results are highlighted in bold.

Table 11. Averaged accuracy by classes obtained by the algorithms.

| Datasets | ONN | TCCS | EIS-RFS | AKH-GA | IN-GA | KJ-GA | FIS-SM |
|---|---|---|---|---|---|---|---|
| breast-w | 0.94 | 0.94 | 0.95 | 0.94 | 0.91 | 0.91 | **0.96** |
| credit-a | 0.81 | 0.78 | 0.78 | 0.79 | 0.64 | 0.63 | **0.85** |
| diabetes | 0.68 | 0.58 | 0.65 | 0.64 | 0.63 | 0.60 | **0.69** |
| heart-c | 0.70 | 0.69 | **0.77** | 0.64 | 0.63 | 0.60 | 0.71 |
| hepatitis | 0.63 | 0.71 | 0.63 | **0.79** | 0.73 | 0.76 | 0.76 |
| tic-tac-toe | 0.76 | 0.73 | 0.53 | 0.75 | 0.70 | **0.84** | 0.79 |
| wine | **0.96** | 0.41 | **0.96** | 0.81 | 0.82 | 0.83 | **0.96** |
| zoo | **0.97** | 0.90 | **0.97** | 0.80 | 0.71 | 0.81 | 0.95 |

The averaged accuracy results over the repository datasets favored the proposed FIS-SM, which obtained the best classifier performance in four datasets. We considered that this behavior was due to FIS-SM being designed to deal with imbalanced data, a key feature that allows it to maintain good classifications in the datasets.

However, according to the instance retention rate (Table 12) the EIS-RFS algorithm was the best. In all datasets it achieved the best instance reduction rates, with over 93% reduction. On the other hand, the proposed FIS-SM had good results, around 35% reduction.

Table 12. Instance retention results of the algorithms.

| Datasets | TCCS | EIS-RFS | AKH-GA | IN-GA | KJ-GA | FIS-SM |
|---|---|---|---|---|---|---|
| breast-w | 0.32 | **0.02** | 0.50 | 0.47 | 0.46 | 0.25 |
| credit-a | 0.51 | **0.01** | 0.49 | 0.49 | 0.48 | 0.32 |
| diabetes | 0.58 | **0.01** | 0.49 | 0.47 | 0.48 | 0.28 |
| heart-c | 0.59 | **0.01** | 0.49 | 0.47 | 0.48 | 0.30 |
| hepatitis | 0.56 | **0.03** | 0.51 | 0.43 | 0.46 | 0.30 |
| labor | 0.75 | **0.07** | 0.52 | 0.51 | 0.48 | 0.39 |
| wine | 0.95 | **0.04** | 0.51 | 0.45 | 0.45 | 0.37 |
| zoo | 0.52 | **0.05** | 0.49 | 0.49 | 0.47 | 0.12 |

According to feature retention (Table 13), the best algorithm was IN-GA, with the best results for six of the eight datasets. TCCS and FIS-SM had a similar performance. This is due to both algorithms using the set of minimal reducts to obtain feature sets. The EIS-RFS algorithm deleted no features, but for only three datasets.

**Table 13.** Feature retention results of the algorithms.

| Datasets | TCCS | EIS-RFS | AKH-GA | IN-GA | KJ-GA | FIS-SM |
|---|---|---|---|---|---|---|
| breast-w | 1.00 | 1.00 | 0.62 | **0.40** | 0.49 | 1.00 |
| credit-a | 0.87 | 1.00 | 0.58 | **0.39** | 0.45 | 0.87 |
| diabetes | 1.00 | 1.00 | 0.63 | **0.31** | 0.40 | 1.00 |
| heart-c | 0.81 | 1.00 | 0.63 | **0.31** | 0.40 | 0.83 |
| hepatitis | 0.67 | 1.00 | 0.60 | **0.43** | 0.54 | 0.73 |
| labor | 0.53 | 0.49 | **0.41** | 0.44 | 0.49 | 0.53 |
| wine | 0.73 | 0.88 | 0.52 | **0.44** | 0.45 | 0.73 |
| zoo | 0.43 | **0.12** | 0.44 | 0.43 | 0.54 | 0.43 |

In addition to the above experiments that supported the excellent performance of the proposed FIS-SM over imbalanced datasets, we carried out a statistical test to determine if there exist significant differences in the performance of FIS-SM with respect to previously reported algorithms.

We used the Wilcoxon test [35] to compare the results. This is a non-parametric statistical test to compare the differences in two related samples. We defined the null hypothesis as the hypothesis that no performance differences exist between FIS-SM and the other algorithm, and we set a significance value of 0.05, for a 95% confidence level. Table 14 shows the statistical results. We highlight in bold the results with statistical differences favoring FIS-SM algorithm, and in italics the results with statistical significance against our proposal. The columns w–l–t state for won–lost–ties.

**Table 14.** Results of the Wilcoxon test comparing the performance of the algorithms over repository data.

| Pair | Avg_Acc | | Instance Retention | | Feature Retention | |
|---|---|---|---|---|---|---|
| | w–l–t | Probability | w–l–t | Probability | w–l–t | Probability |
| FIS-SM vs. ONN | 6-1-1 | 0.075 | 8-0-0 | **0.012** | 6-2-0 | 0.270 |
| FIS-SM vs. TCCS | 6-2-0 | **0.012** | 8-0-0 | **0.012** | 0-2-6 | 0.180 |
| FIS-SM vs. EIS-RFS | 5-2-1 | 0.176 | 0-8-0 | *0.012* | 4-2-2 | 0.463 |
| FIS-SM vs. AKH-GA | 7-1-0 | **0.025** | 8-0-0 | **0.012** | 1-7-0 | *0.017* |
| FIS-SM vs. IN-GA | 7-1-0 | **0.012** | 8-0-0 | **0.012** | 0-7-1 | *0.018* |
| FIS-SM vs. KJ-GA | 6-2-0 | **0.034** | 8-0-0 | **0.012** | 1-7-0 | *0.025* |

Comparing the proposed FIS-SM algorithm with the unprocessed NN, the Wilcoxon test did not find significant differences in Avg_Acc nor in feature retention. However, FIS-SM surpassed ONN according to the instance retention. Compared to TCCS, the test found differences favoring FIS-SM according to both averaged accuracy and instance retention. With respect to EIS-RFS, the test found significant differences according to instance retention and feature retention. The test found that FIS-SM used fewer features, but more instances than EIS-RFS. According to the genetic based algorithms (AKH-GA, IN-GA and KJ-GA), the proposed FIS-SM was significantly better according to averaged accuracy and instance retention. However, the genetic based algorithms outperformed FIS-SM according to feature retention. These results confirm the good performance of the proposed FIS-SM algorithm, which is competitive with state-of-the-art methods for selecting features and instances.

## 5. Conclusions

Predicting the presence or absence of high capabilities for the integral personality development in kindergarten children is a challenge for the Cuban educational system. The results of this study suggest the following findings with respect of the use of data driven approaches for organizational learning: first, the use of feature selection techniques allows an efficient and objective determination of which features may intervene para enhances the prediction in the kindergarten children data. Secondly, the use of a novel preprocessing algorithm for selecting both relevant instances and features, suitable for handling multi-class imbalanced problems, in mixed and incomplete scenarios, facilitates the early detection of highly capable kindergarten children, improving their development possibilities. The proposed algorithm improved the Nearest Neighbor classifier in detecting high capabilities in Cuban kindergarten children and over repository data. These results confirm the adequacy of using Rough Set Theory and similarity relations to determine the relevance of instances and features. In addition, the proposed ensemble-inspired merging strategy was found very suitable for obtained accurately results in selecting both instances and features in multiclass imbalanced problems. Third, the study shows that data integration is a key aspect in the development of educational applications.

It is noteworthy that at the moment of this writing, this research is being currently carried out within the municipality of Ciego de Ávila. As future work, we will continue collecting data until the information from the whole province is obtained. As well, in order to generalize these results to other provinces we need to consider that the characteristics of children may vary from one region to another.

**Author Contributions:** Conceptualization, C.F.R.-B.; methodology, Y.V.-R.; software, Y.V.-R.; formal analysis, C.F.R.-B.; investigation, O.C.-N. and C.Y.-M.; writing—original draft preparation, Y.V.-R.; writing—review and editing, C.Y.-M. All authors have read and agreed to the published version of the manuscript.

**Funding:** This research received no external funding.

**Acknowledgments:** The authors gratefully acknowledge the Instituto Politécnico Nacional (Secretaría Académica, Comisión de Operación y Fomento de Actividades Académicas, Secretaría de Investigación y Posgrado, CIC and CIDETEC), the Consejo Nacional de Ciencia y Tecnología (Conacyt), and Sistema Nacional de Investigadores for their economic support to develop this work.

**Conflicts of Interest:** The authors declare no conflict of interest.

## References

1. Smutny, J.F.; Walker, S.Y.; Meckstroth, E.A. *Teaching Young Gifted Children in the Regular Classroom: Indentifying, Nurturing, and Challenging Ages*; Free Spirit Publishing: Minneapolis, MN, USA, 1997.
2. Mooij, T. Designing instruction and learning for cognitively gifted pupils in preschool and primary school. *Int. J. Incl. Educ.* **2013**, *17*, 597–613. [CrossRef]
3. Dal Forno, L.; Bahia, S.; Veiga, F. Gifted amongst Preschool Children: An Analysis on How Teachers Recognize Giftedness. *Int. J. Technol. Incl. Educ.* **2015**, *5*, 707–715. [CrossRef]
4. Sternberg, R.J.; Ferrari, M.; Clinkenbeard, P.; Grigorenko, E.L. Identification, instruction, and assessment of gifted children: A construct validation of a triarchic model. *Gift. Child Q.* **1996**, *40*, 129–137. [CrossRef]
5. Calero, M.D.; García-Martin, M.B.; Robles, M.A. Learning potential in high IQ children: The contribution of dynamic assessment to the identification of gifted children. *Learn. Individ. Differ.* **2015**, *21*, 176–181. [CrossRef]
6. Walsh, R.L.; Kemp, C.R.; Hodge, K.A.; Bowes, J.M. Searching for Evidence-Based Practice A Review of the Research on Educational Interventions for Intellectually Gifted Children in the Early Childhood Years. *J. Educ. Gift.* **2012**, *35*, 103–128. [CrossRef]
7. Callahan, C.M.; Hertberg-Davis, H.L. *Fundamentals of Gifted Education: Considering Multiple Perspectives*; Taylor & Francis: Abingdon, UK, 2013.
8. Karnes, M.B. *The Underserved: Our Young Gifted Children*; The Council for Exceptional Children, Publication Sales: Reston, VA, USA, 1983.
9. Cline, S.; Schwartz, D. *Diverse Populations of Gifted Children: Meeting Their Needs in the Regular Classroom and Beyond*; Merrill/Prentice Hall: Old Tappan, NJ, USA, 1999.
10. Webb, J.T. *Nurturing Social Emotional Development of Gifted Children*; ERIC, Clearinghouse: Reston, VA, USA, 1994.
11. Galbraith, J.; Delisle, J. *When Gifted Kids Don't Have All the Answers: How to Meet Their Social and Emotional Needs*; Free Spirit Publishing: Minneapolis, MN, USA, 2015.

12. Cover, T.M.; Hart, P.E. Nearest Neighbor pattern classification. *IEEE Trans. Inf. Theory* **1967**, *13*, 21–27. [CrossRef]
13. Villuendas-Rey, Y.; Rey-Benguría, C.; Caballero-Mota, Y.; García-Lorenzo, M.M. Improving the family orientation process in Cuban Special Schools through Nearest Prototype Classification. *Int. J. Artif. Intell. Interact. Multimed. Spec. Issue Artif. Intell. Soc. Appl.* **2013**, *2*, 12–22.
14. Pawlak, Z. Rough Sets. *Int. J. Inf. Comput. Sci.* **1982**, *11*, 341–356. [CrossRef]
15. Martínez-Trinidad, J.F.; Ruiz-Shulcloper, J.; Lazo-Cortés, M.S. Structuralization of universes. *Fuzzy Sets Syst.* **2000**, *112*, 485–500. [CrossRef]
16. Renzulli, J.S.; Reis, S.M. *Identification of Students for Gifted and Talented Programs*; Corwin Press: Thousand Oaks, CA, USA, 2004.
17. Duda, R.O.; Hart, P.E.; Stork, D.G. *Pattern Classification*; John Wiley & Sons: Hoboken, NJ, USA, 2001.
18. García-Laencina, P.J.; Sancho-Gómez, J.-L.; Figueiras-Vidal, A.R. Pattern classification with missing data: A review. *Neural Comput. Appl.* **2010**, *19*, 263–282. [CrossRef]
19. Derrac, J.; Cornelis, C.; García, S.; Herrera, F. Enhancing evolutionary instance selection algorithms by means of fuzzy rough set based feature selection. *Inf. Sci.* **2012**, *186*, 73–92. [CrossRef]
20. Chen, Y.; Zhu, Q.; Xu, H. Finding rough set reducts with fish swarm algorithm. *Knowl. Based Syst.* **2015**, *81*, 22–29. [CrossRef]
21. Villuendas-Rey, Y.; Caballero-Mota, Y.; García-Lorenzo, M.M. Using Rough Sets and Maximum Similarity Graphs for Nearest Prototype Classification. *Lect. Notes Comput. Sci.* **2012**, *7441*, 300–307.
22. Santiesteban, Y.; Pons-Porrata, A. LEX: A new algorithm to calculate typical testors. *Math. Sci. J.* **2003**, *21*, 31–40.
23. García-Borroto, M.; Ruiz-Shulcloper, J. Selecting Prototypes in Mixed Incomplete Data. *Lect. Notes Comput. Sci.* **2005**, *3773*, 450–459.
24. Kuncheva, L.I. *Combining Pattern Classifiers. Methods and Algorithms*; John Wiley & Sons: Hoboken, NJ, USA, 2004.
25. Orrite, C.; Rodríguez, M.; Martínez, F.; Fairhurst, M. Classifier Ensemble Generation for the Majority Vote Rule. *Lect. Notes Comput. Sci.* **2008**, *5197*, 340–347.
26. Kuncheva, L.I.; Whitaker, C.J. Measures of diversity in classifier ensembles and their relationship with the ensemble accuracy. *Mach. Learn.* **2003**, *51*, 181–207. [CrossRef]
27. Bradley, A.P. The use of the area under the ROC curve in the evaluation of machine learning algorithms. *Pattern Recognit.* **1997**, *30*, 1145–1159. [CrossRef]
28. Tsai, C.-F.; Eberle, W.; Chu, C.-Y. Genetic algorithms in feature and instance selection. *Knowl. Based Syst.* **2013**, *39*, 240–247. [CrossRef]
29. Ishibuchi, H.; Nakashima, T. Evolution of reference sets in nearest neighbor classification. In *Simulated Evolution and Learning*; Springer: Berlin, Germany, 1998; pp. 82–89.
30. Kuncheva, L.I.; Jain, L.C. Nearest neighbor classifier: Simultaneous editing and feature selection. *Pattern Recognit. Lett.* **1999**, *20*, 1149–1156. [CrossRef]
31. Ahn, H.; Kim, K.-J.; Han, I. A case-based reasoning system with the two-dimensional reduction technique for customer classification. *Expert Syst. Appl.* **2007**, *32*, 1011–1019. [CrossRef]
32. Villuendas-Rey, Y.; García-Borroto, M.; Ruiz-Shulcloper, J. Selecting features and objects for mixed and incomplete data. *Lect. Notes Comput. Sci.* **2008**, *5197*, 381–388.
33. Lichman, M. *UCI Machine Learning Repository*; School of Information and Computer Science, University of California: Irvine, CA, USA, 2013; Available online: http://archive.ics.uci.edu/ml (accessed on 10 April 2020).
34. Wilson, R.D.; Martinez, T.R. Improved Heterogeneous Distance Functions. *J. Artif. Intell. Res.* **1997**, *6*, 1–34. [CrossRef]
35. Demsar, J. Statistical comparison of classifiers over multiple datasets. *J. Mach. Learn. Res.* **2006**, *7*, 1–30.

36. Fernandez, A.; LóPez, V.; Galar, M.; Del Jesus, M.J.; Herrera, F. Analysing the classification of imbalanced data-sets with multiple classes: Binarization techniques and ad-hoc approaches. *Knowl. Based Syst.* **2013**, *42*, 97–110. [CrossRef]
37. Witten, I.H.; Frank, E.; Trigg, L.E.; Hall, M.A.; Holmes, G.; Cunningham, S.J. *Weka: Practical Machine Learning Tools and Techniques with Java Implementations*; Department of Computer Science, University of Waikato: Hamilton, New Zealand, 1999.

© 2020 by the authors. Licensee MDPI, Basel, Switzerland. This article is an open access article distributed under the terms and conditions of the Creative Commons Attribution (CC BY) license (http://creativecommons.org/licenses/by/4.0/).

Article

# Predicting Students Success in Blended Learning—Evaluating Different Interactions Inside Learning Management Systems

**Luiz Antonio Buschetto Macarini [1], Cristian Cechinel [1,\*], Matheus Francisco Batista Machado [1], Vinicius Faria Culmant Ramos [1] and Roberto Munoz [2,\*]**

[1] Centro de Ciências, Tecnologias e Saúde, Universidade Federal de Santa Catarina, Araranguá 88906072, Brazil; luizbuschetto@gmail.com (L.A.B.M.); matheusmachadoufsc@gmail.com (M.F.B.M.); professor.vinicius.ramos@gmail.com (V.F.C.R.)
[2] Escuela de Ingeniería Civil Informática, Universidad de Valparaíso, Valparaíso 2362835, Chile
\* Correspondence: contato@cristiancechinel.pro.br (C.C.); roberto.munoz@uv.cl (R.M.)

Received: 2 November 2019; Accepted: 11 December 2019; Published: 15 December 2019

**Abstract:** Algorithms and programming are some of the most challenging topics faced by students during undergraduate programs. Dropout and failure rates in courses involving such topics are usually high, which has raised attention towards the development of strategies to attenuate this situation. Machine learning techniques can help in this direction by providing models able to detect at-risk students earlier. Therefore, lecturers, tutors or staff can pedagogically try to mitigate this problem. To early predict at-risk students in introductory programming courses, we present a comparative study aiming to find the best combination of datasets (set of variables) and classification algorithms. The data collected from Moodle was used to generate 13 distinct datasets based on different aspects of student interactions (cognitive presence, social presence and teaching presence) inside the virtual environment. Results show there are no statistically significant difference among models generated from the different datasets and that the counts of interactions together with derived attributes are sufficient for the task. The performances of the models varied for each semester, with the best of them able to detect students at-risk in the first week of the course with AUC ROC from 0.7 to 0.9. Moreover, the use of SMOTE to balance the datasets did not improve the performance of the models.

**Keywords:** at-risk students; machine learning; learning management system; blended learning; introduction to programming

## 1. Introduction

Student dropout and failure are two major problems faced during the teaching-learning process of computer programming at any education level [1]. These disciplines have high failure rates around the world, sometimes achieving over 50% [1–5]. According to the literature, many factors may contribute to this low approval rate, such as difficulties related to the required abstraction for the proper development of algorithms, difficulties in problem-solving, and also the early stage, in which the programming courses are placed inside the curricula [6–8].

In Brazil, for example, there is a huge demand for Information Technology (IT) professionals but the formal teaching-learning environments (schools, courses, universities, etc.) do not account for this demand. The prediction of the IT professionals demand is around 70,000 between 2020 and 2024 [9] but the Brazilian universities are graduating 46 thousand, which leaves a deficit of 24,000 per year. In other parts of the world, the scenario is heavier. It estimates that the deficit of IT professionals in Europe from 2015 until 2020 is roughly 800,000 [10,11].

Beside that market demand, international institutes and organisms consider the computational thinking a knowledge for future generation [12,13]. Resnik [14] says that the consumption of technology by the actual generation do not convert them, automatically, in technology producers or developers. The author state that this generation must understand how technology works to create, update and innovate in hardware, software and so on.

In this context, the early identification of at-risk students can help the educational staff to take some action to mitigate the students' failure. One of the biggest challenges is to develop algorithms and tools to predict the students' behavior, aiming to facilitate the intervention of professors, tutors and educators [15,16].

Educational Data Mining (EDM) is an interdisciplinary research area that deals with the development of methods and techniques to explore data from educational contexts and which has been exploring different techniques to detect at-risk students [17].

Interactions within the learning management systems are used in several works to extract knowledge and discover patterns [18]. For example, Murray et al. [19] shows that the students with the highest rates of access to the study materials within the Learning Management Systems (LMS) received highest grades, and Dickson [20] presents that the number of clicks made by a student is strongly correlated to its final grade in the course.

At the same time that there is an overwhelming amount of studies about the detection of at-risk students, most of the results reported in the literature do not show solutions able of detecting at-risk students until the middle of the course [21]. In this work, the collected data belongs to the whole course (15 weeks) but the prediction is based only on the first 8 weeks of the course.

Nevertheless, in this paper we also compare different types of interactions that took place within the LMS and it is based according to a conceptual framework proposed by Garrison et al. [22]. The authors proposed a framework to identify the critical elements required for a successful computer-mediated educational experience [22]. The critical elements identified are: (1) cognitive presence—representing the extent to which one is able to construct meaning; (2) social presence—representing the ability that the student has to project himself to the others participants of the virtual community as a real person and (3) teaching presence—being the design of an educational experience, facilitating and enhancing cognitive and social presence for the achievement of learning outcomes.

According to Swan [23], each of the critical elements proposed by Garrison et al. [22] represents different types of students' interaction in the LMS. These interactions can affect learning efficiency, that is, with the course (cognitive presence), among peers (social presence) and with teachers/instructors (teaching presence).

In this context, the main goal of this paper is to evaluate whether the use of these three different types of presences significantly influences in the performance of predictive models to early detect at-risk students. To achieve this goal, we evaluate whether a given type of presence in the LMS is more suitable to early predict at-risk students or the data collected through a survey may help to improve the performance of the models.

Since the number of samples is small and unbalanced, we needed to find a solution to overcome this problem. Previous studies have shown that the use of the SMOTE (Synthetic Minority Over-sampling Technique)technique to balance datasets helps on improving the performance of the models [24]. As we are dealing with highly unbalanced datasets, we also applied SMOTE balancing technique to check if its use interferes in the models' performance.

Before initiating the courses, social and demographic data were collected from the students. Since we get only the interaction count from Moodle logs, we included this information in the study to evaluate to which extent this information could help to improve the performances of the models. We base our studies on previous work that use solely the count of interactions to predict students at-risk, with the justification of using information that is not restricted to a given type of learning management system [25]. The idea here is to test the sole use of the interaction count to see if it achieves a satisfactory result.

In this work, we do not distinguish our analysis between students' failure and dropout. Therefore, if it is not explicitly said the difference, the term "at-risk students" means students that got a final grade lower than 6.0 (on a scale from 1.0 to 10.0). In this context, students who dropped out got zero in their final grade and, consequently, are included in this definition.

For those reasons, the present work come up with the following research questions:

**RQ1.** Which are the most appropriate datasets to early predict at-risk students?
**RQ2.** Is the sole use of the count of students interactions sufficient to early predict students' failure in the course?
**RQ3.** Does the use of oversampling techniques (SMOTE) help the models to achieve better performances?
**RQ4.** Does the use of data from questionnaires applied at the beginning of the course help to improve model performance?

The remainder of this paper is divided into 4 sections—Section 2 presents related works. Section 3 presents the methodology, the process of data collection, its description, the dataset generation and the model evaluation. Section 4 reports the results obtained in this study and Section 5 shows the works' conclusion and discussion.

## 2. Related Work

Predicting at-risk students on higher education is a relatively well-established task in the literature, as well as the notion of interactions within the LMS. Some works show that students' performance has often been associated with different measures of LMS interactions and usually has a high correlation with their success in the course. This section presents a non-exhaustive review of the literature that used user interaction data to predict at-risk students.

### 2.1. Programming Courses

In introductory programming course context, Costa et al. [24] presented a comparative study aiming to measure the effectiveness of educational data mining techniques aiming on predicting at-risk students. The results have shown that the techniques used in the study can identify students with the risk of failing, where the best results were achieved using the Support Vector Machine (SVM) algorithm. Azcona et al. [26] present a research methodology to detect at-risk students in computer programming courses too. The authors provide adaptive feedback to students based on weekly generated predictions. The models used students' offline data and information about the activity logs. Results show that the students who followed the personalized guidance and recommendations performed better in exams. The usage of online learning material (in an introductory programming course) was used to predict academic success [27]. The results obtained have shown that the time spent with the material is a moderate predictor of student success. The performances of the models depend on the amount of data used to train them (where the predictions become more accurate during the progress of the course).

### 2.2. Computer Science/IT Courses

In a computer science course, Tillmann et al. [28] used exam results data from the LMS to indicators of academic success. Results show that the use of data of domain-specific skills could help to improve the accuracy and student interaction data almost does not interfere in the results. Using interaction logs from three computer science courses, Sheshadri et al. [29] tried to predict students' performance in a blended course. Results show that the performance can be predicted using data from LMS and also from a forum, version control and homework system. Using a plug-in to capture data from Moodle, Jokhan et al. [30] tried to predict the student's performance in the first year of an IT literacy course. A regression model was used to determine if there is any correlation between students' online behavior and performance. Results show that the performance in this course could be predicted based on their average logins per week and the average completion rates of activities.

*2.3. University*

On an university context, a model to early predict students who are at-risk of failing was presented by Sandoval et al. [31]. The data comes from the university's LMS, that is, activity logs for each user and the administrative information system called DARA, that is, past and current academic status and demographic data. The results outperform other approaches in terms of accuracy, cost and generalization. In Mwalumbwe and Mtebe [32], the authors designed a Learning Analytics tool to determine the causation between LMS usage and students' performance at Mbeya University of Science and Technology. Results show that discussion posts, peer interaction, and exercises are significant factors for students' academic achievement in blended learning at the university.

*2.4. Fully Online*

On a fully online course, Hung et al. [33] used time-series clustering to early identify at-risk online students. Data were collected from an online graduate program in the United States, and results show that the proposed approach could generate models with higher accuracy if it is compared to traditional frequency aggregation approaches. In Soffer and Cohen [34], the authors used learning analytics methods on engagement data from online courses aiming to find their impact on academic achievements. Results showed that there are significant differences between who completes the course and who does not. An example is that the students who complete the course are twice more active than those who do not complete (except for forum activities). In Kostopoulos et al. [35] it was combined classification and regression algorithms for predicting students' performance in a distance web-based course. When the results are compared with some machine learning methods, they show that the proposed model is accurate and remains comprehensive. Baneres et al. [36] propose to identify at-risk students using an adaptive predictive model based on students' grades, trained for each course. They also present an early warning system using dashboards visualization for stakeholders. The results show the effectiveness of the approach on data coming from a fully online university's LMS.

*2.5. Blended Courses*

In a blended course context, Conijn et al. [37] processed data from LMS on 17 courses. Results show that the performance of predictive models strongly varies across courses, even when they are generated with data collected from a single institution. In Sukhbaatar et al. [38], the authors used a decision tree analysis on LMS data with the goal of predict (until the middle of the semester) students that are at-risk of failing or dropout in a blended course. Results showed that this approach worked well to predict the dropouts. However, to predict students that are at risk of failing, the method presented a lousy performance.

*2.6. Multiple Data Sources*

In Adejo & Connolly [39], the authors compared the use of multiple data sources (student record system, LMS and survey) and different classification algorithms aiming to predict student's academic performance. The main result is that using multiple data sources combined with an ensemble of classifierhigh accuracy in the s brought a high accuracy in the prediction of student performance. Umer et al. [40] used machine learning algorithms and the LMS data to predict students at-risk of failing. Results show that those data can be used to predict students' outcomes. However, the count of activities alone is not enough. In other words, the combination of LMS data and assessment scores can improve the accuracy of prediction models. Olivé et al. [41] tried to find which students would likely submit their assignments on time based on LMS data until two days before the deadline. The main goal was to perform an early prediction of at-risk students. The authors added contextual information to improve their predictions using neural networks, achieving satisfactory results.

*2.7. Only Interaction Data/Log Files*

Using only course log files, in Cohen [42], the author used data accumulated in three academic course to check if student activity on course websites may assist in providing early identification of learner dropout. Results show that identifying the changes in student activity during the course period could help in detecting at-risk students. In Kondo et al. [43] was proposed an automatic method to detect at-risk students by using log data of the LMS. Experimental results indicated that using this log data, some characteristics of behavior about learning which affect the student outcomes can be detected. Also, by using interaction data from the LMS, Usman et al. [44] used EDM and pre-processing techniques to predict students' performance. Results show that the Decision Tree achieved the best performance, followed by Naive Bayes and kNN. In Detoni et al. [25], the authors presented a methodology to classify students using only the interaction count in the LMS. Three machine learning methods were tested and results showed that the patterns in the data could provide useful information to classify at-risk students, allowing personalized activities, trying to avoid the student dropout. In Zhou et al. [45], the authors created a feature selection framework to pre-processing the data coming from internet access logs and generate models to predict the students' performance. Results have shown that this approach can identify most of the high-risk students. Some online characteristics were also discovered and can help educational professionals to understand the relation between students' internet use and academic performance.

*2.8. Early Prediction*

Aiming to find the optimal time in a course to apply an early warning system, the authors of Howard et al. [46] examined eight prediction methods to identify at-risk students. The course has a weekly continuous assessment and a large proportion of resources on the LMS. The results show that the optimal time to implement an early warning system is in weeks 5-6 (halfway through the semester). This way, the students can make changes in their study patterns. One of the objectives in Lu et al. [47] was to find the moment that the at-risk students could be predicted. For that, the authors used learning analytics and big educational data approach to predict the students' performance on a blended calculus course. Results show that the performance can be predicted when one-third of the semester is complete. With a similar idea, the authors of Gray and Perkins [48] proposed a new descriptive statistic for student attendance and applied machine learning methods to create a predictive model. Results show how at-risk students can be identified as early as week three in the fall semester. Appendix A presents an overview of the main characteristics of the works discussed in this section.

*2.9. Approach Novelty*

The novelty of our approach is based on the extensive comparison of datasets and classification algorithms, resulting in 65 combinations (13 datasets and 5 classification algorithms). We also used pre-processing techniques (SMOTE) aiming to tackle the lack of samples to train and test the algorithms. Some questionnaire data were used to aggregate more information on the discussion, adding information like social and demographic variables on the analysis. We also used three types of presence (cognitive, teaching and social) aiming to generate more data to predict student at-risk of failing and according to an existing theory about how interactions work inside Virtual Learning Environments.

The idea of making early predictions is to find out as early as possible whether the student is at risk of failing. For that, from the data available, we used just those related to the weeks up to the half of the semester (week 8). In this way, we are testing models that can be used in time to provide information that can help professors to intervene in order to avoid students failure.

## 3. Methodology

This section describes the methods used to achieve the goal of this paper. This research paper investigates thirteen different datasets (set of attributes), for each of the 4 (four) distinct semesters: 2016-1, 2016-2, 2017-1 and 2017-2, of an Introductory Programming Course to evaluate whether the types of presence, presented by Garrison et al. [22], influences in the performance of predictive models to early detect at-risk students. The overview of the adopted methodology is shown in Figure 1 and the four steps of the methodology are shown in Figure 2.

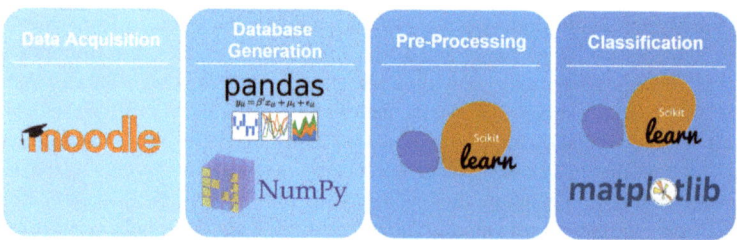

**Figure 1.** Overview of the adopted methodology.

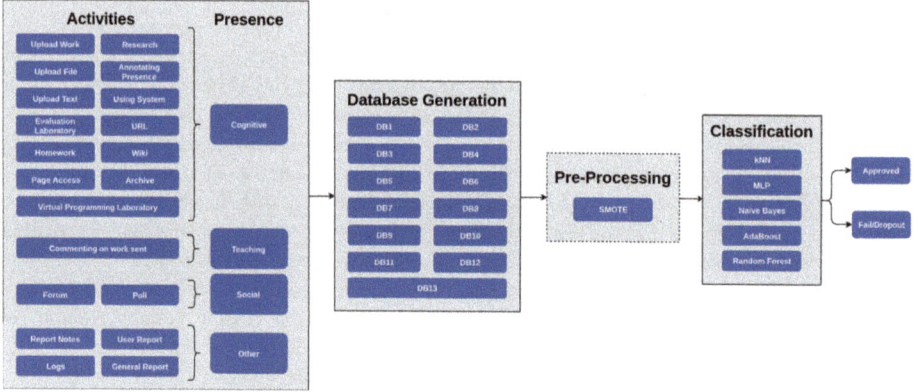

**Figure 2.** Steps of the adopted methodology. The "Pre-Processing" step was showed in dotted lines because it is optional, i.e., applied only in some experiments.

The first step consists of gathering data from Moodle logs, considering that the platform records the interactions that the students make in the VLE. The next step consists of generating the datasets containing different attributes to compare them and verify those which achieve the best results. Next, we employ some pre-processing techniques, such as oversampling, intending to increase the performance of the models. The fourth step consists of the generation and evaluation of the classification models. In the final step, we compare the obtained results to answer the research questions. The next subsections describe, in more detail, the steps followed.

### 3.1. Data Collection and Description

Data was collected from the Moodle logs of Introductory Programming courses of the Information and Communication Technologies (ICT) undergraduate program at the Federal University of Santa Catarina (UFSC). The introductory course is offered at ICT at night and it has 108 hours, in total, over 18 weeks. There are three classes per week, where one of them is an online activity. Every type of activity is computed as an "interaction". In other words, independently of the type the activity (log in, click on a given link, send a file, etc.), the interaction count is incremented by one. Table 1 shows the summary of the data.

Table 1. Summary of data.

| Semester | Interaction Count | Average of Interaction | Students Approved | Students Reproved | Total of Students |
|---|---|---|---|---|---|
| 2016-1 | 10,395 | 547.10 | 6 | 13 | 19 |
| 2016-2 | 11,512 | 605.89 | 6 | 13 | 19 |
| 2017-1 | 23,457 | 902.19 | 9 | 17 | 26 |
| 2017-2 | 33,727 | 1,349.08 | 12 | 13 | 25 |

The Average of Interaction is calculated by the Interaction Count divided by the Total of Students. The lecturer was the same for all four semesters. It is important to note that in 2016, the C programming language was used but in 2017 we started teaching the Python programming language. The activities were gradually developed by the lecturer for each semester and he also instead content from previous semester.

For example, every semester, the old exams are posted in the course. In 2017-1 (first semester of 2017), the lecturer posted new programming exercises, video classes and a bunch of links to other video classes and content. The LMS course became more abundant in the material than before. At the end of the course, in 2017-1, the lecturer created a new LMS course environment, reorganizing the topics and content, describing the environment to assist the student in following instructions and making the course very attractive to the student. In addition to the video classes and content, most of the activities cited here are related to programming exercises that can be developed, executed and evaluated in Moodle by the Virtual Programming Laboratory plugin (VPL) [49].

For all the courses, throughout the semester students had three assessments. In 2016-1 students had two tests—week 10 and 17 and a final assignment in week 18. The tests were handwriting, that is, students did not make it in VPL because the modified Moodle environment for tests (Moodle's Test) that prohibits students access to the internet, was not available at the campus. In 2016-2 the Moodle's test was installed and students had two VPL tests in weeks 8 and 16 and a final assignment in week 15. In 2017-1 students had two VPL tests in week 10 and week 16 and a final assignment in week 17. In 2017-2, it was a bit different, students had three VPL tests in weeks 9, 15 and 17.

It is important to note that in both semesters of 2016, the final assignment was made by a group of maximum 3 students, it was implemented at home, in 4 weeks and posted in Moodle. In 2017-1, the assignment was made by two students per group in two classes (the same double in both days). In 2017-2, all the tests were made within VPL in classes. The final score is calculated as follows: $FS = (T1 * 0.35 + T2 * 0.35 + ASGMT * 0.3)$, where FS is the final score, T1 and T2 are tests and ASGMT is the final assignment or the final test in 2017-2.

Every student interaction in the LMS is saved in the logs together with the description of the activity performed. From that, we calculated the interaction counting for each week during the course for every student. Figure 3 shows a frequency distribution of interactions on each week of the four semesters considered for this work. Regarding the weeks when the first test was applied, it is important to note that one or two weeks before the test, there was a peak of interactions, as seen in 2016-2, 2017-1 and 2017-2. It is also interesting that the students did not use the Moodle in 2016-1, even though there were 53 not-mandatory VPL activities there.

In 2016-1, there is not a peak per se. But the highest number of interaction happens on Week 1. For 2016-2 and 2017-1, most of the interaction happens on Week 7. The 2017-2 semester has the highest number of interactions, where the peak is found on Week 8. From the interactions, we generated thirteen datasets with different sets of derived attributes to compare the performances of the models. Table 2 shows the description of the attributes generated.

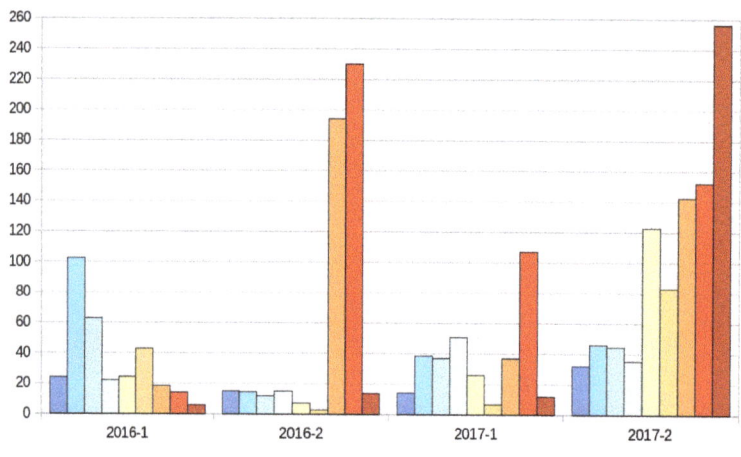

**Figure 3.** Interaction frequency distribution in each week for every semester.

**Table 2.** Description of the attributes.

| Attribute | Description |
| --- | --- |
| Count | Interaction count for each week |
| Average | Average of interactions on the week |
| Median | Median of interactions on the week |
| Zeroed weeks [50] | Number of weeks with zero interactions until the moment |
| Average of the difference [50] | Average of the difference between interactions on week $i$ and week $i + 1$ |
| Commitment factor [50] | Ratio between the student's week interactions and the average class interaction for that week |
| Cognitive count [23] | Number of cognitive interaction on the week |
| Teaching count [23] | Number of teaching interaction on the week |
| Social count [23] | Number of social interaction on the week |
| Other count | Number of other types of interaction on the week |

It is important to point out that each attribute in Table 2 is gathered at student level, that is, every calculation in based on data collected for each student. *Cognitive Count*, *Teaching Count* and *Social Count* are the counting of the Cognitive, Teaching and Social Presences presented in Swan [23]. "Other count" is a category created by us for all the other interactions that do not fit the three previously mentioned categories. In other words, the sum of these four types of interactions result in $Count_i$ (Equation (1)). Table 3 presents how different interactions inside Moodle fall into the three types of presence evaluated in our work.

Table 3. Example of interactions classification.

| Attribute | Description |
|---|---|
| Cognitive count | Interactions involving content access and visualization: File upload/download, VPL exercise, URL access |
| Teaching count | Interactions with the professor: comments to the files sent |
| Social count | Interactions with other students: forum participation |

Students interactions are normally highly correlated to engagement in distance learning settings, reflecting the behaviour students have in relation the their course. According to Moore [51], the interaction with content (cognitive presence), interaction with instructors (teaching presence) and interaction among peers (social presence) are the three kinds of interactivity that affect the learning process. Each of these interaction types supports learning and in practice, none of them works independently [23]. The idea of using these types of interaction is to better discriminate each type of interaction aiming to help on the generation of better predictive models, that better capture students behaviour in those learning settings. The implicit idea is that students who fail present different interactions in the different types of presence than students who succeed and that difference helps to generate better models.

Following, we formalize every attribute contained in the datasets.

$$Count_i = \sum_{j=1}^{7} x_j. \quad (1)$$

Equation (1) represents the sum of interactions on every day $j$ in each week $i$.

$$Average_i = \frac{\sum_{j=1}^{7} x_j}{7}. \quad (2)$$

Equation (2) represents the average number of interactions in week $i$, summing up the interactions on each day $j$, divided by the seven days on the week (to calculate the average, we used the *.mean()* method contained in Pandas library [52] (https://pandas.pydata.org/pandas-docs/stable/reference/api/pandas.DataFrame.mean.html)).

$$Median_i = \begin{cases} Sample_{n/2}, & \text{if } n \text{ is odd} \\ \frac{Sample_{n/2} + Sample_{(n/2)+1}}{2}, & \text{if } n \text{ is even.} \end{cases} \quad (3)$$

Equation (3) represents the *Median*, where $n$ represents the number of samples in the vector. It is the value in the middle of the crescent ordered vector. If the number of samples is even, the median is the mean of the two middle values of the vector (To calculate the median, we used the *.median()* method contained in Pandas library (http://pandas.pydata.org/pandas-docs/stable/reference/api/pandas.DataFrame.median.html)).

$$ZeroedWeek_i = \begin{cases} ZeroedWeek_{i-1} + 1, & \text{if } Count_i = 0 \\ ZeroedWeek_{i-1} + 0, & \text{otherwise.} \end{cases} \quad (4)$$

Equation (4) represents the number of weeks that the students had zero interactions, until week $i$. For example, if he had zero interactions on week $i$, the result is incremented in one. If the student had at least one interaction on week $i$, the result stays the same.

$$AOD_i = \frac{Count_i - Count_{i-1}}{2}. \quad (5)$$

The *Average of the Difference* represents the average of the difference of interactions between week $i-1$ and week $i$.

$$CF_i = \frac{Count_i}{\frac{\sum_{j=1}^{n} Count_{i,j}}{n}}. \tag{6}$$

The *Commitment Factor* represents the ratio between the interaction count of a student on week $i$ divided by the average interaction count of the class, where $j$ represents a student and $n$ the number of students in the class.

Table 4 shows the set of attributes/variables included in each dataset.

Table 4. Attributes of each dataset.

| Dataset | Variables |
|---|---|
| DB1 | Count |
| DB2 | Count, Average, Median |
| DB3 | Count, Cognitive Count, Teaching Count, Social Count, Other Count |
| DB4 | Count, Average, Median, Cognitive Count, Teaching Count, Social Count, Other Count |
| DB5 | Count, Average, Median, Zeroed Week, Commitment factor, Average of the difference |
| DB6 | Cognitive Count, Teaching Count, Social Count |
| DB7 | Cognitive Count, Teaching Count |
| DB8 | Cognitive Count, Social Count |
| DB9 | Teaching Count, Social Count |
| DB10 | Cognitive Count |
| DB11 | Teaching Count |
| DB12 | Social Count |
| DB13 | All variables |

The idea when creating the datasets was to "separate" the derived attributes from each work. For example, in DB3 (dataset 3), we only use the attributes from Swan [23] (together with the interaction count). In DB5, we used attributes similar to Detoni el al. [50]. In DB4, the idea is similar, but with the addition of the average and median. In DB1, there is only the interaction counting, and in DB2, the attributes are derived from the interaction counting only (not using the type of interaction). DB6 contains strictly variables from Swan [23]. In DB7, DB8 and DB9, we created combinations of two variables from the same work [23]. In DB10, DB11 and DB12, the counting of each type of presence were used. DB13 is the datasets that contains all variables shown in Table 2 together.

Information from the logs was used together with a socio-demographic-motivational questionnaire that was applied to the students in the first week of the course. Questions were created to outline students' profiles, such as their usage of computer/smartphone (if, how, and how much they use), the reasons they choose the ICT program, previous skills on computing and computer programming languages, among others. The idea of using data from the questionnaire was to test to which extent the inclusion of socio-demographic-motivational data about/from the students would improve the performances of the models in comparison with using only data coming from students' interactions within the LMS. The motivational part is only one question and it is related to the main reason students choose the ICT program, that is for personal satisfaction, to get a better job/position, for family satisfaction (pressure), to apply for a PhD in the future or to get any degree.

*3.2. Dataset Generation*

The interaction counting was made week by week. It begins on Week 0 (last week before the beginning of the semester) to Week 17 (last week of the semester). However, in this work, we have used only data from Week 0 to Week 8 (middle of the semester) since the objective was to early predict the students that were at-risk of failing. It is important to note that in this work we do not distinguish between fail and dropout. We consider an at-risk student that student that gets a final grade below 6.0, the necessary grade to be approved on this course. So, independently if the student drops the course out in the first weeks, he is considered a failing student.

*3.3. Data Pre-Processing*

Table 1 shows the number of students in each semester and it is clear that there are not a lot of samples. Therefore, we applied the over-sampling technique called *Synthetic Minority Over-sampling Technique* (SMOTE) [53] to generate synthetic data. This allowed us to compare the performances of the models when using the original datasets and balanced datasets. The script was developed in Python using the method in the *Imbalanced-learn* library [54].

*3.4. Generation and Evaluation of the Models*

For classification, we used Naive Bayes, Random Forest, AdaBoost, Multilayer Perceptron (MLP), k-Nearest Neighbor (kNN) and Decision Tree algorithms. However, during the experiments, we removed the last one due to its over-fitting. All these algorithms were implemented using the *Scikit-learn* [55] library in Python.

Since the number of samples to train, validate and test the classifiers is small, we used the *Leave-One-Out Cross-Validation*. The performance was measured using the Area Under Curve (AUC)—ROC Curve [56]. It is a measure of performance for classification tasks at various threshold settings and represents how much a model can distinguish between classes. Consequently, the higher AUC, the better the model is at predicting. AUC has been used as a reference metric by related literature such as Gašević et al. [57].

*3.5. Comparison between Cases*

To compare the results and check if there are differences between performances we applied the *Mann-Whitney U test* [58]. This test is suitable for situations where the requisites for the application of *Student T-test* have not been met. The Mann-Whitney U test is a non-parametric test applied on two independent samples with the same size, checking for the null hypothesis. If the $p$-value is below a threshold (0.05 in this work), the difference between the two samples did not occur by chance.

To answer the research questions, we performed comparisons presented in Section 4. The difference between performances (and the improvement of one configuration versus the other) is considered existent when there is a statistic difference between them (i.e., the $p$-value of the test between the two samples is lower than 0.05).

## 4. Results

As previously mentioned, the ROC curve was calculated for each model generated for each DB. Sixty-five models for each semester were generated. Models were trained with the counting of the weeks. For example, to get the results in the first week, we fed the classifier with interaction data from week 0 only. For the second week, we used the counting of week 0 and week 1 and so on.

We calculated the mean and median of the ROC values until week 8 (middle of the semester) and sorted the results descending by the median, obtaining our Top-5 combinations for each semester. It is essential to say that the interaction count is made individually for each week and are not cumulative. Table 5 shows the Top-5 performances for each semester, considering the combination of the DB and the classifier used. To do this, we need to compute the ROC value for each week. So, we get the predictions on test set for each week using leave-one-out validation, followed by the calculation of the ROC value and computation of the AUC for the week. The median is calculated using the AUC values from Week 0 to Week 8, that is, we get the median of these nine values.

**Table 5.** Five best DB-Classifier combinations for each semester ordered (descending) by median.

| Semester | DB | Classifier | Median |
|---|---|---|---|
| 2016-1 | DB12 | AdaBoost | 0.62820 |
| | DB2 | AdaBoost | 0.55128 |
| | DB5 | AdaBoost | 0.55128 |
| | DB9 | AdaBoost | 0.55128 |
| | DB12 | MLP | 0.55128 |
| 2016-2 | DB2 | AdaBoost | 0.71795 |
| | DB5 | AdaBoost | 0.71795 |
| | DB9 | kNN | 0.71795 |
| | DB12 | kNN | 0.71795 |
| | DB1 | Random Forest | 0.71154 |
| 2017-1 | DB2 | AdaBoost | 0.66013 |
| | DB5 | AdaBoost | 0.63072 |
| | DB6 | kNN | 0.60784 |
| | DB8 | kNN | 0.60784 |
| | DB10 | Random Forest | 0.60784 |
| 2017-2 | DB2 | AdaBoost | 0.83974 |
| | DB5 | AdaBoost | 0.83654 |
| | DB13 | AdaBoost | 0.75641 |
| | DB2 | Random Forest | 0.67949 |
| | DB4 | Random Forest | 0.67628 |

The results show that the AdaBoost classifier appears in 11 of 20 cases, being the most present algorithm. Next, we have the Random Forest and kNN, both appearing four times each. Last, we have the MLP, which appears only one time, in the fifth position at 2016-1. Next section will answer the proposed Research Questions focused on the five best results.

*4.1. Research Questions*

4.1.1. RQ1. Which Are the Most Appropriate Datasets to Early Predict at-Risk Students?

To answer this question, Table 5 provides information about the Top-5 DB-classifier combination for each week, ordered by the median. The combination that presents better results is the DB2 with AdaBoost classifier, followed by the DB5 with the same classifier in almost every semester. The exception is 2016-1, where the DB12 with AdaBoost (again) achieved the best results. However, the two previously cited combinations (DB2 and DB5) are in the second and third positions, respectively. To confirm to what extent the differences between the best performances and the others were significant, we applied the Mann-Whitney test. Table 6 shows the results of the tests for each combination.

According to the results of the Mann-Whitney test, there is no significant statistical difference between the best five results. This means that one could use any of the combinations (model + DB) without loose or gain significant performances in the predictions. From now on, we will use "DB2—AdaBoost" as the best combination, since there was no significant difference between this one and "DB12—AdaBoost". We choose the former because it appears as the best combination also in the other semesters (2016-2, 2017-1 and 2017-2). It is important to highlight though that from these findings, there is no better dataset configuration that one should use to train the models.

We considered the best combination as DB2 with AdaBoost since it brought the best result on almost every semester. However, it is necessary to say that there is no significant statistical difference between this combination the other four on Top-5 (Table 6). So, we may say that this combination is enough to predict at-risk students. The dataset consists of interaction count, with average and median, both derived variables from the first. This dataset may have brought the best results since it has the information on interaction count and, with the other two variables, gives a notion on the behavior of the students in the past weeks, until the moment of the prediction. It can also bring some insights into student's engagement during the weeks.

**Table 6.** Application of the Mann-Whitney test on the five best results, comparing the best with the other four combinations.

| Semester | Combination 1 | Combination 2 | p-Value |
|---|---|---|---|
| 2016-1 | DB12—AdaBoost | DB2—AdaBoost | 0.13032 |
| | DB12—AdaBoost | DB5—AdaBoost | 0.19794 |
| | DB12—AdaBoost | DB9—AdaBoost | 0.48212 |
| | DB12—AdaBoost | DB12—MLP | 0.48224 |
| 2016-2 | DB2—AdaBoost | DB5—AdaBoost | 0.32775 |
| | DB2—AdaBoost | DB9—kNN | 0.50000 |
| | DB2—AdaBoost | DB12—kNN | 0.50000 |
| | DB2—AdaBoost | DB1—Random Forest | 0.42911 |
| 2017-1 | DB2—AdaBoost | DB5—AdaBoost | 0.34448 |
| | DB2—AdaBoost | DB6—kNN | 0.14441 |
| | DB2—AdaBoost | DB8—kNN | 0.14441 |
| | DB2—AdaBoost | DB10—Random Forest | 0.34525 |
| 2017-2 | DB2—AdaBoost | DB5—AdaBoost | 0.41160 |
| | DB2—AdaBoost | DB13—AdaBoost | 0.18712 |
| | DB2—AdaBoost | DB2—Random Forest | 0.32884 |
| | DB2—AdaBoost | DB4—Random Forest | 0.26740 |

4.1.2. RQ2. The Sole Use of the Count of Student Interactions Is Sufficient to Early Predict Students' Failure in the Course?

Considering that there is no statistical difference between the models generated using DB1 and other datasets, one could say that the counting of student interactions could be sufficient to early predict student's failure. In other words, the inclusion of several different derived attributes was not sufficient to improve the performance of the models at a statistically significant level. At the same time, it is essential to point out that the best results were obtained from DB2 and DB5, which are variations of DB1 that do not consider the different types of presence (cognitive, social and teaching).

4.1.3. RQ3. Does the Use of Oversampling Techniques (SMOTE) Help the Models to Achieve Better Performances?

To answer this question, we calculated the median of the performances of the models generated with original DBs (without the application of SMOTE). We compared them with the performances of the models generated with oversampled DBs. SMOTE was applied on the training set after splitting the data in training/testing sets. To check if there is any statistical difference between them, we apply the Mann-Whitney test again. Table 7 summarizes the results.

Table 7. Comparison between the ROC values of the normal and oversampled data.

| Semester | Combination | p-Value | Median (Normal) | Median (Oversample) |
|---|---|---|---|---|
| 2016-1 | DB2—AdaBoost | 0.03123 | 0.55128 | 0.59615 |
|  | DB5—AdaBoost | 0.07874 | 0.55128 | 0.63461 |
|  | DB2—Random Forest | 0.00603 | 0.42308 | 0.50641 |
|  | DB5—Random Forest | 0.01344 | 0.42949 | 0.47436 |
| 2016-2 | DB2—AdaBoost | 0.00280 | 0.71795 | 0.51282 |
|  | DB5—AdaBoost | 0.00038 | 0.71795 | 0.42949 |
|  | DB2—Random Forest | 0.02070 | 0.62820 | 0.67949 |
|  | DB5—Random Forest | 0.36134 | 0.67308 | 0.63461 |
| 2017-1 | DB2—AdaBoost | 0.06606 | 0.66013 | 0.54575 |
|  | DB5—AdaBoost | 0.01047 | 0.63072 | 0.51961 |
|  | DB2—Random Forest | 0.16419 | 0.54902 | 0.57516 |
|  | DB5—Random Forest | 0.00067 | 0.52287 | 0.63399 |
| 2017-2 | DB2—AdaBoost | 0.35254 | 0.83974 | 0.75641 |
|  | DB5—AdaBoost | 0.35279 | 0.83654 | 0.75320 |
|  | DB2—Random Forest | 0.00016 | 0.67949 | 0.91987 |
|  | DB5—Random Forest | 0.00011 | 0.67628 | 0.91987 |

Results show that there is an improvement on the median of ROC values in 9 out of the 16 cases (only for DB5 - AdaBoost on 2016-2 semester the results got worse) but these differences are statistically significant in only 7 out of the 16 cases (p-value is smaller than 0.05).

Figures 4–7 help to better visualize the results for the first 8 weeks of the four evaluated semesters (2016-1, 2016-2, 2017-1 and 2017-2 respectively).

Figures 4 and 5 show similar results for the semesters 2016-1 and 2016-2, respectively, which are when SMOTE is not applied, the results are better. It happens for the two cases, in both figures. It can be seen in Figures 4 and 5 that the AdaBoost achieved the best prediction result with DB5.

In 2017-1 (Figure 6), it can be seen that the use of SMOTE improved the prediction results since the AdaBoost—DB5 combination with SMOTE presented the best results for the eight week. However, in Week 8, we can see that the Random Forest—DB5 combination presented similar results.

In Figure 7 we can see that the application of SMOTE brought the biggest difference if compared to the data without SMOTE. The Random Forest classifier (with DB2 and DB5) presented the best results and the application of SMOTE improved the results. However, in Week 8, results of Random Forest (without the SMOTE application) and AdaBoost—DB2/DB5 were pretty similar.

From the results, one can say that the use of SMOTE helps on improving the performances of the models in only 43.75% of the cases considering all four semesters. Moreover, the use of SMOTE showed the best improvement on 2017-2, where the ROC value for Random Forest with DB2 and DB5 stayed above all the other combinations on all the weeks.

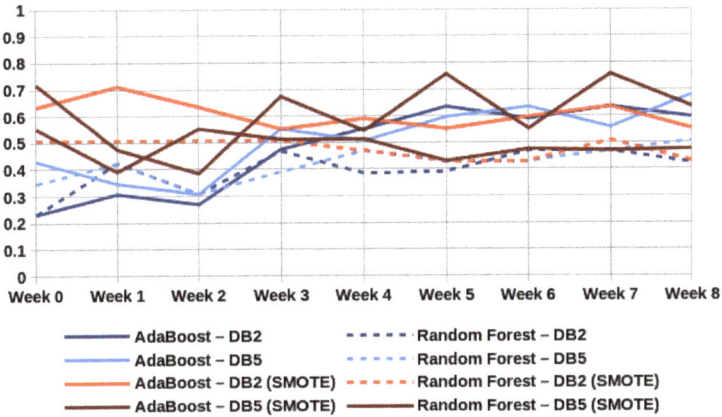

**Figure 4.** ROC Curve: 2016-1.

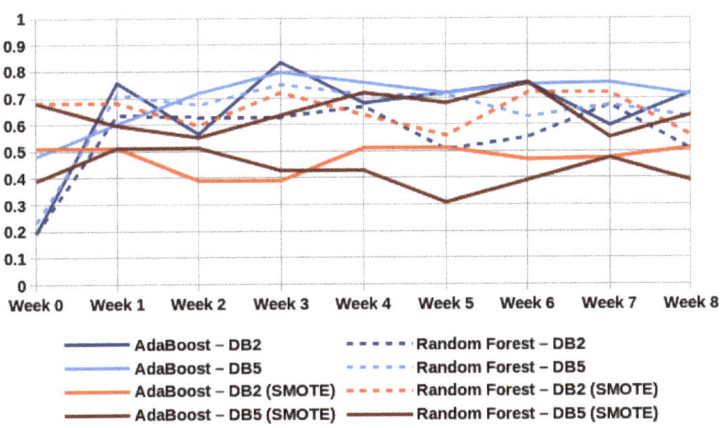

**Figure 5.** ROC Curve: 2016-2.

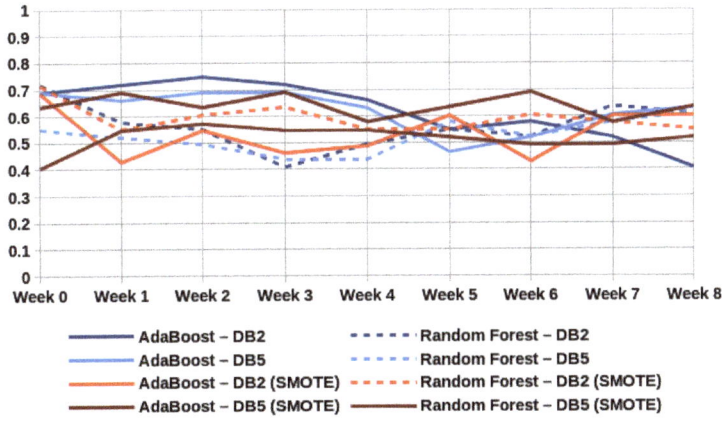

**Figure 6.** ROC Curve: 2017-1.

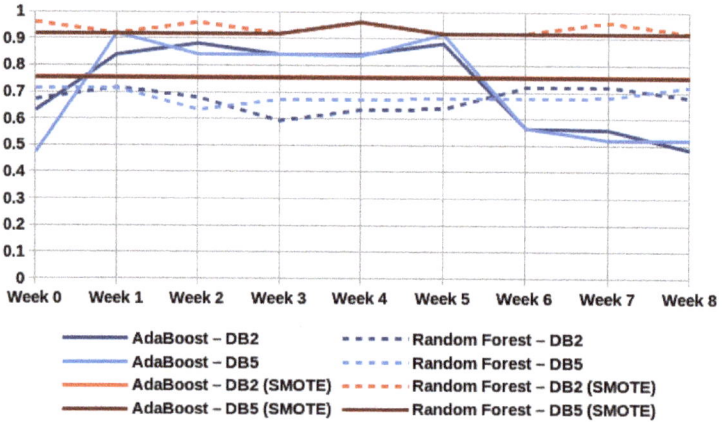

**Figure 7.** ROC Curve: 2017-2.

### 4.1.4. RQ4. Does the Use of Data from Questionnaires Applied at the Beginning of the Course Help to Improve Models Performance?

To answer this question, we used the same methodology of the previous question, initially not including the use of SMOTE and then applying the SMOTE. Table 8 presents the results.

On the one hand, in Table 8 it is possible to see the improvement of the performances (median of ROC values) in only 3 out of 16 cases, where only 2 cases are statistically significant. Both in 2016-1, with DB2 and DB5 with AdaBoost. On the other hand, there are some cases where the inclusion of data from the questionnaire decreases the performances of the models, in which two of them have a statistically significant level. According to these results, we can say that using questionnaire data, without performing feature selection, does not help with the prediction of failing of the students.

**Table 8.** Comparison between the ROC values for the normal data and including questionnaire answers.

| Semester | Combination | $p$-Value | Median (Normal) | Median (Questionnaire) |
|---|---|---|---|---|
| 2016-1 | DB2—AdaBoost | 0.02081 | 0.55128 | 0.67308 |
| | DB5—AdaBoost | 0.03846 | 0.55128 | 0.62820 |
| | DB2—Random Forest | 0.48202 | 0.42308 | 0.42308 |
| | DB5—Random Forest | 0.19819 | 0.42949 | 0.38461 |
| 2016-2 | DB2—AdaBoost | 0.44679 | 0.71795 | 0.67949 |
| | DB5—AdaBoost | 0.05542 | 0.71795 | 0.64103 |
| | DB2—Random Forest | 0.26698 | 0.62820 | 0.62820 |
| | DB5—Random Forest | 0.16124 | 0.67308 | 0.66667 |
| 2017-1 | DB2—AdaBoost | 0.00302 | 0.66013 | 0.49020 |
| | DB5—AdaBoost | 0.01466 | 0.63072 | 0.49346 |
| | DB2—Random Forest | 0.08310 | 0.54902 | 0.44118 |
| | DB5—Random Forest | 0.41219 | 0.52287 | 0.49673 |
| 2017-2 | DB2—AdaBoost | 0.39453 | 0.83974 | 0.79808 |
| | DB5—AdaBoost | 0.29755 | 0.83654 | 0.75641 |
| | DB2—Random Forest | 0.48230 | 0.67949 | 0.71154 |
| | DB5—Random Forest | 0.50000 | 0.67628 | 0.67628 |

We also analyzed the case where over-sampled data was compared with the DBs plus questionnaire data (also over-sampled). Table 9 shows the results.

In Table 9, it is important to point out that the results got better in 8 out of 16 cases. However, in these 8 cases better results, there are statistical differences in six of them. Based on these results, we can reinforce our previous statement that data from the questionnaire does not help to improve the performance of the models (even when the datasets are balanced).

Table 9. Comparison between the ROC values on the normal data with oversample and data with oversampled plus questionnaire.

| Semester | Combination | p-Value | Median (Oversample) | Median (Questionnaire Data with Oversample) |
|---|---|---|---|---|
| 2016-1 | DB2—AdaBoost | 0.06890 | 0.59615 | 0.58974 |
| | DB5—AdaBoost | 0.21254 | 0.63461 | 0.58974 |
| | DB2—Random Forest | 0.00376 | 0.50641 | 0.50641 |
| | DB5—Random Forest | 0.13058 | 0.47436 | 0.46795 |
| 2016-2 | DB2—AdaBoost | 0.00506 | 0.51282 | 0.34615 |
| | DB5—AdaBoost | 0.1488 | 0.42949 | 0.39102 |
| | DB2—Random Forest | 0.0087 | 0.67949 | 0.71795 |
| | DB5—Random Forest | 0.03328 | 0.63461 | 0.71795 |
| 2017-1 | DB2—AdaBoost | 0.28199 | 0.54575 | 0.57189 |
| | DB5—AdaBoost | 0.2510 | 0.51961 | 0.49346 |
| | DB2—Random Forest | 0.0015 | 0.57516 | 0.66013 |
| | DB5—Random Forest | 0.0533 | 0.63399 | 0.60457 |
| 2017-2 | DB2—AdaBoost | 0.0000 | 0.75641 | 0.79487 |
| | DB5—AdaBoost | 0.0000 | 0.75320 | 0.79487 |
| | DB2—Random Forest | 0.2260 | 0.91987 | 0.95833 |
| | DB5—Random Forest | 0.02940 | 0.91987 | 0.96154 |

## 5. Conclusions

This work presented a comparative study aiming to find the best combination between dataset and classification algorithm (using and not using pre-processing algorithms) to early predict at-risk students in introductory programming courses. Thirteen dataset combinations together with five classification algorithms (k-Nearest Neighbor, Multilayer Perceptron, Naive Bayes, AdaBoost and Random Forest) were used in the experiments.

The literature has works that also analyze log data from Moodle for generating predictive models for early identification of at-risk students, though the present work differs from them by providing a categorization of the counting of the logs according to the three elements required for a successful computer-mediated learning experience proposed by Garrison et al. [22], that is, cognitive, social and teaching presences.

We tested to which extent the classification of the counting of the logs into these three dimensions would serve as better datasets for the generation of more accurate predictive models. The main idea was that the different classes of students (Approved versus Reproved) would interact differently in those dimensions of presence and that could help the models to better capture students behavior in the learning settings. However, results have shown that there is no improvement in the performance of the models using those three dimensions: cognitive, social and teaching presences. Because of that, one can assume that the simple counting of interactions can be used to generate predictive models, corroborating with previous work [59]. This contradicts the findings of other authors, such as Conijn et al. [37] that say that predictive models cannot be generalized only by the LMS data logs and additional data sources are needed.

Considering that our interest is to early predict at-risk students, we measured the performances of the models until the middle of the semester (8 weeks). It is possible to say that the models achieved performances that can be considered satisfactory (with AUC ROC values of 90% already in the first week) and it is similar to the results found in the literature, for example, Detoni et al. [25], Howard et al. [46], Sandoval et al. [31], and Lu et al. [47]. These results were found considering the pre-processing of the datasets using SMOTE to balance the classes. Even with datasets being highly unbalanced, the use of SMOTE did not helped on increasing the performance of the models, improving on only 43.75% of the cases. Improvements in the performances of the models to predict at-risk students by applying SMOTE were reported in the literature in Costa et al. [24].

At last, we tested whether the inclusion of general, demographic and motivational information about the students would help to increase the performances of the models. The results show that data coming from the questionnaire did not help to improve the performance, contradicting results of other experiments reported by Tillmann et al. [28] and Adejo and Connolly [39], but corroborating previous findings of Brooks et al. [60].

The performance of the models varied according to the semester and the machine learning algorithm in use. The decision of which model apply and the the best moment for that would depend on the specifics of the semester. For instance, in some cases, it is possible to observe a drop in the performance of the models for some algorithms as the semester approaches to the middle. This is the case, for instance, of Adaboost-DB2 and Adaboost-DB5 at week 5 of semester 2017.2 (e.g., see Figure 7. In this scenario, it is recommended to use models generated by Random Forest with the use of SMOTE). From the figures, one could say that the best moment for predicting with good performances and before any significant loss, would be week 3. Again, for each semester, a given set of configuration should be picked accordingly.

One of the main contributions of our work is the investigation of the effectiveness of EDM techniques to early detect at-risk students and the extensive comparison of different combinations of classifiers and dataset (five classification algorithms with 13 DBs, generating 65 combinations for each semester). We also investigated the effect of pre-processing algorithms, such as SMOTE and the use of questionnaire data.

Regarding the courses' context, activities, tests and assignment, an important discussion that we can provide are about the activities and materials the lecturer provided during the 4 semesters presented in this work. The lecturer gradually improved the quality and the quantity of the resources of the course. It includes VPL exercises, which increased from 53 in 2016-1 to 86 in 2017-2. It also increased the number of other resources (slides, websites, examples, tutorials and so on) from 23 to 60 at the end of 2017-2. A deep analysis of these aspects shows that after the 4th week, students are autonomous to interact with the course's resources, more specifically, they can start programming using VPL. There are a lot of interactions in Moodle within VPL exercises. It seems that the course structure of the 2017-2 version is more intuitive to the students and it let them interact more precisely with the resources. We are able to conclude that a more structured course, with dozens of materials, best fits the students' needs, because they can have good interactions with the course and, consequently, succeed. It also seems that student interaction means engagement, and more engagement leads students to succeed.

The limitation of the work lies on the small number of cases included in each dataset (semester), although this limitation was softened with the use of leave-one-out validation during the training and testing of the models and with the use of SMOTE (that generates and includes new synthetic cases in the samples).

Future works include the test of more pre-processing techniques, aiming to improve the quality of the data, since the number of samples used in this work was small. Also, we intend to use other classification algorithms or even a combination of them. Deep Learning techniques can be also used for classification. When available, we intend to process data from 2018 and 2019 to check if there are any differences in the results.

**Author Contributions:** L.A.B.M.: experimental data analysis, algorithms development, experiments conduction, results description, manuscript writing; C.C.: methodology definition, experiments setup, writing; M.F.B.M.: algorithms development, data pre-processing; V.F.C.R.: course lecturer, conceived and designed the LMS structure, content and evaluation, writing-review and editing; R.M.: writing—review and editing. The manuscript was written and approved to submit by all authors.

**Funding:** This work was supported by CNPq (Brazilian National Council for Scientific and Technological Development) [Edital Universal, proc.404369/2016-2][DT-2 Productivity in Technological Development and Innovative Extension scholarship, proc.315445/2018-1].

**Conflicts of Interest:** The authors declare no conflict of interest.

## Abbreviations

The following abbreviations are used in this manuscript:

| | |
|---|---|
| APA | Average prediction Accuracy |
| BART | Bayesian Additive Regressive Trees |
| DT | Decision Tree |
| e-SVR | e-insensitive Support Vector Regressors |
| EDM | Educational Data Mining |
| IT | Information Technology |
| kNN | k-Nearest Neighbor |
| LA | Learning Analytics |
| LMS | Learning Management Systems |
| MAE | Mean Absolute Error |
| MLP | Multilayer Perceptron |
| NN | Neural Networks |
| PAP | Percentage Accurate Predictions |
| PCR | Principal Components Regression |
| RF | Random Forest |
| RMSE | Root Mean Square Error |
| SVM | Support Vector Machine |
| VLE | Virtual Learning Environment |
| VPL | Virtual Programming Laboratory plugin |

## Appendix A. Related Literature—Overview of Context and Main Characteristics

| Article | Number of Participants | Data-Mining/Machine Learning Techniques | Statistics Packages | Corpus | Measure |
|---|---|---|---|---|---|
| [24] | 423 | Naive Bayes, DT, NN, SVM | Pentaho Data Integration tool, WEKA, SMOTE | Distance education, On campus | F-measure, Precision, Recall |
| [26] | 950 | kNN, DT, RF, Logistic regression, Linear SVM, Gaussian SVM | Scikit-learn | Custom VLE | AUC, F-measure, precision, recall |
| [27] | 271 | Support Vector Classifiers, e-SVR | Not informed | Interaction with HTML elements | F-measure, R-squared |
| [28] | 145 | Multiple backwards stepwise regression, multiple squared correlation, binary logistic regressions | SPSS | LMS and Academic performance | Z-scores |
| [29] | 527 | Logistic regression, DT, and kNN | Not informed | Moodle, Piazza, Github Enterprise, WebAssign. | Kendall rank correlation coefficient, F-Measure |
| [30] | 1403 | Multiple linear regression | SPSS | home-grown EWS (early warning system) plug-in for Moodle | R-squared, ANOVA analysis |

| Article | Number of Participants | Data-Mining/Machine Learning Techniques | Statistics Packages | Corpus | Measure |
|---|---|---|---|---|---|
| [31] | 21,314 | Linear regression, Robust linear regression, RF | Not informed | Student administrative information system, LMS | R2, MAE, RMSE, APA, PAP, Precision, Recall, F-score |
| [32] | 171 | Linear Regression, RF | Developed Analytics Tool and SPSS | VLE Interaction | R-squared |
| [34] | 646 | Logistic Regression, Hierarchical linear regression | SPSS | VLE Interaction and assignment score | ANOVA analysis |
| [35] | 3882 | C4.5 DT, Radial Basis Function, kNN, Naive Bayes, Reduced Error Pruning Tree, SVM (SMO), AdaBoost, LogitBoost, Rotation Forest, Linear Regression, M5' Algorithm, M5' Rules Algorithm, RBF Networks, kNN | Free Implementation | pre-university and performance data (17 attributes) | Accuracy, MAE |
| [36] | 608 courses. Not mention the number of students. | CART DT, kNN, Naive Bayes, SVM | Weka, Python and Scikit-learn | Universitat Oberta de Calanunya Data Mart | precision, recall, F-measure, classification error and RMS |
| [37] | 4989 | multi-level and standard regressions | STATA 14 | VLE Interaction and assignment score | Accuracy, F-measure, R-Squared |
| [38] | 717 | DT | Not informed | VLE Interaction | Accuracy, F-measure |
| [39] | 141 | DT, NN, SVM, Stacking Ensemble (combining the other three) | SPSS, Rapid Miner Studio | student record system, LMS, and survey | Precision, Recall, F-measures, classification error and RMS |
| [40] | 99 | RF, Naive Bayes, kNN, LDA | scikit-learn | VLE Interaction and assignment score | Accuracy, kappa coefficient, F-meassure, AUC |
| [41] | 78,722 | NN | Not informed | VLE Interaction | Accuracy, F-measure |
| [42] | 362 | Not informed | Not informed | VLE Interaction | Accuracy |
| [43] | 202 | Logistic Regression, RF, SVM | Not informed | VLE Interaction | Precision, recall, and F-measure |
| [44] | 515 | kNN, Naive Bayes, DT (Adaboost) | Weka | VLE Interaction | Accuracy |
| [25] | 578 | SVM, Naive Bayes, DT (Adaboost) | Not informed | VLE Interaction | False-Positive, False-Negative, AUC |
| [46] | 136 | BART, RF, PCR, Multivariate Adaptive Regression Splines, kNN, NN, and SVM, XGBoost | R | Students' background information, continuous assessment, and VLE interaction | MAE |
| [47] | 59 | Principal Component Regression | Not informed | student learning profiles, out-of-class practice behaviors, homework and quiz scores, and after-school tutoring | MSE, R2, Q-Q, predictive MSE, predictive mean absolute, percentage correction |
| [48] | 9847 | Floating search, Sequential Forward Selection, C4.5, RF, RF Regression, Random Tree, Random Tree Regression, MLP, SOM, Naive Bayes, Decision Table, C4.5, kNN | Weka | 32 features | F-measure, accuracy, Precision, AUC, Recall |

## References

1. Bennedsen, J.; Caspersen, M.E. Failure rates in introductory programming: 12 years later. *ACM Inroads* **2019**, *10*, 30–36. [CrossRef]
2. Watson, C.; Li, F.W. Failure rates in introductory programming revisited. In Proceedings of the 2014 Conference on Innovation & Technology in Computer Science Education, Uppsala, Sweden, 21–25 June 2014; pp. 39–44.
3. Dasuki, S.; Quaye, A. Undergraduate Students' Failure in Programming Courses in Institutions of Higher Education in Developing Countries: A Nigerian Perspective. *Electron. J. Inf. Syst. Dev. Ctries.* **2016**, *76*, 1–18. [CrossRef]
4. Hawi, N. Causal attributions of success and failure made by undergraduate students in an introductory-level computer programming course. *Comput. Educ.* **2010**, *54*, 1127–1136. [CrossRef]
5. Krpan, D.; Mladenović, S.; Rosić, M. Undergraduate Programming Courses, Students' Perception and Success. *Procedia- Behav. Sci.* **2015**, *174*, 3868–3872. [CrossRef]
6. Jenkins, T. On the difficulty of learning to program. In Proceedings of the 3rd Annual Conference of the LTSN Centre for Information and Computer Sciences, The Higher Education Academy, Loughborough, UK, 27–29 August 2002; Volume 4, pp. 53–58.

7. Dunican, E. Making the analogy: Alternative delivery techniques for first year programming courses. In Proceedings of the 14th Workshop of the Psychology of Programming Interest Group, London, UK, 18 June 2002.
8. Byrne, P.; Lyons, G. The effect of student attributes on success in programming. *Acm Sigcse Bull.* **2001**, *33*, 49–52. [CrossRef]
9. BRASSCOM. Relatório Setorial de TIC. Technical Report, Brasscom, 2019. Available online: https://brasscom.org.br/relatorio-setorial-de-tic-2019/ (accessed on 3 October 2019).
10. Gareis, K.; Hüsing, T.; Birov, S.; Bludova, I.; Schulz, C.; Korte, W. *E-Skills for Jobs in Europe: Measuring Progress and Moving Ahead*; European Commission: Brussels, Belgium, 2014.
11. Korte, W.; Hüsing, T.; Dashja, E. *High-Tech Leadership Skills for Europe-Towards an Agenda for 2020 and Beyond*; European Communities: Brussels, Belgium, 2017.
12. European Political Strategy Centre (EPSC). Global Trends to 2030: The Future of Work and Workspaces. Technical Report, European Strategy and Policy Analysis System, 2018. Available online: https://espas.secure.europarl.europa.eu/orbis/sites/default/files/generated/document/en/Ideas%20Paper%20Future%20of%20work%20V02.pdf (accessed on 3 October 2019).
13. Bughin, J.; Hazan, E.; Lund, S.; Dahlström, P.; Wiesinger, A.; Subramaniam, A. *Skill Shift: Automation and the Future of the Workforce*; McKinsey Global Institute. McKinsey & Company: Brussels, Belgium, 2018.
14. Resnick, M. Mother's Day, Warrior Cats, and Digital Fluency: Stories from the Scratch Online Community. In Proceedings of the Constructionism 2012 Conference: Theory, Practice and Impact, Athens, Greece, 21–25 August 2012; pp. 52–58.
15. Macfadyen, L.P.; Dawson, S. Mining LMS data to develop an 'early warning system' for educators: A proof of concept. *Comput. Educ.* **2010**, *54*, 588–599. [CrossRef]
16. Lakkaraju, H.; Aguiar, E.; Shan, C.; Miller, D.; Bhanpuri, N.; Ghani, R.; Addison, K.L. A machine learning framework to identify students at risk of adverse academic outcomes. In Proceedings of the 21th ACM SIGKDD International Conference on Knowledge Discovery and Data Mining, Sydney, NSW, Australia, 10–13 August 2015; pp. 1909–1918.
17. Romero, C.; Ventura, S. Data mining in education. *Wiley Interdiscip. Rev. Data Min. Knowl. Discov.* **2013**, *3*, 12–27. [CrossRef]
18. Mishra, T.; Kumar, D.; Gupta, S. Mining students' data for prediction performance. In Proceedings of the 2014 Fourth International Conference on Advanced Computing & Communication Technologies (ACCT), Rohtak, India, 8–9 February 2014; pp. 255–262.
19. Murray, M.; Pérez, J.; Geist, D.; Hedrick, A. Student interaction with content in online and hybrid courses: Leading horses to the proverbial water. In Proceedings of the Informing Science and Information Technology Education Conference, Porto, Portugal, 1–6 July 2013; Informing Science Institute: Porto, Portugal, 2013; pp. 99–115.
20. Dickson, W.P. *Toward a Deeper Understanding of Student Performance in Virtual High School Courses: Using qUantitative Analyses and Data Visualization to Inform Decision Making*; Technical Report; NCREL/Learning Point Associates: Naperville, IL, USA, 2005. Available online: https://msu.edu/user/pdickson/talks/DicksonNCREL2005.pdf (accessed on 13 December 2019).
21. Romero, C.; Ventura, S. Educational data mining: A review of the state of the art. *IEEE Trans. Syst. Man Cybern. Part C Appl. Rev.* **2010**, *40*, 601–618. [CrossRef]
22. Garrison, D.R.; Anderson, T.; Archer, W. Critical inquiry in a text-based environment: Computer conferencing in higher education. *Internet High. Educ.* **1999**, *2*, 87–105. [CrossRef]
23. Swan, K. Learning effectiveness online: What the research tells us. *Elem. Qual. Online Educ. Pract. Dir.* **2003**, *4*, 13–47.
24. Costa, E.B.; Fonseca, B.; Santana, M.A.; de Araújo, F.F.; Rego, J. Evaluating the effectiveness of educational data mining techniques for early prediction of students' academic failure in introductory programming courses. *Comput. Hum. Behav.* **2017**, *73*, 247–256. [CrossRef]
25. Detoni, D.; Cechinel, C.; Matsumura, R.A.; Brauner, D.F. Learning to Identify At-Risk Students in Distance Education Using Interaction Counts. *Rev. De Informática Teórica E Apl.* **2016**, *23*, 124–140. [CrossRef]
26. Azcona, D.; Hsiao, I.H.; Smeaton, A.F. Detecting students-at-risk in computer programming classes with learning analytics from students' digital footprints. In *User Modeling and User-Adapted Interaction*; Springer: Berlin, Germany, 2019; pp. 1–30.

27. Leppänen, L.; Leinonen, J.; Ihantola, P.; Hellas, A. Predicting Academic Success Based on Learning Material Usage. In Proceedings of the 18th Annual Conference on Information Technology Education, Rochester, NY, USA, 4–7 October 2017; pp. 13–18.
28. Tillmann, A.; Krömker, D.; Horn, F.; Gattinger, T. *Analysing & Predicting Students Performance in an Introductory Computer Science Course*; Hochschuldidaktik der Informatik HDI 2018; Universität Potsdam: Potsdam, Germany, 2018; pp. 29–46.
29. Sheshadri, A.; Gitinabard, N.; Lynch, C.F.; Barnes, T.; Heckman, S. Predicting student performance based on online study habits: A study of blended courses. *arXiv* **2019**, arXiv:1904.07331.
30. Jokhan, A.; Sharma, B.; Singh, S. Early warning system as a predictor for student performance in higher education blended courses. *Stud. Higher Educ.* **2018**, *44*, 1900–1911. [CrossRef]
31. Sandoval, A.; Gonzalez, C.; Alarcon, R.; Pichara, K.; Montenegro, M. Centralized student performance prediction in large courses based on low-cost variables in an institutional context. *Internet High. Educ.* **2018**, *37*, 76–89. [CrossRef]
32. Mwalumbwe, I.; Mtebe, J.S. Using learning analytics to predict students' performance in moodle learning management system: A case of mbeya university of science and technology. *Electron. J. Inf. Syst. Dev. Ctries.* **2017**, *79*, 1–13. [CrossRef]
33. Hung, J.L.; Wang, M.C.; Wang, S.; Abdelrasoul, M.; Li, Y.; He, W. Identifying at-risk students for early interventions—A time-series clustering approach. *IEEE Trans. Emerg. Top. Comput.* **2017**, *5*, 45–55. [CrossRef]
34. Soffer, T.; Cohen, A. Students' engagement characteristics predict success and completion of online courses. *J. Comput. Assisted Learn.* **2019**, *35*, 378–389. [CrossRef]
35. Kostopoulos, G.; Kotsiantis, S.; Pierrakeas, C.; Koutsonikos, G.; Gravvanis, G.A. Forecasting students' success in an open university. *Int. J. Learn. Technol.* **2018**, *13*, 26–43. [CrossRef]
36. Baneres, D.; Rodriguez-Gonzalez, M.E.; Serra, M. An Early Feedback Prediction System for Learners At-risk within a First-year Higher Education Course. *IEEE Trans. Learn. Technol.* **2019**, *12*, 249–263. [CrossRef]
37. Conijn, R.; Snijders, C.; Kleingeld, A.; Matzat, U. Predicting student performance from LMS data: A comparison of 17 blended courses using Moodle. *IEEE Trans. Learn. Technol.* **2017**, *10*, 17–29. [CrossRef]
38. Sukhbaatar, O.; Ogata, K.; Usagawa, T. Mining Educational Data to Predict Academic Dropouts: a Case Study in Blended Learning Course. In Proceedings of the IEEE TENCON 2018-2018 IEEE Region 10 Conference, Jeju, Korea, 28–31 October 2018; pp. 2205–2208.
39. Adejo, O.W.; Connolly, T. Predicting student academic performance using multi-model heterogeneous ensemble approach. *J. Appl. Res. High. Educ.* **2018**, *10*, 61–75. [CrossRef]
40. Umer, R.; Mathrani, A.; Susnjak, T.; Lim, S. Mining Activity Log Data to Predict Student's Outcome in a Course. In Proceedings of the 2019 International Conference on Big Data and Education, London, UK, 30 March–1 April 2019; pp. 52–58.
41. Olivé, D.M.; Huynh, D.; Reynolds, M.; Dougiamas, M.; Wiese, D. A Quest for a one-size-fits-all Neural Network: Early Prediction of Students At Risk in Online Courses. *IEEE Trans. Learn. Technol.* **2019**, *12*, 171–183. [CrossRef]
42. Cohen, A. Analysis of student activity in web-supported courses as a tool for predicting dropout. *Educ. Technol. Res. Dev.* **2017**, *65*, 1285–1304. [CrossRef]
43. Kondo, N.; Okubo, M.; Hatanaka, T. Early Detection of At-Risk Students Using Machine Learning Based on LMS Log Data. In Proceedings of the 2017 6th IIAI International Congress on Advanced Applied Informatics (IIAI-AAI), Hamamatsu, Japan, 9–13 July 2017; pp. 198–201.
44. Usman, U.I.; Salisu, A.; Barroon, A.I.; Yusuf, A. A Comparative Study of Base Classifiers in Predicting Students' Performance based on Interaction with LMS Platform. *FUDMA J. Sci.* **2019**, *3*, 231–239.
45. Zhou, Q.; Quan, W.; Zhong, Y.; Xiao, W.; Mou, C.; Wang, Y. Predicting high-risk students using Internet access logs. *Knowl. Inf. Syst.* **2018**, *55*, 393–413. [CrossRef]
46. Howard, E.; Meehan, M.; Parnell, A. Contrasting prediction methods for early warning systems at undergraduate level. *Internet High. Educ.* **2018**, *37*, 66–75. [CrossRef]
47. Lu, O.H.; Huang, A.Y.; Huang, J.C.; Lin, A.J.; Ogata, H.; Yang, S.J. Applying Learning Analytics for the Early Prediction of Students' Academic Performance in Blended Learning. *J. Educ. Technol. Soc.* **2018**, *21*, 220–232.
48. Gray, C.C.; Perkins, D. Utilizing early engagement and machine learning to predict student outcomes. *Comput. Educ.* **2019**, *131*, 22–32. [CrossRef]

49. Rodríguez-del Pino, J.C.; Rubio-Royo, E.; Hernández-Figueroa, Z.J. A Virtual Programming Lab for Moodle with automatic assessment and anti-plagiarism features. In Proceedings of the International Conference on e-Learning, e-Business, Enterprise Information Systems, and e-Government (EEE), Las Vegas, ND, USA, 16–19 July 2012; The Steering Committee of The World Congress in Computer Science, CSREA Press: Las Vegas, ND, USA, 2012; pp. 80–85.
50. Detoni, D.; Cechinel, C.; Matsumura Araújo, R. Modelagem e Predição de Reprovação de Acadêmicos de Cursos de Educação a Distância a partir da Contagem de Interações. *Revista Brasileira de Informática na Educação* **2015**, *23*, 1–11.
51. Moore, M.G. Three types of interaction. *Am. J. Distance Educ.* **1989**, *3*, 1–7.
52. McKinney, W. Data structures for statistical computing in python. In Proceedings of the 9th Python in Science Conference, Austin, TX, USA, 28–30 June 2010; Volume 445, pp. 51–56.
53. Chawla, N.V.; Bowyer, K.W.; Hall, L.O.; Kegelmeyer, W.P. SMOTE: Synthetic minority over-sampling technique. *J. Artif. Intell. Res.* **2002**, *16*, 321–357. [CrossRef]
54. Lemaître, G.; Nogueira, F.; Aridas, C.K. Imbalanced-learn: A Python Toolbox to Tackle the Curse of Imbalanced Datasets in Machine Learning. *J. Mach. Learn. Res.* **2017**, *18*, 1–5.
55. Pedregosa, F.; Varoquaux, G.; Gramfort, A.; Michel, V.; Thirion, B.; Grisel, O.; Blondel, M.; Prettenhofer, P.; Weiss, R.; Dubourg, V.; et al. Scikit-learn: Machine Learning in Python. *J. Mach. Learn. Res.* **2011**, *12*, 2825–2830.
56. Bradley, A.P. The use of the area under the ROC curve in the evaluation of machine learning algorithms. *Pattern Recognit.* **1997**, *30*, 1145–1159. [CrossRef]
57. Gašević, D.; Dawson, S.; Rogers, T.; Gasevic, D. Learning analytics should not promote one size fits all: The effects of instructional conditions in predicting academic success. *Internet High. Educ.* **2016**, *28*, 68–84. [CrossRef]
58. Mann, H.B.; Whitney, D.R. On a test of whether one of two random variables is stochastically larger than the other. *Ann. Math. Stat.* **1947**, *18*, 50–60. [CrossRef]
59. Umer, R.; Susnjak, T.; Mathrani, A.; Suriadi, S. A learning analytics approach: Using online weekly student engagement data to make predictions on student performance. In Proceedings of the 2018 International Conference on Computing, Electronic and Electrical Engineering (ICE Cube), Quetta, Pakistan, 12–13 November 2018; pp. 1–5.
60. Brooks, C.; Thompson, C.; Teasley, S. Who you are or what you do: Comparing the predictive power of demographics vs. activity patterns in massive open online courses (MOOCs). In Proceedings of the Second (2015) ACM Conference on Learning@ Scale, Vancouver, BC, Canada, 14–18 March 2015; pp. 245–248.

© 2019 by the authors. Licensee MDPI, Basel, Switzerland. This article is an open access article distributed under the terms and conditions of the Creative Commons Attribution (CC BY) license (http://creativecommons.org/licenses/by/4.0/).

*Article*

# The Machine Learning-Based Dropout Early Warning System for Improving the Performance of Dropout Prediction

**Sunbok Lee [1] and Jae Young Chung [2],\***

1. Department of Psychology, University of Houston, Houston, TX 77004, USA
2. Department of Education, Ewha Womans University, Seoul 03760, Korea
\* Correspondence: jychung@ewha.ac.kr; Tel.: +82-2-3277-2632

Received: 4 July 2019; Accepted: 29 July 2019; Published: 31 July 2019

**Abstract:** A dropout early warning system enables schools to preemptively identify students who are at risk of dropping out of school, to promptly react to them, and eventually to help potential dropout students to continue their learning for a better future. However, the inherent class imbalance between dropout and non-dropout students could pose difficulty in building accurate predictive modeling for a dropout early warning system. The present study aimed to improve the performance of a dropout early warning system: (a) by addressing the class imbalance issue using the synthetic minority oversampling techniques (SMOTE) and the ensemble methods in machine learning; and (b) by evaluating the trained classifiers with both receiver operating characteristic (ROC) and precision–recall (PR) curves. To that end, we trained random forest, boosted decision tree, random forest with SMOTE, and boosted decision tree with SMOTE using the big data samples of the 165,715 high school students from the National Education Information System (NEIS) in South Korea. According to our ROC and PR curve analysis, boosted decision tree showed the optimal performance.

**Keywords:** dropout; machine learning; big data; class-imbalance; oversampling; ensemble

## 1. Introduction

The negative consequences of students' dropping out of school are significant for both the individual and society. The educational deficiencies of dropout students could severely limit economic and social well-being in their later lives [1]. The society also suffers losses because the nation's productive capacity could be undermined by the shortage of the skilled workforce, and also the dropout students are more likely to be frequent recipients of welfare and unemployment subsidies [2]. Because of those negative consequences, students' dropouts have long been considered as a serious educational problem by educators, researchers, and policymakers. A dropout early warning system can help schools to preemptively identify students who are at risk of dropping out of school and to promptly react to them [3]. The students at risk are likely to drop out without carefully considering the negative consequences of their decisions or without having an opportunity to consult with experts. The early intervention informed by the dropout early warning system can redirect potential dropout students onto the path to graduation and lead them to a better future [4]. Because of the great potential, many governments have developed dropout early warning systems. For example, the department of education and early childhood development in the state of Victoria in Australia developed the Student Mapping Tool (SMT) to help schools to identify students at risk of disengagement and dropout [5], and the state of Wisconsin in the United States developed the Dropout Early Warning System (DEWS) to predict students' dropouts [6]. In the United States, about half of public high schools implemented the dropout early warning systems during 2014–2015 [7].

Machine learning is a promising tool for building a predictive model for a dropout early warning system. However, the class-imbalance could be one of the potential difficulties in implementing a dropout early warning system using machine learning. In the binary outcome representing students' dropouts, the proportions of the two classes (i.e., dropouts and non-dropouts) tend to be imbalanced (e.g., 1.4 percent of dropouts vs. 98.6 percent of non-dropouts in Korean high school in 2016). In general, machine learning classifiers trained on datasets with imbalanced classes tend to show a very poor performance in predicting the minor class because the classifiers ignore the minor class as a noise [8,9]. Because the class of interest in dropout prediction is a minor class (i.e., dropouts), the class-imbalance issue could severely degrade the sensitivity of the early warning system in predicting potential dropout students. Another key issue in the presence of class imbalance is to use performance metrics that are sensitive to performance differences. Traditionally, the area under the curve (AUC) in the receiver operating characteristic (ROC) curve has been widely used in machine learning literature. However, in the presence of class imbalance, the ROC curve analysis may not be sensitive enough to differentiate the performances of classifiers, and the precision–recall (PR) curve may perform better [10]. In the literature, Márquez-Vera et al. [11] predicted student failure at school using genetic programming and different machine learning approaches by addressing the class imbalance issue using the synthetic minority oversampling techniques (SMOTE), and identified the best model based on the true positive (TP) rate, true negative (TN) rate, and accuracy. Knowles [6] used machine learning to build a predictive model of student dropout risk, and identified the best statistical model using the ROC curve. Márquez-Vera et al. [12] used various machine learning algorithms for early dropout prediction, and used the TP rate, TN rate, accuracy, and AUC. However, in the previous literature, the class-imbalance issue and the advantage of using the PR curve have not been fully discussed yet. Thus, the present study aimed to improve the performance of a dropout early warning system: (a) by addressing the class imbalance issue using the SMOTE and ensemble methods in machine learning; and (b) by evaluating the trained classifiers with both ROC and PR curves. To that end, we trained random forest, boosted decision tree, random forest with SMOTE, and boosted decision tree with SMOTE using the big data samples of the 165,715 high school students from the National Education Information System (NEIS) in South Korea. Because the class-imbalance issue is prevalent (e.g., cheaters in online education), the implication of this study is relevant to building predictive models for other educational outcomes as well.

## 2. Students' Dropouts in South Korea

In this section, we briefly present the current status and reasons for high school dropouts in South Korea to clarify the types of dropouts we are interested in. We also present the rationale for the goal of our dropout early warning system. Table 1 shows the dropout rates of high school students in South Korea from 2010 to 2016 [13]. The dropout rates have decreased from 2.0 percent in 2010 to 1.4 percent in 2016.

**Table 1.** The Dropout rates of high school students in South Korea from 2010 to 2016.

| Year | The Total Number of Students | The Number of Dropouts Students | Dropouts Rates (%) |
|---|---|---|---|
| 2016 | 1,752,457 | 23,441 | 1.4 |
| 2015 | 1,788,266 | 22,554 | 1.3 |
| 2014 | 1,839,372 | 25,318 | 1.4 |
| 2013 | 1,893,303 | 30,382 | 1.6 |
| 2012 | 1,920,087 | 34,934 | 1.8 |
| 2011 | 1,943,798 | 37,391 | 1.9 |
| 2010 | 1,962,356 | 38,887 | 2.0 |

Table 2 shows the reasons for high school dropouts in South Korea in 2013 and 2016 [13]. Students left schools for various reasons: diseases, family problems, poor academic performance, poor relationship with others, strict school rules, and other reasons (e.g., studying overseas and alternative education). Simply leaving schools does not necessarily mean negative outcomes. Some students leave schools to study overseas, to attend alternative education programs, or to pursue their own career paths earlier. The dropouts due to those positive reasons are not the types of dropouts we are interested in. Chung et al. [14] defined at-risk youths as the youths who are exposed to personal and environmental risks, likely to experience behavioral or psychological problems and find it difficult to achieve normal development without appropriate educational intervention. This group of youths reports high risks of running away from home, dropout, unemployment, violence, prostitution, substance abuse, and other misconducts, crimes, as well as psychological disorders such as depression, anxiety, and suicide. We are interested in predicting the dropouts among those at-risk youths who could benefit from the intervention programs informed by the dropout early warning system.

Table 2. The Reasons for high school dropouts in South Korea in 2013 and 2016.

| | Leaving | | | | | | Expulsion | Total |
|---|---|---|---|---|---|---|---|---|
| | Diseases | Family Problem | Poor Academic Performance | Poor Relationship with Others | Strict School Rules | Other Reasons | | |
| 2013 | 1429 (4.7%) | 2327 (7.7%) | 9887 (32.6%) | 486 (1.6%) | 1019 (3.4%) | 14,094 (46.5%) | 1090 (3.6%) | 30,287 (100%) |
| 2016 | 882 (4.7%) | 503 (2.7%) | 4047 (21.6%) | 222 (1.2%) | 225 (1.2%) | 11,855 (63.3%) | 998 (5.3%) | 18,732 (100%) |

The optimal performance of a classifier is only meaningful in relation to a specific task. In a dropout early warning system, the sensitivity represents the proportion of actual dropout students predicted correctly. In this study, we aimed to maximize the sensitivity of our dropout prediction for the following reason. The primary aim of public schools is to support successful learning of all students without a single failure. UNESCO has placed "Education for All (EFA)" as the international policy agenda [15]. The idea behind the agenda is to ensure all students around the world benefit from education. The United States has been building an accountability system to keep all students from falling behind through the "No Child Left Behind Act" and "Every Study Succeeds Act" [16]. To support successful learning of all students, in South Korea, it was proposed to operate a three-tier dropout prevention programs [17]. In the first-tier, all students participate in the general prevention program designed to prevent school dropouts. In the second-tier, students who were identified as being at-risk of dropouts participate in more specialized group- or individual-based prevention programs. In the third-tier, students who express their intention to dropout have opportunities to deliberate their decisions for two weeks before making their final decisions. During the period of deliberation, students receive personalized counseling and training. In this proposed three-tier prevention programs, it is very important to preemptively identify all the potential dropout students and to promptly react to them in order to reduce the number of students who actually want to drop out. Another important performance metric in a dropout early warning system is the precision (or positive predictive value), which represents the proportion of predicted dropout students who actually dropout. The precision is important because it is directly related to the cost for the intervention.

## 3. Analysis Plan

### 3.1. Supervised Learning

We used supervised learning in machine learning to train our binary classifiers that predict students' dropouts and non-dropouts. The goal of the supervised learning is to estimate the best mapping function $f(.)$ from the set of features ($X$s) to the target label ($Y$) by training a specific machine learning model on a dataset. The learning process in the supervised learning focuses on assuring the capability of a trained model generalizing knowledge learned from the current observations to the future observations. The emphasis on the generalizability of the model makes the overfitting a critical issue in supervised learning. The overfitting is said to occur when a model is more complex than necessary and therefore fits too much noise in the training dataset. The model complexity is controlled by the so-called hyper-parameters of the model (e.g., the strength of the penalty in the regularized regression, the depth of a tree in the decision tree). Therefore, the key task in supervised learning is to determine the optimal values of hyper-parameters to make a balance between bias and variance. In practice, $k$-fold cross-validation is often used to determine (or tune) hyper-parameters. In $k$-fold cross-validation, the training dataset is partitioned into $k$ equal-sized subsets, each of which is called a fold. At each iteration from 1 to $k$, a single fold is retained as the validation dataset, and the remaining $k-1$ folds are retained as the training dataset, and the model trained on the training dataset is evaluated on the validation dataset. Then, $k$ performance metrics from the $k$ iterations are averaged to produce a less biased estimate of the performance of the model. The best hyper-parameters can be determined by comparing the averaged performance metrics from $k$-fold cross-validation of the models with different values of hyper-parameters. We used 10-fold cross-validation for our analysis.

### 3.2. The Problem of Class Imbalance

The focus of our analysis is to train our binary classifiers by addressing the class-imbalance issue. In classification, a classifier predicts categorical labels (or classes). The classes are imbalanced if there are many more instances of some classes than others in a dataset [18]. The class imbalance is prevalent because many real-world applications, such as fraud detection, spam detection, anomaly detection, and psychological diagnosis, are composed of a large number of normal examples with only a small number of abnormal or interesting examples [19]. The ratio between minor and major classes can be 1:100, 1:1000, or even 1:10,000 depending on the applications. For example, fraudulent cases in retail banking are about 0.1 percent [20].

The class imbalance poses a difficulty in classification because the classifiers trained on the imbalance dataset tend to show a higher predictive accuracy on the major classes, but a poorer predictive accuracy on the minor classes. This bias toward the major classes happens because the performance metrics tend to treat the minor classes as the noise, and therefore guide the classifiers to ignore the misclassification of the minor classes during the learning process [9]. Table 3 shows a hypothetical confusion matrix illustrating the case where the accuracy of a binary classifier can be deceptively excellent when the classifier completely ignores the misclassification of the minor classes. In this example, the proportions of dropouts and non-dropouts are imbalanced, i.e., 100 dropouts (1%) vs. 9900 non-dropouts (99%). The accuracy of the binary classifier in this example is 0.99 despite the complete misclassifications of the dropouts. In this way, when classes are imbalanced, the minor classes are often more misclassified than the major classes. Because the minor class is usually the class of interest in classification, the class imbalance has been a challenging problem in data mining community [21,22].

The problem of class imbalance is a well-known issue in the machine learning community. However, less attention has been paid to this issue when developing dropout early warning system. As presented in Table 1, high school dropout rates in South Korea are less than 2%. According to the National Center for Education Statistics, high school dropout rates in the United States have decreased from 27.2% in 1960 to 6.1% in 2016. Because the class of interest in the dropout prediction is a minor class (i.e., dropout), the issue of class imbalance needs to be properly handled when building a predictive model for the dropout early warning system.

**Table 3.** The hypothetical confusion matrix showing the case where the accuracy of a binary classifier can be deceptive for an imbalanced dataset. In this example, the proportions of dropouts and non-dropouts are imbalanced, i.e., 100 dropouts (1%) vs. 9900 non-dropouts (99%). Despite of the complete misclassifications of the dropouts, the accuracy is still $0.99 = (0 + 9900)/(0 + 0 + 100 + 9900) = 9900/10000$ because the correct predictions of the non-dropout dominate the accuracy.

|  |  | True Labels | |
|---|---|---|---|
|  |  | Dropout | Non-Dropout |
| Predicted lables | Dropout | 0 | 0 |
|  | Non-dropout | 100 | 9900 |

### 3.3. SMOTE

Many methods have been proposed to address the problem of class imbalance. In the literature, those methods are typically categorized into four groups: algorithm-level, data-level, cost-sensitive, and ensemble approaches [8,9]. The algorithm-level approaches modify existing classification algorithms to be biased toward the minor classes to improve the performance of the model in predicting the minor classes [23,24]. These approaches require knowledge of the specific classifiers, and why the classifiers fail to modify the algorithms. The data-level approaches rebalance the imbalanced classes by over-sampling the minor classes or under-sampling the major classes to alleviate the effect of imbalanced classes [19]. Because these approaches are implemented in the preprocessing step, they are independent of specific classifiers and also can be more easily implemented. The cost-sensitive approaches combine both the data- and algorithm-level approaches by adding high misclassification costs for the minor classes (data level approaches), and also modifying the classification algorithms to accept the costs ([25], algorithm level approaches). Recently, the ensemble approaches are attracting more and more attention as a solution to the class imbalance problem. Hybridizing the bagging and boosting paradigms in ensemble methods with the algorithm-level, data-level, and cost-sensitive approaches for the imbalanced dataset turned out to be very promising. Readers who are interested in a more compressive review on this topic are referred to the works of Galar et al. [9] and Haixiang et al. [8].

In this study, we used SMOTE [19] from the data-level approaches to address the problem of class imbalance. In the data-level approaches, the under-sampling randomly eliminates some major classes to make the major classes less effective on the learning process. However, the under-sampling could remove major classes which are more representative and informative than others, and therefore the decision boundary could be biased. The over-sampling randomly replicates the minor classes to make the minor classes more effective on the learning process. However, the over-sampling creates repeated copies of the same minor class instances many times, and therefore the classifiers could overfit to these minor class instances. After reviewing previous studies on over- and under-sampling, Chawla et al. [19] summarized that the under-sampling showed better performance than the over-sampling, and the combination of the over- and under-sampling did not outperform the under-sampling. They proposed SMOTE as a new over-sampling technique in which the minor class instances are over-sampled by creating synthetic instances rather than creating the same minor instances multiple times with replacement, and showed that the combination of SMOTE and under-sampling performed better than the plain under-sampling. In SMOTE, the minor class instances are over-sampled by creating synthetic instances along the line segments joining the $k$ nearest neighbor instances with minor classes. The idea behind the SMOTE is to over-sample similar instances rather than to over-sample the same instances multiple times so that the classifiers are not overfitted to the minor class instances.

### 3.4. Ensemble Methods

Machine learning has been successfully applied for predictive modeling in various fields. Especially, ensemble methods have gained considerable attention in recent years because ensemble methods can substantially improve the accuracy of predictions by combining multiple machine learning algorithms [26]. Each algorithm in the ensemble methods is usually called a base (or individual or component) learner. The ensemble of learners has outperformed a single learner in various tasks, such as the object detection [27], lung cancer identification [28], and fraud detection [29]. The superior performance of ensemble methods mainly comes from the better generalizability of the ensemble of learners.

In ensemble methods, bootstrap aggregating (bagging) and boosting are the two popular paradigms. As the name indicates, bagging improves the accuracy of predictions by aggregating predictions from multiple learners. In bagging, the $N$ base learners are trained in parallel on $N$ bootstrap samples from the original dataset, and then the $N$ predictions from the $N$ base learners are combined using majority voting or other synthesizing methods. Because of its aggregating (or averaging) nature, bagging can reduce the variance of a model. The random forest is a popular machine learning algorithm that uses the bagging paradigm. The random forest is the collection of $N$ decision trees, and combines $N$ predictions from the $N$ decision trees trained on the $N$ bootstrap samples to make a final prediction.

Boosting is another ensemble paradigm. The idea behind boosting is to produce a series of weak learners to make a strong learner. Unlike bagging in which learners are trained in parallel and the predictions are aggregated without preference to any learner, boosting sequentially trains learners, and the predictions are aggregated with heavier weights on better learners. For example, the adaptive boosting (AdaBoost) calls a weak or base learner repeatedly in a series of rounds $t = 1, ..., T$ by weighting previously misclassified instances with higher weight, and then combines the $T$ predictions from the $T$ base learners with the weights of learners determined during the training process [30]. Notice that both the instances and learners have their distributions of weights which are updated across the rounds. The weight distribution for instances at round $t$ makes the learner at round $t$ focus on the instances that were misclassified at round $t-1$, whereas the weight distribution for learners determines how to combine the $T$ learners after $T$ rounds. In addition to the variance, the boosting can also reduce the bias because of its adaptive nature. In sum, the bagging trains a set of learners in parallel to reduce the variance by exploiting the independence between learners, whereas the boosting sequentially trains a series of learners to reduce both the bias and variance by exploiting the dependence between learners.

In total, we trained four classifiers using the big data samples of the 165,715 high school students from the NEIS database in South Korea: random forest, boosted decision tree, random forest with SMOTE, and boosted decision tree with SMOTE.

*3.5. Performance Metrics for Binary Classifiers*

A confusion matrix is the cross-tabulation between the true labels from the labeled dataset and the predicted labels from a classifier. Depending on the values of true and predicted labels, the true positive (TP), true negative (TN), false positive (FP), and false negative (FN) can be defined, and these four cases are used to define sensitivity (or recall, TP/(TP + FN)), specificity (TN/(FP + TN)), accuracy ((TP + TN)/(TP + FN + FP + TN)), negative predictive value (TN/(FN + TN)), and positive predictive value (or precision, TP/(TP + FP)).

The area under the curve (AUC) is another popular metric. The AUC is the area under the receiver operating characteristic (ROC) curve [31]. The ROC curve is the curve in the two-dimensional ROC space whose $y$-axis represents a classifier's true positive rate (or sensitivity) and $x$-axis represents a classifier's false positive rates (or $1 -$ specificity). Each point in the ROC space represents a classifier's (false positive rate, true positive rate) pair. If the classifier is the discrete classifier that produces only a class label (e.g., dropout or non-dropout), then the performance of the discrete classifier can be represented as a point in the ROC space. In the ROC space, the upper left point (0, 1) represents a perfect classifier that never predicts the true negative labels as positive (i.e., false positive rate = 0) and predicts all the true positive labels as positive (i.e., true positive rate = 1). Some classifiers produce the probability of the instances being a member of a class, instead of the discrete class label. Such classifiers can be converted into the discrete classifiers by introducing a threshold. The ROC curve for such classifier is the set of (false positive rate, true positive rate) pairs for all possible thresholds. The ROC curve allows us to visualize the trade-off between the true positive rate (or sensitivity) and false positive rates (or 1 − specificity) of a classifier. That is, it shows that a classifier cannot increase the true positive rate without increasing the false positive rate [9].

Although the ROC curve is a popular evaluation metric for binary classifiers, the precision–recall (PR) curve is recommended when evaluating binary classifiers trained on imbalanced datasets [10]. When the number of negative instances is very large, the true negative (TN) is also likely to be very large. Then, the large true negative (TN) makes the specificity less sensitive. Therefore, the precision (or positive predictive value) could be a more sensitive measure for the imbalanced data because the precision is not affected by the large true negative (TN). Notice that recall is just another name for the sensitivity, and therefore the PR curve only replaces the false positive rate in the ROC curve with the precision. In PR curves, good classifiers aim for the upper right corner. In the present study, we used both the ROC and PR curves for model-wide threshold-free evaluation of binary classifiers.

## 4. Methods

### 4.1. Data

**Samples.** Our sample consists of the big data samples of 165,715 high school students from the NEIS database of 2014. Those are students from two big cities and two provinces in South Korea: Seoul, Incheon, Gyeongsangbuk-do, and Gyeongsangnam-do. The proportion of male students is 0.60. The proportions of freshman, sophomore, and senior in high school are 0.33, 0.34, and 0.33, respectively. The NEIS is the web-based integrated administration system that connects South Korean's education organizations including around 12,000 elementary, middle and high schools, 17 city and provincial offices of education, and the Ministry of Education. The NEIS was developed by South Korea's Ministry of Education in the early 2000s for several purposes. The NEIS was designed to reduce teachers' workload. For example, teachers do not need to prepare various reports, statistics, and administrative documents. In addition, the NIES was designed to enhance the conveniences of citizens, especially parents. For example, parents can request 38 types of student information (e.g., school schedule, meal schedule, grades, and absence) and official certificates online. The NEIS was also designed to enhance the efficiency in school administration. For example, the NEIS reduces manual document preparation, enhances information sharing, and improves decision making processes at a policy level. Currently, the NEIS is maintained by the Korea Education & Research Information Service (KERIS) under the Ministry of Education. The NEIS has two databases. The educational affairs database contains information more than six million students, such as academic achievement, absence, health and so on. The school administration database contains information about HR affairs, teacher information, and school information. Ethics Committee/Institutional Review Board approval for this study was not sought because we used the government data that are already collected in the NEIS system, and IRB approval is not required in South Korea in this case.

**Target label.** In this study, the target label for prediction is students' dropouts. The binary target label representing students' dropouts was created based on variables named "the school register change" and "the reasons for the school register change" in the NEIS database. The variable named "the school register change" has 15 categories such as entrance, expulsion, leaving, transfer, and graduation. The variable named "the reasons for the school register change"' describes 43 reasons for the changes. As discussed above, we are interested in the dropouts among those at-risk youths who could benefit from the intervention programs informed by the dropout early warning system. Therefore, in this study, we defined dropout students as the ones who have dropped out of school for the 13 negative reasons presented in Table 4. In total, out of 165,715 students, 1348 students (0.81%) were identified as dropout students in our analysis.

**Table 4.** 13 reasons for the school register changes considered as dropouts.

| Category | Specific Reasons | Counts | Percentages (%) |
|---|---|---|---|
| Behavior | Violation of School Rules | 126 | 9.3 |
| Behavior | Requests from Autonomous Committees | 15 | 1.1 |
| Behavior | Assault/Burglary | 4 | 0.3 |
| Behavior | Others | 5 | 0.4 |
| Family | Family Trouble | 9 | 0.7 |
| Maladjustment | Poor Academic Performance | 690 | 51.2 |
| Maladjustment | Victimization | 1 | 0.1 |
| Maladjustment | Relationship with Friends/Teachers | 23 | 1.7 |
| Maladjustment | Strict Rules | 66 | 4.9 |
| Maladjustment | Others | 375 | 27.8 |
| Disease | Disease | 8 | 0.6 |
| Others | Running away from Home | 21 | 1.6 |
| Others | Others | 5 | 0.4 |
| | | 1348 | 100% |

**Features.** Following the recommendation from the National High School Center, we used the attendance, behavior, and course performance (the "ABCs") as the key indicators for our dropout predictions [32]. Previous studies also showed that low attendance at the beginning of a semester can be an indicator for the dropout prediction [33]. Therefore, we further included the attendance in the first four weeks as indicators. In sum, we used 15 features to predict students' dropouts: the unauthorized absence in the first four weeks, unauthorized early leave in first four weeks, unauthorized class absence in first four weeks, unauthorized lateness in first four weeks, unauthorized absence, unauthorized early leave, unauthorized class absence, unauthorized lateness, number of self-regulated activities, number of club activities, number of volunteer activities, number of career development activities, normalized ranking on Korean, normalized ranking on Math, and normalized ranking on English.

*4.2. Preprocessing, Tuning, Training, and Testing*

We used the caret package in R to preprocess, tune, train, and test the four classifiers.

**Preprocessing.** The original dataset that consists of 165,715 students was divided into training (80%; N = 132,573) and testing (20%; N = 33,142) datasets to train and evaluate the four classifiers. For the preprocessing, the 15 features in the training dataset were centered, scaled, and median imputed using the preProcess() function in the caret package.

**SMOTE.** The preprocessed training dataset was over- and under-sampled using the SMOTE() function in the DMwR package in R.

**Tuning.** The 10-fold cross-validation was used to tune the hyper-parameters of each classifier by setting the method option to cv and number option to 10 in the trainControl() function in the caret package. The optimal hyper-parameters were chosen by comparing the classifiers' ROCs with different values of hyper-parameters.

**Training.** The train() function in the caret package in R was used to train the random forest, boosted decision tree, random forest with SMOTE, and boosted decision tree with SMOTE.

**Testing.** The trained classifiers were evaluated on the testing dataset using the predict() function in the caret package. The testing dataset was not oversampled in any case.

## 5. Results

Figure 1 presents the density plots for the selected eight features. Each plot presents the density plot of a specific feature for both the dropouts (shaded as red) and the non-dropouts (shaded as blue). Figure 1 shows that the dropout students are more likely to be problematic in attendance and achievement, and are less likely to participate in the school activities.

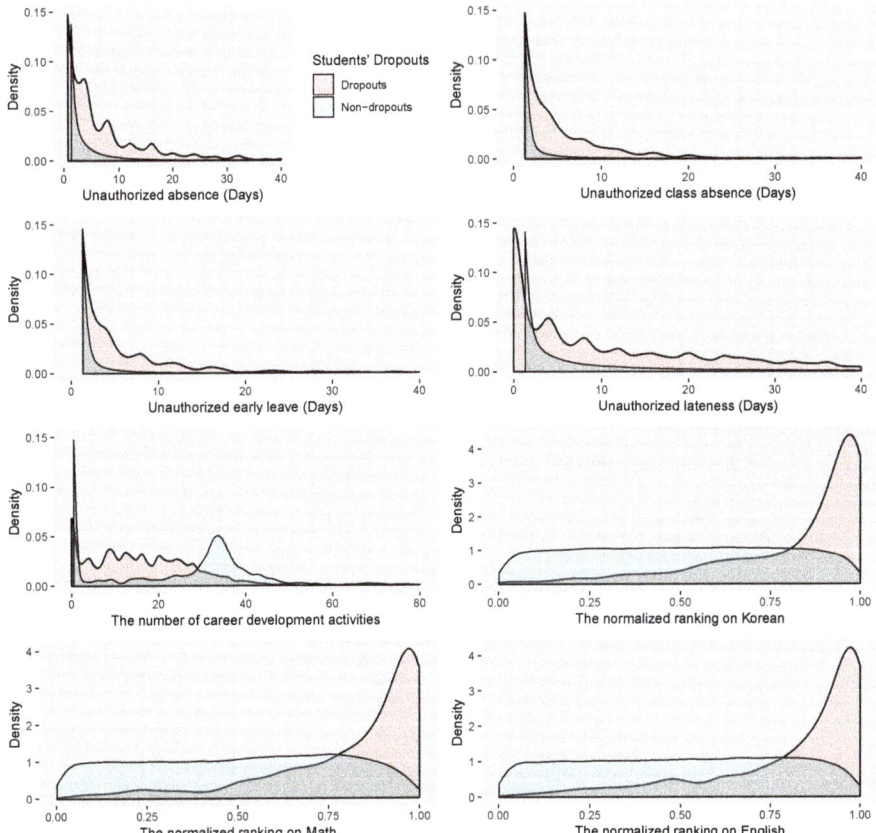

**Figure 1.** The density plots for the selected eight features.

Figure 2 presents the ROC curves for the four binary classifiers used in this study. The AUC of the random forest (RF), boosted decision tree (BDT), random forest with SMOTE (SMOTE + RF), and boosted decision tree with SMOTE (SMOTE + BDT) were 0.986, 0.988, 0.986, and 0.991, respectively.

Figure 3 presents the PR curves for the four binary classifiers used in this study. The AUC of the random forest (RF), boosted decision tree (BDT), random forest with SMOTE (SMOTE + RF), and boosted decision tree with SMOTE (SMOTE + BDT) were 0.634, 0.898, 0.643, and 0.724, respectively.

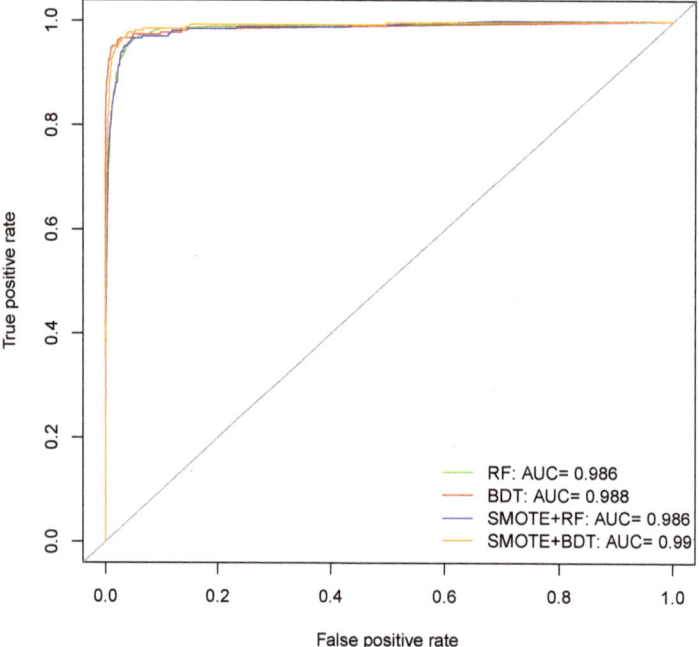

**Figure 2.** The ROC curves.

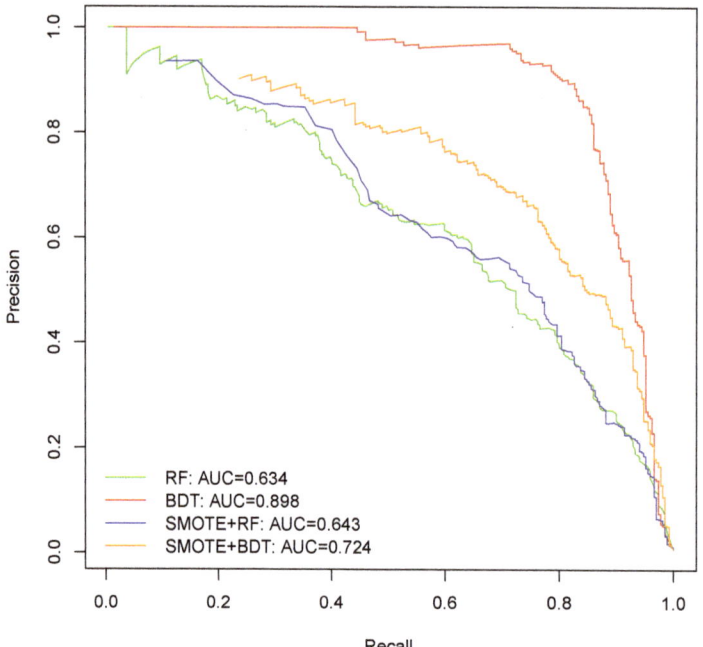

**Figure 3.** The PR curves.

## 6. Discussion

Classifiers trained on class-imbalanced datasets tend to show a poor sensitivity of predicting minor classes because classifiers tend to ignore the misclassification of minor classes. Given our specific goal of maximizing our chance of supporting the successful learning of all students, and minimizing the cost for intervention, the present study aimed to improve the performance of a dropout early warning system: (a) by addressing the class imbalance issue using the SMOTE and ensemble methods in machine learning; and (b) by evaluating the trained classifiers with both receiver operating characteristic (ROC) curves and precision–recall (PR) curves. Using the reliable features from the big data samples of the 165,715 high school students provided by the NEIS database in Korea, we trained four classifiers: random forest (RF), boosted decision tree (BDT), random forest with SMOTE (SMOTE + RF), and boosted decision tree with SMOTE (SMOTE + BDT). Based on our model-wide evaluation based on ROC and PR curves, boosted decision tree showed the best performance.

In Figure 2, the four ROC curves indicate that all four models were excellent in terms of AUCs: the AUC values of RF, BDT, SMOTE + RF, and SMOTE + BDT were 0.986, 0.988, 0.986, and 0.990, respectively. However, this result needs to be interpreted with caution. As previously discussed, the ROC curve may not be a good evaluation metric for imbalanced datasets because the false positive rate (or $1 - $ specificity or $1 - TN/(FP + TN)$) does not change much when the true negative (TN) is huge, which is common for imbalanced datasets. In our analysis, the ROC curves were not informative when comparing the performance of our four classifiers. On the contrary, the PR curves in Figure 3 were more informative in that the PR curves and their corresponding AUC values were more distinctive: the AUC values of RF, BDT, SMOTE + RF, and SMOTE + BDT were 0.634, 0.898, 0.643, and 0.724, respectively. According to the AUC values of the PR curves, the BDT showed the best performance (i.e., AUC = 0.898), indicating that, among the four tested classifiers, the dropout early warning system based on BDT was optimal in maximizing our chance of supporting the successful learning of all students, and minimizing the cost for intervention. Our result is consistent with the recent study on the impact of class rebalancing techniques on the performance of prediction models. Tantithamthavorn et al. [34] recently found that class rebalancing techniques, such as SMOTE, impact recall the most positively and impact precision the most negatively.

The PR curve essentially illustrates the trade-off between recall (or sensitivity) and precision. This trade-off between recall and precision raises an important issue regarding decision making based on machine learning. The predictions made by machine learning are often used to make a policy or plan, which always has a budget constraint. Therefore, the optimal performance of a classifier is only meaningful in relation to a specific task with the consideration of both the benefit from the improved performance and the cost for the improvement. In this study, our task was to build the dropout early warning system that maximizes the sensitivity of predicting potential dropout students to support successful learning of all students, and minimizes the cost for intervention. Even with BDT, the false alarms still exist and will require additional costs in time and money for the interventions. However, we believe that the benefit of preventing dropout students exceeds the cost for interventions. For example, in Ohio in the United States, the median earnings of a high school dropout are $17,748, whereas the ones of high school graduates are $26,207 [35]. The additional earning of $8,459 a year would be accumulated over a lifetime of a single individual.

The results of this study should be interpreted with caution because of the different nature of performance metrics. Sensitivity and specificity are independent of the prevalence of positives in the population, whereas positive and negative predictive values are influenced by the prevalence of positives in the population. Therefore, if our predictive modeling were transported to a population with higher frequencies of dropouts, the sensitivity would remain the same because the sensitivity is the characteristic of a test, but the positive predictive value would increase because the positive predictive value reflects the population.

In machine learning, the quality of training data is a critical factor that determines the performance of predictive models. The NEIS is an ideal database for developing the dropout early warning system in South Korea for several reasons. First, the NEIS database contains information about more than six million students' basic information, academic achievement, absence, health and so on. Therefore, the NEIS can provide various students' features to build an effective dropout early warning system. Second, the NEIS has been used during the past 20 years in South Korea. Therefore, teachers are well trained in using the NEIS system, which also improves the quality of data.

There are some limitations to the present study. First, our access to the NEIS database was limited in this study. Although we included the key risk indicators for dropout prediction in our analysis, we were not able to access many other features in the NEIS database, such as teachers' evaluation of students, at the time of our analysis. We expect that the performance of our prediction model could be improved by adding those additional features in the future. Second, our predictive model only predicts students at risk of dropping out of school. Recent advances in predictive modeling enable us to estimate heterogeneous treatment effects to understand those who can effectively be intervened [36]. Such information would be very useful in designing and implementing prevention programs.

In sum, we aimed to build a dropout early warning system that maximizes our chance of supporting the successful learning of all students, and minimizes the cost for intervention by addressing the class imbalance issue using the SMOTE and ensemble methods in machine learning, and also by evaluating the trained classifiers with both ROC and PR curves. ROC curves were not very informative, whereas PR curves were informative. According to our PR curves, BDT showed the best performance. Considering the prevalence of the class-imbalance issue in other educational outcomes, this study has implications for other educational studies using predictive modeling as well.

**Author Contributions:** Conceptualization, S.L. and J.Y.C.; methodology, S.L.; software, S.L.; validation, S.L. and J.Y.C.; formal analysis, S.L.; investigation, S.L. and J.Y.C.; resources, S.L. and J.Y.C.; data curation, J.Y.C.; writing—original draft preparation, S.L.; writing—review and editing, S.L. and J.Y.C.; visualization, S.L.; supervision, J.Y.C.; and project administration, J.Y.C.

**Funding:** This research received no external funding.

**Conflicts of Interest:** The authors declare no conflict of interest.

## References

1. Rumberger, R.W. High School Dropouts: A Review of Issues and Evidence. *Rev. Educ. Res.* **1987**, *57*, 101. [CrossRef]
2. Catterall, J.S. On the social costs of dropping out of school. *High School J.* **1987**, *71*, 19–30.
3. Balfanz, R.; Herzog, L.; Maciver, D.J. Preventing Student Disengagement and Keeping Students on the Graduation Path in Urban Middle-Grades Schools: Early Identification and Effective Interventions. *Educ. Psychol.* **2007**, *42*, 223–235. [CrossRef]
4. Dynarski, M.; Gleason, P. How Can We Help? What We Have Learned From Recent Federal Dropout Prevention Evaluations. *J. Educ. Stud. Placed Risk (JESPAR)* **2002**, *7*, 43–69. [CrossRef]
5. Lamb, S.; Rice, S. *Effective Strategies to Increase School Completion Report: Report to the Victorian Department of Education and Early Childhood Development*; Communications Division, Department of Education and Early Childhood Development: Melbourne, Australia, 2008.
6. Knowles, J.E. Of needles and haystacks: Building an accurate statewide dropout early warning system in Wisconsin. *JEDM J. Educ. Data Min.* **2015**, *7*, 18–67.
7. Sullivan, R. *Early Warning Signs. A Solution-Finding Report*; Center on Innovations in Learning, Temple University: Philadelphia, PA, USA, 2017.
8. Haixiang, G.; Yijing, L.; Shang, J.; Mingyun, G.; Yuanyue, H.; Bing, G. Learning from class-imbalanced data: Review of methods and applications. *Expert Syst. Appl.* **2017**, *73*, 220–239. [CrossRef]
9. Galar, M.; Fernandez, A.; Barrenechea, E.; Bustince, H.; Herrera, F. A Review on Ensembles for the Class Imbalance Problem: Bagging-, Boosting-, and Hybrid-Based Approaches. *IEEE Trans. Syst. Man Cybern. Part C* **2012**, *42*, 463–484. [CrossRef]
10. Saito, T.; Rehmsmeier, M. The Precision-Recall Plot Is More Informative than the ROC Plot When Evaluating Binary Classifiers on Imbalanced Datasets. *PLoS ONE* **2015**, *10*, e0118432. [CrossRef]

11. Márquez-Vera, C.; Cano, A.; Romero, C.; Ventura, S. Predicting student failure at school using genetic programming and different data mining approaches with high dimensional and imbalanced data. *Appl. Intell.* **2013**, *38*, 315–330. [CrossRef]
12. Márquez-Vera, C.; Cano, A.; Romero, C.; Noaman, A.Y.M.; Mousa Fardoun, H.; Ventura, S. Early dropout prediction using data mining: A case study with high school students. *Expert Syst.* **2016**, *33*, 107–124. [CrossRef]
13. Korean Educational Development Institute. Available online: http://cesi.kedi.re.kr/post/6662567?itemCode=03&menuId=m_02_03_03 (accessed on 1 August 2018).
14. Chung, J.; Kang, T.; Kim, S.K.; Ryoo, J.S.; Lee, D.; Lee, J.; Hwang, J. *Policy Study on the Supporting System for Out-of-School Youth*; Jeollanamdo Office of Education: Jeollanamdo, Korea, 2013.
15. Peters, S.J. "Education for All?". *J. Disabil. Policy Stud.* **2007**, *18*, 98–108. [CrossRef]
16. Mathis, W.J.; Trujillo, T.M. *Lessons from NCLB for the Every Student Succeeds Act*; National Education Policy Center: Boulder, CO, USA, 2016.
17. Chung, J.Y.; Lee, S. Dropout early warning systems for high school students using machine learning. *Child. Youth Serv. Rev.* **2019**, *96*, 346–353. [CrossRef]
18. Chawla, N.V.; Lazarevic, A.; Hall, L.O.; Bowyer, K.W. SMOTEBoost: Improving Prediction of the Minority Class in Boosting. In *Knowledge Discovery in Databases: PKDD 2003*; Springer: Berlin/Heidelberg, Germany, 2003; pp. 107–119. [CrossRef]
19. Chawla, N.V.; Bowyer, K.W.; Hall, L.O.; Kegelmeyer, W.P. SMOTE: Synthetic Minority Over-sampling Technique. *J. Artif. Intell. Res.* **2002**, *16*, 321–357. [CrossRef]
20. Hand, D.J.; Whitrow, C.; Adams, N.M.; Juszczak, P.; Weston, D. Performance criteria for plastic card fraud detection tools. *J. Oper. Res. Soc.* **2008**, *59*, 956–962. [CrossRef]
21. Chawla, N.V. Data Mining for Imbalanced Datasets: An Overview. In *Data Mining and Knowledge Discovery Handbook*; Springer: Berlin/Heidelberg, Germany, 2005; pp. 853–867. [CrossRef]
22. Longadge, R.; Dongre, S. Class imbalance problem in data mining review. *arXiv* **2013**, arXiv:1305.1707.
23. Lin, Y.; Lee, Y.; Wahba, G. Support vector machines for classification in nonstandard situations. *Mach. Learn.* **2002**, *46*, 191–202. [CrossRef]
24. Napierała, K.; Stefanowski, J.; Wilk, S. Learning from Imbalanced Data in Presence of Noisy and Borderline Examples. In *Rough Sets and Current Trends in Computing*; Springer: Berlin/Heidelberg, Germany, 2010; pp. 158–167. [CrossRef]
25. Ling, C.; Sheng, V.; Yang, Q. Test strategies for cost-sensitive decision trees. *IEEE Trans. Knowl. Data Eng.* **2006**, *18*, 1055–1067. [CrossRef]
26. Zhou, Z.H. *Ensemble Methods*; Chapman and Hall/CRC: Boca Raton, FL, USA, 2012. [CrossRef]
27. Viola, P.; Jones, M. Rapid object detection using a boosted cascade of simple features. In Proceedings of the 2001 IEEE Computer Society Conference on Computer Vision and Pattern Recognition, CVPR 2001, Kauai, HI, USA, 8–14 December 2001. [CrossRef]
28. Zhou, Z.H.; Jiang, Y.; Yang, Y.B.; Chen, S.F. Lung cancer cell identification based on artificial neural network ensembles. *Artif. Intell. Med.* **2002**, *24*, 25–36. [CrossRef]
29. Panigrahi, S.; Kundu, A.; Sural, S.; Majumdar, A. Credit card fraud detection: A fusion approach using Dempster–Shafer theory and Bayesian learning. *Inf. Fusion* **2009**, *10*, 354–363. [CrossRef]
30. Freund, Y.; Schapire, R.E. A Decision-Theoretic Generalization of On-Line Learning and an Application to Boosting. *J. Comput. Syst. Sci.* **1997**, *55*, 119–139. [CrossRef]
31. Fawcett, T. An introduction to ROC analysis. *Pattern Recognit. Lett.* **2006**, *27*, 861–874. [CrossRef]
32. Therriault, S.B.; Heppen, J.; O'Cummings, M.; Fryer, L.; Johnson, A. Early Warning System Implementation Guide. Retrieved from the National High School Center Website. 2010. Available online: http://www.betterhighschools.org/documents/NHSCEWSImplementationGuide.pdf (accessed on 1 August 2018).
33. Allensworth, E.M.; Easton, J.Q. *What Matters for Staying On-Track and Graduating in Chicago Public High Schools: A Close Look at Course Grades, Failures, and Attendance in the Freshman Year. Research Report*; Consortium on Chicago School Research: Chicago, IL, USA, 2007.
34. Tantithamthavorn, C.; Hassan, A.E.; Matsumoto, K. The Impact of Class Rebalancing Techniques on the Performance and Interpretation of Defect Prediction Models. *IEEE Trans. Softw. Eng.* **2018**, 1. [CrossRef]

35. Cellini, S.R.; Kee, J.E. Cost-Effectiveness and Cost-Benefit Analysis. In *Handbook of Practical Program Evaluation*; John Wiley & Sons, Inc.: Hoboken, NJ, USA, 2015; pp. 636–672. [CrossRef]
36. Wager, S.; Athey, S. Estimation and Inference of Heterogeneous Treatment Effects using Random Forests. *J. Am. Stat. Assoc.* **2018**, *113*, 1228–1242. [CrossRef]

© 2019 by the authors. Licensee MDPI, Basel, Switzerland. This article is an open access article distributed under the terms and conditions of the Creative Commons Attribution (CC BY) license (http://creativecommons.org/licenses/by/4.0/).

Article

# A Learning Analytics Approach to Identify Students at Risk of Dropout: A Case Study with a Technical Distance Education Course

Emanuel Marques Queiroga [1,2,\*], João Ladislau Lopes [2], Kristofer Kappel [1], Marilton Aguiar [1], Ricardo Matsumura Araújo [1], Roberto Munoz [3,\*], Rodolfo Villarroel [4] and Cristian Cechinel [5]

1. Centro de Desenvolvimento Tecnológico (CDTEC), Universidade Federal de Pelotas (UFPel), Pelotas 96010610, Brazil; kristofer.kappel@gmail.com (K.K.); marilton@inf.ufpel.edu.br (M.A.); ricardo@inf.ufpel.edu.br (R.M.A.)
2. Instituto Federal de Educação, Ciência e Tecnologia Sul-rio-Grandense (IFSul), Pelotas 96015560, Brazil; joao.lblopes@gmail.com
3. Escuela de Ingeniería Informática, Universidad de Valparaíso, Valparaíso 2362735, Chile
4. Escuela de Ingeniería Informática, Pontificia Universidad Católica de Valparaíso, Valparaíso 2362807, Chile; rodolfo.villarroel@ucv.cl
5. Centro de Ciências, Tecnologias e Saúde (CTS), Universidade Federal de Santa Catarina (UFSC), Araranguá 88906072, Brazil; contato@cristiancechinel.pro.br
\* Correspondence: emanuelmqueiroga@gmail.com (E.M.Q.); roberto.munoz@uv.cl (R.M.)

Received: 1 May 2020; Accepted: 28 May 2020; Published: 9 June 2020

**Abstract:** Contemporary education is a vast field that is concerned with the performance of education systems. In a formal e-learning context, student dropout is considered one of the main problems and has received much attention from the learning analytics research community, which has reported several approaches to the development of models for the early prediction of at-risk students. However, maximizing the results obtained by predictions is a considerable challenge. In this work, we developed a solution using only students' interactions with the virtual learning environment and its derivative features for early predict at-risk students in a Brazilian distance technical high school course that is 103 weeks in duration. To maximize results, we developed an elitist genetic algorithm based on Darwin's theory of natural selection for hyperparameter tuning. With the application of the proposed technique, we predicted the student at risk with an Area Under the Receiver Operating Characteristic Curve (AUROC) above 0.75 in the initial weeks of a course. The results demonstrate the viability of applying interaction count and derivative features to generate prediction models in contexts where access to demographic data is restricted. The application of a genetic algorithm to the tuning of hyperparameters classifiers can increase their performance in comparison with other techniques.

**Keywords:** at-risk students; genetic algorithm; learning analytics; educational data mining

## 1. Introduction

Learning analytics (LA) approaches have emerged in the context of the increasing use of digital information and communication technologies in education [1]. LA provides information and knowledge so that institutions can overcome core challenges with the qualification of their teaching and learning processes [2,3]. Student dropout is one of the main problems in e-learning that has received considerable attention from the research community. Early detection of students at risk of dropout plays an essential role in reducing the problem, enabling targeted actions aimed at specific situations [4–6].

According to OECD [7], contemporary education is vast, and there are many concerns about the performance of education systems. Among the various important challenges faced in education, one of the most difficult to tackle is the low completion rates observed in many institutions [8], being the final representation of the high dropout rates and low student performance in courses. These problems are related to many factors other than teaching methodologies, such as the profile of the students and their ability to self-manage time [7,9,10].

Dropout rates in e-learning are generally higher compared with face-to-face education [8]. According to the European Commission on Education and Culture, countries like Poland, Sweden, and Hungary have dropout rates in higher education of 38%, 47%, and 47%, respectively [11]. In Spain, the dropout rate is 50% at the Spanish National Distance Education University (UNED) [12]. In Brazil, the enrolment numbers significantly increased in the last few years, but student dropout rates simultaneously increased. The last census of distance education in Brazil [13] reported dropout rates of 50% in the distance courses offered by the Ministry of Education.

Studies have established that student success in distance courses is directly correlated with their engagement inside virtual learning environments (VLEs). Distance learning technology allows tutors to measure the engagement of students by looking into system logs and evaluating the intensity of students' interactions in the different activities available inside virtual classrooms [9,14,15].

In the educational context, access to data is a considerable challenge [16]. The distribution of institutional and academic data across numerous systems creates challenges for accessing social-demographic and previous academic data. This occurs typically because VLEs are usually unprepared for the storage of this kind of data and because several educational institutions apply different learning modalities, such as face-to-face learning, hybrid learning, and distance learning, thus requiring a central academic system. Data are usually concentrated in a central academic system that has no direct connection with the virtual environment. This situation restricts the automated retrieval of data external to VLE, for example, to use in dashboards for data visualization or in the generation of predictive models. In many institutions, the access to use this kind of data is restricted either due to internal policies or data access legislation [16–18].

One of the main advantages of distance learning courses is the large amount of data generated by interactions between students and the system, which provides new possibilities for studying and understanding the data. In e-learning courses, the interaction between students and teachers is usually mediated by a VLE. Thus, VLEs generate a large volume of data that can be consumed by machine learning models [19]. Machine learning algorithms have been used to build successful classifiers using diverse student attributes [10]. While these models showed promising results in several settings, these results are usually attained using attributes that are not immediately transferable to other courses or platforms.

In machine learning, the parameters are defined by the model generated by the algorithms, unlike regular programming, where the term *parameter* is used to refer to the entry of a given function. The final accuracy of models is directly linked to the quality of the fine-tuning of their hyperparameters on the algorithm input [20]. Thus, more adjusted hyperparameters result in more accurate models [21,22]. The control variables of the classifiers are called hyperparameters, which aim to define relevant issues regarding the model to be trained, such as the number of estimators in a random forest algorithm or the number of layers hidden in a neural network [21]. In a neural network context, parameters are adjusted during the training phase using weights. Hyperparameters are variables set before the training, such as the network topology or learning information [22].

In this context, we previously proposed exploiting students' interaction counts solely over time (and other attributes derived from the counts) to predict at-risk students [23–25]. This approach was tested and produced good results, allowing the early prediction of students at risk of dropout and achieving overall accuracies varying from 65% to 90% in the first eight weeks of a two-year distance courses. These studies produced results comparable to those in the literature. For instance,

Jayaprakash et al. [26] obtained general accuracies varying from 73% to 94% and Manhães et al. [4] reported accuracies from 62.22% to 67.77%.

Maximizing the results obtained by predictions is a considerable challenge [27], as the different algorithms commonly present a wide variation in the performance rates that depend on the combination of several characteristics (e.g., balance among classes, amount of data, input variables, and others) and algorithm hyperparameters [28]. Evolutionary computation, and especially genetic algorithms (GAs), are used for optimization problems and tuning classifiers in several areas such as medicine [20] and emotion recognition [29], producing significant results. Here, we propose the use of an evolutionary GA to tune the hyperparameters of the classifiers, thereby optimizing the performance of the models for the early detection of students at risk of dropping out.

This paper is a continuation of these previous works, now aiming to enhance the results by applying an approach that uses GAs to tune machine learning algorithms' hyperparameters. This paper contrasts the results of two methods for hyperparameter optimization applied on models to detect at-risk students in technical e-learning courses based on the counting of students' interactions inside the VLE. The first method for hyperparameter optimization is based on a GA created by the authors, and the second is the traditional widely used method called grid search [21]. During this study, we aimed to answer the following research questions:

**RQ1.** Does the GA approach to hyperparameter optimization outperform traditional techniques?
**RQ2.** Does the resulting predictive models generated by the use of the GA approach for hyperparameter optimization perform better than models with default hyperparameters?

The remainder of this paper is organized as follows: Section 2 presents the theoretical background and related work about the problem of predicting at-risk students and the use of GAs in this context. Section 3 presents the case study conducted to test the proposed solution, detailing the data gathered, the methodology, the proposed GA for fine-tuning, and the experiments. Section 4 discusses the results, and Section 5 concludes the paper and proposes future work.

## 2. Theoretical Background

This section presents works focused on predicting at-risk students in different scenarios and the use of hyperparameter techniques to improve results. Several works in the field of learning analytics and educational data mining deal with the problem of early predicting at-risk students. The works usually differ according to several aspects, such as (1) the sources of data used to generate the models for prediction (demographic, VLEs, surveys, exams); (2) the level of education of the courses (high school, secondary education); (3) the goal of the predictive models (e.g., to predict performance or evasion); (4) the scope of the prediction focused on an entire program or a specific course or discipline; (5) the modality of the course (formal or informal, face-to-face, blended, or distance learning); and (6) whether or not to use tuning techniques for classifiers.

According to Liz-Domínguez et al. [30], data analysis is the set of techniques used to transform data into information and knowledge, thus revealing correlations and hidden patterns. The data resulting from this process can be used to create early warning systems to predict future events. This process mainly aims to support learning and mitigate some of the problems, such as academic performance, retention, and dropout. The reliability of the predictions by the predictor is one of the main factors established by Liz-Domínguez et al. [30] and Herodotou et al. [31] for their application on a large scale.

According to Liz-Domínguez et al. [30], researchers have experimented with methodologies in different scenarios. However, according to Hilliger et al. [32] and Cechinel et al. [33], in Latin America, these studies are mainly concentrated in the university context, so more applications in other contexts are necessary.

González et al. [34] demonstrated that information and communication technologies have a greater impact on the teaching and education process. González et al. [34], de Pablo González [35] demonstrated the significant impact of the use of VLEs by teachers on student learning. This impact can be maximized using intervention methods based on machine learning, as proposed by Herodotou et al. [36]. Herodotou et al. [31] demonstrated that the classes where teachers used predictive methods produced a performance at least 15% higher than the classes without that use. This improvement was also observed in comparison with classes with the same teachers but from previous years.

In the educational context, traditional research usually uses data from educational systems and virtual environments. The research by Zohair [37] proposed only using data from the academic system (e.g., extracurricular courses, grades, and age) to predict performance in graduate students. Some of the extracted data were extracurricular courses taken and the respective grades, initial training course, and descriptive data about the grades and the age of the student. This study demonstrated that for small groups of students, this is a logical approach that produces good results with few pre-processing steps and a limited set of data. The author focused on the use of algorithms that perform well with low amounts of data, such as support vector machines and multilayer perceptrons (MLP), that produce results with accuracy above 76%.

The search for methods that can be generalized and therefore replicable for other courses represents a significant portion of the research. Thus, studies such as [38] proposed an architecture that is not dependent on a single type of datum, working with the flow of clicks that academics make in a Massive Open Online Course (MOOC). To do so, data are captured from a course and different prediction models are trained and tested in other courses and environments. The experiments showed 87% accuracy when testing in different courses and 90% when tested in the same course, not varying significantly according to the environment.

In [39], several techniques for pre-processing data were compared in terms of interactions with the virtual environment Moodle in risk prediction. Data from the plugin Virtual Programming Laboratory (VPL) were used for risk prediction in algorithm and programming disciplines in undergraduate courses. Data such as weekly interaction count, an average of interactions, median, number of weeks without interactions, standard deviation, and commitment factor are generated based on a previously proposed technique [25,40]. Data added included the teacher interaction count, social count, and cognitive count based on a proposed theory Swan [41]. With naturally unbalanced data, the synthetic minority over-sampling technique (SMOTE) was applied to create balance. Several datasets were generated with different variables to compare the techniques. The results demonstrated that the use of only the interaction count as proposed in [24,25] presented results superior to the other techniques, including their union.

For instance, [5] proposed a students' dropout prediction system that combines outcomes from three different algorithms (neural network, support vector machine (SVM), and probabilistic ensemble simplified fuzzy Adaptive Resonance Theory (ARTMAP—PESFAM)). The authors gathered static demographic data, like sex and place of residence; academic data, like performance and scholar degree; and dynamic data, such as the number of interactions in the virtual environment, grades, and even delivery dates of activities. After applying the algorithms, three distinct approaches to the dropout prediction were generated: (1) A student is considered a dropout case if at least one method classified them as such, (2) a student is considered as a dropout if at least two methods indicated the student to be a dropout and, (3) the student is only presumed as a dropout if all three techniques classified them as a dropout. The accuracy of the results obtained ranged from 75% to 85%, and the best results were achieved using the less restrictive approach, the first one, which achieved accuracies up to 85% on the first section of a given course.

Jayaprakash et al. [26] proposed a warning system focused on student performance to reduce dropout and retention rates. The system provides the student with updated feedback on their potential scholarly performance. To do so, the system uses several types of data, such as demographic (sex and age), student interactions on the VLE, previous academic performance, time passed since the student entered the university, online time spent on the VLE, and outcomes from the scholastic aptitude test (SAT) (verbal and math). Different models of prediction were produced using J48, Bayesian networks with naive Bayes, SVM with minimal sequential optimization (SMO), and logistic regression, considering data from 9938 students. These classifiers presented similar results, with the classifier based on logistic regression producing slightly superior outcomes (94.2% general accuracy and 66.7% precision for identifying students at dropout risk).

A classifier able to early predict student dropout using students' interactions inside a VLE was proposed [42]. They used information such as if the student watched all video tutorials, if the student ignored some given material or activity, if the student was delayed in following the virtual classes, and the student performance in the activities. Students were then classified according to three flags: Green (low dropout risk), yellow (medium dropout risk), and red (high dropout risk). The authors did not mention the types of machine learning algorithms used but reported performance (TP accuracy) varying from 40% to 50% to predict dropout students within two weeks in advance.

Genetic algorithms are widely used in data mining and can be implemented as the classifier or as a result of the optimizer, as proposed in this approach. One of the applications of genetic algorithms for optimization is a method combining the predictions generated by classifiers. To this end, Minaei-Bidgoli and Punch [43] proposed the application of machine learning to predicting student performance in an online physics course at Michigan State University. For this, data derived from the tasks performed by the students were used. Ten different variables were extracted, including success rate, success on the first attempt, the number of attempts, the time between task delivery and deadline, the time involved in solving, and the number of interactions with colleagues and instructors. A principal component analysis (PCA) method was applied to transform the variables, and three different sets with two, three, or nine components were generated. After this, the Bayes classifier, I-nearest neighbor (I-NN), k-nearest neighbor (k-NN), Parzen-window, multilayer perceptron (MLP), and decision tree classifiers were applied. Then, the predictions obtained by the classifiers were combined with the genetic algorithm using 200 individuals with 500 generations. The GA proposed by the author achieved optimization of 10% to 12% depending on the number of components in the input.

Márquez-Vera et al. [6] proposed the evolutionary algorithms Interpretable Classification Rule Mining Algorithm (ICRM) [27] and ICRM2 [6] based on grammar-based genetic programming (GBGP). In Márquez-Vera et al. [6], ICRM was used to predict the dropout of high school students in Mexico. The authors proposed a double-approach prediction on the same algorithm, creating two classification rules: One for identifying students who tend to complete the course and the other for students who tend to drop out. The data used included 60 attributes that range from the entrance test to research data distributed to students. As a comparison method, the algorithm proposed by the author was compared with five classifiers: Naive Bayes, decision tree, Instance-based lazy learning (IBK), Repeated Incremental Pruning (JRip), and SVM. Techniques were also used to reduce the dimensionality of the base. Using the accuracy as an evaluation metric, the results obtained by the proposed algorithm showed that it can be a valid approach, especially considering the ease of interpretation of the generated classification rules.

## 3. Proposed Approach

The proposed approach consists of the use of a GA for the classifier (hyperparameter) optimization and selection of the fittest, to predict dropout in distance learning courses. Figure 1 shows the proposed solution. The following machine learning algorithms were selected to test the solution: Classic decision tree (DT), random forest (RF), multilayer perceptron (MLP), logistic regression (LG), and the meta-algorithm AdaBoost (ADA). The proposed approach was compared against the grid search method regarding hyperparameter optimization and the regular solution without hyperparameter optimization. The proposed approach uses a classification method, where several classifiers with different hyperparameters, such as DT, RF, MLP, LG, and ADA, compete against each other. In the end, the classifier and the hyperparameters with the best results are selected by a fitness function.

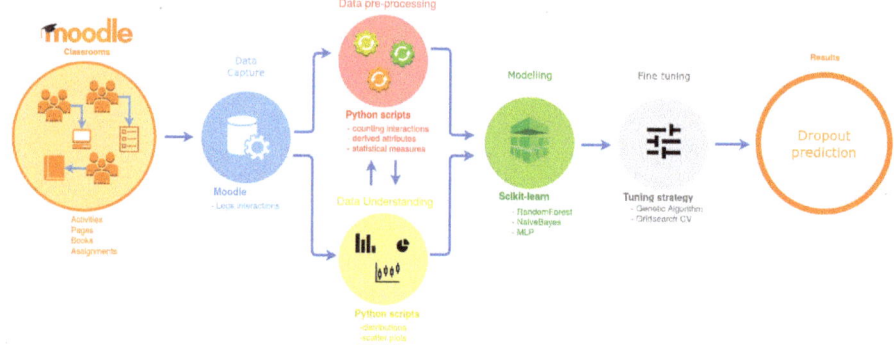

**Figure 1.** Proposed approach.

*3.1. Case Study*

The case study consisted of the following steps: Data capture, data pre-processing, data understanding, and modelling, according to the solution proposed in the Figure 1. These steps occur in parallel, with tests, implementations, and generation of new features for developing models for the early prediction of at-risk students in a technical distance learning course. The methodology to generate the models relies on the counting of interactions of the students inside the VLE, with the use of the proposed solution described in the previous section.

Data related to the student's interactions were collected from the logs of the institutional Moodle platform of a given technical distance course of the Instituto Federal Sul Rio-grandense (IFSul) in Brazil. Table 1 shows the number of logs collected, the number of students enrolled in the course, and the percentages of dropout and success. The course is taught in 18 different cities throughout the state of Rio Grande do Sul and involves weekly activities that are posted on the VLE by the teacher. Students have one week to develop the activities with the help of tutors. The course has a maximum completion time of 103 weeks, with a total workload of 1215 h divided into disciplines. The maximum duration is 24 months, with three breaks also called vacations, and the student's final situation is determined by their performance in the evaluations and their re-enrolment every six months.

The maximum term for completion of the curriculum is four years, and the student may repeat each discipline only once and, therefore, the year. The student has the option of taking up to two subjects for the next year and taking them concurrently with the others. For approval, the student must have a grade of six or higher in each of the disciplines of the curriculum. Students who spend 365 days without interactions with the virtual environment or do not perform their annual re-enrolment are considered absent and are removed from the course. Thus, the student receives a grade from 0 to 10 at the end of a given discipline, and one of two states is associated with the student: Approved or failed. However, we aimed to predict students who drop out during the course. For this, the student will be considered dropped out if they leave, do not perform the activities during the course, and their enrolment in the following semester.

**Table 1.** Dataset summary.

| Number of Log Rows | Number of Students | Dropouts (%) | Success (%) |
|---|---|---|---|
| 1,051,012 | 752 | 354 (47%) | 398 (53%) |

The choice to only use data from the counting of interactions was motivated by previous research that achieved satisfactory results using the same approach [23,25]. This choice was also related to limitations on capturing other kinds of data for the present study. In previous works, we sought to create models that are easy to generalize so that they could be applied to other courses. To accomplish that, we used four courses, where the model created by one was applied to the others, and the models generated with data from three courses were applied to the remaining one. In these experiments, the labeling of the type of interaction was tested and did not show significant results. When testing the models generated with data from one course on data from other courses, this type of labeling negatively impacted the results.

Studies such as Macarini et al. [39] tested the application of different types of interactions and derived data, with their labeling showing no significant differences in performance. Thus, we applied the methodology that presented the best previous results to model other courses in the same educational context, even if the model is derived from data from one course only.

The courses studied here are offered in several cities throughout the interior of Brazil and present a large demographic diversity. Nowadays, the collection of demographic data is a task manually performed by eighteen different teaching centers through a printed questionnaire that is sent to IFSul after completion. This process generates a series of problems, such as lack of data, reading and typing problems, and consequently low diversity and inconsistencies. These factors led to the lack of reliability in these data and their consequent non-use.

Data capture consisted of collecting raw data from student interactions with Moodle VLE. The data initially had the format presented in Table 2. After selection, data were validated. This stage consisted of comparing the student situation data in the VLE to the data on the institutional academic system. Both systems are independent and have no integration. Cases of inconsistency were handled manually by checking other types of internal control.

Table 2. Information contained in the log files.

| Column | Comment |
| --- | --- |
| Course | Name of the virtual classroom accessed |
| Time | Day and time of the access |
| IP Address | IP Address of the machine |
| Full name | User (student) name |
| Action Event Name | The action represents the type of interaction that the student performed in the classroom. For instance: (1) Visualization and participation on chats; (2) Visualization and inclusion of posts in forums; (3) Visualization of resources; and (4) Visualization of the course. |
| Description | Detailed description of the event. Example: Download the .pdf file. |

The course format analyzed in this project consists of 103 weeks divided over two years. As stated by [5], early identification of a risk situation is a fundamental criterion for its reversal. Thus, for this work, we chose to use the methodology based on [4], which consists of the application of data mining on the data of the first subjects of the course. Using this process, we chose to use data from the 50 weeks that compose the first year of the course. Every two weeks starting from the fourth, a prediction model was generated, so the approaches used in this work created 23 models in the period.

After validation, data were anonymized and preprocessed, and variables were generated (features extraction). Table 3 describes the variables extracted to be used as the input for training and testing the predictive models. The table shows that all variables were based on the counting of students' interactions inside the VLE. Figure 2 exemplifies the behavior of the Weekly interactions variable for some weeks of the course and according to the Student Final Status category.

Exploratory data analysis (EDA) seeks to visualize dataset information to better understand the student's behavior when using the VLE. Table 4 shows how dropout rates evolved after every 10 weeks of the course until week 50. The table also shows the dropout rates for the first and second year of the course after week 50. We considered a student as dropped out after a period of six weeks without interactions with the VLE. The idea here was to pinpoint the period where the departure occurs.

The evasion rates between the two years of the course are practically the same (182 dropouts for year 1 and 172 dropouts for year 2). However, if we look proportionally at the number of students enrolled at the beginning of each year, the dropout rate is slightly higher in the second year, with 30.06% compared with 24.20% in the first year. These values differ from the average dropout rates known from higher institutions in Brazil [44] as well as from secondary and technical schools [45]. Unfortunately, there are no national data related to the distance learning modality to enable a more precise comparison.

A total of 86.81% of the course dropouts of the first year are concentrated in the first 20 weeks (152 dropouts of the1 82 in the first year). This shows a tendency of the students to leave at the very beginning of the course, which could be related to difficulties faced in the initial studies. This tendency is also reported in the literature in relation to face-to-face courses where difficulties in the beginning of the course are reported as the most critical factor leading students to drop out.

Figure 2 presents the bi-weekly total count, the means, and the standard deviations of the students' interactions. In the figure, students identified as dropped out in a given week are not counted in the following weeks. As shown in the figure, dropout students present a higher number of interactions than successful students until week 13. One possible explanation for this behavior is that those students are experiencing difficulties during their learning process, so they interact more with the VLE to obtain assistance. The total count of interactions per group is lower for the dropout group (considering the whole period). Figure 3 presents a boxplot of the counting of interactions for each group of students, which highlights the differences in these groups regarding the use of the VLE.

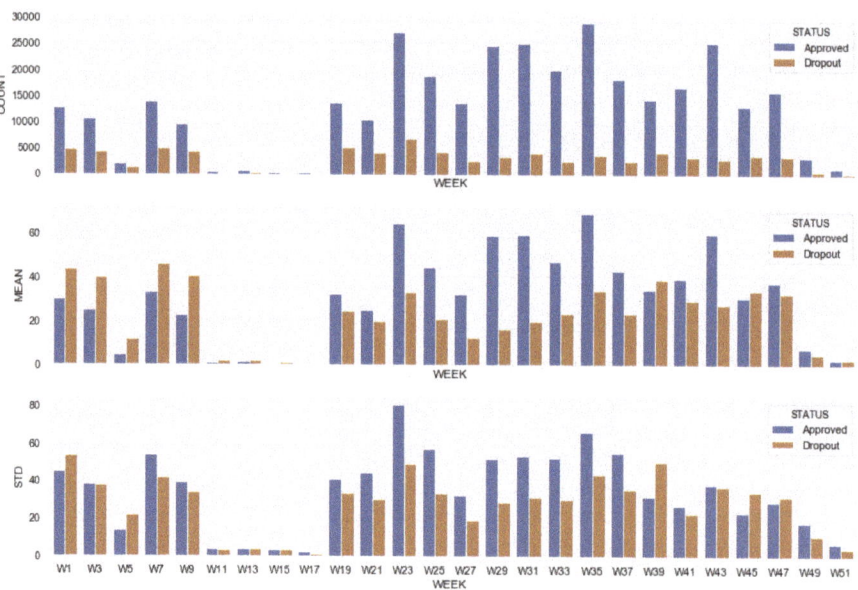

**Figure 2.** Interactions every two weeks.

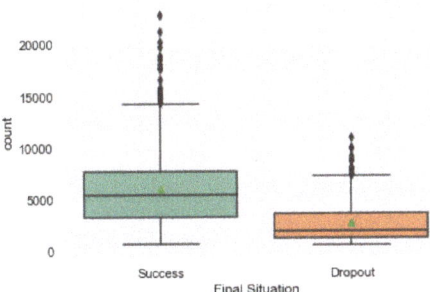

**Figure 3.** Boxplot success X dropout.

**Table 3.** Features extracted to be used as input for the models.

| Variable | Description |
|---|---|
| Daily interactions | Count of interactions of a given day (from 1 to 350 days) |
| Weekly interactions | Count of interactions of a given week (from 1 to 50 weeks) |
| Mean of the week | Average of the count of interactions of a given week |
| Standard deviation of the week | Standard deviation of the count of interactions of a given week |
| Student final status | Dependent variable representing the student final status: Dropout or success |

**Table 4.** Evolution of dropout during the course.

| Year | Period | Number of Students in Course | Number of Dropout Students (NDS) | NDS Rate | Accumulated NDS | Accmulated NDS Rate |
|---|---|---|---|---|---|---|
| Year 1 | Week 10 | 752 | 87 | 11.56 | 87 | 11.56 |
|  | Week 20 | 665 | 71 | 10.67 | 158 | 21.01 |
|  | Week 30 | 594 | 21 | 3.5 | 179 | 23.27 |
|  | Week 40 | 573 | 1 | 0.17 | 180 | 23.4 |
|  | Week 50 | 572 | 2 | 0.34 | 182 | 24.20 |
|  | Total of First 50 Weeks | 752 | 182 | 24.20 | 182 | 24.20 |
| Year 2 | Total after 50 Weeks | 572 | 172 | 22.87 | 354 | 47.07 |
| Final Values | Total | 752 | 354 | 47.07 | 354 | 47.07 |

In Figure 4, the central diagonal presents the density plots of the Weekly Interactions variable for weeks 1, 10, 20, 30, and 40. The two groups of students (dropout and success) initially presented similar behavior at the beginning of the course (weeks 1 and 10), and gradually started to differ after week 20 when the number of weekly interactions of the successful students was slightly higher. The scatterplots help to better visualize the behavior of the interactions and their comparison between the weeks. The scatter plots demonstrate that there is no direct positive correlation between weeks. Students who were successful in the course tended to have more interactions, similar to that observed in Figure 2.

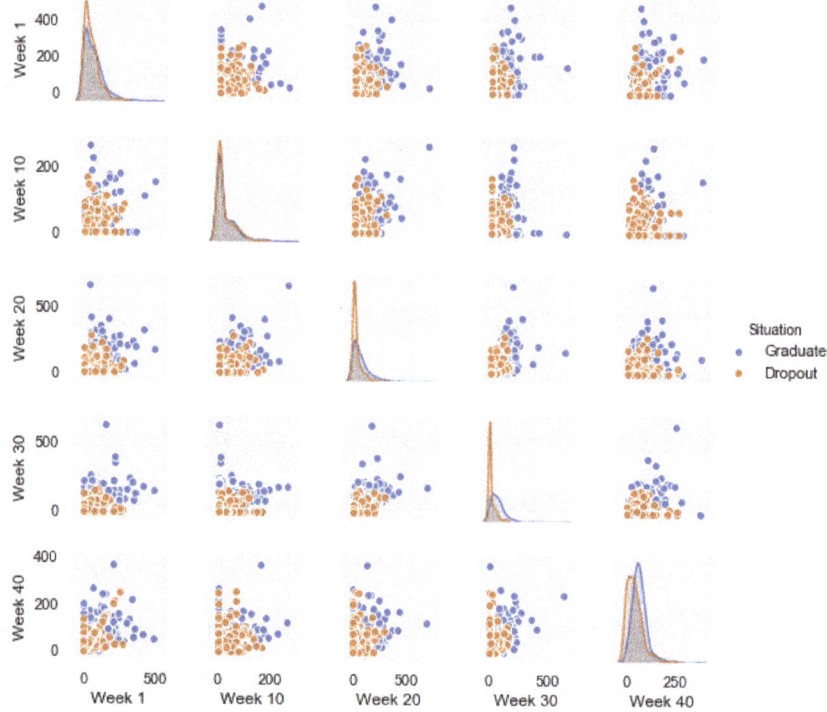

**Figure 4.** Density and scatter plots of weekly interactions.

*3.2. Fine Tuning with Proposed Genetic Algorithm*

In the GA, the solution set is defined by a space where a search for an optimal solution occurs, which may not be the global best solution [46]. This factor is directly dependent on the problem, the time that can be spent searching, the expected result, and the input dataset, among others. These should be considered when the algorithm is designed [47]. In this work, a time-limited search approach is proposed, so the algorithm creates a number $N$ of generations, where $N$ is predefined at the time of configuration. In the end, the algorithm returns a solution with the setting that produced the best performance according to the predefined metric [48]. In this case, a learning machine model together with its hyperparameters were optimized for the prediction of students at risk in technical distance courses. As previously mentioned, this solution can be global or local. The steps of this process are presented in Figure 5.

The proposed approach is executed according to the general steps of classical GA solutions, which are: (1) Generate population, (2) fitness function, (3) selection, (4) crossover, and (5) mutation. For the context of our solution, the following definitions are provided:

(a) Epoch: One complete cycle execution of the GA (from Steps 1 to 5). The proposed approach works with 50 epochs;
(b) Individual (or candidate): A machine learning algorithm/classifier (DT, RF, MLP, LG, and ADA) together with its hyperparameters;
(c) Chromosome: A vector of hyperparameters for a given individual (machine learning algorithm). As different machine learning algorithms have different hyperparameters, the chromosomes in our study have different sizes and meaning according to the machine learning algorithm to which they are referring.

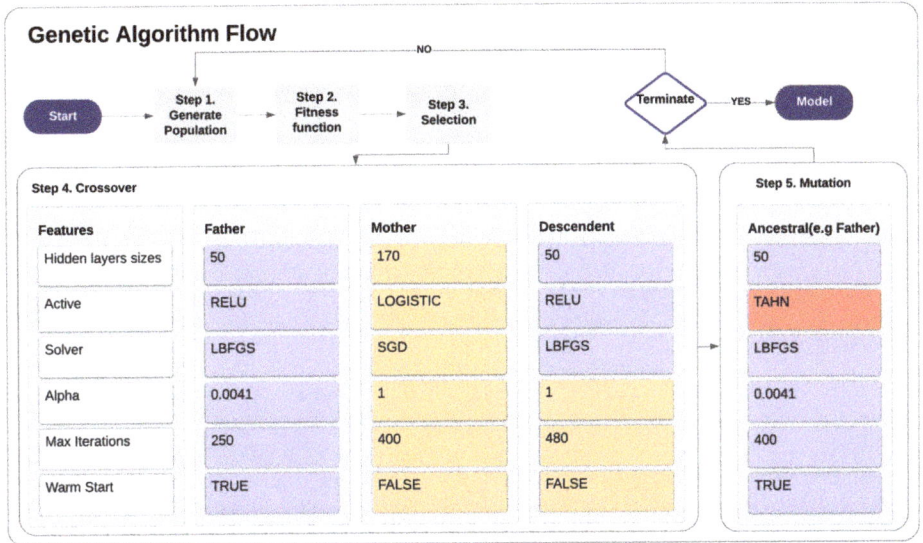

**Figure 5.** Genetic algorithm flow: An example of crossover and mutation with a multilayer perceptrons (MLP) chromosome.

Here, we outline each step of the process in the context of our proposed approach:

- Step 1 (generate population): The GA generates 100 individuals (candidates) for each machine learning algorithm (DT, RF, MLP, LG, and ADA) with hyperparameters (chromosomes) randomly defined considering the available list of options. The classifiers are trained and tested using 10-fold cross-validation and their performances are measured by using the area under the receiver operating characteristic curve metric (AUROC) [49] and as conducted by Gašević et al. [50].
- Step 2 (fitness function): The performance obtained by each of the 100 individuals of each machine learning algorithm are then compared by the fitness function.
- Step 3 (selection): The 25 individuals with the highest AUC for each machine learning algorithm are selected for the next step.
- Step 4 (crossover): The crossover is conducte using the concept based on the genetic inheritance of sexual reproductions, where each descendant receives a part of the genetic code (chromosome) of the father and part of the mother, as exemplified in Figure 5. Thus, the configurations of the fittest individuals of the last step are combined, one being the father and the other the mother. In the implemented algorithm, the individuals who will assign part of their genetic code to form a new member are chosen randomly from among the 25 best placed of that classifier in the last generation. This step results in 25 new individuals for each machine learning algorithm.
- Step 5 (mutation): This step randomly alters the chromosome (hyperparameter) of the 25 best individuals. In other words, a certain characteristic of an individual selected in the previous step receives a randomly generated configuration. As shown in Figure 5, an individual of the MLP type with hyperparameter "Active" set to "RELU" was changed to "TAHN". The mutation is set to change only one hyperparameter of the chromosome.

After Step 5, if the GA did not run the predefined number of epochs (50 for our experiment), a new population is generated in Step 1. The last important factor in generating a new population is randomness. For each generation, 25 new individuals are randomly generated again, even though they may have already been generated in earlier epochs. This seeks to ensure population diversity by narrowing the hypothesis that the solution reaches a local maximum and has no opportunity to evolve to the global maximum. The quantitative formation of the population from the second epoch onwards for each machine learning algorithm is:

- 25 individuals selected from the previous generation from the fitness function (Steps 2 and 3);
- 25 individuals formed by crossover (Step 4);
- 25 individuals formed by mutations (Step 5); and
- 25 new individuals randomly generated (Step 1).

The process is repeated for 50 epochs. In the end, for each of the five machine learning algorithms, the individual with the highest aptitude (highest AUC) is selected. With the selection of the fittest for each machine learning algorithm, the five remaining individuals compete against themselves, and the one with the best AUC is selected.

### 3.3. Experiments

This section outlines the experiments with three different approaches to predict students at risk of dropout in the database described earlier. The first is the proposed genetic algorithm, the second is a grid search method called GridSearchCV, implemented using the Scikit-learn package. The third and last is the use of classifiers with their default hyperparameters. The machine learning techniques implemented in this study used the Python programming language with the Scikit-learn, Pandas, and Numpy libraries.

GridsearchCV allowed the testing of different combinations of hyperparameters for classifiers, facilitating choosing the best one. The hyperparameters needed to be explicitly declared and all possible combinations tested. All available combinations in Table 3 were checked with the same algorithms defined in the GA (DT, RF, MLP, LG, and ADA). For each week of the course, we selected the classifier together with its hyperparameters that achieved the best performance for the given week.

The same machine learning algorithms with their default hyperparameters were also implemented for comparison with the GA and GridsearchCV approaches. All experiments were performed with 10-fold cross-validation, and the number of combinations was approximately 5000 individuals created by the GA. Appendix A shows the quantities tested in each of the classifiers in the Evaluations column.

An essential task in machine learning is choosing the performance appraisal metric. For this work, we decided to use the area under the ROC curve, also known as AUC and AUROC. AUC is calculated from the size of the area under the plotted curve where the y-axis is represented by true positive rate (TPR) or sensitivity (Equation (1)), and the x-axis is true negative rate (TNR) or specificity (Equation (2)):

$$Sensitivity = \frac{TP}{TP + FN} \quad (1)$$

$$Specificity = \frac{TN}{TN + FP} \quad (2)$$

According to Gašević et al. [50], the AUC may be interpreted as follows:

- AUC $\leq$ 0.50: Bad discrimination;
- 0.50 < AUC $\leq$ 0.70: Acceptable discrimination;
- 0.70 < AUC $\leq$ 0.90: Excellent discrimination; and
- AUC > 0.90: Outstanding discrimination.

## 4. Results and Discussion

This section presents the results obtained by the models generated by each of the selected algorithms compared with the application of the GA. Table 5 presents the AUC results for each tested machine learning algorithm without hyperparameter optimization and for the grid search (GRID) and GA approaches.

Table 5. AUC for 50 weeks.

| Approach or Machine Learning Algorithm | Hyperparameter Optimization | AUC Mean | AUC Median | AUC Standard Deviation |
|---|---|---|---|---|
| GA | Yes | 0.8454 | 0.8498 | 0,0637 |
| GRID | | 0.7939 | 0.8288 | 0.1056 |
| ADA | | 0.7509 | 0.8062 | 0.1342 |
| DT | No | 0.6771 | 0.7065 | 0.1008 |
| LG | | 0.6943 | 0.7198 | 0.1110 |
| MLP | | 0.7353 | 0.7946 | 0.1277 |
| RF | | 0.7752 | 0.8243 | 0.1150 |

As can be seen from Table 5, the best AUC results were produced by the GA approach with a mean of 0.8454 and median of 0.8498. GA also produced the lowest AUC standard deviation (0.0637) among all tested approaches. Figure 6 helps visualize the performance of the models for the 50 weeks of the course.

To confirm the research hypothesis in this work (RQ1 and RQ2), two tests of statistical significance were applied. The objective of the tests was to verify if there was a significant difference in the treatments applied and, if so, which method was the most accurate. The central idea involved in the process of statistical significance is to test whether one treatment, in this study GA, presents a significant result concerning the others [51].

The results had a normal distribution, so analysis of variance (ANOVA) was chosen to verify the existence of a significant difference, and Tukey's test to determine in which treatment it occurred. For this, the $p$-value was set to 0.05; thus, values lower than this indicated that the treatment was significant and higher than not significant. In ANOVA, the $p$-value was 0.0006865, which reflects the existence of significant differences between the approaches. In Tukey's test, the results produced a $p$-value of 0.0475 for the GridSearch and 0.0003 for standard RF, indicating a statistically significant difference between the performance. Thus, statistically, the results obtained by GA were superior to the other treatments.

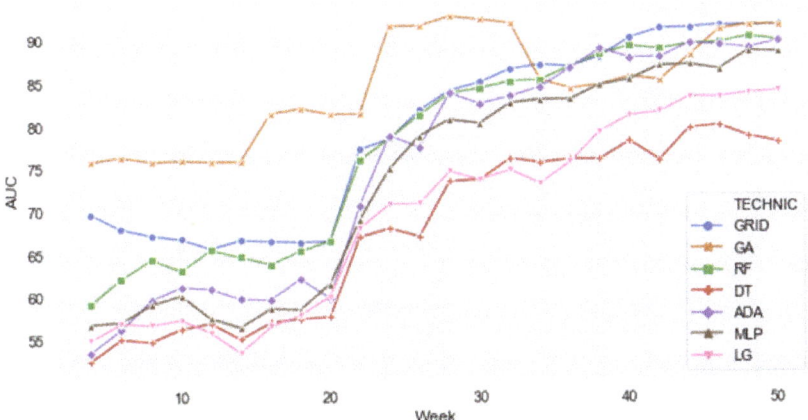

Figure 6. AUC results for each tested technique during the 50 weeks of the course.

The results obtained from the three approaches are presented in Figure 6. The GA achieved excellent discrimination (AUC > 0.7) as early as week 4. This held until week 24, where the GA provides outstanding discrimination (AUC > 0.9). The other approaches still yielded acceptable discrimination results (AUC < 0.7) until week 22. However, from week 30, the performance of the GA considerably decreased, with the other approaches progressing. One of the factors determining this drop in GA performance was the increase in the number of input attributes. In this situation, the GA tends to find a local solution quickly and converge on it. However, this solution is probably a plateau and the GA getting stuck. This is a problem specific to genetic algorithms that does not occur in the other approaches tested. In the proposed algorithm, the reinsertion step tries to soften this, but as verified from weeks 32 to 42, the GA is still susceptible to this failure. However, the GA was considerably better in early prediction and with limited data. This demonstrates that the refinement of the GA is essential for tuning hyperparameters.

Table 6 presents the best configuration obtained by the GA approach for week 25 of the course (individual 37, fourth epoch), with an MLP with an AUC of 91.54, in comparison with the configuration for the same algorithm without hyperparameter optimization. From the first weeks of the courses, satisfactory results were already produced in the prediction of students at risk of dropout.

In general, the results of the models generated by GA per the AUC were satisfactory, allowing the prediction of at-risk students in the early stages of the courses. Data were naturally balanced, with similar percentages of dropout and success students. The models developed here produced similar or better results in comparison to some of the works in the literature that focused on the early prediction of dropout students.

Table 6. Comparison between configurations of models for week 25.

| Hyperparameter Optimization | Hidden Layer Sizes | Activation | Solver | Alpha | max Iter | Warm Start | AUC |
|---|---|---|---|---|---|---|---|
| yes | 30 | logistic | sgd | 0.2855486101 | 353 | False | 0.9154 |
| no | 100 | relu | adam | 0.0001 | 200 | False | 0.849 |

According to [31,52], one of the main factors involved in the acceptance of learning analytics by teachers and students when using prediction models is the correctness rates involved in the process. The GA proposed in this work was able to increase these rates compared to the results obtained in previous works [23,24]. However, direct comparison with these experiments is somewhat complicated, as they used the true positive (TP) and true negative (TN) of the models as metrics, and we used AUCROC.

In these previous experiments, the results obtained in scenarios similar to this experiment showed rates of TP and TN varying between 58 and 82 in the first 25 weeks of the course. However, with the approach proposed in this work, it was possible to reach an initial AUCROC above 0.75, which increased over the first 25 weeks until reaching values above 0.90.

The comparison with prominent works of predictors of educational environments is necessary to situate the results obtained. Some limitations for comparison include the various techniques used to measure the results, such as accuracy, TP, TN, AUC, and AUCROC, among others [32] Cechinel et al. [33] Liz-Domínguez et al. [30]. Still, a significant part of the works on LA are characterized by the exploration of data from disciplines of a specific course or semester, whereas the work presented in this paper is characterized by the use of data from a course of two years in duration [32]. However, even when we compare the results obtained with the related works, the rates are satisfactory. Previous studies Lykourentzou et al. [5], Zohair [37], Whitehill et al. [38] reported rates of 85% and Jayaprakash et al. [26] reported 94% overall accuracy, but only 66.7% dropout prediction.

The results obtained in the optimization with the proposed GA are close to those of the literature Minaei-Bidgoli and Punch [43], which obtained an optimization of 12%. The proposed GA was able to reach values above 10% in the experiments until the 20th week compared to the algorithms in their standard configuration. When compared to the other optimization method, Gridsearch, in that same period, GA obtained values always above 6%, sometimes reaching 15%.

The method followed here is the result of an incremental process of a series of experiments previously performed [23,24]. As such, when comparing the results achieved in this work with the results from previous actions, the hyperparameters generated by the GA allows the generation of more robust models and higher performance. This is also demonstrated in comparison to the other methods tested in this article. Thus, the methodology used both for the development of the GA and for the generation of input data from genetic algorithms demonstrated that it could be used for early prediction of students at risk of dropout. Concerning data modeling, although the use of interaction count is not unprecedented, the methodology used in this study has several attributes that produced the results.

## 5. Final Remarks

This paper presented the results of an approach for the early prediction of students at risk of dropout using the counting of their interactions inside the VLE. This approach uses genetic algorithms for the hyperparameter of classifiers. The methodology of generating a prediction model every two weeks allows every student to be followed throughout the course. This is an approach that differs from the traditional methods [6] that define models that seek to predict dropout using all available data at the end of the course. This difference and, consequently, the results obtained with smaller amounts of data contribute to the early prediction of the risk of dropout.

The proposed approach is based on the premise of allowing greater generalization when replicating the methodology in other courses and platforms, since it only uses the count of interactions within the VLE without distinguishing the types of actions performed and without using information from different data sources (demographic data, questionnaires, curriculum, etc.), the availability of which may vary between e-learning platforms. The results can be considered satisfactory since they allow the identification of students at risk of dropout with reasonable performance rates even before the end of the first semester of the course.

The prediction of academic issues, such as performance and dropout, is concentrated at the university level, with about 70% of the research destined for this purpose [10]. This trend is repeated in Latin America, with few applications considering the context of education at the secondary and technical levels [33]. While not unprecedented, the application of prediction techniques in other contexts, such as technical high school e-learning, is also relevant [10].

**RQ1.** Does the approach for hyperparameter optimization with a GA outperform traditional techniques?

The proposed GA must be evaluated to emphasize that testing different combinations of hyperparameters within the same algorithm is a complicated and time-consuming task that may require a large amount of processing time. However, the accuracy of prediction models is directly linked to the quality of hyperparameter optimization. Thus, the more adjusted they are, the more accurate the rates of the models tend to be. The alternatives to applying exhaustive search methods, such as grid-search, are computationally expensive when searching in large spaces [53]. Thus, the refinement obtained by GA with its mutation and crossover stages produces better results for model generation, surpassing the traditional techniques and grid-search. Compared to standard algorithms, the performance of the proposed method is clearly superior.

**RQ2.** Does the resulting predictive models generated by the use of the GA approach for hyperparameter optimization perform better than models with default hyperparameters?

In comparison with the classifications using the default hyperparameters, the GA produced significantly better results. In the first 20 weeks of the course, the difference between the two methods varies from 10% and 15%. Tukey's test demonstrated that the overall values obtained are significantly different. However, all techniques have advantages and limitations. The drawback of the GA is the lack of assurance that the solution is global; the positive aspect is the number of resultant hyperparameters accepted without significantly altering the processing cost and the final results. In grid-search, the computational cost is the biggest issue, as previously reported; however, it delivers the best possible combination of hyperparameters. Concerning the standard classifiers, we highlight the cost–benefit factor as the method produces satisfactory results in short processing time, which, depending on the project, can be an essential point.

The main limitation of the proposed methodology presents is that for each course analyzed, the calendar must be studied to identify periods without classes, such as holidays. This causes extra work, which does not occur when socio-demographic data are used. Another limitation concerns generalization; although the methodology may be generalized, the models are unlikely to be suitable for courses that do not follow the same timetable as ETec. Models that seek long-term predictions are more susceptible to failures due to external situations, such as economic and epidemiological crises.

An important point to note is that the GA possibly presents slightly different results for each execution. Thus, it may be interesting to run the GA multiple times (e.g., 10). Analysis of other metrics, such as overall accuracy and true positive (TP) and true negative (TN), may provide different perspectives. The application of other hyperparameter search methods, such as random search, and algorithms, such as XGBOOST, can still be explored. These questions will possibly be studied in the future stages of this project, as well as hybrid choice methods such as the vote theory, for final classification selection.

The results obtained in this work enable the development of an early warning system using the proposed approach. Currently, the development of this system is occurring in the form of a plugin integrated with Moodle. Another future work toward improving the results is the application of survival analysis to increase student retention and consequently reduce dropout.

**Author Contributions:** Author Contributions: E.M.Q.: Experimental data analysis, algorithms development, data pre-processing, experiments conduction, results description, and manuscript writing; J.L.L.: Course lecturer, conceived and designed, and methodology definition; K.K.: Algorithms development and writing review; M.A.: manuscript writing and algorithms development; R.M.A.: Algorithms development and data pre-processing; R.V.: writing—review and editing; R.M.: writing—review and editing. C.C.: methodology definition, algorithm developed, experiments setup, manuscript writing, and writing—review and editing. The final manuscript was written and approved by all authors. All authors have read and agreed to the published version of the manuscript.

**Funding:** This work was supported by CNPq (Brazilian National Council for Scientific and Technological Development) [Edital Universal, proc.404369/2016-2][DT-2 Productivity in Technological Development and Innovative Extension scholarship, proc.315445/2018-1]. R.V. and R.M. were funded by Corporación de Fomento de la Producción (CORFO) 14ENI2-26905 "Nueva Ingeniería para el 2030"—Pontificia Universidad Católica de Valparaíso, Chile.

**Conflicts of Interest:** The authors declare no conflict of interest.

**Abbreviations**

The following abbreviations are used in this manuscript:

| | |
|---|---|
| ADA | ADABoost |
| ANOVA | Analysis of Variance |
| AUC | Area Under the Curve |
| AUROC | Area Under the Receiver Operating Characteristic Curve |
| DT | Decision Tree |
| EDA | Exploratory Data Analysis |
| EDM | Educational Data Mining |
| GA | Genetic Algorithm |
| GBGP | Grammar-Based Genetic Programming |
| GRID | Grid SearchCV |
| IBK | Instance-Based Lazy Learning |
| ICRM | Interpretable Classification Rule Mining Algorithm |
| IFSul | Instituto Federal Sul Rio-grandense |

| INN | I-nearest neighbor |
|---|---|
| kNN | k-Nearest Neighbor |
| LA | Learning Analytics |
| LG | Logistic Regression |
| LMS | Learning Management Systems |
| ML | Machine Learning |
| MAE | Mean Absolute Error |
| MLP | Multilayer Perceptron |
| NDS | Number of Dropout Students |
| PCA | Principal Component Analysis |
| RQ | Research Question |
| RF | Random Forest |
| SAT | Scholastic Aptitude Test |
| SMOTE | Synthetic Minority Over-Sampling Technique |
| SVM | Support Vector Machine |
| TNR | True Negative Rate |
| TPR | True Positive Rate |
| VLE | Virtual Learning Environment |

## Appendix A

Table A1. Classifiers, Hyperparameters and Number of Evaluations.

| Alg. | Hyperparameters | Possibi-Lities | Number of Ind. | Grid | Eval. |
|---|---|---|---|---|---|
| DT | criterion: [gini, entropy], max_depth: range (0, 32), min_samples_split: range (1, 15), min_samples_leaf: range (1, 20) | 19.200 | 5.100 | criterion: [gini,entropy], max_depth: [0, 1, 2, 3, 5, 7, 10, 12, 15, 17, 20, 23, 25, 30], min_samples_split: [0, 1, 2, 3, 5, 7, 10, 12, 15] min_samples_leaf: [0, 1, 2, 3, 4, 5, 7, 9, 10, 12, 15, 17, 20] | 3.726 |
| RF | n_estimators: range (1,200), criterion: [gini, entropy], max_features [1, 2, 3,4], min_samples_split: range (2, 21), min_samples_leaf: range (1, 2), bootstrap: [True, False] | 128.000 | 5.100 | n_estimators: [1, 10, 20, 30, 40, 50, 70, 100, 120, 130, 150, 170, 190, 200], criterion: [gini, entropy], max_features [1, 2, 3, 4], min_samples_split: [2, 3, 4, 5, 7, 9, 10, 12, 15, 17, 20], min_samples_leaf: [1, 2], bootstrap: [True, False] | 4.928 |
| ADA | algorithm: [SAMME, SAMME.R], n_estimators: range (1, 200), random_state: range (None, 50), learning_rate: range (1e-2,1) | 2 KK | 5.100 | algorithm: [SAMME, SAMME.R], n_estimators: [1, 10, 20, 30, 40, 50, 70, 100, 120, 130, 150, 170, 190, 200], random_state: [None, 1, 5, 10, 15, 20, 25, 30, 40, 50 ], learning_rate: [1e-2, 5e-2, 7e-2, 1e-1, 3e-1, 5e-1, 7e-1, 1] | 2.240 |
| MLP | hidden_layer_sizes: range (1,200), activation: [identity, logistic, tanh, relu], solver: [lbfgs, sgd, adam], max_iter: range (50, 200), alpha: range (1e-4, 1e-1), warm_start: [True, False] | 720 KK | 5.100 | hidden_layer_sizes: [(50,50,50), (50,100,50), (100,), (50,), (10,), (1), (5)], activation: [identity, logistic, tanh, relu], solver: [lbfgs, sgd, adam], max_iter: [1, 2, 5, 10, 30, 50], alpha: [1e-4, 1e-3, 1e-2, 5e-2, 1e-1], warm_start: [True, False] | 5.040 |
| RL | penalty: [l1, l2, elasticnet], C: [1e-4, 1e-3, 1e-2, 1e-1, 5e-1, 1, 5, 10, 15, 20, 25], dual: [True, False], solver: [newton-cg, lbfgs, lbfgs, sag, saga], multi_class: [ovr, auto], max_iter: range (50,200) | 99.000 | 5.100 | penalty: [l1, l2, elasticnet], C: [1e-4, 1e-1, 5e-1, 1, 5, 15, 25], dual: [True, False], solver: [newton-cg, lbfgs, lbfgs, sag, saga], multi_class: [ovr, auto], max_iter: [1, 10, 20, 30, 40, 50, 70, 100, 120, 130, 150, 170, 190, 200] | 5.800 |

## References

1. Chatti, M.A.; Dyckhoff, A.L.; Schroeder, U.; Thüs, H. A reference model for learning analytics. *Int. J. Technol. Enhanc. Learn.* **2013**, *4*, 318–331. [CrossRef]
2. Siemens, G. Learning analytics: The emergence of a discipline. *Am. Behav. Sci.* **2013**, *57*, 1380–1400. [CrossRef]
3. Sheehan, M.; Park, Y. pGPA: A personalized grade prediction tool to aid student success. In Proceedings of the Sixth ACM Conference on Recommender Systems, Dublin City, Ireland, 9–13 September 2012; pp. 309–310.
4. Manhães, L.M.B.; Cruz, S.d.; Costa, R.J.M.; Zavaleta, J.; Zimbrão, G. Previsão de Estudantes com Risco de Evasão Utilizando Técnicas de Mineração de Dados. In Proceedings of the Anais do XXII SBIE-XVII WIE, Aracaju, Brazil, 21–25 November 2011.
5. Lykourentzou, I.; Giannoukos, I.; Nikolopoulos, V.; Mpardis, G.; Loumos, V. Dropout prediction in e-learning courses through the combination of machine learning techniques. *Comput. Educ.* **2009**, *53*, 950–965. [CrossRef]
6. Márquez-Vera, C.; Cano, A.; Romero, C.; Noaman, A.Y.M.; Mousa Fardoun, H.; Ventura, S. Early dropout prediction using data mining: A case study with high school students. *Expert Syst.* **2016**, *33*, 107–124. [CrossRef]
7. OECD. *Benchmarking Higher Education System Performance*; OECD: Paris, France, 2019; p. 644. [CrossRef]
8. Yukselturk, E. Predicting Dropout Student: An Application of Data Mining Methods in an Online Education Program. *Comput. Educ.* **2014**, *17*, 118–133. [CrossRef]
9. Li, Q.; Baker, R.; Warschauer, M. Using clickstream data to measure, understand, and support self-regulated learning in online courses. *Internet High. Educ.* **2020**, 100727. [CrossRef]
10. Rastrollo-Guerrero, J.L.; Gómez-Pulido, J.A.; Durán-Domínguez, A. Analyzing and Predicting Students' Performance by Means of Machine Learning: A Review. *Appl. Sci.* **2020**, *10*, 1042. [CrossRef]
11. Vossensteyn, J.J.; Kottmann, A.; Jongbloed, B.W.; Kaiser, F.; Cremonini, L.; Stensaker, B.; Hovdhaugen, E.; Wollscheid, S. Dropout and Completion in Higher Education in Europe: Main Report. In *European Commission*; Center for Higher Education Policy Studies and Nordic Institute for Studies in Innovation Research and Education: Enschede, The Nerthland, 2015; doi:10.2766/826962. 2015. [CrossRef]
12. Gregori, E.B.; Zhang, J.; Galván-Fernández, C.; Fernández-Navarro, F.d.A. Learner support in MOOCs: Identifying variables linked to completion. *Comput. Educ.* **2018**, *122*, 153–168. [CrossRef]
13. Censo, E. BR 2018-Relatório Analítico da Aprendizagem a Distância no Brasil. *Acesso Em* **2018**, *16*.
14. Dickson, W.P. Toward a deeper understanding of student performance in virtual high school courses: Using quantitative analyses and data visualization to inform decision making. In *A Synthesis of New Research in K–12 Online Learning*; Michigan Virtual University: Lansing, MI, USA, 2005; pp. 21–23.
15. Murray, M.; Pérez, J.; Geist, D.; Hedrick, A. Student interaction with content in online and hybrid courses: Leading horses to the proverbial water. In Proceedings of the Informing Science and Information Technology Education Conference, Santa Rosa, CA, USA, 30 June–6 July 2013; Informing Science Institute: Santa Rosa, CA, USA, 2013; pp. 99–115.
16. Leitner, P.; Ebner, M.; Ebner, M. Learning Analytics Challenges to Overcome in Higher Education Institutions. In *Utilizing Learning Analytics to Support Study Success*; Springer: Berlin, Germany, 2019; pp. 91–104.
17. Gursoy, M.E.; Inan, A.; Nergiz, M.E.; Saygin, Y. Privacy-preserving learning analytics: Challenges and techniques. *IEEE Trans. Learn. Technol.* **2016**, *10*, 68–81. [CrossRef]
18. Drachsler, H.; Greller, W. Privacy and analytics: It's a DELICATE issue a checklist for trusted learning analytics. In Proceedings of the Sixth International Conference on Learning Analytics & Knowledge, Edinburgh, Scotland, 25–29 April 2016; pp. 89–98.
19. Baker, R.S.; Inventado, P.S. Educational data mining and learning analytics. In *Learning Analytics*; Springer: Berlin, Germany, 2014; pp. 61–75.
20. Olivares, R.; Munoz, R.; Soto, R.; Crawford, B.; Cárdenas, D.; Ponce, A.; Taramasco, C. An Optimized Brain-Based Algorithm for Classifying Parkinson's Disease. *Appl. Sci.* **2020**, *10*, 1827. [CrossRef]
21. Bergstra, J.S.; Bardenet, R.; Bengio, Y.; Kégl, B. Algorithms for hyper-parameter optimization. In *Advances in Neural Information Processing Systems*; Curran Associates Inc.: Granada, Spain, 2011; pp. 2546–2554, ISBN 9781618395993.

22. Li, L.; Jamieson, K.; DeSalvo, G.; Rostamizadeh, A.; Talwalkar, A. Hyperband: A novel bandit-based approach to hyperparameter optimization. *J. Mach. Learn. Res.* **2017**, *18*, 6765–6816.
23. Queiroga, E.; Cechinel, C.; Araújo, R. Predição de estudantes com risco de evasão em cursos técnicos a distância. In Proceedings of the Brazilian Symposium on Computers in Education (Simpósio Brasileiro de Informática na Educação-SBIE), Recife, Brazil, 30 October–2 November 2017; p. 1547.
24. Queiroga, E.; Cechinel, C.; Araújo, R.; da Costa Bretanha, G. Generating models to predict at-risk students in technical e-learning courses. In Proceedings of the IEEE Latin American Conference on Learning Objects and Technology (LACLO), San Carlos, CA, USA, 3–7 October 2016; pp. 1–8.
25. Detoni, D.; Cechinel, C.; Matsumura Araújo, R. Modelagem e Predição de Reprovação de Acadêmicos de Cursos de Educação a Distância a partir da Contagem de Interações. *Revista Brasileira de Informática na Educação* **2015**, *23*, 1.
26. Jayaprakash, S.M.; Moody, E.W.; Lauria, E.J.M.; Regan, J.R.; Baron, J.D. Early Alert of Academically At-Risk Students: An Open Source Analytics Initiative. *J. Learn. Anal.* **2014**, *1*, 6–47. [CrossRef]
27. Márquez-Vera, C.; Cano, A.; Romero, C.; Ventura, S. Predicting student failure at school using genetic programming and different data mining approaches with high dimensional and imbalanced data. *Appl. Intell.* **2013**, *38*, 315–330. [CrossRef]
28. Xing, W.; Guo, R.; Petakovic, E.; Goggins, S. Participation-based student final performance prediction model through interpretable Genetic Programming: Integrating learning analytics, educational data mining and theory. *Comput. Hum. Behav.* **2015**, *47*, 168–181. [CrossRef]
29. Munoz, R.; Olivares, R.; Taramasco, C.; Villarroel, R.; Soto, R.; Barcelos, T.S.; Merino, E.; Alonso-Sánchez, M.F. Using black hole algorithm to improve eeg-based emotion recognition. *Comput. Intell. Neurosci.* **2018**, *2018*, 22. [CrossRef]
30. Liz-Domínguez, M.; Caeiro-Rodríguez, M.; Llamas-Nistal, M.; Mikic-Fonte, F.A. Systematic Literature Review of Predictive Analysis Tools in Higher Education. *Appl. Sci.* **2019**, *9*, 5569. [CrossRef]
31. Herodotou, C.; Rienties, B.; Verdin, B.; Boroowa, A. Predictive learning analytics 'at scale': Towards guidelines to successful implementation in Higher Education based on the case of the Open University UK. *J. Learn. Anal.* **2019**. [CrossRef]
32. Hilliger, I.; Ortiz-Rojas, M.; Pesántez-Cabrera, P.; Scheihing, E.; Tsai, Y.S.; Muñoz-Merino, P.J.; Broos, T.; Whitelock-Wainwright, A.; Pérez-Sanagustín, M. Identifying needs for learning analytics adoption in Latin American universities: A mixed-methods approach. *Internet High. Educ.* **2020**, *45*, 100726. [CrossRef]
33. Cechinel, C.; Ochoa, X.; Lemos dos Santos, H.; Carvalho Nunes, J.B.; Rodés, V.; Marques Queiroga, E. Mapping Learning Analytics initiatives in Latin America. *Br. J. Educ. Technol.* **2020**, doi:10.1111/bjet.12941. [CrossRef]
34. González, P. Factores que favorecen las presencia docente en entornos virtuales de aprendizaje. *Tendencias Pedagógicas* **2017**, *29*, 43–58.
35. de Pablo González, G. *La Importancia de la Presencia Docente en Entornos Virtuales de Aprendizaje*; Universidad Autónoma de Madrid: Madrid, Spain, 2016.
36. Herodotou, C.; Rienties, B.; Boroowa, A.; Zdrahal, Z.; Hlosta, M.; Naydenova, G. Implementing predictive learning analytics on a large scale: The teacher's perspective. In Proceedings of the Seventh International Learning Analytics & Knowledge Conference, Vancouver, BC, Canada, 13–17 March 2017; pp. 267–271.
37. Zohair, L.M.A. Prediction of Student's performance by modelling small dataset size. *Int. J. Educ. Technol. High. Educ.* **2019**, *16*, 27. [CrossRef]
38. Whitehill, J.; Mohan, K.; Seaton, D.; Rosen, Y.; Tingley, D. Delving deeper into MOOC student dropout prediction. *arXiv* **2017**, arXiv:1702.06404.
39. Macarini, B.; Antonio, L.; Cechinel, C.; Batista Machado, M.F.; Faria Culmant Ramos, V.; Munoz, R. Predicting Students Success in Blended Learning—Evaluating Different Interactions Inside Learning Management Systems. *Appl. Sci.* **2019**, *9*, 5523. [CrossRef]
40. Queiroga, E.; Cechinel, C.; Araújo, R. Um Estudo do Uso de Contagem de Interações Semanais para Predição Precoce de Evasão em Educação a Distância. In Proceedings of the Anais dos Workshops do Congresso Brasileiro de Informática na Educação, Maceio, Brazil, 26–30 October 2015; p. 1074.
41. Swan, K. Learning effectiveness online: What the research tells us. *Elem. Qual. Online Educ. Pract. Dir.* **2003**, *4*, 13–47.

42. Halawa, S.; Greene, D.; Mitchell, J. Dropout Prediction in MOOCs using Learner Activity Features. *Eur. MOOC Summit EMOOCs* **2014**, *37*, 1–10.
43. Minaei-Bidgoli, B.; Punch, W.F. Using genetic algorithms for data mining optimization in an educational web-based system. In Proceedings of the Genetic and eVolutionary Computation Conference, Chicago, IL, USA, 12–16 July 2003; Springer: Berlin, Germany, 2003; pp. 2252–2263.
44. Silva Filho, R.L.L.; Motejunas, P.R.; Hipólito, O.; Lobo, M.B.d.C.M. A evasão no ensino superior brasileiro. *Cadernos de Pesquisa* **2007**, *37*, 641–659. [CrossRef]
45. Resende, M.L.d.A. *Evasão Escolar No Primeiro Ano Do Ensino médio Integrado Do Ifsuldeminas-Campus Machado*; Encontro Anual da ANPOCS: Caxambu, Brazil, 2012.
46. Fonseca, C.M.; Fleming, P.J. Genetic Algorithms for Multiobjective Optimization: Formulation Discussion and Generalization. In Proceedings of the ICGA, San Mateo, CA, USA, 17–22 June 1993; pp. 416–423.
47. Hartmann, S. A competitive genetic algorithm for resource-constrained project scheduling. *Nav. Res. Logist. (NRL)* **1998**, *45*, 733–750. [CrossRef]
48. Sebastiani, F. Machine learning in automated text categorization. *ACM Comput. Surv. (CSUR)* **2002**, *34*, 1–47. [CrossRef]
49. Fawcett, T. An introduction to ROC analysis. *Pattern Recognit. Lett.* **2006**, *27*, 861–874. [CrossRef]
50. Gašević, D.; Dawson, S.; Rogers, T.; Gasevic, D. Learning analytics should not promote one size fits all: The effects of instructional conditions in predicting academic success. *Internet High. Educ.* **2016**, *28*, 68–84. [CrossRef]
51. Bruce, P.; Bruce, A. *Practical Statistics for Data Scientists: 50 Essential Concepts*; O'Reilly Media, Inc.: Sebastopol, CA, USA, 2017.
52. Larrabee Sønderlund, A.; Hughes, E.; Smith, J. The efficacy of learning analytics interventions in higher education: A systematic review. *Br. J. Educ. Technol.* **2019**, *50*, 2594–2618. [CrossRef]
53. Zöller, M.A.; Huber, M.F. Survey on automated machine learning. *arXiv* **2019**, arXiv:1904.12054.

© 2020 by the authors. Licensee MDPI, Basel, Switzerland. This article is an open access article distributed under the terms and conditions of the Creative Commons Attribution (CC BY) license (http://creativecommons.org/licenses/by/4.0/).

Article

# An Early Warning System to Detect At-Risk Students in Online Higher Education

David Bañeres [1,2,*], M. Elena Rodríguez [1,2], Ana Elena Guerrero-Roldán [1,2] and Abdulkadir Karadeniz [1,3]

1. eLearn Center, Universitat Oberta de Catalunya, 08018 Barcelona, Spain; mrodriguezgo@uoc.edu (M.E.R.); aguerreror@uoc.edu (A.E.G.-R.); akaradeniz@uoc.edu (A.K.)
2. Faculty of Computer Science, Multimedia and Telecommunications, Universitat Oberta de Catalunya, 08018 Barcelona, Spain
3. Open Education Faculty, Yunus Emre Campus, Anadolu University, 26470 Eskisehir, Turkey; abdulkadirkaradeniz@anadolu.edu.tr
* Correspondence: dbaneres@uoc.edu

Received: 30 May 2020; Accepted: 25 June 2020; Published: 27 June 2020

**Abstract:** Artificial intelligence has impacted education in recent years. Datafication of education has allowed developing automated methods to detect patterns in extensive collections of educational data to estimate unknown information and behavior about the students. This research has focused on finding accurate predictive models to identify at-risk students. This challenge may reduce the students' risk of failure or disengage by decreasing the time lag between identification and the real at-risk state. The contribution of this paper is threefold. First, an in-depth analysis of a predictive model to detect at-risk students is performed. This model has been tested using data available in an institutional data mart where curated data from six semesters are available, and a method to obtain the best classifier and training set is proposed. Second, a method to determine a threshold for evaluating the quality of the predictive model is established. Third, an early warning system has been developed and tested in a real educational setting being accurate and useful for its purpose to detect at-risk students in online higher education. The stakeholders (i.e., students and teachers) can analyze the information through different dashboards, and teachers can also send early feedback as an intervention mechanism to mitigate at-risk situations. The system has been evaluated on two undergraduate courses where results shown a high accuracy to correctly detect at-risk students.

**Keywords:** early warning system; artificial intelligence; predictive models; personalized feedback; online learning

## 1. Introduction

The use of technology in education is getting more and more intensive day by day, and it is becoming a necessity for effective and permanent learning to be updated. Technology has been utilized and continues to be used in many areas such as students' access to course materials, administrators' follow-up management processes, teachers' course control, and activities in education. Particularly in the field of Artificial Intelligence (AI), the technology has moved effectively in education to a different dimension with a significant leap [1]. It is well-known that students benefit not only in material access, but also in monitoring their processes, evaluating their learning, and monitoring their performance, through intelligent tutoring systems (ITS). One of these ITS is developed in the LIS (Learning Intelligent System) project [2], which aims to assist students in their educational processes. LIS is a system formed within the Universitat Oberta de Catalunya (UOC) to develop an adaptive system to be globally applicable at the custom Learning Management System (LMS) implemented at UOC to help students to succeed in their learning process. The project intends to provide help to the student in terms of automatic feedback in assessment activities, recommendations in terms of learning paths, self-regulation or learning resources, and gamification techniques to improve the students' engagement.

The first stage of this project focuses on the development of an Early Warning System (EWS) to detect at-risk students by using data from the past and present and to warn the student and his or her teacher about the situation. Also, the system provides semi-automatic feedback as an early intervention mechanism in order to amend possible conditions of failure. A proof of concept of the EWS was proposed in [3], where sound results in terms of a predictive model and the application of the EWS in a higher education course were presented. Such experiment was used as a pillar to build a functional and enhanced version of the EWS at the UOC where the learning process is held by a custom LMS.

This paper aims at presenting a new system with several contributions. The first contribution is a predictive model denoted as Gradual At-Risk (GAR) model. Such a model is based only on students' grades and predicts the likelihood to fail a course. A deep analysis of the model is performed in the whole set of courses at the university by using the data available in a data mart provided by our institution. Compared to [3], we propose a method to obtain the best classifier and training set for each course and semester. This method was proposed after observing that new data do not always contribute to improving the accuracy and, therefore, sometimes should be discarded.

The second one is a method to determine a threshold to consider the trained GAR model of a course as a high- or low-quality model. The GAR model, when used in a real educational setting, will provide to the student feedback based on her/his risk level. Therefore, a teacher cannot afford to send a wrong message or recommendation to the student. This threshold is used for the EWS to adapt the type of message sent to the student.

The third contribution is the application of the EWS in a real educational setting in two courses. The GAR model is used to provide meaningful information to the students and teachers in terms of dashboards and feedback. In this paper, we analyze the accuracy of identifying at-risk students in such a real learning scenario and the impact on the final performance of the courses. We consider also relevant this last contribution, since it proves the application of the AI in the educational field. These contributions are drawn as a consequence of answering the next research questions underpinning this study:

**RQ1.** How accurate is the predictive model in the whole institution after six semesters of available data?

**RQ2.** Which is the accuracy limit for the predictive model to consider a low-quality model to adapt the intervention measures in the EWS?

**RQ3.** How accurate is the EWS in identifying at-risk students in a real educational setting?

The paper is organized as follows. Section 2 summarizes related work and Section 3 focuses on the methods and context of the institution where the research took place. Section 4 analyzes the process to obtain the best classification algorithm and training set for the GAR model, and Section 5 presents two of the main dashboards provided by the EWS as well as the implemented feedback intervention mechanism. The experimental results on two case studies are described in Section 6, while Section 7 discusses the results. Finally, the conclusions and future work are summarized in Section 8.

## 2. Related Work

### 2.1. Predictive Models

As described in different systematic reviews [4,5], many models can be applied to education. Students' performance [6], students' dropout within an individual course [7,8], program retention [9], recommender systems in terms of activities [10], learning resources, [11] and next courses to be enrolled [12,13] are some examples of the application of those models.

Independently of the desired outcome, models have used many different types of data in order to perform the predictions. Different variables (or features) have been explored ranging from demographic data [14] (e.g., age, gender, ethnic origin, marital status, among others), self-reported questionnaires [15,16], continuous assessment results [17,18], user-generated content [19] to LMS data [20,21].

Numerous classification algorithms have been analyzed through the proposed predictive models. Decision Tree (DT) [22], Naive Bayes (NB) [23], Support Vector Machine (SVM) [24], Logistic Regression [25–27], Hierarchical Mixed models [17,28], K-Nearest Neighbors (KNN) [26], Neural Network models [29], or Bayesian Additive Regressive Trees [30] are some examples of the employed techniques.

As previously mentioned, we focus on identifying at-risk students by checking the likelihood to fail a course following the claims of other researchers [24,25,31] to create specific course predictive models. A simple model based on grades of the continuous assessment activities (named GAR model) is used instead of using a complex model. Activities performed by students throughout their learning process are indicators of the performance they will reach in the future. Although we use this simple model, we have comparable results with other predictive models to detect at-risk students.

Table 1 illustrates a comparison of the predictive GAR model with other related works where more complex models were proposed. The table shows for each comparison, the intervention point in the semester timeline (*Semester Intervention Point*), the compared accuracy metric (*Accuracy Metric*), the value of the metric in the referenced work (*Value Metric Ref.*), the LOESS regression of the GAR model at the intervention point in the complete set of courses at our university (*LOESS Regr. GAR whole institution*), and the percentages of courses with a metric value larger than the metric of the referenced work (*Perc. Courses Metric GAR > Metric Ref.*). Authors in [23] obtained an $F_{1,5}$ (F-score) of 62.00% with Naive Bayes at 40% of the semester timeline; meanwhile, our model reaches a LOESS regression value of 78.55% on average in the whole courses at our university at the same point of the semester timeline. When courses are evaluated individually, we found that more than 70% of the courses have an $F_{1,5}$ larger than 62.00% at this point of the semester. Authors in [25] reached a TNR (True Negative Rate) of 75.40% at the end of the course meanwhile the GAR model reaches a LOESS regression value of 97.56%, and more than 99% of the courses have a TNR larger than 75.40%. Authors in [30] computed the MAE (Mean Absolute Error) at 40% of the semester timeline. They reached a MAE value of 0.07, whereas the GAR model has a LOESS value of 0.08, and more than 64% of the courses have a MAE smaller than 0.07 at this point of the semester. The approach presented in [32] reached a TPR (True Positive Rate) of 81.00% at the 40% of the semester timeline while our model obtained a LOESS regression value of 80.46% but more than 40% of the courses have a TPR larger than 81.00% at this point of the semester. On the approach presented in [33], where SMOTE was used in order to balance classes, the AUC (Area Under The Curve) ROC (Receiver Operating Characteristics) curve was used to evaluate the model. The best model reached a ROC value near to 91.00% at 60% of the semester timeline. The GAR model without SMOTE has a LOESS value near to 93.00% and more than 59% of the courses have a ROC value larger than 91.00% at this point of the semester.

Table 1. Comparison GAR Model with other related work.

| Reference | Semester Intervention Point | Accuracy Metric | Value Metric Ref. | LOESS Regr. GAR Whole Institution | Perc. Courses Metric GAR > Metric Ref. |
|---|---|---|---|---|---|
| Marbouti et al. [23] | 40% | $F_{1,5}$ | 62.00% | 78.55% | 70% |
| Macfadyen et al. [25] | 100% | TNR | 75.40% | 97.56% | 99% |
| Howard et al. [30] | 40% | MAE | 0.07 | 0.08 | 64% |
| Akçapınar et al. [32] | 40% | TPR | 81.00% | 80.46% | 40% |
| Buschetto et al. [33] | 60% | AUC | 91.00% | 93.00% | 59% |

$F_{1,5}$: F-score, TNR: True Negative Rate, MAE: Mean Absolute Error, TPR: True Positive Rate, AUC: Area Under the Curve.

*2.2. Early Warning Systems*

An EWS is a tool used to monitor students' progress. It identifies students at-risk of either failing or dropping out of a course or program [23]. It helps students to be on track and aid in their self-directed learning journey [34]. Also, it can help to reach the necessary information about student engagement and performance to facilitate personalized timely interventions [28].

Based on the predictive models mentioned in the previous section, some examples of EWS are students' dropout detection on face-to-face environments [35], students' dropout on online settings [36–38], or early identification of at-risk students, which may allow some type of intervention to increase retention and success rate [16,25,26,39].

Many of the previously described approaches propose an EWS, but the EWS is just sketched from a conceptual point of view. Therefore, few full-fledged developments can be found. The most referenced one is the Course Signals at Purdue University [17] where different dashboards are available at the student's and teacher's point of view. Moreover, the system triggers a visual warning alert using a Green-Amber-Red semaphore. Other systems can be found where information is available in dashboards for teachers [31,40,41] and students [42].

Personalized feedback [17] is one possible intervention mechanism for these kind of approaches. Other intervention mechanisms can be applied, such as pedagogical recommendations [43], mentoring [44], or academic support environment [45], with a significant impact on performance, dropout, and retention. Feeding students depending on his or her situation will affect students' perception and will impact his or her way of learning and self-regulation. If personalized feedback can be one of the possible intervention mechanisms, nudges can complement it in a very constructive way. Nudges according to the definition provided in [46] (p. 2) are "interventions that preserve freedom of choice that nonetheless influence people's decisions". Nudges have their origin in behavioral economics, which studies the effects of psychological knowledge about human behavior to enhance decision-making processes. In education [47], nudges intend to obtain a higher educational attainment (e.g., improvement of grades, to increase course completion rates and earned credits, or to increase course engagement and participation), and they have been used in primary, secondary, and higher education, including Massive Open Online Courses (MOOC), and involving different stakeholders (parents, students, and teachers). The information provided by nudges includes remainders, deadlines, goal setting, advice, etc. How the information included in nudges is stated can also increase social belonging and motivation.

The EWS we propose is able to provide personalized feedback. First, students receive predictions from the first activity about the minimum grade they should obtain in the activity to succeed in the course prior to the submission deadline date. Thus, the student is knowledgeable about the effort he or she should apply in the activity to have a chance to pass the course. This prediction is updated after each graded activity and a new prediction is generated for the next one. This type of prediction differs from other approaches where the models can only be used after a certain number of activities, denoted as the best point of intervention when enough data have been gathered to have an accurate model. Second, the teacher can complement these predictions with constructive feedback from the very beginning of the course, including recommendations to revert (or even prevent) at-risk situations.

## 3. Methods and Context

*3.1. University Description: Educational and Assessment Model*

The UOC from its origins (1995) was conceived as a purely online university that used the Information and Communication Technologies (ICT) intensively for both the teaching-learning process and management. This implies that most of the interactions between students, teachers, and administrative staff occur within the UOC's own LMS, generating a massive amount of data. Its educational model is centered on the students and the competences they should acquire across their courses. The assessment model is based on continuous assessment and personal feedback is given to students after obtaining a mark when delivering assessment activities. Thus, any student enrolled is having a personalized learning process by means of quantitative, but also qualitative feedback. Although the student profile is aged up to the regular ones with family and full job employed, they devote time to learn in order to get a better position in their job or to enhance their knowledge with another bachelor's degree. Students at UOC are really competence oriented, but usually, they lack daily time for all personal and professional tasks. This student background and their profiles became a cornerstone to developing the EWS to guide them in a personal way when being assessed and when receiving personal feedback.

The assessment process within a course is based on a continuous assessment model combined with summative assessment at the end of the semester. Therefore, there are different assessment activities during the semester and a face-to-face final examination at the end of the course. The final mark is computed based on a predefined formula for each course where each assessment activity has a different weight depending on the significance of the assessment activity contents within the course. The UOC grading system is based on qualitative scores on assessment activities. Each assessment activity is graded with the following scale: A (very high), B (high), C+ (sufficient), C- (low), D (very low), where a grade of C- and D means failing the assessment activity. In addition, another grade (N, non-submitted) is used when a student does not submit the assessment activity. Also, UOC courses are identified by codes, and students are randomly distributed in classrooms. Finally, the semesters are coded by academic year and the number of the semester (i.e., 1 for fall and 2 for spring semester). For instance, 20172 identifies the 2018 spring semester of the academic period 2017/2018.

*3.2. Data Source: The UOC Data Mart*

The UOC provides their researchers and practitioners with data to promote a culture of data evidence-based decision-making. This approach is materialized in a centralized learning analytics database: the UOC data mart [48]. The UOC data mart collects and aggregates data that are transferred from the different operational data sources using ETL (Extract-Transform-Load) processes, solving problems as data fragmentation, duplication, and the use of different identifiers and non-standardized vocabularies for describing the same real-world entities. During the ETL processes, sensitive data are anonymized (personal data are obfuscated, and all internal identifiers are changed to a new one [49]).

UOC uses from its origins a custom LMS [50] that has been improved and upgraded several times during the last 25 years (the current version is version 5.0) according to the new requirements of learners, teachers, and available technology. Although the campus has a high interoperability to add external tools (e.g., Wordpress, Moodle, MediaWiki, among others), mainly the learning process is done in the custom classrooms. Operational data sources include data from the custom LMS and other learning spaces (e.g., data about navigation, interaction, and communication), as well as data from institutional warehouse systems (CRM, ERP, etc.), which include data about enrollment, accreditation, assessment, and student curriculum, among others. As a result, the UOC data mart offers: (1) historical data from previous semesters; (2) data generated during the current semester aggregated by day. Currently, the UOC data mart stores curated data since the academic year 2016–2017.

*3.3. Gradual At-Risk Model*

A GAR model is built for each course, and it is composed of a set of predictive models defined as submodels based only on a student's grades during the assessment process. A course has a submodel for each assessment activity, and each submodel uses the grades of the current and previous graded assessment activities as features to produce the prediction. Note that, there is no submodel for the final exam since there is nothing to produce a prediction from when the final score of the course can be computed straightforwardly from the complete set of grades (i.e., the assessment activities and the final exam) by using the final mark formula.

The prediction outcome for the submodels is to fail the course. This is a binary variable with two possible values: pass or fail. We are interested in predicting whether a student has chances to fail the course, and we denote this casuistic as *at-risk student*. Although a global at-risk prediction taking into account all enrolled courses is an interesting outcome, we focus individually on each course to give simple messages and recommendations to the student on courses in which she or he is at-risk.

**Example 1.** *Let us describe the GAR model for a course with four Assessment Activities (AA). In such a case, the GAR model contains four submodels:*

$Pr_{AA1}(Fail?) = (Grade_{AA1})$
$Pr_{AA2}(Fail?) = (Grade_{AA1}, Grade_{AA2})$
$Pr_{AA3}(Fail?) = (Grade_{AA1}, Grade_{AA2}, Grade_{AA3})$
$Pr_{AA4}(Fail?) = (Grade_{AA1}, Grade_{AA2}, Grade_{AA3}, Grade_{AA4})$

where $Pr_{AAn}(Fail?)$ denotes the name of the submodel to predict whether the student will fail the course after the assessment activity AAn. Each submodel $Pr_{AAn}(Fail?)$ uses the grades ($Grade_{AA1}, Grade_{AA2}, \ldots, Grade_{AAn}$), that is, the grades from the first activity until the activity AAn. Each submodel can be evaluated based on different accuracy metrics. We use four metrics [23]:

$$TNR = \frac{TN}{TN+FP} \quad ACC = \frac{TP+TN}{TP+FP+TN+FN} \quad\quad (1)$$
$$TPR = \frac{TP}{TP+FN} \quad F_{1,5} = \frac{(1+1,5^2)TP}{(1+1,5^2)TP+1,5^2FN+FP}$$

where TP denotes the number of at-risk students correctly identified, TN the number of non-at-risk students correctly identified, FP the number of at-risk students not correctly identified, and FN the number of non-at-risk students not correctly identified. These four metrics are used for evaluating the global accuracy of the model (ACC), the accuracy when detecting at-risk students (true positive rate—TPR), the accuracy when distinguishing non-at-risk students (true negative rate—TNR) and a harmonic mean of the true positive value (precision) and the TPR (recall) that weights correct at-risk identification (F score - $F_{1,5}$). Note that, the area under the ROC curve (AUC) is not considered on this study [51].

### 3.4. Next Activity At-Risk Simulation

The GAR model only provides information about whether the student has the chance to fail the course based on the last graded assessment activities. This model can be used to give information to the student about the likelihood to fail, but it is not very useful when the teacher wants to provide early and personalized feedback concerning the next assessment activities. We define the Next Activity At-risk (NAAR) simulation as the simulation to determine the minimum grade that the student has to obtain in the next assessment activity to have a chance to pass the course.

This prediction is performed by using the submodel of the assessment activity we want to predict. The NAAR simulation uses the grades of the previous activities already graded and simulates all possible grades for the activity we want to predict for identifying when the prediction changes from failing to pass.

**Example 2.** *Let us take the submodel $Pr_{AA1}(Fail?)$ of Example 1. In order to know the minimum grade, six simulations are performed based on the possible grades the student can obtain in AA1. Each simulation will produce an output based on the chances to fail the course. An output example is shown next based on the first assessment activity of the Computer Fundamentals course that will be analyzed in Section 6.*

$Pr_{AA1}(Fail?) = (N) \quad \rightarrow \quad Fail? = Yes$
$Pr_{AA1}(Fail?) = (D) \quad \rightarrow \quad Fail? = Yes$
$Pr_{AA1}(Fail?) = (C-) \quad \rightarrow \quad Fail? = Yes$
$Pr_{AA1}(Fail?) = (C+) \quad \rightarrow \quad Fail? = Yes$
$Pr_{AA1}(Fail?) = (B) \quad \rightarrow \quad Fail? = No$
$Pr_{AA1}(Fail?) = (A) \quad \rightarrow \quad Fail? = No$

*where we can observe that students have a high probability of passing the course when they get a B or an A grade on the first assessment activity. This means that most of the students pass when they obtain these grades.*

However, it is possible to pass the course with a lower mark, but less frequently. Note that, this is for the first assessment activity where there are no previous activities. On further activities, the grades of previous activities are taken into account and the prediction is better personalized for each student based on his or her previous grades.

*3.5. Datasets*

Table 2 describes the datasets used for each semester. As we can observe, the number of registries for training increases each semester that are counted from the 2016 fall semester (20161). This number depends on the number of enrolled students. The number of offered courses also differs on each semester and depends on the opened and extinguished academic programs in the semester taken as testing semester, and a minimum number of ten enrollments per course to open the course stated by the university.

**Table 2.** Description of the dataset.

|  | 20171 | 20172 | 20181 | 20182 |
|---|---|---|---|---|
| Number of courses | 889 | 830 | 968 | 979 |
| Min–Max activities / course | 3–14 | 3–11 | 3–11 | 3–11 |
| Semesters for training (from–to) | 20161–20162 | 20161–20171 | 20161–20172 | 20161–20181 |
| Registries training set | 260153 | 362368 | 474957 | 585936 |
| Semester for testing | 20171 | 20172 | 20181 | 20182 |
| Registries test set | 102215 | 112589 | 110979 | 138746 |

*3.6. Generation and Evaluation of the Predictive Model*

The GAR model is built by using Python and the machine learning Scikit-Learn library [52], while the statistical analysis has been performed by the analytical tool R [53]. The GAR model for a given course is trained based on the historical data of previous semesters from the 2016 fall semester (i.e., 20161), and the test is performed on the data of the last historical available semester from the UOC data mart (that is hosted in Amazon S3). For example, for semester 20171, the models are trained with data from semesters 20161 and 20162 to test it on the semester 20171. During the validation test, four algorithms are tested: NB, DT, KNN, SVM.

In order to evaluate the classification algorithms, the GAR model is built for each course of the institution based on the number of assessment activities (see Example 1 in Section 3.3). Each course has a different number of assessment activities and some courses have a final exam. In such cases, the submodel for the final exam is not generated since the final grade can be straightforwardly computed from all grades of the assessment activities and the final exam, and no prediction is needed. Then, the training and test are performed for each course and submodel. In order to analyze the results globally for the whole institution, the value of each metric described in Section 3.3 is ordered and uniformly distributed among the semester timeline based on the submission date of the respective assessment activity associated with the submodel. For instance, for a course with four assessment activities, the prediction of the first assessment activity is set to the position at 20%, the second at 40%, the third at 60%, and the fourth at 80% of the semester timeline. Note that, this distribution changes on courses with a different number of activities. This distribution helps to identify at each stage of the timeline the average quality of the GAR model based on the submitted assessment activities at that time for the whole institution. Finally, in order to evaluate the different classification algorithms, the LOESS regression [54] is used. Although a linear regression would show a pretty linear perception of the increment of the accuracy, this would not represent the correct relationship between metrics and timeline. The LOESS regression shows a better approximation due to the large number of values.

The NB was selected in [3] as the best classification algorithm to be used in the institution based on the performance observed on the four metrics. Precisely, the selection was mainly done by the results of the TPR and $F_{1.5}$ since these metrics tend to indicate the algorithm that mostly detects at-risk students.

Currently, we have more data in the data mart, and further analysis can be done on how it is evolving the GAR model among the semesters. Specifically, three more semesters can be analyzed (i.e., until 2019 spring semester). We can answer the research questions RQ1 and RQ2 by (1) analyzing how the NB performance evolves during these three semesters; (2) proposing a method to obtain the best classification algorithm and training set for each assessment activity and course; and, finally, (3) determining a method to deduce a threshold to consider the GAR model of a course as a high- or low-quality model.

During the semester, trained models are used by means of an operation that is run on the daily information available at the UOC data mart. A cron-like Python script downloads the data from the UOC data mart and checks whether students have been graded for any assessment activity proposed in the course. When this happens, the corresponding NAAR simulation is executed by getting the respective trained GAR model. All these functionalities (e.g., train, test, statistical analysis, and daily predictions) among others are embedded into the EWS. The full description of the technical architecture and capabilities of the EWS can be found in [55].

*3.7. Case Studies in Real Educational Settings*

The GAR model and the EWS that hosts it have been tested through pilots in two real learning scenarios, as will be presented in Section 6, because LIS project follows a mixed research methodology that combines an action research methodology with a design and creation approach. This mixed research methodology as well as the outputs it produces are depicted in Figure 1.

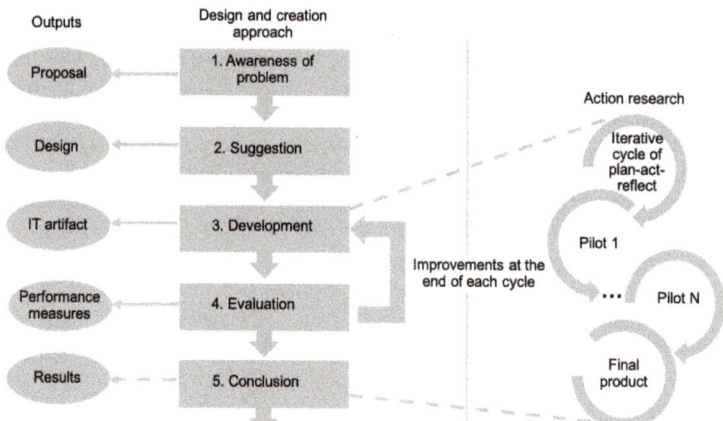

**Figure 1.** Research methodology.

Action research methodology allows to investigate and improve own practices, guided by the next principles [56]: concentration on practical issues, an iterative cycle plan-act-reflect, an emphasis on change, collaboration with practitioners, multiple data generation methods, and finally, action outcomes plus research outcomes and research.

The design and creation approach is especially suited when developing new Information Technology (IT) artifacts. It is a problem-solving approach that uses an iterative process involving five steps [57]: Awareness (the recognition of a problem where actors identify areas for further work looking at findings in other disciplines); Suggestion (a creative leap from curiosity about the problem offering very tentative ideas of how the problem might be addressed); Development (where the idea is implemented, depending on the kind of the proposed IT artifact); Evaluation (examines the developed IT artifact and looks for an evaluation of its worth and deviations from expectations); and Conclusion (where the results of the design process are consolidated and the gained knowledge is identified).

First, the problem to solve (learners' at-risk identification) is detected and shared by teachers and educational institutions. Secondly, a solution (the EWS) is suggested. Thirdly, the EWS is implemented and proved in different real learning scenarios following the iterative cycle of plan-act-reflect. This cycle is done through pilots conducted across courses during several academic semesters by cycles. At the end of each cycle, an evaluation process is done. This will probably cause changes and improvements in the EWS, and the initiation of a new cycle until a final artifact is available and ready to be used in educational institutions.

## 4. Algorithms and Training Dataset Selection for the GAR Model

### 4.1. Naive Bayes Evaluation

In order to evaluate the NB algorithm, we used the datasets described in Section 3.5 and the evaluation process described in Section 3.6 for the four semesters from the 2017 fall semester (20171) to the 2019 spring semester (20182). The results processed with R-based scripts are shown in Figure 2 and Table A1 in Appendix A for the four metrics ACC, TNR, TPR, and F-score 1,5 with a LOESS regression.

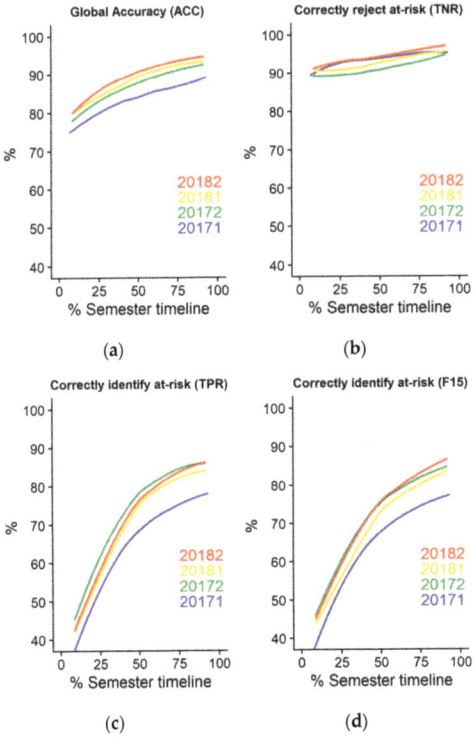

**Figure 2.** LOESS regression plots of the GAR model using Naive Bayes Classifier for (**a**) Accuracy, (**b**) TNR, (**c**) TPR, and (**d**) F-score 1,5 metrics from 20171 to 20182 semesters.

In general, we can observe that adding more training data helps to improve all the metrics with respect to the baseline 20171. However, the last two semesters (i.e., 20181 and 20182) do not impact on getting better TPR results, i.e., correctly detect at-risk students. This is due to mostly the students at UOC tending to pass the courses. The average performance rate in the institution was 78.90% in the 2018/2019 academic year [58]. Thus, more data help to identify new situations when students are not at-risk, and new data have a low impact on detecting new at-risk students.

## 4.2. Algorithm and Training Set Selection

As mentioned previously, we observed that the metrics do not always improve over semesters for specific courses, even though more training data are available. Different factors may impact on these results: 1) The behavior of students in some semesters may add noise to the model that produces worse results; or 2) some academic change such as new resources or changes in the difficulty or the design of the assessment activities may impact the grades of a specific semester. In order to deal with these issues, we propose a method to select the best training set and classification algorithm for each course and activity. This selection can be reduced to an optimization problem with the objective function $L$ to be maximized

$$L(S_{TR}, M) = TPR\left(D_{S_{TR},C,A}, D_{S_{TE},C,A}, M\right) + TNR\left(D_{S_{TR},C,A}, D_{S_{TE},C,A}, M\right) \quad (2)$$

where $S_{TR}$ is the semester to explore as training set, $S_{TE}$ is the semester to perform the validation test, $M$ is the classification algorithm used to perform the training, and $D_{S,C,A}$ is a slice from the whole dataset $D$ based on the semester $S$, course $C$ and activity $A$. After different tests, we found that the best choice is to maximize the sum of the TPR and TNR. This function tends to select classifiers and training sets that achieve good results in both metrics, while maximizing one of the metrics tends to penalize the discarded one.

The method has been split into two algorithms. The first algorithm selects the best classification algorithm, while the second one selects the best training set for each assessment activity of each course. The selection of the best algorithm (see Algorithm 1) searches for the best algorithm based on four available classification algorithms: NB, DT, KNN, and SVM. The process is quite simple but computationally expensive since four training processes are run for each course and assessment activity. However, there is a substantial benefit since each activity (i.e., each submodel for the GAR model associated with the course) has the best-selected algorithm.

---

**Algorithm 1.** Pseudocode of Best_Classification_Algorithm.

---

**Input:**    $S_{TR}$: Semester training dataset, $S_{TE}$: Semester test dataset
**Output:**   $B_{CL}$: Best Classification Algorithm per course and activity
**Steps:**
    Initialize($B_{CL}$)
    **For each** course $C \in S_{TE}$ **do**
        **For each** activity $A \in C$ **do**
            $M_{CL} \leftarrow$ Select best classifier $M \in$ {NB, KNN, DT, SVM} based on opt. function $L(S_{TR}, M)$ (Equation (2))
            $B_{CL}(C, A, S_{TR}) \leftarrow \{S_{TR}, M_{CL}\}$

    **Return** $B_{CL}$

---

The second process is presented in Algorithm 2. In this case, the process goes further, and it explores for the submodel of the activity the surrounding submodels in terms of previous activities within the same course, and the same submodel within the same course in the previous semesters. We observed that sometimes an activity is not mandatory, or it has a low impact on the final grade of the course, or a semester adds noise to the model, and such a semester produces a lower accurate submodel. For example, it is commonly observed in our institution that the behavior of the students is different depending on the spring or fall semester. Thus, in such cases, we suggest selecting the best-known training set within the same course in previous activities or in the same activity among previous semesters. Note that the computational cost is even higher than the former since the evaluation test should be redone with the training set of the selected semester and the test set of last available semester. We are aware that this process will be unfeasible when the number of semesters increases. Thus, a window of training semesters should be defined in the future.

**Algorithm 2.** Pseudocode of Best_Classification_and_Training_Set.

**Input:**   $S_{TE}$: Semester test dataset
**Output:**   $B_{CL}$: Best classification algorithm and training set per course and activity
**Steps:**
    //Train and test all semesters with respect to $S_{TE}$
    $B_{CL} \leftarrow \emptyset$
    **For each** semester $S \in \{20171, \ldots, S_{TE}\}$ **do**
        $B_{CL} \leftarrow B_{CL} \cup$ Best_Classification_ Algorithm $(S, S_{TE})$

    //Compare on same semester
    **For each** semester $S \in \{20171, \ldots, S_{TE}\}$ **do**
        **For each** course $C \in S$ **do**
            **For each** pair $(A_i, A_j) \in C$ st. $i < j$ **do**
                $\{S, M_{Ai}\} \leftarrow B_{CL}(C, A_i, S)$
                $\{S, M_{Aj}\} \leftarrow B_{CL}(C, A_j, S)$
                If $L(S, M_{Ai}) > L(S, M_{Aj})$ then $B_{CL}(C, A_j, S) \leftarrow \{S, M_{Ai}\}$

    //Compare inter semester
    **For each** course $C \in S_{TE}$ **do**
        **For each** activity $A \in C$ **do**
            **For each** pair $(S, S_{TE})$ st. $S \in \{20171, \ldots, S_{TE-1}\}$
                $\{S, M_S\} \quad \leftarrow B_{CL}(C, A, S)$
                $\{S_{TE}, M_{STE}\} \leftarrow B_{CL}(C, A, S_{TE})$
                If $L(S, M_S) > L(S_{TE}, M_{STE})$ then $B_{CL}(C, A, S_{TE}) \leftarrow \{S, M_S\}$

    **Return** $B_{CL}$

In order to analyze the performance of these two algorithms, the evaluation test has been performed only in the last semester 20182 for the different metrics and taking as a baseline the NB classifier results. The results are shown in Figure 3 and Table A2 in Appendix A. The best algorithm selection slightly improves the different metrics since the best selection is only performed within the explored algorithms on an activity. In the case of the TPR, the LOESS regression compared to the NB improves from the range 44.60–86.04% to 47.88–88.43%. However, considerable improvement is obtained with the second algorithm, where the LOESS regression increases until 58.79–93.60%. This result will help to define a more significant threshold to consider a high-quality submodel, as we will see in the next section.

Although the last finding proves that the second process helps to identify the best classifier and training set for each assessment activity, it is not clear which classifier has been mostly selected and from which origin semester. Table 3 summarizes this information with interesting insights. The table shows the percentage of classifiers and from which semester they have been selected. The process mostly selected the DT with more than half of the trained submodels.

Table 3. Distribution of the classification algorithm selection for 2019 spring semester.

|  | 20171 | 20172 | 20181 | 20182 | Total |
|---|---|---|---|---|---|
| Decision Tree | 10.42% | 9.27% | 12.10% | 19.19% | 50.98% |
| K-Nearest Neighbors | 2.47% | 3.43% | 4.80% | 5.19% | 15.89% |
| Naive Bayes | 4.66% | 5.72% | 5.81% | 9.73% | 25.92% |
| Support Vector | 1.43% | 1.54% | 1.66% | 2.58% | 7.21% |
| Total | 18.97% | 19.97% | 24.37% | 36.69% | 100.00% |

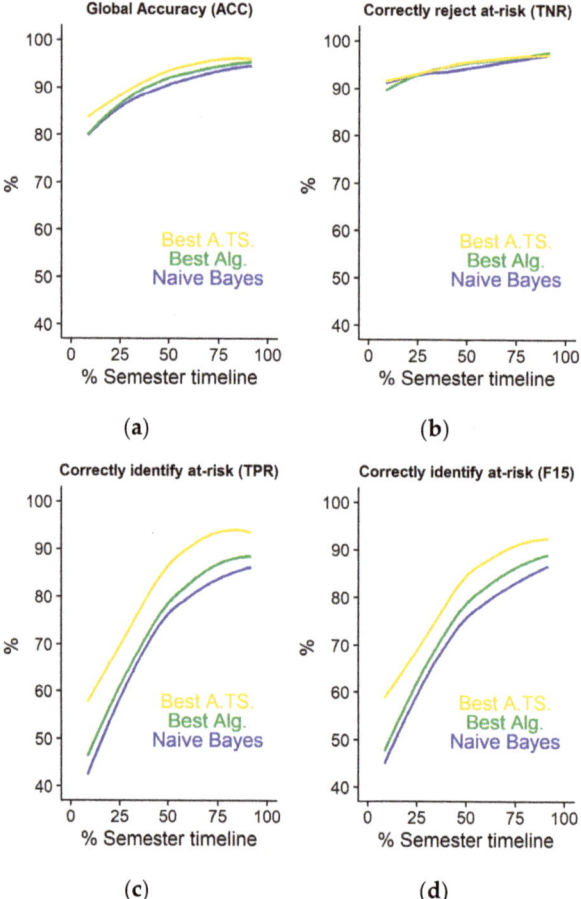

**Figure 3.** LOESS regression plots of the GAR model using Naive Bayes Classifier, selecting best algorithm (Best Alg.) and selecting best algorithm and training set (Best A. TS.) for (**a**) Accuracy, (**b**) TNR, (**c**) TPR, and (**d**) F-score $F_{1.5}$ metrics for 20182 semester.

The NB proposed in [3] is only selected the 25.92% of the total. Thus, we conclude that the NB is not the most appropriate classifier to train the models when more data are available. Finally, we can observe that the distribution among semesters is quite reasonable. The training dataset of the last available semester is the most selected one (36.69%), but for some submodels, the dataset from previous semesters with less training data helps to get more accurate models. Finally, we give an insight about the computational cost of this operation in absolute numbers for semester 20182. The number of training operations for each semester are 26,468 in 20182, 24,996 in 20181, 23,144 in 20172 and 24,184 in 20171. Note that, this number for a semester takes into account the training operation for the four classifiers for all courses and activities.

### 4.3. Quality Threshold Identification

Some predictive models aimed at early identify at-risk students defined the best point of intervention during the semester. This point is deduced from the experimental results [23] or is fixed before the evaluation [59]. Our EWS performs interventions from the first assessment activity. Thus, the concept of intervention point has nonsense. In our system, the submodels (i.e., the training model applied on each assessment activity) are classified based on high- or low-quality models based on the TPR and TNR since the intervention measures are adapted based on the quality of the model. For instance, an intervention action based on a likelihood to fail the course cannot be applied as-it-is when the submodel has a low-quality TPR.

Similarly, a praise message based on a likelihood to pass cannot be applied when the submodel has a low-quality TNR. In those cases, the interventions are adapted when the likelihood to fail or pass cannot be assured (see Section 5 for further details). This classification is performed based on a quality threshold that can be defined globally for the institution or individually for each course based on the teacher's experience.

In this section, we seek the quality threshold globally applicable to demonstrate that the GAR model can be valid with a unique threshold for the whole institution and avoid particular cases. Also, we want to analyze whether the method presented in Algorithm 2 to obtain the best algorithm classifier and training set can improve this threshold with respect to [3] where the threshold selection was performed by observation without any data analysis.

The quality threshold identification can be reduced to an optimization problem since the objective is to maximize the threshold while the number of submodels considered high-quality do not worsen significantly. However, this problem is unfeasible to be solved because there is no optimal solution. Thus, we define a function to be maximized in order to approximate the problem

$$f(x) = x + \frac{\sum_{i \in T} \omega_i \sum_{j \in S_i} j \mid TPR(j) > x}{\sum_{i \in T} \omega_i} \quad (3)$$

where $x$ is the threshold value, $T \in \{0\%, 5\%, 10\%, \ldots, 95\%, 100\%\}$ positions of the semester timeline, $w_i$ is a weight that can be assigned to the position $i$ of the semester timeline, and $S_i$ is the set of all the submodels that the submission deadline is in the position $i$. In summary, the function seeks to sum the threshold value with the weighted average of the number of submodels that their TPR is above the threshold for each position of the semester timeline. We defined a weighted average due to it might being interesting to give more relevancy to some positions of the semester. Note that, we assume in our optimization problem all positions with the same weight (i.e., $w_i = 1$). Moreover, the TPR is used since we are interested to particularly maximize the threshold over submodels for detecting at-risk students.

After solving the optimization problem for the 2019 spring semester with an R-based script, the result is illustrated in Figure 4a where $f(x)$ summands are plotted in the axis. As we can observe, both summands generate a curve of Pareto Points with the optimum on the threshold 75% (i.e., the function $f(x)$ maximized on the threshold 75%). Thus, we define high-quality submodels as all submodels with a TPR higher than 75%.

In order to further compare with [3], we computed the percentage of explored courses where the TPR and TNR are higher than thresholds 70% and 75% (see Figure 4b). Note that, we removed the multiple plots for the TNR because there was only an average increment of 1–3% over each threshold. For the 2019 spring semester, even increasing the threshold to 75%, we obtain better coverage of high-quality submodels compared to the 2017 fall semester, where the threshold was set to 70%. The coverage is quite similar for the TNR at 25% from 70.07% of the courses to 69.80% but there is a considerable increment at 50% from 89.31% to 97.12%. Although only 26.71% of the courses will have a TPR higher than 75% at 25% of the semester timeline (it was 24.01% on 2017 fall semester), this value increases considerably to 74.58% at the 50% of the semester timeline (it was 65.95% in 2017 fall semester).

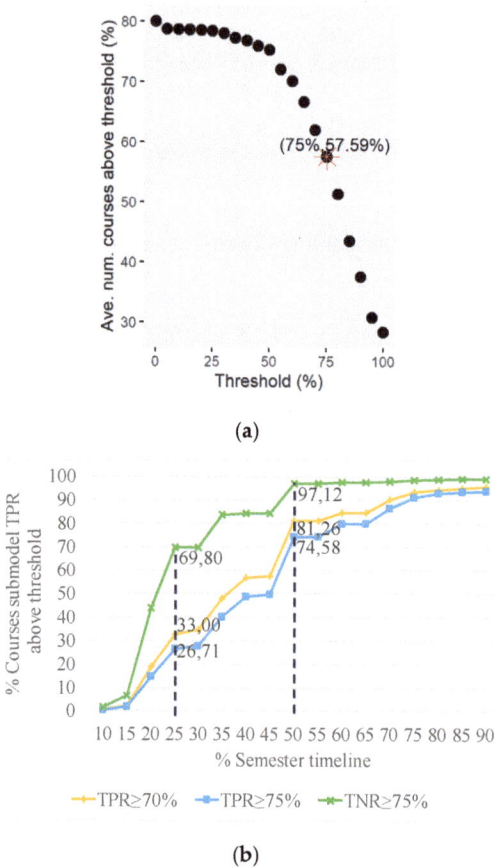

**Figure 4.** (a) Pareto Points distribution of f(x) summands and optimal value. (b) Percentage of courses where the GAR model can be applied with high-quality based on different thresholds for TNR and TPR.

## 5. The Early Warning System: Dashboards and Feedback Intervention Mechanism

The EWS provides data visualization features to teachers and students by means of dashboards. Those features are complemented with a feedback intervention mechanism. The full description of the technical architecture and capabilities of the EWS can be found in [55].

Students and teachers have different dashboards and permissions. Students have a simple dashboard to see the prediction to succeed in the enrolled courses. The prediction is based on the NAAR simulation, and a Green-Amber-Red semaphore (similar to [17]) that warns the students about their warning classification level. A semaphore in green represents that the student is non-at-risk, while a semaphore with a red signal indicates a high likelihood to fail. For an assessment activity, the student gets first the prediction of the minimum grade that she or he should obtain to have a high likelihood to pass the course. This prediction is received while the student is working in the assessment activity (see Figure 5a). When the assessment activity is submitted and assessed, the grade (see the triangles above and below the C- grade in the bar corresponding to the first assessment activity in Figure 5b) and the warning level are updated in the student dashboard, and the prediction for the next assessment activity (the second assessment activity in the case of Figure 5b) is computed and plotted in the dashboard as a new bar.

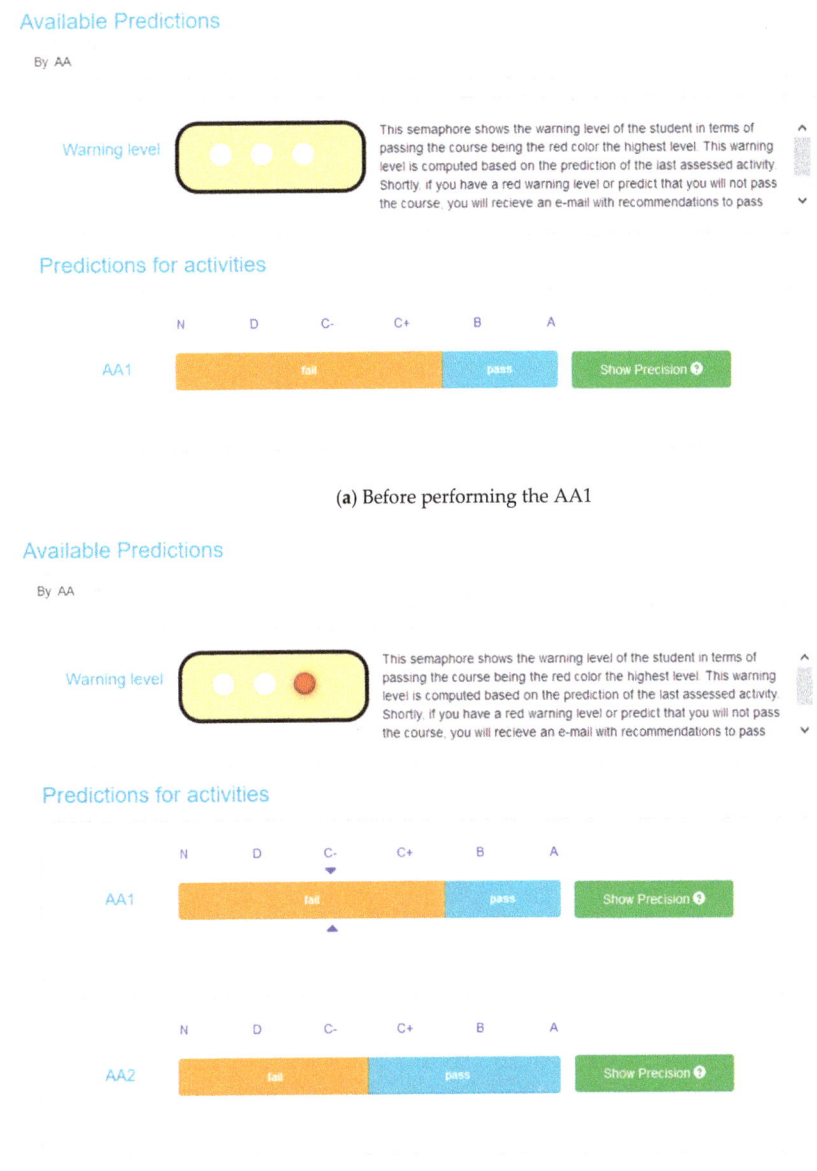

(a) Before performing the AA1

(b) After being graded AA1

**Figure 5.** Early warning dashboard for students.

Teachers have a different dashboard to see the performance of the students and help them in case of trouble. Figure 6 shows a tabular dashboard where all the students of a course are shown. As we can observe, only students who have consented to participate in the study (by signing a consent form) can be reviewed. For those who accepted, the teacher can easily check the progress of the predictions and warning levels. The readability is quite clear based on the same Green-Amber-Red semaphore used for the students. Teachers have a new color classification (the black color) to detect potential students' dropout (i.e., students that do not submit their assessment activities).

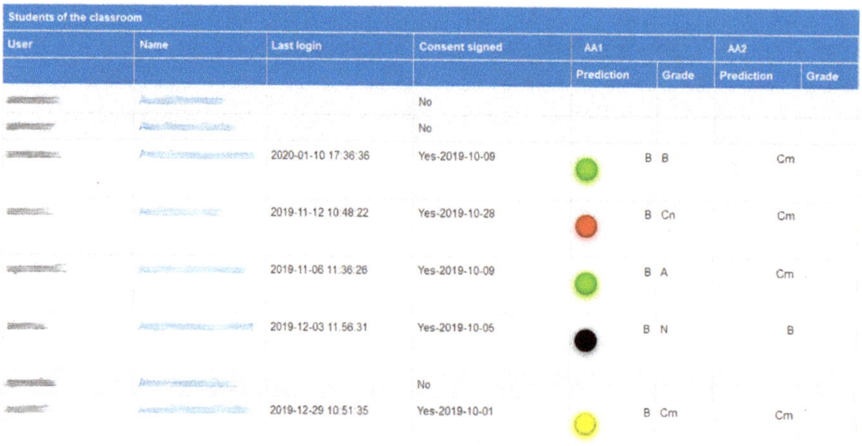

| Students of the classroom | | | | | | | |
|---|---|---|---|---|---|---|---|
| User | Name | Last login | Consent signed | AA1 | | AA2 | |
| | | | | Prediction | Grade | Prediction | Grade |
| | | | No | | | | |
| | | | No | | | | |
| | | 2020-01-10 17:36:36 | Yes-2019-10-09 | 🟢 | B B | | Cm |
| | | 2019-11-12 10:48:22 | Yes-2019-10-28 | 🔴 | B Cn | | Cm |
| | | 2019-11-06 11:36:26 | Yes-2019-10-09 | 🟢 | B A | | Cm |
| | | 2019-12-03 11:56:31 | Yes-2019-10-05 | ⚫ | B N | | B |
| | | | No | | | | |
| | | 2019-12-29 10:51:35 | Yes-2019-10-01 | 🟡 | B Cm | | Cm |

**Figure 6.** Tabular dashboard for teachers to check the predictions for the students.

The EWS is able to provide feedback messages as an early intervention mechanism. Feedback messages contain recommendations, and also nudge students, especially those being at-risk [60]. The intervention mechanism is implemented by means of a feedback messaging system that aims to enhance teachers' actions over students depending on their status, thus providing a better understanding about their own learning process. From the teacher's point of view, the system forces them to provide early and personalized feedback to students when delivering each assessment activity. From the students' point of view, the EWS is providing them the teacher feedback, but also a probabilistic percentage of their success. It is also providing students with richer and valuable information: what they have to do in order to improve their learning process and obtain a better grade and pass the course. They are also simultaneously nudged to better perform the next activity (the importance of the activity on the upcoming activities is provided, as well as the provision of additional learning resources) and the importance for better planning. In summary and according to [47], the information provided in the feedback messages contains nudges that fall in the categories of goal setting, informational nudges, assistance, and reminders.

Figure 7 summarizes in a decision tree the rationale behind the EWS concerning the students' warning level when an assessment activity is graded, which in turn, impacts the feedback message to be sent. When graded, a feedback message is triggered to each student for notifying his or her warning level (predictive statement), as well as the feedback for the next assessment activities. The system distinguishes different situations depending on the warning level, and the feedback message is adapted depending on the specific situation. Green (G) means that the student is not at-risk when the TNR is greater than the minimum threshold of 75% established in Section 4.3 (i.e., the model is considered a high-quality model). In such a case the student receives a comforting message in order to congratulate him or her. Yellow (or amber) means that the student is not considered at-risk, but he or she can be in the near future. The feedback message alerts the student about his or her chances to pass and gives some recommendations to progress successfully in the course. In addition, the feedback message also contains explanations about the accuracy of the prediction because, in some cases, the prediction (may pass or may fail) is under the quality threshold. Therefore, information about the TNR and TPR constitutes one of the differences among the three different types of yellow messages (Y1, Y2, and Y3) that are sent in this case. The distinction of different situations in yellow messages constitutes an enhancement regarding the work presented in [3], where no such distinction existed. This is especially relevant in the case of students that, in spite of passing the assessment activity, the grade obtained is under the grade suggested by the predictive model (message Y2). Red and black represent that the student is at serious risk of failing or dropping out (at-risk student). When the student has submitted and failed the assessment activity, (R) is the most critical situation, although the effort of submitting the activity is positively valued by the teachers. In this case, the feedback message contains recommendations to get out of this situation. Also, the message suggests the student contact his or her teacher in order to talk about the difficulties the student is experiencing in the course. Potentially, this can derive in a more individual support. The case when the student has not submitted the last or the last two assessment activities (B1 and B2) is dealt separately from the previous case, representing a potential dropout student. The feedback message asks for the reasons for not submitting the activities and reminds the student of his or her options to pass the course (information about mandatory assessment activities and the final exam). Unfortunately, and depending on the timeline of the semester, the student can receive a feedback message confirming him or her that has hopelessly failed the course. In such a case, the student receives advice to avoid this situation the next time he or she enrolls in the course, and the proposal of tasks the student can perform before a new semester starts.

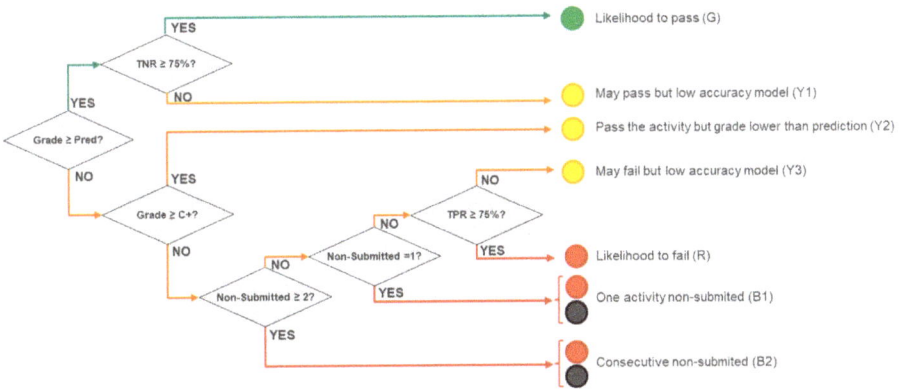

**Figure 7.** Decision tree for warning level classification.

From an educational point of view, the EWS is a powerful tool to reduce dropout and increase students' engagement. It is providing a constructive answer for not disappointing students. In the case of students that are not properly following the course, the system is pointing out how they can improve by showing them new opportunities and even the mandatory assessment activities remaining to successfully pass the course. Finally, students that have not submitted their assessment activities can provide very useful information to the teacher, not only to build better feedback messages for the next edition of the course but also to introduce enhancements in the next course editions (new learning resources, better course design, etc.).

## 6. Case Studies: Computer Fundamentals and Databases

The EWS has been tested in two case studies to answer the research question RQ3. The EWS aims to detect but also support at-risk students, which basically means, to help them to continue their learning process by providing accurate and valuable feedback for not failing or dropping out.

Specifically, the EWS has been introduced in Computer Fundamentals and Databases courses. Both courses are online courses offered in the Computer Science bachelor's degree and in Telecommunication bachelor's degree at UOC. While Computer Fundamentals is a first-semester course, Databases is offered in the fourth one. Thus, students' knowledge and expertise are quite different when performing each one. Both courses are 6 ECTS and their assessment model is based on continuous assessment (several assessment activities are proposed along the semester, some of them are practical activities that imply the development of artifacts) and a final face-to-face exam at the end of the semester.

In Computer Fundamentals (a first-year course), students are devoted to learning the main principles for designing digital circuits and the basis of the computer architecture. In Databases, students are devoted to learning what databases are (and the specialized software that manages them), and how to create and manipulate relational databases using the SQL language (both interactive and embedded SQL). For the Databases course, previous knowledge is required (in programming and logic), so this is the reason to be in the fourth semester. The Computer Fundamentals course has a high number of students enrolled each semester (between 500–600 students) and becomes the first contact with the custom LMS. The Databases course has over 300 students each semester, but students already know very well the UOC educational model as well as how the LMS works. So, they are not as new in Databases as they are in Computer Fundamentals. Thus, both courses are excellent ones to evaluate the EWS and analyze whether at-risk students can be correctly identified and help them through the early feedback system. The system has been tested in both courses during one semester. Previously, a proof of concept was also tested as it can be seen in [3], but now a new version of the EWS is tested with new features and enhancements suggested by teachers and students when collecting their perception, as explained in [60]. As mentioned in Section 3.7, this process has been done following the design and creation research method that uses an iterative model to better develop IT artifacts to solve real problems. This new version of the EWS is the second iteration.

The EWS was tested during the first semester of the academic course 2019/2020 (i.e., 20191 semester). A total of 313 students from Computer Fundamentals (CF) gave their consent to test the system, and a total of 71 students from Databases (DB) gave it too. To sum up, 384 students were testing it. In both courses, and after teachers graded each assessment activity, the EWS was triggering predictions to students, as well as personalized feedback messages, which depended on the warning level classification of the students presented in Section 5. According to the numbers of students taking part in the pilot, and the number of assessment activities performed, the system triggered 1607 predictions (CF: 1252; DB: 355). Feedback messages attached to each prediction and assessment activity were previously designed and analyzed by teachers, with the aim of motivating students for further assessment activities. Feedback messages tended to be as personalized as the system allowed, and they included some nudges to support the students learning process according to their grades.

The quantitative analysis provided below compares both courses involved in the case studies, according to the following criteria: assessment model and performance of GAR model, the performance of the system for correctly classifying students according to their warning level and the statistical significance on the final mark distribution as a consequence of the use of the EWS.

*6.1. Performance of GAR Model*

CF course has four assessment activities starting during the semester timeline at 0% (AA1), 25% (AA2), 50% (AA3) and 75% (AA4) approximately. The formula to compute the final mark (FM) is:

$$FM = MAX(10\% \ Grade_{AA1} + 10\% \ Grade_{AA2} + 10\% \ Grade_{AA3} + 35\% \ Grade_{AA4} + 35\% \ Grade_{EXAM}, \\ 50\% \ Grade_{AA4} + 50\% \ Grade_{EXAM}) \quad (4)$$

where $Grade_{AAn}$ is the grade of the assessment activity AAn and $Grade_{EXAM}$ is the grade of the final exam. The AA4 (which is a practical assessment activity) and the EXAM are mandatory, and they have a significant impact on the final score. Note that, the course can be even passed without performing the three first activities. However, the teachers know by experience that it is difficult to pass the course without the first three activities where fundamental topics are learnt. Thus, most of the students pass the course by completing the four activities.

In the case of DB course, five assessment activities are delivered during the semester timeline at 0% (AA1), 20% (AA2), 40% (AA3), 60% (AA4), and 80% (AA5), approximately. AA2, AA3, and AA5 are practical activities that deal with SQL concepts (basic SQL statements, triggers, and stored procedures, and JDBC, respectively). The final mark (FM) in the DB course is computed as follows. First, a global mark for the practical assessment activities (Grade$_P$) is computed. In case the student delivers AA2, AA3, and AA5, the two best grades are selected, and Grade$_P$ is computed as the average of both grades. Otherwise, the average of the two submitted practical activities is the global mark for the practical assessment activities. Secondly, the final mark for the course (FM) is:

$$FM = MAX(32.5\%\ Grade_{EXAM} + 32.5\%\ Grade_P + 21\%\ Grade_{AA1} + 14\%\ Grade_{AA2},\\ 50\%\ Grade_{EXAM} + 50\%\ Grade_P) \quad (5)$$

Students must perform at least two of three practical activities (AA2, AA3, and AA5) and the final exam (EXAM) in order to pass the course. Although AA1 and AA2 are optional, most of the students pass the course by completing these optional activities too, similarly to CF.

Table 4 shows the performance of the GAR model for both courses. For each submodel, *TP, FP, TN, FN*, and the accuracy metrics *ACC, TNR, TPR*, and $F_{1.5}$ are summarized. The table also shows the best algorithm (*Algorithm*) and the last semester for the training set (*Semester*) that was used to train each submodel (as detailed in Section 4.2). Although, in the case of CF the first submodel (which corresponds to the AA1) is considered a low-quality model for detecting non-at-risk students (i.e., TNR smaller than the threshold of 75%), the quality is good for the rest. In the case of DB, the accuracy is very good from the very beginning of the course in the detection of the students that are likely to pass the course (TNR begins at 89.53%). That means that the grade for AA1 is a very good indicator to predict success in DB. However, the submodel still does not predict correctly students that may fail the course (TPR is 68.18%). This fact is very different in the CF course, where the students at-risk are detected from the AA1 (TPR 82.83%).

**Table 4.** Performance of the GAR model.

| | \multicolumn{9}{c}{COMPUTER FUNDAMENTALS} |
|---|---|---|---|---|---|---|---|---|---|
| | TP | FP | TN | FN | ACC(%) | TNR(%) | TPR(%) | $F_{1.5}$(%) | Algorithm | Semester |
| Pr$_{AA1}$ | 164 | 42 | 92 | 34 | 77.11 | 68.66 | 82.83 | 81.81 | Decision Tree | 20171 |
| Pr$_{AA2}$ | 171 | 10 | 121 | 44 | 84.39 | 92.37 | 79.53 | 83.60 | Decision Tree | 20182 |
| Pr$_{AA3}$ | 327 | 22 | 185 | 27 | 91.27 | 89.37 | 92.37 | 92.78 | Support Vector | 20172 |
| Pr$_{AA4}$ | 187 | 3 | 131 | 11 | 95.78 | 97.76 | 94.44 | 95.63 | K-Nearest Neighbors | 20171 |
| | \multicolumn{9}{c}{DATABASES} |
| | TP | FP | TN | FN | ACC(%) | TNR(%) | TPR(%) | $F_{1.5}$(%) | Algorithm | Semester |
| Pr$_{AA1}$ | 30 | 9 | 77 | 14 | 82.31 | 89.53 | 68.18 | 70.65 | K-Nearest Neighbors | 20182 |
| Pr$_{AA2}$ | 31 | 5 | 81 | 13 | 86.15 | 94.19 | 75.45 | 74.63 | K-Nearest Neighbors | 20182 |
| Pr$_{AA3}$ | 38 | 4 | 82 | 6 | 92.31 | 95.35 | 86.36 | 87.59 | Support Vector | 20182 |
| Pr$_{AA4}$ | 37 | 3 | 83 | 7 | 92.31 | 96.51 | 84.09 | 86.51 | Naive Bayes | 20182 |
| Pr$_{AA5}$ | 39 | 2 | 84 | 5 | 94.62 | 97.67 | 88.64 | 90.54 | K-Nearest Neighbors | 20182 |

### 6.2. Performance of the Warning Level Classification

Regarding the accuracy of the warning level classification, the results for each assessment activity are shown in Table 5 for both courses. On the one hand, the table shows the number of students assigned to each classification level (*No.*) and the final performance of the students for each warning level (*Fail, Pass*). The set of messages to be sent according to the warning level classification (WL) has been previously discussed in Section 5 (see Figure 7). The final performance for each case gives insights about the correct assignation of the students.

As it can be observed, in the case of CF and for the AA1, students were mostly assigned to the yellow warning level. This was due to the low-quality of the submodel, and it is consistent with the results previously discussed (see Table 5). In subsequent assessment activities, all the colors were used. It is worth noting that the accuracy improved, and students assigned to the yellow color were those students that passed the assessment activity, but with a grade lower than the grade suggested by the prediction. The green color was correctly assigned for 74.5% of the students, and the red and black (non-submitted) to 93.5% and 100%, respectively on AA2. Similar results were observed in the AA3 and the AA4. Some students assigned to red color in the AA2 moved to black in the upcoming assessment activities because they did not submit previous activities, causing course dropout. The yellow color only served as medium risk level at first assessment activities, whereas students were progressively moved to the respective correct risk level on the final ones.

**Table 5.** Performance of the warning level where *WL* are the different warning levels defined in Figure 7, *No.* is the number of students identified in that risk, *Fail* is the percentage of students identified in that risk that failed the course and *Pass* is the percentage of students in that risk that passed the course.

| | COMPUTER FUNDAMENTALS | | | | | | | | | | | |
|---|---|---|---|---|---|---|---|---|---|---|---|---|
| | AA1 | | | AA2 | | | AA3 | | | AA4 | | |
| WL | No. | Fail (%) | Pass (%) | No. | Fail (%) | Pass (%) | No. | Fail (%) | Pass (%) | No. | Fail (%) | Pass (%) |
| G | – | – | – | 200 | 25.5 | 74.5 | 194 | 19.6 | 80.4 | 188 | 15.4 | 84.6 |
| Y1 | 221 | 33.0 | 67.0 | – | – | – | – | – | – | – | – | – |
| Y2 | 52 | 78.8 | 21.1 | 33 | 63.6 | 36.4 | 9 | 66.7 | 33.3 | 9 | 66.7 | 33.3 |
| Y3 | – | – | – | – | – | – | – | – | – | – | – | – |
| R | 32 | 87.5 | 12.5 | 31 | 93.5 | 6.4 | 13 | 92.3 | 7.69 | 14 | 92.9 | 7.1 |
| B | 8 | 100 | – | 43 | 100 | – | 49 | 93.9 | 6.12 | 18 | 100 | – |
| B2 | 0 | – | – | 6 | 100 | – | 48 | 100 | – | 84 | 100 | – |

| | DATABASES | | | | | | | | | | | | | | |
|---|---|---|---|---|---|---|---|---|---|---|---|---|---|---|---|
| | AA1 | | | AA2 | | | AA3 | | | AA4 | | | AA5 | | |
| WL | No. | Fail (%) | Pass (%) | No. | Fail (%) | Pass (%) | No. | Fail (%) | Pass (%) | No. | Fail (%) | Pass (%) | No. | Fail (%) | Pass (%) |
| G | 55 | 21.8 | 78.2 | 49 | 10.2 | 89.8 | 47 | 6.3 | 93.6 | 46 | 6.5 | 93.5 | 54 | 13.0 | 87.04 |
| Y1 | – | – | – | – | – | – | – | – | – | – | – | – | – | – | – |
| Y2 | – | – | – | 2 | 100 | – | 2 | 50.0 | 50.0 | 4 | 50.0 | 50.0 | – | – | – |
| Y3 | 9 | 66.6 | 33.3 | – | – | – | – | – | – | – | – | – | – | – | – |
| R | – | – | – | 15 | 73.3 | 26.7 | 5 | 80.0 | 20.0 | 1 | 100 | – | 1 | – | 100 |
| B | 7 | 71.4 | 28.6 | 3 | 100 | – | 13 | 84.6 | 15.3 | 5 | 60.0 | 40.0 | – | – | – |
| B2 | – | – | – | 2 | 100 | – | 4 | 100 | – | 15 | 93.3 | 6.7 | 16 | 100 | – |

Concerning the DB course, and on the contrary of CF, some students were assigned to the green color in AA1. This is consistent with the fact that the grade obtained in AA1 was a good indicator for predicting course success. A percentage of 78.2 of the students were correctly informed about their chances of success, and this ratio increased significantly in the upcoming assessment activities up to 89.8 and 93.6% in AA2 and AA3, respectively. This is consistent with the fact that AA2, AA3, and AA5 were (at least two of them) mandatory activities, and students prioritize the submission of AA2 and AA3 in order to accomplish this requirement as soon as possible in the course timeline. In fact, most of the students assigned to the green color delivered AA2, AA3, and AA5. Similar to CF, yellow color warned students that their performance was under the prediction in all the assessment activities. Students assigned to the red color appear in AA2 (first potentially mandatory assessment activity), and 73.3% were correctly identified at-risk, and this ratio increased until 80.0% in AA3. Clearer than in the case of CF, students assigned to red color in AA2 moved to black color in the subsequent assessment activities.

We also checked whether there is statistical significance on the final mark distribution comparing the semester where the case studies were run concerning the previous semester (20182, i.e., 2019 spring semester). The objective is to see whether the EWS has impacted the performance of the courses. We used the unpaired two-sample Wilcoxon test due to the non-normal distribution of the final mark [61]. Here, we assume as the null hypothesis that the marks are worse or equal than in the previous semester. Note that, the dropout students are not taken into account. For CF, the p-value < 0.04 and, thus, we can reject the null hypothesis, the median of the final mark increases from 7.8 to 7.9, and the dropout decreases from 51% to 31% on the students who signed the consent. The results regarding retention and scoring are slightly better, but we cannot claim that they are only inferred from the utilization of the EWS, since difficulty on the activities may be different, and the percentages were computed based on students who signed. Those students are generally more engaged, and they tend to participate in pilots (i.e., self-selection bias).

Related to DB, the p-value < 0.02 and we can also reject the null hypothesis, the median of the final mark increases from 7 to 7.6, and the dropout decreases from 26 to 17%. A similar claim to CF can be done. However, the difference is significantly better. This course does not have the variability in terms of marks that a first-year course has. The students have already done several courses in an online learning setting. Therefore, they know better how to self-regulate to pass the course compared to new students of a first-year course that do not have this prior experience.

## 7. Discussion

In this section, we discuss the contributions proposed in this paper and we conclude the answers to the research questions. Related to RQ1 and RQ2, we provided a method to select the best algorithm classifier and training set for each assessment activity and course in order to always get one of the best submodels. The results presented in Section 4.2 prove a high accuracy of the GAR predictive model when it is analyzed in the whole institution.

Focusing on RQ1 (How accurate is the predictive model in the whole institution after four semesters of available data?), the GAR model has improved significantly compared to the results presented in [3], by increasing the size of the datasets and selecting the best algorithm and training set. As an example, the LOESS regression of the TPR improved on the NB of the 2017 fall semester from 38.96–77.69% until 58.79–93.60% of the optimal selection in the 2019 spring semester. The GAR model has comparable results to more complex models that take into account other features such as CGPA, enrolled semesters, attempted times, as stated in Section 2.1.

There are still many courses where it is challenging to detect at-risk students in the first half of the semester since there is a low number of failing students. Although resampling methods for imbalance classes [62,63] can be applied, we need to analyze thoroughly if this model is suitable for these courses and maybe other models should be applied to guide the students. Also, the GAR model has a relevant limitation. When the assessment process is changed regarding the number of assessment activities or contents of the activities, the model is invalid for the course. Although other models presented in the literature are also affected by the same limitation [17,18], we solved the problem with the best selection process. In such cases, the method proposed in Section 4.2 tends to select the previous best-known submodel (mostly the previous assessment activity) and such a trained submodel is applied. Even having nearly ten percent of courses (around 100 courses in the 2019 fall semester) with such changes in the assessment model, the results presented in such a section were unaffected. We observed that the behavior of the students is quite similar when only one assessment activity is changed but it starts to fail on major changes. In such limitations, we should consider new features as further research in order to improve the global accuracy of the system.

Related to RQ2 (Which is the accuracy limit for the predictive model to consider a low-quality model to adapt the intervention measures in the EWS?), we increased the intervention threshold to 75% without losing any high-accurate model in terms of TPR with a new method by transforming the search to an optimization problem. Thus, the intervention mechanism can provide more focused early feedback messages based on high accurate TPR and TNR.

Concerning RQ3 (How accurate is the EWS on identifying at-risk students in a real educational setting?), two case studies have been analyzed in order to answer this research question. The EWS is capable to correctly predict the likelihood to fail the course and the Green-Amber-Red risk classification is capable of classifying the risk level correctly in both case studies, even though the courses have different assessment models and the behavior and experience of the students are significantly different. In terms of performance and dropout, there is a slight improvement. However, we cannot assure that it is only based on the EWS utilization.

Related to the early feedback intervention mechanism, the EWS uses feedback messages nudging [46], intervention [64], and counseling [42]. The classification of seven different conditions provides a high personalization. In a fully online setting, early feedback is one of the most appropriate mechanisms in terms of scalability. Also, we found that the feedback sent to the students based on their progress to their email accounts are highly appreciated by the students. These results are consistent with those exposed in [47]. This feedback was part of the intervention mechanism discussed in [60].

Furthermore, some students that were in at-risk situation decided to contact the teacher after receiving this early feedback in order to get additional educational support (i.e., 40 students in Computer Fundamentals and 12 students in Databases during all the semester).

In terms of the results of the case studies, there are some threats to validity to consider. In terms of internal validity, self-selection bias and mortality may affect the quantitative analysis. Students gave their consent to be included in the pilot since this is required in our institution by the Research Ethical Committee [65]. Thus, engaged students tend to participate in such pilots, and performance computed on those students tends to be higher compared to the average of the course. However, it is worth noting that the teachers received replies to the early feedback on dropout students and nobody complained about the system, they congratulated the initiative and even some of them apologized for dropping out of the course and not reaching the course objectives.

## 8. Conclusions and Future Work

AI will be fundamental in the coming years for supporting education and develop new educational systems for supporting online learning. The ongoing pandemic pointed out the deficiencies that we currently have in education (on-site but also online) [66] and the need to improve our learning processes and environments. Tools like those presented in this paper, but also others based on automatic recommendation [67], are some examples of systems that could enhance the way the learning processes are currently done and leverage the work of the teachers on learning contexts with a large number of students.

In this paper, we have presented an EWS from the conceptualization of the predictive model to the complete design of the training and test system and a case study on a real setting. The predictive model has a high accuracy within individual courses, but it has still some deficiencies for identifying at-risk on the first assessment activities. As future piece of work, we are planning to extend the experiments in two directions. On the one hand, the bottleneck mentioned on selecting the most appropriate training set and classifier should be fixed. This process will be prohibitive in the next semesters due to the large exploration and a smarter method should be developed. Inserting a clustering process to detect regions of data with relevant information, applying SMOTE on courses with imbalanced data, or a vote ensemble approach could be different strategies to apply to improve quality and runtime. On the other hand, adding information about the profile of the students can help to better classify students based on their behavior at the institution. This new information can improve the accuracy of the predictions or even detecting students with different needs (i.e., newbie students, repeater students, etc.).

Related to the EWS, we are ready to further analyze the students' behavior within courses in the sense that optimal learning paths can be discovered and proposed to students to improve their learning experience. Also, we plan to start analyzing the students' behavior outside courses in order to check the successful set of enrollment courses within the same semester and discourage the enrollment of conflictive sets. In the end, the aim of the system will be the same: to help students to succeed in their learning process.

**Author Contributions:** Conceptualization, D.B., A.E.G.-R., and M.E.R.; methodology, A.E.G.-R. and M.E.R.; software, D.B.; validation, D.B., A.E.G.-R., M.E.R., and A.K.; formal analysis, D.B., A.E.G.-R., and M.E.R.; investigation, D.B., A.E.G.-R., M.E.R., and A.K.; data curation, D.B; writing—original draft preparation, D.B., A.E.G.-R., M.E.R., and A.K.; writing—review and editing, D.B., A.E.G.-R., M.E.R., and A.K.; visualization, D.B., A.E.G.-R., and M.E.R.; supervision, D.B., A.E.G.-R., M.E.R., and A.K.; project administration, D.B. and A.K. All authors have read and agreed to the published version of the manuscript.

**Funding:** This research has been funded by the eLearn Center at Universitat Oberta de Catalunya through the project New Goals 2018NG001 "LIS: Learning Intelligent System".

**Acknowledgments:** The authors express their gratitude for the technical support received by the eLearn Center staff in charge of the UOC data mart.

**Conflicts of Interest:** The authors declare no conflict of interest.

## Appendix A

**Table A1.** LOESS Regression of the Naive Bayes in the complete set of courses in the different datasets.

| Semester Timeline | ACC | | | | TNR | | | | TPR | | | | $F_{1.5}$ | | | |
|---|---|---|---|---|---|---|---|---|---|---|---|---|---|---|---|---|
| | 20171 | 20172 | 2081 | 20182 | 20171 | 20172 | 2081 | 20182 | 20171 | 20172 | 2081 | 20182 | 20171 | 20172 | 2081 | 20182 |
| 10% | 75.98 | 78.51 | 80.43 | 80.59 | 90.15 | 89.14 | 90.62 | 91.39 | 38.97 | 47.03 | 43.59 | 44.14 | 39.90 | 47.44 | 45.03 | 46.54 |
| 15% | 77.42 | 80.19 | 81.79 | 82.58 | 91.24 | 89.14 | 90.59 | 92.02 | 44.21 | 52.44 | 48.28 | 49.14 | 44.99 | 52.12 | 48.75 | 51.03 |
| 20% | 78.78 | 81.72 | 83.09 | 84.33 | 92.08 | 89.25 | 90.66 | 92.54 | 49.04 | 57.42 | 52.83 | 53.93 | 49.65 | 56.52 | 52.52 | 55.37 |
| 25% | 80.02 | 83.07 | 84.31 | 85.82 | 92.70 | 89.39 | 90.81 | 92.94 | 53.43 | 61.98 | 57.23 | 58.51 | 53.84 | 60.60 | 56.30 | 59.51 |
| 30% | 81.13 | 84.27 | 85.45 | 87.12 | 93.14 | 89.57 | 91.03 | 93.26 | 57.39 | 66.11 | 61.40 | 62.79 | 57.57 | 64.32 | 59.97 | 63.39 |
| 35% | 82.11 | 85.27 | 86.46 | 88.15 | 93.31 | 89.78 | 91.30 | 93.43 | 60.91 | 69.74 | 65.37 | 66.85 | 60.82 | 67.68 | 63.59 | 67.07 |
| 40% | 83.06 | 86.22 | 87.45 | 89.00 | 93.47 | 90.21 | 91.71 | 93.62 | 63.98 | 72.88 | 69.03 | 70.49 | 63.68 | 70.70 | 67.07 | 70.42 |
| 45% | 83.57 | 87.11 | 88.54 | 89.81 | 93.68 | 90.62 | 92.26 | 93.93 | 66.39 | 75.87 | 72.51 | 73.73 | 65.89 | 73.42 | 70.42 | 73.39 |
| 50% | 84.12 | 87.83 | 89.49 | 90.64 | 93.89 | 90.85 | 92.75 | 94.31 | 68.50 | 78.31 | 75.37 | 76.35 | 67.81 | 75.51 | 73.17 | 75.78 |
| 55% | 84.86 | 88.55 | 90.14 | 91.30 | 94.15 | 91.31 | 93.13 | 94.66 | 70.32 | 79.93 | 77.23 | 78.25 | 69.54 | 77.13 | 75.00 | 77.57 |
| 60% | 85.54 | 89.21 | 90.68 | 91.89 | 94.42 | 91.77 | 93.50 | 95.00 | 71.85 | 81.22 | 78.66 | 79.80 | 71.01 | 78.47 | 76.42 | 79.07 |
| 65% | 86.00 | 89.85 | 91.31 | 92.49 | 94.71 | 92.13 | 93.94 | 95.36 | 73.13 | 82.59 | 80.07 | 81.33 | 72.28 | 79.77 | 77.86 | 80.57 |
| 70% | 86.42 | 90.47 | 91.91 | 93.04 | 94.99 | 92.51 | 94.38 | 95.73 | 74.21 | 83.74 | 81.21 | 82.64 | 73.39 | 80.92 | 79.11 | 81.91 |
| 75% | 86.93 | 91.04 | 92.39 | 93.52 | 95.18 | 92.96 | 94.75 | 96.07 | 75.24 | 84.64 | 82.16 | 83.74 | 74.44 | 81.97 | 80.28 | 83.16 |
| 80% | 87.46 | 91.54 | 92.76 | 93.92 | 95.30 | 93.43 | 95.06 | 96.40 | 76.15 | 85.29 | 82.90 | 84.66 | 75.36 | 82.90 | 81.33 | 84.31 |
| 85% | 88.05 | 91.99 | 93.05 | 94.26 | 95.34 | 93.94 | 95.31 | 96.70 | 76.97 | 85.73 | 83.49 | 85.44 | 76.17 | 83.75 | 82.34 | 85.40 |
| 90% | 88.71 | 92.40 | 93.26 | 94.53 | 95.29 | 94.52 | 95.51 | 96.98 | 77.70 | 85.95 | 83.91 | 86.05 | 76.89 | 84.51 | 83.30 | 86.43 |

Table A2. LOESS Regression of the Naive Bayes and methods to select the best algorithm classifier and training set in Semester 2018.2.

| Semester Timeline | ACC | | | TNR | | | TPR | | | F1.5 | | |
|---|---|---|---|---|---|---|---|---|---|---|---|---|
| | NaiveBayes | Best Alg. | Best A. TS | NaiveBayes | Best Alg. | Best A. TS | NaiveBayes | Best Alg. | Best A. TS | NaiveBayes | Best Alg. | Best A. TS |
| 10% | 80.59 | 80.70 | 84.20 | 91.39 | 90.02 | 91.71 | 44.14 | 47.88 | 58.79 | 46.54 | 49.19 | 59.75 |
| 15% | 82.58 | 82.88 | 85.64 | 92.02 | 91.14 | 92.17 | 49.14 | 52.45 | 62.39 | 51.03 | 53.64 | 62.68 |
| 20% | 84.33 | 84.81 | 87.00 | 92.54 | 92.12 | 92.65 | 53.93 | 56.87 | 66.04 | 55.37 | 57.96 | 65.76 |
| 25% | 85.82 | 86.52 | 88.30 | 92.94 | 92.95 | 93.15 | 58.51 | 61.12 | 69.70 | 59.51 | 62.11 | 68.96 |
| 30% | 87.12 | 88.01 | 89.52 | 93.26 | 93.65 | 93.64 | 62.79 | 65.15 | 73.41 | 63.39 | 66.02 | 72.25 |
| 35% | 88.15 | 89.25 | 90.65 | 93.43 | 94.18 | 94.13 | 66.85 | 68.99 | 76.98 | 67.07 | 69.75 | 75.50 |
| 40% | 89.00 | 90.29 | 91.72 | 93.62 | 94.65 | 94.70 | 70.49 | 72.52 | 80.52 | 70.42 | 73.18 | 78.94 |
| 45% | 89.81 | 91.23 | 92.68 | 93.93 | 95.09 | 95.22 | 73.73 | 75.82 | 83.73 | 73.39 | 76.31 | 82.06 |
| 50% | 90.64 | 92.04 | 93.54 | 94.31 | 95.40 | 95.57 | 76.35 | 78.58 | 86.45 | 75.78 | 78.77 | 84.59 |
| 55% | 91.30 | 92.62 | 94.16 | 94.66 | 95.63 | 95.81 | 78.25 | 80.71 | 88.52 | 77.57 | 80.67 | 86.34 |
| 60% | 91.89 | 93.10 | 94.65 | 95.00 | 95.82 | 95.97 | 79.80 | 82.52 | 90.14 | 79.07 | 82.26 | 87.60 |
| 65% | 92.49 | 93.62 | 95.14 | 95.36 | 96.05 | 96.22 | 81.33 | 84.25 | 91.59 | 80.57 | 83.82 | 88.91 |
| 70% | 93.04 | 94.09 | 95.54 | 95.73 | 96.29 | 96.46 | 82.64 | 85.72 | 92.72 | 81.91 | 85.18 | 90.06 |
| 75% | 93.52 | 94.49 | 95.84 | 96.07 | 96.56 | 96.67 | 83.74 | 86.84 | 93.49 | 83.16 | 86.35 | 90.98 |
| 80% | 93.92 | 94.83 | 96.02 | 96.40 | 96.85 | 96.84 | 84.66 | 87.66 | 93.91 | 84.31 | 87.33 | 91.66 |
| 85% | 94.26 | 95.12 | 96.09 | 96.70 | 97.17 | 96.95 | 85.44 | 88.20 | 93.94 | 85.40 | 88.17 | 92.12 |
| 90% | 94.53 | 95.34 | 96.03 | 96.98 | 97.51 | 97.03 | 86.05 | 88.44 | 93.60 | 86.43 | 88.85 | 92.35 |

## References

1. Craig, S.D. *Tutoring and Intelligent Tutoring Systems*; Nova Science Publishers, Incorporated: New York, NY, USA, 2018.
2. Karadeniz, A.; Baneres, D.; Rodríguez, M.E.; Guerrero-Roldán, A.E. Enhancing ICT Personalized Education through a Learning Intelligent System. In Proceedings of the Online, Open and Flexible Higher Education Conference, Madrid, Spain, 16–18 October 2019; pp. 142–147.
3. Baneres, D.; Rodríguez, M.E.; Serra, M. An Early Feedback Prediction System for Learners At-risk within a First-year Higher Education Subject. *IEEE Trans. Learn. Technol.* **2019**, *12*, 249–263. [CrossRef]
4. Zawacki-Richter, O.; Marín, V.I.; Bond, M.; Gouverneur, F. Systematic review of research on artificial intelligence applications in higher education—Where are the educators? *Int. J. Technol. High. Educ.* **2019**, *16*. [CrossRef]
5. Rastrollo-Guerrero, J.; Gámez-Pulido, J.; Durán-Domínguez, A. Analyzing and Predicting Students' Performance by Means of Machine Learning: A Review. *Appl. Sci.* **2020**, *10*, 1042. [CrossRef]
6. Hussain, M.; Zhu, W.; Zhang, W.; Abidi, S.M.R. Student engagement predictions in an e-learning system and their impact on student course assessment scores. *Comput. Intell. Neurosci.* **2018**, *6*, 1–21. [CrossRef]
7. Jokhan, A.; Sharma, B.; Singh, S. Early warning system as a predictor for student performance in higher education blended courses. *Stud. High. Educ.* **2019**, *44*, 1900–1911. [CrossRef]
8. Lee, S.; Chung, J. The Machine Learning-Based Dropout Early Warning System for Improving the Performance of Dropout Prediction. *Appl. Sci.* **2019**, *9*, 3093. [CrossRef]
9. Raju, D.; Schumacker, R. Exploring student characteristics of retention that lead to graduation in higher educationusing data mining models. *J. Coll. Stud. Ret.* **2015**, *16*, 563–591. [CrossRef]
10. Hilton, E.; Williford, B.; Li, W.; Hammond, T.; Linsey, J. Teaching Engineering Students Freehand Sketching with an Intelligent Tutoring System. In *Inspiring Students with Digital Ink*, 1st ed.; Hammond, T., Prasad, M., Stepanova, A., Eds.; Springer: Cham, Switzerland, 2019; pp. 135–148.
11. Duffy, M.C.; Azevedo, R. Motivation matters: Interactions between achievement goals and agent scaffolding for self-regulated learning within an intelligent tutoring system. *Comput. Hum. Behav.* **2015**, *52*, 338–348. [CrossRef]
12. Bydžovská, H. Course Enrollment Recommender System. In Proceedings of the 9th International Conference on Educational Data Mining, Raleigh, NC, USA, 29 Junr–2 July 2016; pp. 312–317.
13. Backenköhler, M.; Wolf, V. Student performance prediction and optimal course selection: An MDP approach. *Lect. Notes Comput. Sci.* **2018**, *10729*, 40–47.
14. Saarela, M.; Kärkkäinen, T. Analyzing student performance using sparse data of core bachelor courses. *JEDM-J. Educ. Data Min.* **2015**, *7*, 3–32.
15. Mishra, T.; Kumar, D.; Gupta, D.S. Mining students data for performance prediction. In Proceedings of the Fourth International Conference on Advanced Computing & Communication Technologies, Rohtak, India, 8–9 February 2014; pp. 255–262.
16. Vandamme, J.P.; Meskens, N.; Superby, J.F. Predicting academic performance by data mining methods. *Educ. Econ.* **2007**, *15*, 405–419. [CrossRef]
17. Pistilli, M.D.; Arnold, K.E. Course signals at Purdue: Using learning analytics to increase student success. In Proceedings of the 2nd International Conference on Learning Analytics and Knowledge, Vancouver, BC, Canada, 29 April–2 May 2012; pp. 2–5.
18. You, J.W. Identifying significant indicators using LMS data to predict course achievement in online learning. *Internet High. Educ.* **2016**, *29*, 23–30. [CrossRef]
19. Saura, J.; Reyes-Menendez, A.; Bennett, D. How to Extract Meaningful Insights from UGC: A Knowledge-Based Method Applied to Education. *Appl. Sci.* **2019**, *9*, 4603. [CrossRef]
20. Romero, C.; López, M.I.; Luna, J.M.; Ventura, S. Predicting students' final performance from participation in on-line discussion forums. *Comput. Educ.* **2013**, *68*, 458–472. [CrossRef]
21. Zacharis, N.Z. A multivariate approach to predicting student outcomes in web-enabled blended learning courses. *Internet High. Educ.* **2015**, *27*, 44–53. [CrossRef]

22. Azcona, D.; Casey, K. Micro-analytics for student performance prediction leveraging fine-grained learning analytics to predict performance. *Int. J. Comput. Sci. Softw. Eng.* **2015**, *4*, 218–223.
23. Marbouti, F.; Diefes-Dux, H.A.; Madhavan, K. Models for early prediction of at-risk students in a course using standards-based grading. *Comput. Educ.* **2016**, *103*, 1–15. [CrossRef]
24. Gašević, D.; Dawson, S.; Rogers, T. Learning analytics should not promote one size fits all: The effects of instructional conditions in predicting academic success. *Internet High. Educ.* **2016**, *28*, 68–84. [CrossRef]
25. Macfadyen, P.L.; Dawson, S. Mining LMS data to develop an early warning system for educators: A proof of concept. *Comput. Educ.* **2010**, *54*, 588–599. [CrossRef]
26. Casey, K.; Azcona, D. Utilizing student activity patterns to predict performance. *Int. J. Educ. Technol. High. Educ.* **2017**, *14*, 4. [CrossRef]
27. Waddington, R.J.; Nam, S.; Lonn, S.; Teasley, S.D. Improving Early Warning Systems with Categorized Course Resource Usage. *J. Learn. Anal.* **2016**, *3*, 263–290. [CrossRef]
28. Joksimović, S.; Gašević, D.; Loughin, T.M.; Kovanović, V.; Hatala, M. Learning at distance: Effects of interaction traces on academic achievement. *Comput. Educ.* **2015**, *87*, 204–217. [CrossRef]
29. Calvo-Flores, M.D.; Galindo, E.G.; Jiménez, M.C.P.; Pérez, O. Predicting students' marks from Moodle logs using neural network models. *Curr. Dev. Technol. Assist. Educ.* **2006**, *1*, 586–590.
30. Howard, E.; Meehan, M.; Parnell, A. Contrasting prediction methods for early warning systems at undergraduate level. *Internet High. Educ.* **2018**, *37*, 66–75. [CrossRef]
31. Wolff, A.; Zdrahal, Z.; Herrmannova, D.; Knoth, P. Predicting student performance from combined data sources. In *Educational Data Mining, Peña-Ayala, A., Ed.*; Springer International Publisher: Cham, Switzerland, 2014; Volume 7, pp. 175–202.
32. Akçapınar, G.; Altun, A.; Aşkar, P. Using learning analytics to develop early-warning system for at-risk students. *Int. J. Educ. Technol. High. Educ.* **2019**, *16*. [CrossRef]
33. Buschetto Macarini, L.A.; Cechinel, C.; Batista Machado, M.F.; Faria Culmant Ramos, V.; Munoz, R. Predicting Students Success in Blended Learning—Evaluating Different Interactions Inside Learning Management Systems. *Appl. Sci.* **2019**, *9*, 5523. [CrossRef]
34. Kovanović, V.; Gašević, D.; Joksimović, S.; Hatala, M.; Adesope, O. Analytics of Communities of Inquiry: Effects of Learning Technology Use on Cognitive Presence in Asynchronous Online Discussions. *Internet High. Educ.* **2015**, *27*, 74–89. [CrossRef]
35. Márquez-Vera, C.; Cano, A.; Romero, C.; Noaman, A.Y.M.; MousaFardoun, H.; Ventura, S. Early dropout prediction using data mining: A case study with high school students. *Expert Syst.* **2016**, *33*, 107–124. [CrossRef]
36. Lykourentzou, I.; Giannoukos, I.; Nikolopoulos, V.; Mpardis, G.; Loumos, V. Dropout prediction in e-learning courses through the combination of machine learning techniques. *Comput. Educ.* **2009**, *53*, 950–965. [CrossRef]
37. Srilekshmi, M.; Sindhumol, S.; Shiffon, C.; Kamal, B. Learning analytics to identify students at-risk in MOOCs. In Proceedings of the IEEE 8th International Conference on Technology for Education, Mumbai, India, 28 November–2 December 2016; pp. 194–199.
38. Xing, W.; Chen, X.; Stein, J.; Marcinkowski, M. Temporal predication of dropouts in MOOCs: Reaching the low hanging fruit through stacking generalization. *Comput. Hum. Behav.* **2016**, *58*, 119–129. [CrossRef]
39. Falkner, N.J.; Falkner, K.E. A fast measure for identifying at-risk students in computer science. In Proceedings of the Ninth Annual International Conference on International Computing Education Research, Auckland, New Zealand, 9–11 September 2012; pp. 55–62.
40. Krumm, A.E.; Waddington, R.J.; Teasley, S.D.; Lonn, S. A learning management system-based early warning system for academic advising in undergraduate engineering. In *Learning Analytics*, 1st ed.; Larusson, J., White, B., Eds.; Springer International Publisher: New York, NY, USA, 2014; pp. 103–119.
41. Najdi, L.; Er-Raha, B. A Novel Predictive Modeling System to Analyze Students at Risk of Academic Failure. *Int. J. Comput. Appl. Tech.* **2016**, *156*, 25–30. [CrossRef]
42. Hu, Y.H.; Lo, C.L.; Shih, S.P. Developing early warning Systems to predict students' online learning performance. *Comput. Hum. Behav.* **2014**, *36*, 469–478. [CrossRef]

43. Jayaprakash, S.M.; Moody, E.W.; Eitel, J.M. Early alert of academically at-risk students: An open source analytics initiative. *J. Learn. Anal.* **2014**, *1*, 6–47. [CrossRef]
44. Vasquez, H.; Azarbayejani, M. Early identification of at-risk students in a lower-level engineering gatekeeper course. In Proceedings of the 2015 IEEE Frontiers in Education Conference (FIE), El Paso, TX, USA, 21–24 October 2015; pp. 1–9.
45. Folger, W.; Carter, J.A.; Chase, P.B. Supporting first generation college freshmen with small group intervention. *Coll. Student J.* **2004**, *38*, 472–476.
46. Sunstein, C.R. Which Nudges Do People Like? A National Survey. Available online: https://ssrn.com/abstract=2619899 (accessed on 24 May 2020).
47. Damgaard, M.T.; Nielsen, H.S. Nudging in education. *Econ. Educ. Rev.* **2018**, *64*, 313–342. [CrossRef]
48. Minguillón, J.; Conesa, J.; Rodríguez, M.E.; Santanach, F. Learning analytics in practice: Providing e-learning researches and practitioners with activity data. In *Frontiers of Cyberlearning: Emerging Technologies for Teaching and Learning*; Springer: Singapore, 2018; pp. 145–164.
49. Drachsler, H.; Hoel, T.; Scheffel, M.; Kismihók, G.; Berg, A.; Ferguson, R.; Manderveld, J. Ethical and privacy issues in the application of learning analytics. In Proceedings of the 5th International Conference on Learning Analytics and Knowledge, ACM, Poughkeepsie, NY, USA, 16–20 March 2015; pp. 390–391.
50. UOC Virtual Campus. Available online: https://www.uoc.edu/estudiant/portal/guia/en/com_estudia/campus_virtual/index.html (accessed on 24 May 2020).
51. Huang, J.; Ling, C.X. AUC and accuracy in evaluating learning algorithms. *IEEE. Trans. Knowl. Data Eng.* **2005**, *17*, 299–310. [CrossRef]
52. Pedregosa, F.; Varoquaux, G.; Gramfort, A.; Michel, V.; Thirion, B.; Grisel, O.; Vanderplas, J. Scikit-learn: Machine learning in Python. *J. Mach. Learn. Res.* **2011**, *12*, 2825–2830.
53. Core Team. R: A Language and Environment for Statistical Computing. R Foundation for Statistical Computing. Available online: https://www.R-project.org/ (accessed on 24 May 2020).
54. Cleveland, W.S.; Grosse, E.H.; Shyu, M.J. Local regression models. In *Statistical Models in S*; Chambers, J.M., Hastie, T.J., Eds.; Chapman and Hall: New York, NY, USA, 1992; pp. 309–376.
55. Baneres, D.; Karadeniz, A.; Guerrero-Roldán, A.E.; Rodríguez, M.E. A predictive system for supporting at-risk students' identification. In Proceedings of the Future Technologies Conference 2020, Vancouver, BC, Canada, 5–6 November 2020.
56. Oates, B.J. *Researching Information Systems and Computing*; SAGE: London, UK, 2005.
57. Vaishnavi, V.; Kuechler, W. Design Research in Information Systems. Last update: 23 October 2013. Available online: http://www.desrist.org/design-research-in-information-systems/ (accessed on 24 May 2020).
58. UOC Performance and Satisfaction Indicators. Available online: https://www.uoc.edu/portal/en/qualitat/resultats/resultats-rendiment/index.html (accessed on 24 May 2020).
59. Hung, J.L.; Wang, M.C.; Wang, S.; Abdelrasoul, M.; Lo, Y.; He, W. Identifying at-risk students for early interventions: A time-series clustering approach. *IEEE. Trans. Emerg. Top. Comput.* **2015**, *5*, 44–55. [CrossRef]
60. Rodríguez, M.E.; Guerrero-Roldán, A.E.; Baneres, D.; Karadeniz, A. Towards an intervention mechanism for supporting learners performance in online learning. In Proceedings of the 12th International Conference of Education, Research and Innovation, Sevilla, Spain, 9–11 November 2019; pp. 5136–5145.
61. Kruskal, W. Historical Notes on the Wilcoxon Unpaired Two-Sample Test. *J. Am. Stat. Assoc.* **1957**, *52*, 356–360. [CrossRef]
62. López, V.; Fernández, A.; García, S.; Palade, V.; Herrera, F. An insight into classification with imbalanced data: Empirical results and current trends on using data intrinsic characteristics. *Inf. Sci.* **2013**, *250*, 113–141. [CrossRef]
63. Sisovic, S.; Matetic, M.; Bakaric, M.B. Clustering of imbalanced moodle data for early alert of student failure. In Proceedings of the IEEE 14th International Symposium on Applied Machine Intelligence and Informatics, Herl'any, Slovakia, 21–23 January 2016; pp. 165–170.
64. Schell, J.; Lukoff, B.; Alvarado, C. Using early warning signs to predict academic risk in interactive, blended teaching environments. *Internet Learn.* **2014**, *3*, 55–67. [CrossRef]
65. UOC Ethical Committee. Available online: https://research.uoc.edu/portal/en/ri/activitat-rdi/comite-etica/funcions/index.html (accessed on 23 May 2020).

66. Zhou, L.; Wu, S.; Zhou, M.; Li, F. School's Out, But Class' On', The Largest Online Education in the World Today: Taking China's Practical Exploration During The COVID-19 Epidemic Prevention and Control As an Example. *Best Evid. Chin. Educ.* **2020**, *4*, 501–519. [CrossRef]
67. Clarizia, F.; Colace, F.; Lombardi, M.; Pascale, F.; Santaniello, D. Chatbot: An education support system for student. In Proceedings of the International Symposium on Cyberspace Safety and Security, Amalfi, Italy, 29–31 October 2018; pp. 291–302.

© 2020 by the authors. Licensee MDPI, Basel, Switzerland. This article is an open access article distributed under the terms and conditions of the Creative Commons Attribution (CC BY) license (http://creativecommons.org/licenses/by/4.0/).

Article

# Automated Assessment and Microlearning Units as Predictors of At-Risk Students and Students' Outcomes in the Introductory Programming Courses

**Jan Skalka * and Martin Drlik**

Department of Informatics, Faculty of Natural Sciences, Constantine the Philosopher University in Nitra, 94974 Nitra, Slovakia; mdrlik@ukf.sk
* Correspondence: jskalka@ukf.sk

Received: 31 May 2020; Accepted: 25 June 2020; Published: 30 June 2020

**Abstract:** The number of students who decided to study information technology related study programs is continually increasing. Introductory programming courses represent the most crucial milestone in information technology education and often reflect students' ability to think abstractly and systematically, solve problems, and design their solutions. Even though many students who attend universities have already completed some introductory courses of programming, there is still a large group of students with limited programming skills. This drawback often increases during the first term, and it is often the main reason why students leave study too early. There is a myriad of technologies and tools which can be involved in the programming course to increase students' chances of mastering programming. The introductory programming courses used in this study has been gradually extended over the four academic years with the automated source code assessment of students' programming assignments followed by the implementation of a set of suitably designed microlearning units. The final four datasets were analysed to confirm the suitability of automated assessment and microlearning units as predictors of at-risk students and students' outcomes in the introductory programming courses. The research results proved the significant contribution of automated code assessment in students' learning outcomes in the elementary topics of learning programming. Simultaneously, it proved a moderate to strong dependence between the students' activity and achievement in the activities and final students' outcomes.

**Keywords:** introductory programming courses; dropout prediction; automated assessment; source code evaluation; microlearning

---

## 1. Introduction

The current demand for experts in information technology (IT) as well as the prognosis of the future development on the labour market cause not only the constant growth of computer science education popularity, but also a continual demand for improving the IT skills of the large group of graduates who enter the labour market every year.

The number of students who decided to study IT-related study programs is continually increasing. Higher educational institutions which train the future IT professionals in different study programs react to this situation differently. Many universities admit as many students to study IT-oriented study programs as their capacities allow, besides considering their current ranking and the position in the country or worldwide. Consequently, they often expect that this number of students will naturally decrease during the first months of the term. Even though this process can be considered natural, it opens the discussion, how to teach this large group of newcomers with a different introductory level of IT skills effectively and how to set up the safety net for the at-risk students with higher predisposition to leave a study too early.

Introductory programming courses represent the most crucial milestone in IT education and often reflect students' ability to think abstractly and systematically, solve problems, and design their solutions. Therefore, the level of knowledge of the developers and similar experts (IT specialists, data science specialists, specialists of Internet of Things (IoT) area, etc.) can be considered a key benefit for the emerging labour market.

The required skills of novice programmers can be described as a set of skills learned simultaneously, e.g., semantics, the syntax of languages, problem-solving, computational thinking etc. [1,2]. Knowledge of one or more programming languages, or algorithmic thinking in general, are considered one of the critical IT skills. Even though many students, who come to the universities, have already attended some introductory courses of programming, there is still a large group of students with limited programming skills. This drawback often increases during the first term and is often the main reason why students leave study too early.

There are many approaches, which can be used for identification of the IT students with a higher predisposition to dropout [3]. Even though weak programming skills are not the only reason for drop out of studies, they often represent the most important one. Therefore, it is natural to assume that the detailed analysis of the students' behaviour in introductory programming courses can lead to some relevant indicators, which can estimate the dropout rate as soon as possible, identify at-risk students, and simultaneously help teachers to find a suitable form of intervention.

There is increasing interest in gathering and analysing this data to learn about how students behave. An understanding of student behaviour has a value to educators in predicting success in examinations and other assessments, identifying student difficulties and interventions designed to mitigate them, designing tools that respond to specific behaviours in a way that is helpful to the students [4].

There is a myriad of technologies and tools which can be successfully involved in this process. They allow a more straightforward application of modern educational approaches also to this area of education. As a result, they can eliminate many problems of teaching and learning introductory programming identified in a previous decade by the implementation of new functions directly into integrated development environment (IDE) or learning environments. As an example, the syntax and basic semantic elements of programming languages are tracked continually and verified during the source code writing. Therefore, the students can use code completion, hints showing parameters, as well as a short explanation and focus directly on developing their programming thinking [4].

Many universities implemented these technologies and tools, e.g., different massive open online courses (MOOCs) or learning management systems (LMSs), to support different learning forms. These systems serve as the repositories of the curated educational content at least. Moreover, in case of more advanced IT courses allow submitting the programming assignments and their automated evaluation, writing programming code directly in the embedded editor with syntax highlighting, code peer-reviewing, advanced testing, etc. The integrated functions of LMS and their extensions usually support not only progress monitoring but also many activities, quizzes and content sources integration. Students' activities and achievements are monitored, analysed with appropriate statistical methods, and suitably visualised on personalised dashboards (Figure 1).

It can be assumed that the activities, which require active student's involvement in learning, can bring more relevant results in comparison with the observation of the passive student's presence in the course.

Current technological advancements that allow automated evaluation of the source code written by the student and provide immediate feedback, integrated with other approaches utilising e-learning and microlearning advantages were selected for these study, while they have a potential to engage the students to be more active during their study in introductory programming courses.

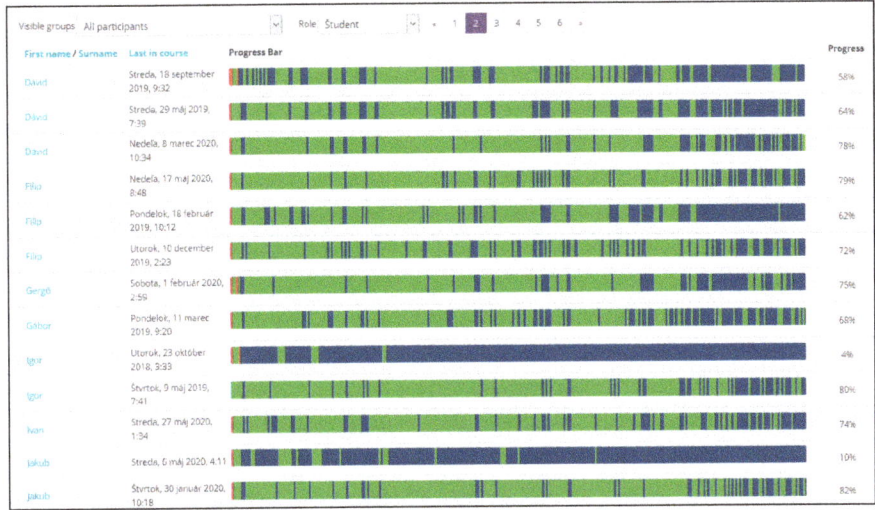

**Figure 1.** An example of the visualisation of the progress monitoring in one of the LMS Moodle courses used in the research. It is possible to identify users with low activity in course.

Therefore, the introductory programming course used in this study has been extended with the automated evaluation of the programming assignments followed by the implementation of a set of suitably designed microlearning units with the following aims:

- To analyse the relationship between the input student's characteristics and his/her final achievements.
- To evaluate the overall contribution of automated evaluation of the programming assignments closely interrelated to the set of suitably designed microlearning units to the students' final grades.
- To research the role of these two elements as possible predictors of identification of at-risk students who fail the introductory programming course.

While the automated programming code evaluation and microlearning units were implemented subsequently during several years, it was possible to collect four different datasets of students' achievements and their activities, which characterise the students' behaviour in the introductory programming course and can be compared with each other.

The structure of the article is as follows. The related work section summarises the current state of the introductory programming education research and emphasises that the understanding the learning process, identifying of the factors, which influence the students' outcomes and the ability to predict the at-risk students are still actual. The third section describes the background of the research, defines the research questions and used methods. The next section is devoted to the obtained results, which are consequently thoroughly discussed in the next section. The conclusion section summarises the main findings and suggests the direction of future research.

## 2. Related Work

Becker et al. [5] analysed the evolution of the introductory programming education research over fifty years thoroughly. They confirmed that the design and structure of the course, as well as automated assessment and student's retention and predicting their success based on course enhancement using new tools and technologies still belong to the main categories of the research with increasing interest.

This statement also confirms a comprehensive report [4], which analyses recent trends across the breadth of introductory programming over the last 15 years. While other authors estimated that the dropout rate among students is about 30–40% [6,7], this study indicates that dropout rates among computing students are not alarmingly high. It has been suggested that the difficulties faced by novices may be a consequence of unrealistic expectations rather than intrinsic complexity of the course irrespective of used educational approaches, tools and technologies.

Many studies have been conducted that tried to identify factors related to success in the learning of programming. Among the identified student characteristics that may contribute to student success in introductory programming courses are prior programming experience, gender, secondary school performance and dislike of programming, intrinsic motivation and comfort level, high school mathematics background, attribution to luck for success/failure, formal training in programming, and perceived understanding of the material [6,8].

Hellas et al. [9] present a systematic literature review of work in the area of predicting student performance. Their analysis shows an increasing amount of research in this area, as well as an increasing variety of techniques used. They did not analyse the relationship between an automated assessment as well as microlearning and predicting students' performance in their review explicitly.

Another systematic review of predicting students' learning outcomes is provided by [10]. The authors identified 14 prediction targets. The student retention/dropout was the second most frequent. Among the feature types used, 151 unique feature types were identified. Student record and performance in the current course, as well as activity and course features and learning behaviour, belong to the most frequent.

Tabanao et al. [6] tried to quantify indicators of novice programmer progress in the task of writing Java programs through the analysis of online protocols of errors. They evaluated the use of these indicators for identifying at-risk students. Even though the derived models could not accurately predict the at-risk students, the authors stated, that described approach can identify the students, who need intervention.

The question of why students drop a computer science course was broadly examined by Kinnunen [7]. The results indicate that several reasons affect students' decision to quit a course. They analysed social, cultural, demographic factors and their impact on students' dropout rate using the interview. The most frequent reasons were the lack of time to make exercises and motivation, firmly joined to the required level of knowledge, which often led to frustration. However, these reasons were also affected by factors such as the perceived difficulty of the course, general difficulties with time managing and planning studies, or the decision to prefer other courses. This study shows that the complexity and extensive variety of factors are involved in students' decision to drop the course. This indicates that simple actions to improve teaching or organisation on a course to reduce the dropout rate may be ineffective. Efficient intervention to the problem requires a combination of many different actions that take into consideration the versatile nature of reasons involved in drop out. They again did not research the impact of educational approach or technology on dropout rate or students' success.

Measuring prior programming knowledge and its impact on the outcomes is the main aim of the paper written by Duran et al. [11]. They proposed and evaluated a novel self-evaluation instrument for measuring prior programming knowledge in introductory programming course to bridge the gap between ad-hoc surveys and standardised tests.

Several groups of researchers developed automated methods for identifying at-risk students early in the semester. Many of these techniques are based on automatically monitoring student activity as the students develop code or advanced data mining and predictive modelling techniques [12]. The research in this area indicates that early success in an introductory programming course is vital for a student's ultimate success. Many researchers have shown that students having difficulty can be identified early in the semester.

An automated assessment (AA), which is in the middle of the interest of this study, represents a tool that allows checking source code automatically and brings a new perspective on learning. The automated assessment of programming assignments has been practised since programming has been taught, especially in the introductory programming courses. It has different features, which are automatically assessed by various assessment tools and systems [13].

Considering the survey about the AA for the novice programmers in the introductory courses [14], the following base conditions should be fulfilled for successful implementation of AA:

- a clear and unambiguous specification should define the requirement for program work and results, with simultaneous checking whether the programs meet the specification or not;
- sufficient testing of the assignment should be ensured, as each bug disturbs and demotivates beginners;
- environmental support for the discovery of syntactic and semantic errors should exist,
- a suitable mechanism for dealing with the programs with syntactic and semantic errors should be created;
- immediate and corrective feedback for the submitted assignments; feedback helps to build students' knowledge, and habits should be available.

According to Skalka et al. [15] and Rodriguez-del-Pino et al. [16], AA is beneficial for the following reasons:

- the student gains immediate feedback whether the program is correct, and students can use their own pace,
- the teacher gains extra time, instead of time wasted by checking the assignment and identifying and re-explaining repeated errors in past,
- it is possible to teach large groups of students without increasing the demands on teachers, which apply especially in the case of MOOC courses,
- the learning process is more efficient and, due to the errors tracking, speed and quality of the solutions, the individual parts of the process can be fragmented, quantified and described (problematic topics, problematic examples, number of necessary attempts, etc.).

Any of the above-mentioned studies did not provide proof that AA has a significant impact on the students' achievements or significantly reduce a student dropout rate. A large number of studies measure the effectiveness of assessment tools in helping students to write the program and perform the solution [17]. Although AA has been extensively used in programming lessons for several years, research focused on their contribution to programming learning is still limited.

Keuning [18] performed a systematic literature review to find out what kind of feedback is provided, which techniques are used to generate the feedback, how adaptable the feedback is, and how these tools are evaluated. They found that feedback, including AA, mostly focuses on identifying mistakes and less on fixing problems.

According to Akahane et al. [19], the practical results of AA implementation in MOOCs are not trivial. The educational goal can only be achieved through the availability of many high-quality assignments, coupled with coaching in the form of guaranteed rapid and accurate feedback. Applying automated assessment itself is not a solution.

Figueiredo [20] stated that there had been an intense research activity in studying the difficulties in teaching and learning introductory programming. Achieving success or failure early in the introductory programming course is directly related to student continuity in the course of computer science. They proposed a system that allows to suggest exercises and to evaluate the results automatically. They did not examine the proposed approach as a suitable predictor of student's dropout or achievement.

Two groups with and without using AA were compared in the research of Pieterse [21]. The scores of the experimental group showed that students who worked with AA gained a more solid grasp of concepts related to debugging, deployment, and versioning. However, the difference between the means of groups was not statistically significant.

The research conducted by Rubio-Sánchez [22] was focused on improving the average final exam scores using an automated grading (particularly AA). It concluded with the result that the automation of key processes such as program grading could save a significant amount of scarce resources in introductory courses without a negative impact on academic performance. The author presented significantly higher exam scores for students who used automated grading.

The next research [23] used the Mooshak system, which did not produce clear results concerning whether it helps to reduce the dropout rate or improve the students' achievements. Students use it for testing their programming code and consider that AA deployment is a good idea.

The microlearning is defined as an action-oriented approach offering bite-sized learning that gets learners to learn, act, and practice [24]. Microlearning refers to a didactic concept and approach that uses digital media to deliver small, coherent and self-contained content for short learning activities [25]. Microlearning has become popular, mainly due to the expansion of mobile devices and brings new possibilities for tracking user activities. The development level of front-end web frameworks has made microlearning no longer limited to mobile devices. Web browsers offer the same comfort and quality not only for content displaying and interacting but also for tracking user activity [24].

The content is organised in short lessons (1–5 min) and consists of two types of activities: provision of information (explanation of one idea, concept, or procedure) and verification of understanding (a simple question usually connected to information presented in the previous step). The idea of microlearning is based on every-where and every-time learning and support of learning in small and concluded parts. The goal is to engage students in deeper learning and encouraging them to think about and work with the content of subject/course in their everyday lives. The learning scenario preparation is the most crucial step in building microlearning content because didactic shortcomings in providing content often mean student failure. Course developers should bear in mind that the student receives the content in a dense form, often without linking to the previous lesson, and the time delay between the lessons can be several days [26].

Predicting learning success based on the usage of learning materials similar to microlearning units is described by Leppänen et al. [27]. The authors explore students' usage of online learning materials as a predictor of academic success. They focused on time spent with each paragraph of the online learning material. The authors found that such time can be considered a moderate predictor of student success even when corrected for student time-on-task and that the information can be used to identify at-risk students. In other words, course material usage can be used to predict academic success.

Although the impact of microlearning on students outcomes has been extensively studied in last decade, i.e., its positive or negative impact on learning programming, consideration of the student dropout rate is quite rare and therefore will be analysed later herein [4,5].

The logs of the students' activity in AA and microlearning units are stored similarly as other resources and activities in the e-learning course created in LMS Moodle. The logs will be used later for a possible explanation of the presented study findings considering the fact, that they can uncover the reason, why AA or microlearning have or have not the expected effect. Different resources, including LMS Moodle, have also been analysed in [3] and the academic performance of students in a blended learning form was also analysed. The authors identified a set of variables with well-known predictive value in dropout courses in general.

Many researchers focused their research on the early prediction of the final grade and identification of the threats of dropout by application of different log mining techniques on introductory programming courses [28–30]. These studies analyse all activities of the stakeholders involved in the e-learning course, research their behaviour in different types of course activities, as well as compare different periods of the term. Although these approaches provide some promising results, they usually catch the real students' activity in the course and their interaction with the content and course activities only partially. Moreover, they often aggregate the students' data with different grades to larger groups and compare the behaviour of these groups.

Ihantola et al. [31] provide an overview of the body of knowledge regarding the use of educational data mining and learning analytics focused on the teaching and learning of programming. They defined five challenges, which provide a framework for systematic research in effective using learning analytics and educational data mining in teaching programming. They identified a learning environment category, which was related to tools and automated testing, grading and feedback, but they did not focus on microlearning or other for educational content.

Sisovic et al. [32] applied educational data mining and learning analytics techniques in order to find out what impacts success in programming. The research was conducted on the dataset compounded of extracted logs from the LMS Moodle and data related to prior knowledge and students' preparation for the study. Classification methods were used to detect connections between prior knowledge and Moodle course activity in relation to final grades. They compared the impact of prior knowledge with the effect of Moodle activity on passing or failing the introductory course of programming. The study showed that some activities and the preparatory seminar contributes to the course success and decreasing of students' dropout rate.

The problem with inactive and low-performance students in e-learning courses was thoroughly analysed in the research conducted by Hussain et al. [33]. They analysed logs from the LMS Moodle and compared several machine learning techniques to predict the low-performance students and identify active and inactive students. The results can have a significant contribution to the LMS Moodle to enable the instructor to focus on groups of the low-performance and inactive students and then give them appropriate feedback. As a result, they assume decreasing student failure and dropout rate in programming courses.

## 3. Materials and Methods

The authors continually investigated various methods, aspects and approaches to teaching introductory programming courses [24,34]. Over the four years, the authors of the Java introductory programming course introduced new elements into the study every year and inspected their impact on student learning outcomes.

Gradual application of new educational objects into programming courses is implemented to eliminate the reduction of admission requirements to cover the needs of the labour market. The main reason for research is the rising dropout of students in this course and the deterioration of the average results of the subject (Table 1).

Table 1. Structure of final grades and dropout.

| Group | Students | A | B | C | D | E | Fx | Dropped Out (%) |
|---|---|---|---|---|---|---|---|---|
| 2016 | 51 | 8 | 6 | 4 | 10 | 8 | 15 | 29.4% |
| 2017 | 70 | 12 | 7 | 18 | 7 | 10 | 16 | 22.9% |
| 2018 | 82 | 8 | 5 | 15 | 12 | 8 | 34 | 41.5% |
| 2019 | 102 | 8 | 3 | 18 | 13 | 10 | 50 | 49.0% |

### 3.1. The Educational Content

The most effective approach to getting the ability on how to solve algorithms and programming problems is training. Ability to acquire these skills depends significantly on the curriculum, and the structure of the programming course, student's willingness and motivation to write many programs. The essential requirement for the long-term quality assurance is the maintenance and continual improvement of the course using instructional design approach, which reflects most of the stakeholders' expectation, divides course content according to the course objectives, types of available resources and course assessments [35]. The suggested approach to reach the best effort is the following:

- develop innovative methodologies in the course;
- make lectures mandatory for the students;
- provide for immediate feedback as soon as possible.

The structure of the introductory programming course is based on the combination of introduction to procedural programming, object-oriented programming, and the graphical user interface (GUI) development.

The procedural programming part lasts five weeks and consists of:

- introduction to Java; variables; input and output;
- conditions; loops; primitive variables;
- string type; nested cycles; syntax and semantic;
- errors and exceptions; indexes and arrays; random numbers; switch structure;
- 2D arrays; streams and files.

The second part is focused on the objects and class type. It lasts four weeks and consists of:

- introduction into the concept of object-oriented programming; classes, methods and parameters;
- setters; constructors; implicit constructor, overloading etc.;
- static variables, static objects manipulation (e.g., counter);
- the definition of inheritance, relationships between objects and classes, superclass; constructor of superclass;
- polymorphism, overriding, application of inheritance and its principles.

The last part of the course is focused on GUI proposal and applications with a simple GUI. This part lasts two weeks and consists of:

- basic components (button, text fields, check and radio buttons);
- components with data models (lists, tables).

The subjects covered programming are educated 6 h per week: 2 h lessons, 2 h for the main exercise, and 2 h for a voluntary programming seminar. The formal study can be complete by individual exercises and/or consultations.

The e-learning course in LMS Moodle fully supports the present form of the study. The educational content is primarily composed of interactive activities that require active student participation. The e-learning lessons usually consist of parts presented in Figure 2:

- ppt presentation—presented on lessons;
- video-lectures and video-exercises—recorded on the lessons divided into more topics or chapters;
- AA activities—contains programming assignments and auto evaluation mechanism;
- microlearning activities implemented as quizzes in the course of 2019/2020;
- forums—placed for some summary chapters.

Two practical tests are required to graduate for the successful completion of the course. The difficulty of the tests is determined to consider the knowledge and programming speed of students. The tasks are designed to be demanding of the best students with the aim to differentiate performance in the group of the best ones. Based on many years of experience and experimentation, the limit for passing the test was set at 40% of points.

The final exam consists of a quiz focused on an understanding of written programs and a few essential questions of programming theory. The students passed quiz successfully proceed to the oral examination consists of debate about random topics of programming lessons.

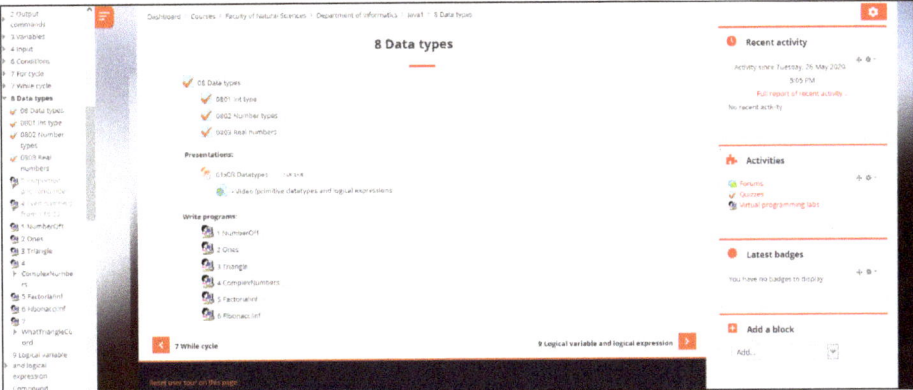

**Figure 2.** The view of the chapter Data types in the English version of the course of 2019/2020. It consists of quizzes, presentation file, link to the video placed on YouTube and automated source code evaluation activities.

The educational material was changed over four years. Students were provided with the following educational materials in the first year of the experiment (2016/2017):

- presentations of lectures; solved assignments (finished source codes); video recordings of selected programs; video lectures.

Interactive elements were represented by:

- every week's quiz focused on the understanding of topics; voluntary bonus tasks (program development); final tests.

The educational materials were extended in the second year of the experiment (2017/2018) by interactive elements represented by automatic assessment with the ability to solve it anytime, anywhere. The part of structural programming was covered.

The interactive content of the courses was enriched in the third year of the experiment (2018/2019) by automatically evaluated assignments were expanded to all lessons of course (more than 170 exercises), and requirements for successful completion of the semester were expanded by the need to obtain at least 50% of the points in these assignments.

Finally, the interactive content was also enriched in the last year of the experiment (2019/2020) by microlearning activities implemented by quiz object (more than 500 microlessons) and requirements for successful completion of the semester were set to obtain at least 80% of the points in these activities. The structure of a typical quiz is presented in Figure 3.

The gradual building of the structure and content of the courses used in the experiment presents Figure 4.

The department of the authors is one of the departments that actively use LMS tools in the present form of study for many years [36]. The student's activity in the course and the use of LMS activities, in general, are easily traceable. Students used e-learning course as a source of educational resources, activities, exercises, and tests. Using an LMS made it possible to monitor their activity, successes and failures, and overall results of a study.

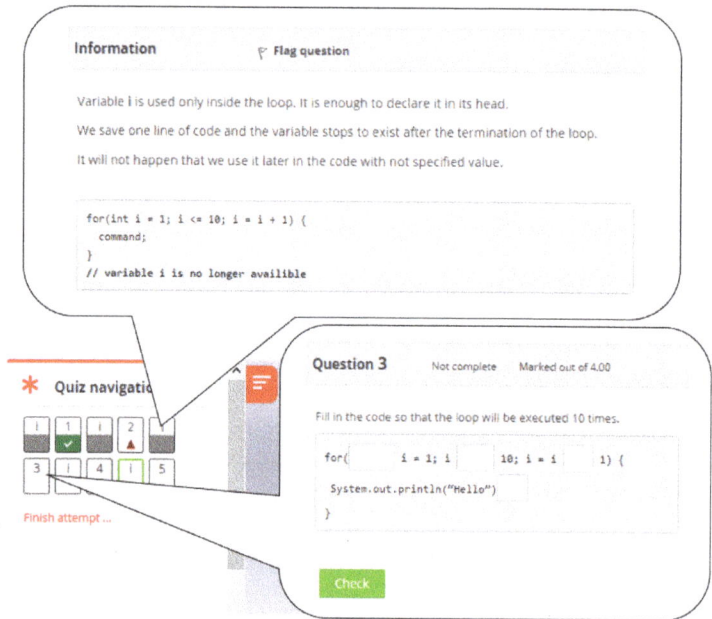

**Figure 3.** View to the microlearning structure and content represented by the quiz. The suitable rotation of content activities and interactive activities is ensured by the sequence of different types of questions in the quiz.

|  | 2016 | 2017 | 2018 | 2019 |
|---|---|---|---|---|
| sources: | presentations<br>video lectures<br>solved programing assignments | presentations<br>video lectures<br>solved programing assignments | presentations<br>video lectures<br>solved programing assignments | presentations<br>video lectures<br>solved programing assignments |
|  |  |  |  | microlessons - content |
| activities: | every-week summarisation quiz | every-week summarisation quiz | every-week summarisation quiz | microlessons - quiz |
|  |  | automated assessment<br>(procedural programming) | automated assessment<br>(procedural programming) | automated assessment<br>(procedural programming) |
|  |  |  | automated assessment<br>(class programming) | automated assessment<br>(class programming) |

**Figure 4.** The process of content building—the changes between inspected years.

Virtual programming Lab for Moodle [21] (VPL) (Figure 5) was selected as the most appropriate tool for source code evaluation. VPL is the system of the third generation of automated assessment with the support of many common programming languages. The validated code is running in a safe sandbox, and VPL is integrated directly into the Moodle as a plugin. Gaining a complete assessment report and history of validated files (what is fundamental in introductory programming courses) are possible using this tool.

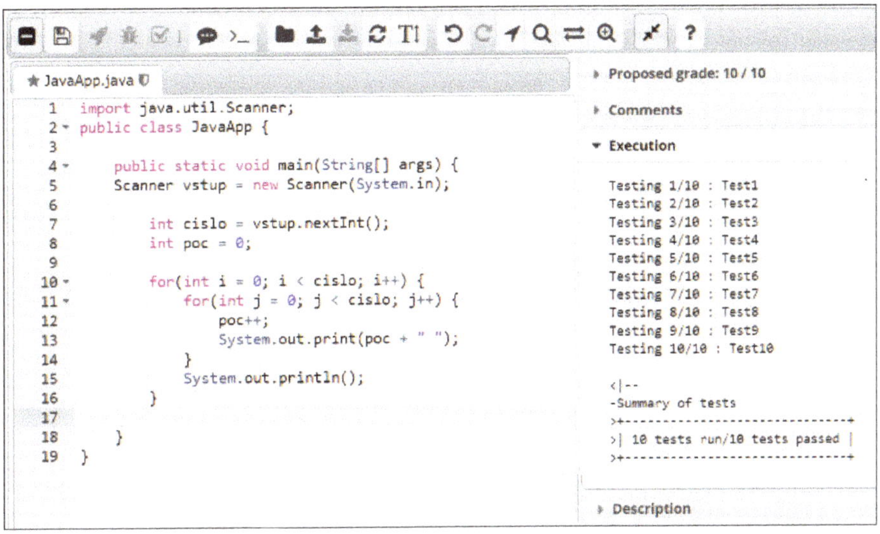

**Figure 5.** Virtual programming lab for Moodle [21].

*3.2. The Goals*

The goals of the research are divided into three consecutive parts focused on the application of the interactive activities of students.

- The identification and estimation of the impact of selected interactive activities in the LMS environment on the final test results. The significance of the automatic evaluation of programs and using microlearning activities are separately investigated.
- The relationship between the achieved results expressed by the obtained points from the tests and the interim results of the writing programs and solving microlearning activities will be identified.
- The possibility of identifying problem students since their activities within interactive activities, or the possibility of estimating their marks on the basis of their results in these activities will be presented.

*3.3. Research Questions*

In accordance with changes in content structure, the research questions are based on a comparison of educational outcomes measured through the tests. The content inspection will be divided into two parts: introductory to programming (structural part) and classes (object-oriented part). The hypotheses inspect approaches to minimise dropout.

**Hypothesis 1 (H1).** *The use of LMS objects for the automatic evaluation of source codes improves students' results in the area of introduction to programming.*

A comparison of 2016 and 2017 groups will be used to verify this hypothesis. In 2017, the LMS object "virtual programming lab" was used for the first time and its scope covered parts of the Java language aimed at explaining the basic control and data structures. This hypothesis should verify the importance of using automatic programs evaluation for students beginning programming.

**Hypothesis 2 (H2).** *The use of LMS objects for the automatic evaluation of source codes improves students' results in object-oriented programming.*

A comparison of groups 2017 and 2018 will be used to verify this hypothesis. In 2018 has been programming course extended by parts covered object-oriented chapters. The number of LMS virtual programming labs increased to 170, which represents a burden on students with 15–20 assignments per week. The hypothesis should verify the contribution of VPL to teaching advanced programming topics.

Following the division of the course into two parts, other hypotheses will be examined to verify the effectiveness of microlearning.

**Hypothesis 3 (H3).** *The use of microlearning principles improves students' results in the area of introduction to programming.*

**Hypothesis 4 (H4).** *The use of microlearning principles improves students' results in object-oriented programming.*

In order to find elements that allow predicting the risk of unsuccessful completion of the course, the existence of dependence between the success of students in individual activities and the overall success of the course will be identified. The following dependencies will be inspected:

- the relationship between the results of entrance exams (points of secondary level of study) and the result of the course,
- the relationship between course activity and course achievement, and
- the relationship between the results in the VPL and microlearning activities and the result in the course.

### 3.4. Characteristics of the Respondents

Comprehensive research has been carried out on a sample of 51–102 students per year. The structure of the student's groups attending the introductory programming courses is rather diverse because of different skills reached in secondary schools, various experience with programming, and different level of computational thinking. It is very complicated to define homogenous groups with optimal size and start teaching on the different entrance level. The students with excellent programming skills as well as students who have never made any program have the same starting position.

The students who participated in the experiment were divided into four groups. Every group consists of computer science first-year students at the age of 18–24. Only students who have studied the subject for the first time are in the groups. Students who repeat the study of programming were excluded from the research.

The entrance results of student groups were obtained from university applications and reflected the grades acquired in high-school study and secondary school competitions. These results are rated on a scale 0–40. The statistical characteristics of the entrance results are presented in Figure 6. A year-on-year decline in students' initial scoring can be seen at first glance. This situation may be partly due to demography and partly to an increase in the number of first-year students.

### 3.5. Measurement Tools

The main tools used for research were:

- the list of admitted students with the number of points awarded in the admission process used primarily in pretest;
- the test results of students in two tests realised after introductory course part and object-oriented course part used for evaluation of used objects and method;
- LMS Moodle log used for the assessment of the activities of the students and dependency identification; the parts of the log were processed to use for relevant calculation.

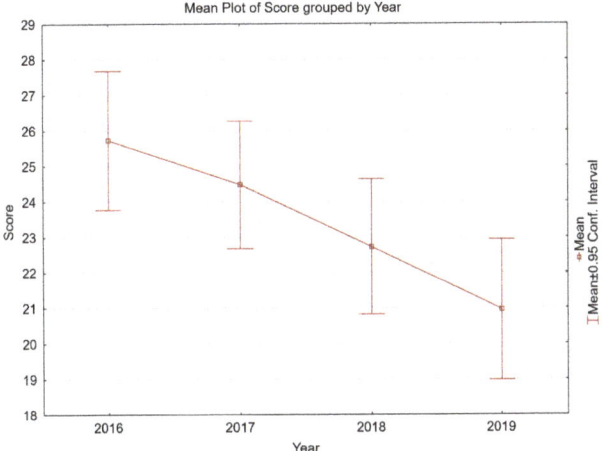

**Figure 6.** Graphical visualisation of statistical characteristics of groups (points awarded in the admission procedure).

## 4. Results

The differences between the results of students' groups for four years were inspected in the following research. The groups learnt via different educational sources, which are described in part as the educational content.

*4.1. Pretest*

The first step before the research is proof that student's groups were well-modelled by a normal distribution according to the level of their performance at the high school. These values are reflected by the score obtained in the admission procedure. Simultaneously, these values do not depend on the previous students' experience in programming and thus do not distort the prerequisites for mastering the course. The range of awarded points was between 0 and 40.

The Kolmogorov–Smirnov test was used to prove that the distributions of groups match the characteristics of a normal distribution. All the essential characteristics are listed in Table 2.

**Table 2.** Proof of normal distribution.

| Group | Count | Mean | Median | Std. Dev. | D (Val. of K-S Test) | $p$-Value |
|---|---|---|---|---|---|---|
| 2016 | 51 | 25.73 | 26 | 6.96 | 0.10 | 0.59 |
| 2017 | 70 | 24.47 | 24 | 7.52 | 0.10 | 0.45 |
| 2018 | 82 | 22.72 | 23 | 8.68 | 0.09 | 0.55 |
| 2019 | 102 | 20.95 | 21.5 | 10.07 | 0.08 | 0.50 |

The data in every group of students do not differ significantly from a normal distribution. The $p$-values prove normal distributions at the 5% significance level. All groups were well-modelled by a normal distribution. Characteristics of the groups were visualised in Figure 6.

Levene's test to assess the variance of two groups was used in the next step. The null hypothesis that two normal populations have the same variance was used to verify the equality of variance for all the pairs of groups. The requirement of homogeneity is met when the result is not significant. The results are presented in Table 3.

The hypothesis about the equality of variance at the 5% significance level was rejected in pairs 2016–2019 and 2017–2019. The equality of variance in other cases is not significantly different. Therefore, it is possible to accept the assumption that the results of the group can be compared.

**Table 3.** The proof of the equality of variance.

|           | Valid N1 | Valid N2 | Std.Dev.1 | Std.Dev.2 | F-Statistic | *p*-Value |                          |
|-----------|----------|----------|-----------|-----------|-------------|-----------|--------------------------|
| 2016–2017 | 51       | 70       | 6.96      | 7.52      | 0.78        | 0.997     |                          |
| 2016–2018 | 51       | 82       | 6.96      | 8.68      | 0.82        | 0.084     |                          |
| 2016–2019 | 51       | 102      | 6.96      | 10.07     | 0.87        | **0.001** | significantly different  |
| 2017–2018 | 70       | 82       | 7.52      | 8.68      | 0.87        | 0.078     |                          |
| 2017–2019 | 70       | 102      | 7.52      | 10.07     | 0.90        | **0.001** | significantly different  |
| 2018–2019 | 82       | 102      | 8.68      | 10.07     | 0.92        | 0.081     |                          |

Normal distribution and homogeneity of variances give assumptions for the analysis of variance (ANOVA test) used for investigating whether the population means of the groups are equal., it is necessary to compare the means of the following pairs to validate hypotheses H1–H4:

- 2016–2017 (H1)—to research the benefit of VPL activities in introductory programming parts,
- 2017–2018 (H2)—to evaluate the benefit of VPL activities in object–oriented programming parts,
- 2018–2019 (H3, H4) – to inspect the benefit of microlearning activities in both (introductory and object-oriented programming) parts.

The descriptive statistic and results are presented in Table 4.

**Table 4.** The proof of the equality of mean.

| Groups    | Valid N1 | Valid N2 | F-Statistic | *p*-Value | Result                      |
|-----------|----------|----------|-------------|-----------|-----------------------------|
| 2016–2017 | 51       | 70       | 0.87        | 0.35      | not significantly different |
| 2017–2018 | 70       | 82       | 1.74        | 0.19      | not significantly different |
| 2018–2019 | 82       | 102      | 1.58        | 0.21      | not significantly different |

The *p*-value corresponding to the F-statistic is higher than 0.05, which means that the results are not significantly different at the 5% significance level. The result identifies comparable characteristics in all monitored pairs at the level of significance of 5%.

As a result, the research intention can be realised, because the differences between the educational outcomes in groups of students can be compared.

*4.2. Post-Tests*

The following hypotheses require a comparison of students' results measured by tests. The tests consist of four or five assignments to write programs. The tasks are only practical and measure the student's ability to write and debug the program. The assignments cover the entire content of the relevant part of the course.

The automatic evaluation of source code is used in the first step of evaluation, followed by the evaluation realised by a human evaluator. Source code of every program is checked and also evaluated by the teacher. If the evaluation is realised by more than one teacher, the rule that one task is checked only by one teacher is followed to ensure the same conditions for all students' solutions.

4.2.1. H1—Using VPL Improves Student Performance in Introductory Chapters of Programming

The assumptions of normal distribution and homogeneity of variances are met. The results of the Kolmogorov–Smirnov test and Levene's test are presented in Table 5.

The data in groups do not differ significantly from a normal distribution. The *p*-values prove normal distributions at the 5% significance level and the groups were well-modelled by a normal distribution. The results of the Levene's test is not significant. It means that the variances of groups are not significantly different.

The ANOVA test was used to compare the results of the student tests. The test compares the means of groups at the 5% significance level. The null hypothesis in ANOVA assumes that there is not a significant difference in means. The alternative hypothesis captures any difference in means. The results are summarised in Table 6.

Table 5. Assumptions of normal distribution and homogeneity of variances.

| The Results of the Kolmogorov-Smirnov Test of Normality | | | | | | |
|---|---|---|---|---|---|---|
| Group | Count | Mean | Median | Std. Dev. | D (Val. of K-S Test) | $p$-Value |
| 2016 | 51 | 235.97 | 227.80 | 153.29 | 0.10 | 0.60 |
| 2017 | 70 | 317.12 | 366.65 | 157.82 | 0.15 | 0.09 |
| The Results of the Levene's Test of Homogeneity of Variance | | | | | | |
| | Valid N1 | Valid N2 | Std.Dev.1 | Std.Dev.2 | F-Statistic | $p$-Value |
| 2016–2017 | 51 | 70 | 6.96 | 7.52 | 0.02 | 0.90 |

Table 6. Assumptions of normal distribution and homogeneity of variances.

| | DF | Sum of Square | Mean Square | F-Statistic | $p$-Value |
|---|---|---|---|---|---|
| Groups (between groups) | 1 | 194,258.95 | 194,258.95 | 7.99 | 0.0055 |
| Error (within groups) | 119 | 2,893,546.19 | 24,315.51 | | |
| Total | 120 | 3,087,805.14 | 25,731.71 | | |

Since $p$-value $< \alpha$, $H_0$ is rejected, the difference between the means of groups can be considered large enough to be statistically significant. While $p$-value equals 0.00552176, [p (x ≤ F) = 0.994478], the chance of type1 error (rejecting a correct $H_0$) is small: 0.005522 (0.55%).

The hypothesis H1 was not rejected, and thus the use of automated evaluation of the students' programs in the introductory programming courses brought significant differences in student outcomes.

4.2.2. H2—Using VPL Improves Student Performance in Advanced Chapters of Programming

The same procedure was applied for testing hypothesis H2. The results of the final test realised at the end of the semester are used. The results of the Kolmogorov–Smirnov test and Levene's test are presented in Table 7.

Table 7. Assumptions of normal distribution and homogeneity of variances.

| The Results of the Kolmogorov-Smirnov Test of Normality | | | | | | |
|---|---|---|---|---|---|---|
| Group | Count | Mean | Median | Std. Dev. | D (Val. of K-S Test) | $p$-Value |
| 2017 | 70 | 228.39 | 225 | 143.17 | 0.083 | 0.68 |
| 2018 | 82 | 231.34 | 250 | 158.88 | 0.099 | 0.37 |
| The Results of the Levene's Test of Homogeneity of Variance | | | | | | |
| | Valid N1 | Valid N2 | Std.Dev.1 | Std.Dev.2 | F-Statistic | $p$-Value |
| 2016–2017 | 70 | 82 | 79.69 | 77.30 | 2.42 | 0.12 |

The data in the observed groups, as well as the variances of groups, are not significantly different from a normal distribution.

Again, the ANOVA test at the 5% significance level was used to compare student test results. The null hypothesis assumes that there is not any significant difference in means. The results are summarised in Table 8.

Since $p$-value $> \alpha$, $H_0$ is accepted. The difference between the means of groups is not large enough to be considered statistically significant. The $p$-value equals 0.905179, [p(x ≤ F) = 0.0948215]. This means that, if $H_0$ were rejected, the chance of type1 error (rejecting a correct $H_0$) would be too high: 0.9052 (90.52%).

Table 8. Assumptions of normal distribution and homogeneity of variances.

|  | DF | Sum of Square | Mean Square | F-Statistic | p-Value |
|---|---|---|---|---|---|
| Groups (between groups) | 1 | 328.32 | 328.32 | 0.014 | 0.91 |
| Error (within groups) | 150 | 3,458,909.89 | 23,059.40 | | |
| Total | 151 | 3,459,238.21 | 22,908.86 | | |

It follows that the hypothesis H2 cannot be accepted. In other words, the use of automated assessment object in the advanced topics of introductory programming course does not cause significant differences in student's outcomes.

4.2.3. H3—The Use of Microlearning Improves Student Performance in Introductory Chapters of Programming

The compared groups are groups of students from 2018 and 2019 year. The results of the test realised in half of the semester are used. The test score distribution of the test is demonstrated in Figure 7.

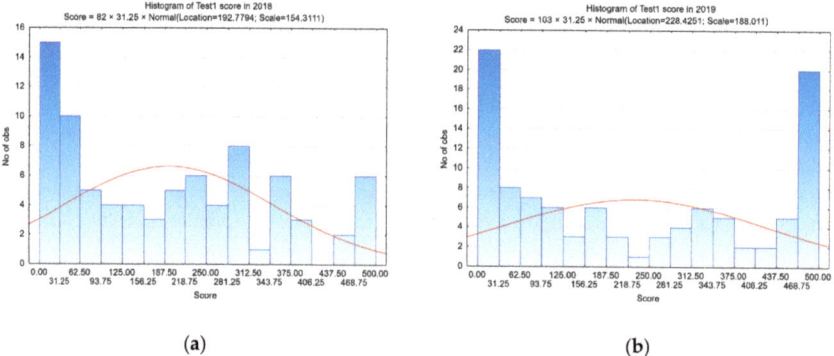

(a)                                      (b)

Figure 7. Histogram of test score distribution in monitored groups: (a) Test score in the group trained without microlearning in 2018; (b) Test score in the group of students taught with microlearning in 2019.

The results of the Kolmogorov-Smirnov test are presented in Table 9.

Table 9. The results of the Kolmogorov-Smirnov test of normality for test results in group 2018 and group 2019.

| Group | Count | Mean | Median | Std. Dev. | D (Val. of K-S Test) | p-Value |
|---|---|---|---|---|---|---|
| 2018 | 82 | 192.78 | 187.61 | 154.31 | 0.13 | 0.130 |
| 2019 | 103 | 228.43 | 177.78 | 188.01 | 0.13 | 0.048 |

The data in 2018 group does not significantly differ from a normal distribution, but the distribution of the test results in the 2019 group is significantly different from a normal distribution. Therefore, a non-parametric Mann–Whitney U-test should be used to investigate if the results are significantly different.

The null hypothesis assumes that the means are not significantly different. The distribution of values is approximately normal. Therefore, the z-score should be used. The values of the test are presented in Table 10.

The U-value is 3820.5, the Z-Score is 1.11105, and the p-value is 0.1335. The result is not significant at $p < 0.05$. Since p-value > $\alpha$, the hypothesis is accepted, the difference between the averages of all groups is not large enough to be statistically significant.

Table 10. Mann-Whitney U-test results.

|  | 2018 | 2019 | Combined |
|---|---|---|---|
| Sum of ranks | 7223.5 | 9981.5 | 17,205 |
| Mean of ranks | 88.09 | 96.91 | 93 |
| Expected sum of ranks | 7626 | 9579 |  |
| Expected mean of ranks | 93 | 93 |  |
| $U$-value | 4625.5 | **3820.5** |  |
| Expected $U$-value | 4223 | 4223 |  |
| Standard Deviation |  |  | 361.82 |

Therefore, the hypothesis H3 cannot be accepted, and it means the implementation of the microlearning activities in the introductory topics of programming courses does not lead to the significant differences in student outcomes.

4.2.4. H4—The Use of Microlearning Improves Student Performance in Advanced Chapters of Programming

The last hypothesis H4 compared groups of students between 2018 and 2019. The results of the final test written at the end of the semester are used. The examined sample does not include students who failed the study of the course during the semester and did not attend the second test.

The graphical presentation of test score distribution is demonstrated in Figure 8.

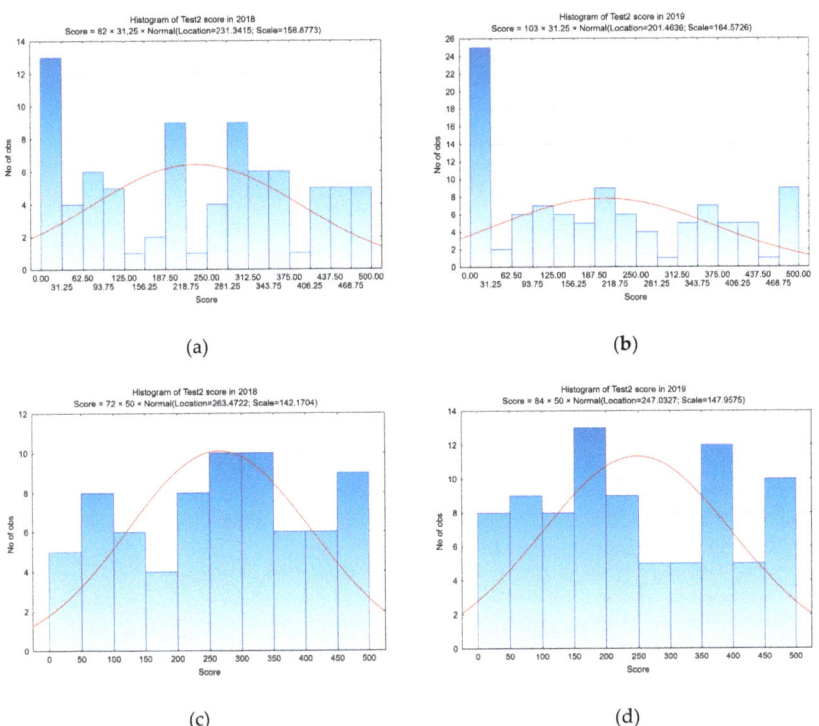

Figure 8. Histogram of test score distribution in monitored groups: (a) Test score in the group trained without microlearning in 2018; (b) Test score in the group taught with microlearning in 2019; (c) Test score in the group trained without microlearning in 2018 without students who failed during the semester; (d) Test score in the group trained with microlearning in 2019 without students who failed during the semester. The red curve represents the outline of the normal distribution of values.

The results of the Kolmogorov–Smirnov test in examined samples are presented in Table 11.

Table 11. Assumptions of normal distribution and homogeneity of variances.

| The Results of the Kolmogorov-Smirnov Test of Normality for Results | | | | | | |
|---|---|---|---|---|---|---|
| Group | Count | Mean | Median | Std. Dev. | D (Val. of K-S Test) | p-Value |
| 2018 | 72 | 263.47 | 292.50 | 142.17 | 0.088 | 0.596 |
| 2019 | 84 | 247.03 | 220.50 | 147.96 | 0.100 | 0.345 |
| The Results of the Levene's Test of Homogeneity of Variance | | | | | | |
| | Valid N1 | Valid N2 | Std.Dev.1 | Std.Dev.2 | F-Statistic | p-Value |
| 2018–2019 | 72 | 84 | 74.28 | 74.43 | 0.32 | 0.57 |

The data in groups is not significantly different from a normal distribution. Their variances do not significantly differ too.

The ANOVA test was used to compare student test results at the 5% significance level. The results are shown in Table 12.

Table 12. Assumptions of normal distribution and homogeneity of variances.

| | DF | Sum of Square | Mean Square | F-Statistic | p-Value |
|---|---|---|---|---|---|
| Groups (between groups) | 1 | 10,477.64 | 10,477.64 | 0.50 | 0.48 |
| Error (within groups) | 154 | 3,252,069.67 | 21,117.34 | | |
| Total | 155 | 3,262,547.30 | 21,048.69 | | |

Since $p$-value > $\alpha$, $H_0$ is accepted. Consequently, the difference between the means of the groups is not considered large enough to be statistically significant. $p$-value equals 0.482255, [p(x ≤ F) = 0.517745]. This means that if $H_0$ were rejected, the chance of type1 error (rejecting a correct $H_0$) would be too high: 0.4823 (48.23%).

Therefore, the hypothesis H4 cannot be accepted. Therefore, the use of microlearning in the advanced chapters of programming course has no significant impact on student's outcomes.

4.2.5. Dependencies Inspection

A revealing of the dependence between individual variables is relatively simple in some cases. However, in others, the expected influence of variables is not proven. Based on simple reasoning, it could be assumed that students who have demonstrated a lower initial assessment in the admission process will have more significant problems in their studies.

The inspection of the relation between the results of entrance exams (points of secondary level of study) and the result of the course showed a low correlation. The results are based on Pearson correlation coefficient, which is used to measure the strength of a linear association between two variables. The results are summarised in Table 13.

Table 13. Pearson correlation coefficient between results of entrance admission process and grades of tests in individual experimental groups.

| Group | Structural Programming Test | | Object-Oriented Programming Test | |
|---|---|---|---|---|
| 2016 | −0.093 | weak | 0.339 | weak |
| 2017 | 0.074 | weak | 0.231 | weak |
| 2018 | 0.362 | weak | 0.379 | weak |
| 2019 | 0.274 | weak | 0.296 | weak |

The dependences between inspected variables in groups are weak. However, it is possible to observe that the dependency between the entrance process values and results of the second test is a little bit stronger. The reason is that some of the students dropped out, while they were students with lower input rating (differences are statistically undetectable).

The LMS allows monitoring of students' activity within the study period by logging the operations performed by the students in the virtual environment (Figure 9).

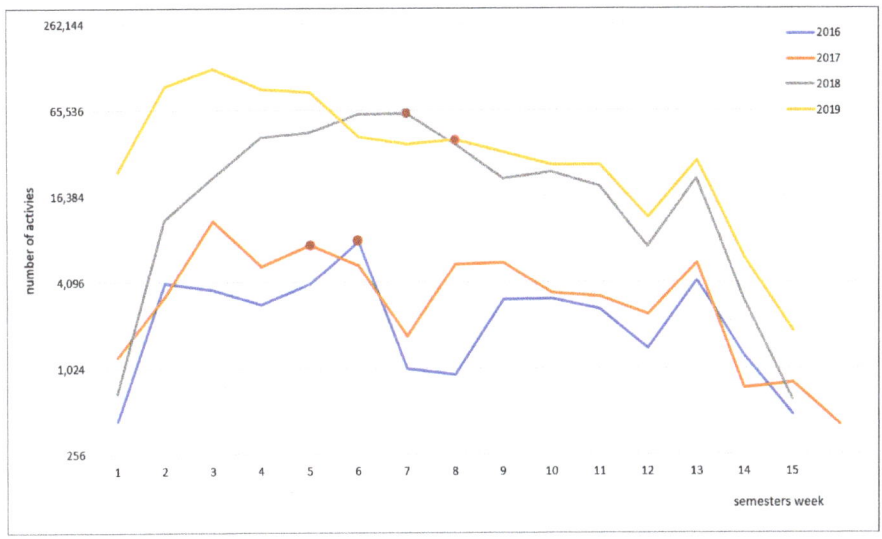

**Figure 9.** The student's activity expressed by the number of interactions performed in the course in the course during the semester - the x-axis shows the weeks of the semester (from the 1st week to the last (14th or 15th) week of the semester). The y-axis represents number of student's activities on a logarithmic scale. The red dots indicate the date of the first test. The last test was realised in the 13th week.

Considering the log visualisation (Figure 9), the students' activity is very similar over the course of all four years. The most significant increase in activity can be observed before the first test. The activity declines subsequently and never reaches the value it had before the first test. The time before the final test also causes the growth of the students' activities, but these activities are not in that quantity as before the first test.

A subjective explanation of this phenomenon is based on communication and feedback with the students using anonymous questionnaires and interviews. The students said that they were afraid of the unknown before the first test, and they studied as much as possible. Later, before the second test, they were with less stress due to the known requirements for the expected skills and practices. Although the students' activity has increased significantly due to the use of VPL in the third and fourth observed year, the curve copies the previous ones.

Therefore, it is useful to visualise the scope of VPL and microlearning activities in 2018 and 2019 to obtain a complete picture of the interactive activities (Figure 10).

The graphs in Figures 9 and 10 confirm that interactive activities represent a significant part of users' activity, and thus represent a suitable tool for identifying the study behaviour of the students.

This statement about the significance of these activities in the educational process is also supported by the identification of dependencies between students' test results and VPL and quiz results presented in Table 14. The dependence between activity in the course and final evaluation has not been proven.

The Pearson correlation coefficient expresses moderate to strong dependence between final students' achievements and results achieved solving interactive activities in courses. It can be argued that the overall success of the students depends on the ongoing results in individual interactive activities, while early warning must be based on the ongoing results in these activities. The influence of the user's activity in the course on his or her success is inconclusive.

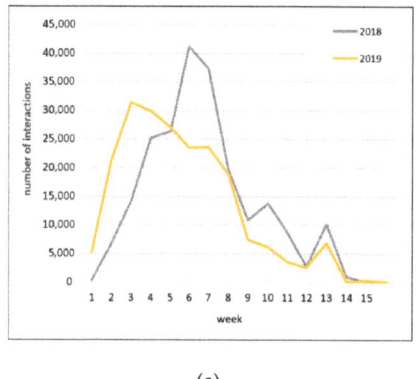
(a)

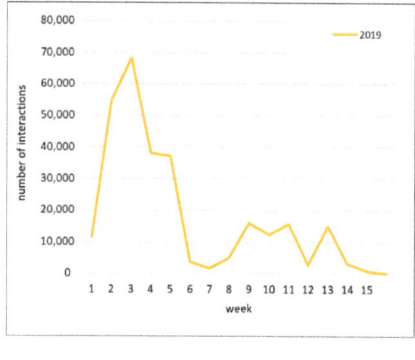
(b)

**Figure 10.** The interactive activities in courses 2018 and 2019 during the weeks of the semester: (**a**) automated source code evaluation activities; (**b**) microlearning activities.

**Table 14.** Pearson correlation coefficient between the test results and interactive student activities results.

| Group | Test 1—VPL1 | Test2—VPL2 | Sum of Tests—Microlearning |
|---|---|---|---|
| 2018 | 0.512 | 0.721 | - |
| 2019 | 0.563 | 0.683 | 0.577 |

## 5. Discussion and Conclusions

Based on the verification of the established hypotheses on the sample of more than 300 students in total, it can be specified that the use of additional interactive concepts in introductory programming courses brings the following benefits:

**Hypothesis 1 (H1).** *The use of LMS objects for the automatic evaluation of source codes improves students' results in the area of introduction to programming.*

The hypothesis was not rejected. The use of automatic evaluation of programs in the introductory chapters of programming courses brought significant differences in student outcomes. These introductory chapters cover essential topics as input/output, variables, data types, nested loops, arrays, exceptions, files, etc. and they are often the reason for students' loss of interest in programming because of a misunderstanding of its principles, problems with memorisation, or loss of the motivation [37,38].

Successful completion of this part of the introductory course is usually a prerequisite for mastering the second part of the course of the programming course, which is oriented to object-oriented programming. It is often (but not always) the case that students who fail the introductory part do not continue their studies. These students repeat the course a year or more often.

The finding that the use of VPL is significant brings these students an increased chance of successful completion of the course. The result is in accordance with the results presented in [21,23,39]. At the same time, it should be noted that applying automated assessment is not a solution itself. The quality of the automated assessment is also essential.

**Hypothesis 2 (H2).** *The use of LMS objects for the automatic evaluation of source codes improves students' results in object-oriented programming.*

The hypothesis cannot be accepted, and the use of automated assessment object in the advanced chapters of introductory programming course does not lead to the significant differences in student's outcomes. The reason for this statement is mainly the fact that this part of the introductory programming course is completed by students who have completed the first part successfully after the most significant dropout occurs. Students who have completed the first part of the course probably have enough motivation to master programming. Their skills have shifted to a matching level to understand the concepts and principles of programming and, in essence, the concept of object-oriented programming. The groups of students in both monitored years have stabilised at approximately the same level of knowledge. As a result, they do not differ significantly between the years.

**Hypothesis 3 (H3).** *The use of microlearning principles improves students' results in the area of introduction to programming.*

The hypothesis cannot be accepted. The use of microlearning activities in the introductory chapters of programming courses does not imply significant differences in student outcomes. Although microlearning in its modern form represents a new approach in university education and can produce better results than traditional methods in various areas, it did not ensure a significant change in the level of knowledge of the experimental group of students [40,41]. The reasons for this can be as follows:

- microlearning was applied in combination with the automatically evaluated assignments and its addition was minimised or overlapped,
- many of the different sources and the obligation to develop microlearning lessons caused overload for weaker students and caused them to resign.

The results of the questionnaire survey presented below support the first claim. The histogram shown in Figure 7b presents the group division into students with excellent and students with weak (resp. zero) results, while the number of students with average results was minimised. The reasons for and real effects of microlearning on the obtained level of knowledge or the dropout rate of the students should be the subject of further research.

**Hypothesis 4 (H4).** *The use of microlearning principles improves students' results in object-oriented programming.*

The hypothesis cannot be again accepted. The use of microlearning in the advanced chapters of introductory programming course does not cause significant differences in students' outcomes. The reasons are similar to the reasons mentioned in a discussion about the hypothesis H2.

The dependencies between the achieved VPL score and the final test score, as well as the dependencies between the microlearning activities and the final score, were identified in a section focused on the verification of the dependencies between the success of students in the inspected activities and the results in the course. The dependencies are identified from the moderate to strong level and place these LMS activities into the position of a tool with the assumptions to identify the risk of dropout.

The 2019 group responded to the questionnaire survey conducted after the end of the semester, and the results collected also correspond to the research findings. Thereby, students evaluated the subjective contribution of the monitored activities to their learning.

The main facts are summarised in Table 15. The students expressed their opinions using a seven-point Likert scale questionnaire.

The questionnaire shows that both types of activities are received positively by more than 70% of users. Activities are identified as resources that play a significant role in building skills and knowledge. Activities with automated code evaluation are accepted more positively. The students identified the main benefits as immediate control and feedback on the submitted program, learning from one's own mistakes, practical learning, and possibility to repeat solutions in the case of error.

Table 15. Subjective perception of VPL and microlearning activities by students.

| Group | 7 | 6 | 5 | 4 | 3 | 2 | 1 |
|---|---|---|---|---|---|---|---|
| VPL assignments helped me understand the curriculum | 42.31 | 11.54 | 15.38 | 17.31 | 1.92 | 5.77 | 5.77 |
| VPL assignments helped me practice the curriculum | 51.92 | 11.54 | 13.46 | 13.46 | 1.92 | 0.00 | 7.69 |
| microlearning assignments helped me understand the curriculum | 34.62 | 21.15 | 25.00 | 11.54 | 3.85 | 1.92 | 1.92 |
| microlearning assignments helped me practice the curriculum | 34.62 | 25.00 | 25.00 | 7.69 | 3.85 | 1.92 | 1.92 |
| microlearning was used as a main way of learning | 34.62 | 25.00 | 13.46 | 15.38 | 1.92 | 7.69 | 1.92 |

The benefits of microlearning activities were most often mentioned: a better understanding of the content, preparation for the following lessons, quick acquisition of information, brief content of the lesson, possibility of practice. Moreover, students would expect similar use of both types of objects in other programming courses.

The research result aimed at verifying the effectiveness of interactive activities for successful completion of the course is the confirmation of a significant benefit of the implementation of automatically evaluated programs into the introductory programming courses. At the same time, it was found that this benefit is not significant in advanced programming topics. The advantage of the educational content transformation into the microlearning form did not bring a significant improvement in the students' results despite the positive perception of this activity by the students.

Even though the significant contribution of interactive elements was confirmed only in the case of automatically evaluated programs in the first half of the course, the dependence between the overall results of students and the results in the activities was proven. Further research will focus on the identification of students at risk of a dropout based on their behaviour during the solving of the mentioned activities.

**Author Contributions:** Conceptualisation, J.S. and M.D.; methodology, J.S. and M.D.; investigation, J.S. and M.D.; resources, J.S. and M.D.; data curation, J.S. and M.D.; writing—original draft preparation, J.S. and M.D.; writing—review and editing, J.S. and M.D.; funding acquisition, J.S. and M.D. All authors have read and agreed to the published version of the manuscript.

**Funding:** This research was funded by European Commission under the ERASMUS+ Programme 2018, KA2, grant number: 2018-1-SK01-KA203-046382 "Work-Based Learning in Future IT Professionals Education" and the Cultural and educational agency of the Ministry of Education of the Slovak Republic, grant number: KEGA 029UKF-4/2018 "Innovative Methods in Programming Education in the University Education of Teachers and IT Professionals."

**Conflicts of Interest:** The authors declare no conflict of interest.

## References

1. Malik, S.I. Improvements in Introductory Programming Course: Action Research Insights and Outcomes. *Syst. Pract. Action Res.* **2018**, *31*, 637–656. [CrossRef]
2. Mason, R.; Cooper, G.; Raadt, M. Trends in introductory programming courses in Australian Universities-Languages, environments and pedagogy. In Proceedings of the Fourteenth Australasian Computing Education Conference (ACE2012), Melbourne, Australia, 31 January–3 February 2012; Volume 123, pp. 33–42.
3. Chango, W.; Cerezo, R.; Romero, C. Predicting academic performance of university students from multi-sources data in blended learning. In Proceedings of the Second International Conference on Data Science, E-Learning and Information Systems, Tromsø, Norway, 2–5 December 2019. [CrossRef]
4. Luxton-Reilly, A.; Albluwi, I.; Becker, B.A.; Giannakos, M.; Kumar, A.; Ott, L.M.; Paterson, J.; Adrir Scott, M.; Sheard, J.; Szabo, C. Introductory programming: A systematic literature review. In Proceedings of the ITiCSE '18 Companion, Larnaca, Cypru, 2–4 July 2018.
5. Becker, B.A.; Quille, K. 50 years of CS1 at SIGCSE: A review of the evolution of introductory programming education research. In Proceedings of the SIGCSE 2019-Proceedings 50th ACM Technical Symposium Computer Science Education, Minneapolis, MN, USA, 27 February–2 March 2019; Volume 1, pp. 338–344. [CrossRef]

6. Tabanao, E.S.; Rodrigo, M.M.T.; Jadud, M.C. Predicting at-risk novice Java programmers through the analysis of online protocols. In Proceedings of the Seventh International Workshop on Computing Education Research, ICER 2011, Providence, RI, USA, 8–9 August 2011. [CrossRef]
7. Kinnunen, P.; Malmi, L. Why Students Drop out CS1 Course? In Proceedings of the Second International Workshop on Computing Education Research, New York, NY, USA, 10–12 September 2006; pp. 97–108. [CrossRef]
8. Bergin, S.; Reilly, R. Programming: Factors That Influence Success. In Proceedings of the 36th SIGCSE Technical Symposium on Computer Science Education, St. Louis, MO, USA, 23–27 February 2005; pp. 411–415. [CrossRef]
9. Hellas, A.; Nam Liao, S.; Ihantola, P.; Petersen, A.; Ajanovski, V.V.; Gutica, M.; Hynninen, T.; Knutas, A.; Leinonen, J.; Messom, C. Predicting academic performance: A systematic literature review. In Proceedings of the 23rd Annual ACM Conference on Innovation and Technology in Computer Science Education, ITiCSE, Larnaca, Cyprus, 2–4 July 2018; pp. 175–199. [CrossRef]
10. Hu, X.; Cheong, C.W.L.; Ding, W.; Woo, M. A Systematic Review of Studies on Predicting Student Learning Outcomes Using Learning Analytics. In Proceedings of the Seventh International Learning Analytics & Knowledge Conference, New York, NY, USA, 13–17 March 2017; pp. 528–529. [CrossRef]
11. Duran, R.; Rybicki, J.M.; Hellas, A.; Suoranta, S. Towards a common instrument for measuring prior programming knowledge. In Proceedings of the 2019 ACM Conference on International Computing Education Research Conference, ITiCSE, London, UK, 11–15 November 2019; pp. 443–449. [CrossRef]
12. Costa, E.B.; Fonseca, B.; Santana, M.A.; de Araújo, F.F.; Rego, J. Evaluating the effectiveness of educational data mining techniques for early prediction of students' academic failure in introductory programming courses. *Comput. Hum. Behav.* **2017**, *73*, 247–256. [CrossRef]
13. Galan, D.; Heradio, R.; Vargas, H.; Abad, I.; Cerrada, J.A. Automated Assessment of Computer Programming Practices: The 8-Years UNED Experience. *IEEE Access* **2019**, *7*, 130113–130119. [CrossRef]
14. Luchoomun, T.; Chumroo, M.; Ramnarain-Seetohul, V. A Knowledge Based System for Automated Assessment of Short Structured Questions. In Proceedings of the 2019 IEEE Global Engineering Education Conference (EDUCON), Dubai, UAE, 8–11 April 2019; pp. 1349–1352. [CrossRef]
15. Skalka, J.; Drlík, M.; Obonya, J. Automated Assessment in Learning and Teaching Programming Languages using Virtual Learning Environment. In Proceedings of the 2019 IEEE Global Engineering Education Conference (EDUCON), Dubai, UAE, 8–11 April 2019; pp. 689–697. [CrossRef]
16. Rodriguez-del-Pino, J. A Virtual Programming Lab for Moodle with automatic assessment and anti-plagiarism features. In Proceedings of the International Conference on e-Learning, e-Business, Enterprise Information Systems, & e-Government, Las Vegas, NV, USA, 16–19 July 2012.
17. Salleh, S.M.; Shukur, Z.; Judi, H.M. Analysis of Research in Programming Teaching Tools: An Initial Review. *Procedia Soc. Behav. Sci.* **2013**, *103*, 127–135. [CrossRef]
18. Keuning, H.; Jeuring, J.; Heeren, B. A Systematic Literature Review of Automated Feedback Generation for Programming Exercises. *ACM Trans. Comput. Educ.* **2018**, *19*, 1–43. [CrossRef]
19. Akahane, Y.; Kitaya, H.; Inoue, U. Design and evaluation of automated scoring Java programming assignments. In Proceedings of the 2015 IEEE/ACIS 16th International Conference on Software Engineering, Artificial Intelligence, Networking and Parallel/Distributed Computing (SNPD), Takamatsu, Japan, 1–3 June 2015; pp. 1–6. [CrossRef]
20. Figueiredo, J.; García-Peñalvo, F.J. Building skills in introductory programming. *ACM Int. Conf. Proc. Ser.* **2018**, 46–50. [CrossRef]
21. Pieterse, V. Automated Assessment of Programming Assignments. In Proceedings of the 3rd Computer Science Education Research Conference on Computer Science Education Research, Arnhem, The Netherlands, 4–5 April 2013; pp. 45–56.
22. Wilcox, C. The Role of Automation in Undergraduate Computer Science Education. In Proceedings of the 46th ACM Technical Symposium on Computer Science Education, Kansas City, MO, USA, 4–7 March 2015; pp. 90–95. [CrossRef]
23. Rubio-Sánchez, M.; Kinnunen, P.; Pareja-Flores, C.; Velázquez-Iturbide, Á. Student Perception and Usage of an Automated Programming Assessment Tool. *Comput. Hum. Behav.* **2014**, *31*, 453–460. [CrossRef]
24. Skalka, J.; Drlík, M. *Conceptual Framework of Microlearning-Based Training Mobile Application for Improving Programming Skills*; Springer: Cham, Switzerland, 2018.

25. Göschlberger, B.; Bruck, P.A. Gamification in Mobile and Workplace Integrated Microlearning. In Proceedings of the 19th International Conference on Information Integration and Web-Based Applications & Services, Salzburg, Austria, 4–6 December 2017; pp. 545–552. [CrossRef]
26. Skalka, J. Data processing methods in the development of the microlearning-based framework for teaching programming languages. In Proceedings of the 12th International Scientific Conference on Distance Learning in Applied Informatics (DIVAI), Štúrovo, Slovakia, 2–4 May 2018; pp. 503–512.
27. Leppänen, L.; Leinonen, J.; Ihantola, P.; Hellas, A. Predicting academic success based on learning material usage. In Proceedings of the SIGITE 2017-Proceedings 18th Annual Conference Information Technology Education, Rochester, NY, USA, 4–7 October 2017; pp. 13–18. [CrossRef]
28. Figueira, Á. Mining moodle logs for grade prediction: A methodology walk-through. *ACM Int. Conf. Proc. Ser.* **2017**. Part F1322. [CrossRef]
29. Félix, I.M.; Ambrósio, A.P.; Neves, P.S.; Siqueira, J.; Brancher, J.D. Moodle predicta: A data mining tool for student follow up. In Proceedings of the CSEDU 2017-Proceedings 9th International Conference Computer Support Education, Porto, Portugal, 21–23 April 2017; Volume 1, no. Csedu. pp. 339–346. [CrossRef]
30. Kadoić, N.; Oreški, D. Analysis of student behavior and success based on logs in Moodle. In Proceedings of the 2018 41st International Convention on Information and Communication Technology, Electronics and Microelectronics (MIPRO), Opatija, Croatia, 21–25 May 2018; pp. 654–659. [CrossRef]
31. Ihantola, P.; Vihavainen, A.; Ahadi, A.; Butler, M.; Börstler, J.; Edwards, S.H.; Isohanni, E.; Korhonen, A.; Petersen, A.; Rivers, K.; et al. Educational Data Mining and Learning Analytics in Programming: Literature Review and Case Studies. In Proceedings of the 20th Annual Conference on Innovation and Technology in Computer Science Education (ITiCSE), Vilnius, Lithuania, 4–8 July 2015; Volume 16. [CrossRef]
32. Sisovic, S.; Matetic, M.; Bakaric, M.B. Mining student data to assess the impact of moodle activities and prior knowledge on programming course success. *ACM Int. Conf. Proc. Ser.* **2015**, *1008*, 366–373. [CrossRef]
33. Hussain, M.; Hussain, S.; Zhang, W.; Zhu, W.; Theodorou, P.; Abidi, S.M.R. Mining moodle data to detect the inactive and low-performance students during the moodle course. *ACM Int. Conf. Proc. Ser.* **2018**, 133–140. [CrossRef]
34. Skalka, J.; Drlík, M. Educational Model for Improving Programming Skills Based on Conceptual Microlearning Framework BT-The Challenges of the Digital Transformation in Education. In *The Challenges of the Digital Transformation in Education*; Springer: Berlin, Germany, 2020; pp. 923–934.
35. Huet, I.; Pacheco, O.R.; Tavares, J.; Weir, G. New challenges in teaching introductory programming courses: A case study. In Proceedings of the 34th Annual Frontiers in Education, Savannah, GA, USA, 20–23 October 2004; Volume 1, pp. T2H/5–T2H/9. [CrossRef]
36. Drlik, M.; Skalka, J. Virtual Faculty Development Using Top-down Implementation Strategy and Adapted EES Model. *Procedia Soc. Behav. Sci.* **2011**, *28*, 616–621. [CrossRef]
37. Jenkins, T. On the difficulty of learning to program. In Proceedings of the 3rd Annual Conference LTSN Centre Information Computer Science, Loughborough, UK, 27–29 August 2002; Volume 4, pp. 53–58.
38. Gomes, A.J.; Santos, A.N.; Mendes, A.J. A Study on Students' Behaviours and Attitudes towards Learning to Program. In *Proceedings of the 17th ACM Annual Conference on Innovation and Technology in Computer Science Education*; ACM: New York, NY, USA, 2012; pp. 132–137. [CrossRef]
39. Aleman, J.L.F. Automated Assessment in a Programming Tools Course. *IEEE Trans. Educ.* **2011**, *54*, 576–581. [CrossRef]
40. Mohammed, G.S.; Wakil, K.; Nawroly, S.S. The Effectiveness of Microlearning to Improve Students' Learning Ability. *Int. J. Res. Rev.* **2018**, *3*, 32–38. Available online: https://www.ijere.com/article/the-effectiveness-of-microlearning-to-improve-students-learning-ability (accessed on 31 May 2020).
41. Kapp, K.M.; Defelice, R.A. *Microlearning: Short and Sweet*; American Society for Training & Development: Alexandria, VA, USA, 2019.

© 2020 by the authors. Licensee MDPI, Basel, Switzerland. This article is an open access article distributed under the terms and conditions of the Creative Commons Attribution (CC BY) license (http://creativecommons.org/licenses/by/4.0/).

Article

# Predicting Students' Behavioral Intention to Use Open Source Software: A Combined View of the Technology Acceptance Model and Self-Determination Theory

F. José Racero, Salvador Bueno * and M. Dolores Gallego

Department of Management and Marketing, Universidad Pablo de Olavide, 41013 Seville, Spain; fjracmon@upo.es (F.J.R.); mdgalper@upo.es (M.D.G.)
* Correspondence: sbueavi@upo.es

Received: 26 February 2020; Accepted: 10 April 2020; Published: 14 April 2020

**Abstract:** This study focuses on students' behavioral intention to use Open Source Software (OSS). The article examines how students, who were trained in OSS, are motivated to continue using it. A conceptual model based on Self-Determination Theory and the Technological Acceptance Model (TAM) was defined in order to test the behavioral intention to use OSS, comprising six constructs: (1) autonomy, (2) competence, (3) relatedness, (4) perceived ease of use, (5) perceived usefulness and (6) behavioral intention to use. A survey was designed for data collection. The participants were recent secondary school graduates, and all of them had received mandatory OSS training. A total of 352 valid responses were used to test the proposed structural model, which was performed using the Lisrel software. The results clearly confirmed the positive influence of the intrinsic motivations; autonomy and relatedness, to improve perceptions regarding the usefulness and ease of use of OSS, and; therefore, on behavioral intention to use OSS. In addition, the implications and limitations of this study are considered.

**Keywords:** Open Source Software (OSS); Technology Acceptance Model (TAM); Self-Determination Theory (SDT); behavioral intention to use; student; secondary school

## 1. Introduction

Information and Communication Technologies (ICT) have become a crucial element for students in their daily educational tasks [1–4]. Nowadays, it is possible to affirm that education without ICT is unimaginable [5]. In fact, many institutions and governments have developed strategies in order to integrate ICT with pedagogical methods [6,7]. In this context, the adaptation of pedagogical systems and the incorporation of ICT innovations are essential to the survival of many educational institutions [8,9]. Nevertheless, the involvement of three factors is required in order to achieve efficient and effective use of ICT for educational purposes [10]: (1) the academic community; (2) educational structures; and (3) legislation.

This study focuses on the adoption of Open Source Software (OSS) in education. According to [11], the three OSS primary drivers in education are: (1) lowered acquisition costs; (2) relaxed licensing agreements; and (3) interoperability. In this respect, OSS is one of the ICT's with the greatest growth potential in the field [12,13]. Indeed, many governments are adapting their regulations or investing in new infrastructures to promote OSS use in education. For instance, OSS adoption in higher education has been popular in the United States [14]. In a similar way, the government of Andalusia (Spain), which exercises regulatory and executive power in different areas, including education, has approved some initiatives to boost the use of OSS in primary and secondary education [15].

Generally, OSS has achieved enormous popularity due to three factors [16]: (1) user-developer interaction; (2) market potential; and (3) development stage. Two key OSS features are highlighted [17,18]: (1) it is developed in a public and collaborative manner; and (2) the source code is accessible for users, and they can modify it, and in most cases, its distribution is even allowed. Therefore, OSS is considered a viable alternative to proprietary software for many institutions [19,20], becoming an innovative global movement where different social, economic, and public agents collaborate, united by the need to control the software design [21]. Consequently, the number of OSS projects in the world has increased significantly in recent decades in all fields [22,23].

Particularly, the implementation of OSS in the educational context is a reality [12,15]. OSS usually increases the quality of education in three aspects [24]: (1) service level; (2) student productivity; and (3) student satisfaction. In addition, OSS shares similar goals with educational principles, such as collectiveness and cooperation [12]. Hence, educational organizations should define OSS strategies considering the different needs of the stakeholders, mainly students, and teachers, in order to spread the OSS principles and benefits [25]. Indeed, according to [26], students and teachers agree that the total cost of ownership is one of the most important factors in OSS adoption.

However, the literature has not sufficiently explored certain issues surrounding the transmission to students regarding the values associated with OSS and its subsequent application in other fields. In this manner, these questions could be the starting point for the present paper: (1) Do students adopt a favorable behavior towards the OSS use as a result of the training received?; (2) Do students consider that OSS provides a solid alternative to proprietary software?; and (3) Are students motivated to use OSS after receiving training focused on OSS?

Consequently, there is a gap in our knowledge concerning the impact of education and the intention to continue using this type of ICT. Thus, this paper seeks to fill part of that gap. Specifically, two research objectives are defined: (1) to explore the motivational determinants of student behavior towards OSS; and (2) to propose a research model to analyze the effect of self-motivation factors in order to gain a deeper understanding of the relationship between human motivation and technology acceptance. In this regard, this research suggests that students will be active in satisfying their basic software needs within the psychological field. Therefore, theories of motivation could provide a relevant view from which to achieve the proposed objectives. Indeed, this study adopts the perspective of Self-Determination Theory (SDT) in combination with the Technological Acceptance Model (TAM).

The remainder of this article is organized as follows: Section 2 provides the theoretical framework based on both theories and the hypotheses; Section 3 presents the preliminary analysis; Section 4 tests the model; Section 5 discusses the findings that emerged from the analysis. Finally, Section 6 contains the conclusions, addressing the limitations and the implications of the findings.

## 2. Theoretical Framework

The ICT literature has always been concerned to understand usage behavior regarding ICT [27,28]. In this respect, many studies have revealed that this behavior can vary among individuals or groups [27–29], and behavioral intention to use is frequently analyzed through the application of certain constructs or approaches to address the acceptance of emergent technologies [30]. The Technology Acceptance Model (TAM) is one of the most influential theoretical frameworks to explain users' acceptance of ICT [31].

The TAM was developed by [32] in order to study the usage intention of technology based on the principles proposed by [33] in the "Theory of Reasoned Action". Ever since, this model has been used intensively by researchers to develop predictive models about the intention to use any technology (i.e., Internet, mobile devices, enterprise systems or open software) in any discipline (i.e., medicine, business, education, economics or psychology), and in many cases, the hypothetical relationships have been widely supported [34]. Nowadays, it continues to be one of the main theoretical frameworks for evaluating the use of technology, and its validity for this purpose has been widely demonstrated [35–37].

In the context of education, TAM has been applied to a huge range of purposes. For instance, [38] sought to measure clinical students' perceptions of simulation-based learning using TAM. Also, [39] developed a research model based on the TAM to evaluate the acceptance of mobile technologies among teachers. Moreover, [40] proposed a TAM based model to understand the motivational factors that influence acceptance of the open-source learning management system Moodle.

In any case, the application of the TAM needs to be adapted to a technology or context. Therefore, specific variables related to social and psychological factors that influence user acceptance must be identified [41] to provide more consistent predictions of ICT use. In fact, TAM is often combined with other theories that support the inclusion of such variables [42]. Hence, TAM has been extended using external factors from other ICT theories depending on technological characteristics, target users, and context [43].

One relevant limitation of the TAM that must be considered in the current study pertains to the omission of intrinsic motivations and social influence [15]. According to [44], the explanation of the TAM may be limited when ICT acceptance and use are not only to achieve tasks or procedures but also to fulfill emotional needs. In fact, some extensions of the TAM, such as TAM2 and TAM3, have been proposed to incorporate these needs in order to improve its predictive capacity.

Additionally, since this study is linked, in part, with students' emotions regarding OSS acceptance, SDT has been used to identify the external variables that complete the acceptance model. This theory is focused on identifying the reason behind an individual's autonomy in the development of any type of activity [45]. Indeed, the combination of the TAM and Self-Determination Theory has been widely used by the literature in recent years [46–48], and the compatibility of both has been robustly demonstrated [49]. Following the foundations of both frameworks, the hypotheses will be shown in two groups: (1) related to the TAM and (2) related to SDT.

## 2.1. Technological Acceptance Model

The original proposal for the TAM [32] is made up of five concepts: perceived usefulness, perceived ease of use, attitude toward using, behavioral intention to use, and actual use. Following Davis' proposal, the relationships between these constructs are illustrated in Figure 1. In fact, the defined model in this study is inspired by this framework whilst adopting a TAM2 and TAM3 perspective. This implies that it is assumed the incorporation of their three key constructs [50,51]: perceived usefulness (PU), perceived ease of use (PEU) and behavioral intention to use (BI), so that the two belief constructs (PU and PEU) are primary determinants of an individual's BI to use an ICT [52]. The TAM literature considers the removal of the construct attitude towards use to be viable, owing to its reduced mediating effect on BI [39].

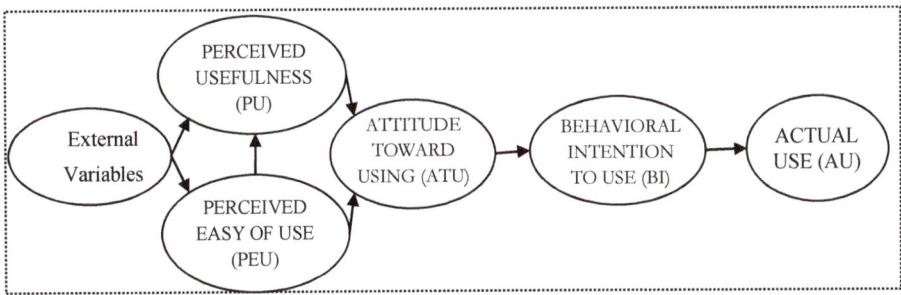

**Figure 1.** Technology Acceptance Model (TAM) original proposal [32].

TAM3, which includes TAM2, was proposed initially as a means of understanding employee use of ICT in a business environment [51]. It emphasizes individual and social factors that influence the individual-level adoption behavior of an ICT [53]. Hence, the user perception of technology determines its level of acceptance. Specifically, TAM3 [50] takes the variables from TAM2 that influence PU (voluntariness, experience, subjective norms, job relevance, output quality and results in demonstrability), proposing that the anchor (computer self-efficacy, perception of external control, computer anxiety and computer playfulness) and adjustment (perceived enjoyment and objective usability) factors impact PEU.

PU is defined by [32] (p. 320) as "the degree to which a person believes that using a particular system would enhance his or her job performance", and PEU is "the degree to which a person believes that using a particular system would be free of effort". Based on the TAM postulates, PEU and PU are factors that influence BI [50], and the impact is assumed to be positive. Hence, in this present study, the greater the students' PEU and PU regarding OSS, the more likely the students' BI. Thereby, the following hypotheses were included in the TAM3 model (Figure 2):

**Hypothesis 1 (H1).** *Perceived ease of use (PEU) has a positive effect on the perceived usefulness (PU) of OSS.*

**Hypothesis 2 (H2).** *Perceived ease of use (PEU) has a positive effect on behavioral intention to use (BI) OSS.*

**Hypothesis 3 (H3).** *Perceived usefulness (PU) has a positive effect on behavioral intention to use (BI) OSS.*

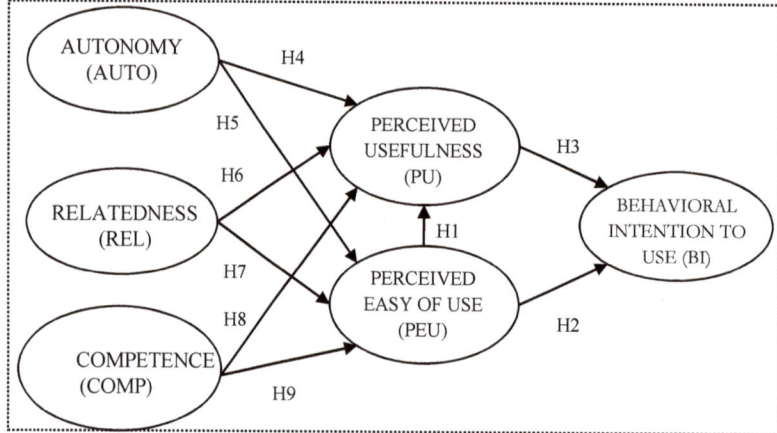

**Figure 2.** Research model.

## 2.2. Self-Determination Theory (SDT)

SDT is a theoretical framework proposed by [54] to help define comprehensive behavioral models. This theory seeks to understand the socio-environmental factors that affect an individual's tendency towards self-motivation. Indeed, SDT affirms that individuals can improve their optimal functioning and well-being by engaging in activities that interest them [55,56].

It is considered one of the leading motivational theories today [57]. SDT has been used to tackle motivational studies across many disciplines, including: healthcare [58], writing [59], human resources [60,61], education [62–64], organizations [65–67], and sport [68], among others.

Three basic psychological needs are identified by this theory: autonomy, relatedness, and competence [69]. They are postulated as central intrinsic motivations, which refer to doing something because it is inherently interesting or enjoyable [70]. Conversely, extrinsic motivations appear when behaviors are performed because of external forces [71,72]. Furthermore, SDT does not differentiate between the strength of these needs, although the literature related to this theory suggests that autonomy is considered more essential than the other two [73].

SDT proposes that individuals try to be motivated to satisfy these needs [58]. In general, SDT considers that competence is related to a sense of self-efficacy or perceived ability to attain objectives. Hence, it is a need to feel effective [74]. Moreover, autonomy refers to the sense of behavior self-regulation [75]. Finally, relatedness is likened to the need to be integrated into a larger group [69]. So, each of these motivations are analyzed in order to complete the research model, considering that educational contexts that are supportive of autonomy, competence, and relatedness help to increase the internalization and integration of these three needs [76].

2.2.1. Autonomy

In contrast to forced regulation by external agents, autonomy is related to regulation by the self [45]. It refers to the need to be autonomous [77], and, therefore, it pertains to those personal acts through which individuals control their own behavior. Obviously, this sense impacts directly on the way of behaving due to its capacity to stimulate voluntary acts, even if they come from external initiatives [78]. In this regard, SDT does not deny the presence of contingencies, although it is focused on a person's endorsement of the act itself [45].

In the educational context, students usually have a sense of learning autonomy [48,79]. It is a psychological state through which students perceive internal control over learning goals and outcomes [80]. In fact, autonomy impacts on student satisfaction. According to [47], motivation based on autonomy has a higher impact on satisfaction than external motivations.

Furthermore, autonomy could lead to greater performance when the tasks are interesting to individuals who are performing them [73]. In addition, evidence shows that the presence of a supportive autonomy environment can increase the tendency to develop a specific behavior [81,82]. Hence, educational systems geared towards the provision of rationale, the provision of choice, and the encouragement of critical thinking are more likely to foster autonomy among students [83]. In fact, entrepreneurship students have a high degree of autonomy and therefore have a greater capacity to initiate actions [79].

Extending this motivational reasoning to an educational context, where the use of OSS is incentivized, autonomous acts would influence the PU and PEU of OSS. Indeed, previous studies have shown the positive relationship between perceived autonomy and perceived usefulness and perceived ease of use in a huge range of ICT contexts [48,84,85]. Based on these, the following hypotheses propose that autonomy exerts an influence on the PU and PEU of OSS (Figure 2):

**Hypothesis 4 (H4).** *Autonomy (AUTO) has a positive effect on the perceived usefulness (PU) of OSS.*

**Hypothesis 5 (H5).** *Autonomy (AUTO) has a positive effect on the perceived ease of use (PEU) of OSS.*

2.2.2. Relatedness

Relatedness refers to the need to establish emotional links with other individuals [75]. In an educational context, relatedness pertains to the capacity to engage in tasks that allow for collaboration and communication with other students [63]. Also, according to SDT, a student can enjoy social interactions and social connections [80].

Educational literature shows that relatedness is the least studied need [84]. Nonetheless, some research has shown that relatedness is a strong predictor of learners' intention to continue in an educational program [85]. Perhaps it is due to the intrinsic characteristics of the educational environment, where a student can develop the ability to initiate connections with others, from which it is possible to foster the generalization of relevant behaviors [45].

In this respect, relatedness can reduce fears and increase the tendency to share with others knowledge related to the OSS features [84]. In the field of ICT, relatedness is one of the most important incentives. People tend to value the opinions of those to whom they feel connected as highly relevant [85]. Therefore, the following hypotheses have been proposed (Figure 2):

**Hypothesis 6 (H6).** *Relatedness (REL) has a positive effect on the perceived usefulness (PU) of OSS.*

**Hypothesis 7 (H7).** *Relatedness (REL) has a positive effect on the perceived ease of use (PEU) of OSS.*

### 2.2.3. Competence

This need refers to effective behavior, the expansion of personal capabilities, and the desire to be enough [48]. In this context, SDT indicates that competence allows individuals to master tasks or achieve aims with ease [55]. When this basic need is satisfied, individuals begin to acquire the feeling of being effective in developing tasks [54].

According to [49], in the field of ICT, the need for competence is associated with factors such as (1) job satisfaction; (2) levels of job burnout; (3) experience in using technology; (4) expectations of the outcomes of using computers; (5) emotional reactions to computers; and (6) actual computer use, among others. Consequently, it is possible to define a relationship between competence and the degree to which people benefit from the use of ICT [86].

In addition, previous studies carried out in the educational context have shown that there is a relationship between competence and the constructs PU and PEU [87]. In our case, students' competence corresponds to the need to become more effective in the use of OSS in order to achieve high academic levels [88]. This is because competence is expected to make students more effective in their OSS use. This anticipation would increase the PU and PEU of OSS. The following hypotheses have been defined (Figure 2):

**Hypothesis 8 (H8).** *Competence (COMP) has a positive effect on the perceived usefulness (PU) of OSS.*

**Hypothesis 9 (H9).** *Competence (COMP) has a positive effect on the perceived ease of use (PEU) of OSS.*

## 3. Methods

### 3.1. Participants and Procedure

The study was conducted at secondary schools within the Education System of Andalusia, Spain, between April 2019 and September 2019. The participants were recent secondary school graduates in order to ensure that all the participants had received enough OSS training before the interviews since OSS use in the classroom was mandatory. The instrument used was a web-based survey developed with Google Form. A web-based survey offers three advantages to the study [89]: (1) it prevents transcription errors, (2) it enables reachability to many participants in a short space of time, and (3) it ensures anonymity. Students were informed of the objectives of the study. A total of 352 students completed the survey. The demographic profile of the respondents is given in Table 1.

**Table 1.** Demographic profile of the participants.

| Characteristic | Statistic (%) |
|---|---|
| Gender | |
| Male | 217 (61.64%) |
| Female | 135 (38.35%) |
| Age | |
| Less than 20 years old | 131 (37.5%) |
| Between 21 and 25 | 100 (28.40%) |
| More than 25 years old | 120 (34.09%) |
| OSS Frequency of use | |
| All software I use | 113 (32.10%) |
| Minimum Once a day | 138 (39.20%) |
| Minimum Once a week | 35 (18.46%) |
| Rarely | 36 (10.22%) |

### 3.2. Measures

The questionnaire was designed considering evidence from prior research on the TAM and SDT. In fact, the scale used to measure the constructs was developed using the measures created by [48,90,91].

Items were identified as indicators for each construct (Appendix A). The questionnaire was composed of two parts. In the first part, responders provided demographic information (Table 1). In the second section, participants were required to indicate their agreement or disagreement with 21 items using a five-point Likert-type scale, ranging from "Not at all/strongly disagree" (1) to "Exactly/strongly agree" (5). The 21 items were grouped into the six constructs of the model.

### 3.3. Data Analysis

A Structural Equation Model (SEM) was proposed. SEMs are frequently used in work related to behavior [92]. The quantitative data analysis included two processes: (1) an analysis of the descriptive statistics and the reliability of the measurement tool using the SPSS version 24 statistical program; and (2) SEM testing. Specifically, Lisrel 8.80 software allowed us to evaluate the correlation coefficient between variables in factor analysis and the path analysis equation model. A detailed explanation of the application of both analytical procedures and results is given in Section 4.

## 4. Results

The first stage involves testing the discriminant validity and reliability of the constructs by applying four analytical procedures: (1) assessment of item loadings; (2) internal consistency reliability (Cronbach's alpha and composite reliabilities); (3) convergent validity; and (4) discriminant validity. The results of applying these analyses are shown in Table 2.

Table 2. Item loadings and measurement reliability.

| Construct | | Mean | Std. Dev. | Factor Loading | Lambda Stand. | Composite Reliability | AVE | Cronbach's α |
|---|---|---|---|---|---|---|---|---|
| Autonomy (AUTO) | AUTO1 | 2.97 | 1.337 | 0.907 | 0.900 | 0.95 | 0.826 | 0.949 |
| | AUTO2 | 2.99 | 1.368 | 0.902 | 0.901 | | | |
| | AUTO3 | 2.75 | 1.339 | 0.931 | 0.934 | | | |
| | AUTO4 | 2.77 | 1.327 | 0.891 | 0.900 | | | |
| Competence (COMP) | COMP1 | 2.64 | 1.315 | 0.939 | 0.941 | 0.972 | 0.867 | 0.96 |
| | COMP2 | 2.69 | 1.275 | 0.929 | 0.932 | | | |
| | COMP3 | 2.50 | 1.274 | 0.916 | 0.917 | | | |
| | COMP4 | 2.73 | 1.265 | 0.917 | 0.921 | | | |
| Relatedness (REL) | REL1 | 3.01 | 1.225 | 0.908 | 0.910 | 0.955 | 0.841 | 0.955 |
| | REL2 | 2.91 | 1.278 | 0.923 | 0.922 | | | |
| | REL3 | 2.83 | 1.226 | 0.936 | 0.931 | | | |
| | REL4 | 2.80 | 1.237 | 0.903 | 0.906 | | | |
| Perceived Ease to USE (PEU) | PEU1 | 3.13 | 1.248 | 0.931 | 0.936 | 0.952 | 0.87 | 0.951 |
| | PEU2 | 3.11 | 1.253 | 0.958 | 0.952 | | | |
| | PEU3 | 3.18 | 1.258 | 0.905 | 0.909 | | | |
| Perceived Usefulness (PU) | PU1 | 2.94 | 1.227 | 0.907 | 0.912 | 0.939 | 0.837 | 0.94 |
| | PU2 | 2.99 | 1.328 | 0.903 | 0.926 | | | |
| | PU3 | 2.92 | 1.296 | 0.906 | 0.907 | | | |
| Behavioral Intention to USE (BI) | BI1 | 3.18 | 1.301 | 0.935 | 0.938 | 0.969 | 0.912 | 0.96 |
| | BI2 | 3.21 | 1.342 | 0.955 | 0.955 | | | |
| | BI3 | 3.24 | 1.356 | 0.974 | 0.972 | | | |

### 4.1. Convergent Validity

To determine whether convergent validity is acceptable, the measurements must fulfill three conditions [93,94]: (1) all item factor loadings with reflective measures must be significant and greater than 0.70, (2) the composite reliability for each construct must surpass 0.70, and (3) the Average Variance Extracted (AVE) for each construct should be higher than 0.5. In this study (Table 2), the factor loadings for all constructs substantially exceeded the threshold of 0.70, and they were statistically significant at the 0.001 level. In addition, composite reliability scores showed good internal consistency for all constructs (Table 2), and the AVE values were between 0.826 and 0.912, considerably higher than the recommended value of 0.5.

### 4.2. Discriminant Validity

On the one hand, the values contained in the Correlation Matrix (Table 3) were used to evaluate the discriminant validity of the constructs. The diagonal elements of this matrix were substituted by the square root of the AVE. In all cases, the square roots of the AVE were larger than the inter-construct correlations, and all shared variances between any two different constructs were less than the amount of variance extracted by one of the two constructs [93]. On the other hand, all items loaded more strongly on their corresponding construct than on other constructs [95]. Therefore, these results confirm the discriminant validity of all constructs.

Table 3. Correlation Matrix [1].

|  | AUTO | COMP | REL | PEU | PU | BI |
|---|---|---|---|---|---|---|
| Autonomy (AUTO) | 0.970 | | | | | |
| Competence (COMP) | 0.660 | 0.930 | | | | |
| Relatedness (REL) | 0.668 | 0.675 | 0.920 | | | |
| Perceived Ease to Use (PEU) | 0.662 | 0.588 | 0.686 | 0.980 | | |
| Perceived Usefulness (PU) | 0.742 | 0.616 | 0.753 | 0.770 | 0.910 | |
| Behavioral Intention to Use (BI) | 0.630 | 0.531 | 0.642 | 0.714 | 0.827 | 0.980 |

[1] Diagonal elements are the square root of the shared variance between the constructs and their measures.

### 4.3. Model Fit

Table 4 shows the fit indices for the research model, together with the suggested values. These results manifest that the research model has an acceptable fit over the minimum/maximum limit defined by [96].

Table 4. Goodness of fit statistics.

| Fit Indexes | Values | Recommended Value |
|---|---|---|
| $\chi^2$/grade of freedom | 0.0206 | ≤3.00 |
| Normed Fit Index (NFI) | 0.966 | ≥0.90 |
| Non-normed Fit Index (NNFI) | 0.981 | ≥0.90 |
| Comparative Fit Index (CFI) | 0.984 | ≥0.90 |
| Adjusted Goodness-of-Fit Index (AGFI) | 0.894 | ≥0.80 |
| Root Mean Square Error of Approximation (RMSEA) | 0.0489 | ≤0.05 |
| Goodness-of-Fit Index (GFI) | 0.918 | ≥0.90 |
| Incremental Fit Index (IFI) | 0.984 | ≥0.90 |

### 4.4. Results of the Structural Equation Model

The structural equations software Lisrel 8.80 was used to test the research model with an estimation method of maximum likelihood [97]. Lisrel fuses factor analysis modeling from psychometric theory with structural equations modeling associated with econometrics [98]. The aim was to evaluate the model based on the significance and effect sizes ($\beta$) for each hypothesized path and to explain the variance (R2) for each dependent variable [99,100].

Table 5 shows an abridgment of the findings, evidencing the statistical significance of the defined hypotheses. Specifically, AUTO and REL were significant predictors of PEU (0.32, $p < 0.001$; and 0.415, $p < 0.001$, respectively), although the relationship between COMP and PEU has not been demonstrated. In a similar way, AUTO (0.276, $p < 0.001$) and REL (0.306, $p < 0.001$) were significantly related to PU. Nevertheless, COMP is not a predictor of PU.

**Table 5.** Research hypotheses test.

| Hypothesis (Path) | Path Coefficient | t-Value [1] | Supported |
|---|---|---|---|
| H1: PEU→PU | 0.35 | 7.196 *** | Yes |
| H2: PEU→BI | 0.197 | 3.392 *** | Yes |
| H3: PU→BI | 0.742 | 11.529 *** | Yes |
| H4: AUTO→PU | 0.276 | 6.007 *** | Yes |
| H5: AUTO→PEU | 0.32 | 5.513 *** | Yes |
| H6: REL→PU | 0.306 | 9.411 *** | Yes |
| H7: REL→PEU | 0.415 | 6.481 *** | Yes |
| H8: COMP→PU | 0.0853 | 1.950 | No |
| H9: COMP→PEU | 0.0973 | 1.742 | No |

[1] Significant at: * $p < 0.05$ t(0.05; ¥) = 1.9670; ** $p < 0.01$; t(0.01; ¥) = 2.5904; *** $p < 0.001$; t(0.001; ¥) = 3.3195.

Furthermore, PEU had a significant positive impact on PU (0.35, $p < 0.001$). Finally, PU (0.742, $p < 0.001$) and PEU (0.197, $p < 0.001$) had a significant positive impact on BI. Considering these results, the percentages of variance explained by the research model for the dependent constructs were as follows: (1) 69.8% for BI, (2) 55% for PEU, and (3) 73.3% for PU.

## 5. Discussion

OSS, together with all other ICT, has begun to change the way of teaching and learning, offering a viable alternative to proprietary educational technologies. The principal aims of this study were to contribute additional evidence regarding motivations to use OSS for educational and non-educational purposes. The findings revealed a measurement and structural model to predict behavioral intention to use OSS among secondary school graduates who had received mandatory OSS training. In this respect, little research has found empirical support to define best teaching practices in secondary school education in order to motivate ICT use.

In this context, the current study incorporated motivational predictors into OSS acceptance in the educational context. Indeed, it proposed a motivational acceptance model of OSS, combining constructs from SDT (autonomy, relatedness, and competence) with the TAM. This model purports to explain the factors that affect behavioral intention to use OSS in order to help fill the gap in the literature about the acceptance of OSS in the educational field. Some researchers have reported [15] active student attitudes towards the use of OSS in a training context, but motivational factors have been largely neglected. In fact, this study is one of the first to explore the interaction between the basic needs of autonomy, competence, and relatedness, and behavioral intention to use OSS.

Specifically, the research presented here explored the connections between the TAM [32,50] and SDT [54,55]. In recent years, both frameworks have drawn the attention of many researchers in educational literature [38–40,62–64]. Consistent with this growing interest in both theories, this study has investigated the relationship between behavioral intention to use OSS among secondary school graduates from education systems that provide intensive OSS training and the following constructs: perceived ease of use, perceived usefulness, autonomy, relatedness, and competence. Specifically, the combination of these two frameworks was adopted in order to: (1) explore the motivational determinants of student behavior towards OSS; and (2) propose a research model to analyze the effect of self-motivation factors in order to gain a deeper understanding of the relationship between human motivation and technology acceptance.

Findings are in line with previous research. According to [101], it is possible to influence three aspects to stimulate self-determination among students: (1) defining interpersonal connections that accentuate choice and flexibility rather than control and rule; (2) explaining to students in a reasoned way why certain attitudes are relevant for their well-being; and (3) accepting adverse feelings towards some activities. Applying these three propositions to this current research, students with OSS training will be more inclined to use OSS in any facet of their life because they perceive that it is easy to use or useful. Indeed, according to [56], individuals can improve their optimal functioning and well-being by engaging in activities that interest them.

Thus, the TAM-SDT model defined offers a useful framework to identify the socio-environmental factors affecting the tendency toward self-motivation and to draw conclusions about why people use OSS to fulfill their needs. In fact, the TAM is the most widely used theoretical approach to study the usage intention of technology, although it is limited when the acceptance and use of ICT are also geared towards fulfilling emotional needs [44]. In this context, based on previous SDT research [58,69,73,74], the proposed model includes the most relevant motivational factors of this theory, and several interesting findings emerged.

Overall, the hypotheses, excluding H8 and H9 related to the factor COMP, were supported, and the model attained acceptable fit indices. As expected, based on the studies of [48,90,91], these results highlight the positive influence of AUTO, REL, PEU, and PU on BI towards OSS. In this respect, this study offers evidence that corroborates the all-purpose combined use of SDT and the TAM, and at the same time, supports the relationship between OSS training and motivational models.

Aligned with the postulates of SDT, this study has demonstrated that autonomy enhances perceived usefulness and ease of use. Hence, the sense of autonomy impacts directly on positive behaviors toward OSS use due to its capacity to stimulate voluntary acts, even if they come from external initiatives. In a similar way, collaborations and communications with others can reduce fears and increase the sharing of knowledge related to OSS features. Hence, relatedness has a positive impact on PU and PEU.

## 6. Conclusions

The findings of this research suggest that intrinsic motivations are crucial for spreading OSS use as an alternative to proprietary software. In this respect, these results emphasize that participating as a student in a training system, in which it is mandatory to use educational software based on OSS, encourages intrinsic motivations, such as autonomy or relatedness. These motivations help activate a positive behavior to continue using OSS, due to an improvement in the perception of this ICT. Bearing this in mind, certain implications and limitations of these findings are described below.

*6.1. Implications*

It is possible to identify certain implications based on the findings. From an academic point of view, this study further develops knowledge regarding the use and adoption of OSS. Hence, the feasibility of combining the TAM and SDT in order to explain ICT adoption has been demonstrated. Moreover, from a managerial perspective, understanding the behavioral intention to use OSS is meaningful for the OSS movement. In fact, some practical implications can be extracted.

First, a better understanding of the motivations of OSS users could be advantageous for OSS developers in determining which software functionalities encourage OSS expansion. Second, with these findings, the OSS movement might achieve segmentation of users in order to identify behaviors that favor OSS use, and thus can anticipate the success of this type of ICT.

*6.2. Limitations*

This research is not without limitations. First, some weaknesses have been identified regarding the sample. On the one hand, data collection was performed in secondary schools from a specific region without considering other geographical areas. On the other hand, this study has not applied a stratified sampling procedure, which would have allowed us to recruit equal sizes of age groups or age groups that mirror the current population. Second, the percentage of explained variance for behavioral intention to use could be improved with the incorporation of other predictors associated with other motivational theories. Finally, the findings from this study are limited to OSS use with an educational purpose. Therefore, it would be helpful to carry out complementary studies that include additional OSS uses.

**Author Contributions:** Conceptualization, F.J.R., S.B. and M.D.G.; methodology, F.J.R., S.B. and M.D.G.; software, S.B., M.D.G.; validation, M.D.G.; formal analysis, F.J.R., S.B. and M.D.G.; investigation, F.J.R., S.B. and M.D.G.; resources, F.J.R., S.B. and M.D.G.; data curation, M.D.G.; writing—original draft preparation, F.J.R., S.B. and M.D.G.; writing—review and editing, S.B. and M.D.G.; visualization, M.D.G.; supervision, S.B. and M.D.G. All authors have read and agreed to the published version of the manuscript.

**Funding:** This research received no external funding

**Conflicts of Interest:** The authors declare no conflict of interest.

## Appendix A

Table A1. Questionnaire.

|  | Items | Source |
|---|---|---|
| AUTO1 | I fell a sense of choice and freedom using OSS | [48,90] |
| AUTO2 | OSS education provides me interesting options and choices | |
| AUTO3 | I have more control while using OSS | |
| AUTO4 | OSS gives me more chances to control my tasks | |
| COMP1 | I am better in OSS than other users | [48,90,91] |
| COMP2 | I have stronger capability than other users thanks OSS | |
| COMP3 | I am superior to others through using OSS | |
| COMP4 | After receiving an OSS training, I felt competent | |
| COMP5 | I have been able to learn an interesting new skill through OSS | |
| REL1 | I really like the OSS users | [90,91] |
| REL2 | OSS gives me more chances to interact with others | |
| REL3 | I feel close to others while using OSS | |
| REL4 | I have more opportunity to be close to other though OSS | |
| PEU1 | My interaction with OSS solutions is clear and under stable | [41,48] |
| PEU2 | It is easy for me to become skillful at using OSS | |
| PEU3 | I find OSS easy to use | |
| PU1 | Using OSS enhances my effectiveness | [41,48] |
| PU2 | OSS is useful for my life/job | |
| PU3 | Using OSS increases my productivity | |
| BI1 | I indent to use OSS in the future | [41,48] |
| BI2 | I plan to use OSS in the future | |
| BI3 | I predict I would use OSS in the future | |

## References

1. Hatlevik, O.E.; Throndsen, I.; Loi, M.; Gudmundsdottir, G.B. Students' ICT self-efficacy and computer and information literacy: Determinants and relationships. *Comput. Educ.* **2018**, *118*, 107–119. [CrossRef]
2. Comi, S.L.; Argentin, G.; Gui, M.; Origo, F.; Pagani, L. Is it the way they use it? Teachers, ICT and student achievement. *Econ. Educ. Rev.* **2017**, *56*, 24–39. [CrossRef]
3. Gil-Flores, J.; Rodríguez-Santero, J.; Torres-Gordillo, J.-J. Factors that explain the use of ICT in secondary-education classrooms: The role of teacher characteristics and school infrastructure. *Comput. Hum. Behav.* **2017**, *68*, 441–449. [CrossRef]
4. Balogh, Z.; Kuchárik, M. Predicting Student Grades Based on Their Usage of LMS Moodle Using Petri Nets. *Appl. Sci.* **2019**, *9*, 4211. [CrossRef]
5. Ramirez, G.M.; Collazos, C.A.; Moreira, F. All-Learning: The state of the art of the models and the methodologies educational with ICT. *Telemat. Inform.* **2018**, *35*, 944–953. [CrossRef]
6. Tondeur, J.; Aesaert, K.; Prestridge, S.; Consuegra, E. A multilevel analysis of what matters in the training of pre-service teacher's ICT competencies. *Comput. Educ.* **2018**, *122*, 32–42. [CrossRef]
7. Vega-Hernández, M.-C.; Patino-Alonso, M.-C.; Galindo-Villardón, M.-P. Multivariate characterization of university students using the ICT for learning. *Comput. Educ.* **2018**, *121*, 124–130. [CrossRef]

8. Picatoste, J.; Pérez-Ortiz, L.; Ruesga-Benito, S.M. A new educational pattern in response to new technologies and sustainable development. Enlightening ICT skills for youth employability in the European Union. *Telemat. Inform.* **2018**, *35*, 1031–1038. [CrossRef]
9. Kang, D.; Park, M.J. Competitive prospects of graduate program on the integration of ICT superiority, higher education, and international aid. *Telemat. Inform.* **2017**, *34*, 1625–1637. [CrossRef]
10. Perbawaningsih, Y. Plus Minus of ICT Usage in Higher Education Students. *Procedia-Soc. Behav. Sci.* **2013**, *103*, 717–724. [CrossRef]
11. Ebardo, R.A. Visibility and Training in Open Source Software Adoption: A Case in Philippine Higher Education. In Proceedings of the 8th International Workshop on Computer Science and Engineering, Bangkok, Thailand, 28–30 June 2018.
12. Lakka, S.; Stamati, T.; Michalakelis, C.; Anagnostopoulos, D. Cross-national analysis of the relation of eGovernment maturity and OSS growth. *Technol. Forecast. Soc.* **2015**, *99*, 132–147. [CrossRef]
13. Lakka, S.; Michalakelis, C.; Varoutas, D.; Martakos, D. Exploring the determinants of the OSS market potential: The case of the Apache web server. *Telecommun. Policy* **2012**, *36*, 51–68. [CrossRef]
14. van Rooij, S.W. Adopting open-source software applications in U.S. higher education: A cross-disciplinary review of the literature. *Rev. Educ. Res.* **2009**, *79*, 682–701. [CrossRef]
15. Gallego, M.D.; Bueno, S.; Racero, F.J.; Noyes, J. Open source software: The effects of training on acceptance. *Comput. Hum. Behav.* **2015**, *49*, 390–399. [CrossRef]
16. Cheruy, C.; Robert, F.; Belbaly, N. OSS popularity: Understanding the relationship between user-developer interaction, market potential and development stage. *Syst. Inf. Manag.* **2017**, *2*, 47–74. [CrossRef]
17. Behfar, S.K.; Turkina, E.; Burger-Helmchen, T. Knowledge management in OSS communities: Relationship between dense and sparse network structures. *Int. J. Inf. Manag.* **2018**, *38*, 167–174. [CrossRef]
18. Sutanto, J.; Kankanhalli, A.; Tan, B.C.Y. Uncovering the relationship between OSS user support networks and OSS popularity. *Decis. Support Syst.* **2014**, *64*, 142–151. [CrossRef]
19. Joia, L.A.; Vinhais, J.C.S. From closed source to open source software: Analysis of the migration process to Open Office. *J. High Technol. Manag. Res.* **2017**, *28*, 261–272. [CrossRef]
20. Spinellis, D.; Giannikas, V. Organizational adoption of open source software. *J. Syst. Softw.* **2012**, *85*, 666–682. [CrossRef]
21. Gamalielsson, J.; Lundell, B. Sustainability of Open Source software communities beyond a fork: How and why has the LibreOffice project evolved? *J. Syst. Softw.* **2014**, *89*, 128–145. [CrossRef]
22. Wang, L.; Huang, M.; Liu, M. How founders' social capital affects the success of open-source projects: A resource-based view of project teams. *Electron. Commer. Res. Appl.* **2018**, *30*, 51–61. [CrossRef]
23. Kuwata, Y.; Miura, H. A Study on Growth Model of OSS Projects to estimate the stage of lifecycle. *Procedia Comput. Sci.* **2015**, *60*, 1004–1013. [CrossRef]
24. Bahamdain, S.S. Open Source Software (OSS) Quality Assurance: A Survey Paper. *Procedia Comput. Sci.* **2015**, *56*, 459–464. [CrossRef]
25. Kemp, R. Open source software (OSS) governance in the organization. *Comput. Law Secur. Rev.* **2010**, *26*, 309–316. [CrossRef]
26. van Rooij, S.W. Higher education sub-cultures and open source adoption. *Comput. Educ.* **2011**, *57*, 1171–1183. [CrossRef]
27. Palvia, P.; Baqir, N.; Nemati, H. ICT for socio-economic development: A citizens' perspective. *Inf. Manag.* **2018**, *55*, 160–176. [CrossRef]
28. Luhan, J.; Novotná, V. ICT Use in EU According to National Models of Behavior. *Procedia-Soc. Behav. Sci.* **2015**, *213*, 80–85. [CrossRef]
29. Areepattamannil, S.; Khine, M.S. Early adolescents' use of information and communication technologies (ICTs) for social communication in 20 countries: Examining the roles of ICT-related behavioral and motivational characteristics. *Comput. Hum. Behav.* **2017**, *73*, 263–272. [CrossRef]
30. Malaquias, R.F.; Malaquias, F.F.O.; Hwang, Y. Understanding technology acceptance features in learning through a serious game. *Comput. Hum. Behav.* **2018**, 395–402. [CrossRef]
31. Xia, M.; Zhang, Y.; Zhang, C. A TAM-based approach to explore the effect of online experience on destination image: A smartphone user's perspective. *J. Destin. Mark. Manag.* **2018**, *8*, 259–270. [CrossRef]
32. Davis, F.D. Perceived Usefulness, Perceived Ease of Use, and User Acceptance of Information Technology. *MIS Q.* **1989**, *13*, 319–340. [CrossRef]

33. Fishbein, M.; Ajzen, I. *Belief, Attitude, Intention, and Behavior: An Introduction to Theory and Research*; Addison-Wesley Reading: Boston, MA, USA, 1975.
34. Chen, C.F.; Chen, P.-C. Applying the TAM to travelers' usage intentions of GPS devices. *Expert Syst. Appl.* **2011**, *38*, 6217–6221. [CrossRef]
35. Okafor, D.J.; Nico, M.; Azman, B.B. The influence of perceived ease of use and perceived usefulness on the intention to use a suggested online advertising workflow. *Can. Int. J. Sci. Technol.* **2016**, *6*, 162–174.
36. Hsiao, C.H.; Yang, C. The intellectual development of the technology acceptance model: A co-citation analysis. *Int. J. Inf. Manag.* **2011**, *31*, 128–136. [CrossRef]
37. Turner, M.; Kitchenham, B.; Brereton, P.; Charters, S.; Budgen, D. Does the technology acceptance model predict actual use? A systematic literature review. *Inf. Softw. Technol.* **2010**, *52*, 463–479. [CrossRef]
38. Lemay, D.J.; Morin, M.M.; Bazelais, P.; Doleck, T. Modeling Students' Perceptions of Simulation-Based Learning Using the Technology Acceptance Model. *Clin. Simul. Nurs.* **2018**, *20*, 28–37. [CrossRef]
39. Sánchez-Prieto, J.C.; Olmos-Migueláñez, S.; García-Peñalvo, F.J. Informal tools in formal contexts: Development of a model to assess the acceptance of mobile technologies among teachers. *Comput. Hum. Behav.* **2016**, *55*, 519–528. [CrossRef]
40. Sánchez, R.A.; Hueros, A.D. Motivational factors that influence the acceptance of Moodle using TAM. *Comput. Hum. Behav.* **2010**, *26*, 1632–1640. [CrossRef]
41. Venkatesh, V.; Morris, M.G.; Davis, G.B.; Davis, F.D. User acceptance of information technology: Toward a unified view. *MIS Q.* **2003**, *27*, 425–478. [CrossRef]
42. Legris, P.; Ingham, J.; Collerette, P. Why do people use information technology? A critical review of the technology acceptance model. *Inf. Manag.* **2003**, *40*, 191–204. [CrossRef]
43. Yoon, C. Extending the TAM for Green IT: A normative perspective. *Comput. Hum. Behav.* **2018**, *83*, 129–139. [CrossRef]
44. Taherdoost, H. A review of technology acceptance and adoption models and theories. *Procedia Manuf.* **2018**, *22*, 960–967. [CrossRef]
45. Arvanitis, A. Autonomy and morality: A Self-Determination Theory discussion of ethics. *New Ideas Psychol.* **2017**, *47*, 57–61. [CrossRef]
46. Khan, I.U.; Hameed, Z.; Yu, Y.; Islam, T.; Sheikh, Z.; Khan, S.U. Predicting the acceptance of MOOCs in a developing country: Application of task-technology fit model, social motivation, and self-determination theory. *Telemat. Inform.* **2018**, *35*, 964–978. [CrossRef]
47. Joo, Y.J.; So, H.-J.; Kim, H.H. Examination of relationships among students' self-determination, technology acceptance, satisfaction, and continuance intention to use K-MOOCs. *Comput. Educ.* **2018**, *122*, 260–272. [CrossRef]
48. Nikou, S.A.; Economides, A.A. Mobile-Based Assessment: Integrating acceptance and motivational factors into a combined model of Self-Determination Theory and Technology Acceptance. *Comput. Hum. Behav.* **2017**, *68*, 83–95. [CrossRef]
49. Leung, L.S.K.; Matanda, M.J. The impact of basic human needs on the use of retailing self-service technologies: A study of self-determination theory. *J. Retail. Consum. Serv.* **2013**, *20*, 549–559. [CrossRef]
50. Venkatesh, V.; Davis, F.D. A theoretical extension of the technology acceptance model: Four longitudinal field studies. *Manag. Sci.* **2000**, *46*, 186–204. [CrossRef]
51. Venkatesh, V.; Bala, H. Technology acceptance model 3 and a research agenda on interventions. *Decis. Sci.* **2008**, *39*, 273–315. [CrossRef]
52. Al-Gahtani, S.S. Empirical investigation of e-learning acceptance and assimilation: A structural equation model. *Appl. Comput. Inform.* **2016**, *12*, 27–50. [CrossRef]
53. Faqih, K.M.S.; Jaradat, M.-I.R.M. Assessing the moderating effect of gender differences and individualism-collectivism at individual-level on the adoption of mobile commerce technology: TAM3 perspective. *J. Retail. Consum. Serv.* **2014**, *22*, 37–52. [CrossRef]
54. Deci, E.L.; Ryan, R.M. *Intrinsic Motivation and Self-Determination in Human Behavior*; Planum: New York, NY, USA, 1985.
55. Ryan, R.M.; Deci, E. *Self-Determination Theory. Basic Psychological Needs in Motivation, Development, and Wellness*; Guilford Press: New York, NY, USA, 2017.
56. Ryan, R.M.; Deci, E.L. Intrinsic and extrinsic motivations: Classic definitions and new directions. *Contemp. Educ. Psychol.* **2000**, *25*, 54–67. [CrossRef] [PubMed]

57. Tagkaloglou, S.; Kasser, T. Increasing collaborative, pro-environmental activism: The roles of Motivational Interviewing, self-determined motivation, and self-efficacy. *J. Environ. Psychol.* **2018**, *58*, 86–92. [CrossRef]
58. France, C.R.; France, J.L.; Carlson, B.W.; Frye, V.; Shaz, B.H. Applying self-determination theory to the blood donation context: The blood donor competence, autonomy, and relatedness enhancement (Blood Donor CARE) trial. *Contemp. Clin. Trials* **2017**, *53*, 44–51. [CrossRef] [PubMed]
59. Enko, J. Creative writers' experience of self-determination: An examination within the grounded theory framework. *Think. Skills Creat.* **2014**, *14*, 1–10. [CrossRef]
60. Lohmann, J.; Muula, A.S.; Houlfort, N.; De Allegri, M. How does performance-based financing affect health workers' intrinsic motivation? A Self-Determination Theory-based mixed-methods study in Malawi. *Soc. Sci. Med.* **2018**, *208*, 1–8. [CrossRef]
61. Friederichs, S.A.H.; Bolman, C.; Oenema, A.; Verboon, P.; Lechner, L. Exploring the working mechanisms of a web-based physical activity intervention, based on self-determination theory and motivational interviewing. *Internet Interv.* **2016**, *3*, 8–17. [CrossRef]
62. Zheng, C.; Liang, J.-C.; Li, M.; Tsai, C.-C. The relationship between English language learners' motivation and online self-regulation: A structural equation modelling approach. *System* **2018**, *76*, 144–157. [CrossRef]
63. Sergis, S.; Sampson, D.G.; Pelliccione, L. Investigating the impact of Flipped Classroom on students' learning experiences: A Self-Determination Theory approach. *Comput. Hum. Behav.* **2018**, *78*, 368–378. [CrossRef]
64. Streb, J.; Keis, O.; Lau, M.; Hille, K.; Spitzer, M.; Sosic-Vasic, Z. Emotional engagement in kindergarten and school children: A self-determination theory perspective. *Trends Neurosci. Educ.* **2015**, *4*, 102–107. [CrossRef]
65. Cho, H.-T.; Yang, J.-S. How perceptions of organizational politics influence self-determined motivation: The mediating role of work mood. *Asia Pac. Manag. Rev.* **2018**, *23*, 60–69. [CrossRef]
66. Lin, X.S.; Chen, Z.X.; Ashford, S.J.; Lee, C.; Qian, J. A self-consistency motivation analysis of employee reactions to job insecurity: The roles of organization-based self-esteem and proactive personality. *J. Bus. Res.* **2018**, *92*, 168–178. [CrossRef]
67. Sheldon, K.M.; Turban, D.B.; Brown, K.G.; Barrick, M.R.; Judge, T.A. Applying Self-Determination Theory to Organizational Research. In *Research in Personnel and Human Resources Management (Research in Personnel and Human Resources Management, 22)*; Emerald Group Publishing Limited: Bingley, UK, 2003; pp. 357–393.
68. Jowett, S.; Adie, J.W.; Bartholomew, K.J.; Yang, S.X.; Gustafsson, H.; Lopez-Jiménez, A. Motivational processes in the coach-athlete relationship: A multi-cultural self-determination approach. *Psychol. Sport Exerc.* **2017**, *32*, 143–152. [CrossRef]
69. Gagné, M.; Vansteenkiste, M. Self-Determination Theory's Contribution to Positive Organizational Psychology. In *Advances in Positive Organizational Psychology (Advances in Positive Organizational Psychology, 1)*; Bakker, A.B., Ed.; Emerald Group Publishing Limited: Bingley, UK, 2013; pp. 61–82.
70. Vallerand, R.J.; Fortier, M.; Guay, F. Self-determination and persistence in a real-life setting: Toward a motivational model of high school dropout. *J. Personal. Soc. Psychol.* **1997**, *72*, 1161–1177. [CrossRef]
71. Howard, J.; Gagné, M.; Morin, A.J.S.; Van den Broeck, A. Motivation profiles at work: A self-determination theory approach. *J. Vocat. Behav.* **2016**, *95–96*, 74–89. [CrossRef]
72. Moran, C.M.; Diefendorff, J.M.; Kim, T.-Y.; Liu, Z.-Q. A profile approach to self-determination theory motivations at work. *J. Vocat. Behav.* **2012**, *81*, 354–363. [CrossRef]
73. Kuvaas, B. A test of hypotheses derived from self-determination theory among public sector employees. *Empl. Relat.* **2008**, *31*, 39–56. [CrossRef]
74. Kelley, J.B.; Alden, D.L. Online brand community: Through the eyes of Self Determination Theory. *Internet Res.* **2016**, *26*, 790–808. [CrossRef]
75. Ryan, R.M.; Deci, E.L. Self-Regulation and the Problem of Human Autonomy: Does Psychology Need Choice, Self-Determination, and Will? *J. Personal.* **2006**, *74*, 1557–1585. [CrossRef]
76. Ryan, R.M.; Deci, E.L. Self-determination theory and the facilitation of intrinsic motivation, social development and well-being. *Am. Psychol.* **2000**, *55*, 68–78. [CrossRef]
77. Russo, S.; Stattin, H. Self-determination theory and the role of political interest in adolescents' sociopolitical development. *J. Appl. Dev. Psychol.* **2017**, *50*, 71–78. [CrossRef]
78. Deci, E.L.; Ryan, R.M. Facilitating optimal motivation and psychological well-being across life's domains. *Can. Psychol.* **2008**, *49*, 14–23. [CrossRef]
79. van Gelderen, M. Autonomy as the guiding aim of entrepreneurship education. *Educ. Train.* **2010**, *52*, 710–721. [CrossRef]

80. Adams, C.; Khojasteh, J. Igniting students' inner determination: The role of a need supportive climate. *J. Educ. Adm.* **2018**, *56*, 382–397. [CrossRef]
81. Engström, J.; Elg, M. A self-determination theory perspective on customer participation in service development. *J. Serv. Mark.* **2015**, *29*, 511–521. [CrossRef]
82. Cooke, A.; Fielding, K. Fun environmentalism!: Potential contributions of autonomy supportive psychology to sustainable lifestyles. *Manag. Environ. Qual. Int. J.* **2010**, *21*, 155–164. [CrossRef]
83. Eyal, O.; Roth, G. Principals' leadership and teachers' motivation: Self-determination theory analysis. *J. Educ. Adm.* **2011**, *49*, 256–275. [CrossRef]
84. Rezvani, A.; Khosravi, P.; Dong, L. Motivating users toward continued usage of information systems: Self-determination theory perspective. *Comput. Hum. Behav.* **2017**, *76*, 263–275. [CrossRef]
85. Roca, J.C.; Gagne, M. Understanding e-learning continuance intention in the workplace: A self-determination theory perspective. *Comput. Hum. Behav.* **2008**, *24*, 1585–1604. [CrossRef]
86. Aesaert, K.; van Braak, J.; van Nijlen, D.; Vanderlinde, R. Primary school pupils' ICT competences: Extensive model and scale development. *Comput. Educ.* **2015**, 326–344. [CrossRef]
87. Jeno, L.M.; Grytnes, J.-A.; Vandvik, V. The effect of a mobile-application tool on biology students' motivation and achievement in species identification: A Self-Determination Theory perspective. *Comput. Educ.* **2017**, *107*, 1–12. [CrossRef]
88. Niemiec, C.P.; Ryan, R.M. Autonomy, competence, and relatedness in the classroom. Applying self-determination theory to educational practice. *Theory Res. Educ.* **2009**, *7*, 133–144. [CrossRef]
89. Gupta, V.; Kapur, P.K.; Kumar, D. Modeling and measuring attributes influencing DevOps implementation in an enterprise using structural equation modelling. *Inf. Softw. Technol.* **2017**, *92*, 75–91. [CrossRef]
90. Lee, Y.; Lee, J.; Hwang, Y. Relating motivation to information and communication technology acceptance: Self-determination theory perspective. *Comput. Hum. Behav.* **2015**, *51*, 418–428. [CrossRef]
91. Sørebø, Ø.; Halvari, H.; Gulli, V.F.; Kristiansen, R. The role of self-determination theory in explaining teachers' motivation to continue to use e-learning technology. *Comput. Educ.* **2009**, *53*, 1177–1187. [CrossRef]
92. Sharmeen, F.; Arentze, T.; Timmermans, H. An analysis of the dynamics of activity and travel needs in response to social network evolution and life-cycle events: A structural equation model. *Transp. Res. Part A Policy Pract.* **2014**, *59*, 159–171. [CrossRef]
93. Fornell, C.; Larcker, D.F. Evaluating Structural Equation Models with Unobservable Variables and Measurement Error. *J. Mark. Res.* **1981**, *18*, 39–50. [CrossRef]
94. Gefen, D.; Straub, D. A Practical Guide to Factorial Validity Using Pls-Graph: Tutorial and Annotated Example. *Commun. ACM* **2005**, *16*, 91–109. [CrossRef]
95. Limayem, M.; Cheung, C.M.K. Understanding Information Systems Continuance: The Case of Internet-Based Learning Technologies. *Inf. Manag.* **2008**, *45*, 227–232. [CrossRef]
96. Hair, J.F.; Black, W.C.; Babin, B.J.; Anderson, R.E. *Multivariate Data Analysis*, 7th ed.; Prentice Hall: Upper Saddle River, NJ, USA, 2010.
97. Jöreskog, K.G.; Sörbom, D. *Lisrel 8.80 for Windows (Computer Software)*; Scientific Software International, Inc.: Lincolnwood, IL, USA, 2006.
98. Reisinger, Y.; Turner, L. Structural equation modeling with Lisrel: Application in tourism. *Tour. Manag.* **1999**, *20*, 71–88. [CrossRef]
99. Lei, P.W. Evaluating estimation methods for ordinal data in structural equation modeling. *Qual. Quant.* **2009**, *43*, 495–507. [CrossRef]
100. Skrondal, A.; Rabe-Hesketh, S. *Generalized Latent Variable Modeling: Multilevel, Longitudinal, and Structural Equation Models*; Chapman & Hall/CRC: Boca Ratón, FL, USA, 2004.
101. Reeve, J. Self-determination theory applied to educational settings. In *Handbook of Self-Determination Research*; Deci, E.L., Ryan, R.M., Eds.; University of Rochester Press: Rochester, NY, USA, 2002; pp. 183–203.

© 2020 by the authors. Licensee MDPI, Basel, Switzerland. This article is an open access article distributed under the terms and conditions of the Creative Commons Attribution (CC BY) license (http://creativecommons.org/licenses/by/4.0/).

Article

# A Multi-Analytical Approach to Predict the Determinants of Cloud Computing Adoption in Higher Education Institutions

Yousef A. M. Qasem [1,*], Shahla Asadi [1,*], Rusli Abdullah [1,*], Yusmadi Yah [1], Rodziah Atan [1], Mohammed A. Al-Sharafi [2] and Amr Abdullatif Yassin [3]

1. Faculty of Computer Science and Information Technology, Universiti Putra Malaysia, Serdang 43400, Malaysia; yusmadi@upm.edu.my (Y.Y.); rodziah@upm.edu.my (R.A.)
2. Faculty of Computer Systems and Software Engineering, University Malaysia Pahang, Kuantan 26600, Malaysia; pcc15013@stdmail.ump.edu.my
3. School of Language Studies and Linguistics, Faculty of Social Sciences and Humanities, Universiti Kebangsaan Malaysia, Bangi 43600, Kajang, Selangor, Malaysia; amryassin84@gmail.com
* Correspondence: gs45505@student.upm.edu.my (Y.A.M.Q.); asadi_shahla@upm.edu.my (S.A.); rusli@upm.edu.my (R.A.)

Received: 30 May 2020; Accepted: 20 June 2020; Published: 17 July 2020

**Abstract:** Cloud computing (CC) delivers services for organizations, particularly for higher education institutions (HEIs) anywhere and anytime, based on scalability and pay-per-use approach. Examining the factors influencing the decision-makers' intention towards adopting CC plays an essential role in HEIs. Therefore, this study aimed to understand and predict the key determinants that drive managerial decision-makers' perspectives for adopting this technology. The data were gathered from 134 institutional managers, involved in the decision making of the institutions. This study applied two analytical approaches, namely variance-based structural equation modeling (i.e., PLS-SEM) and artificial neural network (ANN). First, the PLS-SEM approach has been used for analyzing the proposed model and extracting the significant relationships among the identified factors. The obtained result from PLS-SEM analysis revealed that seven factors were identified as significant in influencing decision-makers' intention towards adopting CC. Second, the normalized importance among those seven significant predictors was ranked utilizing the ANN. The results of the ANN approach showed that technology readiness is the most important predictor for CC adoption, followed by security and competitive pressure. Finally, this study presented a new and innovative approach for comprehending CC adoption, and the results can be used by decision-makers to develop strategies for adopting CC services in their institutions.

**Keywords:** cloud computing; technology adoption; higher education institutions; SEM; neural network

## 1. Introduction

Cloud computing (CC) has emerged as a new technology and popular computing model to deliver access to a huge amount of data and computational resources by utilizing simple interface [1]. There are many characteristics of CC, including flexibility, cost-effectiveness, scalability, and collaboration, which make it crucial for higher education institutes, organizations, and users. According to a CC tracking poll IDC [2], 43% of HEIs had implemented or sustained CC by 2012. This number increased by 10% between 2011 and 2012, and the growth is estimated to increase in the next few years. Besides, the International Data Corporation stated that the industrial field, including the education sector, will witness an increase of $210 billion or about 23.8% in the amount of CC by 2019; hence, there will be an increase rate of 22.5% in five consecutive years to become $370 billion by 2022 [3]. It has been noted that cloud platforms, as well as ecosystems, will function as the launchpad for the drastic rise in the digital innovation pace and scale in the next five years. Additionally, CC is considered to be the fifth utility following the four main utilities, namely water, gas, telephone, and electricity [4]. In the education sector, institutions that provide education to degree-level, tertiary, and HEIs providers [5], will have to keep pace with technological advancement. In the past, investment in IT by these institutions has traditionally been expensive, yet the provided education services to the community are expected to be affordable and maintain excellent quality [6]. To rise to this challenge, HEIs must become more efficient through focusing on the delivery of excellent services, and they need to look for ways to maximize their resources in order to maintain providing excellent services [7]. Although HEIs need to deliver good standards of education through factual knowledge and more practical skills, they have a unique opportunity to graduate skillful and professional students, who are solution-focused and adept at problem-solving [5].

For higher education institutions, CC presents an ideal opportunity to lower their IT costs with increasing efficiency, which has a positive impact on their long-term sustainability. As suggested by Thomas [8], CC is not only a learning tool for HEIs but also an important platform in more general terms as it will encourage educators to improve their practice and encourage partnership in order to improve their productivity. Moreover, CC will be able to save both costs and energy output because the same cloud infrastructure can be utilized by a wide range of users in teaching, learning, and research [9]. Besides, the successful adoption of CC and delivery for cloud-based education services requires understanding of these processes from the side of HEIs [10,11].

Although CC suggests excessive aids to organizations, there are some challenges that might impact its adoption. Several studies on CC have been carried out in developed nations. Studies on CC in educational institutions in developing nations are scarce [12], especially in Malaysia [13,14]. The successful adoption of any novel technology such as CC does not depend only on universities and cloud service providers' support but also on users' willingness and intention to adopt and utilize these services [12,15,16]. Therefore, the adoption of any new technology depends on the innovativeness of the decision-makers. That is, the role of decision-makers plays an essential role because they are the main contributors to CC adoption, especially that they can support the required CC services and types in HEIs [17,18].

Many challenges are facing HEIs in sustaining the education process such as delivering affordable education services, improving education quality, increasing budgets and participants, and getting the requirement of infrastructure IT [19,20]. Therefore, HEIs keep struggling in managing their resources and improving their service [21]. CC is a favorable solution for HEIs that supports cost reduction and improves education quality [22]. Besides, the sustainability of HEIs can be achieved by providing the required infrastructure, software, and storage through CC adoption [21,23,24]. Thus, the emergence of CC and the advantages it provides can help bridge this technological gap. Generally, CC in HEIs is increasing in popularity, but it is still lagging behind the commercial, government, and other sectors [25]. Past literature has shown that productivity at the organizational-level increases significantly for organizations that have invested in ICTs for their operations [26]. Besides, the Coronavirus 2019 (COVID-19) pandemic affected HEIs not just in Wuhan, China where the virus originated but all other HEIs in 188 countries as of 6 April 2020. CC as a technology of the fourth industrial revolution (IR 4.0) could enable educational countermeasures to continue the education process despite the COVID-19 predicaments [27,28]. Therefore, CC in this case is not only an alternative option for HEIs but also an essential solution.

In the current study, the unit of analysis is the organization level because the primary focus is on decision-makers, who are responsible for CC adoption. Individuals are considered to be the observers for the phenomenon at the organizational level [29].

Besides, most of the prior studies have primarily focused on CC technology, costs, applications, security, and benefits in small and medium organizations [30]. However, a limited number of studies have focused on CC adoption and its usage in HEIs [3]. Furthermore, several studies have looked at

CC from different perspectives in various developing countries such as sub-Saharan Africa [30–32], Malaysia [33,34], and Saudi Arabia [18,35,36]. Other studies discussed CC implementation in academic libraries [37,38] and the enhancement of overall awareness regarding CC migration issues [18]. Moreover, organization-based studies have evaluated the readiness of HEIs to implement CCs [32,39,40], and other studies have examined the impacts of technology on HEIs [14,41].

Even though a substantial amount of consideration is given to the CC, few studies have been carried out to identify the influential factors in adopting CC in HEIs from the perspective of decision-makers [3,30]. Meanwhile, in spite of the efficiency and usefulness of advanced artificial neural networks (ANN) as a soft computing technique in identifying and ranking determinants in technology adoption [42], application of this technique in the context of CC remains mainly unexplored, especially in education atmosphere. Taking into consideration these points, the current study aimed to develop and test a proposed adoption model and to examine the key factors, influencing decision-makers' intention of CC adoption in Malaysian higher education institutions. Therefore, the key objectives of the current study are as follow:

To analyze the factors that influence the adoption of CC in HEIs.

To propose an appropriate model for evaluating the adoption of CC in HEIs, validated by using two analytical approaches (i.e., PLS-SEM and ANN).

To contribute to the body of knowledge on the organizational-level adoption, this research will first merge two well-established theories which are the Technology-Organizational-Environmental (TOE) framework [43] and the diffusion of innovations (DOI) [44], to fill the gap in previous literature. Drawing on the organizational level adoption theories, our research model is built on the TOE framework and DOI model which is in line with the objectives of this study. Furthermore, the research model constructs are grounded by the literature taking into account the context of the study. The study also implemented variance-based structural equation modeling (PLS-SEM) for assessing the factors impacting CC adoption, and a neural network is used for predicting how CC is adopted in HEIs. For this, the sequential multi-method research design, suggested by Scott and Walczak [45], was implemented as it is suitable for enabling a deeper understanding of the subject under investigation. In this study, PLS-SEM is applied for corroborating the validity of the causal relationships through the assessment of the goodness of the model's fit. Following this, PLS-SEM analysis of supported relationships along with PLS-SEM analysis of significant variables were utilized as the neural network structure inputs for estimating how CC is adopted in HEIs. Merging these two approached provides a significant benefit for utilizing a new method to evaluate CC adoption in which one method benefits help in balancing out the other method drawbacks [45].

Generally, we contribute to research in different ways. First, this research contributes to the body of knowledge within information systems (IS) field surrounding technology adoption. This study provided empirical literature within IS, especially CC, and it provided an extensive model that integrates the TOE framework and DOI model. Second, this study provided an assessment for CC adoption in HEIs, and more revitalization of the CC and intent of decision-makers to utilize CC in HEIs. Third, the DOI model and TOE framework incorporation improved the ability to explain the proposed model with 81% of the dependent variable's variance, which shows that the model's ability for prediction is powerful and remarkable. Fourth, this research used a hybrid approach for the integration of PLS-SEM and ANN to validate the proposed model and to give priority to the factors that impact CC adoption, through the identification of the relative importance of every factor. Conventional statistical approaches are valid and necessary; thereby, offering a powerful foundation in previous IS adoption studies. The suggestion of this research is the need to reinterpret past works on IS adoption through the combination of linear and non-linear approaches in order to provide outstanding strength to technology adoption. Fifth, since HEI is a promising market for cloud service providers, this study is remarkably impactful for cloud providers and technology practitioners as it will help in the recognition of the factors that influence the adoption of CC. Likewise, cloud providers need to provide a clear instruction or navigation system in guiding users in HEIs to operate the services smoothly, thereby increasing the assurance that cloud technology is used. Finally, the research results will help decision-makers with the assessment of cloud technology, organization, and environments during the decision of the adoption of CC. Furthermore, decision-makers may use this proposed framework for the investigation of other IT/IS adoption procedures.

The rest of this study is arranged as follows: Section 2 reviews previous studies on CC adoption. Section 3 presents the hypotheses of the study and discusses the model development. Section 4 highlights the research methodology and Section 5 explains the analytical approaches, including PLS-SEM and neural network. The discussion of the study is presented in Section 6, and Implications are presented in Section 7. Conclusion, limitations, and future research directions are discussed at the end of the study.

## 2. Literature Review

### 2.1. Cloud Computing Concept

The concept of CC does not have a single definition that has been accepted universally as there is still an ongoing discussion and debate about this term. This might be due to some parallels between other types of high-performance computing and CC, such as peer-to-peer computing, cluster computing, market and service-oriented computing, and grid computing [24]. As technology continues to make advancements, the debate around CC continues, and studying the existing literature does reveal some common characteristics for CC across the various available definitions [46].

According to the National Institute of Standards and Technology (NIST), CC is a model that allows wide-ranging, on-demand, network access to shared configurable computing resources such as services, storage, applications, and networks. These resources can be provided quickly and with little effort by either the provider or the customer [47] as they are essentially a way of integrating existing technologies, but provide them in a new way to help businesses make a fundamental change to their operations [48]. This is achieved by connecting existing technology, including software as a service (SaaS), utility computing, and grid computing [49]. Next-generation data centers that combined virtual services such as database, hardware, application logic, and user interface in a network was an objective for the application of cloud technology [50]. Crucially, these new data centers have allowed users to access their applications not only from a singular location but also from any place.

### 2.2. Cloud Computing Services and Deployment Models

According to [47], CC comprises a tripartite of services, infrastructure as a service (IaaS), platform as a service (PaaS) and software as a service (SaaS). The latter enables users to access applications via a cloud-based infrastructure. SaaS means that the infrastructure such as the servers, operating systems, and networks are essentially removed from the consumer, who no longer need to be concerned with this or with other issues such as data storage. To access the services, the customer uses either a direct interface, which is used for web-based emails such as Gmail, or a program interface such as Dropbox. Meanwhile, the IaaS model means that consumers can deploy and run the software, which they choose, through the provision of computing resources such as networks, storage, and processing. This can be achieved through varies softwares, which might be an application or even an entire operating system such as Microsoft Azure and Amazon Web Services, which are two examples of providers within this sphere. Finally, PaaS provides a platform for users to deploy applications on a broader cloud infrastructure and allows them to create and modify their applications by using libraries, services, and languages that have already been developed by a cloud platform provider such as Google App Engine or Heroku.

A description of the four deployment models in cloud technology applications is seen in [47], where these cloud types are named as private, community, public, and hybrid. The private cloud, as the name suggests, is used solely within one organization and its infrastructure may be either self-managed or operated by a third party [51]. This model is usually chosen when security issues are a concern for a particular organization, so in the academic sector, this may be due to ownership of certain resources or to cultivate an online community [51].

Concerning the community model, many institutions may use the same basic infrastructure that is hosted either by a third party or by one of the organizations that is part of the community. Organizations may consider this model to be an advantage either through shared costs and resources or because perceived risks are lessened when the model is shared [52]. This model may work well when used by cooperating organizations, or when institutions have a close relationship or are interlinked in some way but can be an issue in higher education sector where many similar institutions are essentially in competition with each other for students, funding and other resources.

The public cloud is probably the most popular form of cloud deployment and is managed by the provider of the service, and the most well-known providers are Microsoft One Drive, Dropbox, and Google Drive as well as those provided by Amazon. In the field of education, users such as students, lecturers and faculty staff will probably be familiar with the system, which is one of its advantages.

The final model of deployment is the hybrid cloud, which combines two or more models. Utilizing more than one model harnesses the benefits of each model and aims to mitigate the disadvantages of every single model as well as to provide a more flexible and wide-ranging approach.

*2.3. Cloud Computing in HEIs*

In the education environment, CC can provide both teachers and students with numerous advantages. Whether in education or research, the ability to store big data and to collaborate on projects and share materials is an attractive proposition [52]. Besides, because CC can be used remotely, users can take advantage of the ability to access these materials on any device at any time and from any place. HEIs and universities have chosen to bypass old-style IT set-ups and software systems in favor of CC, and they have been attracted to its efficiency and rapid implementation [21].

Collaborate approaches to learning are one of the key benefits that CC technology offers, which makes it an ideal choice for the institutions, looking for computer-based technologies to enhance more socially-oriented and cooperative learning styles [53]. Cloud computing also facilitates e-learning in human computing interaction as they are able to utilize facilities such as data access monitoring and storage through a cloud platform, which also provides its infrastructure [54].

Cloud computing is increasing in popularity in HEIs, although it is considered to be in its infancy in this sector of the market, as it is unable to surpass the commercial sector or government organizations [25]. However, it is increasingly becoming a necessary part of the educational offer rather than a choice, and this is due to the increasing competition in the higher education marketplace and the pressures on performance, student successes, and income [55]. HEIs can benefit from the CC features and surpass its limitations so that CC services can be accessible to the practicing educational community [56].

Table 1 illustrates how scientific contributors have discussed this subject from a range of perspectives and how they have attempted to capture the services that CC offers in the higher education sector. Despite this evidence, gaps in research are still clear at the organizational level [57], as many of the existing studies lack empirical findings about CC usage in HEIs [30,31]. This lack of evidence at the organizational level necessitates conducting further studies about CC adoption in HEIs and exploring in depth the factors that affect this process of adoption. Although Table 1 shows the previous literature on adoption of the CC in HEIs that includes the TOE, DOI, and technology acceptance model (TAM) models (TAM1, TAM3), this study is built on the organizational level theories (i.e., TOE and DOI) which is in line with the objectives of the study.

**Table 1.** The adoption of CC in HEIs: a summary of prior research studies.

| Study | Title | Theory | Methodology | Country |
|---|---|---|---|---|
| [31] | "A cross-country model of contextual factors impacting CC adoption at universities in sub-Saharan Africa" | DOI theory and TAM | Quantitative research. A survey concerning university-level ICT experts as well as decision makers. 355 valid responses. | HEIs in sub-Saharan Africa |
| [30] | "Conceptualizing a model for adoption of CC in education" | DOI theory TAM | Conceptual Model | HEIs in sub-Saharan Africa |
| [58] | "The Effectiveness of Cloud-Based E-Learning towards Quality of Academic Services: An Omanis' Expert View" | N/A | Qualitative approach/Semi-structured interviews. | HEIs in Oman. |
| [18] | "An exploratory study for investigating the critical success factors for cloud migration in the Saudi Arabian higher education context" | N/A Success factors based on literature | Structured online questionnaire | HEIs in Saudi Arabia |
| [54] | "Using CC for E-learning systems" | LR | | HEIs in Saudi Arabia |
| [24] | "Student perceptions of cloud applications effectiveness in higher education" | N/A | Survey | University in Southeast Michigan USA |
| [5] | "A conceptual model of e-learning based on CC adoption in higher education institutions" | DOI; FVM | Conceptual Model | HEIs in Oman |
| [59] | "Examining CC Adoption Intention in Higher Education: Exploratory Study" | TAM | A survey utilizing a questionnaire on paper. | Politehnica University of Bucharest, Romania. |
| [60] | "Investigating the structural relationship for the determinants of CC adoption in education" | TAM | A quantitative method/administer a survey | Universities in Thailand |
| [61] | "Cloud for e-Learning: Determinants of Its Adoption by University Students in a Developing Country" | TAM3 | An empirical study and a survey questionnaire | Saudi Arabia |
| [62] | "Determinants and their causal relationships affecting the adoption of CC in science and technology institutions" | DOI | Focus group discussion and DEMATEL | Science and technology institutions, Taiwan |
| [35] | "CC adoption by HEIs in Saudi Arabia: an exploratory study" | TOE | Survey | HEIs in Saudi Arabia |
| [63] | "CC adoption and usage in community colleges" | TAM3 | Virtual Computing Lab and focus groups concerning instructors as well as interviews of other stakeholders such as IT support staff and college administrators | Rural and urban community colleges, USA |

*2.4. Technology Adoption Theories*

The adoption process refers to the decision-making individual (the adopter) or unit undergoing the process of taking a new product, service, or idea into account [44]. There are numerous phases involved in this process, and the outcome is the decision of whether the new item should be selected. According to [64], the decision is made by an entity regarding the adoption of a particular object and in a specific context. Moreover, various factors are affecting this decision, and in the present study, HEI is the entity while CC adoption is the object. After analyzing previous studies, it was found that many studies considered constructs influencing the CC adoption at an individual level ([24,59–61,63,65–77]); however, there was a dearth of material concerning this at the organizational level [31,32,35]. As mentioned above, the two most dominant hypotheses used for considering technology adoption from an organizational perspective are the TOE framework, and the DOI model [31,32,35,78–84].

### 2.4.1. TOE Framework

TOE framework can define the innovation process within an enterprise context because TOE considers three aspects of an enterprise, namely technology, organization, and environment, that affect the adoption of emerging technologies [43]. In this framework, technology refers to the internal and external technical knowledge of an organization, as well as the mechanization that may influence the adoption decision. Besides, the characteristics of the company, including its particular communications channels and resources, are under the organization aspects, while the external forces such as competition and the regulatory and market conditions sit within the environment aspect [43,85,86].

### 2.4.2. DOI Model

DOI theory uses five phases to explain how the innovation process works within an organization [25]. The five phases are knowledge, persuasion, decision, implementation, and confirmation [55]. This theory is broad-based and provides a persuasive explanation for the process of adopting innovation by any organization. By focusing on this process, DOI theory offers a complementary perspective because it focuses more on the technological aspects of the TOE framework, and the use of the two frameworks makes everyone has a complementary advantage.

The TOE framework and the DOI model are used widely to examine the adoption of technology at the organizational level [31,32,35,78–84]. We carry out an analysis of the adoption theories used in the literature. Table 2 shows that authors apply one or more theoretical models to build their research models. Nevertheless, it is not possible to apply a single theory to all types of innovations [87]. Therefore, an incorporated model of theories is desirable, to be used in deciding the adoption process of certain types of innovation.

**Table 2.** Mapping matrix of the model theories.

| Theory/Model | Definition | Justification | Limitation | Previous Studies | |
|---|---|---|---|---|---|
| | | | | IT Adoption (Dependent Variable) | Source |
| TOE | The aim of TOE framework [43] is to clarify the procedure for innovation adoption at the organizational level. It looks into three contexts that affect the use of an innovation in a firm—the organization, the technology, and the environment context. | TOE model has a wide power across a number of technological, industrial, and national/cultural contexts [88–90]. TOE framework can be applied in empirical research since new technologies are developed, especially when novel contexts for adoption can be identified [91]. | TOE does not offer a robust model for relating the factors that affect the organizational acceptance decision making; instead, it gives a taxonomy for classifying adoption factors in their individual contexts. Researchers are advised to take a wider context into consideration in which improvement takes place [92]. | Mobile supply chain | [93] |
| | | | | Radio frequency identification (RFID) | [94–96] |
| | | | | Green IT | [92,97] |
| | | | | Interorganizational business process standards | [98] |
| | | | | E-business | [86,99,100] |
| | | | | SaaS | [101] |
| | | | | Cloud computing | [102,103] |
| DOI | DOI theory [104] gives a detailed explanation on the diffusion of innovation within an organization. According to DOI theory, an innovation undergoes a number of stage procedures until it thrives in the firm [105]. | DOI theory gives a broader standpoint on the diffusion incident and gives a good explanation on how new innovations are applied. Therefore, DOI enriches the technological context of the TOE framework, and thus gains value when applied in conjunction with the TOE framework [84]. | It is not possible to apply a single theory to all types of innovations [87]. | Internet | [106] |
| | | | | E-procurement | [107] |
| | | | | RFID | [108] |
| | | | | E-business | [100,109] |
| | | | | Cloud computing | [103] |
| TOE and DOI | | DOI theory makes a wide standpoint available on the diffusion phenomenon, and it gives excellent explanations on how new innovations are chosen. Therefore, DOI enriches the technological context of the TOE structure, and thereby obtain value when applied in conjunction with TOE framework [84]. | | Benchmarking | [107] |
| | | | | Collaborative commerce | [110] |
| | | | | E-commerce | [79] |
| | | | | Open source | [111] |
| | | | | Digital transformation | [112] |
| TOE and INT | | INT benefits TOE by enriching the environmental context of TOE framework [28–30], so it gains value when used in combination with the TOE structure [21]. | | Scope of ecommerce use | [113] |
| TOE, DOI and INT | | A combination of DOI theory, TOE framework, and INT theory thus gives a theoretically solid basis to evaluate the technology, organization, and environment characteristics [84]. | | E-procurement | [63] |
| | | | | SaaS diffusion in firms | [84] |
| TOE and ECM | | It is imperative to incorporate not only technology-level factors from the IS continuance literature, but also new constructs and relationships that capture the complex nature of organization-level decisions [114,115]. | | Enterprise 2.0 post-adoption | [115] |

231

## 2.5. Analysis Techniques

Statistical analysis has been an essential tool for researchers for more than a century to extend their ability to develop, explore, and confirm research findings. Statistical methods' applications have expanded recently with the advent of computer technologies [116]. In this section, we explain two analytical approaches, and why the purpose of their employment in this study.

### 2.5.1. Structural Equation Modeling

Structural equation modeling (SEM) is a second-generation multivariate data analysis method that is used to either explore or confirm theory [116]. There are two types of SEM—one is covariance-based, and the other is variance-based. CBSEM is used to confirm (or reject) theories. Variance-based structural equation modeling (i.e., PLS-SEM) is primarily used for exploratory research and the development of theories [116]. To validating the measurement and structural model, Variance-based structural equation modeling (PLS-SEM) was applied to the collected data with SmartPLS 3.0.

### 2.5.2. Neural Network

The neural network can be explained as a significant parallel distributed processor, consisting of simple processing units that are naturally inclined to store experimental knowledge and to provide access for use [117]. Moreover, a neural network is considered to be similar to the human brain and is capable of attaining new knowledge from its surroundings by implementing the learning process. Then, the synaptic weights store this acquired knowledge [117]. Following this, the learning algorithm uses sample data for altering the synaptic weights of the neural network in an orderly fashion in order to achieve the design objective [117]. Moreover, the neural network offers numerous benefits than traditional statistical methods. Such benefits include non-linear and linear neural networks to enable the assessment of non-compensatory decision processes, and it can help attain the input and output mapping without requiring specific distribution concerning the output or input [118]. Furthermore, the adaptivity of the neural network suggests that it is able to address the data generation process in terms of structural changes and that it is not difficult to re-train it according to environmental changes [118,119]. It has also been noted that neural networks surpass traditional compensatory models such as multiple, discriminant, and logistic regression analyses [118,119]. However, despite the fact that neural network has been implemented in studies in different fields such as economics [120], customer loyalty [121], wearable healthcare devices [122], and consumer choice [119,123], few studies have focused on its information systems applications [124]. Hence, the present study will first utilize PLS-SEM to determine the constructs that have strong relationships with the adoption of CC in HEIs, and then implement the non-compensatory neural network model for foreseeing the adoption of CC in HEIs according to the critical adoption variables.

## 3. Hypotheses and Model Development

A research hypothesis is defined as a "logically conjectured relationship between two or more variables expressed in the form of a testable statement" [125]. For this reason, the assumptions of the current study are discussed below.

### 3.1. Compatibility

In DOI theory, compatibility is the first variable that is expected to be able to foresee CC adoption. This is also called the extent to which an innovation matches the past practices, current values, and present needs of the potential adopter [104]. Moreover, compatibility examined how much innovation can conform to the existing systems. It has also been noted that the characteristics of a new technology innovation can impact potential innovation adopters. Further, DOI studies have accentuated how significant compatibility is when assessing the disposition of organizations for implementing new technology [104,126].

Several studies have examined compatibility as an important addition to the variance concerning IT managers' inclination to adopt CC [30,31,35,127,128]. Hence, the following hypothesis is devised:

**Hypothesis 1 (H1).** *Compatibility positively impacts CC adoption in HEIs.*

*3.2. Competitive Pressure*

Competitive pressure is the perceived pressure by the leaders of an institution when CC services help competitors to achieved substantial competitive advantage in teaching and learning effectiveness [115,129,130]. Literature has studied competitive pressure as a significant construct, affecting the use of CC in various contexts [100,112,115,131–133]. Therefore, the second hypothesis is as follows:

**Hypothesis 2 (H2).** *Competitive pressure positively influences CC adoption in HEIs.*

*3.3. Complexity*

Complexity refers to the perceived difficulty of the organization regarding comprehending and utilizing an innovation [134]. If the relevant innovation is deemed to be difficult to use, it reduces the possibility of adoption [104]. A meta-analysis study was conducted by Tornatzky and Klein [135] where they observed that compatibility and complexity formed the major attributes concerning technology innovation behavior. The DOI literature also highlights the importance of determining the complexity of organizations in their tendencies to implement new technologies [104,126].

Previous literature has studied complexity as the most significant construct, influencing CC adoption [30,31,35,127,128]. It is, therefore, hypothesized that:

**Hypothesis 3 (H3).** *Complexity negatively influences CC adoption in HEIs.*

*3.4. Cost Savings*

Cost savings refer to the decreased capital investment needed in an institution for IT service leased resources and hardware solutions [136]. The storage and delivery services provided by CC have significantly reduced the cost [137], which has made it a valuable solution in the current financial crisis to maintain the quality of services by the institutions [138]. Cloud computing technology is based on Internet technologies and cost-effectiveness as key distinguishing characteristics of CC [139] which can influence its adoption. Researchers found that perceived higher cost saving led to higher intention to adopt an innovation [140,141]. Based on the literature, it is postulated that:

**Hypothesis 4 (H4).** *Cost saving positively influences CC adoption in HEIs.*

*3.5. Vendor Support*

Top management literature suggests that IT service provider or vendor also plays a very important role in the decision of IT services adoption [142,143]. Vendor support in the case of CC services is far more crucial because cloud-based IT services from a capable vendor may enhance the internal capabilities of an organization [144]. Vendors provide cloud-based services, which can be dynamically priced and can be scaled up/down according to the requirements. This flexibility enables the client institution to develop and enhance their capabilities. However, only capable service providers will be able to provide these benefits. Therefore, it is hypothesized that:

**Hypothesis 5 (H5).** *Vendor support positively influences CC adoption in HEIs.*

*3.6. Technology Readiness*

Technology Readiness captures the internal technical resources of the organization [112]. A meta-analysis [145] asserted the technology readiness importance for IS adoption and impact. Mata, Fuerst [146] recommended technology readiness to be composed of technology infrastructure and IT skills.

Before adopting CC technology, it is important to know the readiness of an HEI. The HEI needs to promote the technology readiness of CC, and the Internet bandwidth should be sufficient for cloud access by all students and teachers. Instructional content should be ready to run on the cloud. Teachers and students need to have appropriate devices and an adequate internet connection to support the CC initiative [147].

Recent studies on CC adoption using DOI did find that technological readiness still has a significant impact on the adoption of CC [18,33,39,84,147]. Therefore, it is hypothesized that:

**Hypothesis 6 (H6).** *Technology readiness positively influences CC adoption in HEIs.*

*3.7. Top Management Support*

Top management support [18] refers to the top management's attitude regarding the concerned technology as well as the extent of support given to the adoption. In terms of a strategic perspective, the successful implementation of CC in HEIs depends on the capabilities of top leadership or management to drive the change from traditional deployment to CC through an official pro-cloud strategy [148]. The decision-makers' awareness and consensus are vital. Their support will ensure what cloud services are needed and what type of cloud deployment is best for HEIs settings. To do that, the decision-makers have to understand the benefits of cloud-based services, the value they can add to the educational services, and how to migrate to the CC environment [149]. Accordingly, it is hypothesized that:

**Hypothesis 7 (H7).** *Top management support positively influences CC adoption in HEIs.*

*3.8. Security*

Despite the boom in CC with new features and market access, security in CC remains the biggest problem hindering the adoption of CC services [31,37].

Security is one of the crucial technical problems concerning CC adoption. Cloud vendors are trying to simulate the classic principles of confidentiality, availability, and integrity, which are commonly found in physical systems for distributed, virtualized, and dynamic cloud systems that are accessed online [150]. Three service models are used in CC (SaaS, PaaS, and IaaS) and four deployment models (public, private, community, and hybrid), which require different levels of security for each model to protect the user's data [151]. Internet security vulnerabilities have been an issue for users for years, such as e-commerce and online banking. Hence, the importance of security in IT environment of HEIs is critical [148,152,153]. Because CC is based on Internet technology, the same security issues hinder its adoption. However, the advanced security algorithms used in CC have been identified as the main differentiators of CC [139] that can influence its adoption. Previous studies have considered security as an influencing factor in adopting CC services [31,33,37,38,147]. Accordingly, it is hypothesized that:

**Hypothesis 8 (H8).** *Data security negatively influences CC adoption in HEIs.*

*3.9. Research Model*

Based on the theoretical and conceptual background outlined previously, this research used a method that complements existing constructs in the DOI model through the lens of the TOE framework using constructs from the previous empirical literature on adoption research (see Table 2) to the context of IS adoption in HEIs. The importance of using these theoretical perspectives gives a theoretical basis to assess the task, organization, technology, and environment characteristics that affect CC adoption in HEIs, and this has received empirical support consistently [71,82–84,93,97,110,154,155]. To be able to include the various and wide list of factors from past search and filter them, we undertook a process of collaborating, matching, filtering, and consolidating for all the information and ideas from the past studies, discussed in the literature review [156,157]. Eventually, the most frequent factors were selected. Table 3 shows the mapping matrix of the related adoption theories and factors, obtained from previous literature.

**Table 3.** Mapping matrix of the model factors from TOE framework and DOI theory.

| Model/ Theory | Technology/ Dependent Variable | Source | Compatibility | Complexity | Security | Technology Readiness | Cost Savings | Top mgmt. Support | Competitive Pressures | Vendor Support |
|---|---|---|---|---|---|---|---|---|---|---|
| TOE | Cloud migration | [18] | | | | × | | × | | |
| DOI and others | CC adoption | [30,31] | × | × | × | × | × | | | |
| TOE | Open systems | [158] | | × | | | | | | |
| TOE | Electronic data interchange | [159] | | | | × | × | | | |
| TOE | E-business use | [85] | | | | | × | | | |
| DOI and TOE | E-business use | [112] | × | × | × | | × | | | |
| TOE | E-business adoption | [100] | | | | | × | | | |
| TOE | E-business | [80] | × | | | | | | | |
| TOE | Knowledge management and enterprise systems | [81] | × | × | | | | × | | |
| DOI and TOE | Collaborative commerce | [110] | × | × | | | | × | | |
| DOI, TOE, and others | Internet utilization | [106] | | | | × | × | × | | |
| DOI, TOE, and others | Cloud-based services adoption | [144] | | | | | | × | | × |
| DOI and TOE | Benchmarking | [107] | × | × | | | | | | |
| DOI | RFID | [108] | | × | | | | × | | |
| TOE and others | E-business adoption | [86] | | | | × | | | | |
| TOE | E-commerce | [160] | × | | | | × | × | | |
| TOE | Internet/E-business | [109] | × | × | | | | × | | |
| TOE | RFID adoption | [161] | × | × | | | × | × | | |
| DOI and TOE | CC adoption | [103] | × | × | | × | × | × | × | |
| DOI | Internet-based purchasing application assimilation | [162] | × | × | | | | | | |
| DOI | CC adoption | [163] | × | × | | | | | | |
| TOE | CC adoption | [164] | × | × | × | | × | | | |
| TOE | CC adoption | [165] | × | × | | | × | × | × | × |
| TOE | CC adoption | [102] | × | × | | × | × | × | × | |
| DOI and others | CC adoption | [166] | × | × | | | | | | |
| TOE and DOI | CC adoption | [84] | × | × | × | × | × | × | × | |
| TOE, DOI, and INT | SaaS diffusion in firms | [84] | × | × | × | × | × | × | × | |
| TOE and TAM | CC adoption | [167] | × | × | × | | | | × | × |
| TOE and TAM | CC adoption | [167] | × | × | | | | × | × | |
| TOE and TAM | CC adoption | [89] | × | × | | | | × | × | |
| DOI and FVM | CC adoption | [82] | × | × | × | × | × | | | |
| FVM, TOE and DOI | Cloud ERP Adoption | [168] | × | | × | | × | × | | |
| This study | | | × | × | × | × | × | × | × | × |

We also formulated a related hypothesis to specify the purpose of the research, highlight future areas of research, and to consolidate knowledge relating to CC adoption. Figure 1 provides an overview of the research proposed model. The research model demonstrates that compatibility, complexity, security, technology readiness, cost savings, top management support, competitive pressure, and vendor support factors will have a significant relationship with the CC adoption in HEIs. The model is grounded at the organizational level of analysis [157], and the smallest unit of analysis is an individual of CC.

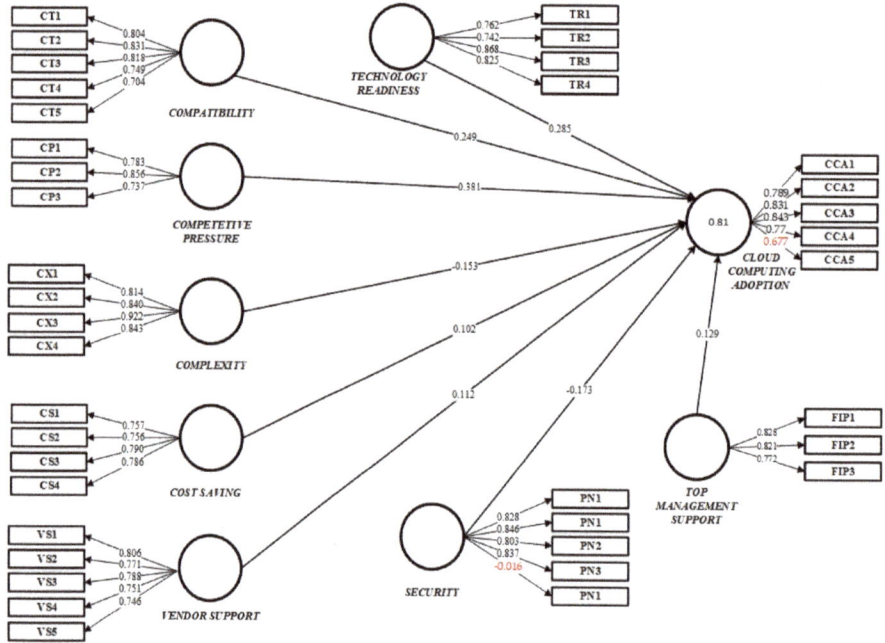

**Figure 1.** Proposed model.

## 4. Methodology

The proposed study applied two stages of analysis methods, namely variance-based structural equation modeling (PLS-SEM) and artificial neural networks (ANN). The reliability and validity of the measurement model and also hypotheses were tested by SEM, while the neural network was employed for the predictors and antecedents of CC adoption [45]. As indicated by Chan and Chong [169], to validate the relationship of hypotheses in behavioral and social science, PLS-SEM is frequently used; however, it is seldom integrated with other artificial intelligence algorithms. As PLS-SEM is employed for the linear model, it may often simplify the complications in making technology adoption decisions [170]. To solve this issue, the neural network method was used to recognize the non-linear relationships between predictors in the proposed research model. According to Chan and Chong [169], ANN helps to learn complex linear and non-linear associations between the factors of technology adoption and adoption decisions. Moreover, the ANN makes it possible to perform more precise anticipation in comparison to the general regression procedure [171]. However, some researchers applied a combination of ANN and PLS-SEM analysis in diverse adoption settings, such as CRM adoption Ahani, Rahim [172], CC Sharma, Al-Badi [66], and wearable healthcare devices and IOS adoption Chong and Bai [173]. Therefore, at the main phase, to find the factors that have an important influence on the adoption of CC, this study applied SEM. The ANN approach was employed in the second phase for predicting the CC adoption, based on the considerable factors resulted from the PLS-SEM analysis.

*Sampling and Data Collection*

Quantitative studies can utilize probability as well as non-probability sampling approaches. However, the non-probability sampling approach is mainly used for qualitative studies [174]. Generalizing the results driven from a small group of people to large groups is the key advantage of the quantitative research method. [175]. Daniel [174] declared that "in purposive sampling researcher purposely selects the elements because they satisfy specific inclusion and exclusion criteria for participation in the study." Purposive sampling is suitable for the initial phases of study where subjects have not much experience with a particular event under investigation [176]. Therefore, this study adopted a purposive sampling approach, and the target population of the study is the individuals who are related to the decision of adopting CC services in the institution (e.g., ICT directors, administrators, information technology officers, etc.) and can provide recommendations regarding the adoption of CC services. The summary of the respondent's characteristics in Table 2 shows that most of the respondents have advance or expert level in computer literature (i.e., 57.46% and 35.07% respectively) and 1–5 years or 6–10 years of experience in the field (i.e., 81.34% and 15.67% respectively). Face validity, content validity, and a pilot study were performed to ensure the validity and reliability of the questionnaire. For most scholars, a pilot study sample size of 20–40 is reasonable [177–182]. In this regard, our pilot study's reliability statistic was based on 30 online completed questionnaires. Structural equation modeling (SEM) was applied to the pilot data with SmartPLS 3.0 [116]. The results of a pilot study, conducted through a survey with ICT decision-makers, and based on the proposed conceptual model, indicate that the instrument is both reliable and valid, and so point the way towards further research. It is worth drawing attention to the fact that the questions were adapted from prior empirical literature that had been validated by previous researchers (see Appendix A). Data were collected online from May to July 2019. After three months, a total of 148 responses to the survey questionnaire were received by researchers. After data screening, some questionnaires with a missing value were excluded, and a total of 134 responses were found valid for the analysis. The demographic information of the respondents is presented in Table 4.

**Table 4.** Characteristics of the respondents.

| Respondents Information | | |
|---|---|---|
| | Frequency | Percentage |
| **Computer literacy level** | | |
| Beginner | 1 | 0.75% |
| Intermediate | 9 | 6.72% |
| Advanced | 77 | 57.46% |
| Expert | 47 | 35.07% |
| **Experience** | | |
| 1–5 years | 109 | 81.34% |
| 6–10 years | 21 | 15.67% |
| 11–15 years | 4 | 2.99% |
| More than 15 years | 0 | 0 |
| **Job title** | | |
| Administrator | 19 | 14.17% |
| Lecturer | 13 | 9.70% |
| Teaching staff | 3 | 2.38% |
| ICT director | 26 | 19.40% |
| Chief information officer | 11 | 8.21% |
| IT specialist | 4 | 2.98% |
| Business analyst | 2 | 1.49% |
| Researcher | 53 | 39.55% |
| Associate professor | 3 | 2.23% |

## 5. Data Analysis and Results

This study applied two analytical approaches, namely variance-based structural equation modeling (PLS-SEM) and artificial neural network (ANN). First, the PLS-SEM approach has been used for analyzing the proposed model and extracting the significant relationships among the identified factors. The obtained result from PLS-SEM analysis revealed that factors identified significant in influencing decision-makers' intention towards adopting CC. Second, the normalized importance among those significant predictors was ranked utilizing the ANN. This section explains the data analysis and results in detail.

### 5.1. Analysis of PLS-SEM Results

A variance-based technique (i.e., PLS-SEM) was used to analyze the structural model, and this decision was made for several reasons: firstly, the partial least squares (PLS) method is effective for small-to-moderately-sized samples, and it provides parameter estimates even at reduced sample sizes [183,184]; secondly, PLS is viable for exploratory research [185], particularly when examining new structural paths in the context of incremental studies that extend previous models [186], or when the relationships and measures proposed are new or have not been extensively examined in prior literature [187,188]; and thirdly, the variance-based approach in PLS is effective for predictive applications. Therefore, since the study's objective was to identify the factors underlying CC adoption, PLS was a suitable choice [189].

#### 5.1.1. Measurement Model Assessment

SEM is composed of two-step process measurement and structural model assessments. The measurement model assessment is the first step of the model assessment, to ensure that every construct is measured correctly. Reliability and validity are the primary requirement for measurement model assessment to measure the strength of the suggested model. According to Hair Jr, Hult [116], "for internal consistency of the measurement model composite reliability and Cronbach's α were applied." The validity of the constructs was evaluated by applying "average variance extracted (AVE)" and "cross-factor loadings." The reliability and validity results of the specified constructs were summarized in Table 5. As recommended by Hair Jr, Hult [116] for the reliability of the constructs, the value above 0.7 is a satisfactory score for the internal consistency of the survey. For all defined constructs, the results showed that composite reliability and Cronbach's α are above the satisfactory value of 0.7, which surpasses the suggested score, except CCA5 and VS5. Furthermore, the minimum score of 0.50 is considered to be an acceptable value of AVE for each construct [116]. As depicted in Table 5, the validity of scale items was above 0.5, which exceeded the threshold value. The next step after convergent validity verification is discriminant validity. The "discriminant validity" was evaluated by analyzing correlations between the constructs [190]. As revealed in Table 6, the Square root of AVE for defined constructs had a higher value in comparison to correlation co-efficient with other latent constructs. Therefore, "convergent and discriminant validity" was approved in the assessment of the measurement model [190]. Consequently, based on the above assessments, the validity and reliability of the constructs for the measurement model have been accepted and meet the recommended values.

**Table 5.** Constructs' reliability and validity.

| Constructs | Items | OL (>0.7) | CA (>0.6) | CR (>0.7) | AVE (>0.5) |
|---|---|---|---|---|---|
| CC Adoption | CCA1 | 0.789 | 0.842 | 0.888 | 0.615 |
| | CCA2 | 0.831 | | | |
| | CCA3 | 0.843 | | | |
| | CCA4 | 0.77 | | | |
| | CCA5 | 0.677 | | | |
| Compatibility | CT1 | 0.804 | 0.842 | 0.887 | 0.612 |
| | CT2 | 0.831 | | | |
| | CT3 | 0.818 | | | |
| | CT4 | 0.749 | | | |
| | CT5 | 0.704 | | | |

Table 5. Cont.

| Constructs | Items | OL (>0.7) | CA (>0.6) | CR (>0.7) | AVE (>0.5) |
|---|---|---|---|---|---|
| Competitive pressure | CP1 | 0.783 | 0.71 | 0.836 | 0.63 |
|  | CP2 | 0.856 |  |  |  |
|  | CP3 | 0.737 |  |  |  |
| Complexity | CX1 | 0.814 | 0.879 | 0.916 | 0.732 |
|  | CX2 | 0.84 |  |  |  |
|  | CX3 | 0.922 |  |  |  |
|  | CX4 | 0.843 |  |  |  |
| Cost saving | CS1 | 0.757 | 0.772 | 0.852 | 0.59 |
|  | CS2 | 0.756 |  |  |  |
|  | CS3 | 0.79 |  |  |  |
|  | CS4 | 0.768 |  |  |  |
| Vendor support | VS1 | 0.806 | 0.832 | 0.881 | 0.597 |
|  | VS2 | 0.771 |  |  |  |
|  | VS3 | 0.788 |  |  |  |
|  | VS4 | 0.751 |  |  |  |
|  | VS5 | 0.746 |  |  |  |
| Technology readiness | TR1 | 0.762 | 0.812 | 0.877 | 0.642 |
|  | TR2 | 0.742 |  |  |  |
|  | TR3 | 0.868 |  |  |  |
|  | TR4 | 0.825 |  |  |  |
| Top Manager's support | TMS1 | 0.828 | 0.734 | 0.849 | 0.652 |
|  | TMS2 | 0.821 |  |  |  |
|  | TMS3 | 0.772 |  |  |  |
| Security | SC1 | 0.828 | 0.74 | 0.829 | 0.55 |
|  | SC2 | 0.846 |  |  |  |
|  | SC3 | 0.803 |  |  |  |
|  | SC4 | 0.837 |  |  |  |
|  | SC5 | −0.016 |  |  |  |

OL = Outer loading, CA = Cronbach's alpha, CR = Composite reliability, AVE = Average variance extracted.

Table 6. Fornell–Larckers criterion analysis construct.

|  | CC | CT | CP | CX | CS | VS | TR | TMS | SC |
|---|---|---|---|---|---|---|---|---|---|
| CCA | 0.784 |  |  |  |  |  |  |  |  |
| CT | 0.684 | 0.783 |  |  |  |  |  |  |  |
| CP | 0.78 | 0.62 | 0.794 |  |  |  |  |  |  |
| CX | 0.369 | 0.613 | 0.417 | 0.856 |  |  |  |  |  |
| CS | 0.586 | 0.489 | 0.475 | 0.331 | 0.768 |  |  |  |  |
| VS | 0.677 | 0.621 | 0.637 | 0.545 | 0.492 | 0.773 |  |  |  |
| TR | 0.721 | 0.509 | 0.577 | 0.356 | 0.479 | 0.535 | 0.801 |  |  |
| TMS | 0.669 | 0.549 | 0.615 | 0.36 | 0.486 | 0.643 | 0.474 | 0.807 |  |
| SC | 0.547 | 0.569 | 0.682 | 0.4 | 0.499 | 0.535 | 0.509 | 0.521 | 0.741 |

Note: CC adoption (CCA); Compatibility (CT); Competitive pressure (CP); Complexity (CX); Cost saving (CS); Vendor support; Technology readiness (TR); Top manager's support (TMS); Security (SC).

5.1.2. Structural Model Assessment

In the PLS-SEM analysis, after analyzing the measurement model for getting approval for the reliability and validity of the defined constructs, the next step was the structural model assessment. In PLS-SEM as recommend by Hair Jr, Hult [116], for testing the predictive power of the structural model, researchers measured R-Square, and path coefficient between the constructs was used. Total predicted $R^2$ for the dependent variable (intention) is 0.81, which represents substantial coefficients of determination [116]. The result of the hypothesis testing and path coefficients for the structural model was measured, and the findings are shown in Table 7. The values for "$t = 3.091$" and "$p < 0.001$", "$t = 2.326$" and "$p < 0.01$", and "$t = 1.645$" and "$p < 0.05$" can be accepted for $t$-value at various significance levels [138]. The result of the hypotheses calculation by running bootstrapping shows that all the proposed CC adoption antecedent factors had a significant influence on it, except vendor support. Based on the analysis, CC adoption is positively influenced by compatibility ($\beta = 0.249$, $t$-value = 4.311, $p < 0.01$). Thus, this hypothesis supported. Competitive pressure ($\beta = 0.381$, $t$-value = 5.516, $p < 0.01$) has positive significant influence on CC adoption. The complexity has a negative significant influence on CC adoption (β = −0.153, *t*-value = 2.887, *p* < 0.01); therefore, this hypothesis is also supported. Cost saving is another factor which had significant and positive influence on CC adoption (β = 0.102, *t*-value = 2.266, *p* < 0.05). However, vendor support (β = 0.112, *t*-value = 1.447, *p* > 0.05) does not have a significant influence on CC adoption, and this hypothesis is not supported. Furthermore, from the analysis, CC adoption is positively influenced by technology readiness (β = 0.285, *t*-value = 4.888, *p* < 0.01). The results indicated that the top manager's support has a positive and significant influence on CC adoption (β = 0.129, *t*-value = 1.978, *p* < 0.05). Meanwhile, from the analysis, it shows that CC adoption is negatively and significantly influenced by security (β = −0.173, *t*-value = 2.226, *p* < 0.05). It is clear from the result that among all the constructs, competitive pressure had the highest significant level and was the most significant factor that was selected and influenced the individuals' intention for the adoption of CC in higher education, followed by the technology readiness, which had higher significance in bootstrapping analysis. As depicted in Figure 2, the result of the proposed model showed that 81% of the variance in CC adoption can be described by the technological, environmental, and organizational factors (TOE) factors.

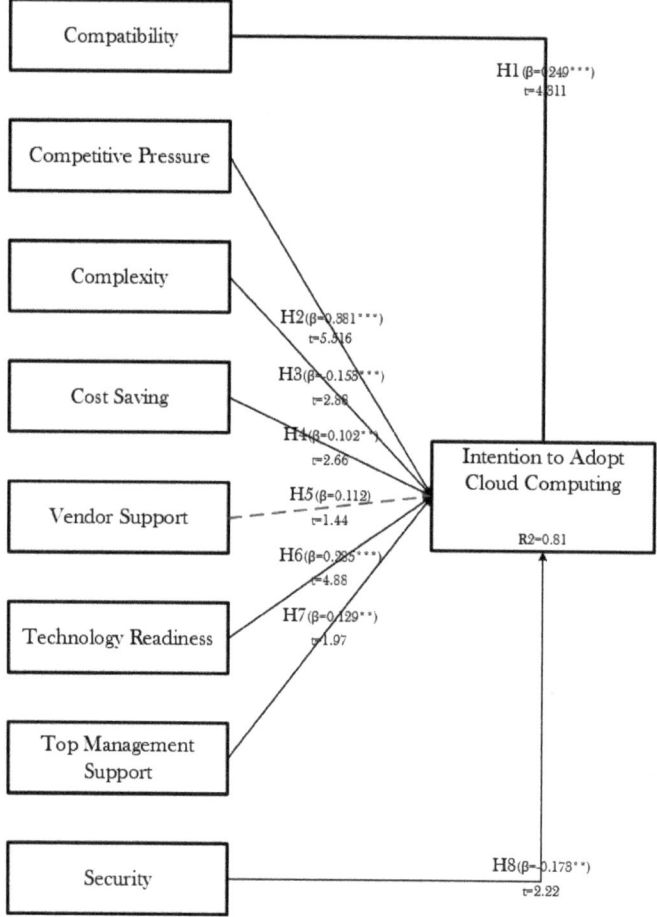

**Figure 2.** Results of structural model. Note: ** < 0.05, *** < 0.01.

Table 7. Summary of hypothesis tests.

| | Original Sample (O) | Sample Mean (M) | Standard Deviation (STDEV) | t Value (|O/STDEV|) | p Values | Result |
|---|---|---|---|---|---|---|
| Compatibility -> CC adoption | 0.249 | 0.243 | 0.058 | 4.311 | 0 *** | Supported |
| Competitive pressure -> CC adoption | 0.381 | 0.375 | 0.069 | 5.516 | 0 *** | Supported |
| Complexity -> CC adoption | −0.153 | −0.15 | 0.053 | 2.887 | 0.004 *** | Supported |
| Cost saving -> CC adoption | 0.102 | 0.102 | 0.045 | 2.266 | 0.023 ** | Supported |
| Vendor support -> CC adoption | 0.112 | 0.117 | 0.077 | 1.447 | 0.148 | NS |
| technology readiness -> CC adoption | 0.285 | 0.277 | 0.058 | 4.888 | 0 *** | Supported |
| Top manager's support -> CC adoption | 0.129 | 0.13 | 0.065 | 1.978 | 0.048 ** | Supported |
| Security-> CC adoption | −0.173 | −0.167 | 0.078 | 2.226 | 0.026 ** | Supported |

Note: ** < 0.05, *** < 0.01.

*5.2. Analysis of Neural Network for Cloud Computing Adoption*

The proposed study has combined the two analytical approaches, namely PLS-SEM as a statistical approach and neural network as an artificial intelligence technique. Multiple regression analysis (MRA) and PLS-SEM are considered to be a conventional linear statistical technique, which is used for identifying the linear relationship between variables and simplify the complex decision-making process [191]. To solve this issue, it is suggested to apply the artificial neural network, which can easily recognize the non-linear relationship. According to Chan and Chong [169], the advantage of using the neural network model is that it can learn complex linear and non-linear relationships between predictors and the adoption decision. Also, the ANN is more flexible and can give better prediction accuracy as compared to the linear model(s), and it may surpass the usual statistical technique (such as MRA) [172]. However, because of its "black-box" nature, ANN is not suitable for checking the hypothesis and determining the causal relationship [191]. Thus, this paper adopted a two-stages approach, similar to [66]. In the first stage of the study, the research model is tested, and the important hypothesized predictors are analyzed using SEM. The result of the PLS-SEM is then given as input to the model of ANN, which is employed to analyze the relative significance of each predictor variable in the second stage. Hence, the results of selected factors from Smart-PLS analysis were employed to improve ANN analysis. The applied ANN has three layers: "Input layer, hidden layer, and output layer". The hidden nodes have no direct connection with the outside world (thus the name "hidden") [192]. These nodes are responsible for performing computations and transferring information from the input nodes to the output nodes [193]. As depicted in Figure 3, seven independent substantiation factors, derived from PLS-SEM analysis, are considered as the input section for ANN; whereas one dependent variable (CC adoption) is considered as the output section of ANN (see Figure 3). Wang and Elhag [194] recommended that ANNs should be calculated by varying the number of hidden nodes from one to ten. To detect the hidden nodes (H1-H10 in Figure 3), researchers such as Ahani, Rahim [172] have recommended testing the ANN model by modifying the number of hidden nodes from one to ten. The proposed research has been applied to the 10 hidden nodes to create the relative significance of the predictors. The proposed study established ANN by using R programming, as it helps to simplify and give effective results. A multilayer perception training algorithm was applied for the preparation of the ANN model (see Table 8). Hence, 70 % of the data have been used as the train network model, and the remaining 30% of the data were used to test the proposed research model. Seven predicting factors, namely compatibility, competitive pressure, complexity, cost saving, technology readiness, security, and top management support, were tested. The factor "intention", which is the dependent variable in the proposed study, has been calculated in the output layer of the ANN model. The root-mean-square error (RMSE) was used to assess the precision of the ANN model that was developed [195] in both the training and testing datasets. As shown in Table 8, the average RMSE values of the training and testing procedures are relatively small at 0.1101 and 0.1022, respectively. Therefore, this confirms that there is an excellent model fit. Besides, the importance of variable is verified based on the number of non-zero synaptic weights connected to relevant hidden parts (see Table 8), which displays that the model has a high predicting accuracy, based on minor RMSE scores and it shows that the model is reliable in depicting the relationship between predictors and output.

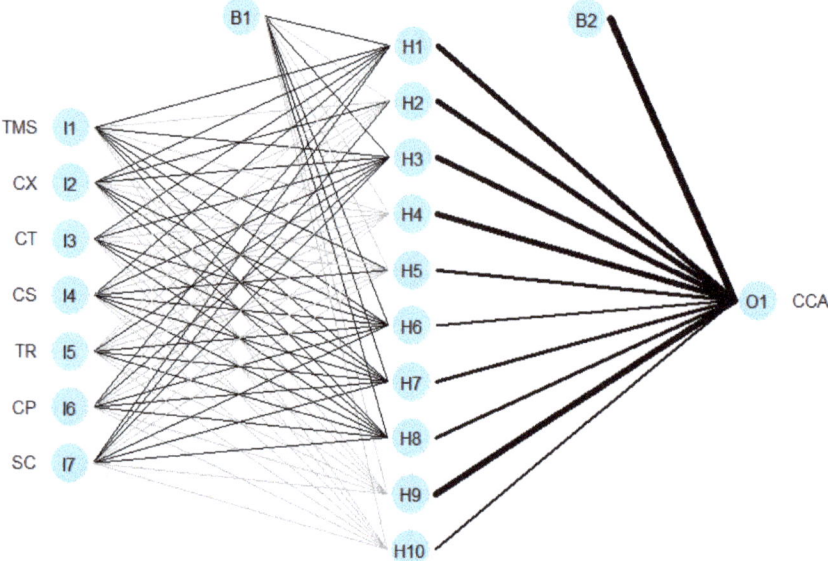

**Figure 3.** The anticipated ANN architect for 10 neurons. Note: CC adoption (CCA); Compatibility (CT); Competitive pressure (CP); Complexity (CX); Cost saving (CS); Technology readiness (TR); Top manager's support (TMS); Security (SC).

**Table 8.** RMSE values of artificial neural networks.

| Network Configures | Testing | Training |
|---|---|---|
| ANN1 | 0.1174 | 0.0994 |
| ANN2 | 0.1079 | 0.1004 |
| ANN 3 | 0.1132 | 0.1013 |
| ANN 4 | 0.1105 | 0.1015 |
| ANN 5 | 0.1137 | 0.105 |
| ANN 6 | 0.1054 | 0.1015 |
| ANN 7 | 0.1069 | 0.1029 |
| ANN 8 | 0.1124 | 0.1045 |
| ANN 9 | 0.1066 | 0.1053 |
| ANN 10 | 0.1141 | 0.0973 |
| Average | 0.1101 | 0.1022 |
| Standard deviation | 0.0034 | 0.0026 |

Therefore, all the factors are suitable for forecasting CC adoption as a dependent variable. The normalized importance is the ratio of the relative importance of each factor with its maximum relative significance, and it is stated in percentage form. Based on the PLS-SEM examination, just significant linear factors have been employed in the input parts of the ANN model. In this regard, just linear relationships have been checked. The normalized importance was calculated in the sensitivity analysis according to relative factor importance weights (see Table 9). The variable "technology readiness" resulted as the most significant factor in predicting the CC adoption, and "security" is the second important factor.

Table 9. Normalized importance of variables.

| Variables | Importance | Normalized Importance |
|---|---|---|
| TMS | 0.077 | 39.50% |
| CX | 0.11 | 56.20% |
| CT | 0.129 | 66.00% |
| CS | 0.13 | 66.40% |
| TR | 0.196 | 100.00% |
| CP | 0.171 | 87.30% |
| SC | 0.188 | 96.00% |

Note: Compatibility (CT); Competitive pressure (CP); Complexity (CX); Cost saving (CS); Technology readiness (TR); Top manager's support (TMS); Security (SC).

## 6. Discussion

Our study examined the influence of eight constructs obtained from the literature. Our research model explained 81% of the dependent variable's variance, higher than other studies that examined the adoption of cloud computing (e.g., [31,196]). Sabi, Uzoka [196] study found that their model could explain only 43%, while Sabi, Uzoka [31] study found that their model could explain only 44.7%. The results of the previous studies and the current investigations are compared on variously considered factors.

According to the hypotheses test, compatibility has a positive and significant impact on CC adoption. The β, t-value, and p-value of the test result are 0.249, and 4.311 respectively, which is significant at the level of $p < 0.01$. These values demonstrate support for this hypothesis. Besides, the ANN output revealed that the variable "compatibility" is the fourth crucial factor in the prediction of the CC adoption. Hence, the adoption of CC is significantly affected by compatibility and H1 is supported. The result corroborates what was observed in past studies ([80,81,107,110,112]). According to this research, compatibility refers to the degree to which an innovation equates the previous practices, present values, and current needs of the likely adopter [104]. In addition, compatibility looked into the extent to which an innovation can attune to available systems.

The output of the measurement model shows that competitive pressure has a significant and positive impact on CC adoption. The β, t-value, and p-value of the test result are 0.381, 5.516, respectively, which is significant at the level of $p < 0.01$. These values demonstrate support for this hypothesis. Besides, the ANN output revealed that the variable "competitive pressure" is the third crucial factor in the prediction of CC adoption. Hence, the adoption of CC is significantly affected by competitive pressure. The result corroborates what was observed in past studies ([100,112,115,131–133]). According to this research, competitive pressure refers to the pressure observed by the leaders of an institution concerning the competitors' attainment of remarkable competitive advantage through CC services, such as the effectuality of teaching and learning ([115,129,130]).

The stipulation of hypothesis H3 is that complexity possesses a negative impact on CC adoption. According to [134], complexity shows the observed difficulty of an institution in understanding and using innovation. If a useful innovation appears difficult to be utilized, then there will be a reduction in the likelihood of adoption [104]. As portrayed in the results of the current study, there is a significant effect of complexity on CC adoption in HEIs, because the β, t-value, and the p-value of complexity are −0.153, 2.887 respectively, which is significant at the level of $p < 0.01$. Therefore, complexity has a significant effect on CC adoption in HEIs. This result is in line with previous studies [30,31,35,127,128].

The output of the measurement model shows a positive impact on cost saving with CC adoption. The β, t-value, and p-value of the result are 0.102, 2.266 respectively, which is significant at the level of $p < 0.05$. These values support the hypothesis that cost saving has a significant effect on the adoption of CC in HEIs. This result supports the findings of previous studies ([82–84,102,103,106,112,159–161,164,168]).

According to this research, cost savings is the reduced capital investment required in an institution for IT service in terms of leased resources and hardware solutions [136].

The stipulation of hypothesis H5 is that vendor support has a positive impact on the adoption of CC in HEIs. According to [142,143], vendors or IT service providers are important in deciding the adoption of IT services. As shown in the results of this study, there is no significant impact of vendor support on CC adoption in HEIs, because β, *t*-value, and *p*-value of the result are 0.112, 1.447 respectively, which is not significant as $p > 0.05$. Hence, H5 significance was unconfirmed, and the output of vendor support was insignificant, which might be due to the indicators utilized in measuring this factor being feeble. Accordingly, the study output is suggesting that further studies need to focus on the selection of powerful indicators of this construct.

The output of this measurement model shows a positive influence of technology readiness on CC adoption. The β, *t*-value, and *p*-value of the result is 0.285, 4.888, respectively, which is significant at the level of $p < 0.01$. These values demonstrate support for this hypothesis. Besides, the ANN output revealed that the variable "technology readiness" is the second crucial factor in the prediction of the CC adoption in HEIs. Therefore, the adoption of CC is significantly affected by technology readiness. The result corroborates what was observed in past studies [18,33,39,84,147]. According to this research, technology readiness secures the internal technical resources of an organization [112]. Before the adoption of CC technology, the readiness of the institution needs to be determined. That is, HEIs must facilitate the readiness of CC technology so that the internet bandwidth needs to be adequate for student and teacher cloud accessibility.

The output of this measurement model shows a positive influence of top management support on CC adoption (H7). The β, *t*-value, and *p*-value of the result are 0.129, 1.978 respectively, which is significant at the level of $p < 0.05$. These values demonstrate support for this hypothesis. Hence, the adoption of CC is significantly affected by top management support. This result is in line with the findings of past studies [81–84,102,103,106,108–110,160,161,168]. According to this research, the attitude of top management is important in terms of the technology involved and the degree of support provided for the adoption [18]. The knowledge and agreement of decision-makers are crucial. When they provide the necessary support, it will facilitate the needs of cloud services and the appropriate cloud deployment for HEIs settings.

Hypothesis H8 stipulates that security possesses a negative impact on the adoption of CC in HEIs. According to [31,37], security in CC is still the most remarkable challenge in adopting CC services. Security is a critical technical problem when it comes to adopting CC. Cloud vendors are making attempts towards the simulation of the typical principles of confidentiality, availability, and integrity usually within physical systems for distributed, virtualized, and dynamic cloud systems that users access online [150]. As shown in the results of this study, there is a significant impact of security on CC adoption in HEIs as the β, *t*-value, and *p*-value of the result are −0.173, 2.226 respectively, which is significant at the level of $p < 0.05$. Therefore, H5 significance was confirmed, and the output of security was significant.

## 7. Implications

### 7.1. Theoretical Contribution

This study provided empirical literature within IS, especially CC, and it provided an extensive model that integrates the TOE framework and DOI model. Also, this study provided an assessment for CC adoption in HEIs, and more revitalization of the CC and intent of decision-makers to utilize CC in HEIs.

The DOI model and TOE framework incorporation improved the ability to explain the proposed model. The proposed model was able to explain 81% of CC adoption variation, which shows that the model's ability for prediction is powerful and remarkable. Hair, Ringle [197] maintained that the $R^2$ values of 0.75, 0.50, or 0.25 for endogenous variables show significant, moderate, or weak coefficients of determination. This study extends the original TOE framework regarding CC as well as the generalizability; hence, this model is useful in the assessment of the intent to adopt any other innovation. This study was able to test whether the scales utilized in the survey instrument are valid and reliable.

In conclusion, this research used a hybrid approach for the integration of PLS-SEM and ANN to validate the proposed model and to give priority to the factors that impact CC adoption, through the identification of the relative importance of every factor. PLS-SEM determines linear association and ANN determines nonlinear association among predictors and target variables. According to the claim by past scholars, ANN is more accurate in prediction than PLS-SEM [45,66,169]. However, this study recognized that conventional statistical approaches are valid and necessary; thereby offering a powerful foundation in previous IS adoption studies. The suggestion of this research is the need to reinterpret past works on IS adoption through the combination of linear and non-linear approaches in order to provide outstanding strength to technology adoption.

*7.2. Practical Implications*

7.2.1. Implications for Practitioners and Cloud Providers

HEIs are a promising market for cloud service providers. Hence, this study is remarkably impactful for cloud providers and technology practitioners as it will help in the recognition of the factors that influence the adoption of CC. The research results show the essentiality of compatibility, competitive pressure, complexity, cost saving, security, technology readiness, and top management support in adopting CC in HEIs. CC is a new technology and remains thought-out as disruptive. HEIs still lack awareness of the benefits of using cloud services, especially in developing nations. Hence, cloud providers need to consider a variety of approaches in increasing the understanding of HEIs for this technology via workshops and seminars. There is a need to emphasize functional utilities and simple interfaces in the design of cloud services for HEIs towards easy usage of these services, even with little technological knowledge. Likewise, cloud providers need to provide a clear instruction or navigation system in guiding users in HEIs to operate the services smoothly, thereby increasing the assurance that cloud technology is used.

7.2.2. Implications for Decision-Makers

This study emphasizes that top management and ICT department support are important in adopting CC at the HEIs. Likewise, it was discovered that enhancing situations like technology readiness and security with the process in place is the impactful antecedent of adopting CC in HEIs. Hence, there is a need for decision-makers to concentrate on the development of these organizational resources towards gaining the highest merits of cloud services. Besides, top managers pay more attention to the assessment of cloud technology and its assimilation into IT infrastructure effectively and efficiently. In summary, the research results will help decision-makers with the assessment of cloud technology, organization, and environments during the decision of the adoption of CC. Furthermore, decision-makers may use this proposed framework for the investigation of other IT/IS adoption procedures.

## 8. Conclusions, Limitations and Future Research Directions

This current study utilized the notion of adopting CC in HEIs and likewise assessed how the research model created from the DOI mode and TOE framework correlates. This study demonstrates that there is consistency between the proposed model and the data. Apart from the direct influence of vendor support on the intention of adopting CC, the basic factors on decision-makers' intention have a significant influence on the adoption of CC in HEIs. The study outputs have theoretical effects on the identification of the factors influencing the decision-makers' intention to adopt CC and the crucial function of managerial awareness and competitive edges in the research model. The results of the current study affirmed that technology readiness is the most remarkable factor that determines the intention to adopt CC. Therefore, the results suggest that technology readiness has a remarkable and direct correlation regarding the adoption of CC in HEIs. Therefore, the results of the study were able to demonstrate that the theories are useful for pro-environmental behavior and to forecast the intention of adopting CC. Besides, the research model is useful for the improved explanation of the intention of decision-makers in adopting CC.

This study has some limitations that will bring about the focus of subsequent research. First, data were collected only in Malaysia. Therefore, subsequent studies can use data from other nations for the validation of the results in the current study. Second, the development of the model in this study was carried out using some critical factors within TOE framework dimensions; hence, future studies may include other critical factors within the three major dimensions. Third, one-time cross-sectional data was used in testing the model, so subsequent studies may work on the validation of the model introduced here with longitudinal data within some time. Fourth, this study tried the investigation of CC adoption in HEIs, based on the context of decision-makers; hence, subsequent studies can pay attention to the context of the cloud provider for a wider comprehension of the intention to adopt CC. Finally, this study looked into only the intent of an organization in adopting CC from the perspective of HEIs. Future studies can use the evaluation of the post-adoption phase, and the successful establishment of this common technology.

A world with current modern technologies that keep evolving requires organizations and individuals to keep adapting to the evolved technologies. Thus, researchers are required to always remain ahead of these innovations by investigating future technologies. In this regard, the fourth industrial (IR 4.0) revolution provides a dialectical, intricate, and intriguing opportunity to higher education (HE 4.0), in which the society would be changed for the better. Education in the IR 4.0 era (Education 4.0) is driven by biller technologies as artificial intelligence (AI), augmented reality (AR), internet of things (IoT), big data analysis, CC, and mobile devices, which can promote a way of teaching, research, and service and change the work area from task-centered to human-based [198]. To the best of the researchers' knowledge, no empirical study has been revealed on the adoption and use of HE 4.0. Therefore, further investigations on the adoption and use of HE 4.0 may gain the attention of the researchers.

**Author Contributions:** Conceptualization, Y.A.M.Q. and R.A. (Rusli Abdulah); Data curation, Y.A.M.Q. and M.A.A.-S.; Formal analysis, S.A.; Methodology, Y.A.M.Q. and S.A.; Project administration, R.A. (Rusli Abdulah), Y.Y. and R.A. (Rodziah Atan); Resources, Y.Y. and A.A.Y.; Supervision, R.A. (Rusli Abdulah) and R.A. (Rodziah Atan); Validation, M.A.A.-S.; Writing—original draft, Y.A.M.Q.; Writing—review & editing, A.A.Y. All authors have read and agreed to the published version of the manuscript.

**Funding:** This research was funded by Research Management Center (RMC), Universiti Putra Malaysia (UPM), grant number 95223100.

**Conflicts of Interest:** The authors declare no conflict of interest.

Appendix A

Table A1. Factors' Items and Definition.

| Factors | Definitions | | Measurement Items | | |
|---|---|---|---|---|---|
| | Definition | Source(s) | Items | Adapted Source | Previous Studies |
| CC Adoption (CCA) | The intention to adopt cloud computing services in higher education institutions. | [44,103,165,200] | (1 = Strongly Disagree to 7 = Strongly Agree)<br>CCA1. My institution intends to continue using our cloud computing solutions rather than discontinue.<br>CCA2. My intentions are to continue using our cloud computing service rather than use any alternative means (traditional software).<br>CCA3. If I could, I would like to *discontinue* my use of our cloud computing service. (**reverse coded**). | [199] | [114,115] |
| Compatibility (CT) | The extent to which the value of the cloud computing is consistent with existing values, beliefs, and the needs of a potential adopter. | [44,103,165,200] | CT1. The continuous use of cloud computing will be compatible with all aspects of my institution work.<br>CT2. The continuous use of cloud computing fits well with the way I like to work at the institution.<br>CT3. The continuous use of cloud computing is completely compatible with my current work requirements at the institution.<br>CT4. It is easy to integrate cloud computing with our other existing systems (e.g., LMS, Finance, ERP, CRM, SCM, etc.).<br>CT5. Cloud computing is compatible with our culture and values. | [83,94,112,160] | [31,84,133,134,161] |
| Complexity (CX) | The degree of difficulty to understand, use, or continue using the cloud computing. | [44,103,201] | Cx1. The continuous use of cloud computing requires a lot of mental effort.<br>Cx2. The continuous use of cloud computing is frustrating.<br>Cx3. The continuous use of cloud computing is too complex.<br>Cx4. The skills needed to continue using cloud computing are too complex for the users. | [83,126] | [31,94,133] |
| Security (SC) | The degree to which cloud computing is appropriate for HEIs systems security requirements. | [44,202,203] | SC1. The confidentiality and security of my institution data are guaranteed when using cloud computing solutions.<br>SC2. In case of damage, present liability law is clear about who will bear the liability.<br>SC3. The cloud computing service provider will not exploit contractual loopholes (i.e., incomplete contracting) to the detriment of my institution.<br>SC4. The institution's data stored on cloud computing is secure.<br>SC5. The institution's data will be adequately protected through cloud computing systems.<br>SC6. Cloud computing providers have stronger security systems to safeguard the institution's data. | [204] | [83,84,112,205,206] |
| Technology Readiness (TR) | The technological characteristics available in the institution, such as the IT professionals and the IT infrastructure. | [83,85] | TR1. My institution knows how cloud computing can be used to support our operations.<br>TR2. The technology infrastructure of my institution is available to support cloud computing for continuous use.<br>TR3. My institution is dedicated to ensuring that the users are familiar with cloud computing.<br>TR4. My institution has good knowledge of cloud computing. | [93] | [83,84] |

247

Table A1. *Cont.*

| Factors | Definitions | | Measurement Items | | |
|---|---|---|---|---|---|
| | Definition | Source(s) | Items | Adapted Source | Previous Studies |
| Cost saving (CS) | Cloud computing creates an opportunity for innovation, reduces infrastructure costs, decreases energy consumption, and lowers maintenance expenditures. | [84,207,208] | CS1. Cloud computing is more effective than the alternative.<br>CS2. Cloud computing saves time and effort.<br>CS3. Institutions can avoid unnecessary cost and time by continuous use of cloud computing. | [93] | [83,84] |
| Top Management Support (TMS) | The vision, support, and commitment provided to foster the desired environment for the continuous adoption of cloud computing in HEIs. | [83,209] | TMS1. Top management is likely to take risk involving the continuous use of cloud computing.<br>TMS2. Top management actively participates in establishing a vision and formulating strategies for the continuous use of cloud computing.<br>TMS3. Top management communicates its support for the continuous use of cloud computing. | [93] | [83,84] |
| Competitive Pressure (CP) | The pressure perceived by an institution's leaders that competitors have achieved substantial competitive advantage by using cloud computing services (for example, in terms of teaching and learning effectiveness). | [114,129,130] | CP1. More and more institutions are conducting teaching activities and communication through cloud computing.<br>CP2. More and more institutions are conducting knowledge management and sharing though cloud computing.<br>CP3. More and more institutions are conducting project and learning management though cloud computing. | [85,112] | [114] |
| Vendor Support (VS) | Refers to the supplier activities that can significantly influence the probability to continue using cloud computing | [210] | VS1. Vendors actively market cloud computing.<br>VS2. There is a service level agreement (SLA), guaranteed by the vendor.<br>VS3. There is adequate technical support for cloud computing provided by vendors.<br>VS4. Support is easily available from cloud computing vendors during implementation.<br>VS5. Training for cloud computing is adequately provided by vendors. | [160,167,211] | [134,167] |

## References

1. Moscato, F.; Aversa, R.; Di Martino, B.; Petcu, D.; Rak, M. An Ontology for the Cloud in mOSAIC. In *Cloud Computing*; CRC Press: Boca Raton, FL, USA, 2017; pp. 467–485.
2. IDC. IDC Forecasts Worldwide Public Cloud Services Spending. Available online: https://www.idc.com/getdoc.jsp?containerId=prUS44891519 (accessed on 17 June 2020).
3. Qasem, Y.A.M.; Abdullah, R.; Jusoh, Y.Y.; Atan, R.; Asadi, S. Cloud Computing Adoption in Higher Education Institutions: A Systematic Review. *IEEE Access* **2019**, *7*, 63722–63744. [CrossRef]
4. Sayuti, Y.; Albattat, A.; Ariffin, A.N.; Nazrin, N.S.; Silahudeen, T. Food safety knowledge, attitude and practices among management and science university students, Shah Alam. *Manag. Sci. Lett.* **2020**, *10*, 929–936. [CrossRef]
5. AlAjmi, Q.; Arshah, R.A.; Kamaludin, A.; Sadiq, A.S.; Al-Sharafi, M. A conceptual model of e-learning based on cloud computing adoption in higher education institutions. In Proceedings of the 2017 International Conference on Electrical and Computing Technologies and Applications (ICECTA), Aurak, UAE, 21–23 November 2017.
6. Abdullah, R.; Eri, Z.D.; Talib, A.M. A model of knowledge management system for facilitating knowledge as a service (KaaS) in cloud computing environment. In Proceedings of the 2011 International Conference on Research and Innovation in Information Systems (ICRIIS, 2011), Kuala Lumpur, Malaysia, 23–24 November 2011; IEEE: Piscataway, NJ, USA, 2011.
7. Monroy, C.R.; Arias, C.A.; Guerrero, Y.N. The new cloud computing paradigm: The way to IT seen as a utility. *Lat. Am. Caribb. J. Eng. Educ.* **2012**, *6*, 24–31.
8. Thomas, P.Y. Cloud computing: A potential paradigm for practising the scholarship of teaching and learning. *Electron. Libr.* **2011**, *29*, 214–224. [CrossRef]
9. Razak, S.F.A. Cloud computing in Malaysia Universities. In Proceedings of the 2009 Innovative Technologies in Intelligent Systems and Industrial Applications, Kuala Lumpur, Malaysia, 25–26 July 2009.
10. Abdullah, R.; Alsharaei, Y.A. A Mobile Knowledge as a service (mKaaS) model of knowledge management system in facilitating knowledge sharing of cloud education community environment. In Proceedings of the 2016 Third International Conference on Information Retrieval and Knowledge Management (CAMP), Melaka, Malaysia, 23–24 August 2016; IEEE: PIscataway, NJ, USA, 2016.
11. Qasem, Y.A.; Abdullah, R.; Atan, R.; Jusoh, Y.Y. Towards Developing A Cloud-Based Education As A Service (CEAAS) Model For Cloud Computing Adoption In Higher Education Institutions. *Complexity* **2018**, *6*, 7. [CrossRef]
12. Njenga, K.; Garg, L.; Bhardwaj, A.K.; Prakash, V.; Bawa, S. The cloud computing adoption in higher learning institutions in Kenya: Hindering factors and recommendations for the way forward. *Telemat. Inf.* **2019**, *38*, 225–246. [CrossRef]
13. Rahimah, K.; Aziati, N. The Integrated Framework of Cloud Computing Implementation in Higher Education Institution: A Review of Literature. *Adv. Sci. Lett.* **2017**, *23*, 1475–1479. [CrossRef]
14. Shakeabubakor, A.A.; Sundararajan, E.; Hamdan, A.R. Cloud Computing Services and Applications to Improve Productivity of University Researchers. *Int. J. Inf. Electron. Eng.* **2015**, *5*, 153. [CrossRef]
15. Rahman, M.M.; Suhaimi, A.; Shah, A. A Model of Factors Influencing Cloud Computing Adoption Among Faculty Members and Students of Higher Educational Institutions of Bangladesh. In Proceedings of the 2018 IEEE 5th International Conference on Engineering Technologies and Applied Sciences (ICETAS), Bangkok, Thailand, 22–23 November 2018; IEEE: Piscataway, NJ, USA, 2018.
16. Odeh, M.; Garcia-Perez, A.; Warwick, K. Cloud computing adoption at higher education institutions in developing countries: A qualitative investigation of main enablers and barriers. *Int. J. Inf. Educ. Technol.* **2017**, *7*, 921–927. [CrossRef]
17. Wilson, B. A Framework to Support Cloud Adoption Decision-Making by SMEs in Tamil Nadu. Ph.D. Thesis, Sheffield Hallam University, Sheffield, UK, 2017.
18. Alharthi, A.; Alassafi, M.O.; Walters, R.J.; Wills, G.B. An exploratory study for investigating the critical success factors for cloud migration in the Saudi Arabian higher education context. *Telemat. Inf.* **2017**, *34*, 664–678. [CrossRef]
19. Alexander, B. Social networking in higher education. In *The Tower and the Cloud*; EDUCAUSE: Louisville, CO, USA, 2008; pp. 197–201.

20. Katz, N. *The Tower and the Cloud. Higher Education in the Age of Cloud Computing*; EDUCAUSE: Louisville, CO, USA, 2008; p. 9.
21. Sultan, N. Cloud computing for education: A new dawn? *Int. J. Inf. Manag.* **2010**, *30*, 109–116. [CrossRef]
22. Arpaci, I. Antecedents and consequences of cloud computing adoption in education to achieve knowledge management. *Comput. Hum. Behav.* **2017**, *70*, 382–390. [CrossRef]
23. Vaquero, L.M. EduCloud: PaaS versus IaaS Cloud Usage for an Advanced Computer Science Course. *IEEE Trans. Educ.* **2011**, *54*, 590–598. [CrossRef]
24. Ashtari, S.; Eydgahi, A. Student perceptions of cloud applications effectiveness in higher education. *J. Comput. Sci.* **2017**, *23*, 173–180. [CrossRef]
25. Katz, R.; Goldstein, P.; Yanosky, R. Cloud Computing in Higher Education. In EDUCAUSE. 2010. Available online: http://net.educause.edu/section_params/conf/CCW (accessed on 5 October 2010).
26. Commander, S.; Harrison, R.; Menezes-Filho, N. ICT and productivity in developing countries: New firm-level evidence from Brazil and India. *Rev. Econ. Stat.* **2011**, *93*, 528–541. [CrossRef]
27. Javaid, M.; Haleem, A.; Vaishya, R.; Bahl, S.; Suman, R.; Vaish, A. Industry 4.0 technologies and their applications in fighting COVID-19 pandemic. *Diabetes Metab. Syndr. Clin. Res. Rev.* **2020**, *14*, 419–422. [CrossRef]
28. Toquero, C. Challenges and Opportunities for Higher Education amid the COVID-19 Pandemic: The Philippine Context. *Pedagog. Res.* **2020**, *5*, 1–5. [CrossRef]
29. Walther, S.; Sedera, D.; Urbach, N.; Eymann, T.; Otto, B.; Sarker, S. Should we stay, or should we go? Analyzing continuance of cloud enterprise systems. *J. Inf. Technol. Theory Appl.* **2018**, *19*, 57–88.
30. Sabi, H.M.; Uzoka, F.; Langmia, K.; Njeh, K. Conceptualizing a model for adoption of cloud computing in education. *Int. J. Inf. Manag.* **2016**, *36*, 183–191. [CrossRef]
31. Sabi, H.M.; Uzoka, F.; Langmia, K.; Njeh, F.; Tsuma, C. A cross-country model of contextual factors impacting cloud computing adoption at universities in sub-Saharan Africa. *Inf. Syst. Front.* **2018**, *20*, 1381–1404. [CrossRef]
32. Dahiru, A.A.; Bass, J.M.; Allison, I.K. Cloud computing adoption in sub-Saharan Africa: An analysis using institutions and capabilities. In Proceedings of the International Conference on Information Society, i-Society 2014, London, UK, 10–12 November 2014.
33. Md Kassim, S.S.; Salleh, M.; Zainal, A. Cloud Computing: A General User's Perception and Security Awareness in Malaysian Polytechnic. In *Pattern Analysis, Intelligent Security and the Internet of Things*; Abraham, A., Muda, A.K., Choo, Y.-H., Eds.; Springer International Publishing: Cham, Switzerland, 2015; pp. 131–140.
34. Asadi, S.; Yadegaridehkordi, E. Customers perspectives on adoption of cloud computing in banking sector. *Inf. Technol. Manag.* **2017**, *18*, 305–330. [CrossRef]
35. Tashkandi, A.N.; Al-Jabri, I.M. Cloud computing adoption by higher education institutions in Saudi Arabia: An exploratory study. *Clust. Comput.* **2015**, *18*, 1527–1537. [CrossRef]
36. Shi, Y.; Yang, H.; Yang, Z.; Wu, D. Trends of Cloud Computing in Education, in Hybrid Learning. Theory and Practice. In Proceedings of the 7th International Conference, ICHL 2014, Shanghai, China, 8–10 August 2014; Simon, K.S.C., Fong, J., Zhang, J., Kwan, R., Eds.; Springer International Publishing: Cham, Switzerland, 2014; pp. 116–128.
37. Yuvaraj, M. Determining factors for the adoption of cloud computing in developing countries: A case study of Indian academic libraries. *Bottom Line* **2016**, *29*, 259–272. [CrossRef]
38. Yuvaraj, M. Problems and prospects of implementing cloud computing in university libraries: A case study of Banaras Hindu University library system. *Libr. Rev.* **2015**, *64*, 567–582. [CrossRef]
39. Surya, G.S.F.; Fajar, S.; Surendro, K. E-Readiness Framework for Cloud Computing Adoption in Higher Education. In Proceedings of the 2014 International Conference of Advanced Informatics: Concept, Theory and Application (ICAICTA), Bandung, Indonesia, 20–21 August 2014; IEEE: Piscataway, NJ, USA, 2014; pp. 278–282.
40. Lal, P. Organizational learning management systems: Time to move learning to the cloud! *Dev. Learn. Organ.* **2015**, *29*, 13–15. [CrossRef]
41. Koch, F.; Assunção, M.D.; Cardonha, C.; Netto, M.A. Optimising resource costs of cloud computing for education. *Future Gener. Comput. Syst.* **2016**, *55*, 473–479. [CrossRef]
42. Petković, D. Prediction of laser welding quality by computational intelligence approaches. *Optik* **2017**, *140*, 597–600. [CrossRef]

43. Tornatzky, L.G.; Fleischer, M.; Chakrabarti, A.K. *Processes of Technological Innovation*; Lexington Books: Lexington, MA, USA, 1990.
44. Rogers Everett, M. *Diffusion of Innovations*; The Free Press: New York, NY, USA, 1995; p. 12.
45. Scott, J.E.; Walczak, S. Cognitive engagement with a multimedia ERP training tool: Assessing computer self-efficacy and technology acceptance. *Inf. Manag.* **2009**, *46*, 221–232. [CrossRef]
46. Al-Sharafi, M.A.; Arshah, R.A.; Abu-Shanab, E.A. Factors Influencing the Continuous Use of Cloud Computing Services in Organization Level. In Proceedings of the International Conference on Advances in Image Processing—ICAIP 2017, Bangkok, Thailand, 25–27 August 2017; pp. 189–194.
47. Mell, P.; Grance, T. *The NIST Definition of Cloud Computing*; U.S. Department of Commerce, National Institute of Standards and Technology: Gaithersburg, MD, USA, 2011.
48. Jing, S.-Y.; Ali, S.; She, K.; Zhong, Y. State-of-the-art research study for green cloud computing. *J. Supercomput.* **2013**, *65*, 445–468. [CrossRef]
49. Zissis, D.; Lekkas, D. Addressing cloud computing security issues. *Future Gener. Comput. Syst.* **2012**, *28*, 583–592. [CrossRef]
50. Beloglazov, A.; Abawajy, J.; Buyya, R. Energy-aware resource allocation heuristics for efficient management of data centers for cloud computing. *Future Gener. Comput. Syst.* **2012**, *28*, 755–768. [CrossRef]
51. Dillon, T.; Wu, C.; Chang, E. Cloud computing: Issues and challenges. In Proceedings of the 2010 24th IEEE International Conference on Advanced Information Networking and Applications (AINA), Perth, WA, Australia, 20–23 April 2010; IEEE: Piscataway, NJ, USA, 2010.
52. Qasim, A.; Sadiq, A.; Kamaludin, A.; Al-Sharafi, M. E-learning models: The effectiveness of the cloud-based E-learning model over the traditional E-learning model. In Proceedings of the 2017 8th International Conference on Information Technology (ICIT), Amman, Jordan, 17–18 May 2017; IEEE: Piscataway, NJ, USA, 2017.
53. Thorsteinsson, G.; Page, T.; Niculescu, A. Using virtual reality for developing design communication. *Stud. Inf. Control* **2010**, *19*, 93–106. [CrossRef]
54. Pocatilu, P.; Alecu, F.; Vetrici, M. Using cloud computing for E-learning systems. In Proceedings of the 8th WSEAS International Conference on Data Networks, Communications, Computers, Baltimore, MD, USA, 7–9 November 2009; World Scientific and Engineering Academy and Society (WSEAS): Athens, Greece, 2009.
55. Sasikala, S.; Prema, S. Massive Centralized Cloud Computing (MCCC) Exploration in Higher Education. 2011. Available online: http://14.139.186.108/jspui/handle/123456789/1528 (accessed on 30 May 2020).
56. Qasem, Y.A.; Abdullah, R.; Atan, R.; Jusoh, Y. Mapping and Analyzing Process of Cloud-based Education as a Service (CEaaS) Model for Cloud Computing Adoption in Higher Education Institutions. In Proceedings of the 2018 Fourth International Conference on Information Retrieval and Knowledge Management (CAMP 2018), Sabah, Malaysia, 26–28 March 2018; IEEE: Piscataway, NJ, USA, 2018.
57. Al-Sharafi, M.A.; Arshah, R.A.; Abu-Shanab, E.A. Factors affecting the continuous use of cloud computing services from expert's perspective. In Proceedings of the TENCON 2017 IEEE Region 10 Conference, Penang, Malaysia, 5–8 November 2017.
58. Alajmi, Q.A.; Kamaludin, A.; Arshah, R.A.; Al-Sharafi, M.A. The Effectiveness of Cloud-Based E-Learning towards Quality of Academic Services: An Omanis' Expert View. *Int. J. Adv. Comput. Sci. Appl.* **2018**, *9*, 158–164. [CrossRef]
59. Militaru, G.; Purcărea, A.A.; Negoiță, O.D.; Niculescu, A. Examining Cloud Computing Adoption Intention in Higher Education: Exploratory Study. In Proceedings of the International Conference on Exploring Services Science 2016, Bucharest, Romania, 25–27 May 2016; Springer: Cham, Switzerland, 2016.
60. Bhatiasevi, V.; Naglis, M. Investigating the structural relationship for the determinants of cloud computing adoption in education. *Educ. Inf. Technol.* **2016**, *21*, 1197–1223. [CrossRef]
61. Almazroi, A.A.; Shen, H.; Teoh, K.K.; Babar, M.A. Cloud for e-Learning: Determinants of Its Adoption by University Students in a Developing Country. In Proceedings of the 2016 IEEE 13th International Conference on e-Business Engineering (ICEBE), Macau, China, 4–6 November 2016; IEEE: Piscataway, NJ, USA, 2016.
62. Hwang, B.-N.; Huang, C.-Y.; Yang, C.-L. Determinants and their causal relationships affecting the adoption of cloud computing in science and technology institutions. *Innovation* **2016**, *18*, 164–190. [CrossRef]
63. Behrend, T.S.; Wiebe, E.N.; London, J.E.; Johnson, E.C. Cloud computing adoption and usage in community colleges. *Behav. Inf. Technol.* **2011**, *30*, 231–240. [CrossRef]

64. Li, Y.-H. An empirical investigation on the determinants of e-procurement adoption in Chinese manufacturing enterprises. In *2008 International Conference on Management Science and Engineering 15th Annual Conference Proceedings*; IEEE: Piscataway, NJ, USA, 2008.
65. Shiau, W.L.; Chau, P.K. Understanding behavioral intention to use a cloud computing classroom: A multiple model comparison approach. *Inf. Manag.* **2016**, *53*, 355–365. [CrossRef]
66. Sharma, S.K.; Al-Badi, A.; Govindaluri, S.M.; Alkharusi, M. Predicting motivators of cloud computing adoption: A developing country perspective. *Comput. Hum. Behav.* **2016**, *62*, 61–69. [CrossRef]
67. Gurung, R.K.; Alsadoon, A.; Prasad, P.W.C.; Elchouemi, A. Impacts of Mobile Cloud Learning (MCL) on Blended Flexible Learning (BFL). In Proceedings of the 2016 International Conference on Information and Digital Technologies (IDT) 2016, Rzeszów, Poland, 5–7 July 2016.
68. Arpaci, I. Understanding and predicting students' intention to use mobile cloud storage services. *Comput. Hum. Behav.* **2016**, *58*, 150–157. [CrossRef]
69. Tan, X.; Kim, Y. User acceptance of SaaS-based collaboration tools: A case of Google Docs. *J. Enterp. Inf. Manag.* **2015**, *28*, 423–442. [CrossRef]
70. Arpaci, I.; Kilicer, K.; Bardakci, S. Effects of security and privacy concerns on educational use of cloud services. *Comput. Hum. Behav.* **2015**, *45*, 93–98. [CrossRef]
71. Yadegaridehkordi, E.; Iahad, N.A.; Ahmad, N. Task-Technology Fit Assessment of Cloud-Based Collaborative Learning Technologies. Remote Work and Collaboration: Breakthroughs in Research and Practice: Breakthroughs in Research and Practice. *Int. J. Inf. Syst. Serv. Sect. (IJISSS)* **2016**, *8*, 58–73. [CrossRef]
72. Stantchev, V.; Colomo-Palacios, R.; Soto-Acosta, P.; Misra, M. Learning management systems and cloud file hosting services: A study on students' acceptance. *Comput. Hum. Behav.* **2014**, *31*, 612–619. [CrossRef]
73. Pinheiro, P.; Aparicio, M.; Costa, C. Adoption of cloud computing systems. In Proceedings of the 2014 International Conference on Information Systems and Design of Communication, Lisbon, Portugal, 16–17 May 2014; ACM Digital Library: New York, NY, USA, 2014; pp. 127–131.
74. Nguyen, T.D.; Nguyen, T.M.; Pham, Q.-T.; Misra, S. Acceptance and Use of E-Learning Based on Cloud Computing: The Role of Consumer Innovativeness. In *Computational Science and Its Applications—ICCSA 2014*; Murgante, B., Misra, S., Rocha, A.M.A.C., Torre, C., Rocha, J.G., Eds.; Springer: Cham, Switzerland, 2014; Volume Pt V, pp. 159–174.
75. Atchariyachanvanich, K.; Siripujaka, N.; Jaiwong, N. What Makes University Students Use Cloud-based E-Learning? Case Study of KMITL Students. In Proceedings of the 2014 International Conference on Information Society (I-Society 2014), London, UK, 12 November 2014; pp. 112–116.
76. Wu, W.W.; Lan, L.W.; Lee, Y.T. Factors hindering acceptance of using cloud services in university: A case study. *Electron. Libr.* **2013**, *31*, 84–98. [CrossRef]
77. Park, S.C.; Ryoo, S.Y. An empirical investigation of end-users' switching toward cloud computing: A two factor theory perspective. *Comput. Hum. Behav.* **2013**, *29*, 160–170. [CrossRef]
78. Oliveira, T.; Martins, M.F. Literature review of information technology adoption models at firm level. *Electron. J. Inf. Syst. Eval.* **2011**, *14*, 110–121.
79. Leinbach, T.R. *Global E-Commerce: Impacts of National Environment and Policy*; Kraemer, K.L., Dedrick, J., Melville, N.P., Zhu, K., Eds.; Cambridge University Press: Cambridge, UK, 2006; p. xxii+444. ISBN 0-521-84822-9.
80. Lin, H.-F.; Lin, S.-M. Determinants of e-business diffusion: A test of the technology diffusion perspective. *Technovation* **2008**, *28*, 135–145. [CrossRef]
81. Ramdani, B.; Kawalek, P.; Lorenzo, O. Predicting SMEs' adoption of enterprise systems. *J. Enterp. Inf. Manag.* **2009**, *22*, 10–24. [CrossRef]
82. Mohammed, F.; Ibrahim, O.; Nilashi, M.; Alzurqa, E.A. Cloud computing adoption model for e-government implementation. *Inf. Dev.* **2017**, *33*, 303–323. [CrossRef]
83. Martins, R.; Oliveira, T.; Thomas, M.A. An empirical analysis to assess the determinants of SaaS diffusion in firms. *Comput. Hum. Behav.* **2016**, *62*, 19–33. [CrossRef]
84. Oliveira, T.; Thomas, M.; Espadanal, M. Assessing the determinants of cloud computing adoption: An analysis of the manufacturing and services sectors. *Inf. Manag.* **2014**, *51*, 497–510. [CrossRef]
85. Zhu, K.; Kraemer, K.L. Post-adoption variations in usage and value of e-business by organizations: Cross-country evidence from the retail industry. *Inf. Syst. Res.* **2005**, *16*, 61–84. [CrossRef]

86. Oliveira, T.; Martins, M.F. Understanding e-business adoption across industries in European countries. *Ind. Manag. Data Syst.* **2010**, *110*, 1337–1354. [CrossRef]
87. Zmud, R.W. Diffusion of modern software practices: Influence of centralization and formalization. *Manag. Sci.* **1982**, *28*, 1421–1431. [CrossRef]
88. Borgman, H.P.; Bahli, B.; Heier, H.; Schewski, F. Cloudrise: Exploring cloud computing adoption and governance with the TOE framework. In Proceedings of the 2013 46th Hawaii International Conference on System Sciences (HICSS), Maui, HI, USA, 7–10 January 2013; IEEE: Piscataway, NJ, USA, 2013.
89. Gangwar, H.; Date, H.; Ramaswamy, R. Understanding determinants of cloud computing adoption using an integrated TAM-TOE model. *J. Enterp. Inf. Manag.* **2015**, *28*, 107–130. [CrossRef]
90. Reza Bazi, H.; Hassanzadeh, A.; Moeini, A. A comprehensive framework for cloud computing migration using Meta-synthesis approach. *J. Syst. Softw.* **2017**, *128*, 87–105. [CrossRef]
91. Baker, J. The technology–organization–environment framework. In *Information Systems Theory*; Springer: New York, NY, USA, 2012; pp. 231–245.
92. Bose, R.; Luo, X. Integrative framework for assessing firms' potential to undertake Green IT initiatives via virtualization–A theoretical perspective. *J. Strateg. Inf. Syst.* **2011**, *20*, 38–54. [CrossRef]
93. Chan, F.T.; Chong, A.Y.-L. Determinants of mobile supply chain management system diffusion: A structural equation analysis of manufacturing firms. *Int. J. Prod. Res.* **2013**, *51*, 1196–1213. [CrossRef]
94. Chong, A.Y.-L.; Chan, F.T. Structural equation modeling for multi-stage analysis on Radio Frequency Identification (RFID) diffusion in the health care industry. *Expert Syst. Appl.* **2012**, *39*, 8645–8654. [CrossRef]
95. Kim, S.; Garrison, G. Understanding users' behaviors regarding supply chain technology: Determinants impacting the adoption and implementation of RFID technology in South Korea. *Int. J. Inf. Manag.* **2010**, *30*, 388–398. [CrossRef]
96. Wang, Y.-M.; Wang, Y.-S.; Yang, Y.-F. Understanding the determinants of RFID adoption in the manufacturing industry. *Technol. Forecast. Soc. Chang.* **2010**, *77*, 803–815. [CrossRef]
97. Thomas, M.; Costa, D.; Oliveira, T. Assessing the role of IT-enabled process virtualization on green IT adoption. *Inf. Syst. Front.* **2016**, *18*, 693–710. [CrossRef]
98. Venkatesh, V.; Bala, H. Adoption and impacts of interorganizational business process standards: Role of partnering synergy. *Inf. Syst. Res.* **2012**, *23*, 1131–1157. [CrossRef]
99. Zhu, K.; Kraemer, K.; Xu, S. Electronic business adoption by European firms: A cross-country assessment of the facilitators and inhibitors. *Eur. J. Inf. Syst.* **2003**, *12*, 251–268. [CrossRef]
100. Zhu, K.; Kraemer, K.L.; Xu, S. The process of innovation assimilation by firms in different countries: A technology diffusion perspective on e-business. *Manag. Sci.* **2006**, *52*, 1557–1576. [CrossRef]
101. Yang, Z.; Sun, J.; Zhang, Y.; Wang, Y. Understanding SaaS adoption from the perspective of organizational users: A tripod readiness model. *Comput. Hum. Behav.* **2015**, *45*, 254–264. [CrossRef]
102. Abdollahzadegan, A.; Che Hussin, A.R.; Moshfegh Gohary, M.; Amini, M. The organizational critical success factors for adopting cloud computing in SMEs. *JISRI* **2013**, *4*, 67–74.
103. Low, C.; Chen, Y.; Wu, M. Understanding the determinants of cloud computing adoption. *Ind. Manag. Data Syst.* **2011**, *111*, 1006–1023. [CrossRef]
104. Rogers, E.M. *Diffusion of Innovations*; Simon and Schuster: New York, NY, USA, 2010.
105. Sharma, M.K. Receptivity of India's small and medium-sized enterprises to information system adoption. *Enterp. Inf. Syst.* **2009**, *3*, 95–115. [CrossRef]
106. Shah Alam, S. Adoption of internet in Malaysian SMEs. *J. Small Bus. Enterp. Dev.* **2009**, *16*, 240–255. [CrossRef]
107. Azadegan, A.; Teich, J. Effective benchmarking of innovation adoptions: A theoretical framework for e-procurement technologies. *Benchmark. Int. J.* **2010**, *17*, 472–490. [CrossRef]
108. Tsai, M.-C.; Lee, W.; Wu, H.-C. Determinants of RFID adoption intention: Evidence from Taiwanese retail chains. *Inf. Manag.* **2010**, *47*, 255–261. [CrossRef]
109. Ifinedo, P. An empirical analysis of factors influencing Internet/e-business technologies adoption by SMEs in Canada. *Int. J. Inf. Technol. Decis. Mak.* **2011**, *10*, 731–766. [CrossRef]
110. Chong, A.Y.-L.; Lin, B.; Ooi, K.-B.; Raman, M. Factors affecting the adoption level of c-commerce: An empirical study. *J. Comput. Inf. Syst.* **2009**, *50*, 13–22.

111. Dedrick, J.; West, J. Why firms adopt open source platforms: A grounded theory of innovation and standards adoption. In Proceedings of the Workshop on Standard Making: A Critical Research Frontier for Information Systems, Seattle, WA, USA, 12–14 December 2003.
112. Zhu, K.; Dong, S.; Xu, S.X.; Kraemer, K.L. Innovation diffusion in global contexts: Determinants of post-adoption digital transformation of European companies. *Eur. J. Inf. Syst.* **2006**, *15*, 601–616. [CrossRef]
113. Gibbs, J.L.; Kraemer, K.L. A cross-country investigation of the determinants of scope of e-commerce use: An institutional approach. *Electron. Mark.* **2004**, *14*, 124–137. [CrossRef]
114. Obal, M. What drives post-adoption usage? Investigating the negative and positive antecedents of disruptive technology continuous adoption intentions. *Ind. Mark. Manag.* **2017**, *63*, 42–52. [CrossRef]
115. Jia, Q.; Guo, Y.; Barnes, S.J. Enterprise 2.0 post-adoption: Extending the information system continuance model based on the technology-Organization-environment framework. *Comput. Hum. Behav.* **2017**, *67*, 95–105. [CrossRef]
116. Hair, J.F., Jr.; Hult, G.T.M.; Ringle, C.M.; Sarstedt, M. *A Primer on Partial Least Squares Structural Equation Modeling (PLS-SEM)*; Sage Publications: Los Angeles, CA, USA, 2016.
117. Haykin, S. *Neural Networks: A Comprehensive Foundation*; Prentice Hall: New Dehli, India, 1994.
118. Garson, G.D. *Neural Networks: An Introductory Guide for Social Scientists*; Sage: London, UK, 1998.
119. Chiang, W.-Y.K.; Zhang, D.; Zhou, L. Predicting and explaining patronage behavior toward web and traditional stores using neural networks: A comparative analysis with logistic regression. *Decis. Support Syst.* **2006**, *41*, 514–531. [CrossRef]
120. Kaastra, I.; Boyd, M. Designing a neural network for forecasting financial and economic time series. *Neurocomputing* **1996**, *10*, 215–236. [CrossRef]
121. Hsu, C.-I.; Shih, M.L.; Huang, B.W.; Lin, B.Y.; Lin, C.N. Predicting tourism loyalty using an integrated Bayesian network mechanism. *Expert Syst. Appl.* **2009**, *36*, 11760–11763. [CrossRef]
122. Asadi, S.; Abdullah, R.; Safaei, M.; Nazir, S. An Integrated SEM-Neural Network Approach for Predicting Determinants of Adoption of Wearable Healthcare Devices. *Mob. Inf. Syst.* **2019**, *2019*. [CrossRef]
123. Hu, M.Y.; Shanker, M.; Hung, M.S. Estimation of posterior probabilities of consumer situational choices with neural network classifiers. *Int. J. Res. Mark.* **1999**, *16*, 307–317. [CrossRef]
124. Shmueli, G.; Koppius, O.R. Predictive analytics in information systems research. *Mis Q.* **2011**, *35*, 553–572. [CrossRef]
125. Sekaran, U.; Bougie, R. *Research Methods for Business: A Skill Building Approach*; John Wiley & Sons: Hoboken, NJ, USA, 2016.
126. Moore, G.C.; Benbasat, I. Development of an instrument to measure the perceptions of adopting an information technology innovation. *Inf. Syst. Res.* **1991**, *2*, 192–222. [CrossRef]
127. Taweel, A. *Examining the Relationship between Technological, Organizational, and Environmental Factors and Cloud Computing Adoption*; UMI Dissertations Publishing; ProQuest: Ann Arbor, MI, USA, 2012.
128. Tashkandi, A.; Al-Jabri, I. Cloud Computing Adoption by Higher Education Institutions in Saudi Arabia: Analysis Based on TOE. In Proceedings of the 2015 International Conference on Cloud Computing, ICCC 2015, Riyadh, Saudi Arabia, 26–29 April 2015.
129. Bughin, J.; Chui, M.; Manyika, J. Clouds, big data, and smart assets: Ten tech-enabled business trends to watch. *McKinsey Q.* **2010**, *56*, 75–86.
130. Lin, H.-F. Understanding the determinants of electronic supply chain management system adoption: Using the technology–organization–environment framework. *Technol. Forecast. Soc. Chang.* **2014**, *86*, 80–92. [CrossRef]
131. Shah Alam, S.; Ali, M.Y.; Jani, M.F.M. An empirical study of factors affecting electronic commerce adoption among SMEs in Malaysia. *J. Bus. Econ. Manag.* **2011**, *12*, 375–399. [CrossRef]
132. Wang, M.W.; Lee, O.-K.; Lim, K.L. Knowledge management systems diffusion in Chinese enterprises: A multi-stage approach with the technology-organization-environment framework. In Proceedings of the 2007 Pacific Asia Conference on Information Systems (PACIS), Auckland, New Zealand, 4–6 July 2007; p. 70.
133. Ifinedo, P. Internet/e-business technologies acceptance in Canada's SMEs: An exploratory investigation. *Internet Res.* **2011**, *21*, 255–281. [CrossRef]
134. Klug, W.; Bai, X. The determinants of cloud computing adoption by colleges and universities. *Int. J. Bus. Res. Inf. Technol.* **2015**, *2*, 14–30.

135. Tornatzky, L.G.; Klein, K.J. Innovation characteristics and innovation adoption-implementation: A meta-analysis of findings. *IEEE Trans. Eng. Manag.* **1982**, *1*, 28–45. [CrossRef]
136. Opala, O.J. An Analysis of Security, Cost-Effectiveness, and it Compliance Factors Influencing Cloud Adoption by it Managers. Ph.D. Thesis, Capella University, Minneapolis, MN, USA, 2012.
137. Broberg, J.; Buyya, R.; Tari, Z. Creating aCloud Storage'Mashup for High Performance, Low Cost Content Delivery, Service-Oriented Computing—ICSOC 2008 Workshops. In Proceedings of the International Conference on Service-Oriented Computing ICSOC 2008 International Workshops, Sydney, Australia, 1 December 2008; Springer: Berlin/Heidelberg, Germany, 2008.
138. Mircea, M. SOA, BPM and cloud computing: Connected for innovation in higher education. In Proceedings of the 2010 International Conference on Education and Management Technology, Cario, Egypt, 2–4 November 2010; IEEE: Piscataway, NJ, USA, 2010.
139. Saya, S.; Pee, L.G.; Kankanhalli, A. "THE IMPACT OF INSTITUTIONAL INFLUENCES ON PERCEIVED TECHNOLOGICAL CHARACTERISTICS AND REAL OPTIONS IN CLOUD COMPUTING ADOPTION" (2010). ICIS 2010 Proceedings. 24. Available online: https://aisel.aisnet.org/icis2010_submissions/24 (accessed on 30 May 2020).
140. Hossain, M.A.; Quaddus, M. Radio frequency identification (RFID) adoption: A cross-sectional comparison of voluntary and mandatory contexts. *Inf. Syst. Front.* **2015**, *17*, 1057–1076. [CrossRef]
141. Asadi, S.; Nilashi, M.; Safaei, M.; Abdullah, R.; Saeed, F.; Yadegaridehkordi, E.; Samad, S. Investigating factors influencing decision-makers' intention to adopt Green IT in Malaysian manufacturing industry. *Resour. Conserv. Recycl.* **2019**, *148*, 36–54. [CrossRef]
142. Bunduchi, R.; Weisshaar, C.; Smart, A.U. Mapping the benefits and costs associated with process innovation: The case of RFID adoption. *Technovation* **2011**, *31*, 505–521. [CrossRef]
143. Gagnon, Y.-C.; Toulouse, J.-M. The behavior of business managers when adopting new technologies. *Technol. Forecast. Soc. Chang.* **1996**, *52*, 59–74. [CrossRef]
144. Lal, P.; Bharadwaj, S.S. Understanding the impact of cloud-based services adoption on organizational flexibility: An exploratory study. *J. Enterp. Inf. Manag.* **2016**, *29*, 566–588. [CrossRef]
145. Kwon, T.H.; Zmud, R.W. Unifying the fragmented models of information systems implementation. In *Critical Issues in Information Systems Research*; John Wiley & Sons, Inc.: Hoboken, NJ, USA, 1987.
146. Mata, F.J.; Fuerst, W.L.; Barney, J.B. Information technology and sustained competitive advantage: A resource-based analysis. *Mis Q.* **1995**, 487–505. [CrossRef]
147. Mokhtar, S.A.; Ali, S.H.S.; Al-Sharafi, A.; Al-Sharafi, A. Organizational Factors in the Adoption of Cloud Computing in E-learning. In Proceedings of the 3rd International Conference on Advanced Computer Science Applications and Technologies Acsat, Amman, Jordan, 26 December 2014; pp. 188–191.
148. Albalawi, M.S. Critical Factors Related to the Implementation of Web-Based Instruction by Higher-Education Faculty at Three Universities in the Kingdom of Saudi Arabia. Ph.D. Thesis, University of West Florida, Pensacola, FL, USA, 2007.
149. Mansour, A.J. The Adoption of Cloud Computing Technology in Higher Education Institutions: Concerns and Challenges (Case Study on Islamic University of Gaza'iug'), IUG dissertation. 2013. Available online: http://hdl.handle.net/20.500.12358/17670 (accessed on 30 May 2020).
150. Sathyanarayana, T.; Sheela, L.M.I. Data security in cloud computing. In Proceedings of the 2013 International Conference on Green Computing, Communication and Conservation of Energy (ICGCE), Chennai, India, 12–14 December 2013; IEEE: Piscataway, NJ, USA, 2013.
151. Subashini, S.; Kavitha, V. A survey on security issues in service delivery models of cloud computing. *J. Netw. Comput. Appl.* **2011**, *34*, 1–11. [CrossRef]
152. Wheeler, B.; Waggener, S. Above-campus services: Shaping the promise of cloud computing for higher education. *Educ. Rev.* **2009**, *44*, 52–67.
153. Weber, A.S. Cloud computing in education in the Middle East and North Africa (MENA) Region: Can barriers be overcome? In *Conference Proceedings of «ELearning and Software for Education» (eLSE)*; Carol, I., Ed.; National Defence University Publishing House: Bucharest, Romania, 2011.
154. Ciganek, A.P.; Haseman, W.; Ramamurthy, K. Time to decision: The drivers of innovation adoption decisions. *Enterp. Inf. Syst.* **2014**, *8*, 279–308. [CrossRef]
155. Yoon, T.E.; George, J.F. Why aren't organizations adopting virtual worlds? *Comput. Hum. Behav.* **2013**, *29*, 772–790. [CrossRef]

156. Wymer, S.A.; Regan, E.A. Factors influencing e-commerce adoption and use by small and medium businesses. *Electron. Mark.* **2005**, *15*, 438–453. [CrossRef]
157. Rousseau, D.M. Issues of level in organizational research: Multi-level and cross-level perspectives. *Res. Organ. Behav.* **1985**, *7*, 1–37.
158. Chau, P.Y.; Tam, K.Y. Factors Affecting the Adoption of Open Systems: An Exploratory Study. *MIS Q.* **1997**, *21*, 1–24. [CrossRef]
159. Kuan, K.K.; Chau, P.Y. A perception-based model for EDI adoption in small businesses using a technology–organization–environment framework. *Inf. Manag.* **2001**, *38*, 507–521. [CrossRef]
160. Ghobakhloo, M.; Arias-Aranda, D.; Benitez-Amado, J. Adoption of e-commerce applications in SMEs. *Ind. Manag. Data Syst.* **2011**, *111*, 1238–1269. [CrossRef]
161. Thiesse, F.; Staake, T.; Schmitt, P.; Fleisch, E. The rise of the "next-generation bar code": An international RFID adoption study. *Supply Chain Manag. Int. J.* **2011**, *16*, 328–345. [CrossRef]
162. Klein, R. Assimilation of Internet-based purchasing applications within medical practices. *Inf. Manag.* **2012**, *49*, 135–141. [CrossRef]
163. Lin, A.; Chen, N.-C. Cloud computing as an innovation: Percepetion, attitude, and adoption. *Int. J. Inf. Manag.* **2012**, *32*, 533–540. [CrossRef]
164. Nkhoma, M.Z.; Dang, D.P.; De Souza-Daw, A. Contributing factors of cloud computing adoption: A technology-organisation-environment framework approach. In Proceedings of the European Conference on Information Management & Evaluation, Gdansk, Poland, 12–13 September 2013.
165. Alshamaila, Y.; Papagiannidis, S.; Li, F. Cloud computing adoption by SMEs in the north east of England: A multi-perspective framework. *J. Enterp. Inf. Manag.* **2013**, *26*, 250–275. [CrossRef]
166. Wu, Y.; Cegielski, C.G.; Cegielski, B.T.; Hall, D.J. Cloud computing in support of supply chain information system infrastructure: Understanding when to go to the cloud. *J. Supply Chain Manag.* **2013**, *49*, 25–41. [CrossRef]
167. Cheng, X.; Bounfour, A. The determinants of Cloud Computing Adoption by Large European Firms. *Inf. Syst. Chang. Econ. Soc.* **2015**, *50*.
168. Salum, K.H.; Rozan, M.Z.A. Conceptual model for cloud erp adoption for smes. *J. Theor. Appl. Inf. Technol.* **2017**, *95*, 743.
169. Chan, F.T.S.; Chong, A.Y.L. A SEM–neural network approach for understanding determinants of interorganizational system standard adoption and performances. *Decis. Support Syst.* **2012**, *54*, 621–630. [CrossRef]
170. Venkatesh, V.; Goyal, S. Expectation Disconfirmation and Technology Adoption: Polynomial Modeling and Response Surface Analysis. *Mis Q.* **2010**, *34*, 281–303. [CrossRef]
171. Joshi, R.; Yadav, R. An integrated SEM neural network approach to study effectiveness of brand extension in Indian FMCG industry. *Bus. Perspect. Res.* **2018**, *6*, 113–128.
172. Ahani, A.; Rahim, N.Z.A.; Nilashi, M. Forecasting social CRM adoption in SMEs: A combined SEM-neural network method. *Comput. Hum. Behav.* **2017**, *75*, 560–578. [CrossRef]
173. Chong, A.Y.-L.; Bai, R. Predicting open IOS adoption in SMEs: An integrated SEM-neural network approach. *Expert Syst. Appl.* **2014**, *41*, 221–229. [CrossRef]
174. Daniel, J. *Sampling Essentials: Practical Guidelines for Making Sampling Choices*; Sage: Thousand Oaks, CA, USA, 2011.
175. Kotrlik, J.; Higgins, C. Organizational research: Determining appropriate sample size in survey research appropriate sample size in survey research. *Inf. Technol. Learn. Perform. J.* **2001**, *19*, 43.
176. Sibona, C.; Walczak, S. Purposive Sampling on Twitter: A Case Study. In Proceedings of the 2012 45th Hawaii International Conference on System Sciences, Maui, HI, USA, 4–7 January 2012.
177. Hertzog, M.A. Considerations in determining sample size for pilot studies. *Res. Nurs. Health* **2008**, *31*, 180–191. [CrossRef]
178. Saunders, M.N. *Research Methods for Business Students*; Pearson Education India: Upper Saddle River, NJ, USA, 2011.
179. Sekaran, U.; Bougie, R. *Research Methods for Business, A Skill Building Approach*; John Willey & Sons, Inc.: New York, NY, USA, 2003.
180. Tellis, W.M. Introduction to Case Study. The Qualitative Report, 3, 1-14. 1997. Available online: https://nsuworks.nova.edu/tqr/vol3/iss2/4 (accessed on 30 May 2020).

181. Whitehead, A.L.; Julious, A.S.; Cooper, C.L.; Campbell, M.J. Estimating the sample size for a pilot randomised trial to minimise the overall trial sample size for the external pilot and main trial for a continuous outcome variable. *Stat. Methods Med Res.* **2016**, *25*, 1057–1073. [CrossRef]
182. Straub, D.; Boudreau, M.-C.; Gefen, D. Validation guidelines for IS positivist research. *Commun. Assoc. Inf. Syst.* **2004**, *13*, 24. [CrossRef]
183. Chin, W.W.; Marcolin, B.L.; Newsted, P.R. A partial least squares latent variable modeling approach for measuring interaction effects: Results from a Monte Carlo simulation study and an electronic-mail emotion/adoption study. *Inf. Syst. Res.* **2003**, *14*, 189–217. [CrossRef]
184. Hulland, J. Use of partial least squares (PLS) in strategic management research: A review of four recent studies. *Strateg. Manag. J.* **1999**, *20*, 195–204. [CrossRef]
185. Gefen, D.; Rigdon, E.E.; Straub, D. Editor's Comments: An Update and Extension to SEM Guidelines for Administrative and Social Science Research. *MIS Q.* **2011**, *35*, iii–xiv. [CrossRef]
186. Chin, W.W. How to write up and report PLS analyses. In *Handbook of Partial Least Squares*; Springer: Berlin/Heidelberg, Germany, 2010; pp. 655–690.
187. Ainuddin, R.A.; Beamish, P.W.; Hulland, J.S.; Rouse, M.J. Resource attributes and firm performance in international joint ventures. *J. World Bus.* **2007**, *42*, 47–60. [CrossRef]
188. Henseler, J.; Ringle, C.M.; Sinkovics, R.R. The use of partial least squares path modeling in international marketing. In *New Challenges to International Marketing*; Emerald Group Publishing Limited: Bradford, UK, 2009; pp. 277–319.
189. Urbach, N.; Ahlemann, F. Structural equation modeling in information systems research using partial least squares. *J. Inf. Technol. Theory Appl.* **2010**, *11*, 5–40.
190. Fornell, C.; Larcker, D.F. Structural Equation Models with Unobservable Variables and Measurement Error: Algebra and Statistics. *J. Mark. Res.* **1981**, *18*, 382–388. [CrossRef]
191. Liébana-Cabanillas, F.; Marinković, V.; Kalinić, Z. A SEM-neural network approach for predicting antecedents of m-commerce acceptance. *Int. J. Inf. Manag.* **2017**, *37*, 14–24. [CrossRef]
192. El-Amir, H.; Hamdy, M. A Tour through the Deep Learning Pipeline. In *Deep Learning Pipeline*; Springer: Berlin/Heidelberg, Germany, 2020; pp. 57–84.
193. Jaafar, K.; Ismail, N.; Tajjudin, M.; Adnan, R.; Rahiman, M.H.F. Artificial Neural Networks for Water Level Prediction Based on Z-Score Technique in Kelantan River. *Int. J. Electr. Electron. Syst. Res.* **2018**, *13*.
194. Wang, Y.-M.; Elhag, T.M. A comparison of neural network, evidential reasoning and multiple regression analysis in modelling bridge risks. *Expert Syst. Appl.* **2007**, *32*, 336–348. [CrossRef]
195. Asadi, S.; Abdullah, R.; Jusoh, Y.Y. An Integrated SEM-Neural Network for Predicting and Understanding the Determining Factor for Institutional Repositories Adoption. In Proceedings of the SAI Intelligent Systems Conference, London, UK, 5–6 September 2019; Springer: Cham, Switzerland, 2019.
196. Sabi, H.M.; Uzoka, F.-M.E.; Mlay, S.V. Staff perception towards cloud computing adoption at universities in a developing country. *Educ. Inf. Technol.* **2018**, *23*, 1–24. [CrossRef]
197. Hair, J.F.; Ringle, C.M.; Sarstedt, M. Partial least squares structural equation modeling: Rigorous applications, better results and higher acceptance. *Long Range Plan.* **2013**, *46*, 1–12. [CrossRef]
198. Qasem, Y.A.; Abdullah, R.; Jusoh, Y.; Atan, R. Cloud-Based Education As a Service (CEAAS) System Requirements Specification Model of Higher Education Institutions in Industrial Revolution 4.0. *Int. J. Adv. Technol. Eng. Explor.* **2019**, *8*, 1382–1386.
199. Nuseibeh, H. Adoption of Cloud Computing in Organizations. AMCIS 2011 Proceedings—All Submissions. 372. 2011. Available online: http://aisel.aisnet.org/amcis2011_submissions/372 (accessed on 30 May 2020).
200. Bhattacherjee, A. Understanding Information Systems Continuance: An Expectation-Confirmation Model. *MIS Q.* **2001**, *25*, 351–370. [CrossRef]
201. Morgan, L.; Conboy, K. Factors affecting the adoption of cloud computing: An exploratory study. In Proceedings of the ECIS 21st European Conference on Information Systems 2013, Utrecht, The Netherlands, 5–8 June 2013; pp. 1–12. Available online: http://hdl.handle.net/10344/3209 (accessed on 30 May 2020).
202. Rieger, P.; Gewald, H.; Schumacher, B. Cloud-computing in banking influential factors, benefits and risks from a decision maker's perspective. In Proceedings of the AMCIS 2013, Chicago, IL, USA, 15–17 August 2013; pp. 1–12.
203. Lian, J.-W.; Yen, D.C.; Wang, Y.-T. An exploratory study to understand the critical factors affecting the decision to adopt cloud computing in Taiwan hospital. *Int. J. Inf. Manag.* **2014**, *34*, 28–36. [CrossRef]

204. Benlian, A.; Hess, T. Opportunities and risks of software-as-a-service: Findings from a survey of IT executives. *Decis. Support Syst.* **2011**, *52*, 232–246. [CrossRef]
205. Luo, X.; Gurung, A.; Shim, J.P. Understanding the determinants of user acceptance of enterprise instant messaging: An empirical study. *J. Organ. Comput. Electron. Commer.* **2010**, *20*, 155–181. [CrossRef]
206. Wu, W.-W. Mining significant factors affecting the adoption of SaaS using the rough set approach. *J. Syst. Softw.* **2011**, *84*, 435–441. [CrossRef]
207. Cervone, H.F. An overview of virtual and cloud computing. *OCLC Syst. Serv. Int. Digit. Libr. Perspect.* **2010**, *26*, 162–165. [CrossRef]
208. Marston, S.; Li, Z.; Bandyopadhyay, S.; Zhang, J.; Ghalsasi, A. Cloud computing—The business perspective. *Decis. Support Syst.* **2011**, *51*, 176–189. [CrossRef]
209. Lee, S.; Kim, K.-J. Factors affecting the implementation success of Internet-based information systems. *Comput. Hum. Behav.* **2007**, *23*, 1853–1880. [CrossRef]
210. Frambach, R.T.; Barkema, H.G.; Nooteboom, B.; Wedel, M. Adoption of a service innovation in the business market: An empirical test of supply-side variables. *J. Bus. Res.* **1998**, *41*, 161–174. [CrossRef]
211. Yap, C.-S.; Thong, J.Y.; Raman, K. Effect of government incentives on computerisation in small business. *Eur. J. Inf. Syst.* **1994**, *3*, 191–206. [CrossRef]

 © 2020 by the authors. Licensee MDPI, Basel, Switzerland. This article is an open access article distributed under the terms and conditions of the Creative Commons Attribution (CC BY) license (http://creativecommons.org/licenses/by/4.0/).

Article

# Predicting Student Grades Based on Their Usage of LMS Moodle Using Petri Nets

Zoltán Balogh * and Michal Kuchárik

Department of Informatics, Faculty of Natural Sciences, Constantine the Philosopher University in Nitra, 94974 Nitra, Slovakia; mkucharik@ukf.sk
* Correspondence: zbalogh@ukf.sk

Received: 21 August 2019; Accepted: 3 October 2019; Published: 9 October 2019

**Abstract:** This paper deals with the possibility of predicting student's grades based on their usage of Learning Management System (LMS) Moodle. It is important to know what materials would be best suited in LMS as study materials and what materials could be improved or removed based on the student's usage of the materials and the final grade. In order to do this, the correlations between access to materials and the final grade were observed. These correlations could also be used to predict the grades of the student. Therefore, a model with Petri nets was created that based on the highest correlation would be able to predict what grade the student would get based on his usage of LMS. Obviously, it would not be possible to predict every result with certainty, however, more precise predictions could be obtained with higher correlations.

**Keywords:** petri nets; simulation; transitions; probability; concurrency; LMS

## 1. Introduction

The implementation of new technologies and practices into education currently represents the greatest support for the development of learner's cognitive and intellectual abilities. A virtual university system enables to create a virtual classroom on the web. Such systems combine learning management skills with student collaboration capabilities to support learning abilities such as exercises, discussions and grading. Due to the increasing popularity of distance learning, a number of software tools for distance learning for web browsers have been developed. These systems have been used at various universities and departments.

The static structure of information on the web, whose task is to provide information, has long been succeeded. More and more web software systems are being created that are more complex than ever. From a usage point of view of these systems, the need to enrich the information space of the heterogeneous resources under which these systems work is becoming increasingly important, with elements of user adaptation and/or user experience. The goal is to present personalized information to the user, in other words, information that is relevant to the user in a way that is best suited for that user [1].

This paper focuses on the educational processes that happen inside the Learning Management System (LMS) Moodle. The open-source LMS Moodle is useful for creating an effective online learning community. It also encourages learners to participate in the learning process and helps teachers who aim to improve the learning performance of their students through creative collaboration [2].

Moodle (Modular Object-Oriented Dynamic Learning Environment) is an open source LMS developed in Australia in 2002 and has been available since the 1.0 version was released in March 2011. Moodle is used for blended learning, distance education, flipped classroom, and other e-learning projects in schools, universities, workplaces, and other sectors [3]. As a famous learning LMS, Moodle is a diversified technical tool that supports an evaluation of blended learning. Authors in the paper

*Engaging Asian students through game mechanics: Findings from two experiment studies* [4] used Moodle to report the effects of game mechanics to foster users' engagement in blended learning and found that the digital implementation of game mechanics automatically kept track of students' activities in Moodle. Moodle provides a number of ways to express and share the knowledge that learners possess. Moodle also provides a good tool for monitoring community learning activities. Through these collaborative activities, learners can create new knowledge on their own and further develop critical thinking and flexible creative problem-solving skills through mutual cooperation between members [5].

The Moodle LMS is customized and has several features available for teachers to assist them in teaching. The LMS is generally used for delivering course content, course progression plan, grading, creating activities, collecting course feedback, and communicating with course participants. Among several features, only a few of them such as assignment, feedback, quiz, and workshop modules are considered very essential and are heavily used [6].

The aim of this paper is to use modeling with Petri nets to predict the student's success based on his/her passage through the e-course and thus to design models that could be used to create better e-courses for LMS Moodle.

## 2. Related Work

The introduction of information and communication technologies (ICT) into practice has brought changes in all areas of society including in the field of education [7]. However, in order to fully utilize the potential of these technologies, a new approach to education is needed. This, in turn, requires a new model of the educational institution whose processes would be changed by the use of ICT [8]. Without changing the existing educational process, it is unlikely to achieve a different learning outcome. Information and Communication Technologies have become one of the pillars of modern society and a natural part of the everyday life of most people. Education is no exception. Today, the use of ICT in education varies depending on the countries and types of educational institutions, as well as between institutions. However, the use of technology is a standard in most universities. Examples include LMS and Virtual Learning Environments (VLE) [9].

The great potential of these methods lies in the ability to open the black box and "see" what education actually looks like in online learning environments. Although the use of LMS in teaching is relatively common in many colleges, teachers using LMS in their classroom often do not have many opportunities to see exactly what is happening in their online courses, how students behave, or how they access online materials or progress when engaging in learning activities. Generally, LMS does not automatically include advanced data acquisition tools, while the external data acquisition tools are too complex for teachers and their features to go beyond what the educator may require [10,11].

Regarding the process extraction, the first reference to the method is defined in the process mining in the first Handbook of Educational Data Mining (EDM) [12] as one of the basic EDM techniques. It was, however, mentioned as a technique that had been used rather sparsely until then, as the existing EDM approaches have rarely focused on the process as a whole [13]. Nevertheless, process mining in education is attracting increased research attention. Its potential use in education has been discussed by Reimann and Yacef [14] among others. Reimann et al. [15] dedicated their critical article to process mining from the perspective of methodological challenges in data-intensive research methods.

A browsing behavior model based on High-Level Petri Nets (HLPN) to generate behavioral patterns for e-learning was written by authors Yi-ChunChang et al. [16]. Many researchers have made great efforts to promote high-quality e-learning environments such as adaptive learning environments, customized/adaptive guidance mechanisms, etc. These studies must collect a large number of behavioral patterns for verification and/or experimentation. Collecting sufficient behavioral patterns usually takes a lot of time and effort. To solve this problem, Yi-ChunChang et al. proposed a Model of Browsing Behavior (B2model) based on High Level Petri Networks to model and generate student behavior patterns.The established behavioral patterns are compared with the actual behavioral patterns collected from primary school pupils. The results confirm that the generated behavioral patterns are analogous to the actual behavioral patterns.

An example of the use of Petri nets in education could be described by authors Balogh et al. in the article *The possibilities of using Petri Nets for realization of a universal model of educational process* [17]. This work summarized the results obtained from the design, creation and implementation of a universal model of educational processes with the use of Petri nets. Based on the created models in Petri nets, it was possible to verify and simulate individual processes through which the student passes through the e-course in LMS. The universal model was implemented at the Department of Informatics in 2009/2010. The module is used in technically oriented courses, mainly in the field of applied informatics. The results obtained from the use of the module are mentioned in the debate and show that in this way it was possible to find certain rules of behavior of students in the e-course in terms of use and compare them with the created process models. In the resulting effect, it was possible to remove all disturbing elements from the e-courses and make them more efficient and attractive. The universal model of educational processes supported by Petri nets has thus contributed to improve student abilities and skills without them knowing it.

In the article *Possibilities of Modeling Web-based Education Using IF-THEN Rules and Fuzzy Petri Nets in LMS* and in the book *Process Modeling Using Petri Nets*, there was an example of a fuzzy Petri network which described the modeling of student knowledge that was used in the following example [18,19].

Serial machines, commonly used to describe the behavior of learning processes, have several limitations in modeling complex processes such as the number of states. Therefore, Petri nets are used for given purposes derived from the expanding modeling capabilities of series machines.

One of the advantages of modeling educational processes using Petri nets is their formal description enriched with graphical representation. It allows the precise and exact specification of the educational process and elimination of design ambiguities, uncertainties and contradictions. In addition to the visual representation, Petri nets also have a mathematical basis that is well used in software tools to specify and analyze computer-based educational processes [20]. The article described the creation of a rule-based model. With TransPlaceSim, the rules could be recovered.

The publication *Finding learning paths using Petri nets modeling applicable to e-learning platforms* [21] presents an approach to model courses with the help of Petri nets. The method can be used to support the development of electronic learning platforms, such as LMS, allowing student guidance in a decision to achieve a particular goal. This goal can be simple, such as passing a course, or even complex, such as combining different modules from different courses to get a qualification. Each course is characterized by a group of modules and the relationships between them. Each module is represented by a Petri net model, and the structure of the module that represents the course dependency is shifted to the next Petri net. Additional courses or modules can be added as their associated Petri Network models can be easily assigned using additional operations. The contribution of this work lies in the use of common techniques to analyze Petri nets to limit student possibilities to optimize his/her path towards grades and qualifications. A simple example with a scenario of a few courses and modules was used to illustrate the approach.

There are many examples where Petri nets are used to model educational systems. They are used in systems where the teacher becomes the main element of the process of learning, modeling a course or using higher-level Petri nets to group materials in e-learning. The work has focused on creating a complete model of an e-learning system that would provide several courses and modules and it would encourage students to find a specific way to achieve their goals in accordance with their needs [22,23].

*The Basic Concept of Petri Nets*

Petri Net (PN) is a graphical and mathematical modeling tool that has the advantages of graphical notation and simple semantics [24]. Petri nets designate a wide class of mathematical models that allow modeling and describing control flows and information dependencies within a system.

A PN is a 5-tuple [24,25]: PN = $(P,T,A,W,M_0)$, where

- $P = \{p_1, p_2, \ldots, p_m\}$ is a finite set of places. A place represents a circle, such as $p_1, p_2$ and $p_3$ in Figure 1.
- $T = \{t_1, t_2, \ldots, t_n\}$ is a finite set of transitions. A transition represents a bar, such as $t_1$ in Figure 1. The intersection of P and T is an empty set, while the union of P and T is not an empty set, i.e., $P \cap T = \emptyset$ and $T \cup P \neq \emptyset$.
- $A \subseteq (P \times T) \cup (T \times P)$ is a set of arcs connecting places and transitions, such as the arrowhead from $p_1$ to $t_1$ depicted in Figure 1.
- $W: A \rightarrow \{1, 2, 3, \ldots\}$ is a weight function, whose weight value is positive integers. Arcs, i.e., arrowhead, are labeled with weights. For example, in Figure 1, the arrowhead from $t_1$ to $p_3$, which is labeled with "2", is denoted as $W(t_1, p_3) = 2$. When the weight is unity and/or "1", the label of arc is usually omitted, e.g., $W(p_1, t_1) = 1$ is omitted in Figure 1.
- $M_0: P \rightarrow \{0, 1, 2, 3, \ldots\}$ is the initial marking. If there are k tokens inside place $p_i$, it is said that $p_i$ is marked with k tokens. For example, in Figure 1a, $p_1$ is marked with one token, which is denoted as $M(p_1) = 1$. $p_2$ is marked with two tokens, which is denoted as $M(p_2) = 2$. If Figure 1a is the initial status, the initial marking is denoted as $M_0(p_1, p_2, p_3) = \{1, 2, 0\}$.

A transition t is said to be fired if all its input places $p_i$ are marked with at least $W(p_i, t)$ tokens, where $W(p_i, t)$ is called the firing condition of transition t. For example, in Figure 1, the firing conditions of $t_1$ are $W(p_1, t_1) = 1$ and $W(p_2, t_1) = 2$.

A firing transition t removes $W(p_i, t)$ tokens from each input place $p_i$ and adds $W(t, p_j)$ tokens to each output place $p_j$. For instance, since $M(p_1) = 1$ and $M(p_2) = 2$ have satisfied the firing conditions of $t_1$ in Figure 1a, $t_1$ is fired. After $t_1$ is fired as Figure 1b depicts, $t_1$ has removed $W(p_1, t_1) = 1$ token from input place $p_1$ of $t_1$ and $W(p_2, t_1) = 2$ tokens from input place $p_2$ of $t_1$, respectively, and then added $W(t_1, p_3) = 2$ tokens to output place $p_3$ of $t_1$ [16].

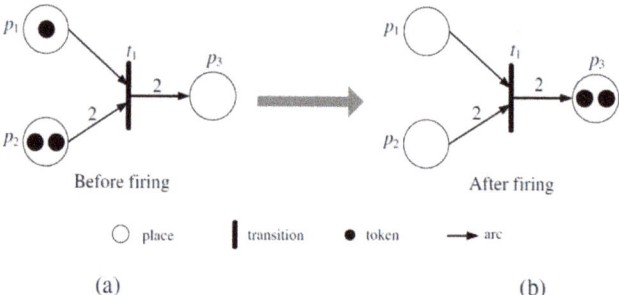

**Figure 1.** Example of Petri Nets: (**a**) Before firing tokens, (**b**) After firing tokens [16].

## 3. Materials and Methods

The aim of the work was to model using Petri nets to predict the student success based on his/her passage through the virtual learning environment and thus to design models that could be used to create better e-courses for LMS Moodle. Based on the created educational models in Petri nets, the individual processes could be verified and simulated that were performed when the student passed through the virtual learning environment. An important phase of the work was the mathematical formalization of created models and the implementation of uncertainties that were found in learning and acquiring knowledge using LMS into the created models. The efficiency of the created models would be verified using statistical methods of cluster and correlation analysis.

Workflow was as follows:

- A design of student behavior models in a virtual learning environment, i.e., study of materials in individual parts of the course, models of logical functions, loop models, condition models,

deadlocks, etc. that could simulate the student behavior in the virtual education system and its subsequent rating.
- After creating the appropriate educational models, it was possible to create a new e-course and test it with the models created for the e-course.
- A creation of an e-course from the proposed Petri Network models.
- After result evaluation of the real e-course using models designed for the e-course, it was possible to find out which parts of the e-course were most used for study and especially which parts contributed the most to the better grades of the students.

Real values, learning outcomes from previous years of student evaluations, could be implemented into created educational models and thus verify and subsequently predict student behavior. Models could be completed that required real student ratings to verify their veracity.

Figure 2 shows how the results of the research were achieved. Using the conceptual models of Petri nets from the previous chapter, an e-course was created that would also deploy in the classroom and an e-course model that would be used to simulate the behavior of students in the e-course. From the e-course, log files would be obtained to know how students behaved in the e-course and which parts they used. In addition, information about students passing the test would be acquired. Predicted results from the e-course model would be obtained and then compared with real results.

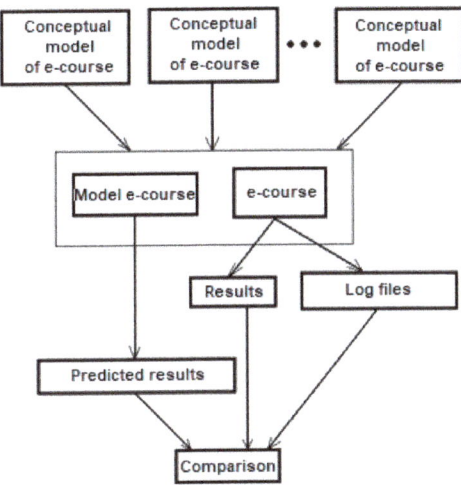

**Figure 2.** Conceptual model.

*3.1. Modeling Uncertainty with Petri Nets*

The Uncertainty is present everywhere in the real world as well as in the teaching process. No matter how the student behaves in the e-course, how he/she learns, it is not possible to determine precisely how successful he/she will be in the final exam. Its result is always determined by factors that are not possible to be accurately determined. For this reason, it was appropriate to propose the principle of modeling uncertainties and processes that commonly occur in the real world. This would enable to model situations where the outcome was not precisely predetermined, or situations where the outcome was only a probability and not an obvious truth or falsehood.

So far, if a higher chance of an event using Petri nets was needed to be simulated, one way was to add multiple transitions between the places with higher probability of the given event (Figure 3).

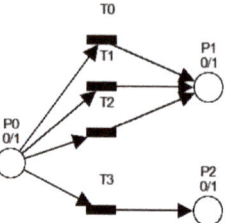

**Figure 3.** Example of a Petri Net model with random selection.

When the weight was added to transitions, the first three transitions could be swapped for one transition with a weight of 3. Then there was a chance that the token would move to P1 is 3:1 [26,27]. The approach was useful in calculating the final probabilities of multiple branched events.

The weights were used in stochastic Petri nets when multiple transitions were active but the firing of one prevented the firing of the others. With the weighted transitions, the model from Figure 3 could be changed to the model from Figure 4.

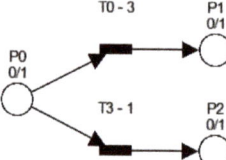

**Figure 4.** Petri Net model with weighted transitions.

In Figure 4, transition T0 had a weight of three and a transition T3 had a weight of one. The likelihood that a token would pass from P0 to P1 was the same for both models [28]. For the simple decision example, the probability of a result could be calculated by dividing the weight of the firing transition with the sum of the weights of the concurrently active transitions.

$$p = \frac{w_0}{\sum_{i=0}^{n} w_i} \quad (1)$$

$w_0$ was the weight of the firing transition and, $w_i$ was the weight of the $i$-th active transition. In the case of the parallel models of Figure 5, the probability of the final state depended on the combination of the final state probabilities of all concurrent models.

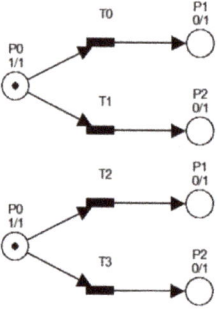

**Figure 5.** Petri Net model with concurrent parts.

For concurrent models, the probability of activating two independent transitions was calculated as follows:

$$p = \frac{w_0 w_3}{\sum_{i=0}^{n} w_{0i} \sum_{j=0}^{m} w_{3j}} \qquad (2)$$

$w_0$ was the weight of the first transition, and $w_3$ was the weight of the second transition, where both could fire simultaneously without deactivating each other. $w_{0i}$ and $w_{3j}$ were the weights of the $i$-th and $j$-th group of active transition, where the firing of one deactivated others. The transitions for which firing of one deactivated the others were called the group of transitions of transition T. The weight of this transition was called $w$ and the weights of transitions from the group were called $w_s$. Therefore, the previous formula could be generalized to:

$$p = \prod_{i=0}^{n} \frac{w_i}{\sum_{j=0}^{m} w_{ij}} \qquad (3)$$

$p$ was the probability of the state to which the model could get out of the current state by firing the correct transitions, $w_i$ was the transition weight of the transition group that fired during this step, and $w_{ij}$ was the transition weight from the transition group Ti. The formula only worked where the models were concurrent and independent. If models were linked, other formulas needed to be used. In this case, the problem was the increasing number of possible combinations of active transitions. For the example in Figure 6, it was necessary to use two different types of formulas for two different activation options.

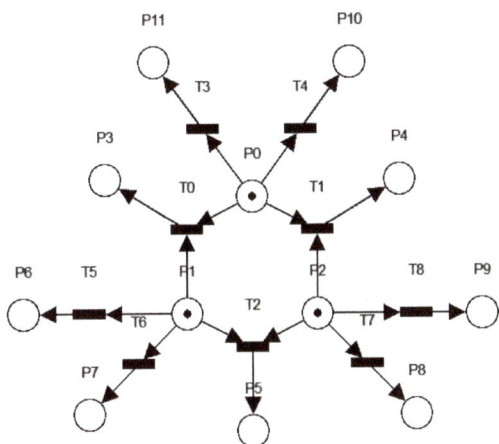

**Figure 6.** Petri Net model with concurrent parts.

For the model in Figure 6, two different situations needed to be considered: Only independent transitions (T3, T4, T5, T6, T7, T8) would fire, or one dependent transition (T0, T1, T2) and two independent transitions would fire. A dependent transition was one that had more than one entry place.

The sum of weights for all active transitions was defined as:

$$s = \sum_{i=0}^{n} w_i \qquad (4)$$

Then, the probability of activating one dependent transition and two independent transitions, such as T0 and T7 or T8, was calculated as:

$$p = \frac{w_n}{s} \cdot \frac{w_i}{\sum_{k=0}^{n} w_{ik}} \tag{5}$$

$w_n$ was the weight of the dependent transition, $w_{ij}$ was the weight of the independent transition, and $w_{ik}$ was the weights of the transition from group Ti.

The probability of firing of all independent transitions was calculated as:

$$p = \prod_{i=0}^{n} \frac{w_i}{\sum_{j=0}^{m} w_{ij}} \cdot \frac{s - \sum_{k=0}^{o} w_k}{s} \tag{6}$$

$w_i$ was the weight of the $i$-th independent transition, $w_{ij}$ was the weight of all independent transitions from transition group Ti, and $w_k$ was the weight of the dependent transitions.

Another approach that worked for all types of models, but only in the case where the weights were ignored, was to find out all the variants of firing transitions. If the permutations of all possible transition firings were taken, the number of options through which the model could get into the next states would be obtained. Taking into consideration the number of states the model can get into and the sum of the permutations of all the transitions firing, the number of all the transition firings could be obtained. If the numbers were divided now, the probability of that state would be aquired.

$$p = \frac{n!}{\left(\sum_{i=0}^{m} n_i!\right)} \tag{7}$$

In this case, $n$ was the number of transitions that fired, and $n_i$ was the number of transitions that were active for each state acquired from the state [29].

### 3.2. Observing Student Movement in LMS

Moodle log files were used to track the movement of students in the e-course. Moodle is used for four primary purposes: (1) making course materials available for browsing when describing class contents, (2) performing a quiz during class, (3) referring to an external web page, and (4) submitting a report at the end of the term. To analyze learning history, it is desirable to clarify the purpose of collecting Moodle course logs [30]. Moodle provided an easy way to get student access logs. With just a few clicks in the Moodle administration page, Moodle would export the log files in .csv format. The logs contained:

- Time
- User name
- Affected user
- Event context
- Component
- Event name
- Description
- Source
- IP

Time, user name, event name, and context were essential for the purposes of the research. It was also necessary to remove teacher access from the log files, as they were also written to the log files, but were not needed to model the student behavior. The logs were organized as follows: The main unit was a student. The student contained a session number. Each session contained links to the Moodle logs that displayed which parts of Moodle the student had visited during that session. The sessions were obtained from the Moodle logs. To get a session, the data were organized by name and time. Based on the work [24], an upper time limit was created – θ. Exceeding this time limit meant a new session. If the time on the first page in one session was $t_0$ and the user's current URL was t, then this page was considered as one session if the inequality $t - t_0 \leq \theta$ was true. While for the next page, it was inequality $t_0 + \theta > t$.

This was the first page of the next session. Normally, θ was set to 30 min. The time of the following accesses were important. If the following access was created sooner than 45 min from the previous one, it was assumed to be a single session. If the time interval was greater than 45 min, it was a new session. An interval of 45 min was chosen because normally one lesson took 1.5 hours. In this case, if the student did not attend the course at least twice during one lesson, we could assume that they did not use the e-course during that lesson [31–33]. Based on these times, the sessions were removed that contained only one entry, as this was not a session but only one login per class.

However, in addition to observing the sections visited, the focus was on the number of visits in the "Book", "Lecture" and "Assignment" sections. The log files showed that only these items were used by students to study. The aim was to find out how the number of study material visits would affect the final grade of students. First of all, attention was payed to visits to materials used to study the principles of operating systems as the exam itself was largely theoretical.

## 4. Results and Discussion

After entering the data from log files, grades and attendance into Excel, graphs were obtained that in detail described the following section. In the charts, the correlation between the grade and the number of visits was observed.

In Figure 7, it was obvious what grade the students got based on access to the study materials "Lecture". The horizontal axis represents the number of visits and the vertical axis the final grade of the student. The lectures were in PDF format. These contained the most information to help students to pass the exam. The correlation of attendance and final ranking was −0.48723, the highest for this section, which represented a moderate correlation rate. The correlation analysis examines the tightness of the statistical dependence between the quantitative variables. The correlation coefficient is the extent of the linear dependence of the two variables. The coefficient is calculated by dividing the covariance with the standard deviation. The value of the coefficient is in the interval from −1 to 1 where −1 represents the indirect proportion, 1 is the direct proportion, and 0 represents the independence of X and Y. According to Cohen, the interpretation of the correlation coefficient is divided from 0.0 to 1.0 (trivial correlation, small, medium, big, very big, almost complete).

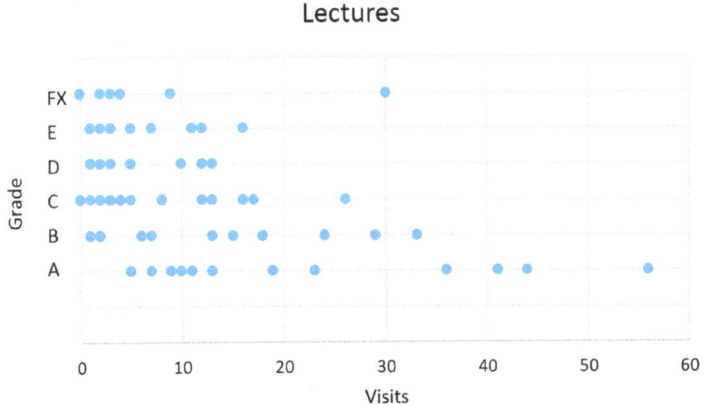

**Figure 7.** Grades based on visits in "Lecture" materials.

Figure 8 presents what grade the students got based on access to the study materials in "Book". The horizontal axis represents the number of visits and the vertical axis the final evaluation of the student. It was the Book module in Moodle that enabled to easily create multi-page resources with a book-like format. The book module made it possible to divide the curriculum into main chapters and subchapters as this module was intended to be a simple source of information for both students and teachers. It also contained the amount of information required for the test. The correlation of traffic and final ranking for this section was −0.43531, the second-highest, which represented a moderate correlation rate.

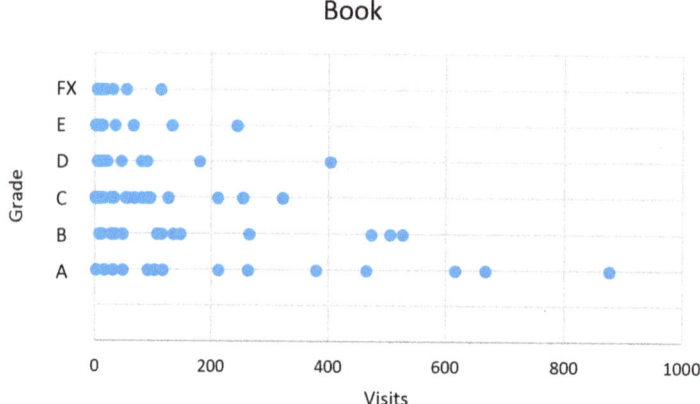

**Figure 8.** Grades based on visits in "Book" material.

Figure 9 shows what grades students got based on assignments submitted during exercises or at home. The horizontal axis represents the number of submitted assignments and the vertical axis represents the final grade of the student. The correlation for this figure was −0.33359, and the correlation was also classified as a moderate correlation rate.

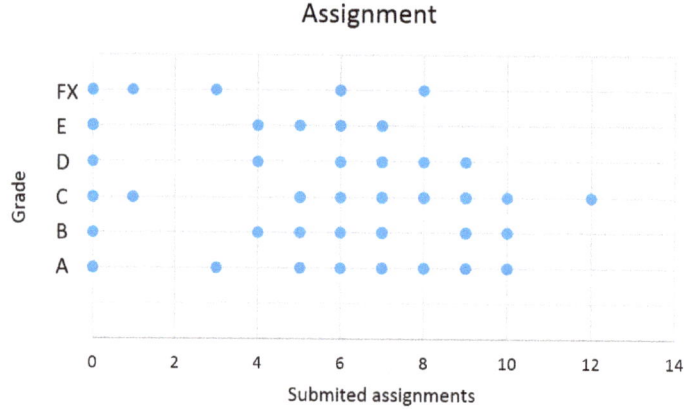

**Figure 9.** Grades based on visits in "Assignment" material.

The last statistic to be observed was the student attendance. For the Figure 10, the correlation was −0.26355, the lowest, which already represented a low correlation rate.

*Appl. Sci.* **2019**, *9*, 4211

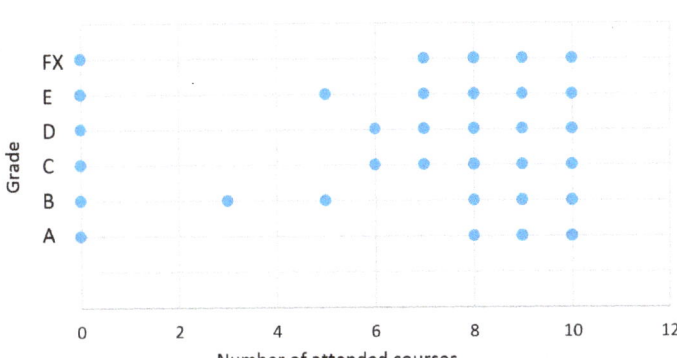

**Figure 10.** Grades based on attendance.

*4.1. Model of the Final Exam in Petri Nets*

Each student was allowed two attempts for the final exam if he/she failed to pass the exam the first time. Based on student grading, a model in Petri Nets was created that showed how students proceeded with passing the exam.

The "Start" location represented the number of students who took the exam this year. The model (Figure 11) also used transition weights to display the distribution of grades from a single exam. Transitions in which "Exam", "Exam 2", and "Exam 3" places were entered, had weights set according to the number of students who received a grade for the exam, as determined by the exit points of these places. In the model, weights were displayed by transition weights so it was shown that four students after the first exam did not come to the next exam, and five students did not take the third exam after failure, but the students who came to the third exam all succeeded. Observing the model, the question arose whether it would be possible to see any improvements in the grade among exams in terms of visits to study materials.

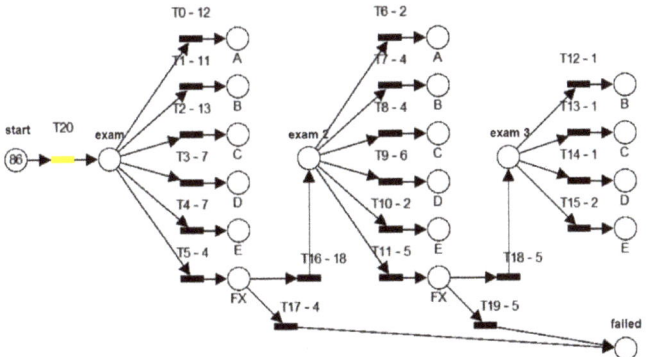

**Figure 11.** Model of the final exam in Petri Nets.

In the model of Figure 12, "Mat 1" and "Mat 2" were added to serve as an e-course visit counter. "The Book" and "Lectures" were the chosen materials to observe. In the previous graphs, they displayed the most significant correlations and they were the only materials that could be used to study between the exams. The tracking data from the model produced interesting results. For students who failed the first attempt, the correlations between their grade obtained after successfully completing the second or third attempt and their time spent studying in the e-course were insignificant. For students who completed the exam after the second attempt, these correlations were −0.24551 for Book visits and −0.13365 for Lecture visits, both of which represented a small correlation. For students who completed the exam on the third attempt, correlations were positive, 0.555851 for "Book" visits and 0.610275 for "Lectures", which would mean that the less they studied, the better grade they got. It could be assumed that these correlations could be explained by the possibility that students cheated on the test or having only a small sample of students for the test (five students).

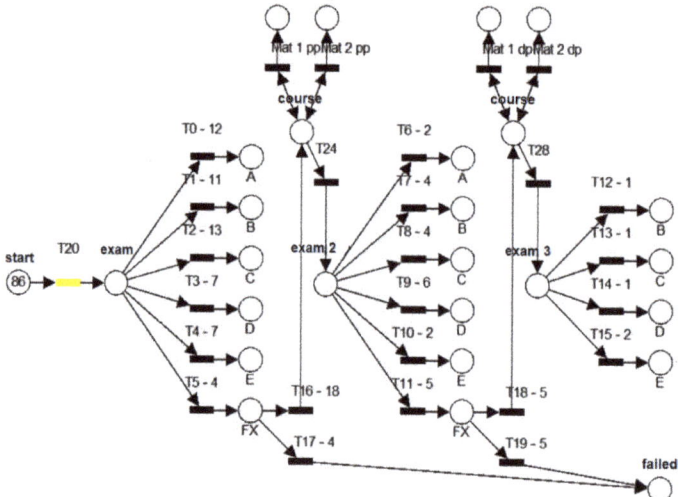

**Figure 12.** Model of the final exam with the observation of the study.

For this reason, the students who passed the exam on their first attempt or did not come to the next dates were observed more. For them, the correlation of the final grade and the time spent studying in the course was most striking, as explained below.

For students who succeeded on the first attempt or gave up after the first attempt, correlation based on Moodle"Book" visit was −0.43742. Their arrangement can be seen in Figure 13.

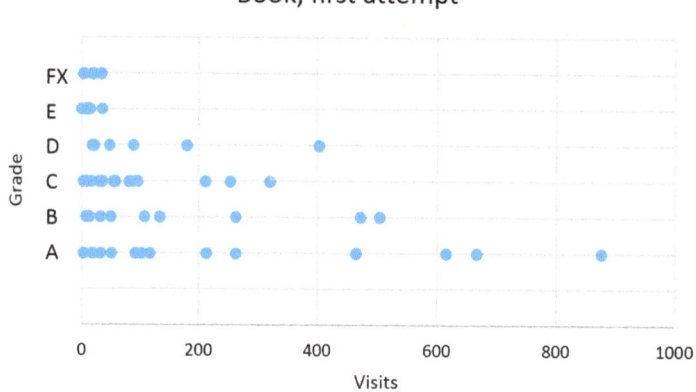

**Figure 13.** Grades based on visits in "Book" material, at the first attempt.

For students who succeeded on the first attempt or gave up after the first attempt, the correlation based on Moodle"Lecture" visit was −0.58561, which represented a greater correlation. This is shown in Figure 14. This was the most significant correlation of all.

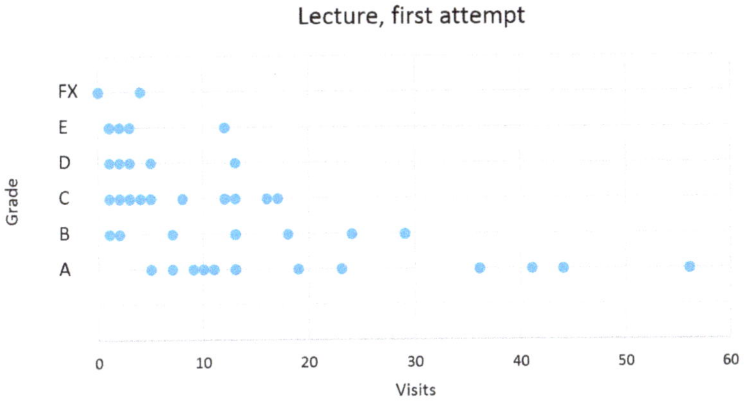

**Lecture, first attempt**

Figure 14. Grades based on visits in "Lecture" material on the first attempt.

To sum up, it is not possible to conclude that the only contributing part to improve student grades was the PDF lectures that students could view in Moodle. Neither participation in the exercises nor the practical assignments submitted to the exercises had a significant impact on the final evaluation of students.

*4.2. Model of Grade Prediction*

Based on the obtained graphs, it could be presumed that the parameter that influenced the students' success the most in the final exam was their visit in "Lectures" material in Moodle. Therefore, the graph in Figure 14 was created.

The graph shows what final grade students received when they accepted the course. According to the number of hits, they could be divided as follows:

In the first row of Table 1, there are ranges of visit counts. They were obtained from Figure 14 by looking at the ranges of visits in "Lecture" material for each grade. The maximum range was determined by the highest visit number for that grade, and the minimum was determined by the last visit number that did not figure for a lower grade. The second row shows the number of students for the given lecture visit ranges. The numbers of students who received a certain grade for a given number of visits can be seen in the rest of the table. Based on the table, the following model of Petri nets could be created:

Table 1. The number of students based on lecture visits and final grade.

| Visits | 0..4 | 5..12 | 13 | 14..17 | 18..29 | 30..56 |
|---|---|---|---|---|---|---|
| Students | 22 | 18 | 6 | 2 | 6 | 4 |
| A | 0 | 5 | 2 | 0 | 2 | 4 |
| B | 2 | 1 | 2 | 0 | 4 | 0 |
| C | 6 | 4 | 1 | 2 | 0 | 0 |
| D | 4 | 1 | 1 | 0 | 0 | 0 |
| E | 6 | 1 | 0 | 0 | 0 | 0 |
| FX | 4 | 0 | 0 | 0 | 0 | 0 |

From the start place (Figure 15), the token got to one of the categories selected based on the number of student visits to the lecture. These places were selected according to the graph in Figure 14.

In this model, transition weights were used that were set according to the number of students assigned to the categories. Subsequently, the token got to the grade place through a transition whose weight was set according to the number of students in the given visit range who received the grade. Using the model, it was possible to simulate the prediction of student grades based on their access to the lecture material [34].

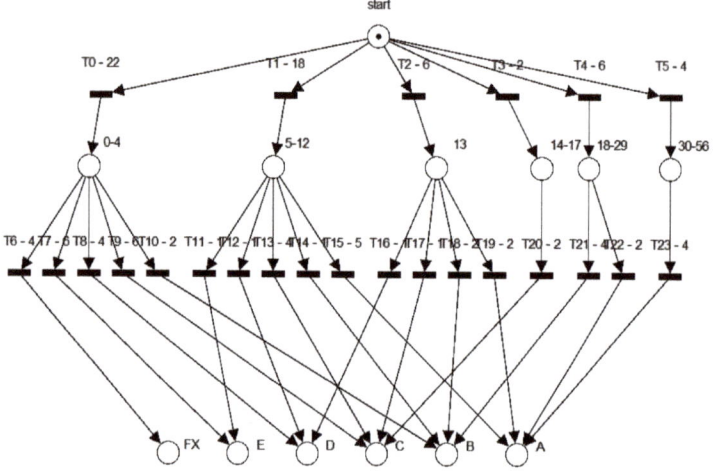

**Figure 15.** Model of grade probability for a single student.

The probability of selecting a category and consequently the probability of selecting a grade for that category was calculated using Formula (8).

$$p = \frac{w_a}{\sum_{i=0}^{n} w_i} \qquad (8)$$

$w_a$ was the weight of the fired transition, $w_i$ was the weight of the $i$-th transition, $n$ was the number of active transitions, and $p$ was the final probability.

## 5. Conclusions

The aim of the paper was to propose a way of predicting student success based on his behavior in Moodle. The method of predicting the student's grade could also be used to modify the course or the method of grading students based on the correlation between the attendance of study materials and the grade. If there was a significant impact of one type of study material on the final grade, it could be assumed that it was these study materials that helped the students to master the curriculum the most. If an activity did not have a significant impact on the student's grade, it might be removed or there would be an option to explore why the activity did not affect the student's grade.

The method of predicting the grade from the paper could be used for any type of material in the LMS with any correlation between the use of the material and the final grade. However, for lower correlations, it would not be possible to predict the grade with sufficient accuracy, so it was recommended to use the method for materials for which the correlation was the highest. This article gave a suggestion of a way of predicting student success based on this behavior in Moodle. Together with the method of grading students based on the correlation between the attendance of study materials and the grade, it could also be used to modify the course.

**Author Contributions:** Conceived and designed the experiments, Z.B.; performed the experiment, M.K.; analyzed the experimental data, Z.B. and M.K.; validation, Z.B.; data curation, M.K.; writing—review and editing, Z.B.; methodology, Z.B.; supervision, Z.B.; project administration, Z.B.; The manuscript was written and approved to submit by all authors.

**Acknowledgments:** This paper was created with the financial support of the project KEGA 036UKF-4/2019, Adaptation of the learning process using sensor networks and the Internet of Things.

**Conflicts of Interest:** The authors declare no conflict of interest.

## References

1. Holub, M.; Bieliková, M. An inquiry into the utilization of behavior of users in personalized Web. *J. Univers. Comput. Sci.* **2011**, *17*, 1830–1853.
2. Kim, E.; Park, H.; Jang, J. Development of a Class Model for Improving Creative Collaboration Based on The Online Learning System (Moodle) in Korea. *J. Open Innov. Technol. Mark. Complex.* **2019**, *5*, 67. [CrossRef]
3. Costello, E. Opening up to open source: Looking at how Moodle was adopted in higher education. *Open Learn. J. Open Distance e-Learn.* **2013**, *28*, 187–200. [CrossRef]
4. Hew, K.F.; Huang, B.; Chu, K.W.S.; Chiu, D.K. Engaging Asian students through game mechanics: Findings from two experiment studies. *Comput. Educ.* **2016**, *92*, 221–236. [CrossRef]
5. Zhou, L.; Chen, L.W.; Fan, Q.M.; Ji, Y.L. Students' Perception of Using Digital Badges in Blended Learning Classrooms. *Sustainability* **2019**, *11*, 18. [CrossRef]
6. Kc, D. Evaluation of Moodle Features at Kajaani University of Applied Sciences—Case Study. *Procedia Comput. Sci.* **2017**, *116*, 121–128. [CrossRef]
7. Molnar, G. The Impact of Modern ICT-Based Teaching and Learning Methods in Social Media and Networked Environment. In Proceedings of the 11th International Scientific Conference on Distance Learning in Applied Informatic (DiVAi), Sturovo, Slovakia, 2–4 May 2016; Wolters Kluwer Cr a S: Strašnice, Czechia, 2016; pp. 341–350.
8. Molnár, G.; Benedek, A. ICT related tasks and challenges in the new model of technical teacher training. In Proceedings of the Eighth International Multi-Conference on Computing in the Global Information Technology (ICCGI), Nice, France, 21–26 July 2013; IARIA: Barcelona, Spain, 2013; pp. 40–44.
9. Juhaňák, L.; Zounek, J.; Rohlíková, L. Using process mining to analyze students' quiz-taking behavior patterns in a learning management system. *Comput. Hum. Behav.* **2019**, *92*, 496–506. [CrossRef]
10. Romero, C.; Cerezo, R.; Bogarín, A.; Sánchez-Santillán, M. Educational process mining: A tutorial and case study using Moodle data sets. In *Data Mining and Learning Analytics: Applications in Educational Research*; John Wiley & Sons, Inc.: Hoboken, NJ, USA, 2016; pp. 1–28.
11. Romero, C.; Ventura, S. Educational data mining: A review of the state of the art. *IEEE Trans. Syst. Man Cybern. Part C (Appl. Rev.)* **2010**, *40*, 601–618. [CrossRef]
12. Romero, C.; Ventura, S.; Pechenizkiy, M.; Baker, R.S. *Handbook of Educational Data Mining*; CRC Press: Boca Raton, FL, USA, 2010.
13. Trcka, N.; Pechenizkiy, M.; van der Aalst, W. Process mining from educational data. In *Handbook of Educational Data Mining*; CRC Press: Boca Raton, FL, USA, 2010; pp. 123–142.
14. Reimann, P.; Yacef, K. Using process mining for understanding learning. In *Handbook of Design in Educational Technology*; Routledge: Abingdon, UK, 2013; pp. 472–481.
15. Reimann, P.; Markauskaite, L.; Bannert, M. e-R esearch and learning theory: What do sequence and process mining methods contribute? *Br. J. Educ. Technol.* **2014**, *45*, 528–540. [CrossRef]
16. Chang, Y.-C.; Huang, Y.-C.; Chu, C.-P. B2 model: A browsing behavior model based on High-Level Petri Nets to generate behavioral patterns for e-learning. *Expert Syst. Appl.* **2009**, *36*, 12423–12440. [CrossRef]
17. Balogh, Z.; Turcani, M.; Magdin, M. The possibilities of using Petri Nets for realization of a universal model of educational process. In Proceedings of the 2013 IEEE 14th International Conference on Information Reuse and Integration (IRI), San Francisco, CA, USA, 14–16 August 2013; pp. 162–169.
18. Balogh, Z.; Turcani, M. Possibilities of Modelling Web-Based Education Using IF-THEN Rules and Fuzzy Petri Nets in LMS. In *Informatics Engineering and Information Science, Pt I*; AbdManaf, A., Zeki, A., Zamani, M., Chuprat, S., ElQawasmeh, E., Eds.; Springer: Berlin, Germany, 2011; Volume 251, pp. 93–106.

19. Klimeš, C.; Balogh, Z. *Modelovanie Procesov Pomocou Petriho Sietí*; Fakulta prírodných vied; UKF Nitra: Nitra, Slovakia, 2012.
20. Kucharik, M.; Balogh, Z. Evaluation of fuzzy Petri nets with the tool TransPlaceSim. In Proceedings of the 10th IEEE International Conference on Application of Information and Communication Technologies (AICT), Baku, Azerbaijan, 12–14 October 2016.
21. Campos-Rebelo, R.; Costa, A.; Gomes, L. Finding learning paths using Petri nets modeling applicable to e-learning platforms. In Proceedings of the 3rd IFIP WG 5.5/SOCOLNET Doctoral Conference on Computing, Electrical and Industrial Systems, DoCEIS 2012, Costa de Caparica, Portugal, 27–29 February 2012; Volume 372, pp. 151–160.
22. Chen, S.M. Representing fuzzy knowledge using extended fuzzy Petri nets. In Proceedings of the 2nd International Symposium on Uncertainty Modeling and Analysis, College Park, MD, USA, USA, 25–28 April 1993; pp. 339–346.
23. Mtibaa, S.; Tagina, M. A Petri-Net model based timing constraints specification for e-learning system. In Proceedings of the 2012 International Conference on Education and e-Learning Innovations, Sousse, Tunisia, 1–3 July 2012.
24. Murata, T. Petri Nets: Properties, Analysis and Applications. *Proc. IEEE* **1989**, *77*, 541–580. [CrossRef]
25. Jensen, K. Colored petri nets. *Lect. Notes Comput. Sci.* **1987**, *254*, 248–299. [CrossRef]
26. Kodamana, H.; Raveendran, R.; Huang, B. Mixtures of Probabilistic PCA with Common Structure Latent Bases for Process Monitoring. *IEEE Trans. Control Syst. Technol.* **2019**, *27*, 838–846. [CrossRef]
27. Tian, Y.; Wang, X.Z.; Jiang, Y.; You, G.H. *A Distributed Probabilistic Coverage Sets Configuration Method for High. Density WSN*; Ieee: New York, NY, USA, 2017; pp. 2312–2316.
28. Dehban, A.; Jamone, L.; Kampff, A.R.; Santos-Victor, J. *A Deep Probabilistic Framework for Heterogeneous Self-Supervised Learning of Affordances*; Ieee: New York, NY, USA, 2017; pp. 476–483.
29. Kuchárik, M.; Balogh, Z. Modeling of Uncertainty with Petri Nets. In *11th Asian Conference on Intelligent Information and Database Systems (ACIIDS 2019)*; Nguyen, N.T., Gaol, F.L., Nguyen, N.T., Trawinski, B., Hong, T.P., Eds.; Springer: Berlin, Germany, 2019; Volume 11431, pp. 499–509.
30. Dobashi, K. Automatic data integration from Moodle course logs to pivot tables for time series cross section analysis. In *Knowledge-Based and Intelligent Information & Engineering Systems*; ZanniMerk, C., Frydman, C., Toro, C., Hicks, Y., Howlett, R.J., Jain, L.C., Eds.; Elsevier Science Bv: Amsterdam, The Netherlands, 2017; Volume 112, pp. 1835–1844.
31. Fang, Y.; Huang, Z. An improved algorithm for session identification on web log. In Proceedings of the 2010 International Conference on Web Information Systems and Mining (WISM 2010), Sanya, China, 23–24 October 2010; Volume 6318, pp. 53–60.
32. Benko, L.; Reichel, J.; Munk, M. Analysis of student behavior in virtual learning environment depending on student assessments. In Proceedings of the 13th IEEE International Conference on Emerging eLearning Technologies and Applications (ICETA), Stary Smokovec, Slovakia, 26–27 November 2015.
33. Maheswara Rao, V.V.R.; Valli Kumari, V.; Raju, K.V.S.V.N. An intelligent system for web usage data preprocessing. In Proceedings of the 1st International Conference on Computer Science and Information Technology, CCSIT 2011, Bangalore, India, 2–4 January 2011; Volume 131, pp. 481–490.
34. Štencl, M.; Šťastný, J. Neural network learning algorithms comparison on numerical prediction of real data. In Proceedings of the 16th International Conference on Soft Computing Mendel, Brno, Czech Republic, 23–25 June 2010; pp. 280–285.

© 2019 by the authors. Licensee MDPI, Basel, Switzerland. This article is an open access article distributed under the terms and conditions of the Creative Commons Attribution (CC BY) license (http://creativecommons.org/licenses/by/4.0/).

*Article*

# The Relationship between the Facial Expression of People in University Campus and Host-City Variables

**Hongxu Wei [1], Richard J. Hauer [2] and Xuquan Zhai [3],***

[1] Northeast Institute of Geography and Agroecology, Chinese Academy of Sciences, Changchun 130102, China; weihongxu@iga.ac.cn
[2] College of Natural Resources, University of Wisconsin–Stevens Point, 800 Reserve St., Stevens Point, WI 54481, USA; rhauer@uwsp.edu
[3] China Center for Public Sector Economy Research, Jilin University, Room 3007, Kuang, Yaming Building, 2699 Qianjin Road, Chaoyang District, Changchun 130012, China
* Correspondence: zhaixuquan@sina.com; Tel.: +86-431-8516-8829

Received: 1 February 2020; Accepted: 19 February 2020; Published: 21 February 2020

**Featured Application:** This work supplies a theoretical approach to evaluate public attitude towards university campuses and to detect the relationship with host-city variables using data about facial expression scores on social network services at the national scale.

**Abstract:** Public attitudes towards local university matters for the resource investment to sustainable science and technology. The application of machine learning techniques enables the evaluation of resource investments more precisely even at the national scale. In this study, a total number of 4327 selfies were collected from the social network services (SNS) platform of Sina Micro-Blog for check-in records of 92 211-Project university campuses from 82 cities of 31 Provinces across mainland China. Photos were analyzed by the FireFACE$^{TM}$-V1.0 software to obtain scores of happy and sad facial expressions and a positive response index (PRI) was calculated (happy-sad). One-way analysis of variance indicated that both happy and PRI scores were highest in Shandong University and lowest in Harbin Engineering University. The national distribution of positive expression scores was highest in Changchun, Jinan, and Guangzhou cities. The maximum likelihood estimates from general linear regression indicated that the city-variable of the number of regular institutions of higher learning had the positive contribution to the happy score. The number of internet accesses and area of residential housing contributed to the negative expression scores. Therefore, people tend to show positive expression at campuses in cities with more education infrastructures but fewer residences and internet users. The geospatial analysis of facial expression data can be one approach to supply theoretical evidence for the resource arrangement of sustainable science and technology from universities.

**Keywords:** machine learning; GIS; mental stress; multiple regression; face reading

## 1. Introduction

Since 2008 more than half of the world population lived in cities and this is expected to reach 70% by 2050 [1]. Cities are widely regarded as important areas in the pursuit of global sustainability [2]. A sustainable society comprises five distinct elements for every human-being such as the proper education, a clean environment, a well-balanced safety, abundant resources for future generation, and contribution to a sustainable world [3]. Easy to collect metrics that rate environmental, economic, educational, and social variables are important to evaluate the global strategies for urban transformation towards sustainability that builds upon national and local scales [4]. A sustainable city should respond to residents' needs through sustainable solutions for social and economic aspects [1]. The tradeoff between resource consumption and citizens' demand can be sustainably solved by the use of information and communication technologies (ICT) and the internet of things (IoT), which can be accessed in a smart local university campus [5,6]. Therefore, a future-like relationship emerges between city variables and public attitude towards local university campuses.

Universities have a central role to create knowledge and tools to transfer information for societal transformations towards sustainability [2,7]. Universities can be a driving force to provide urban sustainable development by embedding knowledge to the local social and economic networks [8–10]. Besides the responsibilities of teaching and research, universities are increasingly expected to turn knowledge into innovation [11]. Universities can also be a partner with their host-city to develop the transformation to a smart community [1,5–7]. To test design principles, a university campus can be taken as a socioeconomic organization like a mini-city and the management and demands for resources therein can be acquired by the using data through the IoT. In China a model is being implemented to construct cities that are famous due to universities therein, but many of these programs are not successful as expected because of the poor educational outcomes and economic productivity [12]. The shortage of objective evaluation on local universities was at least partly responsible for the failure. People around the campus are frontiers that can give a precise evaluation on universities hence their attitude is the key to evaluate the university in its host-city.

City variables are known to affect the satisfaction of residents towards local universities [13,14]. An investigation using self-reported scores revealed that most undergraduates indicated satisfaction with settings of the city where their campus was located [13]. The group of variables out of these settings includes socializing [2,14], resident environment [2,13–16], socio-economic status [8,13,17], and industrialization [8] that have all been detected to have some relationship with perceived satisfaction towards campus although the magnitude was ever either positive or negative. The model of multiple city variables was proposed to measure the performance in the creativity of universities in cities [18]. This means that the multivariable model may also have contributions to the perceived satisfaction of people in university campuses. In addition, the current development of ICT can enable new methods and metrics to assess perceived satisfaction instead of questionnaire methodology. However, results about public attitude towards university campus were limited by the testing method and information that have been published on this matter.

Traditionally, questionnaires provided a common method to evaluate people perception. Evaluation through self-reported scores has several apparent biases from subjective emotion of respondents, real-time mood, problematic questions, and social-role restricted results [19]. Facial expression represents an emotional response to a stimulus and/or a communicative behavior in a social situation, which can be termed as Duchenne (a felt expression with an emotion cue) and non-Duchenne ways (an unfelt expression with a communicative cue), respectively [20]. The facial expression of a visitor's photo at a place provides a novel way to show performative emotional satisfaction in the location. A selfie taken and shared by a person through social media is one way to collect the information of emotional expressions that would like to be exposed to the public. Facial expression scores with a check-in-recorded location enable geographical analysis of posed emotion towards environments in a visited location. Highly popularized social networking service (SNS) results in millions of facial-expression images uploaded to the data-cloud [21,22]. Therefore, to collect and analyze facial images from SNS with check-in locations supplies a new approach to assess satisfaction of people with a wide range of geographical locations. Regarding that people expose their selfies with check-in records to show posed facial expression at the location, all variables about the city where visitors is located can be used as the explanatory independent factors in a regression model together to build the relationship with expressional scores. To utilize data from SNS enables the precise evaluation of public attitude towards universities at the large geographical scale. However, to the best of our knowledge, the use of this methodology has not been tested.

In mainland China, 116 universities are classified in the '211-Project'. These universities were authorized by Ministry of Education of the People's Republic of China (MEPRC) and are being distributed in 82 cities from 31 Provinces [23]. All universities within the 211-Project derive more financial and political support than other universities with an expectation of greater corresponding outcomes of science and technology. Therefore, cities with 211-Project universities are generally promoted by an enhanced scholar population, public services, daily livelihood, and social infrastructures. In this study, campuses of key universities in the 211-Project from mainland China were chosen as the research plots wherein selfies at check-in locations at campuses were collected and analyzed for intended facial expressions. We aimed to assess scores of happy and sad expressions of people in 211-Project universities and map them at the national scale. It was hypothesized that (i) people would pose more positive facial expressions at university campuses in cities with more development in economy and technology, and (ii) city variables about socializing and socio-economy had contrasting contributions to intended positive and negative expressions in university campuses.

## 2. Materials and Methods

### 2.1. Universities

In this study, key universities in the 211-Project were chosen as study locations. A total of 96 campuses of key universities were included in this study (Table S1). Campuses of some universities were also excluded in this study because the sample size of suitable images (as described below) was too small to support the data collection and therefore 96 universities in the 211-Project were included in this study. Overall, a total of 92 campuses of 211-Project universities were selected as the check-in-recorded locations exited for these from 82 cities in 31 provinces across mainland China. These 92 universities are also top scholar institutions in mainland China.

### 2.2. Photo Collection

The Sina Micro-Blog (SMB; Sina Inc., Beijing, China) was chosen as the platform of SNS to collect facial photos using the method of Wei et al. [19]. SMB is widely used by Chinese web-users and functions similar to Twitter (NYSE: TWTR, San Francisco, CA, USA) that supplies a platform to pose real-time mini-blogs to the internet with comments and images (photos). Both personal computer and mobile device terminals can enable users to pose blogs, but only mobile terminals can attach check-in location records. According to the policy of SMB, the use of text and photos in blogs published in SMB are open to the public if no private limit was claimed by the user. As of August 2018, SMB had 0.43 billion active users with 0.19 billion daily submissions of micro-blogs by active users [24]. SMB supplied an open platform to upload photos with check-in data through microblogs and to check and download images. All university campuses chosen in this study had been listed in the location records of SMB.

Photos were collected in the process following three phases:

(i) All microblogs with uploaded photos with check-in data about geography of target university campuses were blocked by time between 15 February and 15 June 2019. This time was chosen because it covered the spring semester period for most universities we studied.

(ii) Blogs with selfies were screened and only photos with young adult portraits were collected. Age of subjects in selfies was visually evaluated through the photo. Many users' age information was hidden by a classified statement in SMB. This resulted in only a few of users' age information published, but the number of revealed ages was too small to support a meaningful statistical analysis. Nearly all (95%) of initially collected selfies were uploaded by young adults. Therefore, we chose to use this part of photos for further analysis to keep the uniformity of age among users. Significant differences of perception and habit between international and Chinese students exist [25], thus, selfies with western-style faces were excluded. It was hard to distinguish nationalities among Eastern Asia countries in photos, hence it was assumed that all Asian faces were Chinese.

(iii) Only photos clearly showing facial features were selected for analysis. Photos were excluded when makeup obscured facial expression (e.g., excessively beautified, over whitened, additionally decorated) or the face feature was twisted.

## 2.3. Face Expression Analysis

Collected photos were modified by cropping and rotating before analysis. Since some photos included more than one face, each face was separated from the original photo by cropping to generate a new photo file with one unique face. It was necessary to rotate photos to make the nose axis vertical to the horizon. Rotating was necessary for analysis precision of facial expressions. Photos were analyzed by the FireFACE$^{TM}$-V1.0 software (Zhilunpudao Agric. Sci. Inc., Changchun, China). This software was calibrated by training the computer program to recognize faces using the independent variables of oriental faces with posed facial expressions. Initially, about 30,000 photos were documented for training the machine to recognize basic expressions (happy, sad, and neutral) with about 10,000 photos for each of them. Photos were recognized and classified into files of known expressions manually then engineers wrote codes to enable the communication between computer and these files. The training was terminated until the machine has been tested to pass the aimed accuracy of 85% for happy and sad expressions and 80% for neutral expression (Figures S1 and S2). To train the software with high accuracy for recognizing faces of Chinese people, posed photos were recognized and classified into perceived expressions by Chinese experts. A total number of 4327 selfies (one person per photo) were analyzed for facial expressional scores.

## 2.4. Data about City Variables

Data depicting the variables of all 82 cities were obtained from the latest database of National Bureau of Statistics of China [26]. We employed city variables that were documented officially for all cities since the time of July 2019. As a result, four parameters (e.g., economy, public facility, habitation, and environments) were used in this study (Table 1). Economic parameters included government expenditure and resident income, which may affect financial status of local universities through tax investment at the national and local scales, respectively [27,28]. Public facilities covered aspects of communication, transportation, health care, education, and regional culture, which were all related to university students [29–31]. Parameters of habitation included the aspects that reflected the socializing and life utilities, which were found to be closely related to perceived satisfaction at campus [2,14]. Environment parameters (e.g., air pollution, water pollution, and garbage disposal) that may impact satisfaction under some given industrialization were extracted from databases of each local bureau [2,13–16].

**Table 1.** Specific parameters used in city variables about economy, public facility, habitation, and environment.

| Variables | Unit | Parameter |
|---|---|---|
| Economy | Yuan | GDP per capita |
| | ×10$^4$ Yuan | Public financial expenditure |
| | ×10$^4$ Yuan | Corporate profit of enterprises above designated scale [1] |
| | Individuals | Population of employees of C&T work-units [2] |
| | Yuan | Average wage of enrolled employees of work-units |
| Public facility | ×10$^4$ Households | Number of internet wideband accesses |
| | Individuals | Real number of end-of-year taxicabs |
| | Individuals | Numbers of hospitals and health-centers |
| | Individuals | Number of regular institutions of higher education [3] |
| | ×10$^3$ Individuals | Collection of books in public libraries |
| Habitation | km$^2$ | Total area of residential lands |
| | ×10$^4$ Individuals | End-of-year population of registered residents |
| | ha | Total area of green space in C&T parks |
| | ×10$^4$ Tons | Domestic water consumption by residents |
| | ×10$^4$ Kilowatt-hour | Electricity consumption of C&T residents |

Table 1. *Cont.*

| Variables | Unit | Parameter |
|---|---|---|
| Environment | ×10⁴ Tons | Discharge of industrial sewage |
| | Tons | Emission of industrial $SO_2$ |
| | Tons | Emission of industrial dust |
| | Percent | Centralized disposal of sewage |
| | Percent | Disposal of household garbage |

Note: [1] Enterprises above designated scale, annual revenue over 20 million Yuan from the primary business of industrial enterprises; [2] C&T, city and town; [3] institutions of higher education, educational institutions that can grant degrees that are higher than high-school education, including university, college, vocational technique university/college, etc.

## 2.5. Statistical Analysis

In addition to happy and sad expressions, we involved the positive response index (PRI) as a scoring metric to evaluate the net positive emotion [32]. PRI is defined as the difference between scores for happy and sad expressions.

SAS (ver. 9.4 64-bit, SAS Institute, Cary, NC, USA) software was used for data analysis. Data about happy and sad scores and PRI values were tested for the normal distribution, which was not found across universities campuses. Therefore, data were ranked to obtain a new set of distribution-free scores [33]. Ranked data were further analyzed by one-way analysis of variance (ANOVA) with the variation of universities as a source of variance. When a significant effect was found, means were arranged and compared by the Duncan Multiple Comparison test at $\alpha = 0.05$ level. To detect the relationship between multiple city-variables and facial expressions, a model of maximum likelihood estimate on the general linear regression was made using the GENMOD procedure with multiple city-variables as the independent variables and facial expression scores as the dependent variables. Data used for the regression were pooled using averaged means for cities ($n = 32$); thereafter dependent variables were found to be normally distributed across cities and independent variables were log-transformed. The probability of a chi-square test was determined to be significant at $\alpha = 0.05$ level for every estimated parameter. We did not distinguish observations from subjects therefore the negative effect of pseudoreplication on our results might happen [34,35]. To assess the possible impact of collinearity on regression, variance inflation (VIF) was detected in SAS by the REG procedure in advance.

## 3. Results

### 3.1. Facial Expressoin Scores among Universities

Results about analysis of one-way ANOVA on facial expression scores across university campuses are shown in Table 2. Happy expression scores were higher in Shandong University, Xi'an Jiaotong University, and South China University than those in most of other universities (Figure 1). Harbin Engineering University had the lowest happy score. On the other hand, Ocean University of China, Inner Mongolia University, and Harbin Engineering University tended to have the highest sad expression scores, while sad scores appeared to be lower in Shandong University, Zhejiang University, and Xi'an Jiaotong University (Figure 1). The PRI generally showed the similar trend of happy score but had some distinctive inverses (Figure 1). For example, PRI in China Pharmaceutical University, Xinjiang University, and Ocean University of China were reduced by the relatively higher level of sad scores. In contrast, the sudden increase of PRI, such as that in Northwestern Polytechnical University, was caused by the relatively lower sad scores.

**Table 2.** Results of one-way analysis of variance (ANOVA) on ranked scores of happy and sad expressions, and positive response index (PRI) in visitors at university campuses across mainland China.

| Variable | Degree of Freedom | | | Sum of Squares | F Value | p Value |
|---|---|---|---|---|---|---|
| | Model | Error | Correction | | | |
| Happy | 95 | 4231 | 4326 | 354,720,095 | 2.49 | <0.0001 |
| Sad | | | | 276,605,667 | 1.94 | <0.0001 |
| PRI | | | | 328,290,197 | 2.28 | <0.0001 |

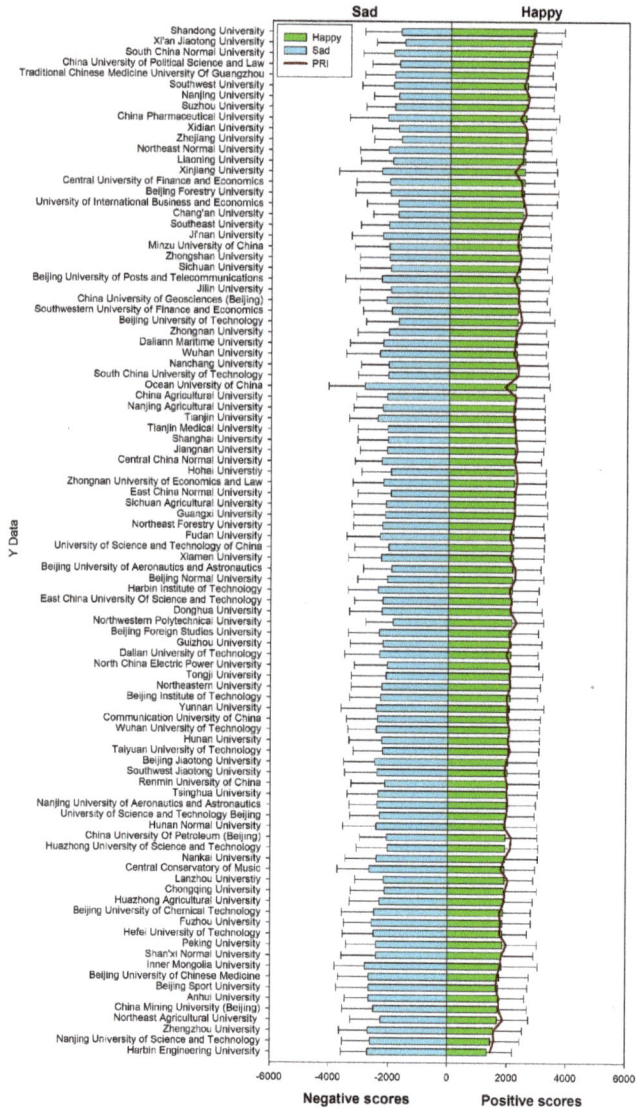

**Figure 1.** Ranked scores of happy and sad expressions and the positive response index (PRI) among selected 211-Project university campuses across mainland China. Universities are ordered by the growing score of happy expression. Different letters marked for significant difference are shown in Tables S2–S4.

*3.2. Geographical Distribution of Expression Scores among Host-Cities*

Happy scores were distributed divisionally with higher values in central-northeast, northern East-China, and Southern China (Figure 2A). Cities of Changchun, Jinan, Wulumuqi, Xi'an, and Hangzhou tended to have higher happy scores, while those of Harbin, Huhetaote, and Chongqing tended to have low happy scores. Cities of Huhetaote, Zhengzhou, and Kunming tended to have high sad scores (Figure 2B). Cities of Hangzhou, Suzhou, and Xi'an tended to have low sad scores. As a result of interplay between happy and sad scores, PRI was highest in Cities of Jinan, and moderately higher in Changchun, Xi'an, Hangzhou, Shanghai, and Guangzhou.

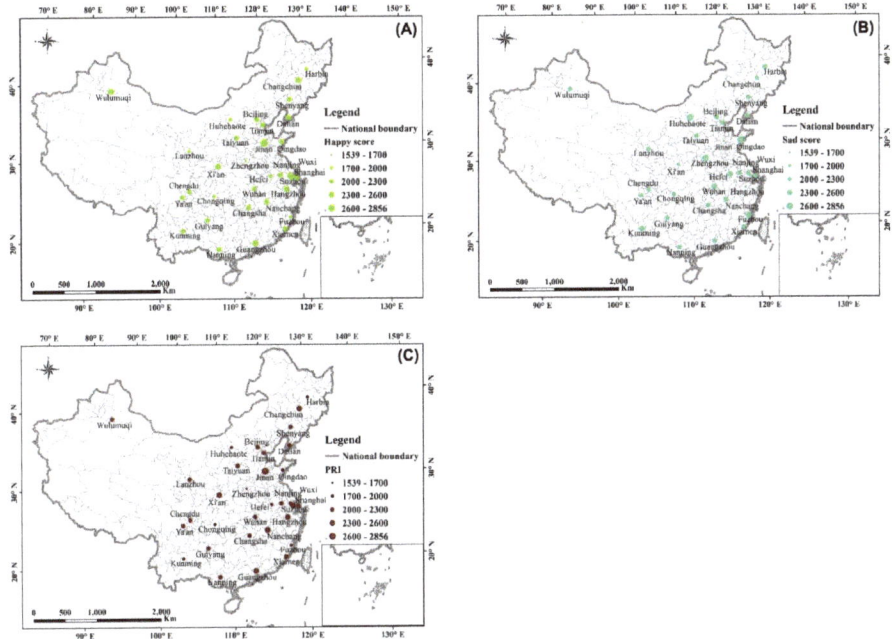

**Figure 2.** The geographical distribution of happy (**A**), sad (**B**), and positive response index (PRI; (**C**)) in cities with 211-Project universities across mainland China.

*3.3. The Bias of Collinearity*

Analysis on VIF shows that the happy expression scores had the high risk of collinearity from variables of public financial expenditure, corporate profit of enterprises above designated scale, and average wage of enrolled employees of work-units (Table 3). Sad expression scores showed possible collinearity from variables of corporate profit of enterprises above designated scale and disposal of household garbage. PRI exhibited potential collinearity from public financial expenditure and average wage of enrolled employees of work-units.

Table 3. The analysis of collinearity among city variables on ranked scores of happy and sad expressions, and positive response index (PRI) in visitors at university campuses across mainland China.

| Variable | DF [1] | Happy | | Sad | | PRI | |
|---|---|---|---|---|---|---|---|
| | | Pr > |t| | VIF [2] | Pr > |t| | VIF | Pr > |t| | VIF |
| Intercept | 1 | 0.3208 | 0 | 0.7825 | 0 | 0.0192 | 0 |
| GDP per capita | 1 | 0.1992 | 8.5949 | 0.5681 | 8.5949 | 0.134 | 8.5949 |
| Public financial expenditure | 1 | **0.0024** [3] | 264.95976 | 0.1355 | 264.95976 | **0.0033** | 264.95976 |
| Corporate profit of enterprises above designated scale [4] | 1 | **0.0361** | 59.3944 | **0.0344** | 59.3944 | 0.0719 | 59.3944 |
| Population of employees of C&T work-units [5] | 1 | 0.0511 | 221.303 | 0.0547 | 221.303 | 0.0945 | 221.303 |
| Average wage of enrolled employees of work-units | 1 | **0.0395** | 107.13049 | 0.9147 | 107.13049 | **0.0262** | 107.13049 |
| Number of internet wideband accesses | 1 | 0.1082 | 45.01435 | 0.953 | 45.01435 | 0.0897 | 45.01435 |
| Real number of end-of-year taxicabs | 1 | 0.826 | 174.32891 | 0.8198 | 174.32891 | 0.7701 | 174.32891 |
| Numbers of hospitals and health-centers | 1 | 0.1418 | 58.34608 | 0.3605 | 58.34608 | 0.1692 | 58.34608 |
| Number of regular institutions of higher education [6] | 1 | 0.1438 | 14.73109 | 0.1323 | 14.73109 | 0.2172 | 14.73109 |
| Collection of books in public libraries | 1 | 0.5681 | 187.98365 | 0.316 | 187.98365 | 0.4092 | 187.98365 |
| Total area of resident lands | 1 | 0.6997 | 112.74508 | 0.0511 | 112.74508 | 0.9902 | 112.74508 |
| End-of-year population of registered residents | 1 | 0.3431 | 79.37711 | 0.4805 | 79.37711 | 0.3929 | 79.37711 |
| Total area of green space in C&T parks | 1 | 0.4886 | 69.92869 | 0.0783 | 69.92869 | 0.7245 | 69.92869 |
| Domestic water consumption by residents | 1 | 0.7263 | 63.86034 | 0.8968 | 63.86034 | 0.7279 | 63.86034 |
| Electricity consumption of C&T residents | 1 | 0.5377 | 178.41355 | 0.8228 | 178.41355 | 0.5412 | 178.41355 |
| Discharge of industrial sewage | 1 | 0.3671 | 22.32038 | 0.8054 | 22.32038 | 0.3135 | 22.32038 |
| Emission of industrial $SO_2$ | 1 | 0.777 | 14.73447 | 0.3799 | 14.73447 | 0.9083 | 14.73447 |
| Emission of industrial dust | 1 | 0.7675 | 10.03224 | 0.2676 | 10.03224 | 0.5754 | 10.03224 |
| Centralized disposal of sewage | 1 | 0.0942 | 5.49206 | 0.5721 | 5.49206 | 0.0562 | 5.49206 |
| Disposal of household garbage | 1 | 0.9116 | 1.58069 | **0.0156** | 1.58069 | 0.5084 | 1.58069 |

Note: [1] DF, degree of freedom; [2] VIF, variance inflation; [3] Values in bold font indicate significant VIF; [4] Enterprises above designated scale, annual revenue over 20 million Yuan from the primary business of industrial enterprises; [5] C&T, city and town; [6] institutions of higher education, educational institutions that can grant degrees that are higher than high-school education, including university, college, vocational technique university/college. etc.

## 3.4. The Regression Analysis

Nearly all parameters about the economy had significant contribution to the happy score but their estimated coefficients were too small to be detectable (Table 4). Among variables of public facilities, number of internet wideband access had a negative contribution to the happy score while number of regular institutions of higher learning had a positive contribution. Neither of these two variables exhibited issues with collinearity. None of the rest of parameters was indicated to have any significant contributions.

In the economic field, parameters of the corporate profit of enterprises above designated scale and number of employees of city and town (C&T) work-units were indicated to have significant contributions to the sad scores but their estimated coefficients were too small to be detected (Table 5). The variable of corporate profit of enterprises above designated scale also suffered showed collinearity. In the field of habitation, the parameter of area of resident lands had a positive contribution to sad scores.

The variable of public financial expenditure showed collinearity (Table 6). Area of resident lands and numbers of regular institutions of higher learning from the public facility had negative and positive contributions to PRI, respectively (Table 6). The absolute value of estimated number of regular institutions of higher learning was about 10-time higher than that of residential area.

Table 4. Maximum likelihood estimation of multiple city variables on happy expression scores of students from key universities of cities across mainland of China.

| Parameter | Degree of Freedom | Estimate | Standard Error | Wald 95% Confidence | | Wald Chi-Square | Pr > Chi-Square |
|---|---|---|---|---|---|---|---|
| Intercept [1] | 1 | −2.986 | 0.9664 | −4.8802 | −1.0918 | **9.55** | **0.002** |
| GDP per capita | 1 | 0 | 0 | 0 | 0 | 2.04 | 0.1536 |
| **Public financial expenditure** | 1 | 0 | 0 | 0 | 0 | **12.06** | **0.0005** |
| **Corporate profit of enterprises above designated scale** [2] | 1 | 0 | 0 | 0 | 0 | **5.76** | **0.0164** |
| **Population of employees of C&T work-units** [3] | 1 | 0 | 0 | 0 | 0 | **5.88** | **0.0153** |
| **Average wage of enrolled employees of work-units** | 1 | 0 | 0 | 0 | 0 | **5.72** | **0.0168** |
| **Number of internet wideband accesses** | 1 | −0.0016 | 0.0008 | −0.0031 | 0 | **4.08** | **0.0435** |
| Real number of end-of-year taxicabs | 1 | 0 | 0 | 0 | 0 | 0 | 0.9914 |
| Numbers of hospitals and health-centers | 1 | −0.001 | 0.0005 | −0.002 | 0.0001 | 3.33 | 0.068 |
| **Number of regular institutions of higher education** [4] | 1 | 0.0066 | 0.003 | 0.0006 | 0.0125 | **4.72** | **0.0299** |
| Collection of books in public libraries | 1 | 0 | 0 | 0 | 0 | 0.61 | 0.4358 |
| Total area of resident lands | 1 | −0.0004 | 0.0013 | −0.003 | 0.0022 | 0.07 | 0.7845 |
| End-of-year population of registered residents | 1 | 0.0004 | 0.0004 | −0.0003 | 0.0011 | 1.55 | 0.2127 |
| Total area of green space in C&T parks | 1 | 0 | 0 | 0 | 0 | 0.99 | 0.3188 |
| Domestic water consumption by residents | 1 | 0 | 0 | 0 | 0 | 0.08 | 0.7836 |
| Electricity consumption of C&T residents | 1 | 0 | 0 | 0 | 0 | 0.32 | 0.5745 |
| Discharge of industrial sewage | 1 | 0 | 0 | 0 | 0 | 1.32 | 0.251 |
| Emission of industrial $SO_2$ | 1 | 0 | 0 | 0 | 0 | 0.12 | 0.7286 |
| Emission of industrial dust | 1 | 0 | 0 | 0 | 0 | 0.07 | 0.7971 |
| Centralized disposal of sewage | 1 | 0.0095 | 0.005 | −0.0002 | 0.0192 | 3.66 | 0.0556 |
| Disposal of household garbage | 1 | −0.0001 | 0.0037 | −0.0074 | 0.0072 | 0 | 0.9788 |
| Scale | 1 | 0.0756 | 0.0053 | 0.0659 | 0.0867 | | |

Note: [1] Values in bold font indicate significant contribution; [2] Enterprises above designated scale, annual revenue over 20 million Yuan from the primary business of industrial enterprises; [3] C&T, city and town; [4] institutions of higher education, educational institutions that can grant degrees that are higher than high-school education, including university, college, vocational technique university/college, etc.

Table 5. Maximum likelihood estimation of multiple city variables on sad expression scores of students from key universities of cities across mainland of China.

| Parameter | Degree of Freedom | Estimate | Standard Error | Wald 95% Confidence | | Wald Chi-Square | Pr > Chi-Square |
|---|---|---|---|---|---|---|---|
| Intercept [1] | 1 | −3.6837 | 1.2682 | −6.1693 | −1.1982 | **8.44** | **0.0037** |
| GDP per capita | 1 | 0 | 0 | 0 | 0 | 0.24 | 0.6208 |
| Public financial expenditure | 1 | 0 | 0 | 0 | 0 | 2.92 | 0.0873 |
| **Corporate profit of enterprises above designated scale [2]** | **1** | **0** | **0** | **0** | **0** | **6.3** | **0.0121** |
| **Population of employees of C&T work-units [3]** | **1** | **0** | **0** | **0** | **0** | **5.4** | **0.0201** |
| Average wage of enrolled employees of work-units | 1 | 0 | 0 | 0 | 0 | 0.01 | 0.9366 |
| Number of internet wideband accesses | 1 | 0 | 0.0009 | −0.0017 | 0.0018 | 0 | 0.9621 |
| Real number of end-of-year taxicabs | 1 | 0 | 0 | 0 | 0 | 0.08 | 0.7727 |
| Numbers of hospitals and health-centers | 1 | 0.0007 | 0.0007 | −0.0006 | 0.0019 | 1 | 0.3182 |
| Number of regular institutions of higher education [4] | 1 | −0.0066 | 0.004 | −0.0145 | 0.0013 | 2.68 | 0.1018 |
| Collection of books in public libraries | 1 | 0 | 0 | 0 | 0 | 1.95 | 0.1624 |
| **Total area of resident lands** | **1** | **0.0041** | **0.0016** | **0.0009** | **0.0073** | **6.46** | **0.0110** |
| End-of-year population of registered residents | 1 | −0.0003 | 0.0004 | −0.0011 | 0.0005 | 0.59 | 0.4429 |
| **Total area of green space in C&T parks** | **1** | **0** | **0** | **0** | **0.0001** | **4.13** | **0.0421** |
| Domestic water consumption by residents | 1 | 0 | 0 | 0 | 0 | 0.01 | 0.9139 |
| Electricity consumption of C&T residents | 1 | 0 | 0 | 0 | 0 | 0.12 | 0.7326 |
| Discharge of industrial sewage | 1 | 0 | 0 | 0 | 0 | 0.22 | 0.6418 |
| Emission of industrial $SO_2$ | 1 | 0 | 0 | 0 | 0 | 1.32 | 0.2498 |
| Emission of industrial dust | 1 | 0 | 0 | 0 | 0 | 1.41 | 0.2345 |
| Centralized disposal of sewage | 1 | 0.0045 | 0.006 | −0.0073 | 0.0162 | 0.55 | 0.4565 |
| Disposal of household garbage | 1 | 0.0155 | 0.0079 | −0.0001 | 0.031 | 3.79 | 0.0515 |
| Scale | 1 | 0.0307 | 0.0021 | 0.0268 | 0.0352 | | |

Note: [1] Values in bold font indicate significant contribution; [2] Enterprises above designated scale, annual revenue over 20 million Yuan from the primary business of industrial enterprises; [3] C&T, city and town; [4] institutions of higher education, educational institutions that can grant degrees that are higher than high-school education, including university, college, vocational technique university/college, etc.

Table 6. Maximum likelihood estimation of multiple city variables on PRI expression scores of students from key universities of cities across mainland of China.

| Parameter | Degree of Freedom | Estimate | Standard Error | Wald 95% Confidence | | Wald Chi-Square | Pr > Chi-Square |
|---|---|---|---|---|---|---|---|
| Intercept | 1 | 0.5661 | 1.9418 | −3.2396 | 4.3719 | 0.09 | 0.7706 |
| GDP per capita | 1 | 0 | 0 | 0 | 0 | 0.87 | 0.3512 |
| Public financial expenditure [1] | 1 | 0 | 0 | 0 | 0 | 9.99 | **0.0016** |
| Corporate profit of enterprises above designated scale [2] | 1 | 0 | 0 | 0 | 0 | 7.23 | **0.0072** |
| Population of employees of C&T work-units [3] | 1 | 0 | 0 | 0 | 0 | 7.86 | **0.0051** |
| Average wage of enrolled employees of work-units | 1 | 0 | 0 | 0 | 0.0001 | 3.36 | 0.067 |
| Number of internet wideband accesses | 1 | −0.0028 | 0.0015 | −0.0057 | 0.0001 | 3.54 | 0.0599 |
| Real number of end-of-year taxicabs | 1 | 0 | 0 | 0 | 0 | 0.14 | 0.7117 |
| Numbers of hospitals and health-centers | 1 | −0.0022 | 0.0025 | −0.0072 | 0.0027 | 0.77 | 0.3798 |
| Number of regular institutions of higher education [4] | 1 | 0.0147 | 0.0056 | 0.0037 | 0.0256 | 6.93 | **0.0085** |
| Collection of books in public libraries | 1 | 0 | 0 | 0 | 0 | 0.24 | 0.6262 |
| Total area of resident lands | 1 | −0.0021 | 0.0011 | −0.0042 | 0 | 4.03 | **0.0448** |
| End-of-year population of registered residents | 1 | 0.0011 | 0.0007 | −0.0003 | 0.0024 | 2.26 | 0.1326 |
| Total area of green space in C&T parks | 1 | 0 | 0 | −0.0001 | 0 | 3 | 0.0831 |
| Domestic water consumption by residents | 1 | 0 | 0 | 0 | 0 | 0.08 | 0.7752 |
| Electricity consumption of C&T residents | 1 | 0 | 0 | 0 | 0 | 0.02 | 0.8823 |
| Discharge of industrial sewage | 1 | 0 | 0 | 0 | 0.0001 | 0.78 | 0.3771 |
| Emission of industrial $SO_2$ | 1 | 0 | 0 | 0 | 0 | 0.5 | 0.4802 |
| Emission of industrial dust | 1 | 0 | 0 | 0 | 0 | 0.11 | 0.7397 |
| Centralized disposal of sewage | 1 | 0.0129 | 0.0096 | −0.0059 | 0.0317 | 1.81 | 0.1781 |
| Disposal of household garbage | 1 | −0.0067 | 0.0062 | −0.0189 | 0.0054 | 1.19 | 0.2751 |
| Scale | 1 | 9.2193 | 0.6455 | 8.0371 | 10.5753 | | |

Note: [1] Values in bold font indicate significant contribution; [2] Enterprises above designated scale, annual revenue over 20 million Yuan from the primary business of industrial enterprises; [3] C&T, city and town; [4] institutions of higher education, educational institutions that can grant degrees that are higher than high-school education, including university, college, vocational technique university/college, etc.

## 4. Discussion

The most significant result in our study is that the happy score in Shandong university (Shandong Province) was highest among universities while geographical distribution also revealed that positive scores tended to be higher in Jinan City (Shandong Province). We surmise that the high happy expression score in a city was the result of the happy expression score in the campus therein. Another example is Changchun City, which obtained a medium-high happy score while the happy scores in the two universities in Jilin Province were medium or high. However, the facial expression score for the city may be null to be indicated by that for the universities therein. For example, overall universities in Beijing City showed a moderate score of positive expressions although some university campuses therein obtained higher happy expression scores (e.g., China University of Political Science and Law). In contrast, the positive expression score in some other universities at Beijing City was lower than the average level (e.g., China Mining University and Beijing Sport University). Changchun, Jinan, and Guangzhou were three cities with high scores for both happy expression and PRI and hence university campuses in these three cities result can be taken to have the highest perceived satisfaction.

Student satisfaction with a university can affect student enrollment and retention. Hajrasouliha [36] investigated quality scores of university campuses in the United States and the scores were associated with freshman retention and graduation rates. The authors also revealed the geographical distribution of scores in selected campuses across the United States and found higher scores in the northeastern cities. Thus, both results from our study and Hajrasouliha [36] revealed no response of distribution to a geographical gradient.

Several public facility parameters were tested for a relationship with facial expression scores. The number of regular institutions of higher education within a city was one parameter that had positive contribution to values of both a happy score and PRI. From the SNS platform of SMB we aimed to collect selfies about young people who can mainly come from students or a new teacher enrolled in the university. Undergraduates and most mater candidates look young, but some PhD candidates may look old as they may have spent several years to earn their degree. For students, it was found that faculty, advising staff, and the class itself all had significant impact on their perceived satisfaction in higher learning institutions [37]. Some lecturers and even associate and full-time professors can also look young if they achieved high scholar scores at young age. Therefore, all young adults who would like to pose their selfies in a campus are likely to feel the emotional cue that originated from campus-life. Our results can be interpreted that young adults as either students or tutors would enjoy the city with more educational institutions where they may show Duchenne expressions as they felt being accompanied by large group of other youths. Other studies also reported that variables about the learning organization could account for the significant satisfaction for both teachers and researchers of higher learning institution [38]. A concentration of university campuses may result in more socializing opportunities, leading to greater satisfaction with a campus through more socializing of young people in their generation group [2,14].

It is surprising that a number of internet accesses had a negative contribution to the happy score. This suggests more internet users in a host-city decreased the ratio of showing happy expression of youths in university campuses. Youths of intense internet users were found to have overconfidence in the web-world, but they were also reported depressive symptomatology, problem behavior, and targeting of traditional bullying in the real world [39]. Another investigation reported that adolescents as frequent internet users reported depression by isolation from their family members [40]. In addition, more internet access may result in a user's habitual internet use and might result in a greater population of "internet addicts". Internet addiction tended to evoke perceived stress, which our results were consistent with less happy expressions [41]. People with an internet gaming disorder manifested in above average time spent with this activity were found to have different kinds of unconscious neutral facial expressions, which depressed the expression of a smiling face [42]. Thus, these studies were all consistent with our results with the higher probability of a reduction with a happy expression in a population with higher ratio of internet users. More direct and explanatory evidence is needed to further verify these results and it is also possible the concentration on an activity itself depresses a happy face.

In our study, the sad expression score was positively correlated with the area of residential lands adjoining a university. These findings concur with those found in England [43] and South Africa [44], where residential housing-density was negative to the perceived satisfaction of neighbors. This negative relationship should be more apparent for a residence-surrounded university campus because of more open space in the campus than in resident communities. However, we detected a weak effect of the area of green space in urban parks on sad expression. Urban green space has been shown to alleviate perceived stress [16]. This may be because people in our study were mainly grouped in the university campus rather than spending time in the green space of parks at the city scale. Or if they did any residual affect was not detected in this study.

We found no environmental variables were associated with our scores of happy, sad, or the PRI. This is because our data showed an obvious ceiling that cities with heavy contamination were unlikely to be included to the database. It is not recommended to install industries with heavy contamination for a city, which has been assigned to develop mainly through intellectual promotion of local universities. A sustainable and healthy community has effective ways to dispose of garbage and sewage, which can increase human disease if not abated [45,46]. Likewise, excessive levels of air pollution and particulate matter from industrial dust can reduce human health [47]. In this study, it is likely that a person would not see these variables and as such no effect on facial images seems reasonable.

This study may have been limited by several aspects. The first may come from the number of users in the selfies. The initially collected selfies were either taken by a single person in a photo or a person cropped from selfies with a group of people. Since individuals can more accurately perceive emotions expressed than in-group members [48], our facial expressions that were analyzed from selfies should have been controlled by the individual and in-group participants. However, this was not available in this study because many factors failed to be concerned, such as the number of people that were separated from a group, genders of them (this probably matters), failure of selfies for cropping (un-intact image of face, unclear face, deflected faces), group of young and mature adults, etc. Therefore, our results may have suffered some bias from the difference between faces of individual and in-group persons. As we omitted this bias for all check-in locations, it was reasonable to assume the technical error was uniform for all campuses.

Another limit to this study comes from the negative impact from pseudoreplication on our data, which resulted in a pretended independence. According to Waller et al. [34], pseudoreplication can occur when more than one datum was observed per individual. It can also occur when data points result from the same stimulus. Both situations were also found in ecological studies [35]. Our data may have suffered a pseudoreplication impact because different types of facial expressions may have been rated from the same subject. More than one facial expression score may have been collected from the same person in a university campus. This would impact the significance of difference of facial expression scores across universities and city variables because some of the replicated observations were not independent. A gross summary suggested that the incidence of pseudoreplication ranged between 12% and 40% in studies on primate communication research [34]. The incidence in our study was far lower than this range by manual screening of selfies. Therefore, it is reasonable to assume the impact from pseudoreplication on our data points can be negligible due to the review of each person. However, we still suggest future work can employ a process of excluding more than one observation from the same individual or at the same location to eliminate any potential pseudoreplication bias.

## 5. Conclusions

In this study, we examined how facial expressions of young adults varied at key universities in the 211-Project across mainland China. Selfies were downloaded from SMB and photos were analyzed by the FireFACE$^{TM}$-V1.0 software to obtain scores of happy and sad expressions. Our results indicated that the geographical distribution of facial expression scores showed divisional patterns and higher positive scores were distributed in Changchun, Jinan, and Guangzhou cities. The formation of facial expression distribution among cities was related to that in universities within host-cities. Regression analysis indicated that number of regular institutions of higher learning had the positive contribution to the happy score and a number of internet accesses and area of resident lands contributed to the negative expression scores. Therefore, if the city planner aimed to promote the perceived satisfaction of young people in the campus of universities, the promotion of educational institution numbers with confining resident communities and broadband accesses would benefit the positively emotional expressions. Our study can be applied for budget and regime planners to establish sustainable development of universities with efficient evaluation using current techniques.

**Supplementary Materials:** The following are available online at http://www.mdpi.com/2076-3417/10/4/1474/s1, Figure S1: The panel of FireFACE™-V1.0 software to recognize photos with typically happy, sad, and neutral facial expressions. Figure S2: The copyright of the FireFACE™-V1.0 software that is authorized in mainland China. Table S1: The list of key universities in the 211-Project of mainland China with province and city names. Table S2: Letters that are marked for different means of ranked happy scores in visitors in university campuses across mainland China. Table S3: Letters that are marked for different means of ranked sad scores in visitors in university campuses across mainland China. Table S4: Letters that are marked for different means of ranked positive response index (PRI) scores in visitors in university campuses across mainland China.

**Author Contributions:** Conceptualization, H.W. and X.Z.; methodology, H.W.; software, H.W.; validation, X.Z.; formal analysis, X.Z. and H.W.; investigation, X.Z.; resources, X.Z.; data curation, X.Z.; writing—original draft preparation, H.W.; writing—review and editing, R.J.H. and X.Z.; visualization, X.Z. All authors have read and agreed to the published version of the manuscript.

**Funding:** This research was funded by the Secondary-Class Support of China Postdoctoral Science Foundation Grants (grant number 2019M651220), the National Natural Science Foundation of China (grant number 41971122; 41861017; 31600496), the Strategic Priority Research Program of the Chinese Academy of Sciences (grant number XDA23070503), the Regional Key Project in S&T Services Network Program of Chinese Academy of Sciences (grant number KFJ-STS-QYZD-044; KFJ-STS-ZDTP-048), the National Key Research and Development Program of China (grant number 2016YFC0500300), and the Fund for Jilin Environmental Science (grant number 2017-16).

**Acknowledgments:** Authors acknowledge Xin Chen for her contribution to use the software of facial analysis. Feng Zhu (Zhilunpudao Agric. S&T Ltd., Changchun, China) is kindly acknowledged for his authorization for us to use the FireFACE™-V1.0 software.

**Conflicts of Interest:** The authors declare no conflict of interest.

## References

1. Albino, V.; Berardi, U.; Dangelico, R.M. Smart cities: Definitions, dimensions, performance, and initiatives. *J. Urban Technol.* **2015**, *22*, 3–21. [CrossRef]
2. Trencher, G.; Bai, X.M.; Evans, J.; McCormick, K.; Yarime, M. University partnerships for co-designing and co-producing urban sustainability. *Glob. Environ. Chang.* **2014**, *28*, 153–165. [CrossRef]
3. De Kerk, G.V.; Manuel, A.R. A comprehensive index for a sustainable society: The SSI—the sustainable society index. *Ecol. Econ.* **2008**, *66*, 228–242. [CrossRef]
4. Nevado-Pena, D.; Lopez-Ruiz, V.R.; Alfaro-Navarro, J.L. The effects of environmental and social dimensions of sustainability in response to the economic crisis of European cities. *Sustainability* **2015**, *7*, 8255–8269. [CrossRef]
5. Fortes, S.; Santoyo-Ramon, J.A.; Palacios, D.; Baena, E.; Mora-Garcia, R.; Medina, M.; Mora, P.; Barco, R. The campus as a smart city: University of Malaga environmental, learning, and research approaches. *Sensors* **2019**, *19*, 23. [CrossRef]
6. Villegas-Ch, W.; Palacios-Pacheco, X.; Lujan-Mora, S. Application of a smart city model to a traditional university campus with a big data architecture: A sustainable smart campus. *Sustainability* **2019**, *11*, 28. [CrossRef]
7. Keeler, L.W.; Beaudoin, F.; Wiek, A.; John, B.; Lerner, A.M.; Beecroft, R.; Tamm, K.; Seebacher, A.; Lang, D.J.; Kay, B.; et al. Building actor-centric transformative capacity through city-university partnerships. *Ambio* **2019**, *48*, 529–538. [CrossRef]
8. Aguilar, R.M.M. The relationship university-city epistemological approach. *Bitacora Urbano Territ.* **2011**, *18*, 127–138.

9. Kolesova, O.V.; Minaev, N.N.; Oplakanskaya, R.V. Siberian university cities: Trends of development, challenges, opportunities. *Tomsk State Univ. J.* **2019**, 106–111. [CrossRef]
10. Russo, A.P.; van den Berg, L.; Lavanga, M. Toward a sustainable relationship between city and university—A stakeholdership approach. *J. Plan. Educ. Res.* **2007**, *27*, 199–216. [CrossRef]
11. Romein, A.; Fernandez-Maldonado, A.M.; Trip, J.J. Delft blues: The long road from university town to knowledge city. *Int. J. Knowl. Based Dev.* **2011**, *2*, 148–165. [CrossRef]
12. Sum, C.Y. A great leap of faith: Limits to China's university cities. *Urban Stud.* **2018**, *55*, 1460–1476. [CrossRef]
13. Chow, H.P.H. Life satisfaction among university students in a Canadian prairie city: A multivariate analysis. *Soc. Indic. Res.* **2005**, *70*, 139–150. [CrossRef]
14. Insch, A.; Sun, B. University students' needs and satisfaction with their host city. *J. Place Manag. Dev.* **2013**, *6*, 178–191. [CrossRef]
15. Espinosa-Garcia, A.C.; Diaz-Avalos, C.; Gonzalez-Villarreal, F.J.; Val-Segura, R.; Malvaez-Orozco, V.; Mazari-Hiriart, M. Drinking water quality in a Mexico city university community: Perception and preferences. *EcoHealth* **2015**, *12*, 88–97. [CrossRef]
16. Grahn, P.; Stigsdotter, U.K. The relation between perceived sensory dimensions of urban green space and stress restoration. *Landsc. Urban Plan.* **2010**, *94*, 264–275. [CrossRef]
17. Moos, M.; Revington, N.; Wilkin, T.; Andrey, J. The knowledge economy city: Gentrification, strudentification and youthification, and their connections to universities. *Urban Stud.* **2019**, *56*, 1075–1092. [CrossRef]
18. Rodrigues, M.; Franco, M. Measuring the performance in creative cities: Proposal of a multidimensional model. *Sustainability* **2018**, *10*, 21. [CrossRef]
19. Wei, H.X.; Hauer, R.J.; Chen, X.; He, X.Y. Facial expressions of visitors in forests along the urbanization gradient: What can we learn from selfies on social networking services? *Forests* **2019**, *10*, 14. [CrossRef]
20. Surakka, V.; Hietanen, J.K. Facial and emotional reactions to Duchenne and non-Duchenne smiles. *Int. J. Psychophysiol.* **1998**, *29*, 23–33. [CrossRef]
21. Nakashima, Y.; Koyama, T.; Yokoya, N.; Babaguchi, N. Facial expression preserving privacy protection using image melding. In Proceedings of the 2015 IEEE International Conference on Multimedia & Expo, Turin, Italy, 29 June–3 July 2015; The IEEE Press: New York, NY, USA, 2015; pp. 13–29.
22. D'Ambrosio, S.; de Pasquale, S.; Iannone, G.; Malandrino, D.; Negro, A.; Patimo, G.; Scarano, V.; Spinelli, R.; Zaccagnino, R. Privacy as a proxy for Green Web browsing: Methodology and experimentation. *Comput. Netw.* **2017**, *126*, 81–99.
23. China Education On-line Retrieved from 2019. Available online: https://daxue.eol.cn/211.shtml (accessed on 12 July 2019).
24. Sina Technology Retrieved from 2018. Available online: https://tech.sina.com.cn/i/2018-08-08/doc-ihhkuskt9903395.shtml (accessed on 8 August 2018).
25. Fincher, R.; Shaw, K. Enacting separate social worlds: 'International' and 'local' students in public space in central Melbourne. *Geoforum* **2011**, *42*, 539–549. [CrossRef]
26. National Bureau of Statistics of China. *Annals of Cities in China*, 2017 ed.; China Statistics Press: Beijing, China, 2017.
27. Daim, T.U.; Ozdemir, D. Impact of US economic crises on university research and development investments. *J. Knowl. Econ.* **2015**, *6*, 13–27. [CrossRef]
28. Goodspeed, T.J. The relationship between state income taxes and local property taxes: Education finance in New Jersey. *Natl. Tax J.* **1998**, *51*, 219–238.
29. Upadhyay, U.D.; Cartwright, A.F.; Johns, N.E. Access to medication abortion among California's public university students. *J. Adolesc. Health* **2018**, *63*, 249–252. [CrossRef]
30. Levey, R.L.; Connors, A.W.; Martin, L.L. Public university use of social infrastructure public-private partnerhips (P3s): An exploratory examination. *Public Works Manag. Policy* **2020**. [CrossRef]
31. Babatunde, S.O.; Perera, S. Public-private partnership in university female students' hostel delivery analysis of users' satisfaction in Nigeria. *Facilities* **2017**, *35*, 64–80. [CrossRef]
32. Kerrihard, A.L.; Khair, M.B.; Blumberg, R.; Feldman, C.H.; Wunderlich, S.M. The effects of acclimation to the United States and other demographic factors on responses to salt levels in foods: An examination utilizing face reader technology. *Appetite* **2017**, *116*, 315–322. [CrossRef]
33. SAS Institute Inc. Nonparametric analysis of variance. In *SAS/STAT®14.3 User's Guide*; SAS Institute Inc.: Cary, NC, USA, 2017; p. 113.

34. Waller, B.M.; Warmelink, L.; Liebal, K.; Micheletta, J.; Slocombe, K.E. Pseudoreplication: A widespread problem in primate communication research. *Anim. Behav.* **2013**, *86*, 483–488. [CrossRef]
35. Ramage, B.S.; Sheil, D.; Salim, H.M.W.; Fletcher, C.; Mustafa, N.Z.A.; Luruthusamay, J.C.; Harrison, R.D.; Butod, E.; Dzulkiply, A.D.; Kassim, A.R.; et al. Pseudoreplication in tropical forests and the resulting effects on biodiversity conservation. *Conserv. Biol.* **2013**, *27*, 364–372. [CrossRef]
36. Hajrasouliha, A. Campus score: Measuring university campus qualities. *Landsc. Urban Plan.* **2017**, *158*, 166–176. [CrossRef]
37. Hammeed, A.; Amjad, S. Students' satisfaction in higher learning institutions: A case study of COMSATS Abbottabad, Pakistan. *Iran. J. Manag. Stud.* **2011**, *4*, 63–77.
38. Ali, A.K. Academic staff's perceptions of characteristics of learning organization in a higher institution. *Int. J. Educ. Manag.* **2012**, *26*, 55.
39. Ybarra, M.L.; Mitchell, K.J. Online aggressor/targets, aggressors, and targets: A comparison of associated youth characteristics. *J. Child Psychol. Psychiatry* **2004**, *45*, 1308–1316. [CrossRef] [PubMed]
40. Sanders, C.E.; Field, T.M.; Diego, M.; Kaplan, M. The relationship of Internet use to depression and social isolation among adolescents. *Adolescence* **2000**, *35*, 237–242. [PubMed]
41. Chen, Z.; Poon, K.T.; Cheng, C. Deficits in recognizing disgust facial expressions and Internet addiction: Perceived stress as a mediator. *Psychiatry Res.* **2017**, *254*, 211–217. [CrossRef]
42. Peng, X.Z.; Cui, F.; Wang, T.; Jiao, C. Unconscious processing of facial expressions in individuals with internet gaming disorder. *Front. Psychol.* **2017**, *8*, 9. [CrossRef]
43. McCulloch, A. Housing density as a predictor of neighbourhood satisfaction among families with young children in urban England. *Popul. Space Place* **2012**, *18*, 85–99. [CrossRef]
44. Landman, K.; du Tolt, J. Residents' perceptions of the importance of outdoor spaces and neighbourliness for medium-density mixed-housing in South Africa. *Town Region. Plan.* **2014**, *65*, 23–34.
45. Knudsen, A.B.; Slooff, R. Vector-borne disease problems in rapid urbanization - New approaches to vector control. *Bull. World Health Organ.* **1992**, *70*, 1–6.
46. McLellan, S.L.; Newton, R.J.; Vandewalle, J.L.; Shanks, O.C.; Huse, S.M.; Eren, A.M.; Sogin, M.L. Sewage reflects the distribution of human faecal Lachnospiraceae. *Environ. Microbiol.* **2013**, *15*, 2213–2227. [CrossRef] [PubMed]
47. Dockery, D.W.; Pope, C.A.; Xu, X.P.; Spengler, J.D.; Ware, J.H.; Fay, M.E.; Ferris, B.G.; Speizer, F.E. An association between air-pollution and mortality in 6 United-states cities. *N. Engl. J. Med.* **1993**, *329*, 1753–1759. [CrossRef] [PubMed]
48. Kang, S.M.; Lau, A.S. Revisiting the out-group advantage in emotion recognition in a multicultural society: Further evidence for the in-group advantage. *Emotion* **2013**, *13*, 203–215. [CrossRef] [PubMed]

© 2020 by the authors. Licensee MDPI, Basel, Switzerland. This article is an open access article distributed under the terms and conditions of the Creative Commons Attribution (CC BY) license (http://creativecommons.org/licenses/by/4.0/).

Article

# How to Extract Meaningful Insights from UGC: A Knowledge-Based Method Applied to Education

Jose Ramon Saura [1], Ana Reyes-Menendez [1,*] and Dag R. Bennett [2]

[1] Department of Business Economics, Faculty of Social Sciences and Law, Rey Juan Carlos University, Paseo Artilleros s/n, 28032 Madrid, Spain; joseramon.saura@urjc.es
[2] Ehrenberg Centre for Research in Marketing, London South Bank University, 103 Borough Rd., London SE1 0AA, UK; bennetd@lsbu.ac.uk
* Correspondence: ana.reyes@urjc.es

Received: 3 September 2019; Accepted: 21 October 2019; Published: 29 October 2019

**Abstract:** New analysis and visualization techniques are required to glean useful insights from the vast amounts of data generated by new technologies and data sharing platforms. The aim of this article is to lay a foundation for such techniques so that the age of big data may also be the age of knowledge, visualization, and understanding. Education is the keystone area used in this study because it is deeply affected by digital platforms as an educational medium and also because it deals mostly with digital natives who use information and communication technology (ICT) for all manner of purposes. Students and teachers are therefore a rich source of user generated content (UGC) on social networks and digital platforms. This article shows how useful knowledge can be extracted and visualized from samples of readily available UGC, in this case the text published in tweets from the social network Twitter. The first stage employs topic-modeling using LDA (latent dirichlet allocation) to identify topics, which are then subjected to sentiment analysis (SA) using machine-learning (developed in Python). The results take on meaning through an application of data mining techniques and a data visualization algorithm for complex networks. The results obtained show insights related to innovative educational trends that practitioners can use to improve strategies and interventions in the education sector in a short-term future.

**Keywords:** knowledge-based method; topic-modeling; sentiment analysis; machine learning; complex networks

## 1. Introduction

Millions of consumers center their consumption habits and daily activities around mobile technologies, apps, social networks, and digital platforms. These, in turn, generate a bewildering profusion of data about users' activity in and use of digital devices [1,2] and it is now becoming ever clearer that data, particularly data sharing, is a dominant paradigm in an interconnected world [1]. This sharing is fostered by customer or client-centric platforms that support and encourage user generated content (UGC) [2], defined as content distributed via social networks by users who share publicly their opinions and comments on topics of interest [3].

At the same time, the mass of UGC data overwhelms the means to extract timely, high-quality information-based insights that are meaningful, useful, efficient or applicable to managerial interventions [3–6]. Nevertheless, the desire to benefit from such data is driving researchers to seek new tools and analysis techniques that focus on identifying knowledge and insight generation [1,7].

Particularly, desirable techniques are those that can be applied to databases that come from social networks and digital platforms where UGC proliferates [8,9]. Previous attempts focused on new technologies and methodological approaches using artificial intelligence, machine learning, topic-modeling, data visualization, sentiment analysis, and business intelligence, among others [10,11], with varying degrees of success. However, extracting useful knowledge from large amounts of data from varied public, private, industrial, and commercial platforms remains an imperfect science with much room for improvement [12–15]. This is particularly true for some markets such as education that include millions of customers (students, teachers, administrators, schools, education systems, regulatory bodies and commercial networks) huge numbers of providers and interested parties, and baffling varieties of ICT systems and procedures [16,17].

Accordingly, in the present study, we focus on the analysis of UGC in the education sector with the aim of developing and demonstrating reliable and re-usable techniques for understanding the users, issues, and trends in the education [18]. Similar techniques for analyzing social network data have been applied in various research areas and market sectors [2,18] with promising results, especially for improving understanding of how users are grouped into communities [19–21]. The refined approach used provides an overview of social media around the education sector, giving us the possibility to focus on key themes, especially around innovation [21–23]. The present study therefore aims to improve understanding of innovation in the education sector. Our main source of information is the verbal content published by users on Twitter [24,25].

As indicated above, a contribution of this research is to identify trends related to innovation in the education sector by applying methods to extract knowledge and as importantly, to communicate it effectively through the application of data visualization algorithms [2,26–30]. This objective also includes detecting and systematizing thematics that characterize the education sector, at least in the short-term [30–32].

Specifically, this study develops a topic-modeling technique known as LDA (latent Dirichlet allocation) on which SA via machine-learning developed in Python, is applied. The results generated are then tested against Krippendorf's alpha value (KAV) which sets a meaningful threshold of 0.8 or better [33,34] to be considered as reliable on a sample of $n$ = 9801 tweets [35]. The information analyzed is the text content of tweets that together with the indicators obtained from the applied methods, as well as the study of their groupings in communities, allow us to derive insights related to innovation in education [17,21]. Comparison of findings with the results of other investigations then aid in the verification of these insights and the identification of new knowledge relevant to the education sector [25,26].

Finally, the results are given meaning by applying data mining techniques and a data visualization algorithm for complex networks, developed by Blondel et al. [36] and known as modularity report (MR). This uses the open source software Gephi, with which different image resolutions are applied to visualize and identify communities in the sample as they relate to education innovation [37]. Then, the results of the discovered topics are compared with UGC communities on Twitter concerned with innovation in education. It is important to note that the primary purpose of this study is discovery, and not hypothesis testing [21]. There are no a priori assumptions about variables in this approach. Instead, the intent is to identify variables that will be useful to further research, and that therefore add value to the literature [38].

This article is structured as follows: first, following the introduction, we present methodology and research questions used in the analysis. Next, the results are presented followed by a discussion and then conclusions and references.

## 2. Methodology and Research Questions

### 2.1. Research Questions

Shelton et al. [18] demonstrated the importance of studying new trends in education, concluding that progress and quality depend on continuous learning. Likewise, Reyes [19] pointed out the need to apply data-based techniques to Big Data to identify trends in education and to learn new teaching skills by applying learning analytics techniques. Furthermore, Anshari et al. [20] concluded that research focused on the discovery of trends for the improvement of education, can be developed with techniques based on knowledge extraction, data mining, or Big Data. Following these investigations, we propose the following research question.

Is it possible to identify trends in the education sector by analyzing the UGC on Twitter and representing them in topics? (RQ1)

This work is based on the work by Huda et al. [21] who showed that insights can be extracted by analyzing the databases to help improve active agents in the education sector through discovering new online learning resources. In addition, in their review, Sin and Muthu [22] analyzed the use of data mining-based techniques in the learning sector, discovering that the sentiment analysis technique—among others—are a rich source of content for the education sector. Likewise, Pang and Lee [23] used sentiment analysis as a technique to extract insights in education, highlighting the need to study content to extract insights based on the feelings expressed in UGC. Based on these findings, our second research question is.

Is it possible to extract insights related to the education sector by analyzing the sentiment (positive, negative, and neutral) in UGC topics published on Twitter? (RQ2)

Previous studies of UGC and social networks in the education sector include, Kogan [24] who highlighted the identity and quality of content that can be extracted from communities of higher educations. Likewise, Jongbloed et al. [25] analyzed the interconnections within the scope of communities in education, highlighting the influence of social networks. Furthermore, La Velle et al. [26] emphasized that communities of teachers in education are a source of quality content related to education and teaching. Based on these previous studies, the third research question addressed here is as follows:

Is it possible to detect user communities that publish UGC on Twitter in the education sector and extract quality insights relevant to these online communities? (RQ3)

### 2.2. Data Sampling Extraction and Collection

For the data extraction process the authors connected to the public Twitter API. The time horizon analyzed was from 10–17 June 2019, allowing the download of a total of $n = 10,786$ tweets under the search term #Education. Following Sherman et al. [39] and Banerjee et al. [40], we used a randomized controlled process to select this term by focusing on the education sector and the proposed research questions. This process allows researchers to systematically select a sample based on the social media content—in this study, in the form of tweets with a specific hashtag. To this end, the authors choose a term for the extraction of the sample that describes the study subject and encompasses each of the proposed research questions, removing any other terms that do not have these characteristics [11,27]. This exploratory process is based on previous study results from other investigations [11,23,25] that groups the sample around the same label—in this case, on Twitter.

Data collection was performed using the MAC version of Python software 3.7.0. [17]. Other investigations have used this same sequence and sample based on the quality of the content and not on the UGC number of samples [11,35,38,41].

After data collection, the tweets were filtered to exclude images and videos which are not part of this study [11]. This was a simple data cleaning exercise to exclude data that was not suitable for analysis using the developed method. Also, the extraneous URLs that contained the tweets were removed. The data cleaning process was performed using Python and Pandas software library. For this filtering we used commands to elect or replace columns and indices to reshape lost or empty values and to debug repeated or unnecessary data. In addition, any retweets, that is, a tweet from one user that is repeated by another user, were treated as independent tweets [42,43]. Repeated tweets from the same user, as well as URLs and references with links to other web pages, were removed with the aim of increasing the quality of the included content and avoiding noise [41]. Also, emojis were not analyzed in this study, as we focused on natural language processing (NLP), rather than on the graphic icons analysis techniques. Our decision to omit emoticons in our analysis was based on the fact that the analysis techniques used in the present study were not meant for the analysis of graphics or graphic icons and were associated with the analysis of feelings in NLP datasets [38]. This filtering process resulted in a final sample of $n$ = 9801 total tweets with direct relevance to the education sector [2,36,37].

## 2.3. Knowledge-Based Method to Extract Insights from UGC

To make sense of the content generated by users, a methodology proposed by Saura and Bennett [2] was applied to the data. This process uses three different approaches based on data mining and topic modeling.

The first step is the development of a mathematical model to detect topics from a series of inputs on which this algorithm is applied. Pritchard and Stephens [44] created the model, and Blei et al. improved it [45]. The improved model is known as LDA. The model has been successfully used in various studies before [46,47]. The objective of the model is to identify the number of times a word is repeated in a sample. Sometimes this sample can be represented by phrases or by documents [46]. The mathematical model developed in Python applies the observation of variables including the number of documents or databases on which the analysis will be carried out; these are the latent variables [44]. The variables then are used to determine the number of topics that the algorithm will find based on the importance of the total database [46].

Once the algorithm has detected the total number of words and the number of repeated words, the researcher must give names or labels to the topics [41]. This name is specified by the researcher and can be based on a phrase creation using the last words that are repeated in the analysis of a document or a database after applying the LDA model. This is an open coding method which is routinely used in research studies based on grounded theory [42].

On LDA results we apply a sentiment analysis, in this case one developed in Python that works with machine learning and that must be trained through a process in which the different samples are classified [47,48] by the researchers; here, tweets from Twitter are classified as positive, negative, and neutral [49] manually. This sentiment-centered analysis can identify connotations and feelings with respect to the subject of study. The SA methodology aims to classify the feelings expressed in a sample. That is, using SA, researchers can analyze the feelings within a community regarding a specific theme. This analysis is based on studying the set of connotations in texts that compose the sample [50].

To determine the number of iterations required to train this algorithm so that it is ready to be used, we focus on the resulting KAV measurement [50]. This measure indicates what the level of significance is in terms of machine learning success [33,34]. Note that in applying the threshold levels of KAV, the results must be equal to or greater than 0.667 to have an average of success that is minimally reliable [50]. A good measure that allows conclusions to be analyzed with confidence that they are meaningful would be to set the acceptable KAV equal to or greater than 0.800 [34].

In the present study, the KAV value is applied to support vector machine (SVM) algorithms. This type of trainable algorithm has an easy application for other academics, and researchers in the educational sector. The SA algorithms that work with SVMs make it possible to train SVMs with a sample (in this case, a collection of tweets), indicating through a user interface whether the sample is negative, positive, or neutral. This training is performed until the model's ability to succeed, as indicated by the KAV, is sufficient [2]. As indicated by Krippendorff [51] and replicated by Saura et al. [38], the basic formula for KAV is the relationship characterized by observed disagreement/expected disagreement. The calculation method is computationally very complex, the process involves resampling methods such as bootstrapping [51].

Therefore, the proposed approach is a data analysis technique that should be useful to those who seek to use UGC to improve their communication or marketing strategies. Also, it should be useful to educational institutions that may be able to enhance their offerings by identifying needs and trends based on technologies previously investigated [52–55].

Figure 1 shows the training process of the SVM algorithm and the classification according to the feelings that (a) represents the training process of a sentiment analysis algorithm with a feature extractor and a machine learning algorithm, and (b) represents the prediction process of a sentiment analysis algorithm with a feature extractor and a classifier model [2].

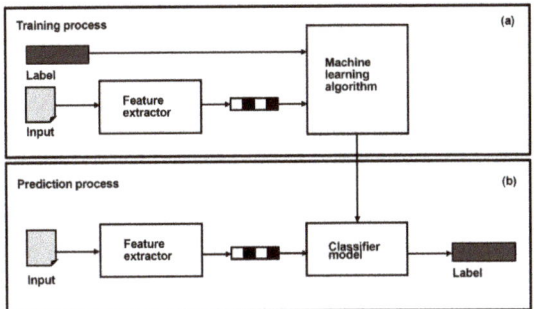

**Figure 1.** Process of sentiment analysis (SA). Source: Reproduced with permission from Saura and Bennett [2], Symmetry; published by MDPI, 2019.

Finally, a textual analysis also known as data text mining is carried out. In this case, a study of the databases resulting from these processes is outlined. That is, as a result of the two processes executed previously, the databases obtained are divided according to the feelings or sentiments labeled positive, negative, and neutral [56].

These textual databases were analyzed using Nvivo [2]. Following Saura and Bennett [2] each database was filtered into groups of nodes and then classified based on the weight of repetition of words and the metric known as weighted percentage (WP) [51,57,58]. This metric identifies the phrases and words that are repeated the most, classified by sentiment as well as by topic, and allows phrases to be classified so that groups of main indicators can be identified. The equations used for this process can be consulted in detail in Saura and Bennett [2]. Figure 2 details each phase of the TA process which (a) represents input data collection and preprocessing, and (b) represents the output process by text mining and text analysis.

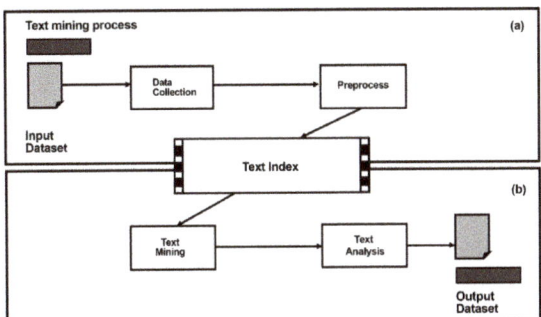

**Figure 2.** Text mining process. Source: Reproduced with permission from Saura and Bennett [2], Symmetry; published by MDPI, 2019.

*2.4. Data Visualization Algorithms*

This technique uses an algorithm for the visualization of complex communities [36,37] developed by Blondel et al. [36] that enables communities to be identified within complex networks called modularity reports (MR) [36,37]. In addition, the technique uses a resolution enhancer to improve visualization of the algorithm created by Lambiotte et al. [37].

Note that the visual representation of communities has been used in previous investigations [58–61]. In the current research, the objective was to detect communities related to education and also to detect new technologies and future trends that can then be compared to topics identified from the study sample. To allow this analysis, the sample is structured in nodes [62]. A node is a neuron that represents the link between different users or different communications in Twitter [2,35]. The links between these nodes and their weight and relevance determine their relationship with respect to the subject. The nodes therefore indicate both communities and topics of communication. In addition, they can be visually represented to detect the number of people or nodes, or users, who are talking about this issue across social networks [63].

With regard to the resolution of the algorithm and its application, the next step is to identify the number of sub-communities based on their weight [61]. Following Lambiotte et al. [37], a higher visualization resolution when using the algorithm will allow us to obtain fewer, but more specific, communities, while lower resolutions will allow us to identify more communities in which more nodes participate.

Blondel et al. [36] and Lambiotte et al. [37] explain that node networks can be visually understood as a community with systematically organized unions. The usefulness of this organizational system is illustrated in Figure 3 which shows how nodes may present simple linkages (a) or may present unions in a community (b).

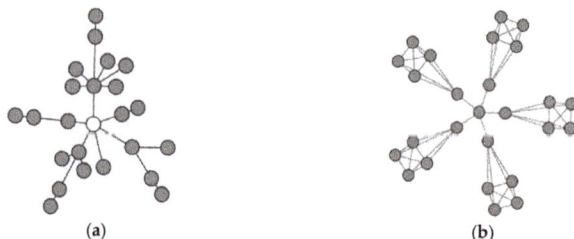

**Figure 3.** Community visual identification. Source: Reproduced with permission from Matta et al. [3], Applied Sciences; published by MDPI, 2018.

Note that each node is identifiable by various descriptors that enable the researcher to demonstrate that topics on the social network are grouped around communities and how different nodes group with other nodes. These systematic organizations make it possible to visually present understandable communities and connections [36] (see Figure 4a–c).

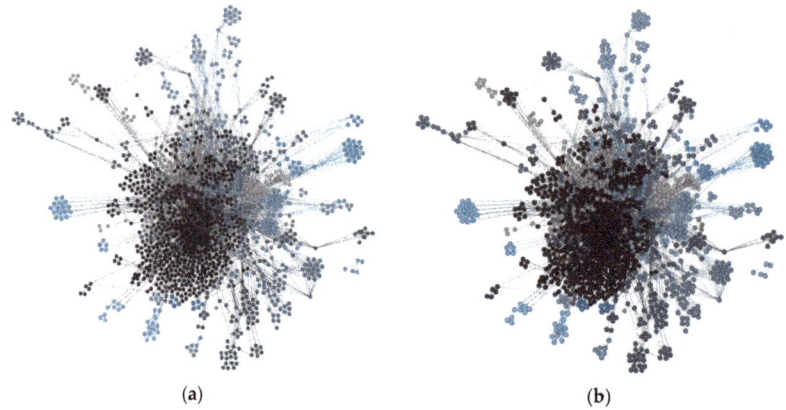

**Figure 4.** *Cont.*

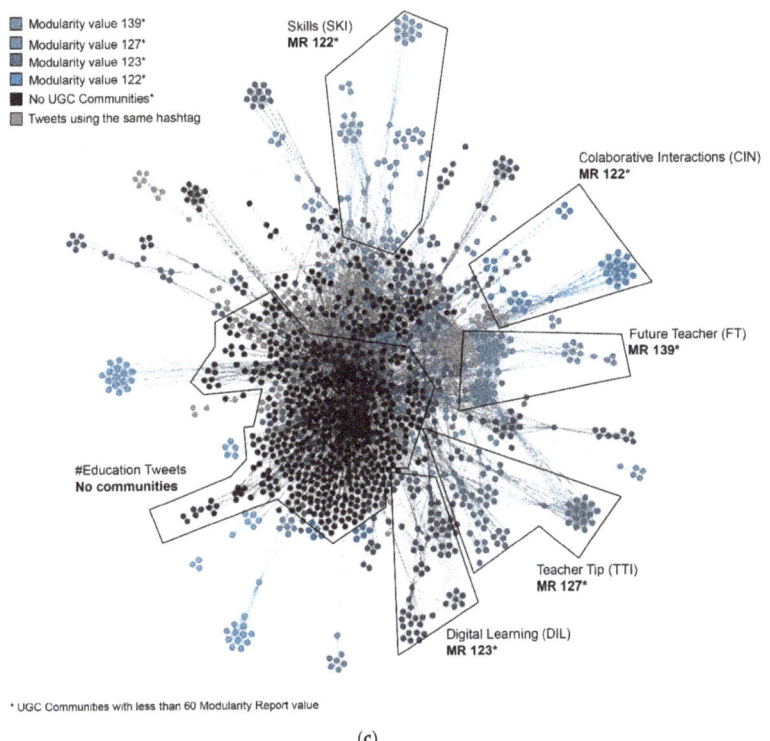

**Figure 4.** (a) Communities visualization resolution 1 (b) Modularity report communities visualization resolution 2 (c) Modularity report communities visualization. Source: The authors.

## 3. Results

*3.1. Knowledge-Based Method Results*

With respect to the LDA process the following results were obtained in which five main topics related to education were defined; three of these topics were associated with a positive sentiment, one topic was negative, and another topic was neutral.

Topic descriptions and sentiments are shown in Table 1, which shows that new technologies play a fundamental role, both directly and indirectly, in innovation and education. On the one hand, new teaching processes based on innovation emerge, along with habits for obtaining online information or tools and tutorials that facilitate the understanding of these new processes. Furthermore, there is a two-way communication between communities that comment on the skills that teachers must have to develop new teaching methodologies based on technology and innovation.

The topics were then rated using sentiment analysis and the algorithm trained with machine-learning processes. The results of applying KAV analysis are shown in Table 2, [64,65]. For positive tweets, KAV values were 0.876, (above the reliability threshold of 0.8) [51]. The same was true for negative tweets with 0.882 KAV but neutral tweets had an average KAV of 0.641.

Table 1. Mean latent Dirichlet allocation (LDA) topics results description.

| N° | Name | Description | Sentiment |
|---|---|---|---|
| 1 | Innovative teaching (IT) | Learning models based on new teaching innovation processes. | Positive |
| 2 | Tutorials and tips for teaching (TTE) | Tutorials and tips for new tools for teaching. | Neutral |
| 3 | Digital teaching and learning (DLE) | New platforms related to education in digital environments. | Positive |
| 4 | Innovative teaching skills (ITS) | Skills related to new information technologies for teaching and tutoring. | Negative |
| 5 | Digital interaction and engagement (DIE) | Thematic linked to engagement and the reciprocal connection of communication through digital environments in the field of education. | Positive |

Table 2. LDA topics results description.

| Conclusion Reliability | Krippendorff's Alpha Value | This Research Study | Average KAV |
|---|---|---|---|
| High | $\alpha \geq 0.800$ | Positive Sentiment | 0.876 |
| Tentative | $\alpha \geq 0.667$ | Negative Sentiment | 0.882 |
| Low | $\alpha < 0.667$ | Neutral Sentiment | 0.641 |

Table 3 makes clear the statements related to education and the trends that have been identified can now be represented as insights [2,25,26]. These insights were identified by simply dividing the nodes (Count) by feelings (positive, negative, neutral) to calculate the WP and then applying data mining analysis [2].

Table 3. LDA topics insight descriptions.

| N° | Topic | Insight | Count | WP |
|---|---|---|---|---|
| 1 | IT | Innovative learning processes increase positive results in teaching. | 273 | 0.302 |
| 2 | TTE | Tutorials and tips on new teaching tools are a useful internet resource for teachers | 213 | 0.291 |
| 3 | DLE | The platforms for online education are an efficient resource for teachers. | 209 | 0.283 |
| 4 | ITS | There is a gap in the digital skills of teachers regarding the use of digital tools for teaching. | 179 | 0.209 |
| 5 | DIE | The communication between teachers on social networks is enriching and attracts new ideas and teaching tools. | 141 | 0.199 |

These results show that the main concerns expressed in the UGC sample are related to the skills that teachers should develop. Likewise, enthusiasm for new learning models and teaching methodologies strengthens the teacher's profile. Furthermore, social networks are being used as channels to share information related to teaching innovation and tutorials or tools that help teachers to develop their educational work. These insights provide an overview of possible motivations or concerns of teaching professionals in the education area.

*3.2. Data Visualization MR*

After applying the MR algorithm, it was possible to preview the communities with different resolutions [36]. The objective was to obtain the largest number of communities related to education and innovation in the sector so that a comparison of results of different tests enables identification of communities that are most relevant [2,16]. Table 4 shows the results of different tests performed according to the number of communities identified, their modularity, and the resolution applied to detect them.

Table 4. Modularity report (MR) communities' measurements.

| Test | Communities | Modularity | MR * | Resolution | MMC * | MiMC * |
|---|---|---|---|---|---|---|
| 1 | 42 | 0.213 | 0.175 | 1.0 | 140 | 0 |
| 3 | 153 | 0.098 | −0.012 | 0.1 | 136 | 0 |
| 3 | 978 | 0.007 | −0.011 | 0.001 | 124 | 0 |

* MR—modularity resolution. * MMC—maximum modularity class. * MiMC—minimum modularity class.

For the visualization of the neural networks and the corresponding communities, visualization filters were implemented using the open source Gephi software. The filters, following the application of the MR algorithm at selected resolution levels, use Force Atlas and Force Atlas 2 as shown in Table 5 [37]. These are the settings that are generally applicable and are used to enhance results visualizations.

Table 5. Communities definition.

| Data Visualization Filters | Value |
|---|---|
| Threads number | 1 |
| Tolerance | 1.0 |
| Approximation | 0.1 |
| Scaling | 0.2 |
| Gravity | 1.0 |
| Prevent Overlap | True |
| Edge Weight Influence | 4.0 |

Note that the visualization and resolution regarding the size of each node is 10 and nodes are grouped by communities according to their weight and relation to the main community. In addition, communities are arranged in color scales as shown in Figure 4a–c.

In (a) the results of the communities identified with the filters from Table 5 are presented. In (b) a network contraction filter is applied to help visualize the different modularities. Finally, in (c), the distance between each content community is observed with greater resolution to highlight the communities with the highest MR relative to the chosen subject (i.e., innovation in education), (see also Table 6).

Table 6. Outstanding communities around education and innovation according to MR results.

| N° | Community | Modularity |
|---|---|---|
| 1 | GradStudent | 140 |
| 2 | Future Teacher (FT) | 139 * |
| 3 | School Reform | 139 |
| 4 | Wanna Be Teacher | 139 |
| 5 | Scholarships | 135 |
| 6 | Special Education | 131 |
| 7 | Teacher Tip (TTI) | 127 * |
| 8 | Teacher Hack | 125 |
| 9 | Education Spaces | 125 |
| 10 | Collaborative Interactions (CIN) | 122 * |
| 11 | Digital Learning (DIL) | 123 * |
| 12 | Education Reform | 123 |
| 13 | Skills (SKI) | 122 * |

* Communities highlighted for their links to education in innovation.

Figure 4a–c shows that the center of all identified communities obtains a high MMC, represented here by dark blue. This highlights the relevance of the communities. In addition, the UGC content published without being grouped in a community is shown in black.

However, some small communities with very high MMC's are composed of few nodes, as compared with the communities with a high MiMC value and many nodes. This can be interpreted to mean that although there are more nodes around a community, in reality communities with a high

MMC, even when they have few node connections, are more relevant to the identified issue. That is, the results of the UGC analysis indicate that in the field of education, there are small communities that are very relevant, while other, sometimes larger communities are of minor importance. In the latter communities, while many users participate, their relevance in Twitter is small and only creates noise around the content so there is little interaction among the communities and no user engagement.

The choice of using a higher or lower resolution for the individual analysis of the UGC communities is up to the researcher [37]. In the present study, the aim is to explain the application of the algorithm of Lambiotte et al. [37] so that it can be understood and applied by other researchers in different industries.

To this end, Figure 4a shows the results of applying the filters from Table 5. Figure 4b shows how the space between the nodes is smaller with a shrink filter that allows us to visually detect or measure the size of communities based on labels, colors, or visual measurement values, as well as to understand whether they are really communities or simply UGC. Unlike Figure 4a,b, Figure 4c uses a different resolution to visualize the node communities.

In Figure 4c, it is easier to visually understand what the MMC and MiMC values of each community are, as well as their labeling in colors or names. The idea is that according to objective-specific research aims, the researcher increases the resolution of the algorithm to find the most relevant communities. Once identified, different labels can be added in chronological order, by MR, or engagement level. It is also be possible to visually sort the network of nodes based on the number of nodes (active actors in social networks) that make up each community, regardless of the MR obtained in the analysis.

In this study, while applying the Lambiotte et al. algorithm [37] made it possible to identify a total of 978 UGC communities, in this iteration only those linked to innovation in education were selected, eliminating any that obscure the results by adding noise or that have been mistakenly identified as being related to education but really are not, using the resolution level of 0.1 points.

Once graphs or figures are created, researchers can increase the resolution to label each community one by one and display a specific topic or name in a tag cloud, or make a table showing the most relevant communities (see, e.g., Table 6 [36]).

When a topic goes viral on Twitter, there are usually no communities of UGC [6], as users tend to participate only once or twice. When an opinion or influencer raises a question or requests participation in an initiative, UGC communities may be established around the initiative, where users comment and participate repeatedly, which appears as engagement with that topic. For instance, Figure 4 shows different UGC communities focused on innovation in education. Likewise, the number of nodes within each community can be shown along with values for MR. Researchers can manipulate the graphics to visually show the objectives they want to focus on [37].

Using the same datasets, it is possible to generate contrasting but complementary results. In this study the main communities identified by their connection to innovation in education were selected based on their subject matter and their weight. In this case they are: future teacher (FT), teacher tip (TTI), collaborative interactions (CIN), digital learning (DIL) and skills (SKI). Having identified the communities, it is now possible to compare and analyze them.

## 4. Discussion

The knowledge extraction process identified five topics, of which three were positive, one negative, and one neutral. The analysis identified a subject related to IT with comments regarding learning models based on new teaching innovation processes (see McLoughlin and Lee [66]). This topic was graded as positive based on the diversity of positive opinions related to the improvement of teaching processes based on innovation.

Likewise, DLE also had a positive sentiment rating from positive comments grouped around new social networks and platforms that aim to teach and improve education through technology in digital environments, as confirmed by other research such as Quercia et al. (2012) [67] and Sluban et al. [68]. DIE was a positive topic characterized by the communication between equal parts through digital environments based on innovation. In summary, such results, and the specific insights, should enable teachers to use these features to improve teaching approaches as in Williamson and Piattoeva et al. [30].

With regard to TTE, a neutral sentiment was obtained for a subject composed mainly of tutorials and tricks for using educational tools on the Internet. The sentiment was neutral because of the diversity of comments regarding the user experience or improvements of the tools themselves (see Saura et al. [38]). A negative sentiment was obtained for STIs, a topic associated with a gap in the teachers' technological skills, particularly their ability to teach based on learning methods in innovation. This result was generally in line with those of Brush et al. [69]. In sum, the main insights that can be drawn from these themes according to sentiment analysis ranked in order of weight are summarized in Table 3 above [2].

If these results are compared with the visualization approach of communities within the same topics and with the same sample, it is clear that one of the topics with higher modularity is education itself, followed by the communities summarized in Table 6. Note that five of these communities coincide, in part, with the topics identified as a result of the LDA. The first, FT, is a community with interactions related to the future teachers and their future in digital society. Likewise, a community was found with a modularity of 127 points that deals with advice for teachers linked to education and technological tools was labeled TTI.

Another community with a modularity of 123 points was labelled CIN where opinions, experiences, and learning center activities are shared, and feedback communicated. There is also a community based exclusively on digital education, labelled DIL. Finally, a community speaking specifically about teachers' abilities was identified as SKI.

The communities and issues identified here indicate that future teachers should be proficient in digital communications coinciding with other researchers who propose these lines of research for the future such as Jongbloed et al. [25]. Moreover, as stated by Bonk [70], their communications in collaborative, interactive digital ecosystems should be supported by digital education platforms.

The visualization of data allowed for a detailed understanding of a number of communities on Twitter built around the same topic and that all are linked. Some, however, are more relevant than others and allow the extraction of more industry-specific insights. In addition, visualization of the communities allows for a more granular understanding of their relative importance, their interactions with one another, and how they are related [2].

The visualization of these communities of UGC highlights the importance of social networks for the discovery and extraction of knowledge (see also Goh et al. [71] or Yannopoulou et al. [72]).

Likewise, if we consider the identified communities as topics of users' interest, educational organizations or institutions can focus their content generation strategies on these topics, since the interest of users has been verified through the communities according to the interactions and communications of users [71,72].

## 5. Conclusions

This research developed two distinct processes for extracting information-based knowledge from a database composed of Twitter tweets. In conducting this analysis, it became clear that the study of UGC can lead to valuable insight that should make it possible to enhance and improve strategies for any organization involved in this area of enterprise.

This research outlined different study topics for the education sector applying technologies based on data visualization and data mining. First, an LDA was used to organize samples of tweets into topics, then a SA was applied to these results. The sentiment analysis algorithm was trained with machine learning and data mining processes to obtain an adequate KAV that allows for the analysis of reliable results. Then, an approximation was made with data mining to extract insights and to discover knowledge from the dataset. Next, data visualization algorithms were applied to identify communities, which helped to establish themes linked to education and identify those that contribute to knowledge [73]. This research may also improve understanding of how the networks of nodes and communities exist through UGC publication. This analysis shows that communities can be identified and studied in social networks.

With respect to RQ1, we have demonstrated that it is possible to identify short-term trends for the education sector by analyzing UGC on Twitter under the #Education hashtag, thus showing the effective application of knowledge discovery techniques in UGC. Likewise, insights have been obtained regarding the education sector specifically to which an analysis of sentiment has been applied in the discovered topics (RQ2). This fact allows us to better understand positive, negative, and neutral sentiments held by identified UGC communities regarding specific trends in the education sector, such as tools, capacities, skills, or new development perspectives.

Finally, we have successfully detected user communities that publish UGC on Twitter around the same content theme (RQ3). The relevance of such communities and their interconnectedness has been demonstrated through visualization of nodes. Such analysis and visualization techniques can be used by researchers and educational institutions, e.g., in training courses focused on key topics for teachers. There is also scope to improve skill-sets and to highlight the reasons to be active members of online communities.

The important new contribution of the present study is the application of the Blondel et al.'s [36] algorithm to Twitter UGC to generate useful and actionable insights. The education sector is used as an example of how the technique can be used, and the results generate insights related to innovative education trends that practitioners in the industry can use to improve marketing strategies and refine analyses of markets related to education. An important theoretical implication of the processes outlined is the identification of ten topics directly linked to innovation and education.

*5.1. Theoretical Implications*

As indicated, an important new theoretical implication is the study of the ten topics directly linked to the innovation and education sectors discovered in the UGC. These are specific results of the first process: innovative teaching (IT); tutorials and tips for teaching (TTE); digital teaching and learning (DLE); innovative teaching skills (ITS), and digital interaction and engagement (DIE). The results of the second process include future teacher (FT); teacher tip (TTI); collaborative interactions (CIN); digital learning (DIL), and skills (SKI).

If researchers could take these insights as variables and constructs for their models, they may be able to enhance their understanding of whether positive links exist between them by developing, for example, models based on partial least squares structural equation modeling (PLS-SEM) or SPSS, analysis of moment structures (AMOS) among others, thus contributing to a field of research that emerges from approaches that extract information-based knowledge from large amounts of data. Academics could use these topics in the future in their studies in order to measure the influence they have on teaching innovation, teaching skills, or teaching skills based on new technologies.

Also, academics can use this research to better understand the education sector and to focus on the development of research within the field by focusing on the discovered topics. In addition, they can also focus on content analysis by users of different social networks to better understand what the main habits are when sharing information publicly in digital ecosystems.

*5.2. Practical Implications*

Companies or centers of higher education such as universities or postgraduate centers can use the results of this research to enhance teacher training in the areas that were identified with a high MR. Likewise, educational institutions can use this research to implement knowledge extraction methodologies and thus understand UGC data generated in their own areas.

Further, practitioners can use the research results to improve those areas of teacher education that were identified as key elements for innovation.

Likewise, non-profit institutions or associations that want to improve the future of education, such as focusing on technology or new generations, can use this research to get ideas for their educational communication and marketing plans.

*5.3. Limitations and Future Research*

The limitations of the research are related to the size of the sample and the time horizon analyzed, as well as the credibility of the UGC limited to the Twitter social network. This study can be expanded by focusing on the combined study of several social networks in which a GCE is shared, such as Facebook, Instagram, YouTube, TripAdvisor, or Booking.com. In addition, there are also limitations regarding the number of methodologies used and the approximations carried out by researchers according to the number of findings consulted to carry out this study. In the present study, because of the chosen analysis techniques, we analyzed only the text, excluding emoticons. Therefore, in future research, it would be necessary to use mixed analysis methods based on NLP and iconographic methods so as to enrich the results.

In addition, the use of SVM that work with machine learning must be taken into account; a technique that is constantly improving and that may have failures in measuring the results as it improves over time and the number of samples trained. Finally, within the developed processes of LDA and TA there are exploratory steps analyzed manually by the researchers that could have implied some failure in the measurement or analysis.

**Author Contributions:** Conceptualization, J.R.S., A.R.-M. and D.R.B.; Methodology, J.R.S.; Software J.R.S.; Formal Analysis, A.R.-M. and D.R.B.; Investigation, J.R.S., A.R.-M. and D.R.B; Data Curation, J.R.S. and A.R.-M.; Writing—Original Draft Preparation, J.R.S., A.R.-M. and D.R.B.; Writing—Review & Editing, J.R.S., A.R.-M. and D.R.B.; Visualization, J.R.S.; Supervision, J.R.S., A.R.-M. and D.R.B.

**Funding:** This research received no external funding.

**Acknowledgments:** This article is a scientific result of the contract signed under the protection of Article 83 signed between the Rey Juan Carlos University and the Institute of Business Executives (IDE-CESEM) with reference code 2019/00054/001 entitled: "Los nuevos retos e la formación de postgraodo (on line) en el ámbito de la economía de la empresa y el marketing".

**Conflicts of Interest:** The authors declare no conflict of interest.

## References

1. Reyes-Menendez, A.; Saura, J.R.; Martinez-Navalon, J.G. The impact of e-WOM on Hotels Management Reputation: Exploring TripAdvisor Review Credibility with the ELM model. *IEEE Access* **2019**, *8*. [CrossRef]
2. Saura, J.R.; Bennett, D.R. A Three-Stage method for Data Text Mining: Using UGC in Business Intelligence Analysis. *Symmetry* **2019**, *11*, 519. [CrossRef]
3. Matta, J.; Obafemi-Ajayi, T.; Borwey, J.; Sinha, K.; Wunsch, D.; Ercal, G. Node-Based Resilience Measure Clustering with Applications to Noisy and Overlapping Communities in Complex Networks. *Appl. Sci.* **2018**, *8*, 1307. [CrossRef]
4. Wiemer, H.; Drowatzky, L.; Ihlenfeldt, S. Data Mining Methodology for Engineering Applications (DMME)—A Holistic Extension to the CRISP-DM Model. *Appl. Sci.* **2019**, *9*, 2407. [CrossRef]
5. Van den Broek-Altenburg, E.M.; Atherly, A.J. Using Social Media to Identify Consumers' Sentiments towards Attributes of Health Insurance during Enrollment Season. *Appl. Sci.* **2019**, *9*, 2035. [CrossRef]
6. Herráez, B.; Bustamante, D.; Saura, J.R. Information classification on social networks. Content analysis of e-commerce companies on Twitter. *Rev. Espac.* **2017**, *38*, 16.
7. Saura, J.R.; Rodriguez Herráez, B.; Reyes-Menendez, A. Comparing a traditional approach for financial Brand Communication Analysis with a Big Data Analytics technique. *IEEE Access* **2019**, *7*. [CrossRef]
8. Barbu, M.; Vilanova, R.; Vicario, J.; Pereira, M.J.; Alves, P.; Podpora, M.; Fontana, L. Data mining tool for academic data exploitation: Publication report on engineering students profiles. *ESTiG-Relatórios Técnicos/Científicos* **2019**.

9. Siemens, G.; Baker, R.S.J. DLearning analytics and educational data mining: Towards communication and collaboration. In Proceedings of the 2nd International Conference on Learning Analytics and Knowledge, Vancouver, BC, Canada, 29 April–2 May 2019; pp. 252–254.
10. Wang, Y.; Youn, H.Y. Feature Weighting Based on Inter-Category and Intra-Category Strength for Twitter Sentiment Analysis. *Appl. Sci.* **2019**, *9*, 92. [CrossRef]
11. Reyes-Menendez, A.; Saura, J.R.; Alvarez-Alonso, C. Understanding# World Environment Day User Opinions in Twitter: A Topic-Based Sentiment Analysis Approach. *Int. J. Environ. Res. Public Health.* **2018**, *15*, 2537. [CrossRef]
12. Reyes-Menendez, A.; Saura, J.R.; Palos-Sanchez Alvarez, J.M. Understanding User Behavioral Intention to adopt a Search Engine that promotes Sustainable Water Management. *Symmetry* **2018**, *10*, 584. [CrossRef]
13. Romero, C.; Ventura, S. Educational data mining: A review of the state of the art. *IEEE Trans. Syst. Man Cybern. Part C* **2010**, *40*, 601–618. [CrossRef]
14. Glaser, R. Education and thinking: The role of knowledge. *Am. Psychol.* **1984**, *39*, 93. [CrossRef]
15. George, E.S. Positioning higher education for the knowledge based economy. *High. Educ.* **2006**, *52*, 589–610. [CrossRef]
16. Bennett, D.; Yábar, D.P.B.; Saura, J.R. University Incubators May Be Socially Valuable, but How Effective Are They? A Case Study on Business Incubators at Universities. In *Entrepreneurial Universities. Innovation, Technology, and Knowledge Management*; Peris-Ortiz, M., Gómez, J., Merigó-Lindahl, J., Rueda-Armengot, C., Eds.; Springer: Cham, Switzerland, 2017. [CrossRef]
17. Shelton, M.W.; Lane, D.R.; Waldhart, E.S. A review and assessment of national educational trends in communication instruction. *Commun. Educ.* **1999**, *48*, 228–237. [CrossRef]
18. Reyes, J.A. The skinny on big data in education: Learning analytics simplified. *TechTrends* **2015**, *59*, 75–80. [CrossRef]
19. Anshari, M.; Alas, Y.; Sabtu, N.P.H.; Hamid, M.S.A. Online Learning: Trends, issues and challenges in the Big Data Era. *J. e-Learn. Knowl. Soc.* **2016**, *12*.
20. Huda, M.; Maseleno, A.; Atmotiyoso, P.; Siregar, M.; Ahmad, R.; Jasmi, K.; Muhamad, N. Big data emerging technology: Insights into innovative environment for online learning resources. *Int. J. Emerg. Technol. Learn.* **2018**, *13*, 23–36. [CrossRef]
21. Sin, K.; Muthu, L. Application of Big Data in Education Data Mining and Learning Analytics—A Literature Review. *ICTACT J. Soft Comput.* **2015**, *5*. [CrossRef]
22. Pang, B.; Lee, L. A sentimental education: Sentiment analysis using subjectivity summarization based on minimum cuts. In Proceedings of the 42nd annual meeting on Association for Computational Linguistics, Barcelona, Spain, 21–26 July 2004; p. 271.
23. Kogan, M. Higher education communities and academic identity. *High. Educ. Q.* **2000**, *54*, 207–216. [CrossRef]
24. Jongbloed, B.; Enders, J.; Salerno, C. Higher education and its communities: Interconnections, interdependencies and a research agenda. *High. Educ.* **2008**, *56*, 303–324. [CrossRef]
25. La Velle, L.; Kendall, A. Building Research-Informed Teacher Education Communities: A UCET Framework. *Profession* **2019**, *18*, 19.
26. Reyes-Menendez, A.; Saura, J.R.; Filipe, F. The importance of behavioral data to identify online fake reviews for tourism businesses: A systematic review. *PeerJ Comput. Sci.* **2019**, *5*, e219. [CrossRef]
27. Baker, R.S.J.D. Data mining for education. *Int. Encycl. Educ.* **2010**, *7*, 112–118.
28. Alban, M.; Mauricio, D. Predicting University Dropout through Data Mining: A Systematic Literature. *Indian J. Sci. Technol.* **2019**, *12*, 4. [CrossRef]
29. Williamson, B.; Piattoeva, N. Objectivity as standardization in data-scientific education policy, technology and governance. *Learn. Media Technol.* **2019**, *44*, 64–76. [CrossRef]
30. Zou, X.; Zou, S.; Wang, X. New Approach of Big Data and Education: Any Term Must Be in the Characters Chessboard as a Super Matrix. In Proceedings of the 2019 International Conference on Big Data and Education, Bangkok, Thailand, 14–16 September 2019; pp. 129–134.
31. Daniel, B.K. Big Data and data science: A critical review of issues for educational research. *Br. J. Educ. Technol.* **2019**, *50*, 101–113. [CrossRef]
32. Krippendorff, K. Bivariate Agreement Coefficients for Reliability Data. *Sociol. Methodol.* **1970**, *2*, 139–150. [CrossRef]

33. Krippendorff, K. Measuring the reliability of qualitative text analysis data. *Qual. Quant.* **2004**, *38*, 787–800. [CrossRef]
34. Saura, J.R.; Reyes-Menendez, A.; Alvarez-Alonso, C. Do online comments affect environmental management? Identifying factors related to environmental management and sustainability of hotels. *Sustainability* **2018**, *10*, 3016. [CrossRef]
35. Blondel, V.D.; Guillaume, J.; Lambiotte, R.; Lefebvre, E. Fast unfolding of communities in large networks. *J. Stat. Mech.* **2008**, *2008*. [CrossRef]
36. Lambiotte, R.; Delvenne, J.C.; Barahona, M. Random walks, Markov processes and the multiscale modular organization of complex networks. *IEEE Trans. Netw. Sci. Eng.* **2014**, *1*, 76–90. [CrossRef]
37. Saura, J.R.; Reyes-Menendez, A.; Palos-Sanchez, P. Are Black Friday Deals Worth It? *Mining Twitter Users' Sentiment and Behavior Response. J. Open Innov.* **2019**, *5*, 58.
38. Sherman, K.J.; Cherkin, D.C.; Erro, J.; Miglioretti, D.L.; Deyo, R.A. Comparing yoga, exercise, and a self-care book for chronic low back pain: A randomized, controlled trial. *Ann. Intern. Med.* **2005**, *143*, 849–856. [CrossRef] [PubMed]
39. Banerjee, S.; Chua, A.Y.; Kim, J. Using supervised learning to classify authentic and fake online reviews. In Proceedings of the 9th International Conference on Ubiquitous Information Management and Communication—IMCOM, Bali, Indonesia, 8–10 January 2015.
40. Saura, J.R.; Palos-Sanchez, P.R.; Grilo, A. Detecting Indicators for Startup Business Success: Sentiment Analysis using Text Data Mining. *Sustainability* **2019**, *15*, 553. [CrossRef]
41. Bifet, A.; Frank, E. Sentiment knowledge discovery in twitter streaming data. In Proceedings of the International Conference on Discovery Science, Canberra, Australia, 6–8 October 2010.
42. Lai, L.S.; To, W.M. Content analysis of social media: A grounded theory approach. *J. Electron. Commer. Res.* **2015**, *16*, 138.
43. Pritchard, J.K.; Stephens, M.; Donnelly, P. Inference of population structure using multilocus genotype data. *Genetics* **2000**, *155*, 945–959.
44. Blei, D.M.; Ng, A.Y.; Jordan, M.I.; Lafferty, J. Latent Dirichlet Allocation. *J. Mach. Learn. Res.* **2003**, *3*, 993–1022.
45. Jia, S. Leisure Motivation and Satisfaction: A Text Mining of Yoga Centres, Yoga Consumers, and Their Interactions. *Sustainability* **2018**, *10*, 4458. [CrossRef]
46. Saif, H.; Fernandez, M.; He, Y.; Alani, H. Evaluation datasets for Twitter sentiment analysis: A survey and a new dataset, the STS-Gold. In Proceedings of the 1st Interantional Workshop on Emotion and Sentiment in Social and Expressive Media: Approaches and Perspectives from AI (ESSEM 2013), Turin, Italy, 3 December 2013.
47. Pang, B.; Lee, L. Opinion mining and sentiment analysis. *Found. Trends® Inf. Retr.* **2008**, *2*, 1–135. [CrossRef]
48. Saura, J.R.; Reyes-Menendez, A.; Filipe, F. Comparing Data-Driven Methods for Extracting Knowledge from User Generated Content. *J. Open Innov. Technol. Mark. Complex.* **2019**, *5*, 74. [CrossRef]
49. Krippendorff, K. (Ed.) Reliability Chapter 11. In *Content Analysis; An Introduction to its Methodology*, 2nd ed.; Sage Publications: Thousand Oaks, CA, USA, 2004; pp. 211–256.
50. Krippendorff, K. *Content Analysis: An Introduction to Its Methodology*, 3rd ed.; Sage: Thousand Oaks, CA, USA, 2013; pp. 221–250.
51. Gil, M.; El Sherif, R.; Pluye, M.; Fung, B.C.; Grad, R.; Pluye, P. Towards a Knowledge-Based Recommender System for Linking Electronic Patient Records with Continuing Medical Education Information at the Point of Care. *IEEE Access* **2019**, *7*, 15955–15966. [CrossRef]
52. Al-Rahmi, W.M.; Yahaya, N.; Aldraiweesh, A.A.; Alturki, U.; Alamri, M.M.; Saud, M.S.B.; Alhamed, O.A. Big Data Adoption and Knowledge Management Sharing: An Empirical Investigation on Their Adoption and Sustainability as a Purpose of Education. *IEEE Access* **2019**, *7*, 47245–47258. [CrossRef]
53. Fernandes, E.; Holanda, M.; Victorino, M.; Borges, V.; Carvalho, R.; Van Erven, G. Educational data mining: Predictive analysis of academic performance of public school students in the capital of Brazil. *J. Bus. Res.* **2019**, *94*, 335–343. [CrossRef]
54. West, D.M. Big data for education: Data mining, data analytics, and web dashboards. *Gov. Stud. Brook.* **2012**, *4*.
55. Jabreel, M.; Moreno, A. A Deep Learning-Based Approach for Multi-Label Emotion Classification in Tweets. *Appl. Sci.* **2019**, *9*, 1123. [CrossRef]

56. Saura, J.R.; Palos-Sanchez, P.; Blanco-González, A. The importance of information service offerings of collaborative CRMs on decision-making in B2B marketing. *J. Bus. Ind. Mark.* **2019**. ahead-of-print(ahead-of-print). [CrossRef]
57. Vassileva, J. Toward social learning environments. *IEEE Trans. Learn. Technol.* **2008**, *1*, 199–214. [CrossRef]
58. Novak, J.; Wurst, M. Collaborative knowledge visualization for cross-community learning. In *Knowledge and Information Visualization*; Springer: Berlin/Heidelberg, Germany, 2005; pp. 95–116.
59. Chen, B.J.; Ting, I.H. Applying social networks analysis methods to discover key users in an interest-oriented virtual community. In *7th International Conference on Knowledge Management in Organizations: Service and Cloud Computing*; Springer: Berlin/Heidelberg, Germany, 2013; pp. 333–344.
60. Tsvetovat, M.; Kouznetsov, A. *Social Network Analysis for Startups: Finding Connections on the Social Web*; O'Reilly Media, Inc.: Sevastopol, CA, USA, 2011.
61. Wilson, T.; Wiebe, J.; Hoffmann, P. Recognizing contextual polarity in phrase-level sentiment analysis. In Proceedings of the Human Language Technology Conference and Conference on Empirical Methods in Natural Language Processing, Lisboa, Portugal, 17 September 2005.
62. Mazzoni, E. Social Network Analysis to support interactions in virtual communities for the construction of knowledge. *Ital. J. Educ. Technol.* **2005**, *13*, 54.
63. Liu, B. Sentiment Analysis and Subjectivity. *Handb. Nat. Lang. Process.* **2010**, *2*, 627–666.
64. Liu, B.; Zhang, L. A survey of opinion mining and sentiment analysis. In *Mining Text Data*; Springer: Boston, MA, USA, 2012; pp. 415–463.
65. McLoughlin, C.; Lee, M. Mapping the digital terrain: New media and social software as catalysts for pedagogical change. *Ascilite Melb.* **2008**, *12*, 641–652.
66. Quercia, D.; Ellis, J.; Capra, L.; Crowcroft, J. Tracking gross community happiness from tweets. In Proceedings of the ACM 2012 Conference on Computer Supported Cooperative Work, Washington, DC, USA, 11–15 February 2012.
67. Sluban, B.; Smailović, J.; Battiston, S.; Mozetič, I. Sentiment leaning of influential communities in social networks. *Comput. Soc. Netw.* **2015**, *2*, 9. [CrossRef]
68. Brush, T.; Glazewski, K.D.; Hew, K.F. Development of an instrument to measure preservice teachers' technology skills, technology beliefs, and technology barriers. *Comput. Sch.* **2008**, *25*, 112–125. [CrossRef]
69. Bonk, C.J. *The World is Open: How Web Technology is Revolutionizing Education*; Association for the Advancement of Computing in Education (AACE): Morgantown, WV, USA, 2009; pp. 3371–3380.
70. Goh, K.Y.; Heng, C.S.; Lin, Z. Social media brand community and consumer behavior: Quantifying the relative impact of user-and marketer-generated content. *Inf. Syst. Res.* **2013**, *24*, 88–107. [CrossRef]
71. Yannopoulou, N.; Moufahim, M.; Bian, X. User-generated brands and social media: Couchsurfing and AirBnb. *Contemp. Manag. Res.* **2013**, *9*. [CrossRef]
72. Christensen, C.M.; Eyring, H.J. *The Innovative University: Changing the DNA of Higher Education from the Inside Out*; John Wiley & Sons: Hoboken, NJ, USA, 2011.
73. Pereira, E.T.; Villas-Boas, M.; Rebelo, C.C. Does Entrepreneurship and Innovative Education Matter to Increase Employability Skills?: A Framework Based on the Evidence From Five European Countries. In *Global Considerations in Entrepreneurship Education and Training*; IGI Global: Hershey, PA, USA, 2019; pp. 218–231.

© 2019 by the authors. Licensee MDPI, Basel, Switzerland. This article is an open access article distributed under the terms and conditions of the Creative Commons Attribution (CC BY) license (http://creativecommons.org/licenses/by/4.0/).

Article

# Short CFD Simulation Activities in the Context of Fluid-Mechanical Learning in a Multidisciplinary Student Body

Manuel Rodríguez-Martín [1,*], Pablo Rodríguez-Gonzálvez [2], Alberto Sánchez-Patrocinio [1] and Javier Ramón Sánchez [3]

1. Department of Mechanical Engineering, Universidad de Salamanca, 37008 Salamanca, Spain; aspatrocinio@usal.es
2. Department of Mining Technology, Topography and Structures, Universidad de León, 24071 León, Spain; p.rodriguez@unileon.es
3. Department of Chemical and Textile Engineering, Universidad de Salamanca, 37008 Salamanca, Spain; jrsm@usal.es
* Correspondence: ingmanuel@usal.es; Tel.: +34-923-408080

Received: 29 October 2019; Accepted: 8 November 2019; Published: 10 November 2019

**Featured Application: Improved training of engineers in the industrial branch and instruction of students in fluid simulation tools.**

**Abstract:** Simulation activities are a useful tool to improve competence in industrial engineering bachelors. Specifically, fluid simulation allows students to acquire important skills to strengthen their theoretical knowledge and improve their future professional career. However, these tools usually require long training times and they are usually not available in the subjects of B.Sc. degrees. In this article, a new methodology based on short lessons is raised and evaluated in the fluid-mechanical subject for students enrolled in three different bachelor degree groups: B.Sc. in Mechanical Engineering, B.Sc. in Electrical Engineering and B.Sc. in Electronic and Automatic Engineering. Statistical results show a good acceptance in terms of usability, learning, motivation, thinking over, satisfaction and scalability. Additionally, a machine-learning based approach was applied to find group peculiarities and differences among them in order to identify the need for further personalization of the learning activity.

**Keywords:** Computational Fluid Dynamic (CFD); fluid-mechanics; teaching-learning; engineering education; computer applications; classification problem; machine learning

## 1. Introduction

Computational strategies such as Computational Fluid Dynamic (CFD) are usually applied to simulate fluids (gas and liquids) to obtain different physical variables such as pressure, velocity, mass rate, turbulence energy, temperature, turbulence intensity, vorticity, and others. Based-on CFD applications work over a computational domain using partial differential equations (PDE) and ordinary differential equations (ODE) to describe the relationship among different physical variables to understand the characteristics of fluid flow. The specific applications of the method can be very diverse, depending on the objectives of the analysis, the required accuracy and other factors, such as computing times (which can be high, namely, from hours to days) [1]. The main applications of CFD encompass aerodynamic analyses, multi-phase flows, transport, compressible flows, phenomena and chemical processes involving transfer heat phenomenon, dissipative phenomenon, rotary, mixing of different fluids and chemical reactions [1–5].

Furthermore, specific CFD software can be difficult to handle and, sometimes, unintuitive for students without previous experience. Carrying out processing tasks using CFD can become a long, hard and intense work when it is performed for specific applications [1], for example, optimization [3,6], model calibration [7], sensitivity analysis and consequence analysis [8]).

As it is established in [9], within the CFD context, the Finite Volume Method (FVM) is a specific numerical iterative technique that involves partial differential equations (mainly representing conservation laws) applied over differential volumes. This discretization process is similar to the Finite Element Method (FEM) [9]. The meshing procedure is highly important in the FVM method because it strongly affects the accuracy and stability of the flow predictions [10]. The meshing consists of the generation of a grid over the fluid computational domain. This grid can be generated for the computational model with different typologies (mainly structured, non-structured and hybrid) being a quality mesh essential for a quality simulation [11]. Through the mesh, the discretization of the volume is obtained and the partial differential equations are discretized into algebraic equations by integrating them over each discrete volume element. As a result, a discrete number of algebraic equations are established over a finite number of volumes from application of the meshing process to the whole study volume. These algebraic equations are solved as an algebraic equation system to calculate and compute the values of the dependent variable of each discrete volume element. An adequate mesh design is critical, since the accuracy of the results of the simulation process highly depends on how well the equation system or the mathematical model captures the flow physics [1].

*1.1. CFD Method in the Learning Context*

The CFD method has been used as a teaching resource for university studies, specifically, for undergraduate courses in engineering [12–14]. Nevertheless, simulation methods such as CFD and FEM are frequently offered as specific elective course in many academic institutions around the world for the acquisition of competence in simulation [1]. However, the assimilation of the learning of these types of tools involves long training times and it could be an impediment in the context of basic courses in engineering programs, considering the usual intensity of the scholarship for students and professors [15]. In this way, specific strategies can be used to integrate CFD in basic courses in engineering, specifically in the fluid-mechanics course [15].

The calculation of energy losses in pipes is an important skill which students must achieve in the fluid-mechanical course. Pressure drop in a pipe system is caused by fluid rising in elevation, shaft work, friction, and turbulence from sudden changes in direction or cross-sectional area [16]. Specifically, the calculation and application of pressure loss coefficients for different pipe sizes is important to calculate the energy loss and pressure drop in pipes and specific hydraulic elements installed in the line and, in this way, determine important parameters for engineering tasks, such as determining the correct pump size [17]. A summary of the published literature about pipes fitting in the learning context is established in [1]. When the pipe has a complex internal geometry or specific elements are installed in the pipelines (nozzles, valves, elbows, filters, etc.), the energy losses can be obtained experimentally or through simulation tools such as CFD. However, pressure drop in singular elements can be also calculated using empirical tables and/or graphics, available in the literature (e.g., [11]). Unfortunately, the casuistry of this method based on the literature is reduced for several reasons: Limited number of head loss elements and also limited since ideal conditions are considered as ideal geometries for the elements, single-phase flow, Newtonian fluids, no consideration of the material type of the solids, etc. [15]. However, fluid-mechanical industry problems are sometimes more complex, including multiple phases, complex boundary conditions and complex geometry of the volume. These problems cannot be addressed using only the classic equations and empirical tables and/or graphics; nevertheless, they can be addressed using computer methods based on CFD. Thus, it is important that students, as future professionals, understand the scope and significance of this issue and the limitations of theoretical methods explained in the classroom [15].

Students tend to identify pressure drop with the concept of pressure drop "in line" (caused by friction with respect to the pipe). However, pressure drop is a wider concept which includes the local pressure loss caused by specific elements located in the fluid line, such as contractions or expansions, valves, etc. Due to this simplification of a complex reality, students sometimes ignore the fact that pressure drop can be caused by apparently insignificant anomalies in the geometry of the pipeline.

Teaching this concept in a laboratory using experimental equipment is often expensive because some sophisticated stations and instruments are required [1]. Taking into account the high economic cost of the specific instrumentation, the amount of time spent doing the experimental tasks with the students, and operational limitations (e.g., presence of large groups of students) justifies the creation of virtual laboratory resources to support teaching activities [18]. These initiatives share many objectives with respect to simulation activities, insofar as they replace or complement experimental laboratory lessons. Besides, CFD could be an adequate tool to explain concepts that complement the theoretical classes to understand the pressure drop phenomenon, while we are providing the student with very useful software skills which can be important for their future professional career. The fluid-mechanical course is a subject common to all engineering degrees in the industrial teaching program, but, as has been mentioned, learning times for the CFD method of the tool are normally long. Concurrently, machine-learning based methodologies have shown great potential for pattern recognition and predicting results for multiple types of datasets, in spite of the field using supervised algorithms for most of these works. The results of these methods can be incorporated into the decision-making process [19], even for strategic decision making at higher educational institutions [20], predicting the performance of the students in blended learning [21] or prediction of early dropout [22].

*1.2. Research Question*

The research question can be divided in two parts: First, we want to know if the specific use of short practical activities using the CFD module of Solidworks® [23] is appropriate for the goals raised. Mainly, we want to know whether its use is adequate in terms of usability, satisfaction scalability, learning, thinking over and motivation, which are the most analyzed issues in education [24–26]. Please note that we study the activity's motivation since it is linked with academic performance [27]).

Secondly, by means of a machine-learning approach, we want to know whether the response to the activity is independent of the bachelor's degree of origin or, on the contrary, there are questionnaire response patterns. The presence of a pattern that differentiates the activity's response depending on the bachelor degree will justify future modification to adapt the learning activity.

## 2. Academic Context of the Research and Sample

This research was implemented in the fluid-mechanical subject. This subject is established as mandatory in the second year for the following three bachelor degrees: Mechanical Engineering, Electrical Engineering and Electronical and Automatic Engineering, at the Higher Technical School of Industrial Engineering of Béjar of the University of Salamanca (Spain).

The specific competences (Table 1) of the subject are based on the Spanish regulation [28] which derives from the regulations of the European Higher Education Area (EHEA). The three degrees belong to the industrial engineering field (Figure 1), so the first two courses are common for the three bachelor's degrees while the last two courses are considered as specialization courses and they are different for each one. Some colleges offer double degrees. In this case, students enrolled in the double degree in Electrical and Mechanical Engineering are contemplated in the sample. According to Spanish regulations for the engineers, some engineering tasks can be done indistinctly by any of the engineers of the industrial field, while other more specialized tasks can be done specifically by only one of them (e.g., under Spanish regulation, electrical low voltage projects can be carried out by any industrial engineer, but high voltage projects can only be carried out by electrical engineers). Please note that the B.Sc. in Chemical Engineering is not offered by the High School of Industrial Engineering of the University of Salamanca, so it was not analyzed in the present work.

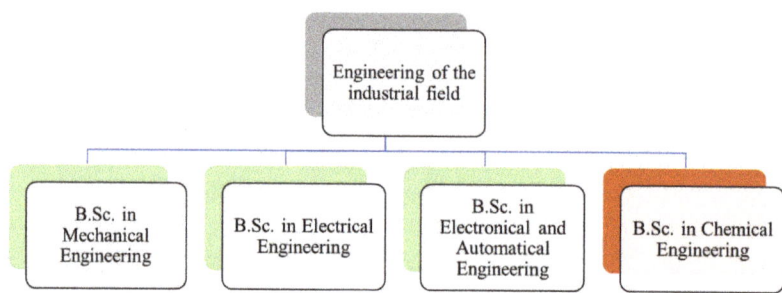

**Figure 1.** Different bachelor degrees belonging to the industrial engineering field. The studies B.Sc are marked in green.

**Table 1.** Competences for the fluid-mechanical subject, common for the three bachelor degrees addressed.

| Competence | Type | Code [29] |
|---|---|---|
| Knowledge of the basic principles of fluid-mechanics and their application to solving problems in the field of engineering. Calculation of pipes, channels and fluid systems. | Specific | CC2 |
| Knowledge and skills for calculating, designing and testing machines. | Specific | CE2 |
| Applied knowledge of the fundamentals of fluid-mechanical systems and machines. | Specific | CE6 |
| Capacity for analysis and synthesis. | Basic | GI1 |
| Basic knowledge of the profession. | Basic | IG4 |
| Problem solving. | Basic | IG8 |
| Ability to apply knowledge in practice. | Basic | GS1 |
| Ability to plan and organize personal work. | Transversal | CT1 |
| Capacity for analysis, criticism, synthesis, evaluation and problem solving. | Transversal | CT6 |

The research was addressed over a sample of 59 students of the fluid-mechanical subject. In spite of the fact that the students came from different grades, they were grouped together in the same classroom since it is a common subject. The distribution of the sample is shown in Table 2.

**Table 2.** Distribution of the sample of 59 students.

| Degree Program | ECTS | Students | |
|---|---|---|---|
| | | Number | Percentage of Study Case |
| B.Sc. in Mechanical Engineering. | 240 | 27 | 45.8% |
| B.Sc. in Electrical Engineering. | 240 | 15 | 25.4% |
| B.Sc. in Electronic and Automatic Engineering | 240 | 12 | 20.3% |
| Double Degree. | 276 | 5 | 8.5% |

## 3. Materials and Methods

### 3.1. Materials

In [15], a previous requirement and potentialities study about the learning activity was raised. As a result, Solidworks® [23] was chosen as teaching software. It is a CAD/CAM/CAE commercial package software with extensive functionalities within the context of mechanical engineering. In summary, this software was chosen for three reasons: (i) Ease of use of the CFD module compared to other CFD software alternatives. The simplicity of use was established as a critical factor to reduce the time assigned for the activity (please note that one of the factors which will be evaluated is the usability); (ii) the object's geometry can be modeled using the same software in an easy way without the need to use other applications, saving time; (iii) the software can be used in other subjects and by other professors in their teaching. Solidworks® was installed in one of the computer classrooms of the Higher Technical School of Industrial Engineering, which is equipped with individual work station posts.

Additionally, to distribute the different activity materials to the students, the documents and files were uploaded to the institutional Learning Management System (LMS) of the University of Salamanca (*Studium*).

*3.2. Methods*

A specific methodology to evaluate the performance of the activity in different terms was raised for this research in an ad hoc manner (Figure 2). The different phases of the methodology will be described in the following paragraphs.

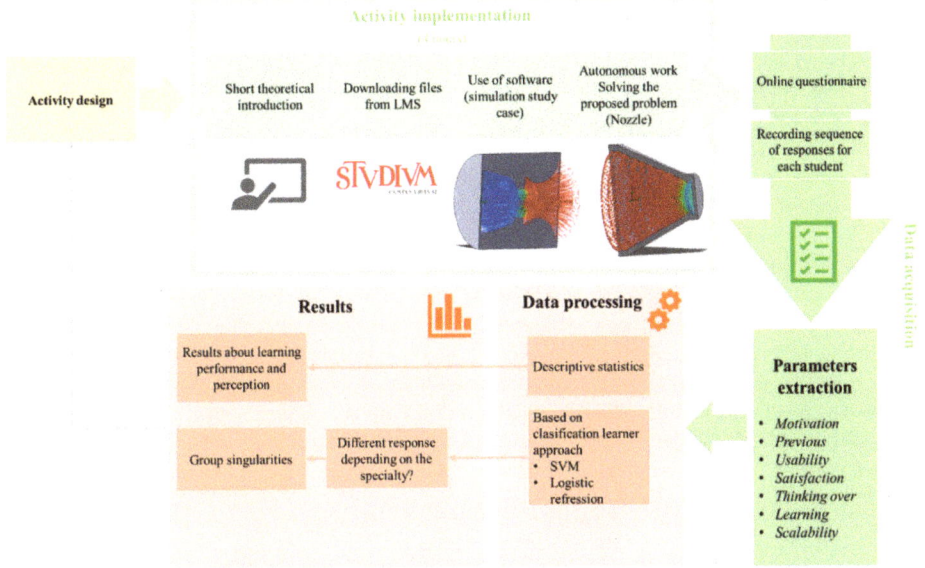

**Figure 2.** Ad hoc methodology proposed for the present research.

3.2.1. Activity Design and Completion

The learning activity was designed through a deep reflection under three important criteria, which were established as a reference for the creation of the learning resources and virtual models for the activity: Quality, economy and reality criteria [15]. These were established in the literature for the virtual environments [18,29,30] and, as has been previously indicated, the authors consider that simulation tasks share objectives and needs with respect to virtual laboratories: The common mission to provide to the student a practical vision about the physical phenomena without using, or complementing, a real laboratory for experimental tasks. According to the reality criterion, the activity is intended to be clear enough to simulate a real behavior of the fluid with adequate visualization results, based on the study of trajectories or particles, as well as maps of the distribution of different variables. The economy criterion refers to the balance between available resources and needs. In this respect, it is required for the simulation process to be as short as possible, so there is no wasted time in computation tasks. This is due to the high concentration of activities that must be completed in the subject and the fact that the simulation process has to be carried out entirely using the available workstations, without acquiring new ones. Toward this goal, various preliminary tests were carried out by the authors to find the simulation case that balanced processing times and results accuracy and met these conditions without affecting the other criteria. The processing times obtained for an adequate accuracy were between 180 and 350 s. Finally, the quality criterion implies that the results have an acceptable accuracy for learning tasks, and all the resources and documents necessary for the activity and for its evaluation can be distributed in LMS (please note that the upload file size limitation is a considered constraint parameter for the activity design).

Due to the proposed reflection, the activity was designed in four phases. Students were divided into two heterogeneous groups in order to achieve a better teacher-student ratio. The same activity was carried out with each of the groups in consecutive weeks. The first three phases (Figure 2) were oriented to the explanation of the activity and the basic concepts: Firstly, a short theoretical lesson about the CFD method was explained; next, students downloaded from the LMS the archives and documents for the activity; and finally, a simulation of an irregular conduit (Figure 3) was presented by the professor while the students were following the steps at the same time.

The fourth phase (Figure 2) was oriented to the autonomous work of the student (practical case), which consisted of the simulation of two hydraulic nozzle models: Smooth and obstructed ones. The obstructed hydraulic nozzle model was designed with respect to the smooth one to compare the obtained results for the two simulations and to compare those with the theoretical results obtained with the Bernoulli equation.

A hydraulic nozzle is really a single hydraulic device used to increment the velocity of the incompressible fluid through a reduction of the effective section. When the nozzle is smooth and clean, the fluid flows in the usual way, following a behavior close to the Bernoulli equation, which is established under ideal flow conditions in the absence of dissipative phenomena. Nevertheless, if the nozzle has an obstructed zone, a significant pressure drop is generated and, in this way, the velocity, pressure, turbulence and other parameters of the fluid differ from the results obtained using the Bernoulli equation for the same initial parameters. Therefore, this situation allows the students to think about the limitations of theoretical methods with respect to experimental methods. Please note that the design of the obstructed nozzle model does not respond to a real case but is an example that has been generated so that the simulation activity would meet the criteria indicated above. The parameters for the simulation indicated to the students in the problem statement are shown in Table 3 and all of them have been established to accomplish the established criteria for the creation of learning resources.

**Table 3.** Simulation setting established for the autonomous work of the students.

| Simulation Setting | |
|---|---|
| Parameter | Value/Description |
| Fluid | Water (Solidworks Newtonian fluid library) |
| Temperature (K) | 293.2 |
| Static pressure inlet (Pa) | 301,325 |
| Static pressure outlet (Pa) | 101,325 |
| Solid material | Steal Stainless 302 (Solidworks® material library) |
| Roughness (µm) | 15 |
| Mesh | Structured (tetrahedral) |
| Mesh refinement level | 5 |
| Turbulence intensity | 2% |
| Turbulence length (mm) | 38 |
| Simulation configuration | Heat transfer consideration Automatic type flow (laminar/turbulent) |

The activity was implemented in the classroom following the established plan for four hours, of which 200 min were used in the students' autonomous work. Two professors were present during the activity, observing the behavior of the students and resolving any doubts they may have. The professor–student rate was 15 students per professor.

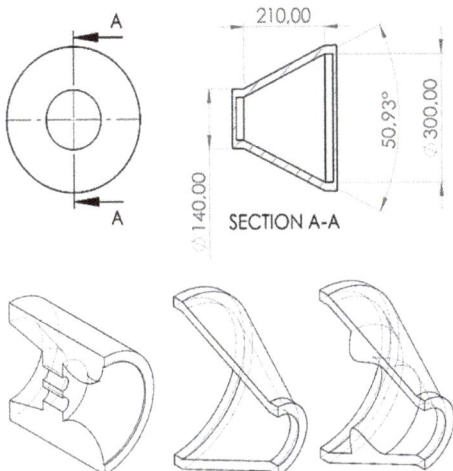

**Figure 3.** Above: Geometrical features of the nozzle. Below: Irregular conduit used for the study case developed in the classroom (left). The two nozzles used for the autonomous work of the student (center and right).

3.2.2. Data Gathering

Once the activity was implemented in the classroom, the data gathering process was carried out to obtain the results to evaluate the suitability and acceptance of the learning activity. An anonymous online questionnaire, which can be fulfilled in 5 min, was designed. The questions are shown in Table 4. The response type is yes/no for the three first questions and for the rest a Likert scale is used [18,29,30]. For the analysis, each question was grouped into one of the categories described in Table 5. The complete pattern of responses for each student was obtained anonymously.

**Table 4.** Questionnaire items.

| ID | Response | Category | Question |
|---|---|---|---|
| P1 | Yes/No | Pretest | Have you used any CFD tools before? |
| P2 | Yes/No | Pretest | Have you used mechanical design tools like Solidworks, Inventor or similar before? |
| P3 | Yes/No | Pretest | Did you previously know the CFD method for fluid analysis? |
| Q1 | 1–5 | Previous (informatic) | I consider that my level of computer knowledge is high. |
| Q2 | 1–5 | Satisfaction | I believe that the practice with CFD software has been satisfactory. |
| Q3 | 1–5 | Usability | I think it is a good practice to explain the use of CFD tools in the classroom. |
| Q4 | 1–5 | Previous (perception) | Before activity, I had the idea that handling such applications was complicated. |
| Q5 | 1–5 | Usability | I think the software handling is easy. |
| Q6 | 1–5 | Learning | The information provided by the program is enough to know the behavior of fluids. |
| Q7 | 1–5 | Learning | This practice has helped me to strengthen the theoretical knowledge taught in class. |
| Q8 | 1–5 | Learning | This practice has helped me to strengthen the practical knowledge taught in the laboratory. |

Table 4. *Cont.*

| ID | Response | Category | Question |
|---|---|---|---|
| Q9 | 1–5 | Thinking over | The activity has made me realize that the theoretical equations do not always correspond to reality. |
| Q10 | 1–5 | Learning | I believe that after doing this practice I have learned more about fluid mechanics. |
| Q11 | 1–5 | Motivation | I would like to do more activities of this kind in class. |
| Q12 | 1–5 | Scalability | I think that activities like this, based on simulation, should also be applied in other subjects. |

Table 5. Categories evaluated through the questions and the description for each of them.

| Categories | Description |
|---|---|
| Pretest | Students' previous knowledge about the tools to be use. |
| Previous (informatic) | Knowledge of the level of ability and experience with the computer applications that the student believes he/she has. |
| Previous (perception) | Knowledge of the perception of the difficulty of the tools used. |
| Satisfaction | Conformity of the student with the activity carried out. |
| Usability | Perception of the level of difficulty of the program and whether its use in class is considered appropriate. |
| Learning | Level of academic achievement the student considers about the activity. |
| Thinking over | Measures whether the activity has awakened critical thinking in the student with respect to the contents explained in class, especially with respect the theoretical methods and their limitations. |
| Motivation | Student's intention to return to this type of activity in class. |
| Scalability | Student's perception of the use of similar tools in other subjects. |

3.2.3. Descriptive Statistical Analysis

The instrumentation applied was an online short questionnaire (Table 4) with two response types: A yes/no answer and a Likert scale. Twelve of the fifteen items of the questionnaire were designed based on a 5-point Likert scale [31]. All answers were raised in terms of the level of agreement (1-Strongly disagree, 2-Disagree, 3-Neither agree or disagree, 4-Agree, and 5-Strongly agree). The scale was chosen to seek simplicity and homogeneity in the answers so as not to generate erroneous or confused answers while making an accurate interpretation of the data.

The results for each question whose response is yes/no was statistically computed using the frequency of each response. The results for each question that used the Likert scale were statistically analyzed through the mean and standard deviation values. Parametric statistics were chosen as they are sufficiently robust to yield correct results when Likert scale answers are analyzed [32]. The same process was applied for the results obtained for the different categories: Average of the questions' answers for each category. For this analysis, the response of each student for each question was analyzed individually by means of a classic statistical approach; therefore, questionnaire response patterns are not taken into account in the descriptive analysis.

3.2.4. Based on ML Approach to Detect Group Characteristics

Once the descriptive analysis was addressed, differences of the mean values for each question among the different groups were identified. A machine-learning classification strategy was implemented to corroborate if there were differences between the responses to the activity for each group (Table 3). For this, the individual questionnaire response pattern of each student was included in the analysis.

The results obtained for each student are classified in function of the B.Sc. degree (mechanical, electrical and electronic, and automatic engineering) in order to analyze if the machine-learning classifier would be able to detect a significant pattern that allows us to classify each student to their degree in function of the questionnaire responses. The set of students' responses for each bachelor degree will be two-to-two compared using four different classification learners. These methods have been chosen based on the literature for similar cases [33] and also considering the adequacy of success indicators: Support machine vectors (SVM), logistic regression (habitually used in social sciences), random forest, and Bayesian network.

Firstly, SVMs are algorithms built on the theory of statistical learning aimed at minimizing structural risk. In pattern recognition, classification and regression analysis, it is expected that SVMs outperform other machine-learning methodologies [34]. An SVM is a discriminative classifier that looks for the optimal hyper plane that categorizes the training data. Secondly, the classifier based on logistic regression identifies specific parameters of the logistic function linked features with respect to binary target variables [33]. Its prediction function (logistic/sigmoid function) depicts the curvilinear relationship between the inputs and outputs. Therefore, the output's coefficients provide the relationship between a binary variable and several independent variables. Thirdly, random forest is an ensemble classifier that produces many classification and regression-like trees where each tree is generated from different bootstrapped samples of training data [35]. Random forest enables many weak or weakly-correlated classifiers to form a strong classifier [36]. Finally, the Bayesian network is one of the most effective classifiers [37] and is very useful tool to define logical relationships among variables in complex models. It is a probabilistic graphical model that expresses the relationships among a set of variables that quantify the links between variables based on their conditional probabilistic relationship [38].

For the machine learning analysis, the open software Weka [39] was used. Different training experiments were implemented in order to choose the most adequate prediction features and the optimum machine learning parameters. For the assessment of the classification $k$-fold cross-validation was employed, which splits the training data into $k$ equal-sized partitions [40]. If the applied machine learning algorithm can classify successfully, this implies that there is a questionnaire response pattern for each group (mechanical, electrical or electronic engineering). Namely, it will be possible to predict the student's degree as a function of the different measured characteristics.

The machine learning classification results are evaluated in terms of the overall accuracy, the Cohen's Kappa index and the receiving operating characteristic (ROC) curve area. The Kappa statistic measures the degree of agreement of categorized data [41]. It is defined in the range of −1–1, with zero being the expected value for a random classification, 1 being a perfect agreement, and negative values indicating no agreement, although they are unlikely in practice. The area under the ROC curve (AUC) provides a comparison between the predicted and actual instance values in a classification by measuring the precision and the recall [42]. It measures the probability that randomly chosen instances will be correctly classified. It is widely used for model comparison, since it describes the model performance for a complete range of classification thresholds. The ROC area is defined in the range 0–1, with 0.5 being the expected value for a random classification. Therefore, AUC values equal to or less than 0.5 imply that the classifier has an efficiency that is not superior to randomness, not being effective in this case.

## 4. Results

### 4.1. Descriptive Analysis

As the reader can see in Table 6, the 54.2% of students have worked previously using a parametric design application as Solidworks® or similar CAD tools, but only 10.2% of students had used a CFD method before. This means that for the majority of the sample, it is the first time that they used this technology, which excludes biases due to possible previous experiences. Considering the results of the previous answer, approximately half of students have used CAD/CAM/CAE tools for 3D design, but not for fluid simulation, although 91.5% of the students knew about the existence of CFD applications.

**Table 6.** Results of the pretest questions.

| Pretest Question | Yes | No |
|---|---|---|
| P1 | 6 (10.2%) | 53 (89.8%) |
| P2 | 32 (54.2%) | 27 (45.8%) |
| P3 | 54 (91.5%) | 5 (8.5%) |

The statistical results (mean and standard deviation) for each question are shown in Figure 4 and Table 7. It can be seen that the main values for all of the questions are above 3 out of 5, while the standard deviation values shows a low dispersion with respect to the mean value (close to 1 in all cases). This assessment is supported by the Z-test of the 66 possible combinations for the 12 questions, with a $p$-value always higher than 0.05 (95% confidence). Namely, there is no significant difference among all answers.

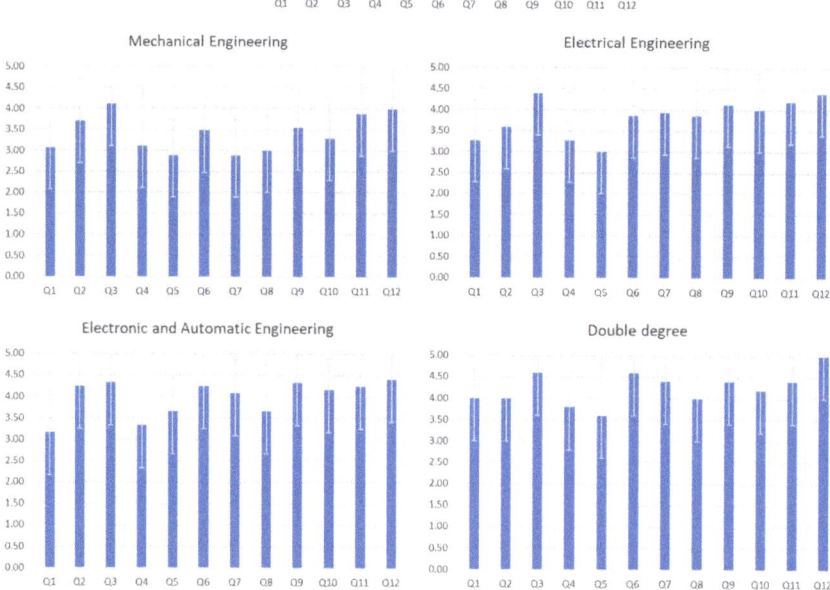

**Figure 4.** Results obtained for each raised question for all of the students (global results) and particularized for each bachelor degree.

Table 7. Statistical results of the rest of the questions.

| Question | Mean | Standard Deviation |
|---|---|---|
| Q1 | 3.22 | 0.892 |
| Q2 | 3.81 | 1.181 |
| Q3 | 4.27 | 0.784 |
| Q4 | 3.25 | 1.240 |
| Q5 | 3.14 | 0.937 |
| Q6 | 3.83 | 0.894 |
| Q7 | 3.53 | 1.006 |
| Q8 | 3.44 | 1.005 |
| Q9 | 3.93 | 0.907 |
| Q10 | 3.73 | 0.962 |
| Q11 | 4.08 | 1.005 |
| Q12 | 4.27 | 0.887 |

Additionally, the analysis will be carried out from the characteristics extracted from each question (Table 4). In this manner, eight important characteristics are extracted from the results of the questions for each student. Mean and standard deviation of the distribution are show in Figure 5 and Table 8. All the results for the eight characteristics have a mean value above the 3 over 5. In global terms, it points outs a good acceptance of the activity in all the measured aspects. Furthermore, the standard deviation is also close to 1 for each case, which indicates that the dispersion tend in the responses are low. Motivation and scalability are the results which higher mean values while the usability result is slightly lower than the rest. This last issue was predictable due to the usual difficulty to handle CFD software; even though the software chosen for the learning activity has an easy handling compared to other CFD alternative applications.

When the results are analyzed by groups (from each B.Sc. degree) the reader can observe both differences and trends in the results. For all the groups, the scalability is the characteristic that achieves the greatest mean value (greater than 4 for all the groups). The second characteristic which greater results obtain is the motivation for Mechanical Eng., Electrical Eng. and double degree but for Electronic and Automatic Eng., the second place is for the thinking over. However, the mean values for Mechanical are slightly lower than the rest, especially in learning (3.17).

Table 8. Statistical results of the categories.

| B.Sc. | | Parameters | | | | | | | |
|---|---|---|---|---|---|---|---|---|---|
| | | Previous (Level) | Previous (Complexity Perception) | Satisfaction | Usability | Learning | Thinking over | Motivation | Scalability |
| Global | Mean | 3.22 | 3.25 | 3.81 | 3.70 | 3.63 | 3.93 | 4.08 | 4.27 |
| | Std. dev. | 0.892 | 1.240 | 1.181 | 0.644 | 0.805 | 0.907 | 1.005 | 0.887 |
| Mechanical Eng. | Mean | 3.07 | 3.11 | 3.70 | 3.50 | 3.17 | 3.56 | 3.89 | 4.00 |
| | Std. dev. | 0.781 | 1.450 | 0.993 | 0.693 | 0.693 | 0.934 | 1.086 | 1.000 |
| Electrical Eng. | Mean | 3.27 | 3.27 | 3.60 | 3.70 | 3.92 | 4.13 | 4.20 | 4.40 |
| | Std. dev. | 0.961 | 1.163 | 1.502 | 0.528 | 0.777 | 0.834 | 1.146 | 0.828 |
| Electronical & automatic Eng. | Mean | 3.17 | 3.33 | 4.25 | 4.00 | 4.04 | 4.33 | 4.25 | 4.42 |
| | Std. dev. | 1.030 | 0.985 | 1.138 | 0.477 | 0.638 | 0.651 | 0.754 | 0.669 |
| Double degree | Mean | 4.00 | 3.80 | 4.00 | 4.10 | 4.30 | 4.40 | 4.40 | 5.00 |
| | Std. dev. | 0.707 | 0.837 | 1.225 | 0.742 | 0.447 | 0.894 | 0.548 | 0.000 |

Appl. Sci. 2019, 9, 4809

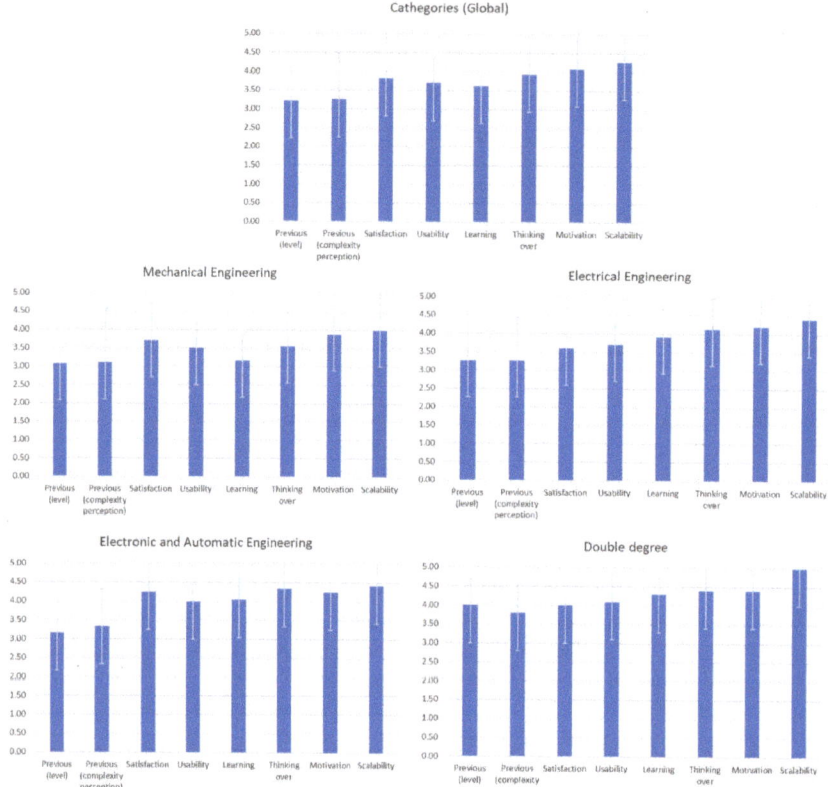

**Figure 5.** Results grouped for each category for all the students (global) and for each bachelor degree.

### 4.2. Machine Learning Classification Approach

The machine learning approach aims to analyze whether the answers provided by the students are conditioned or not by their particular degree. The comparison is carried out for each two degrees as shown in Figure 6. If the classifier provided an adequate classification on the basis of success indicators (precision, overall accuracy, Kappa index and AUC), there is an effective different response pattern for each of the degrees.

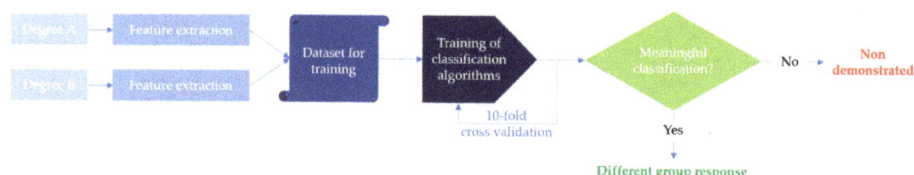

**Figure 6.** Workflow for the analysis based-on machine learning from the questionnaire response patterns.

Machine learning algorithms are trained using different variables to obtain the best results using the prediction features stated in Table 9, which showed better indicators of success. The most effective parameter to evaluate the prediction capacity of each method is the AUC. If this value is 0.5 or less, the algorithm is making predictions with an accuracy close to randomness. It means that a classification is not possible for the algorithm.

As is shown in Table 10, based on features applied (Table 9), the AUC is above 0.5 for the comparison between the B.Sc. degrees in electrical engineering and the B.Sc. degree in mechanical engineering. For the comparison between the B.Sc. degree in electronic and automatic engineering with respect to the B.Sc. degree in mechanical engineering.

However, for the comparison between the B.Sc. degree in electrical engineering with respect to the B.Sc. degree in electronic and automatic engineering. Therefore, the classifier could not predict successfully (lowest values for the four indicators of Table 9).

Please note that the data collection is limited, and very different subjective parameters are being evaluated, so the AUC and Kappa values do not show the high accuracy typical of other applications of machine learning [43,44]. However, this analysis is not oriented to establish a high accuracy predictive algorithm, but this approach is oriented to demonstrate differences in the questionnaire response patterns for each student. If it is possible to predict the degree, then it is demonstrated that degree conditioning factors to the activity in a non-homogeneous sample with students from different B.Sc. degrees who carried out the same activity at the same time. Different experiments were carried out in order to find the predictor features which provide better Kappa and AUC results.

When the questionnaire answers are compared between the B.Sc. degrees in electrical engineering and the B.Sc. degree in mechanical engineering, the best results are obtained with the Bayesian network classifier, achieving an overall accuracy of 80.9% and a Kappa index of 0.530. These results are significant for the quality of the success of the classification between the two groups. Regarding the AUC, for all four tested classifiers the value obtained is higher than 0.5, being the most optimal AUC result (0.768) obtained for the random forest classifier.

In the comparison between the B.Sc. degrees in mechanical engineering and the B.Sc. degree in electronic and automatic engineering, the Bayesian network classifier achieved the best results, with an overall accuracy of 84.6%, a Kappa index of 0.581 and an AUC of 0.728. The rest of the classifiers achieve lower performance results, but always higher than the randomness threshold (0 for Kappa, and 0.5 for AUC).

While for the two comparisons mentioned above the algorithm test can classify with acceptable accuracy the response patterns (results parameters with a success rate higher than randomness), when the same classifier algorithms are trained and applied between the B.Sc. degree in electrical engineering and the B.Sc. Degree in electronic and automatic engineering, all classifications cannot classify satisfactorily the degree based on the chosen features. More specifically, three of the classifiers show a negative Kappa index, and the highest AUC is 0.44 (lower than the 0.5 threshold). In this case, we cannot demonstrate that there are differences between both groups based on the questionnaire response pattern.

Using the predictors features applied, we can indicate that, studying the questionnaire response patterns of responses for each student, there are differences among the response to the activity.

Table 9. Prediction features applied for the training.

| Predictor Features Applied |
|---|
| P2 (yes/no) |
| P3 (yes/no) |
| Previous (informatic) (1–5) |
| Satisfaction (1–5) |
| Usability (1–5) |
| Learning (1–5) |

Table 10. Training quality indicators for the based-on classification learner approaches.

|  |  | Electrical Engineering vs. Mechanical Engineering | Electronical Engineering vs. Mechanical Engineering | Electrical Engineering vs. Electronical Engineering |
|---|---|---|---|---|
| SVM linear | Kappa | 0.222 | 0.210 | −0.200 |
|  | Precision | 0.685 | 0.694 | 0.407 |
|  | Overall Acc. | 69.0% | 71.8% | 40.7% |
|  | AUC | 0.596 | 0.588 | 0.400 |
| Logistic regression | Kappa | 0.421 | 0.446 | −0.050 |
|  | Precision | 0.735 | 0.764 | 0.481 |
|  | Overall Acc. | 73.8% | 76.9% | 48.1% |
|  | AUC | 0.738 | 0.713 | 0.406 |
| Random forest | Kappa | 0.412 | 0.369 | −0.286 |
|  | Precision | 0.735 | 0.734 | 0.364 |
|  | Overall Acc. | 73.8% | 74.4% | 37.0% |
|  | AUC | 0.768 | 0.671 | 0.444 |
| Bayes network | Kappa | 0.530 | 0.581 | 0.195 |
|  | Precision | 0.853 | 0.874 | 0.607 |
|  | Overall Acc. | 80.9% | 84.6% | 59.3% |
|  | AUC | 0.659 | 0.728 | 0.447 |

## 5. Conclusions

In global terms, analyzing the results for each individual question, it is demonstrated that students think that it is a good practice to explain the use of CFD tools in the classroom and that the activity has made them realize that the theoretical equations do not always correspond to reality (thinking over). The indicators associated with them are particularly high, which confirms that the initial objectives of the learning activity were met.

If the results are analyzed by groups according to the bachelor degree, the answers indicated a good acceptance of the activity regardless of the bachelor degree. In relation to this, the most widely accepted characteristic is scalability, indicating that students want to do more of this type of activity. However, there are slight differences for the activity: The second characteristic in terms of score is the motivation for the B.Sc. degree in Mechanical Engineering, in Electrical Engineering, and double degree. Motivation results for the activity are clearly positive, as was the case for research on virtual laboratories and virtualization of materials [18,30]. On the contrary, for the B.Sc. degree in Electronic and Automatic Engineering, the second place was for the thinking over. It is of note that the mean values for the B.Sc. Degree in Mechanical Engineering was slightly lower than the rest, especially in learning. This could be hypothetically justified from the affinity of the studies, since mechanical engineering is most related to fluid mechanics and hydraulic systems, which is why the learning obtained after the activity the knowledge acquired might be less novel to them.

Using the questionnaire response pattern given by each student, we can detect differences between the response sequence pattern given by the B.Sc. degree in mechanical engineering students with respect to both electricity engineering and electronics and automatic engineering students. The machine learning algorithms applied were capable of classifying the students as groups according to the predictor variables. This is an indication that there are peculiarities in the results that differentiate some groups from others, as far as the response pattern to the activity is concerned, extracted from the sequences of responses given for the six prediction features. In other words, it is shown that the response to the learning activity from the questions raised is different for students of B. Sc. degree in mechanic engineering with respect to those of electronic and automatic or electricity engineering, but the existence of these differences could not be demonstrated between the latter two. Namely, the same analysis is not successful when the classification algorithm is applied to classify between B.Sc. degree in electrical engineering students and B. Sc. degree in electronic and automatic engineering. This behavior is justified from the curriculum similarity between both B.Sc degrees (especially in comparison with the B.Sc. degree in mechanical engineering). The aforementioned group's results are compatible with the differences observed in the descriptive statistical results. However, please note that the machine learning approach was implemented over a small dataset; therefore, we can obtain hints and/or indications to generate new hypotheses but not scientific statements derived solely from the machine learning analysis. This would require a much larger sample, on which the possible inter-relationships of the different intervening variables could be drawn. Nevertheless, since the proposed methodology is adapted to the student, a larger sample could be operationally unapproachable in this context.

In conclusion, the learning activity has been satisfactory, and the results show that there has been a good acceptance on the part of the students in terms of usability, learning, thinking over, motivation and scalability.

There are indications of a different group response that could justify similar learning activities aimed exclusively at the group in order to adapt the activity to the specialty as much as possible. Futures works will address this issue and new research will be conducted to continue proposing new methodologies oriented to the acquisition of competence in subjects of high complexity and abstraction, like fluid-mechanical learning.

**Author Contributions:** Conceptualization, M.R.-M. and P.R.-G.; methodology, M.R.-M.; data gathering, M.R.-M., A.S.-P. and J.R.S.; formal analysis, M.R.-M. and P.R.-G.; investigation, M.R.-M. and P.R.-G.; resources, A.S.-P., M.R.-M. and J.R.S.; writing—original draft preparation, M.R.-M. and P.R.-G.; writing—review and editing, M.R.-M. and P.R.-G.; project administration, M.R.-M.; funding acquisition, M.R.-M.

**Funding:** This research was funded by Universidad de Salamanca, grant number ID2018/134 in the context of the Innovation Project entitled *"Improvement of competences in fluid engineering through the integration of CFD simulation applications* (Ref. ID2018/134)".

**Acknowledgments:** The authors acknowledge the support provided by the Higher Technical School of Industrial Engineering of Béjar and the Department of Mechanical Engineering.

**Conflicts of Interest:** The authors declare no conflict of interest.

## References

1. Perumal, K.; Ganesan, R. CFD modeling for the estimation of pressure loss coefficients of pipe fittings: An undergraduate project. *Comput. Appl. Eng. Educ.* **2016**, *24*, 180–185. [CrossRef]
2. Franchina, N.; Kouaissah, O.; Persico, G.; Savini, M. Three-Dimensional CFD Simulation and Experimental Assessment of the Performance of a H-Shape Vertical-Axis Wind Turbine at Design and Off-Design Conditions. *Int. J. Turbomach. Propuls. Power* **2019**, *4*, 30. [CrossRef]
3. Chuang, Y.-C.; Chen, C.-T. Mathematical modeling and optimal design of an MOCVD reactor for GaAs film growth. *J. Taiwan Inst. Chem. Eng.* **2014**, *45*, 254–267. [CrossRef]
4. Chen, C.-T.; Tan, W.-L. Mathematical modeling, optimal design and control of an SCR reactor for NOx removal. *J. Taiwan Inst. Chem. Eng.* **2012**, *43*, 409–419. [CrossRef]
5. Pan, H.; Chen, X.-Z.; Liang, X.-F.; Zhu, L.-T.; Luo, Z.-H. CFD simulations of gas–liquid–solid flow in fluidized bed reactors—A review. *Powder Technol.* **2016**, *299*, 235–258. [CrossRef]
6. Boukouvala, F.; Ierapetritou, M.G. Derivative-free optimization for expensive constrained problems using a novel expected improvement objective function. *AIChE J.* **2014**, *60*, 2462–2474. [CrossRef]
7. Kajero, O.T.; Thorpe, R.B.; Yao, Y.; Wong, D.S.H.; Chen, T. Meta-Model-Based Calibration and Sensitivity Studies of Computational Fluid Dynamics Simulation of Jet Pumps. *Chem. Eng. Technol.* **2017**, *40*, 1674–1684. [CrossRef]
8. Loy, Y.; Rangaiah, G.; Lakshminarayanan, S. Surrogate modelling for enhancing consequence analysis based on computational fluid dynamics. *J. Loss Prev. Process. Ind.* **2017**, *48*, 173–185. [CrossRef]
9. Moukalled, F.; Mangeni, L.; Darwish, M. *The Finite Volume Method in Computational Fluid Dynamics*; Springer: Cham, Switzerland, 2015. [CrossRef]

10. Perumal, K.; Bing, M.W.M. A CFD study of low pressure wet gas metering using slotted orifice meters. *Flow Meas. Instrum.* **2011**, *22*, 33–42. [CrossRef]
11. Yunus, A.Ç; Cimbala, J.M. *Fluid Mechanics: Fundamentals and Applications*, 4th ed.; McGraw-Hill Education: New York, NY, USA, 2004.
12. Pujol, A.; Montoro, L.; Pelegri, M.; Gonzalez, J.R. Learning Hydraulic Turbomachinery with Computational Fluid Dynamics (CFD) codes. *Comput. Appl. Eng. Educ.* **2013**, *21*, 684–690. [CrossRef]
13. Aradag, S.; Cohen, K.; Seaver, C.A.; McLaughlin, T. Integration of computations and experiments for flow control research with undergraduate students. *Comput. Appl. Eng. Educ.* **2010**, *18*, 727–735. [CrossRef]
14. Rabi, J.A.; Cordeiro, R.B.; Oliveira, A.L. Introducing natural-convective chilling to food engineering undergraduate freshmen: Case studied assisted by CFD simulation and field visualization. *Comput. Appl. Eng. Educ.* **2009**, *17*, 34–43. [CrossRef]
15. Rodríguez-Martín, M.; Rodríguez-Gonzálvez, P.; Sánchez, A.; Sánchez, J.R. Short Simulation Activity to Improve the Competences in the Fluid-Mechanical Engineering Classroom Using Solidworks® Flow Simulation. In Proceedings of the Seventh International Conference on Technological Ecosystems for Enhancing Multiculturality (TEEM'19), Léon, Spain, 16–18 October 2019; ACM: New York, NY, USA, 2019; pp. 72–79. [CrossRef]
16. Coker, A.K. *Ludwig's Applied Process Design for Chemical and Petrochemical Plants*, 4th ed.; Gulf Professional Publishing: Houston, TX, USA, 2007.
17. Massey, B. *Mechanics of Fluids*, 7th ed.; Van Nostrand Reinhold: London, UK, 1970.
18. Rodríguez, D.V.; Martin, M.R.; Cavero, M.P.R.; Garcia, F.J.N.; Cobo, L.M. Formación de Personal Técnico en Ensayos no Destructivos por Ultrasonidos Mediante Realidad Virtual. *DYNA Ing. E Ind.* **2018**, *94*, 150–154. [CrossRef]
19. Lounis, H.; Fares, T. Using Efficient Machine-Learning Models to Assess Two Important Quality Factors: Maintainability and Reusability. In Proceedings of the Joint Conference of the 21st International Workshop on Software Measurement and the 6th International Conference on Software Process and Product Measurement, Nara, Japan, 3–4 November 2011; pp. 170–177. [CrossRef]
20. Nieto, Y.; Gacia-Diaz, V.; Montenegro, C.; Gonzalez, C.C.; Crespo, R.G. Usage of Machine Learning for Strategic Decision Making at Higher Educational Institutions. *IEEE Access* **2019**, *7*, 75007–75017. [CrossRef]
21. González, C.; Elhariri, E.; El-Bendary, N. Machine Learning Based Classification Approach for Predicting Students Performance in Blended Learning. In Proceedings of the 1st International Conference on Advanced Intelligent System and Informatics (AISI2015), Beni Suef, Egypt, 28–30 November 2015; Springer: Cham, Switzerland, 2015. [CrossRef]
22. Lee, S.; Chung, J.Y. The Machine Learning-Based Dropout Early Warning System for Improving the Performance of Dropout Prediction. *Appl. Sci.* **2019**, *9*, 3093. [CrossRef]
23. Dassault Systemes. Available online: https://www.solidworks.com (accessed on 1 October 2019).
24. LaForce, M.; Noble, E.; Blackwell, C. Problem-Based Learning (PBL) and Student Interest in STEM Careers: The Roles of Motivation and Ability Beliefs. *Educ. Sci.* **2017**, *7*, 92. [CrossRef]
25. Arango-López, J.; Valdivieso, C.C.C.; Collazos, C.A.; Vela, F.L.G.; Moreira, F. CREANDO: Tool for creating pervasive games to increase the learning motivation in higher education students. *Telemat. Inform.* **2019**, *38*, 62–73. [CrossRef]
26. Conradty, C.; Bogner, F.X. Hypertext or Textbook: Effects on Motivation and Gain in Knowledge. *Educ. Sci.* **2016**, *6*, 29. [CrossRef]
27. Vergara, D.; Rubio, M.P.; Lorenzo, M. A Virtual Resource for Enhancing the Spatial Comprehension of Crystal Lattices. *Educ. Sci.* **2018**, *8*, 153. [CrossRef]
28. Ministry of Science and Innovation, Government of Spain. Orden CIN/351/2009, de 9 de Febrero, por la Que se Establecen los Requisitos Para la Verificación de los Títulos Universitarios Oficiales que Habiliten Para el Ejercicio de la Profesión de Ingeniero Técnico Industrial, Madrid, 2009. Published in Boletín Oficial del Estado, 44; 20 February 2019. Available online: https://www.boe.es/diario_boe/txt.php?id=BOE-A-2009-2893 (accessed on 1 October 2019).
29. Rodríguez-Martín, M.; Rodríguez-Gonzálvez, P. Learning based on 3D photogrammetry models to evaluate the competences in visual testing of welds. In Proceedings of the 2018 IEEE Global Engineering Education Conference, Santa Cruz de Tenerife, Spain, 17–20 April 2018; pp. 1582–1587. [CrossRef]

30. Rodríguez-Martín, M.; Rodríguez-Gonzálvez, P. Learning methodology based on weld virtual models in the mechanical engineering classroom. *Comput. Appl. Eng. Educ.* **2019**, *27*, 1113–1125. [CrossRef]
31. Albaum, G. The Likert scale revisited. *Int. J. Mark. Res. Soc.* **1997**, *39*, 1–21. [CrossRef]
32. Norman, G. Likert scales, levels of measurement and the "laws" of statistics. *Adv. Heal. Sci. Educ.* **2010**, *15*, 625–632. [CrossRef] [PubMed]
33. Stimpson, A.J.; Cummings, M.L. Assessing Intervention Timing in Computer-Based Education Using Machine Learning Algorithms. *IEEE Access* **2014**, *2*, 78–87. [CrossRef]
34. Mosavi, A.; Salimi, M.; Ardabili, S.F.; Rabczuk, T.; Shamshirband, S.; Varkonyi-Koczy, A.R. State of the Art of Machine Learning Models in Energy Systems, a Systematic Review. *Energies* **2019**, *12*, 1301. [CrossRef]
35. O'Neil, G.L.; Goodall, J.L.; Watson, L.T. Evaluating the potential for site-specific modification of LiDAR DEM derivatives to improve environmental planning-scale wetland identification using Random Forest classification. *J. Hydrol.* **2018**, *559*, 192–208. [CrossRef]
36. Mao, W.; Wang, F.Y. Chapter 8—Cultural Modeling for Behavior Analysis and Prediction. In *New Advances in Intelligence and Security Informatics*; Academic Press: Cambridge, MA, USA, 2013; pp. 91–102. [CrossRef]
37. Madden, M.G. On the classification performance of TAN and general Bayesian networks. *Knowledge-Based Syst.* **2009**, *22*, 489–495. [CrossRef]
38. Molina, J.-L.; Zazo, S.; Rodríguez-Gonzálvez, P.; González-Aguilera, D. Innovative Analysis of Runoff Temporal Behavior through Bayesian Networks. *Water* **2016**, *8*, 484. [CrossRef]
39. Weka. Weka 3: Data Mining Software in Java Machine learning. 2018. Available online: https://www.cs.waikato.ac.nz/ml/weka/ (accessed on 1 October 2019).
40. Rymer, H.; Brown, G. Gravity fields and the interpretation of volcanic structures: Geological discrimination and temporal evolution. *J. Volcanol. Geotherm. Res.* **1986**, *27*, 229–254. [CrossRef]
41. Cohen, J. A Coefficient of Agreement for Nominal Scales. *Educ. Psychol. Meas.* **1960**, *20*, 37–46. [CrossRef]
42. Bradley, A.P. The use of the area under the ROC curve in the evaluation of machine learning algorithms. *Pattern Recognit.* **1997**, *30*, 1145–1159. [CrossRef]
43. Rodríguez-Gonzálvez, P.; Rodríguez-Martín, M. Weld Bead Detection Based on 3D Geometric Features and Machine Learning Approaches. *IEEE Access* **2019**, *7*, 14714–14727. [CrossRef]
44. Lago-González, D.; Rodríguez-Gonzálvez, P. Detection of Geothermal Potential Zones Using Remote Sensing Techniques. *Remote Sens.* **2019**, *11*, 2403. [CrossRef]

© 2019 by the authors. Licensee MDPI, Basel, Switzerland. This article is an open access article distributed under the terms and conditions of the Creative Commons Attribution (CC BY) license (http://creativecommons.org/licenses/by/4.0/).

Article

# Technology-Enhanced Learning for Graduate Students: Exploring the Correlation of Media Richness and Creativity of Computer-Mediated Communication and Face-to-Face Communication

Shan-Hui Chao [1], Jinzhang Jiang [1,2], Chia-Hsuan Hsu [3,*], Yi-Te Chiang [4], Eric Ng [5] and Wei-Ta Fang [4,*]

1. School of Media & Communication, Shanghai Jiao Tong University, Shanghai 200240, China; rogershc@ms43.hinet.net (S.-H.C.); jinzhangphd@sjtu.edu.cn (J.J.)
2. USC-SJTU Institute of Cultural and Creative Industry, Shanghai Jiao Tong University, Shanghai 200240, China
3. School of Forestry and Resource Conservation, National Taiwan University, Taipei 106, Taiwan
4. Graduate Institute of Environmental Education, National Taiwan Normal University, Taipei 116, Taiwan; faratajiang@gmail.com
5. School of Management and Enterprise, University of Southern Queensland, Toowoomba QLD 4350, Australia; eric.ng@usq.edu.au
* Correspondence: d05625002@ntu.edu.tw (C.-H.H.); wtfang@ntnu.edu.tw (W.-T.F.); Tel.: +886-2-7749-6558 (W.-T.F.)

Received: 10 January 2020; Accepted: 23 February 2020; Published: 28 February 2020

**Abstract:** The objective of the research was to explore and compare the differences in potential creative thinking that media richness had on learners in creativity training through two different types of communication formats; computer-mediated communication, and face-to-face communication. The results indicated that the computer-mediated communication format performed better than the face-to-face in terms of the fluency, flexibility, and originality dimensions of creative thinking. The computer-mediated communication format also had a greater level of media richness perception (i.e., use of multiple cues, language diversity, and personal focus of the medium) than the face-to-face format. In terms of the combined effectiveness of computer-mediated communication, and face-to-face formats, the use of multiple cues, language variety of perception of media richness had direct effects on the fluency of creativity. There was also a positive correlation between the elaboration of creativity and the use of multiple cues, language variety, and personal focus of the medium in the perception of media richness. Furthermore, language variety was correlated with creativity and flexibility. The research findings highlighted the importance of the availability of immediate feedback on media richness, whereas creativity cognition should focus on the breadth and depth of the information, which contributes to enhancing the creativity of individuals or a group of employees.

**Keywords:** creativity; computer mediated communication; face-to-face; media richness; organizational learning

## 1. Introduction

In response to ever-changing technological development and globalization, corporations continue to build capacity in organizational learning and team innovation in order to maintain sustainable operations and competitiveness. Organization innovation relies on the creativity of the employees [1] and the focus has been on the sharing of knowledge and encouraging creative thinking that seek to develop innovative solutions to address existing or future business challenges [2,3]. While a corporation's sharing of internal knowledge through organizational learning can increase the individual employee's skill and learning effectiveness, it also helps to drive a collective innovation process that will contribute towards the corporation's overall sustainable efficacy and development [4–6]. Such an emerging trend has prompted the need to review the relationship between sustainable business development and management education that seek to facilitate effective communication of key abilities such as adaptability to face uncertainty, creativity, or detection and processing emotions, confidence, respect, dialogue, critical thinking and systematic thinking [7].

Perry-Smith (2006) states that creativity involves the attitude and action of an employee to take risks [8]. However, it is imperative that managers provide a supportive environment, and incentives to encourage their employees to think creatively and explore innovative solutions to assist in making more informed strategic decisions [9]. An individual employee's ability to be creative is directly influenced by factors such as diverse skills and autonomy in the organization [10]. Brown and Fridman [11] indicate that feedback (e.g., audio-visual, written) also plays an important role in encouraging creativity. Computer-mediated communication (CMC) and face-to-face (FtF) communication are two forms of feedback communication format that are used to foster creativity whereby CMC is considered having greater media richness than the traditional FtF approach [12]. Although studies [13–15] have revealed that CMC is a more relaxing and engaging feedback communication format than FtF, but there has been a lack of investigation into the correlation between communication formats and creativity.

The research attempts to fill this gap by combining the media richness theory and creativity to explore the relationship between the features of media richness and creative thinking by focusing on creativity training via two different communication formats (i.e., CMC and FtF). The following research questions are proposed:

1. Will the use of different communication formats (i.e., CMC and FtF) have an impact on potential creative thinking?
2. What is the correlation between media richness and potential creative thinking through the use of the above two types of communication format?

## 2. Literature Review and Hypotheses

*2.1. Media Richness*

Media richness theory believes that the richness of information relies on the capacity of communicating information by the media. A communicating media is considered as a 'rich media' when the targeted audiences can better understand the information transmitted. Conversely, if more time is required to understand the information received, then it is considered as a 'lean media' [16,17]. The level of media richness has four key features; namely the availability of immediate feedback; use of multiple cues; language variety; and personal focus which have significant effects on information equivocality and uncertainty [16,17]. Handke et al. [18] state that the efficacy of the organization depends on the extent to which media richness conforms to the information required by the task and further propose that the use and cognition of media are the dynamic combinations of people and technology. On the other hand, Chidambaram and Jones [19] argue that while a greater level of media richness has the ability to better manage uncertain information, it has limited effect on reducing the equivocality of the information. Instead this may increase the complexity and diversity of the communication process and content.

Previous studies [20–23] reveal that the FtF (e.g., communication with language, non-verbal cues) communication format has the highest level of media richness, and this is followed by CMC (e.g., audio-visual), media with only audio and written media. However, as the difficulty and cost of information transmission is reduced due to the advancement of modern technologies, CMC has increasingly been utilized as a communication format. This is particularly evident with the introduction of mobile immediate messaging software, which can be customized to facilitate interactive communication that occurs anytime and anywhere. Its ability for data storage, indexing, searching, and the convenience of using the media by an individual is also greatly enhanced [24].

The synchronized interaction in CMC can offer the similar effect of real-time communication as that of FtF through instant text, voice, and video transmission [24,25]. Studies [26–28] suggest that learners were more likely to perform better in generating new ideas for new product development under the FtF communication format than their counterparts who undertook the CMC format. However, CMC may have potential advantage in terms of creativity learning and performance within a team context [29]. In a study conducted by Hatem et al. [30], the production rate, communication efficiency, and level of cooperation of CMC indicated by the total quantity of information exchange is much higher than that of FtF because users have experienced more interactions under the CMC format. It is the relatively higher equivocality that enables CMC users to exhibit a greater level of active participation and effort, given that space and time barriers have been broken down that enable team members to cooperate more effectively and efficiently on a common task [20,29]. CMC communication via the virtual world is regarded as more fun, and pleasurable than FtF [15]. Croes et al. [13] also suggest that selecting between FtF or CMC is significantly influenced by the perception of the user on controllability, anonymity, and co-existence. As compared to CMC, FtF communicators deliver more facial expressions and any changes in tone of voice may increase the level of tension during communication [14].

The CMC interactive environment also offers more personalized information and differential interactive communication, which has a higher degree of freedom, giving more time and space to the learners to review the appropriateness and completeness of their opinions before they put forward their views [31,32]. Furthermore, CMC provides more time to the users to contemplate on the transmitted information during the interaction and to have a considered response by integrating the information with existing knowledge [29]. On the other hand, FtF does not allow much time for analysis and discussion of different viewpoints, especially when participants are shy or are not ready to share which will lower the participation interaction and affect creativity performance [33]. Furthermore, a relaxing learning situation will help elicit a greater level of creative thinking from the learners. Research [34] shows that creativity rarely emerges under stressful circumstances and thus it is important to keep learners in a relaxed mental state where the subconscious can do the nurturing and forming thoughts that give rise to creative thinking. Therefore, considering the interactivity and advances of the CMC communication format, its media richness has grown significantly in recent years [35,36].

*2.2. Creativity*

Some studies [37–39] suggest that creativity derives from the structure of intelligence that includes cognition, memory, divergent thinking, convergent thinking, and assessment, but other researchers [8,40–45] take on a broader definition. Creativity can be perceived as the ability to generate new viewpoints, relationships, or meanings to produce an innovative idea that is different from the original by reprocessing, amending, integrating or recombining linkable factors based on the original knowledge structure that satisfies a special need or meaningful purpose and exhibits a new originality which has its own unique values [37,46,47]. While studies [48] indicate that knowledge sharing can limit creativity, other researchers [49] argue that the sharing of such knowledge enhances creation skill, openness, and independence which are key characteristics of creativity. Therefore, creativity is the foundation of innovative knowledge; and innovation is the result of expressed creativity.

Creativity is the process of developing innovative solutions to solve problems, but such a process usually differs as a result of differing contexts [50–53]. Accordingly, the need for assessing creativity is well supported by several studies [54,55], and one of the different techniques used is cognitive assessment [56]. The most commonly used cognitive assessment examines the level of fluency, flexibility, elaboration, and originality of the thought process as an assessment index [37,57]. The Torrance Tests of Creative Thinking (TTCT), developed by Torrance [58] adopt a more stringent graphic and language written testing that measures creativity potential.

Prior studies [59–62] have indicated that through well-designed training, creativity can be elevated and further enhances the skill and efficacy of individual employee, which will have a flow on effect to the collective innovation process. This can significantly contribute to the overall effectiveness and growth of sustainable operations in a corporation [4–6]. This study will focus on investigating the impact of communication formats (specifically CMC and FtF) in creativity training on potential creativity, which seek to address the two proposed research questions identified earlier.

## 2.3. Research Hypotheses of Media Richness and Creativity

Media richness and creativity have been researched extensively within their respective contexts, and this has been evident in the extant literature. Media richness has gained much attention in recent years given the advancement of modern technologies that facilitated the enhancement of media delivery and quality, influence, and outreach. Some of the key domains that have been previously explored include: the effects of media richness on social media [63], education learning [64], trust and loyalty [65], organizational learning [66], information quality [67], marketing [68], and communication [69].

On the other hand, creativity has been a longstanding research theme from both an individual and organizational perspectives where the focus has been on instigating new ideas, new ways of thinking, and problem-solving. Previous studies have investigated creativity in different aspects, including: the influence of creativity on business performance [70], education teaching and learning [71], personal development and growth [72], marketing and new product development [73], and creativity assessment [54].

However, there have been limited studies that explore the correlation between media richness and creativity. This research will explore specifically the relationship between the availability of immediate feedback of media richness, use of multiple cues, language variety, and personal focus of the medium with the four indices of fluency, flexibility, elaboration, and originality of creativity. The definitions of these key terms are briefly outlined in Tables 1 and 2.

Table 1. Definitions of key terms related to media richness.

| Term | Definition |
|---|---|
| The availability of immediate feedback | The speed at which the user of communication media can receive immediate response when transmitting information and amend and revise the information. |
| Use of multiple cues | The degree of closeness to the actual situation of the language and non-verbal cues covered in the transmitted information through communication media. |
| Language variety | The degree of ease of interpretation or thinking without spending extra effort by the user when transmitting meanings of the language and symbols through the communication media. |
| Personal focus of the medium | The flexibility and adjustability of the communication media for the user. |

Adapted from Daft and Lengel (1984) and Ishii, Lyons and Carr (2019) [16,17].

Table 2. Definitions of key terms related to creativity.

| Term | Definition |
|---|---|
| Fluency | The ability to generate large quantity of thoughts. |
| Flexibility | The ability to look at familiar thought or situation in different ways. |
| Elaboration | The ability to add more details to existing thought. |
| Originality | The ability to produce new concept that others cannot think of. |

Adapted from Guilford (1967), Torrance (1968) and Chen (2005) [37,39,57].

Given the above discussion, the following variables are proposed to be investigated in the research and are briefly explained accordingly. Figure 1 presents a hypothetical model for this research study.

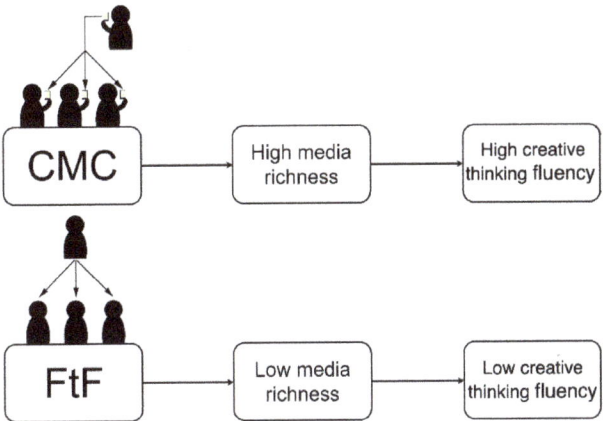

**Figure 1.** Research hypothetical model (e.g., media richness vs. creative thinking fluency) of the hypnotized impact on creativity potential after creative training by media richness.

2.3.1. Independent Variable

The independent variables of the research are the creativity training by different communication types. The experimental group adopts the CMC method that involves using a software (i.e., WeChat), which is most widely used social media in China. As for the control group, participants will receive traditional FtF creativity training.

2.3.2. Dependent Variable

The dependent variables in this study are derived from the 'Abbreviated Torrance Test for Adults (ATTA)' which is a projective assessment of potential creative thinking abilities that included key indicators such as fluency, flexibility, originality, and elaboration [37,57,74].

2.3.3. Intervening Variable

In this research, media richness perception is used as the intervening variable to determine if there is an impact on potential creativity by the creativity training through different communication types.

2.3.4. Control Variable

The control variables adopted in this study during the preparation and experiment stages are the uniform content, procedure, time, and lecturers.

2.3.5. Hypotheses

Based on the above discussion and the research from Guilford, Torrance, Wu, et. al., Hatem, et. al. and Smith [37,57], this research posits the following hypotheses to be investigated:

**Hypothesis 1 (H1):** *The potential creativity cognition performance of the CMC learners in the experimental group is better than the FtF learners in the control group.*

**Hypothesis 1a (H1a):** *The fluency performance of the CMC learners in the experimental group is better than the FtF learners in the control group.*

**Hypothesis 1b (H1b):** *The flexibility performance of the CMC learners in the experimental group is better than the FtF learners in the control group.*

**Hypothesis 1c (H1c):** *The originality performance of the CMC learners in the experimental group is better than the FtF learners in the control group.*

**Hypothesis 1d (H1d):** *The elaboration performance of the CMC learners in the experimental group is better than the FtF learners in the control group.*

**Hypothesis 2 (H2):** *The overall media richness perception of the CMC learners of the experimental group is better than the FtF learners of the control group.*

**Hypothesis 2a (H2a):** *The perception of the availability of immediate feedback by the CMC learners in the experimental group is better than the FtF learners in the control group.*

**Hypothesis 2b (H2b):** *The perception of the use of multiple cues by the CMC learners in the experimental group is better than the FtF learners in the control group.*

**Hypothesis 2c (H2c):** *The perception of language variety by the CMC learners in the experimental group is better than the FtF learners in the control group.*

**Hypothesis 2d (H2d):** *The perception of personal focus of the medium by the CMC learners in the experimental group is better than the FtF learners in the control group.*

**Hypothesis 3 (H3):** *The perception of media richness is significantly correlated to potential creative thinking.*

## 3. Materials and Methods

*3.1. Preparation Stage*

The research, based on the hypotheses, use common creativity methods that have undergone an experiment of creativity training [49]. Next, the Abbreviated Torrance Test for Adults (ATTA) projective assessment of potential creative thinking abilities measurement was employed to evaluate the result of creativity potential after the learning process [74]. A survey was also conducted with postgraduate students (who were also currently working as full-time business professionals in organizations) about their perception on media richness (Table 3) and has adopted a five-point Likert scale (i.e., 1 = strongly disagree; 2 = disagree; 3 = neutral; 4 = agree; 5 = strongly agree) as a measurement to the respondents' answers about their perception of media richness.

*3.2. Experimental Stage (Quasi-Experiment)*

The research was conducted at Shanghai where it has been regarded as having one of the most conductive and open business environments in China. The subjects selected for this study were specifically targeted at postgraduate students who were also currently working as full-time business professionals in organizations within the master's program (major in communication management, business administration, and public relations and advertising) at the Shanghai College of Shih Hsin University.

Two groups of a total of 67 students (i.e., CMC experimental group, $n = 33$; FtF control group, $n = 34$) from the communication management, business administration, and public relations and advertising major studies were randomly selected to participate in this study. The two groups were taught by the same lecturer for creativity training that involved a three-hour class session whereby the CMC experimental group used the mobile communication software (i.e., WeChat) for communication, whereas the FtF control group utilized traditional communication format. Upon finalizing the subjects and experimental methods, as well as setting the time for rehearsal, the official training and surveys were subsequently conducted with the two groups separately.

Table 3. Media richness perception measurement items.

| Dimension | Survey Content | Source |
|---|---|---|
| Availability of immediate feedback | 1. The design of the learning process provides me with effective information to help me communicate quickly.<br>2. The design of the learning process allows me to ask and understand immediately.<br>3. The design of the learning process makes it easier for me to communicate and exchange ideas with others.<br>4. The design of the learning process makes it easier for me to understand the content when I am communicating with others.<br>5. The design of the learning process allows me to grasp the status of information transmission immediately. | Carlson and Zmud (1999), Dennis, Kinney and Hung (1999), Rice, et al. (1987) [75–77] |
| Use of multiple cues | 6. The design of the learning process offers the option of attaching elements like pictures and graphs that can help with understanding the information when transmitting the information.<br>7. The design of the learning process allows me to use, besides language and numbers, other non-verbal cues when communicating with others (such as facial expression, body language, audio-visuals, pictures, graphs).<br>8. The design of the learning process allows me to provide more detailed non-verbal cues as auxiliary information when I am communicating with others. | Carlson and Zmud (1999), Johnson et al. (2006), Rice, et al. (1987) [75,77,78] |
| Language Variety | 9. The design of the learning process provides a more flexible way of expression that allows me to freely use the language with which I am familiar, such as Chinese, English, digital, graphics, symbols, that can help convey clearly the intended message.<br>10. The design of the learning process offers me richer and more diverse ways to accentuate the meaning of the words (such as punctuations, font size, color). | Carlson and Zmud (1999), Johnson et al. (2006) [75] |
| Personal focus of the medium | 11. The design of the learning process is a medium where I can exhibit my personal features such as looks, forms.<br>12. The design of the learning process offers me the ability to display and edit personalized information. | Carlson and Zmud (1999), Johnson et al. (2006), Rice et al. (1987) [75,77,78] |

Written consent forms were delivered to all students to obtain their agreement to participate in this study, and at the same time informed them about their rights to withdraw from the research at any time without penalty. The questionnaire survey proceeded after permissions to participate had all been received and was conducted in the classroom setting at the respective classes. The participants were given approximately 30 minutes in class to complete the questionnaire and the class teacher collated them when completed.

*3.3. Analysis*

The research has adopted the Cronbach's $\alpha$ to examine the reliability of the questionnaire in order to understand the consistency of the questions in it (Table 4). The result of the internal consistency reliability test indicated that the Cronbach's $\alpha$ value for the availability of immediate feedback was 0.866; use of multiple cues was 0.650; language variety was 0.776; and personal focus of the medium was 0.833, which were all at an acceptable level. In addition, the Cronbach's $\alpha$ values of the entire questionnaire ranges between 0.650 to 0.886, with an overall reliability value of 0.883. As such, this questionnaire has passed the reliability test since a Cronbach's $\alpha$ value of 0.8 and above denotes excellent reliability [79–82].

**Table 4.** The questionnaire reliability of media richness.

| Dimension | Survey Content | Mean (M) | SD (Standard Deviation) | Cronbach's α |
|---|---|---|---|---|
| Availability of immediate feedback | 1. The design of the learning process provides me with effective information to help me communicate quickly. | 4.35 | 0.63 | 0.866 |
| | 2. The design of the learning process allows me to ask and understand immediately. | 4.24 | 0.69 | |
| | 3. The design of the learning process makes it easier for me to communicate and exchange ideas with others. | 4.16 | 0.71 | |
| | 4. The design of the learning process makes it easier for me to understand the content when I am communicating with others. | 4.19 | 0.65 | |
| | 5. The design of the learning process allows me to grasp the status of information transmission immediately. | 4.27 | 0.66 | |
| Use of multiple cues | 6. The design of the learning process offers the option of attaching elements like pictures and graphs that can help with understanding the information when transmitting the information. | 3.56 | 1.30 | 0.650 |
| | 7. The design of the learning process allows me to use, besides language and numbers, other non-verbal cues when communicating with others (such as facial expression, body language, audio-visuals, pictures, graphs). | 3.24 | 1.18 | |
| | 8. The design of the learning process allows me to provide more detailed non-verbal cues as auxiliary information when I am communicating with others. | 3.71 | 0.88 | |
| Language variety | 9. The design of the learning process provides a more flexible way of expression that allows me to freely use the language with which I am familiar, such as Chinese, English, digital, graphics, symbols, that can help convey clearly the intended message. | 3.40 | 1.15 | 0.776 |
| | 10. The design of the learning process offers me richer and more diverse ways to accentuate the meaning of the words (such as punctuations, font size, color). | 3.11 | 1.10 | |
| Personal focus of the medium | 11. The design of the learning process is a medium where I can exhibit my personal features such as looks, forms. | 3.53 | 0.74 | 0.833 |
| | 12. The design of the learning process offers me the ability to display and edit personalized information. | 3.65 | 0.70 | |
| Overall reliability | | | | 0.883 |

In terms of validity, three communication scholars from Shanghai Jiao Tong University and Taiwan's Shih Hsin University were invited to examine the validity of the questionnaire. The convergent validity, which is used to examine the degree of correlation between each dimension and its question [83], of this research had reached par level because the Pearson Correlation Coefficient for every item has attained a significant level, indicating a good convergent validity. As for the discriminate validity, which is used to examine the result of discrimination among the dimensions for which regular factor analysis is employed [83], this research has adopted the factor analysis method. The factor loading for every item (except for questions 6, 7 and 10) was greater than 0.5, and the Pearson correlation coefficient for all questions have reached significant level ($p < 0.0001$). The results of the convergent validity and discriminate validity of media richness perception were outlined in Table 5, which suggested that the research questionnaire had attained a satisfactory overall validity.

The Statistical Package for the Social Sciences (SPSS v.22) was used to analyze the information collected in this study, and tests such as the independent sample *t*-test and Pearson correlation coefficient were conducted to examine if correlations existed between the key constructs in this study.

Table 5. The questionnaire validity of media richness.

| Dimension | Item | Factor Loading | Pearson Correlation Coefficient | p-Value |
|---|---|---|---|---|
| Availability of immediate feedback | 1 | 0.653 | 0.764 ** | $p < 0.0001$ |
| | 2 | 0.713 | 0.830 ** | $p < 0.0001$ |
| | 3 | 0.734 | 0.834 ** | $p < 0.0001$ |
| | 4 | 0.773 | 0.875 ** | $p < 0.0001$ |
| | 5 | 0.688 | 0.733 ** | $p < 0.0001$ |
| Use of multiple cues | 6 | 0.422 | 0.821 ** | $p < 0.0001$ |
| | 7 | 0.276 | 0.761 ** | $p < 0.0001$ |
| | 8 | 0.720 | 0.734 ** | $p < 0.0001$ |
| Language variety | 9 | 0.526 | 0.908 ** | $p < 0.0001$ |
| | 10 | 0.376 | 0.900 ** | $p < 0.0001$ |
| Personal focus of the medium | 11 | 0.746 | 0.930 ** | $p < 0.0001$ |
| | 12 | 0.603 | 0.922 ** | $p < 0.0001$ |

\*\* Denotes significant level less than 0.01.

## 4. Results

### 4.1. Distribution of Demographic Profiles

A total of 67 students participated in the experiment, of which 41 were males (61.2%) and 26 were females (38.8%). A majority of the respondents were aged between 41 to 50 years old (50.7%), and this was followed by over 50-year-olds (28.4%), between 31 to 40 years old (13.4%), and under 30 years old (7.5%). Table 6 below briefly presented the overall demographic distribution of the respondents.

Table 6. Overall demographic distribution.

| Variable | Item | Number | Percentage |
|---|---|---|---|
| Gender | Male | 41 | 61.2% |
| | Female | 26 | 38.8% |
| Age | Under 30 | 5 | 7.5% |
| | 31–40 | 9 | 13.4% |
| | 41–50 | 34 | 50.7% |
| | Over 50 | 19 | 28.4% |
| Total | | 67 | 100% |

In terms of the demographic distribution for the CMC experimental group, there were a total of 33 students (18 males and 15 females). The respondents in this experimental group were represented by the following age groups: between 41- to 50-year-old (54.5%), over 50-year-old (27.3%), between 31- to 40-year-old (9.1%), and under 30-year-old (9.1%). As for the FtF control group, there were more males (67.6%) than females (32.4%) with a total of 34 students. A majority of the respondents of this control group were aged between 41 to 50 years old (47.1%), with the others in the following age categories: over 50-year-old (29.4%), between 31- to 40-year-old (17.6%), and under 30-year-old (5.9%). Tables 7 and 8 below briefly outline the demographic distribution of the respondents for both the CMC experimental and FtF control groups, respectively.

### 4.2. Torrance Creativity Cognitive Performance

The research adopted ATTA as the tool to measure creativity potential, with score based on norm of fluency, flexibility, originality, and elaboration. The results (as shown in Table 9) of the independent sample $t$-test for the Torrance creativity cognitive performance ATTA indicated that the overall mean score of the CMC experimental group was higher than the FtF control group in terms of creativity cognition ($p = 0.012$, $t$-test). This signified that participants in the CMC group had a greater creativity than those in the FtF group. Although there was no significant difference ($p = 0.052$, $t$-test) in the elaboration performance between the CMC and FtF groups, the CMC group (mean = 16.79) had a slightly higher mean score than the FtF group (mean = 15.70). On the other hand, the findings revealed that there were significant differences in the performance of the fluency, flexibility, and originality variables between the CMC group and the FtF group. The CMC group had a better fluency performance that suggested a greater level of ability to generate a larger quantity and meaningful thoughts than the FtF group. The CMC group also performed better in the flexibility performance than the FtF group whereby they could better describe more capabilities to easily modify their willingness to change their existing thoughts. In terms of originality performance, the CMC group outperformed the FtF group with a greater ability to produce new concepts and unique ideas toward problem solving. Therefore, Hypotheses H1 ($p = 0.012$, $t$-test), H1a ($p < 0.0001$, $t$-test), H1b ($p = 0.039$, $t$-test), and H1c ($p = 0.014$, $t$-test) were supported, whereas Hypothesis H1d ($p = 0.06$, $t$-test) was rejected.

**Table 7.** Demographic distribution for the computer-mediated communication (CMC) experimental group.

| Variable | Item | Number | Percentage |
|---|---|---|---|
| Gender | Male | 18 | 54.5% |
| | Female | 15 | 45.5% |
| Age | Under 30 | 3 | 9.1% |
| | 31–40 | 3 | 9.1% |
| | 41–50 | 18 | 54.5% |
| | Over 50 | 9 | 27.3% |
| Total | | 33 | 100% |

**Table 8.** Demographic distribution for the face-to-face (FtF) communication control group.

| Variable | Item | Number | Percentage |
|---|---|---|---|
| Gender | Male | 23 | 67.6% |
| | Female | 11 | 32.4% |
| Age | Under 30 | 2 | 5.9% |
| | 31–40 | 6 | 17.6% |
| | 41–50 | 16 | 47.1% |
| | Over 50 | 10 | 29.4% |
| Total | | 34 | 100% |

**Table 9.** Torrance potential creativity cognitive performance in an original-score evaluation.

| | CMC ($n = 33$) | | FtF ($n = 34$) | | | |
|---|---|---|---|---|---|---|
| Variable | Mean | SD | Mean | SD | $t$ value | $p$ |
| H1a: Fluency | 16.60 | 1.77 | 14.79 | 1.72 | 4.25 *** | $p < 0.0001$ |
| H1b: Flexibility | 15.97 | 2.19 | 14.85 | 2.16 | 2.10 * | $p = 0.039$ |
| H1c: Originality | 17.45 | 1.77 | 16.29 | 2.01 | 2.50 * | $p = 0.014$ |
| H1d: Elaboration | 16.79 | 2.22 | 15.70 | 2.46 | 1.90 | $p = 0.06$ |
| H1: Potential creativity cognition performance | 16.70 | 1.99 | 15.41 | 2.09 | 2.58 * | $p = 0.012$ |

***: $p < 0.001$, two-tailed test; **: $p < 0.01$, two-tailed test; *: $p < 0.05$, two-tailed test.

*Appl. Sci.* **2020**, *10*, 1602

### 4.3. Independent Sample t-Test Analysis of Media Richness Perception

Findings (Table 10) of the independent sample *t*-test for media richness perception indicated that the overall mean score of the CMC experimental group was significantly higher than the FtF control group. The outcomes implied that the CMC group had a higher level of perceived media richness in which they attained a more effective understanding of the information through the communication media used, while there was no significant difference between the CMC group and FtF group in terms of availability of immediate feedback ($p < 0.094$, *t*-test), and personal focus of the medium ($p < 0.028$, *t*-test); however, significant differences existed between the groups for the use of multiple cues ($p < 0.001$, *t*-test), and language variety ($p < 0.001$, *t*-test).

**Table 10.** Independent sample *t*-test analysis of media richness perception in a norm-referenced evaluation.

| Dimension | CMC (*n* = 30) | | FtF (*n* = 32) | | *t* Value | *p* |
|---|---|---|---|---|---|---|
| | Mean | SD | Mean | SD | | |
| Availability of immediate feedback | 4.13 | 0.61 | 4.36 | 0.44 | −1.70 | 0.094 |
| Use of multiple cues | 4.04 | 0.64 | 3.00 | 0.75 | 5.88 *** | < 0.001 |
| Language variety | 3.88 | 0.77 | 2.67 | 0.87 | 5.79 *** | < 0.001 |
| Personal focus of the medium | 3.68 | 0.65 | 3.50 | 0.68 | 1.08 * | 0.028 |
| Media richness perception | 3.99 | 0.59 | 3.59 | 0.43 | 3.01 ** | < 0.01 |

***: $p < 0.001$, two-tailed test; **: $p < 0.01$, two-tailed test; *: $p < 0.05$, two-tailed test.

### 4.4. Correlation between Media Richness Perception and Potential Creativity Cognition Performance Variables

As shown in Table 11, the findings revealed no significant correlation ($r = 0.23$, $p = 0.079$) between the overall media richness perception and potential creativity cognition. However, there were significant correlations between the "fluency" variable of the potential creativity cognition performance and two media richness dimensions; namely the "use of multiple cues" ($r = 0.42$, $p < 0.001$), and "language variety" ($r = 0.38$, $p < 0.001$). Results also indicated that significant correlations were not only present between the "elaboration" variable of the potential creativity cognition performance and the overall media richness ($r = 0.30$, $p < 0.05$) but also with three media richness dimensions; "use of multiple cues" ($r = 0.29$, $p < 0.05$), "language variety" ($r = 0.33$, $p < 0.001$), and "personal focus of the medium" ($r = 0.34$, $p < 0.001$. Furthermore, the findings also suggested significant relationships existed between the "language variety" dimension of the media richness with the overall potential creativity cognition performance ($r = 0.39$, $p < 0.001$) and its "flexibility" variable ($r = 0.36$, $p < 0.001$).

Research Hypotheses

There were 12 hypotheses examined in this study (see Table 12). The findings (as shown in Table 10) revealed support for eight hypotheses and rejected the remaining four hypotheses. The overall potential creativity cognition performance of the CMC learners in the experimental group was deemed to be better than the FtF learners in the control group (H1 supported). In terms of the fluency, originality, and elaboration variables of the potential creativity cognition performance, the CMC learners of the experimental group performed better than the FtF learners of the control group (H1a, H1c, H1d supported). However, the CMC learners of the experimental group did not perform better than the FtF learners of the control group with regards to the flexibility variable of the potential creativity cognition performance (H1b rejected).

Table 11. Correlation between media richness perception and potential creativity cognition performance variables.

| | Fluency | Originality | Elaboration | Flexibility | Overall Potential Creativity Cognition Performance | The Availability of Immediate Feedback | Use of Multiple Cues | Language Variety | Personal Focus of the Medium | Overall Media Richness Perception |
|---|---|---|---|---|---|---|---|---|---|---|
| Fluency | - | | | | | | | | | |
| Originality | 0.55 ** | - | | | | | | | | |
| Elaboration | 0.42 ** | 0.21 | - | | | | | | | |
| Flexibility | 0.37 ** | 0.10 | 0.44 ** | - | | | | | | |
| Overall potential creativity cognition performance | 0.77 ** | 0.65 ** | 0.69 ** | 0.56 ** | - | | | | | |
| The availability of immediate feedback | 0.03 | −0.08 | 0.05 | −0.12 | −0.09 | - | | | | |
| Use of multiple cues | 0.42 ** | 0.16 | 0.29 * | 0.18 | 0.27 * | 0.31 * | - | | | |
| Language variety | 0.38 ** | 0.09 | 0.33 ** | 0.36 ** | 0.39 ** | 0.24 | 0.57 ** | - | | |
| Personal focus of the medium | 0.12 | −0.11 | 0.34 ** | 0.23 | 0.19 | 0.50 ** | 0.55 ** | 0.50 ** | - | |
| Overall media richness perception | 0.32 * | 0.04 | 0.30 * | 0.18 | 0.23 | 0.71 ** | 0.81 ** | 0.74 ** | 0.78 ** | - |

Note: Two-tailed test was deployed on the correlation coefficients, * $p < 0.05$; ** $p < 0.01$.

Table 12. Research hypothesis results.

| Hypothesis | Result |
|---|---|
| H1: The overall potential creativity cognition performance of the CMC learners in the experimental group is better than the FtF learners in the control group. | Supported |
| H1a: The fluency performance of the CMC learners of the experimental group is better than the FtF learners of the control group. | Supported |
| H1b: The flexibility performance of the CMC learners of the experimental group is better than the FtF learners of the control group. | Supported |
| H1c: The originality performance of the CMC learners of the experimental group is better than the FtF learners of the control group. | Supported |
| H1d: The elaboration performance of the CMC learners of the experimental group is better than the FtF learners of the control group. | Not Supported |
| H2: The overall media richness perception of the CMC learners of the experimental group is better than the FtF learners of the control group. | Supported |
| H2a: The perception of the availability of immediate feedback of the CMC learners of the experimental group is better than the FtF learners of the control group. | Not Supported |
| H2b: The perception of use of multiple cues of the CMC learners of the experimental group is better than the FtF learners of the control group. | Supported |
| H2c: The perception of language variety of the CMC learners of the experimental group is better than the FtF learners of the control group. | Supported |
| H2d: The perception of personal focus of the medium of the CMC learners of the experimental group is better than the FtF learners of the control group. | Supported |
| H3: Media richness perception is significantly correlated to potential creative thinking. | Not Supported |

As for the overall media richness perception, the CMC learners of the experimental group had performed better than the FtF learners of the control group (H2 supported). In addition, the CMC learners of the experimental group also did better in their perception of use of multiple cues, language variety, and personal focus of the medium as compared to the FtF learners of the control group (H2b, H2c, H2d supported). Conversely, the FtF learners of the control group performed better than the CMC learners of the experimental group in their perception of the availability of immediate feedback (H2a rejected). Hypothesis 3 was also rejected since there was no evidence to suggest a significant correlation between media richness perception and potential creative thinking.

## 5. Discussion

The aim of this research was to explore the correlation between media richness and potential creativity through the use of the CMC and FtF communication formats. In relation to the first research question: "Will the use of different communication formats (i.e., CMC and FtF) have an impact on potential creative thinking?", the research results showed that the CMC communication format had achieved a higher potential creativity in fluency, flexibility, and originality than the FtF communication format. This suggested that the relatively higher communication equivocality by the CMC communication format had helped individuals to overcome the limitations of space and time, and could more actively focus on the exchange of transmitted information [20,29,31]. This outcome aligned with studies in the past that supported CMC communication format in delivering remarkable production and communication efficiency for potential creativity thinking [29,30]. Furthermore, the virtual communication environment of the CMC format offered more relaxing, anonymous, and less tense facial expression and change in tone of voice than that of FtF [13–15]. However, other research studies found that the performance of innovative thinking via the FtF communication format to be better than that of the CMC format, particularly in the context of education research and new product development [26–28,84].

For the second research question: "What is the correlation between media richness and potential creative thinking through the use of the CMC and FtF communication formats?", the research findings discovered that the perception of CMC communication format was stronger than the FtF format in terms of media richness, use of multiple cues, language variety and personal focus of the medium. This outcome was supported by the previous studies [37,57]. In contrast, the perception of the availability of immediate feedback through the CMC communication format was not evident. This could be explained by learners who considered the use of such a format to be a more flexible way of communication that enhanced their understanding and way of thinking about the information received. Such an outcome corresponded with the study by Culnan and Markus [24].

Other researchers also pointed out that the synchronized interaction in CMC communication format had a similar effect to real time face-to-face communication. The combination of text, voice, and video would also remedy what was lacking in oral conversation. Therefore, the CMC communication format might not necessarily be less effective than the FtF format [24,25]. However, this finding was different from some earlier studies in the 1970s, which argued that the FtF format had the highest communication richness [20–23]. While the research findings revealed no significant difference between the CMC and FtF communication formats in the perception of the availability of immediate feedback, previous studies did argue that the CMC media richness for interactivity was still behind the FtF format [11,35].

The research findings indicated that of the four dimensions of media richness, only the availability of immediate feedback had no significant correlation with potential creativity cognition performance. This outcome was supported by previous studies [37,57]. However, the use of multiple cues, and language variety dimensions of media richness, did have an effect on the fluency variable of the potential creativity cognition performance. The three media richness dimensions; use of multiple cues, language variety, and personal focus of the medium also had a positive correlation with the elaboration variable of the potential creativity cognition performance, whereas the language variety dimension was correlated to the flexibility variable of the potential creativity cognition performance. These findings suggested that it would be easier for the learners of creativity to interpret and contemplate language and symbols transmitted by the media format that had better performance of fluency, flexibility, and originality in creative thinking. The availability of immediate feedback focused on the speed of information, meaning it has the ability to receive immediate response and to make corrections, as in FtF when transmitting and receiving information. The creativity cognition focused on the breadth and depth of the information, which contributed to enhancing potential creative thinking. Therefore, the CMC and FtF media influenced the result of creativity cooperation and new product development [29–33,84,85].

Although there were studies [12,29,30,84] conducted to explore the creative results and communication satisfaction of different groups of people through different media, very few were related to media richness and creativity. This research study had attempted to fill this gap whereby the findings suggested that the CMC communication format could transmit better language variety and use of multiple cues of media richness that helped with fluency and elaboration of creative thinking. This result was different to previous studies that argued FtF is more effective in this space. Therefore, the findings on the four dimensions of media richness and the four variables of creativity brought forth by this research had further expanded the relevant research field and the extended the depth of other original similar prior studies.

In conclusion, the research explored the impact on potential creative thinking by media richness perception through creativity training via the CMC and FtF communication formats. The result provided a theoretical and practical reference for corporations facing future challenges, method of utilizing media to acquire effective information, promoting education of sustainable development, and enhancing the individual or group creativity of the employees to help with maintaining sustainable operational competitiveness by social communication activities.

## 6. Limitation

### 6.1. Limitation of Subjects

The research selected students who had actual business administration experience and enrolled in the master's degree program at the Shanghai Shih Hsin University as experimental subjects. This study was limited by the time and resources provided by the corporations that coordinated with the scholastic research institution and by the limited number of experimental subjects (i.e., 67). Therefore, the results could not be generalized to the population at large. In addition, the samples did not represent students without a master degree or non-managers. Also, the research could not extend the deduction to students at different stages of learning, different corporate organizations, or all workers, to verify the correlation between the theory and research structure. A more representative sample would be required for any future research.

*6.2. Limitations of Research Method and Tools*

The study focused on exploring the impact of creativity training of different types of communication formats on potential creative thinking. It was limited to only creativity training as planned in the social-media experiment. Thus, the results could not be interpreted for other contexts. The research chose the more frequently used face-to-face method and mobile communication software, WeChat, for the experiment. Therefore, the research results can be compared less with other traditional or new media. The relevance of the results to other computer-mediated communication media would require further verification. The experiment of the research had no control over the actions of the experimental subjects, the status of the internet, and disturbances by environmental factors during the investigation even though the researcher executed procedure control over the plan before and during the experiment being conducted.

**Author Contributions:** Author contributions are indicated as follows: conceptualization, S.-H.C. and J.J.; methodology, S.-H.C. and J.J.; software, C.-H.H., Y.-T.C., E.N. and W.-T.F.; validation, C.-H.H., Y.-T.C., E.N. and W.-T.F.; formal analysis, S.-H.C.; investigation, S.-H.C.; resources, C.-H.H.; data curation, S.-H.C.; writing—original draft preparation, E.N. and W.-T.F.; writing—review and editing, Y.-T.C.; visualization, J.J.; supervision, J.J.; project administration, S.-H.C. All authors have read and agreed to the published version of the manuscript.

**Funding:** This research received no external funding, instead only in-kind of the laboratory supports in the Master's program at the Shanghai College of Shih Hsin University.

**Acknowledgments:** We thank members of the Graduate Institute of Environmental Education, National Taiwan Normal University (NTNU) and members of the College of Journalism and Communications, Shih Hsin University (Taiwan) and Shanghai College of Shih Hsin University for their contributions to the manuscript.

**Conflicts of Interest:** The authors declare no conflict of interest.

## References

1. Amabile, T.M.; Hadley, C.N.; Kramer, S.J. Creativity under the gun. *Harv. Bus. Rev.* **2002**, *80*, 52–63. [PubMed]
2. Scott, S.G.; Bruce, R.A. Determinants of innovative behavior: A path model of individual innovation in the workplace. *Acad. Manag. J.* **1994**, *37*, 580–607.
3. Zhou, J.; George, J.M. When job dissatisfaction leads to creativity: Encouraging the expression of voice. *Acad. Manag. J.* **2001**, *44*, 682–696.
4. Hackman, J.R.; Wageman, R. A theory of team coaching. *Acad. Manag. Rev.* **2005**, *30*, 269–287.
5. Obstfeld, D. Social networks, the *Tertius Iungens* orientation, and involvement in innovation. *Adm. Sci. Q.* **2005**, *50*, 100–130.
6. Abbas, J.; Hussain, I.; Hussain, S.; Akram, S.; Shaheen, I.; Niu, B. The impact of knowledge sharing and innovation on sustainable performance in Islamic banks: A mediation analysis through a SEM approach. *Sustainability* **2019**, *11*, 4049. [CrossRef]
7. López-Alcarria, A.; Olivares-Vicente, A.; Poza-Vilches, F. A systematic review of the use of agile methodologies in education to foster sustainability competencies. *Sustainability* **2019**, *11*, 2915. [CrossRef]
8. Perry-Smith, J.E. Social yet creative: The role of social relationships in facilitating individual creativity. *Acad. Manag. J.* **2006**, *49*, 85–101.
9. Lee, J.; Kim, S.; Lee, J.; Moon, S. Enhancing employee creativity for a sustainable competitive advantage through perceived human resource management practices and trust in management. *Sustainability* **2019**, *11*, 2305. [CrossRef]

10. Yoo, S.; Jang, S.; Ho, Y.; Seo, J.; Yoo, M.H. Fostering workplace creativity: Examining the roles of job design and organizational context. *Asia Pac. J. Hum. Resour.* **2019**, *57*, 127–149.
11. Brown, K.; Fridman, I. Transforming feedback: An application framework for group feedback videos in design. *Int. J. Art Des. Educ.* **2020**, *39*, 139–152.
12. Zhao, R. Analysis of implementing hybrid teaching in international cruise talents education illustrated by ESP teaching. In Proceedings of the 2019 4th International Conference on Humanities Science and Society Development (ICHSSD 2019), Xiamen, China, 24–26 May 2019.
13. Croes, E.A.; Antheunis, M.L.; Schouten, A.P.; Krahmer, E.J.; Bleize, D.N. The effect of interaction topic and social ties on media choice and the role of four underlying mechanisms. *Communications* **2018**, *43*, 47–73.
14. Croes, E.A.; Antheunis, M.L.; Schouten, A.P.; Krahmer, E.J. Social attraction in video-mediated communication: The role of nonverbal affiliative behavior. *J. Soc. Pers. Relatsh.* **2019**, *36*, 1210–1232.
15. York, J. Language Learning in Complex Virtual Worlds: Effects of Modality and Task Complexity on Oral Performance between Virtual World and Face-to-Face Tasks. Doctoral Thesis, University of Leicester, Lester, UK, 2019.
16. Daft, R.L.; Lengel, R.H. *Information Richness. A New Approach to Managerial Behavior and Organization Design*; Department of Management, Texas A & M University: College Station, TX, USA, 1983.
17. Ishii, K.; Lyons, M.M.; Carr, S.A. Revisiting media richness theory for today and future. *Hum. Behav. Emerg. Technol.* **2019**, *1*, 124–131.
18. Handke, L.; Schulte, E.-M.; Schneider, K.; Kauffeld, S. The medium isn't the message: Introducing a measure of adaptive virtual communication. *Cogent Arts Humanit.* **2018**, *5*, 1514953.
19. Chidambaram, L.; Jones, B. Impact of communication medium and computer support on group perceptions and performance: A comparison of face-to-face and dispersed meetings. *MIS Q.* **1993**, *17*, 465–491.
20. Walther, J.B. Theories of computer-mediated communication and interpersonal relations. *Handb. Interpers. Commun.* **2011**, *4*, 443–479.
21. Short, J.; Williams, E.; Christie, B. *The Social Psychology of Telecommunications*; John Wiley & Sons: Hoboken, NJ, USA, 1976.
22. Daft, R.L.; Lengel, R.H. Organizational information requirements, media richness and structural design. *Manag. Sci.* **1986**, *32*, 554–571.
23. Wei, R. Motivations for using the mobile phone for mass communications and entertainment. *Telemat. Inform.* **2008**, *25*, 36–46.
24. Culnan, M.; Markus, M.L. Information technologies. In *Handbook of Organizational Communication: An Interdisciplinary Perspective*; Sage: Newbury Park, CA, USA, 1987; pp. 420–443.
25. Litosseliti, L.; Marttunen, M.; Laurinen, L.; Salminen, T. Computer-based and face-to-face collaborative argumentation in secondary schools in England and Finland. *Educ. Commun. Inf.* **2005**, *5*, 131–146.
26. Tichavsky, L.P.; Hunt, A.N.; Driscoll, A.; Jicha, K. "It's just nice having a real teacher": Student perceptions of online versus face-to-face instruction. *Int. J. Scholarsh. Teach. Learn.* **2015**, *9*, 2. [CrossRef]
27. Liu, J.; Zhang, R.; Geng, B.; Zhang, T.; Yuan, D.; Otani, S.; Li, X. Interplay between prior knowledge and communication mode on teaching effectiveness: Interpersonal neural synchronization as a neural marker. *NeuroImage* **2019**, *193*, 93–102. [PubMed]
28. Tang, X. The effects of task modality on 12 Chinese learners' pragmatic development: Computer-mediated written chat vs. Face-to-face oral chat. *System* **2019**, *80*, 48–59.
29. Wu, Y.; Chang, K.; Sha, X. Creative performance in the workplace: The roles of Simmelian ties and communication media. *Comput. Hum. Behav.* **2016**, *63*, 575–583.
30. Hatem, W.A.; Naji, H.I.; Alkreem, Z.A.A. Using of advanced communication technology in the construction projects during the implementation stage. *Diyala J. Eng. Sci.* **2018**, *11*, 14–23.
31. Smith, B. Computer-mediated negotiated interaction and lexical acquisition. *Stud. Second Lang. Acquis.* **2004**, *26*, 365–398.
32. Smith, B. The relationship between negotiated interaction, learner uptake, and lexical acquisition in task-based computer-mediated communication. *Tesol Q.* **2005**, *39*, 33–58.
33. Erhart, J. The RRelationship between the Amount of Ftf-Interaction and Conflict in Virtual Teams: The Moderating Role of a Shared Identity. Doctoral Thesis, Catholic University of Portugal, Lisbon, Portugal, 2018.
34. Parnes, S.J. *Creative Behavior Guidebook*; Scribner: New York, NY, USA, 1967.

35. Kushlev, K.; Heintzelman, S.J. Put the phone down: Testing a complement-interfere model of computer-mediated communication in the context of face-to-face interactions. *Soc. Psychol. Personal. Sci.* **2018**, *9*, 702–710.
36. Brown, V.L.; Sidgman, J.; Brazel, J.F. The Multitasking Audit Environment: The Effect of Alternative Modes of Communication on Team Performance. Available online: https://ssrn.com/abstract=3310579 (accessed on 8 October 2019).
37. Guilford, J.P. *The Nature of Human Intelligence*; McGraw-Hill: New York, NY, USA, 1967.
38. Guilford, J.P. *Creative Talents: Their Nature, Uses and Development*; Bearly Limited: New York, NY, USA, 1986.
39. Chen, L. Strategies and techniques for creating thinking. *Educ. Mater. J.* **2005**, *30*, 201–265.
40. Amabile, T.M. The social psychology of creativity: A componential conceptualization. *J. Personal. Soc. Psychol.* **1983**, *45*, 357–376.
41. Amabile, T.M.; Conti, R.; Coon, H.; Lazenby, J.; Herron, M. Assessing the work environment for creativity. *Acad. Manag. J.* **1996**, *39*, 1154–1184.
42. George, J.M.; Zhou, J. When openness to experience and conscientiousness are related to creative behavior: An interactional approach. *J. Appl. Psychol.* **2001**, *86*, 513–524. [PubMed]
43. Perry-Smith, J.E.; Shalley, C.E. A social composition view of team creativity: The role of member nationality-heterogeneous ties outside of the team. *Organ. Sci.* **2014**, *25*, 1434–1452.
44. Soda, G.; Stea, D.; Pedersen, T. Network structure, collaborative context, and individual creativity. *J. Manag.* **2019**, *45*, 1739–1765.
45. Koednok, S.; Sungsanit, M. The influence of multilevel factors of human resource practices on innovative work behavior. *J. Behav. Sci.* **2018**, *13*, 37–55.
46. Mednick, S. The associative basis of the creative process. *Psychol. Rev.* **1962**, *69*, 220–232.
47. Runco, M.A.; Jaeger, G.J. The standard definition of creativity. *Creat. Res. J.* **2012**, *24*, 92–96.
48. Zhang, W.; Sun, S.L.; Jiang, Y.; Zhang, W. Openness to experience and team creativity: Effects of knowledge sharing and transformational leadership. *Creat. Res. J.* **2019**, *31*, 62–73.
49. Niezabitowska, A.; Oleszkiewicz, A.; Pieniak, M. Does the frequency of using emoticons in computer-mediated communication signal creativity? *Creativity. Theor. Res. Appl.* **2019**, *6*, 66–76.
50. Tan, A.-G.; Tsubonou, Y.; Oie, M.; Mito, H. Creativity and Music Education: A State of Art Reflection. In *Creativity in Music Education*; Springer: Berlin/Heidelberg, Germany, 2019; pp. 3–16.
51. Wakefield, J.F. Creativity and cognition some implications for arts education. *Creat. Res. J.* **1989**, *2*, 51–63.
52. Lin, W.-L.; Hsu, K.-Y.; Chen, H.-C.; Wang, J.-W. The relations of gender and personality traits on different creativities: A dual-process theory account. *Psychol. Aesthet. Creat. Arts* **2012**, *6*, 112–123.
53. Lin, W.-L.; Lien, Y.-W. The different role of working memory in open-ended versus closed-ended creative problem solving: A dual-process theory account. *Creat. Res. J.* **2013**, *25*, 85–96.
54. Cramond, B. *The Audacity of Creativity Assessment*; Torrance Center, The University of Georgia: Athens, GA, USA, 2011.
55. Isaksen, S.G.; Puccio, G.J.; Treffinger, D.J. An ecological approach to creativity research: Profiling for creative problem solving. *J. Creat. Behav.* **1993**, *27*, 149–170.
56. Piirto, J. *Understanding Those Who Create*; Great Potential Press: Tucson, AZ, USA, 1998.
57. Torrance, E.P. A longitudinal examination of the fourth grade slump in creativity. *Gift. Child Q.* **1968**, *12*, 195–199.
58. Torrance, E. *Torrance Test of Creative Thinking [Measurement Instrument]*; Personnel Press: Lexington, MA, USA, 1974.
59. Karpova, E.; Marcketti, S.B.; Barker, J. The efficacy of teaching creativity: Assessment of student creative thinking before and after exercises. *Cloth. Text. Res. J.* **2011**, *29*, 52–66.
60. Kienitz, E.; Quintin, E.-M.; Saggar, M.; Bott, N.T.; Royalty, A.; Hong, D.W.-C.; Liu, N.; Chien, Y.-H.; Hawthorne, G.; Reiss, A.L. Targeted intervention to increase creative capacity and performance: A randomized controlled pilot study. *Think. Ski. Creat.* **2014**, *13*, 57–66.
61. Perry, A.; Karpova, E. Efficacy of teaching creative thinking skills: A comparison of multiple creativity assessments. *Think. Ski. Creat.* **2017**, *24*, 118–126.
62. Vally, Z.; Salloum, L.; AlQedra, D.; El Shazly, S.; Albloshi, M.; Alsheraifi, S.; Alkaabi, A. Examining the effects of creativity training on creative production, creative self-efficacy, and neuro-executive functioning. *Think. Ski. Creat.* **2019**, *31*, 70–78.

63. Lodhia, S.; Stone, G. Integrated reporting in an internet and social media communication environment: Conceptual insights. *Aust. Account. Rev.* **2017**, *27*, 17–33.
64. Shepherd, M.M.; Martz, W.B., Jr. Media richness theory and the distance education environment. *J. Comput. Inf. Syst.* **2006**, *47*, 114–122.
65. Tseng, F.-C.; Cheng, T.; Li, K.; Teng, C.-I. How does media richness contribute to customer loyalty to mobile instant messaging? *Internet Res.* **2017**, *27*, 520–537.
66. Labafi, S.; Khajeheian, D.; Williams, I. Impact of Media Richness on Reduction of Knowledge-Hiding Behavior in Enterprises. In *Evaluating Media Richness in Organizational Learning*; IGI Global: Hershey, PA, USA, 2018; pp. 135–148.
67. Chen, C.-C.; Chang, Y.-C. What drives purchase intention on airbnb? Perspectives of consumer reviews, information quality, and media richness. *Telemat. Inform.* **2018**, *35*, 1512–1523.
68. Alamäki, A.; Pesonen, J.; Dirin, A. Triggering effects of mobile video marketing in nature tourism: Media richness perspective. *Inf. Process. Manag.* **2019**, *56*, 756–770.
69. Peltokorpi, V. Corporate language proficiency and reverse knowledge transfer in multinational corporations: Interactive effects of communication media richness and commitment to headquarters. *J. Int. Manag.* **2015**, *21*, 49–62.
70. Khedhaouria, A.; Gurău, C.; Torrès, O. Creativity, self-efficacy, and small-firm performance: The mediating role of entrepreneurial orientation. *Small Bus. Econ.* **2015**, *44*, 485–504.
71. Tan, O.S. Flourishing creativity: Education in an age of wonder. *Asia Pac. Educ. Rev.* **2015**, *16*, 161–166.
72. Barbot, B.; Lubart, T.I.; Besançon, M. "Peaks, slumps, and bumps": Individual differences in the development of creativity in children and adolescents. *New Dir. Child Adolesc. Dev.* **2016**, *2016*, 33–45.
73. Dayan, M.; Ozer, M.; Almazrouei, H. The role of functional and demographic diversity on new product creativity and the moderating impact of project uncertainty. *Ind. Mark. Manag.* **2017**, *61*, 144–154.
74. Goff, K. *Abbreviated Torrance Test for Adults: Manual*; Scholastic Testing Service: Bensenville, IL, USA, 2002.
75. Carlson, J.R.; Zmud, R.W. Channel expansion theory and the experiential nature of media richness perceptions. *Acad. Manag. J.* **1999**, *42*, 153–170.
76. Dennis, A.R.; Kinney, S.T.; Hung, Y.-T.C. Gender differences in the effects of media richness. *Small Group Res.* **1999**, *30*, 405–437.
77. Rice, R.E.; Love, G. Electronic emotion: Socioemotional content in a computer-mediated communication network. *Commun. Res.* **1987**, *14*, 85–108.
78. Johnson, G.J.; Bruner, G.C., II; Kumar, A. Interactivity and its facets revisited: Theory and empirical test. *J. Advert.* **2006**, *35*, 35–52.
79. Cohen, J. A power primer. *Psychol. Bull.* **1992**, *112*, 155–159. [PubMed]
80. DeVellis, R.F. *Scale Development: Theory and Applications*, 4th ed.; Sage Publications: Los Angles, CA, USA, 2017.
81. Mallery, P.; George, D. *SPSS for Windows Step by Step: A Simple Guide and Reference*; Allyn & Bacon: Boston, MA, USA, 2003.
82. Kline, P. *Handbook of Psychological Testing*; Routledge: Abingdon upon Thames, UK, 2013.
83. Campbell, D.T.; Fiske, D.W. Convergent and discriminant validation by the multitrait-multimethod matrix. *Psychol. Bull.* **1959**, *56*, 81–105.
84. Ko, C.-H.; Wu, S.-C.; Chen, C.-Y. Novel and practical idea generation: Consumer-to-consumer interactive behaviors and brand knowledge. *Int. J. Innov. Sci.* **2019**, *11*, 325–343.
85. Sørensen, J.K. Exploring constrained creative communication: The silent game as model for studying online collaboration. *Int. J. E Serv. Mob. Appl.* **2017**, *9*, 1–23.

© 2020 by the authors. Licensee MDPI, Basel, Switzerland. This article is an open access article distributed under the terms and conditions of the Creative Commons Attribution (CC BY) license (http://creativecommons.org/licenses/by/4.0/).

*Review*

# Analyzing and Predicting Students' Performance by Means of Machine Learning: A Review

Juan L. Rastrollo-Guerrero, Juan A. Gómez-Pulido * and Arturo Durán-Domínguez

Escuela Politécnica, Universidad de Extremadura, 10003 Cáceres, Spain; juanluisrg@unex.es (J.L.R.-G.); arduran@unex.es (A.D.-D.)
* Correspondence: jangomez@unex.es

Received: 25 November 2019; Accepted: 23 January 2020; Published: 4 February 2020

**Abstract:** Predicting students' performance is one of the most important topics for learning contexts such as schools and universities, since it helps to design effective mechanisms that improve academic results and avoid dropout, among other things. These are benefited by the automation of many processes involved in usual students' activities which handle massive volumes of data collected from software tools for technology-enhanced learning. Thus, analyzing and processing these data carefully can give us useful information about the students' knowledge and the relationship between them and the academic tasks. This information is the source that feeds promising algorithms and methods able to predict students' performance. In this study, almost 70 papers were analyzed to show different modern techniques widely applied for predicting students' performance, together with the objectives they must reach in this field. These techniques and methods, which pertain to the area of Artificial Intelligence, are mainly Machine Learning, Collaborative Filtering, Recommender Systems, and Artificial Neural Networks, among others.

**Keywords:** prediction; students' performance; dropout; machine learning; supervised learning; unsupervised learning; collaborative filtering; recommender systems; artificial neural networks; deep learning

## 1. Introduction

There is often a great need to be able to predict future students' behavior in order to improve curriculum design and plan interventions for academic support and guidance on the curriculum offered to the students. This is where Data Mining (DM) [1] comes into play. DM techniques analyze datasets and extract information to transform it into understandable structures for later use. Machine Learning (ML), Collaborative Filtering (CF), Recommender Systems (RS) and Artificial Neural Networks (ANN) are the main computational techniques that process this information to predict students' performance, their grades or the risk of dropping out of school.

Nowadays, there is a considerable amount of research and studies that follow along the lines of predicting students' behaviour, among other related topics of interest in the educational area. Indeed, many articles have been published in journals and presented in conferences on this topic. Therefore, the main goal of this study is to present an in depth overview of the different techniques and algorithms proposed that have been applied to this subject.

## 2. Methodology

This article is the result of a qualitative research study of 64 recent articles (almost 90% were published in the last 6 years) related to the different techniques applied for predicting students' behaviour. The literature considered for this study stems from different book chapters, journals and conferences. IEEE, Science Direct, Springer, IEEE Computer Society, iJET, ACM Digital Library,

Taylor & Francis Online, JEO, Sage Journals, J-STAGE, Inderscience Publishers, WIT Press, Science Publications, EJER, and Wiley Online Library were some of the online databases consulted to extract the corresponding literature.

We have excluded papers without enough quality or contribution. The journal papers without an impact factor listed in the ISI Journal Citation Report or not peer-reviewed were excluded. The conference papers corresponding with conferences not organized/supported/published by IEEE, ACM, Springer or renowned organizations and editorials were excluded too. As a result, 35% of the papers analyzed correspond to journal articles; of these, 64% have JCR impact factor and the rest correspond to peer-reviewed journals indexed in other scientific lists.

For the search processes used for these databases we mainly considered the following descriptors: "Predicting students' performance", "Predicting algorithm students", "Machine learning prediction students", "Collaborative filtering prediction students", "Recommender systems prediction students", "Artificial neural network prediction students", "Algorithms analytics students" and "Students analytics prediction performance", among other similar terms.

The literature review provided throughout this article is mainly classified from two points of view: techniques and objectives. We describe the techniques first in this article, since they are applied to reach the objectives considered in each reference. These techniques, in turn, are implemented by means of several algorithmic methods.

Table 1 summarizes the main features of the literature review, showing four groups of columns: students' level, objectives, techniques, and algorithms and methods.

- Students' level: Each reference analyzes datasets built from students of a particular level. We consider a classification of wide levels, corresponding to School (S), High School (HS) and University (U).
- Objectives: The objectives are connected to the interests and risks in the students' learning processes.
- Techniques: The techniques consider the different algorithms, methods and tools that process the data to analyze and predict the above objectives.
- Algorithms and methods: The main algorithms and computational methods applied in each case are detailed in the Table 1. Other algorithms with related names or versions not shown in this table could be also applied. The shadowed cells corresponds with the best algorithms found when several methods were compared for the same purpose.

Figure 1 presents graphically the basic statistics about the techniques, objectives, type of students, and algorithms considered in the literature review. These graphs are built from Table 1 in order to understand better the impact of the literature review that is explained in the next sections.

A first consideration about predicting students' performance by means of ML is the academic level of the students. This information can be useful to know because the datasets built from the students' behaviour imply latent factors that can be different according to the academic level. As we can see in Figure 1, most of the cases correspond to the university level, followed by the high-school level.

**Table 1.** Summary of the main features of the literature review.

| Reference | Students' Level (1) | Objectives | | | | Techniques | | | | | Algorithms and Methods (2)(3) |
|---|---|---|---|---|---|---|---|---|---|---|---|
| | | Students' Dropout | Students' Performance | Recommend Activities and Resources | Students' Knowledge | Supervised Learning | Unsupervised Learning | Recommender Systems (C. Filtering) | Artificial Neural Networks | Data Mining Techniques | (See matrix below) |

Algorithms/Methods columns (left to right): AB, ANN, AT, BART, BBN, BKT, BMF, BN, BSLO, C4.5, CBN, CF, DL, DM, DT, ELM, EM, GBT, JMLM, KNN, LDA, LR, LRMF, LM, MDP, MF, MLP, MLR, NB, One-R, PGPA, RBN, RF, RS, SA, SFS, SL, SLO, SMOTE, SVD, SVM, TL

References [2]–[37] with Students' Level values (U = University, HS = High School, S = School) and × marks indicating applicable objectives, techniques, and algorithms for each study.

Table 1. Cont.

This table is rotated 90° in the source. It contains the following columns (reading the rotated headers):

- **Reference**: [38], [39], [40], [41], [42], [43], [44], [45], [46], [47], [48], [49], [50], [51], [52], [53], [54], [55], [56], [57], [58], [59], [60], [61], [62], [63], [64], [65]
- **Students' Level (1)**: U, U, U, U, U, U, U, U, U, U, U, U, U, U, U, U, U, U, S, U, U, S, U, S, U, U, U, U
- **Objectives**:
  - Students' Dropout: [50], [63], [64]
  - Students' Performance: [38], [40], [41], [42], [43], [44], [45], [46], [48], [51], [52], [53], [54], [55], [56], [57], [58]
  - Recommend Activities and Resources: [41], [46]
  - Students' Knowledge: [59], [60], [61], [62]
- **Techniques**:
  - Supervised Learning: [59]
  - Unsupervised Learning:
  - Recommender Systems (C. Filtering): [38], [39], [40], [41], [42], [43], [44], [45], [46], [47], [48], [49], [50], [51]
  - Artificial Neural Networks: [52], [53], [54], [55], [56], [57], [58]
  - Data Mining Techniques: [59], [60], [62], [63], [64], [65]
- **Algorithms and Methods (2)(3)**: (columns AB, ANN, AT, BART, BBN, BKT, BNF, BN, BSLO, C4.5, CBN, CF, DL, DM, DT, ELM, EM, GBT, jMWM, KNN, LDA, LR, LRMF, LM, MDP, MF, MLP, MLR, NB, One-R, pGPA, RBN, RF, RS, SA, SFS, SL, SLO, SMOTE, SVD, SVM, UL)

Notable marked cells (× in the table):

- ANN column: [52], [53], [54], [55], [56], [57], [58]
- BART column: [61]
- BKT column: [42]
- BNF column: [51]
- BSLO column: [51]
- CF column: [38], [39], [40], [41], [42], [44], [47], [48], [49], [51]
- DM column: [59], [60], [63], [64], [65]
- ELM column: [60]
- EM column: [44]
- GBT column: [62]
- KNN column: [51], [52]
- LR column: [60]
- LRMF column: [44]
- MF column: [42], [44], [50], [51], [52]
- pGPA column: [44]
- RS column: [38]
- SLO column: [51]
- SVD column: [42], [50], [51]

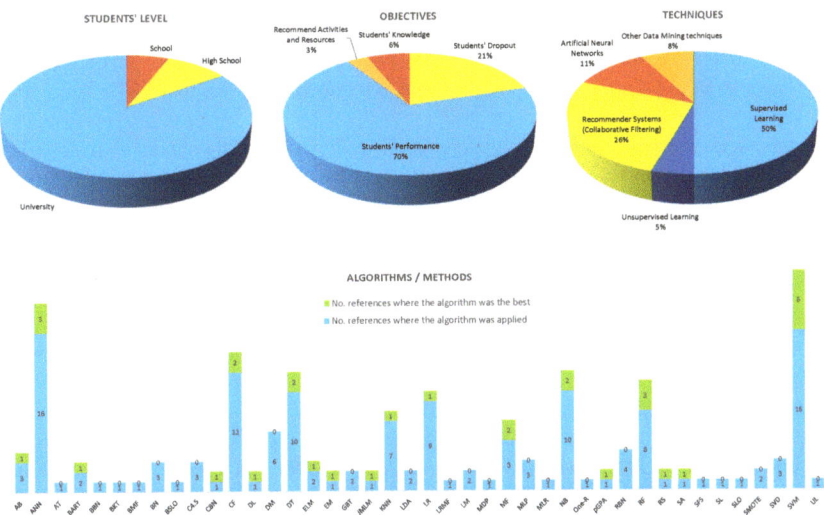

**Figure 1.** Basic statistics about the techniques, objectives and algorithms tackled in the literature review.

## 3. Techniques

The application of techniques such as ML, CF, RS, and ANN to predict students' behavior take into account different types of data, for example, demographic characteristics and the grades from some tasks. A good starting point was the study conducted by the Hellenic Open University, where several machine-supervised learning algorithms were applied to a particular dataset. This research found that the Naïves Bayes (NB) algorithm was the most appropriate for predicting both performance and probability of student dropout [2]. Nevertheless, each case study has its own characteristics and nature, hence different techniques can be selected as the best option to predict students' behaviour.

We have gathered the different techniques into main four groups: supervised ML, unsupervised ML, CF and ANN. An additional group dealing with other DM techniques is added in order to include some works where similar objectives were tackled. Figure 1 shows the weight amount of each of these groups of techniques in the literature, which can indicate the number of problems and cases where each technique is more suitable. In this sense, supervised ML makes up almost half of the cases, followed by CF with a quarter. On the contrary, unsupervised ML has been applied in very few cases.

### 3.1. Machine Learning

Machine Learning is a set of techniques that gives computers the ability to learn without the intervention of human programming [3]. ML has supported a wide range of applications such as medical diagnostics, stock market analysis, DNA sequence classification, games, robotics, predictive analysis, etc. We are particularly interested in the area of predictive analysis, where ML allows us to implement complex models that are used for prediction purposes. These models can be of great help to users by providing relevant data to facilitate decision-making.

ML algorithms are classified into two main streams: supervised and unsupervised.

#### 3.1.1. Supervised Learning

Supervised Learning (SL) seeks algorithms able to reason from instances externally supplied in order to produce general hypotheses, which then make predictions about future instances [66]. In other words, the goal of SL is to build a clear model of the distribution of class labels in terms of predictor characteristics.

Rule Induction is an efficient SL method to make predictions, which was able to reach an accuracy level of 94% when predicting dropout of new students in nursing courses, from 3978 records on 528 students [4].

When using classification techniques, it is necessary to be careful if there are unbalanced datasets, since they can produce misleading predictive accuracy. For this purpose, several improvements were proposed in [5] when predicting dropout, such as exploring a wide range of learning methods, selecting attributes, evaluating the effectiveness of theory, and studying factors between dropout and non-dropout students. The classifier algorithms explored in this study were One-R, C4.5, ADTrees, NB, BN, and Radial Basis Networks (RBN). In this sense, applying several algorithms and comparing their results will be always very useful, as in [6], where four classification algorithms (Logistic Regression (LR) [67], DT, ANN, and SVM) were compared with three data balancing techniques: Over-Sampling, Under-Sampling, and Synthetic Minority Over-Sampling (SMOTE). In this case, SVM with SMOTE gave the best accuracy (90.24%) for retention prediction.

A promising technique was proposed in [7] for predicting the risk of dropout at early stages in online courses, where high dropout rate is a serious problem for this kind of courses at university level. This technique is based on a parallel combination of three ML techniques (K-Nearest Neighbor (KNN), RBN, and SVM), which make use of 28 attributes per student. Considering students' attributes, in [8] a set of ML algorithms (ANN, DT, and BN) took into account the personal characteristics of the students and their academic performance together with input attributes for building prediction models. The effectiveness of the prediction was evaluated using indicators such as the accuracy rate, recovery rate, overall accuracy rate and a particular measure. Moreover, if we take into account the cognitive characteristics of the students, the prediction accuracy improves using DT [9].

An SA framework for early identification of at-risk students was compared to other ML approaches [10], since more than 60% of dropouts occur in the first 2 years, especially in the areas of Science, Technology, Engineering, and Mathematics. Other ML algorithms (DT, NB, KNN, Gradient Boosted Tree (GBT), linear models, and Deep Learning (DL)) were proposed in [11] with similar purposes. Among them, DL and GBT showed the best accuracy. Other studies highlight the quality of SL techniques in predicting dropout: NB and SVM were proposed to predict of individual dropouts [12]; and Sequential Forward Selection (SFS), C4.5, RF, KNN and NB, among other classifiers, were proposed to identify students with difficulties in the third week with 97% accuracy [13]. Along these lines, the use of Random Forests (RF) showed excellent performance in predicting school dropout in terms of various performance metrics for binary classification [14]. Finally, ANN, SVM, LR, NB, and DT were analyzed in [15] for similar purposes by using the data recorded by e-learning tools. In this case, ANN and SVM achieved the highest accuracies.

Several ML algorithms were compared in [2] to predict the performance of new students, where NB showed the best behaviour in a web tool. SVM was the best of the four techniques analyzed in [16] for predicting academic performance. Also Bayesian Belief Network (BNN) was used to predict the students' performance (grade point average) early [17]. Also LR and SVM were applied for this purpose [18]. Nevertheless, the accuracy of the prediction systems can be improved through careful study and implementing different algorithmic features. Thus, preprocessing techniques have been applied together with classification algorithms (SVM, DT and NB) to improve prediction results [19].

A different focus on students' performance can be found in [20], where the main characteristics for observing performance are deduced from students' daily interaction events with certain modules of Moodle. For this purpose, RF and SVM developed the prediction models, and the best results were obtained by RF. With a similar focus, other SL algorithms analyzed datasets directly from websites to evaluate students' performance [21]. Also software platforms in e-learning made it possible to analyze and take advantage of the results of DM and ML algorithms in order to make decisions and justify educational approaches [22].

A data analysis approach to determine next trimester's courses was proposed in [23]. Here, different ML techniques predicted students' performance, which was used to build transition probabilities of a Markov Decision Process (MDP). The Jacobian Matrix-Based Learning Machine (JMLM) was used to analyze the students' learning performance [24], and AdaBoost assembly algorithm was proposed to predict student classification and showed best performance against techniques as DT, ANN, and SVM [25]. Adaboost was also the best meta-decision classifier for predicting student results [26].

SL algorithms are useful for a wide variety of predicting purposes. Predicting whether a student can successfully obtain a certificate was tackled by LR, SVM, NB, KNN, and BN [27]. Predicting graduation grade point averages was tackled by ANN, SVM, and Extreme Learning Machine (ELM) [28], where SVM gave the highest accurate prediction (97.98%). Student performance in the previous semester along with test grades from the current semester were used as input attributes for a series of algorithms (SVM, NB, RF and Gradient Boosting) that predict student grades [29].

Finally, other SL approaches were satisfactorily applied for predicting students' performance. Bayesian Additive Regressive Trees (BART) was used to predict the final grade of students in the sixth week [30]. A model based on SVM weekly predicted the probability of each student belonging to one of these three types: high, medium or low performance [31]. Latent Dirichlet Allocation (LDA) predicted student grades according to how the students described their learning situations after each lesson [32].

3.1.2. Unsupervised Learning

Unsupervised Learning (UL) is also known as class discovery. One of the main differences between UL and SL is that there is no training dataset in UL. As a consequence, there is no obvious role for cross validation [68]. Another important difference is that, although most clustering algorithms are expressed in terms of an optimal criterion, there is generally no guarantee that the optimal solution has been obtained.

A method based on a UL Sparse Auto-Encoder developed a classification model to predict students' performance by automatically learning multiple levels of representation [33]. Classification and clustering algorithms such as K-means and Hierarchical Clustering can be applied to evaluate students' performance [34]. Along these lines, Recursive Clustering was applied in [35] to group students from the programming course into performance-based groups.

*3.2. Recommender Systems*

Recommender systems collect information on the users' preferences for a set of elements (e.g., books, applications, websites, travel destinations, e-learning material, etc.). In the context of students' performance, the information can be acquired explicitly (by collecting users' scores) or implicitly (by monitoring users' behaviour, such as visits to teaching materials, documents downloaded, etc) [69]. RS consider different sources of information to provide predictions and recommendations. They try to balance factors such as precision, novelty, dispersion and stability in recommendations.

Collaborative Filtering

Collaborative Filtering methods play an important role in recommendation, although they are often used together with other filtering techniques such as content-based, knowledge-based or social [69]. Just as humans base their decisions according to past experiences and knowledge, CF acts in the same way to perform predictions.

Some studies predicted different issues with regard to students' performance through CF approaches. Thus, similarities among students were found in [36,37], where students' knowledge was represented as a set of grades from their previous courses. In this case, CF demonstrated a effectiveness similar to ML. Personalized predictions of student grades in required courses were generated from CF using improved similarities [38]. A typical CF method was compared to an article recommendation method based on student's grade in order to recommend personalized articles in an online forum [39]. Students groups, defined by academic characteristics and course influenced matriculation patterns, can be used to design predictive grade models for CF based on neighborhood and MF, and approaches to classification based on popularity [40]. Most of these research studies for predicting students' performance tackle large data matrices. This is the reason why prediction accuracy was not so good when CF was applied for this purpose at small universities [41].

We can find some studies where CF inspires novel methods and tools that try to improve the results in particular environments. A novel student performance prediction model called PSFK combines user-based CF and the user modeling method called Bayesian Knowledge Tracing (BKT) [42]. A method called Hints-Model predicts students' performance [43]. It is combined with a factorization method called Regularized Single-Element-Based Non-Negative Matrix Factorization, achieving a significant improvement in predicting performance. A tool called Grade Prediction Advisor (pGPA) is based on CF and predicts grades in upcoming courses [44]. Two variants of the Low Range Matrix Factorization (LRMF) problem as a predictive task, weighted standard LRMF and non-negative weighted LRMF, were solved by applying the Expectation-Maximization procedure to solve it [45]. A CF technique (matrix decomposition) allows performance prediction of grades for combinations of student courses not observed so far, allowing personalized study planning and orientation for students [46]. A CF tool predicts the unknown performances by analyzing the database that contains students' performances for particular tasks [47]. The optimal parameters of this tool (learning rate and regularization factor) were selected with different metaheuristics in order to improve prediction accuracy. A prototype of RS for online courses improves the performance of new students. It uses CF and knowledge-based techniques to make use of the experience and results of old students in order to be able to suggest resources and activities to help new students [48].

Matrix factorization is a well proven technique in this field. A study conducted at the University of KwaZulu-Natal investigated the efficacy of MF in solving the prediction problem. In this study, an MF technique called Singular Value Decomposition (SVD) was successfully applied [49]. This method was compared with simple baselines (Uniform Random, Global Mean and Mean of Means) when predicting retention [50]. MF and biased MF were compared with other CF methods when predicting whether or not students would answer multiple choice questions: two reference methods (random and global average), two memory-based algorithms (User-kNN and Item-kNN), and two Slope One algorithms (Slope One and Bipolar Slope One) [51]. Probabilistic MF and Bayesian Probabilistic MF using Markov Chain Monte Carlo were used for predicting grades for courses not yet matriculated in by the students, which can help them to make decisions [52].

*3.3. Artificial Neural Networks*

An ANN consists of a set of highly interconnected entities, called Processing Elements. The structure and function of the network is inspired by the biological central nervous system, particularly the brain. Each Processing Element is designed to mimic its biological counterpart, the neuron [53], which accepts a weighted set of inputs and responds with the corresponding output.

ANNs have been applied to different prediction approaches, basically by considering the evaluation results of students, as the following cases show. A feedforward ANN was trained to predict the scores of evaluation tests considering partial scores during the course [54]. An ANN that uses the Cumulative Grade Point Average predicted the academic performance in the eighth semester [55]. Two models of ANN (Multilayer Perceptron and Generalized Regression Neural Network) were compared in order to identify the best model to predict academic performance of students [56]. Lastly, the potential of ANNs to predict learning results was compared to the multivariate LR model in the area of medical education [57].

Not only mere evaluation results, but also additional information from students can improve prediction performed by ANNs. Thus, basic students' information, along with cognitive and non-cognitive measures, were used to design predictive models of students' performance by using three ANN models [58]. The non-linear relationship between cognitive and psychological variables that influence academic performance was analyzed by an ANN, which efficiently grouped students into different categories according to their level of expected performance [53]. Finally, an ELM (which is a particular type of ANN) predicted students' performance by considering the value of the subjects that focus on the final national exam [59].

*3.4. Impact of the Techniques*

The techniques described before had different efficiencies with regard to the students' behaviour. As shown in the bar graph of Figure 1, the different algorithms were not only applied to a greater or lesser extent (blue bars), but also had different performance (green bars) when compared to others. Thus, we check that ANN and SVM were more the most applied, followed by CF, DT, and NB.

On the other hand, SVM was the best method in performance terms. This conclusion should be taken with caution, since it is necessary to consider which algorithms were involved in the comparison, as well as the particular case where they were applied. However, these results may show some guidance in making decisions about which techniques to use for particular scenarios.

## 4. Objectives

We have gathered the different objectives into four wide groups: student dropout, students' performance, recommend recommended activities and resources, and students' knowledge. Figure 1 shows the weight of each of these objectives in the literature, which can indicate their importance or interest for research. In this sense, students' performance collect the majority of the prediction efforts (70%), followed by student dropout (21%). Students' knowledge and recommend activities and resources were low-demand objectives (6% and 3% respectively).

*4.1. Student Dropout*

Several studies focused on the dropout rate in nursing courses have tried to find the causes rather than predicting the likelihood of students dropping out. A useful method for trying to make this type of prediction is the induction of rules, using IBM SPSS Answer Tree (AT) software [4] for this purpose. The authors [5] found that the following factors are highly informative in predicting school dropout: family history, socioeconomic status of families, high school grade and exam results.

It was noticed that unbalanced class data was a common problem for prediction [6]. In addition, classification techniques with unbalanced datasets can provide deceptively high prediction accuracy. To solve this problem, the authors compared different data balancing techniques (including SMOTE) to improve accuracy. All these techniques improved the accuracy of predictions, although Support Vector Machine (SVM) combined with SMOTE data balancing technique achieved the best performance.

Nowadays, higher education institutions are attempting to use data collected in university systems to identify students at risk of dropping out [64]. This study uses the data to validate the Moodle Engagement Analytics Plugin learning analysis tool. High dropout rates are a very important problem for e-learning. The authors propose a technique that considers a combination of multiple classifiers to analyze a set of attributes of students' activities over time [7]. Other authors [8] selected students' personal characteristics and academic performance as input attributes. They developed prediction models using ANN, Decision Trees (DT) and Bayesian Networks (BN). Along these lines, another study [65] identified the most important factors for predicting school dropout risk: those that showed student commitment and consistency in the use of online resources. For this purpose, Exploratory Data Analysis was applied.

In particular, higher education institutions in the United States faced a problem of university student attrition, especially in the areas of Science, Technology, Engineering and Mathematics. More than 60% of the dropouts occurred in the first two years. One study develops and evaluates a Survival Analysis (SA) framework for early identification of students at risk of dropping out of school and early intervention to improve student retention [10].

## 4.2. Student Performance

One of the essential and most challenging issues for educational institutions is the prediction of students' performance. Particularly, this issue could be very useful in e-learning environments at university level. We can find several approaches in the literature for this purpose.

The demographic characteristics of the students and their grades in some tasks can build a good training set for a machine-supervised learning algorithm [2]. Adding other characteristics such as the cumulative grade point of the students, the grades obtained in other courses and the ratings of several exams, can build accurate models. Pursuing this goal, four mathematical models were compared to predict students' performance in a basic course, a high-impact course and a high-enrollment course in engineering dynamics [16]. In this sense, it is advisable to consider several more characteristics, since a relationship among different factors may appear after a detailed analysis of the prediction results. Thus, an analysis of different characteristics of the data obtained from the results of primary school exams in Tamil Nadu (India) showed the relationship between ethnicity, geographic environment, and students' performance [3].

If we focus on the students' history, in [36,37] the performance is predicted considering particular first semester courses. Our goal was to represent the knowledge as a set of grades from their passed courses and to be able to find similarity among students to predict their performance. In small universities or in courses with few students [41], the research was carried out with large sparse matrices, which represented students, assignments, and grades. The result obtained in this research showed that prediction accuracy was not as good as expected; therefore more information from students or homework was needed. Accuracy is important since it can be very useful in planning educational interventions aimed at improving the results of the teaching-learning process, saving government resources and educators' time and effort [51]. Moreover, the additional use of pre-processing techniques along with classification algorithms has improved performance prediction accuracy [19].

It is possible to predict final students' performance beforehand thanks to behavioural data supplemented with other more relevant data (related to learning results). The system proposed in [31] obtained a weekly ranking of each student's probability of belonging to one of these three classification levels: high, medium or low performance. This performance could have something to do with non-cognitive characteristics which can have a significant impact on the students [9]. This research concluded that the prediction mechanism improves by exploiting the cognitive and non-cognitive characteristics of students, thereby increasing accuracy. In any case, the data obtained from previous records seem to be important, even better than applying course-dependent formulas to predict performance [26].

ML Clustering techniques have been satisfactorily applied in this field. For example, recursive clustering groups the students into specific courses according to their performance. Each of these groups receives a set of programs and notes automatically, depending on which group they belong to. The goal of this technique is to move the majority of the students from lower to higher groups [35]. Nevertheless, each student has particular features to be taken into account. A personalized prediction of the student's performance will aid in finding the right specialization for each student. For example, a method of personalized prediction is presented in [38], where specific characteristics such as basic courses, prerequisites and course levels were analyzed for computer specialization courses.

## 4.3. Recommender Activities and Resources

Recommender systems have been used to improve the experience of students and teachers. Most of the studies based on RS consider demographics, interests or preferences of the students to improve their systems. For example, an RS was developed considering the experiences previously stored and classified by former students, which were compared with the current students' competencies [48]. Another example is an RS based on student's performance, which recommends personalized articles to students in an online forum, using a "Like" button similar to the one on Facebook for this purpose [39].

*4.4. Students' Knowledge*

The trend in the use of learning systems aims to analyse the information generated by students [60]. This approach seeks to improve the effectiveness of the education process through the recognition of patterns in students' performance. Along these lines, an automatic approach that detects students' learning styles is proposed in [61] to offer adaptable courses in Moodle. It is based on students' response to the learning style and the analysis of their behavior within Moodle.

In this context, it is very important to discover which students' characteristics are associated with test results, and which school characteristics are associated with the added value of the school [62]. For example, machine learning applications were proposed to acquire knowledge about students' learning in computer science, develop optimal warning models, and discover behavioural indicators from learning analytical reports [63].

## 5. Discussion

In this article, we have reviewed many papers aimed at predicting student behavior in the academic environment. We can draw some conclusions from the analysis of these papers.

We have noted that there is a strong tendency to predict student performance at the university level, as around 70% of the articles included in this review are intended for this purpose. This may encourage us to consider complementary research efforts to fill gaps in other areas. Thus, we consider that it would be interesting to promote working lines to apply these predictions at school level, which would contribute to identify the low performance of students at early ages. The analysis of student dropout during the early stages of their levels is very interesting, as there are still opportunities to research about helpful predictive tools to enable prevention mechanisms. In this sense, a good approach to research would be to apply the same predictive techniques used for academic performance (and other novel ones) to this case, in addition to considering non-university levels.

Based on the data collected in this review, the most widely used technique for predicting students' behavior was supervised learning, as it provides accurate and reliable results. In particular, the SVM algorithm was the most used by the authors and provided the most accurate predictions. In addition to SVM, DT, NB and RF have also been well-studied algorithmic proposals that generated good results.

Recommender systems, in particular collaborative filtering algorithms, have been the next successful technique in this field. However, it should be clarified that success has been more in recommending resources and activities than in predicting student behavior.

As for the neural networks, they are a less used technique, but they obtain a great precision in predicting the students' performance. We believe that a good line of research with these techniques would be to apply them to other related types of predictions in the educational field, different from the strict students' performance.

We emphasize that unsupervised learning is an unattractive technique for researchers, due to the low accuracy of predicting students' behavior in the cases studied. However, this fact can be an incentive for research, as it provides the opportunity to further improve these techniques in order to obtain more reliable and accurate results.

This review can be useful to obtain a wide insight of the possibilities to apply ML for predicting students' performance and related problems. In this regard, Table 1 and Figure 1 may be useful to researchers in planning how to approach the initial stages of their studies. Nevertheless, many researchers will probably tackle this problem in the coming years considering other and new ML tools, since this problem has attarcted a high degree of interest nowadays.

**Author Contributions:** Search, classification, and analysis of bibliographic resources, J.L.R.-G.; work methodology, writing and editing of original manuscript, J.A.G.-P.; supervision and access to resources, A.D.-D. All authors have read and agreed to the published version of the manuscript.

**Funding:** This research was partially funded by the Government of Extremadura (Spain) under the project IB16002, and by the ERDF (European Regional Development Fund, EU) and the AEI (State Research Agency, Spain) under the contract TIN2016-76259-P.

**Acknowledgments:** We express our gratitude to the staff of the Service of Library of the University of Extremadura, Spain, for their support and ease in accessing to the different bibliographic resources and databases.

**Conflicts of Interest:** The authors declare no conflict of interest. The funders had no role in the design of the study; in the collection, analyses, or interpretation of data; in the writing of the manuscript, or in the decision to publish the results.

## Abbreviations

The following abbreviations are used in this manuscript:

| | |
|---|---|
| AB | AdaBoost |
| ANN | Artificial Neural Networks |
| AT | Answer Tree |
| BART | Bayesian Additive Regressive Trees |
| BBN | Bayesian Belief Network |
| BKT | Bayesian Knowledge Tracing |
| BMF | Biased-Matrix Factorization |
| BN | Bayesian Networks |
| BSLO | Bipolar Slope One |
| CBN | Combination of Multiple Classifiers |
| CF | Collaborative Filtering |
| DL | Deep Learning |
| DM | Data Mining |
| DT | Decision Tree |
| ELM | Extreme Learning Machine |
| EM | Expectation-Maximization |
| GBT | Gradient Boosted Tree |
| JMLM | Jacobian Matrix-Based Learning Machine |
| KNN | K-Nearest Neighbor |
| LDA | Latent Dirichlet Allocation |
| LR | Logistic Regression |
| LRMF | Low Range Matrix Factorization |
| LM | Linear Models |
| MDP | Markov Decision Process |
| MF | Matrix Factorization |
| ML | Machine Learning |
| MLP | Multilayer Perception |
| MLR | Multiple Linear Regression |
| NB | Naïves Bayes |
| pGPA | Grade Prediction Advisor |
| RBN | Radial Basis Networks |
| RF | Random Forests |
| RS | Recommender Systems |
| SA | Survival Analysis |
| SFS | Sequential Forward Selection |
| SL | Supervised Learning |
| SLO | Slope One |
| SMOTE | Synthetic Minority Over-Sampling |
| SVD | Singular Value Decomposition |
| SVM | Support Vector Machine |
| UL | Unsupervised Learning |

## References

1. Han, J.; Kamber, M.; Pei, J. *Data Mining: Concepts and Techniques*, 3rd ed.; Morgan Kaufmann Publishers Inc.: San Francisco, CA, USA, 2011.
2. Kotsiantis, S.; Pierrakeas, C.; Pintelas, P. Predicting Students' Performance in Distance Learning using Machine Learning Techniques. *Appl. Artif. Intell.* **2004**, *18*, 411–426. [CrossRef]
3. Navamani, J.; Kannammal, A. Predicting performance of schools by applying data mining techniques on public examination results. *Res. J. Appl. Sci. Eng. Technol.* **2015**, *9*, 262–271. [CrossRef]
4. Moseley, L.; Mead, D. Predicting who will drop out of nursing courses: A machine learning exercise. *Nurse Educ. Today* **2008**, *28*, 469–475. [CrossRef] [PubMed]

5. Nandeshwar, A.; Menzies, T.; Nelson, A. Learning patterns of university student retention. *Expert Syst. Appl.* **2011**, *38*, 14984–14996. [CrossRef]
6. Thammasiri, D.; Delen, D.; Meesad, P.; Kasap, N. A critical assessment of imbalanced class distribution problem: The case of predicting freshmen student attrition. *Expert Syst. Appl.* **2014**, *41*, 321–330. [CrossRef]
7. Dewan, M.; Lin, F.; Wen, D.; Kinshuk. Predicting dropout-prone students in e-learning education system. In Proceedings of the 2015 IEEE 12th Intl Conference on Ubiquitous Intelligence and Computing and 2015 IEEE 12th Intl Conference on Autonomic and Trusted Computing and 2015 IEEE 15th Intl Conference on Scalable Computing and Communications and Its Associated Workshops (UIC-ATC-ScalCom), Beijing, China, 14 August 2016; pp. 1735–1740. [CrossRef]
8. Tan, M.; Shao, P. Prediction of student dropout in E-learning program through the use of machine learning method. *Int. J. Emerg. Technol. Learn.* **2015**, *10*, 11–17. [CrossRef]
9. Sultana, S.; Khan, S.; Abbas, M. Predicting performance of electrical engineering students using cognitive and non-cognitive features for identification of potential dropouts. *Int. J. Electr. Eng. Educ.* **2017**, *54*, 105–118. [CrossRef]
10. Chen, Y.; Johri, A.; Rangwala, H. Running out of STEM: A comparative study across STEM majors of college students At-Risk of dropping out early. In Proceedings of the 8th International Conference on Learning Analytics and Knowledge, Sydney, Australia, 7–9 March 2018; pp. 270–279.
11. Nagy, M.; Molontay, R. Predicting Dropout in Higher Education Based on Secondary School Performance. In Proceedings of the 2018 IEEE 22nd International Conference on Intelligent Engineering Systems (INES), Las Palmas de Gran Canaria, Spain, 21 June 2018; pp. 000389–000394. [CrossRef]
12. Serra, A.; Perchinunno, P.; Bilancia, M. Predicting student dropouts in higher education using supervised classification algorithms. *Lect. Notes Comput. Sci.* **2018**, *10962 LNCS*, 18–33. [CrossRef]
13. Gray, C.; Perkins, D. Utilizing early engagement and machine learning to predict student outcomes. *Comput. Educ.* **2019**, *131*, 22–32. [CrossRef]
14. Chung, J.; Lee, S. Dropout early warning systems for high school students using machine learning. *Child. Youth Serv. Rev.* **2019**, *96*, 346–353. [CrossRef]
15. Hussain, M.; Zhu, W.; Zhang, W.; Abidi, S.; Ali, S. Using machine learning to predict student difficulties from learning session data. *Artif. Intell. Rev.* **2018**, *52*, 1–27. [CrossRef]
16. Huang, S.; Fang, N. Predicting student academic performance in an engineering dynamics course: A comparison of four types of predictive mathematical models. *Comput. Educ.* **2013**, *61*, 133–145. [CrossRef]
17. Slim, A.; Heileman, G.L.; Kozlick, J.; Abdallah, C.T. Predicting student success based on prior performance. In Proceedings of the 2014 IEEE Symposium on Computational Intelligence and Data Mining (CIDM), Singapore, 16 April 2015; pp. 410–415. [CrossRef]
18. Zhao, C.; Yang, J.; Liang, J.; Li, C. Discover learning behavior patterns to predict certification. In Proceedings of the 2016 11th International Conference on Computer Science & Education (ICCSE), Nagoya, Japan, 23 August 2016; pp. 69–73. [CrossRef]
19. Chaudhury, P.; Mishra, S.; Tripathy, H.; Kishore, B. Enhancing the capabilities of student result prediction system. In Proceedings of the Second International Conference on Information and Communication Technology for Competitive Strategies, Udaipur, India, 4–5 March 2016. [CrossRef]
20. Nespereira, C.; Elhariri, E.; El-Bendary, N.; Vilas, A.; Redondo, R. Machine learning based classification approach for predicting students performance in blended learning. *Adv. Intell. Syst. Comput.* **2016**, *407*, 47–56. [CrossRef]
21. Sagar, M.; Gupta, A.; Kaushal, R. Performance prediction and behavioral analysis of student programming ability. In Proceedings of the 2016 International Conference on Advances in Computing, Communications and Informatics (ICACCI), Jaipur, India, 21 September 2016; pp. 1039–1045. [CrossRef]
22. Verhun, V.; Batyuk, A.; Voityshyn, V. Learning Analysis as a Tool for Predicting Student Performance. In Proceedings of the 2018 IEEE 13th International Scientific and Technical Conference on Computer Sciences and Information Technologies (CSIT), Lviv, Ukraine, 11 September 2018; Volume 2, pp. 76–79. [CrossRef]
23. Backenköhler, M.; Wolf, V. Student performance prediction and optimal course selection: An MDP approach. *Lect. Notes Comput. Sci.* **2018**, *10729 LNCS*, 40–47. [CrossRef]
24. Hsieh, Y.Z.; Su, M.C.; Jeng, Y.L. The jacobian matrix-based learning machine in student. *Lect. Notes Comput. Sci.* **2017**, *10676 LNCS*, 469–474. [CrossRef]

25. Han, M.; Tong, M.; Chen, M.; Liu, J.; Liu, C. Application of Ensemble Algorithm in Students' Performance Prediction. In Proceedings of the 2017 6th IIAI International Congress on Advanced Applied Informatics (IIAI-AAI), Hamamatsu, Japan, 16 November 2017; pp. 735–740. [CrossRef]
26. Shanthini, A.; Vinodhini, G.; Chandrasekaran, R. Predicting students' academic performance in the University using meta decision tree classifiers. *J. Comput. Sci.* **2018**, *14*, 654–662. [CrossRef]
27. Ma, C.; Yao, B.; Ge, F.; Pan, Y.; Guo, Y. Improving prediction of student performance based on multiple feature selection approaches. In Proceedings of the ICEBT 2017, Toronto, ON, Canada, 10–12 September 2017; pp. 36–41. [CrossRef]
28. Tekin, A. Early prediction of students' grade point averages at graduation: A data mining approach [Öğrencinin mezuniyet notunun erken tahmini: Bir veri madenciliği yaklaşidotlessmidotless]. *Egit. Arastirmalari Eurasian J. Educ. Res.* **2014**, 207–226. [CrossRef]
29. Pushpa, S.; Manjunath, T.; Mrunal, T.; Singh, A.; Suhas, C. Class result prediction using machine learning. In Proceedings of the 2017 International Conference On Smart Technologies For Smart Nation (SmartTechCon), Bengaluru, India, 19 August 2018; pp. 1208–1212. [CrossRef]
30. Howard, E.; Meehan, M.; Parnell, A. Contrasting prediction methods for early warning systems at undergraduate level. *Internet High. Educ.* **2018**, *37*, 66–75. [CrossRef]
31. Villagrá-Arnedo, C.; Gallego-Duran, F.; Compan-Rosique, P.; Llorens-Largo, F.; Molina-Carmona, R. Predicting academic performance from Behavioural and learning data. *Int. J. Des. Nat. Ecodyn.* **2016**, *11*, 239–249. [CrossRef]
32. Sorour, S.; Goda, K.; Mine, T. Estimation of Student Performance by Considering Consecutive Lessons. In Proceedings of the 4th International Congress on Advanced Applied Informatics, Okayama, Japan, 12 June 2016, pp. 121–126. [CrossRef]
33. Guo, B.; Zhang, R.; Xu, G.; Shi, C.; Yang, L. Predicting Students Performance in Educational Data Mining. In Proceedings of the 2015 International Symposium on Educational Technology (ISET), Wuhan, China, 24 March 2016; pp. 125–128. [CrossRef]
34. Rana, S.; Garg, R. Prediction of students performance of an institute using ClassificationViaClustering and ClassificationViaRegression. *Adv. Intell. Syst. Comput.* **2017**, *508*, 333–343. [CrossRef]
35. Anand, V.K.; Abdul Rahiman, S.K.; Ben George, E.; Huda, A.S. Recursive clustering technique for students' performance evaluation in programming courses. In Proceedings of the 2018 Majan International Conference (MIC), Muscat, Oman, 19 March 2018; pp. 1–5. [CrossRef]
36. Bydžovská, H. Student performance prediction using collaborative filtering methods. *Lect. Notes Comput. Sci.* **2015**, *9112*, 550–553. [CrossRef]
37. Bydžovská, H. Are collaborative filtering methods suitable for student performance prediction? *Lect. Notes Comput. Sci.* **2015**, *9273*, 425–430. [CrossRef]
38. Park, Y. Predicting personalized student performance in computing-related majors via collaborative filtering. In Proceedings of the 19th Annual SIG Conference on Information Technology Education, Fort Lauderdale, FL, USA, 3 October 2018; p. 151. [CrossRef]
39. Liou, C.H. Personalized article recommendation based on student's rating mechanism in an online discussion forum. In Proceedings of the 2016 49th Hawaii International Conference on System Sciences (HICSS), Koloa, HI, USA, 5–8 January 2016; pp. 60–65. [CrossRef]
40. Elbadrawy, A.; Karypis, G. Domain-aware grade prediction and top-n course recommendation. In Proceedings of the 10th ACM Conference on Recommender Systems, Boston, MA, USA, 15 September 2016, pp. 183–190. [CrossRef]
41. Pero, v.; Horváth, T. Comparison of collaborative-filtering techniques for small-scale student performance prediction task. *Lect. Notes Electr. Eng.* **2015**, *313*, 111–116. [CrossRef]
42. Song, Y.; Jin, Y.; Zheng, X.; Han, H.; Zhong, Y.; Zhao, X. PSFK: A student performance prediction scheme for first-encounter knowledge in ITS. *Lect. Notes Comput. Sci.* **2015**, *9403*, 639–650. [CrossRef]
43. Xu, K.; Liu, R.; Sun, Y.; Zou, K.; Huang, Y.; Zhang, X. Improve the prediction of student performance with hint's assistance based on an efficient non-negative factorization. *IEICE Trans. Inf. Syst.* **2017**, *E100D*, 768–775. [CrossRef]
44. Sheehan, M.; Park, Y. pGPA: A personalized grade prediction tool to aid student success. In Proceedings of the sixth ACM conference on Recommender systems, Dublin, Ireland, 3 September 2012, pp. 309–310. [CrossRef]

45. Lorenzen, S.; Pham, N.; Alstrup, S. On predicting student performance using low-rank matrix factorization techniques. In Proceedings of the 9th European Conference on E-Learning—ECEL 2010 (ECEL 2010), Porto, Portugal, 5 November 2010; pp. 326–334.
46. Houbraken, M.; Sun, C.; Smirnov, E.; Driessens, K. Discovering hidden course requirements and student competences from grade data. In Proceedings of the UMAP '17: Adjunct Publication of the 25th Conference on User Modeling, Adaptation and Personalization, Bratislava, Slovakia, 9–10 July 2017; pp. 147–152. [CrossRef]
47. Gómez-Pulido, J.; Cortés-Toro, E.; Durán-Domínguez, A.; Crawford, B.; Soto, R. Novel and Classic Metaheuristics for Tunning a Recommender System for Predicting Student Performance in Online Campus. *Lect. Notes Comput. Sci.* **2018**, *11314 LNCS*, 125–133. [CrossRef]
48. Chavarriaga, O.; Florian-Gaviria, B.; Solarte, O. A recommender system for students based on social knowledge and assessment data of competences. *Lect. Notes Comput. Sci.* **2014**, *8719 LNCS*, 56–69. [CrossRef]
49. Jembere, E.; Rawatlal, R.; Pillay, A. Matrix Factorisation for Predicting Student Performance. In Proceedings of the 2017 7th World Engineering Education Forum (WEEF), Kuala Lumpur, Malaysia, 16 November 2018; pp. 513–518. [CrossRef]
50. Sweeney, M.; Lester, J.; Rangwala, H. Next-term student grade prediction. In Proceedings of the 2015 IEEE International Conference on Big Data (Big Data), Santa Clara, CA, USA, 1 November 2015; pp. 970–975. [CrossRef]
51. Adán-Coello, J.; Tobar, C. Using collaborative filtering algorithms for predicting student performance. *Lect. Notes Comput. Sci.* **2016**, *9831 LNCS*, 206–218. [CrossRef]
52. Rechkoski, L.; Ajanovski, V.; Mihova, M. Evaluation of grade prediction using model-based collaborative filtering methods. In Proceedings of the 2018 IEEE Global Engineering Education Conference (EDUCON), Santa Cruz de Tenerife, Spain, 17 April 2018; pp. 1096–1103. [CrossRef]
53. Adewale Amoo, M.; Olumuyiwa, A.; Lateef, U. Predictive modelling and analysis of academic performance of secondary school students: Artificial Neural Network approach. *Int. J. Sci. Technol. Educ. Res.* **2018**, *9*, 1–8. [CrossRef]
54. Gedeon, T.; Turner, H. Explaining student grades predicted by a neural network. In Proceedings of the 1993 International Conference on Neural Networks, Nagoya, Japan, 25 October 1993; Volume 1, pp. 609–612.
55. Arsad, P.M.; Buniyamin, N.; Manan, J.A. A neural network students' performance prediction model (NNSPPM). In Proceedings of the 2013 IEEE International Conference on Smart Instrumentation, Measurement and Applications (ICSIMA), Kuala Lumpur, Malaysia, 27 November 2013; pp. 1–5. [CrossRef]
56. Iyanda, A.; D. Ninan, O.; Ajayi, A.; G. Anyabolu, O. Predicting Student Academic Performance in Computer Science Courses: A Comparison of Neural Network Models. *Int. J. Mod. Educ. Comput. Sci.* **2018**, *10*, 1–9. [CrossRef]
57. Dharmasaroja, P.; Kingkaew, N. Application of artificial neural networks for prediction of learning performances. In Proceedings of the 2016 12th International Conference on Natural Computation, Fuzzy Systems and Knowledge Discovery (ICNC-FSKD), Changsha, China, 13 August 2016; pp. 745–751. [CrossRef]
58. Musso, M.; Kyndt, E.; Cascallar, E.; Dochy, F. Predicting general academic performance and identifying the differential contribution of participating variables using artificial neural networks. *Frontline Learn. Res.* **2013**, *1*, 42–71. [CrossRef]
59. Mala Sari Rochman, E.; Rachmad, A.; Damayanti, F. Predicting the Final result of Student National Test with Extreme Learning Machine. *Pancar. Pendidik.* **2018**, *7*. [CrossRef]
60. Villegas-Ch, W.; Lujan-Mora, S.; Buenano-Fernandez, D.; Roman-Canizares, M. Analysis of web-based learning systems by data mining. In Proceedings of the 2017 IEEE Second Ecuador Technical Chapters Meeting (ETCM), Guayas, Ecuador, 16 October 2018; pp. 1–5. [CrossRef]
61. Karagiannis, I.; Satratzemi, M. An adaptive mechanism for Moodle based on automatic detection of learning styles. *Educ. Inf. Technol.* **2018**, *23*, 1331–1357. [CrossRef]
62. Masci, C.; Johnes, G.; Agasisti, T. Student and school performance across countries: A machine learning approach. *Eur. J. Oper. Res.* **2018**, *269*, 1072–1085. [CrossRef]

63. Johnson, W. Data mining and machine learning in education with focus in undergraduate cs student success. In Proceedings of the 2018 ACM Conference on International Computing Education Research, Espoo, Finland, 13–15 August 2018; pp. 270–271. [CrossRef]
64. Liu, D.; Richards, D.; Froissard, C.; Atif, A. Validating the effectiveness of the moodle engagement analytics plugin to predict student academic performance. In Proceedings of the 21st Americas Conference on Information Systems (AMCIS 2015), Fajardo, Puerto Rico, 13 August 2015.
65. Saqr, M.; Fors, U.; Tedre, M. How learning analytics can early predict under-achieving students in a blended medical education course. *Med Teach.* **2017**, *39*, 757–767. [CrossRef] [PubMed]
66. Kotsiantis, S. Supervised machine learning: A review of classification techniques. *Informatica* **2007**, *31*, 249–268.
67. Hosmer, D.; Lemeshow, S.; Sturdivant, R. *Applied Logistic Regression*; Wiley Series in Probability and Statistics; Wiley: Hoboken, NJ, USA, 2013.
68. Gentleman, R.; Carey, V.J. Unsupervised Machine Learning. In *Bioconductor Case Studies*; Springer: New York, NY, USA, 2008; pp. 137–157. [CrossRef]
69. Bobadilla, J.; Ortega, F.; Hernando, A.; Gutiérrez, A. Recommender systems survey. *Knowl. Based Syst.* **2013**, *46*, 109–132. [CrossRef]

© 2020 by the authors. Licensee MDPI, Basel, Switzerland. This article is an open access article distributed under the terms and conditions of the Creative Commons Attribution (CC BY) license (http://creativecommons.org/licenses/by/4.0/).

MDPI  
St. Alban-Anlage 66  
4052 Basel  
Switzerland  
Tel. +41 61 683 77 34  
Fax +41 61 302 89 18  
www.mdpi.com

*Applied Sciences* Editorial Office  
E-mail: applsci@mdpi.com  
www.mdpi.com/journal/applsci